THE ROUGH GUIDE TO

Vienna

There are more than two hundred Rough Guide titles
covering destinations from Alaska to Zimbabwe
and subjects from Acoustic Guitar to Travel Health

Forthcoming travel guides include

The Algarve • The Bahamas • Cambodia • Caribbean Islands
Costa Brava • New York Restaurants • South America • Zanzibar

Forthcoming reference guides include

Children's Books • Online Travel • Videogaming • Weather

Rough Guides Online

www.roughguides.com

Rough Guide Credits

Text Editors:	Ruth Blackmore and Alison Murchie
Series Editor:	Mark Ellingham
Editorial:	Martin Dunford, Jonathan Buckley, Jo Mead, Kate Berens, Ann-Marie Shaw, Paul Gray, Helena Smith, Judith Bamber, Orla Duane, Olivia Eccleshall, Geoff Howard, Claire Saunders, Gavin Thomas, Alexander Mark Rogers, Polly Thomas, Joe Staines, Richard Lim, Duncan Clark, Peter Buckley, Sam Thorne, Lucy Ratcliffe, Clifton Wilkinson, David Glen, Matthew Teller, Andrew Dickson (UK); Andrew Rosenberg, Stephen Timblin, Yuki Takagaki, Richard Koss (US)
Online:	Kelly Cross, Anja Mutić-Blessing, Jennifer Gold, Audra Epstein, Suzanne Welles (US)
Production:	Susanne Hillen, Andy Hilliard, Link Hall, Helen Prior, Julia Bovis, Michelle Draycott, Katie Pringle, Mike Hancock, Zoë Nobes, Rachel Holmes, Andy Turner
Cartography:	Melissa Baker, Maxine Repath, Ed Wright, Katie Lloyd-Jones
Picture Research:	Louise Boulton, Sharon Martins
Finance:	John Fisher, Gary Singh, Edward Downey, Mark Hall, Tim Bill
Marketing & Publicity:	Richard Trillo, Niki Smith, David Wearn, Chloë Roberts, Claire Southern (UK); Simon Carloss, David Wechsler, Kathleen Rushforth (US)
Administration:	Tania Hummel, Demelza Dallow, Julie Sanderson

Acknowledgements

The author would like to thank Val for the biblio and general surfing, Kate, Andy and Simon for plenty of positive input during updating, and, of course, Petr for coming down from Brno. The editors would like to thank Andy Turner for production, Ed Wright for cartography and Laurence Larroche for proofreading.

The publishers and authors have done their best to ensure the accuracy and currency of all information in The Rough Guide to Vienna; however, they can accept no responsibility for any loss, injury, or inconvenience sustained by any traveller as a result of information or advice contained in the guide.

This third edition published September 2001 by Rough Guides Ltd, 62–70 Shorts Gardens, London WC2H 9AH.

Distributed by the Penguin Group:
Penguin Books Ltd, 27 Wrights Lane, London W8 5TZ.
Penguin Putnam, Inc. 375 Hudson Street, New York, NY 10014, USA.
Penguin Books Australia Ltd, 487 Maroondah Highway, PO Box 257, Ringwood, Victoria 3134, Australia.
Penguin Books Canada Ltd, 10 Alcorn Avenue, Toronto, Ontario M4V 1E4, Canada.
Penguin Books (NZ) Ltd, 182–190 Wairau Road, Auckland 10, New Zealand.
Printed in England by Clays Ltd, St Ives PLC.
Typography and original design by Jonathan Dear and The Crowd Roars.
Illustrations throughout by Edward Briant.

THE ROUGH GUIDE TO

Vienna

Written and researched by

Rob Humphreys

ROUGH GUIDES

Help us update

We've gone to a lot of trouble to ensure that this third edition of *The Rough Guide to Vienna* is accurate and up to date. However, things inevitably change, and if you feel we've got it wrong or left something out, we'd like to know: any suggestions, comments or corrections would be much appreciated. We'll credit all contributions and send a copy of the next edition – or any other Rough Guide if you prefer – for the best correspondence.

Please mark letters "Rough Guide to Vienna" and send to:
Rough Guides, 62–70 Shorts Gardens, London WC2H 9AH or
Rough Guides, 4th Floor, 345 Hudson St, New York, NY 10014.

Email should be sent to:
mail@roughguides.co.uk

Online updates about Rough Guide titles can be found on our website at www.roughguides.com

The Author

Rob Humphreys joined Rough Guides in 1989, having worked as a failed actor, taxi driver and male model. He has travelled extensively in central and eastern Europe, writing guides to Prague, the Czech and Slovak Republics, and St Petersburg, as well as London. He has lived in London since 1988.

Readers' letters

We'd like to thank the following readers who wrote in with comments and suggestions: Mark & Sue Campbell, Rebecca Gilbert, E. A. Thwaite, Chris Pond, Mr S. Rouchotas, Professor Henry H. Y. Wong.

Rough Guides

Travel Guides • Phrasebooks • Music and Reference Guides

We set out to do something different when the first Rough Guide was published in 1982. Mark Ellingham, just out of University, was travelling in Greece. He brought along the popular guides of the day, but found they were all lacking in some way. They were either strong on ruins and museums but went on for pages without mentioning a beach or taverna. Or they were so conscious of the need to save money that they lost sight of Greece's cultural and historical significance. Also, none of the books told him anything about Greece's contemporary life – its politics, its culture, its people, and how they lived.

So with no job in prospect, Mark decided to write his own guidebook, one which aimed to provide practical information that was second to none, detailing the best beaches and the hottest clubs and restaurants, while also giving hard-hitting accounts of every sight, both famous and obscure, and providing up-to-the-minute information on contemporary culture. It was a guide that encouraged independent travellers to find the best of Greece, and was a great success, getting shortlisted for the Thomas Cook travel guide award, and encouraging Mark, along with three friends, to expand the series.

The Rough Guide list grew rapidly and the letters flooded in, indicating a much broader readership than had been anticipated, but one which uniformly appreciated the Rough Guides' mix of practical detail and humour, irreverence and enthusiasm. Things haven't changed. The same four friends who began the series are still the caretakers of the Rough Guide mission today: to provide the most reliable, up-to-date and entertaining information to independent-minded travellers of all ages, on all budgets.

We now publish 150 titles and have offices in London and New York. The travel guides are written and researched by a dedicated team of more than 100 authors, based in Britain, Europe, the USA and Australia. We have also created a unique series of phrasebooks to accompany the travel series, along with the acclaimed series of music guides, and a best-selling pocket guide to the Internet and World Wide Web. We also publish comprehensive travel information on our Web site: *www.roughguides.com*

Contents

Map List

Colour maps (at back of book):
U- and S-Bahn lines
Vienna
Tram, bus and U-Bahn routes

MAP SYMBOLS

--- ---	Chapter division boundary	∴	Ruin
■-■-■	International boundary	✈	Airport
═══	Road	✝	Church
⦙⦙⦙⦙⦙	Steps	✡	Synagogue
▪▪▪▪	Wall	☪	Mosque
■-■	Gate	⊞	Christian cemetery
───	Railway	⊡	Jewish cemetery
░░░	River/canal	⊠	Post office
▓▓▓	Urban area	ⓘ	Information office
▒▒▒	Park	Ⓤ	U-Bahn
░░░	Forest	Ⓢ	S-Bahn
▲	Peak		

Introduction

Most people visit Vienna with a vivid image of the city in their minds: a monumental vision of Habsburg palaces, trotting white horses, old ladies in fur coats and mountains of fat cream cakes. And they're unlikely to be disappointed in this city that positively feeds off imperial nostalgia – High Baroque churches and aristocratic piles pepper the old town, or Innere Stadt, monumental projects from the late nineteenth century line the Ringstrasse, and postcards of the Emperor Franz-Josef and his beautiful wife Elisabeth still sell by the sackful. Just as compelling as the old Habsburg stand-bys are the wonderful Jugendstil and early modernist buildings, products of *fin-de-siècle* Vienna, when the city emerged as one of Europe's great cultural centres. This was the era of Freud, Klimt, Schiele, Mahler and Schönberg, when the city's famous coffeehouses were filled with intellectuals from every corner of the empire. In a sense, this was Vienna's golden age, after which all has been in decline: with the end of the empire in 1918, the city was reduced from a metropolis of over two million, capital of a vast empire of fifty million, to one of barely more than one-and-a-half million, federal capital of a small country of just eight million souls.

Given the city's twentieth-century history, it's hardly surprising that the Viennese are as keen as anyone to continue plugging the good old days. This is a place, not unlike Berlin, which has had the misfortune of serving as a weather vane of European history. Modern anti-Semitism as a politically viable force was invented here, in front of Hitler's very eyes, in the first decade of the century. It was the assassination of an arrogant Austrian archduke that started World War I, while the battles between Left and Right fought out in the streets of Vienna mirrored those in Berlin in the 1930s. The weekend Hitler enjoyed his greatest electoral victory in the Reichstag was the day the Austrians themselves invented Austro-fascism. In 1938, the country became the first victim of Nazi expansion, greeting the Führer with delirious enthusiasm. And after the war, for a decade, Vienna was divided, like Berlin, into French, American, British and Soviet sectors.

The visual scars from this turbulent history are few and far between – even Hitler's sinister Flacktürme are confined to the suburbs – but the destruction of the city's once enormous Jewish community is a wound that has proved harder to heal. Vienna's Jewish intellectuals and capitalists were the driving force behind much of the city's *fin-de-siècle* culture. Little surprise then, that the city has since struggled to live up to its glorious past achievements. After the war Vienna lost its cosmopolitan character and found itself stuck in a monocultural straightjacket. Since the end of the Cold War, however, this has begun to change, with the arrival of a second wave of immigrants from the former provinces of the old empire. Whether Vienna will learn to accept its new, multicultural identity remains to be seen.

For all its problems, Vienna is still an inspiring city to visit, with one of the world's greatest art collections in the Kunsthistorisches Museum, world-class orchestras, and a superb architectural heritage. It's also an eminently civilized place, clean, safe (for the most part) and peopled by a courteous population who do their best to live up to their reputation for *Gemütlichkeit* or "cosiness". And despite its ageing population, it's also a city with a lively nightlife, of late-opening cafés and drinking holes. Even Vienna's traditional restaurants, long famous for quantity over quality, have discovered innovative methods of cooking and presentation, and are now supplemented by a wide range of ethnic restaurants.

When to go

Lying at the centre of Europe, Vienna experiences the extremes of temperature typical of a continental climate with hot summers and correspondingly cold winters. In terms of weather, therefore, late spring and early autumn are by far the best times to visit. There are other reasons, too, for avoiding July and August in particular, as this is when many of the city's theatres and concert halls close down. Sure, there's enough cultural activity to keep the tourists amused, but the Viennese tend to get the hell out. In contrast, Christmas and New Year are peak season in Vienna. Not only does the city look great in the snow – and you can be sure that the Viennese are very efficient about keeping the paths clear – but also the ball season, known as *Fasching*, gets underway, along with the glittering Christmas markets and, of course, the world-famous New Year's Day concert.

Basics

Basics

Getting there from Britain

The easiest way to get to Vienna from Britain is by plane with daily direct flights from London to Vienna taking around two hours. Trains take around eighteen hours and present a viable alternative if you're keen on overland travel. Travelling by bus is the cheapest option, but also the most time-consuming at about twenty-two hours.

By air

A **scheduled flight** is the most obvious way to go as Vienna is Austria's chief international gateway. The principal **carriers** are Austrian Airlines, British Airways, Lauda Air, and the ticketless airline Buzz, all of which offer nonstop flights from London to Vienna. Lauda Air and Austrian Airlines also fly direct from Manchester. Flights operated by KLM, Air France and Lufthansa require you to make at least one stop on the ground at their hubs, but can – along with BA – offer enormous flexibility of UK departure points.

The most competitive **fares** nowadays are almost always with the new discount airlines, which don't offer free inflight meals or other creature comforts (such as newspapers or airline magazines). Buzz regularly offer fares of around £100 return from Stansted to Vienna. The more established airlines regularly try and compete with these fares with special offers, but at other times, a standard economy fare from London or Manchester to Vienna with British Airways, Austrian Airlines or Lauda Air will cost more like

---

SPECIALIST OPERATORS

Austrian Holidays, 5th Floor, Swiss Centre, 10 Wardour St, London W1 ☎ 020/7434 7399, *www.austrianholidays.co.uk*. Austrian package-tour specialist run by Austrian Airlines. City breaks to Vienna.

Habsburg Heritage Cultural Tours, 158 Rosendale Rd, London SE21 8LG ☎ 020/8761 0444. Highbrow cultural tours, including tailor-made visits to Eisenstadt for the International Haydn Festival (September) or to the Vorarlberg for the Schubertiade festival (June).

Made to Measure, 57 East St, Chichester, West Sussex PO19 1HL ☎ 01243/533333, *www.madetomeasureholidays.com*. Luxury package-tour specialist with retail and "romantic escape" (off-the-peg) packages based in Vienna, as well as more specialized "made-to-measure" tours.

Martin Randall Travel, 10 Barley Mow Passage, London W4 ☎ 020/8742 3355, *www.martinrandall.com*. Small-group cultural tours, led by experts on art, archeology or music. Tours include a cruise down the Danube, the Haydn Festival in Eisenstadt and a Christmas visit to Vienna.

Mondial Travel, The Four Wents, Goudhurst Rd, Cranbrook, Kent TN17 2QD ☎ 01580/714714, *www.mondialtravel.co.uk*. Specialists in flights and accommodation for central and eastern Europe, with two-, three- and four-night city breaks to Vienna.

Page & Moy, 136–140 London Rd, Leicester LE2 ☎ 0116/250 7979. Short breaks to Vienna including tickets to the opera.

Travelscene, 11–15 St Ann's Rd, Harrow, Middlesex ☎ 020/8427 8800, *www.travelscene.co.uk*. City breaks to Vienna.

Worldwide Journeys/Eurocity Breaks, 243 Stevenson Way, London NW1 2HD ☎ 020/7388 0888, *www.j.uk.com*. City breaks to Vienna.

£200 return. Fares can vary slightly according to **season**, tending to be highest from April to October and around Christmas. However, price is determined more by the flexibility of the ticket and the time of the day and week in which you travel. The cheapest tickets tend to be non-changeable, non-refundable, mid-week flights, valid for one month, and including a Saturday night away.

Finding the best fare involves ringing round a few of the discount flight agents listed in the box below, comparing prices and routings, or consulting Buzz by telephone or via the internet (they don't deal with agents, thus cutting out any

---

AIRLINES

Air France ☎0845/084 5111, *www.airfrance.fr*. Flights to Vienna from London (and elsewhere in the UK) via Paris.

Austrian Airlines ☎0845/601 0948, *www.aua.com*. Direct flights from London Heathrow to Vienna.

British Airways ☎0385/722 2111, *www.britishairways.com*. Daily nonstop flights from London Heathrow to Vienna.

Buzz ☎0870/240 7070, *www.buzzaway.com*. Daily nonstop flights from London Stansted to Vienna. Booking by phone and internet only, ticketless travel, no free inflight meals.

KLM Direct ☎0870/507 4074, *www.klmuk.com*. Flights from virtually all UK airports to Amsterdam, with easy connections to Vienna.

Lauda Air ☎0845/434 7383, *www.laudaair.com*. Daily nonstop flights from London Gatwick and Manchester to Vienna.

Lufthansa ☎0845/773 7747, *www.lufthansa.co.uk*. London Heathrow, London City, London Stansted, Birmingham and Manchester to Frankfurt, with onward flights to Vienna.

Swissair ☎020/7434 7300, *www.swissair.com*. Nonstop flights into Zürich from London Heathrow, Stansted and around the UK, and onward flights to Vienna.

DISCOUNT FLIGHT AGENTS

Flightbookers – *www.ebookers.com*: 177–178 Tottenham Court Rd, London W1P 0LX ☎020/7757 2000; Gatwick Airport, South Terminal inside the train station ☎01293/568300, daily 8am–10pm. Low fares on an extensive offering of scheduled flights.

North South Travel, Moulsham Mill Centre, Parkway, Chelmsford, Essex CM2 7PX ☎01245/608291, *www.northsouthtravel.co.uk*. Friendly, competitive travel agency, offering discounted fares worldwide – profits are used to support projects in the developing world, especially the promotion of sustainable tourism.

STA Travel – *www.statravel.co.uk*: 86 Old Brompton Rd, London SW7 3LH; 117 Euston Rd, London NW1 2SX; 38 Store St, London WC1E 7BZ; 11 Goodge St, London W1P ☎020/7361 6145; 25 Queen's Rd, Bristol BS8 1QE ☎0117/929 4399; 38 Sidney St, Cambridge CB2 3HX ☎01223/366966; 75 Deansgate, Manchester M3 2BW ☎0161/834 0668; 88 Vicar Lane, Leeds LS1 7JH ☎0113/244 9212; 36 George St, Oxford OX1 2OJ ☎01865/792800; and other branches in Aberdeen, Birmingham, Canterbury, Cardiff, Coventry, Durham, Glasgow, Liverpool, Loughborough, Newcastle-upon-Tyne, Nottingham, Sheffield and Warwick. Worldwide specialists in low-cost flights and tours for students and under-26s, though other customers also welcome. Also offices abroad.

Trailfinders – *www.trailfinders.com*: 215 Kensington High St, London W6 6BD ☎020/7937 1234; 58 Deansgate, Manchester M3 2FF ☎0161/839 6969; 254–284 Sauchiehall St, Glasgow G2 3EH ☎0141/353 2224; 22–24 The Priory Queensway, Birmingham B4 6BS ☎0121/236 1234; 48 Corn St, Bristol BS1 1HQ ☎0117/929 9000. One of the best-informed and most efficient agents for independent travellers; all branches open daily until 6pm. Student/youth travel specialists, with over fifty branches (some in YHA shops and on university campuses) all over Britain.

USIT Campus ☎0870/240 1010, *www .usitcampus.co.uk*. Discounted flights for students, under 26s and some special deals for everybody.

commission). **Students and those under 26** can take advantage of discounted tickets – STA Travel and Usit Campus are your best bet for these, and they're worth calling even if you're not under 26, since they also offer highly competitive budget fares to all-comers.

In your pursuit of a cheap deal, it also worth checking out the following **websites**: www.cheaptickets.com, www.cheapflights.com, www.lastminute.com and www.deckchair.com.

Packages and city breaks

Package holiday deals can be worth considering, saving you the hassle of having to organize things for yourself. As a general rule, your accommodation will cost less when booked as a package than arranged independently. That said, you won't always get the most imaginative choice of hotel if you book through a travel agent.

Several tour operators offer **city breaks** to Vienna (see box on p.3). Most of these are simple flight-and-accommodation deals, with prices depending on the grade of hotel you choose (most companies offer a choice). Three nights' accommodation in a three-star hotel in Vienna, plus return flights from London, can cost anything from £200 to £350 depending on the season. If you've more money to spend, it's worth checking agents specializing in **cultural or historical tours** (such as Martin Randall and Habsburg Heritage) who arrange such extras as opera and theatre tickets and visits to music festivals – for which, of course, you pay a hefty (if all-inclusive) price.

By train

Travelling **by train** is a pleasantly old-fashioned, and extremely leisurely way to reach Vienna. However, you're unlikely to save any money on the airfare; in fact, you may end up paying a bit more.

The routes

From **London to Vienna** takes around eighteen hours by train via the Channel Tunnel. By catching a Eurostar train at around 2pm from London Waterloo International, you can arrive at Brussels Midi with an hour to spare before taking the Brussels–Vienna overnight service, which will get you into Vienna at around 9.45am.

Although you can simply crash out on the seats, you won't get much sleep as the ticket inspectors wake you up at regular intervals. To travel in more comfort, it's best to book a **couchette** (around £12–17 extra each way on top of the price of the ticket) before you leave. Couchettes are mixed sex and allow little privacy, but you do get the chance of an unbroken night and free rolls and coffee in the morning. For your very own compartment, you'll need to book a berth in a **sleeper** (around £50 extra each way) – and take a friend to share it with. Sleeper compartments are either two-berth or three-berth (the latter being slightly cheaper). If you're travelling alone, however, you will not be required to share with passengers of the opposite sex. For sole occupancy of a sleeper, you must first purchase a first-class ticket.

If you don't want to travel on Eurostar, it is still possible to travel from London to Brussels **via the**

TRAIN INFORMATION

European Rail ☎ 020/7387 0444, www .europeanrail.com. Travel agency specializing in getting the best deal on international rail tickets.

Eurostar ☎ 0990/186186, www.eurostar.com. Latest fares and youth discounts (plus online booking) on the London–Paris and London–Brussels Eurostar service, but no bookings for through trains to Austria.

German Railways ☎ 0870/243 5363, www.bahn.de. Competitive discounted fares for any journey from London across Europe with very reasonable prices for those journeys that pass through the German railway system.

Rail Europe ☎ 0870/584 8848, www.raileurope.co.uk. SNCF-owned informa-

tion and ticket agent for all European passes and journeys from London or Ashford.

Thomas Cook Publishers of the famous red *Thomas Cook European Timetable* ($9.50), detailing schedules of over 50,000 trains in Europe, as well as timings of over 200 ferry routes and rail-connecting bus services. Updated monthly; main changes are in June and October editions. Available from P.O. Box 227, Peterborough PE3 6PU ☎ 01733/503571, or from high-street branches or main train stations across the UK.

USIT Campus ☎ 0870/240 1010, www.usitcampus.co.uk. Discounted fares on rail passes and Eurostar tickets only.

---

ferry to Ostend, though you may not save any money and it does take longer. Trains leave from Charing Cross for Dover Priory at about 8am, and use the catamaran service from Dover to Ostend. To get from London to Brussels using this route takes about eight hours.

Tickets and passes

Fares for continental rail travel are much more flexible than they used to be, so it's worth shopping around for the best deal rather than taking the first offer you get. European Rail (see box on p.5) are adept at working out the cheapest deal available, which is usually with German Railways, who regularly offer a return ticket London–Vienna at around £200 (including couchettes). To qualify for the most heavily discounted fares, however, there are usually various restrictions: you will probably have to stay over a Saturday night, and your Eurostar ticket may be non-exchangeable and non-refundable. If you're travelling with one or more companions, you could also be eligible for a further discount.

Virtually the only way **to buy** an international train ticket at the moment is via a travel agent or over the phone through European Rail, Rail Europe or German Railways. Note that the latter two can only book you a ticket from London or Ashford; for the connecting journey within the UK you must contact the relevant private train company – if you don't know which one phone National Rail Enquiries (☎ 08457/484950). The only British train stations that can sell you an international train ticket over the counter are London's Euston and Charing Cross stations, though their prices are far from competitive. If you're travelling **via Ostend**, either of the above stations can sell you a return from London to Brussels (including the catamaran) for £65 return, as can Hoverspeed (☎ 0990/240241) and Network Leisure Travel (☎ 0870/001 0174). The train journey from Brussels to Vienna, costs about £135 return.

Those **under 26** can purchase discounted tickets from Rail Europe or German Railways, thus saving up to 25 percent on the return fare. The above companies, USIT Campus and European Rail, also offer a range of **Euro Domino passes**, which allow unlimited travel within Austria. These range from £68 for three (non-consecutive) days (£53 for under 26s) to £108 for eight days (£83 for under 26s). Travellers over 60 also get small discounts on all tickets, and can get further discounts between, but not within, European countries by purchasing a

Rail Plus card at a cost of £12. However, before you can buy this card, you must already possess a British Senior Card (£18); both are valid for a year.

If you're planning to visit Vienna as part of a more extensive trip round Europe, it may be worth buying an **InterRail Pass**, which gives you unlimited rail travel within certain countries; you must, however, have been resident in Europe for at least six months (if you haven't, see p.12 for other options). InterRail tickets are currently zonal: to travel to Vienna and back from the UK, you'll need at least a two-zone pass, costing £169 for one month for those under 26, and £235 a month for those aged 26 and over. Passes are not valid in the UK (or whichever country you bought the pass in), though you're entitled to discounted fares at your country of origin, and on Eurostar and cross-Channel ferries. Either way, you're really only going to get your money's worth if you do a lot of travelling. For the latest information, visit the InterRail website at *www.inter-rail.co.uk*.

By bus

The cheapest way to get to Vienna is **by bus**. There's a direct service run by Eurolines from London's Victoria Coach Station more or less daily. The bus sets off at around 10.30am, arriving in Wien-Mitte/Landstrasse roughly 22 hours later. The trip is bearable (just about), but only really worth it if you absolutely can't find the extra cash for the cheap flight. A flexible return (valid for six months) costs £111 return, whereas a non-exchangeable, non-refundable return bought fourteen days in advance and valid for one month costs just £79 return. Under 26s and over 60s get a ten percent discount.

Another option worth considering if you're heading for other parts of Europe as well as Vienna is a **Eurolines pass**. The pass, which covers all the major cities in Europe (including Vienna) is valid for either thirty days (low season Nov–March: £139/£175 under 26/26 & over; shoulder season April, May, Sept & Oct: £153 under 26/£191 26 & over; high season

---

Bus Information

Busabout ☎ 020/7950 1661, *www.busabout.com*. European bus passes.

Eurolines ☎ 0870/514 3219, *www.gobycoach.com*. Tickets can also be purchased from any National Express agent.

June–Aug: £195 under 26/£245 26 & over) or sixty days (low season: £175/£219; shoulder season: £189/£237; high season: £227/£283). Alternatively, a **Euro Explorer** ticket allows you to travel on a Eurolines circuit comprising London–Vienna–Budapest–Prague–London for £116; tickets are valid for six months.

From April to October **Busabout** offers a hop-on, hop-off bus service, which calls in at Vienna (as well as Salzburg and Innsbruck within Austria), plus numerous other cities in western Europe (and Prague). The **Consecutive Pass** allows unlimited travel from two weeks (£169) to seven months (£699); the **Flexible Pass** gives you ten days' travel in two months (£259) or thirty days' travel in four months (£659). The buses travel along pre-determined circular routes in one direction only, so for instance you can only travel from Vienna to Venice and not vice versa. None of the Austrian cities are connected directly with one another, and buses depart only every two to four days. If you're travelling from London, you must add on the price of a London to Paris return (£30).

By car

With two or more passengers, **driving to Vienna** can work out relatively inexpensive. However, it is not the most relaxing option, unless you enjoy pounding along the motorway systems of Europe for the best part of a day and a night.

The quickest way of taking your car over to the continent is to drive to the Channel Tunnel, near Folkestone, where **Eurotunnel** operates a 24-hour service carrying cars, motorcycles, buses and their passengers to Coquelles, near Calais. At peak times services run every fifteen minutes and the journey lasts about 35 minutes. It is possible to turn up unannounced and buy your ticket at the toll booths (after exiting the M20 at junction 11a), but you'll save yourself money and a possible wait if you book in advance. Rates depend on the time of year, time of day and length of stay; for example, in peak season (weekends in July and August), it can be cheaper to travel between 10pm and 6am. A standard period return (valid for 12 months) at an off-peak time starts at around £180 (passengers included) in the low season and goes up to as much as £370 in the peak period. You can often save money by buying in advance; such tickets can be amended up to a day before travel, but are not refundable.

The alternative cross-Channel options for most travellers are the conventional **ferry and catamaran** links between Dover and Calais or Ostend. Fares are pretty similar to those via Eurotunnel, and vary enormously with the time of year, month and even day that you travel, and the size of your car. The standard off-peak fare on the Dover–Calais run, for example, is around £180 return for a carload (including passengers). On an August weekend, with no advance booking, you could pay £350 or more return. But, if you book far enough in advance (before March or April), you can reduce that fare by as much as fifty percent; tickets bought in advance are flexible, too, so you can change the timing of your crossing should you need to.

Once you've made it onto the continent, you've got something in the region of **1200km of driving** ahead of you. For Vienna, the most direct route from Ostend or Calais is via Brussels, Köln, Frankfurt and Nürnberg. It costs nothing to drive on motorways in Belgium and Germany, but to go on an Austrian autobahn, you must buy and display a sticker or *Vignette* (available at border crossings and petrol stations); the cheapest version is valid for one week and costs öS70/€5.09.

If you're travelling by car you'll need proof of ownership or a letter from the owner giving you permission to drive the car. A British or EU driving licence is fine; all other drivers must hold an International Driving Licence. You also need a country identification sticker, a red warning triangle in case you break down, a first-aid kit (all these are compulsory in Austria), and a "Green Card" for third-party insurance cover at the very least. An even better idea is to sign up with one of the national motoring organizations like the AA or the RAC, who offer continental breakdown assistance for an additional fee, and in extreme circumstances will get you and your vehicle brought back home.

Getting there from Ireland

Airlines in Ireland

Aer Lingus – *www.aerlingus.ie*: Northern Ireland ☎ 0845/973 7747; Irish Republic ☎ 01/886 8888. Aer Lingus fly direct from Dublin to London.

British Airways – *www.britishairways.com* : Northern Ireland ☎ 0845/773 3377; Irish Republic ☎ 1-800/626747. No direct flights from Ireland to Austria, but they will take you there via London (and elsewhere).

Ryanair – *www.ryanair.com*: Northern Ireland ☎ 0870/333 1231; Irish Republic ☎ 01/609 7800. Useful for cheap flights from all over the Irish Republic to London.

There are no direct flights to Vienna from Ireland. British Airways offer a Belfast–Vienna round trip via Heathrow for £300, and a Dublin–Vienna fare, also via Heathrow, of IR£300/€236 return. Low-cost flight agents such as Joe Walsh Tours and USIT can sometimes get cheaper deals with other carriers (such as Air France, KLM, Lufthansa or Aer Lingus).

The other option is to pick up a cheap flight to London for around £60 return on one of the new **discount airlines**. Regular cheap flights are available from Easyjet (*www.easyjet.com*), who fly from Belfast to Luton, Go (*www.go-fly.com*), who fly Belfast to Stansted and Ryanair (*www.ryanair.com*), who fly from all over the Republic to London. You can book online with all the above airlines and then pick up a cheap deal on to Vienna (see p.3). Given the lack of direct scheduled flights from Ireland, **city breaks** can work out pretty good value. Liffey Travel, for example, offer three nights in a three-star hotel in Vienna for IR£400/€315.

TRAVEL AGENTS AND TOUR OPERATORS IN IRELAND

Crystal Holidays, *www.crystalholidays.co.uk*: Northern Ireland ☎ 0870/848 7000; Irish Republic ☎ 01/670 8444. City breaks in Vienna.

Joe Walsh Tours, *www.joewalshtours.ie*: 69 Upper O'Connell St, Dublin 2 ☎ 01/872 2555; 8–11 Baggot St, Dublin 2 ☎ 01/676 3053; 117 Patrick St, Cork ☎ 021/277 959. General budget-fares agent.

Liffey Travel, 12 Upper O'Connell St, Dublin ☎ 01/878 8322. Package tour specialists with city breaks to Vienna.

Neenan Travel, 12 South Leinster St, Dublin 2 ☎ 01/676 5181, *www.neenantrav.ie*. General travel agent.

Thomas Cook, *www.thomascook.co.uk*: 11 Donegal Place, Belfast ☎ 028/9088 3900; 118 Grafton St, Dublin 2 ☎ 01/677 1721. Package-holiday and flight agent, with occasional discount offers.

Trailfinders, 4–5 Dawson St, Dublin 2 ☎ 01/677 7888, *www.trailfinders.com*. Competitive fares out of all Irish airports, as well as deals on hotels, insurance, tours and car rental worldwide.

USIT Now, *www.usitnow.ie*: Fountain Centre, College St, Belfast BT1 6ET ☎ 028/9032 4073; 10–11 Market Parade, Patrick St, Cork ☎ 021/270 900; 33 Ferryquay St, Derry ☎ 01504/371 888; 19 Aston Quay, Dublin 2 ☎ 01/602 1600; Victoria Place, Eyre Square, Galway ☎ 091/565 177; Central Buildings, O'Connell St, Limerick ☎ 061/415 064; 36–37 Georges St, Waterford ☎ 051/872 601. Student and youth specialists for flights and trains.

Getting there from North America

The quickest and easiest way to get to Vienna from the US or Canada is by air. Austrian Airlines and United fly direct to Vienna from several US cities, and many other airlines have flights to Vienna via other major European cities. A direct flight from the east coast of the States takes nine hours. Another option is to buy a cheap flight to London or Frankfurt and make your way overland from there (see p.3 for details of getting to Vienna from Britain).

Although in the account that follows we've quoted fares that are offered direct from the airlines, it's always worth checking out cheaper flight

---

NORTH AMERICAN SPECIALIST TOUR OPERATORS

All prices quoted below exclude taxes and are subject to change. Where applicable, accommodation quoted is for double occupancy, and round-trip flights are from New York.

Blue Danube Tours ☎1-800/268 4155, *www.bluedanubeholidays.com.* Extensive range of customized tours operating out of Toronto. Offered excursions include an eight-day Austrian panoramic tour (CDN$1965 including return flights), a twelve-day Eastern Europe tour, taking in Berlin, Prague, Budapest and Vienna (CDN$1500 land only) and an eight-day Danube cruise (CDN$870–$1900 also land only).

Delta Vacations ☎1-800/872 7786, *http://delta-air.deltavacations.com.* Fly-drives and city breaks to Vienna.

Elderhostel ☎1-877/426 8056, *www.elderhostel.org.* Specialists in educational and activity programmes, cruises and homestays for senior travellers aged 55 and up (companions may be younger). They offer courses in Vienna, as well as a Danube study cruise, all under the auspices of UNESCO.

Eastern Europe Tours ☎1-800/641 3456 or 206/448 8400, *www.imp-world-tours.com/.* Three-night city packages to Vienna start around $270 (land only).

Europe Train Tours ☎1-800/551 2085 or 914/758 1777, *www.etttours.com.* Packages centred around Vienna. Their speciality is customized tours.

Fugazy International ☎1-800/828 4488, *www.fugazytravel.com.* Group tours that include Vienna, or personalized packages to Vienna with guided tours.

Herzerl Tours ☎1-800/684 8488, *www.herzerltours.com.* Food, wine, spas and music are the focus of some of the many cultural tours on offer. A week-long Viennese cooking tour (including air fare, accommodation, classes, some meals, concert tickets and various other sundries) is $2300.

International Gay and Lesbian Travel Association ☎1-800/448 8550 or 954/776 2626, *www.iglta.com.* Trade group that will provide lists of gay-owned or gay-friendly travel agents, accommodation and other organizations.

Smolka Tours ☎1-800/722 0057 or 732/576 8813, *www.smolkatours.com.* Specialists in Austrian group or fully independent travel, including cultural, hiking and biking itineraries, music packages and opera tours.

Van Gogh Tours ☎1-800/435 6192 or 781/721-0850, *www.vangoghtours.com.* Nine-day guided bicycle tour taking in Vienna and Salzburg, at $1000 for bike rentals, meals, and accommodation in three- and four-star hotels.

FLIGHTS FROM THE USA ■ AIRLINES IN NORTH AMERICA

Air Canada ☎ 1-888/247 2262, *www.aircanada.ca*. One-stop flights from Toronto and Montréal via Frankfurt or Paris.

Air France US ☎ 1-800/237 2747, *www.airfrance.com*; Canada ☎ 1-800 /667 2747, *www.airfrance.ca*. Good-value flights daily from Toronto, New York and other major North American hubs to Vienna via Paris.

Alitalia US ☎ 1-800/223 5730, *www.alitaliausa.com*; Canada ☎ 1-800/361 8336, *www.alitalia.ca*. Flights from New York (JFK or Newark), Boston, Miami, Chicago, Los Angeles and San Francisco to Vienna with stopovers in Rome and Milan.

Austrian Airlines ☎ 1-800/843 0002, *www.austrianair.com*. The most comprehensive service to Austria, with nonstop daily flights from New York, Washington DC and Chicago. From Vienna, you can fly onwards for free to Graz, Innsbruck, Klagenfurt or Salzburg.

British Airways ☎ 1-800/247 9297, *www.britishairways.com*. Offers a frequent, reasonable service from Toronto, New York and other major cities with a stopover in London.

Delta Airlines ☎ 1-800/2 41 4141, *www.delta.com*. Very reasonably priced flights

from New York to Vienna via Paris and from New York to Munich (with onward connections).

KLM/Northwest – *www.nwa.com*: US ☎ 1-800/374 7747; Canada ☎ 1-800/361 5073. Frequent but rather pricey flights from Toronto and Montréal and major US cities to Vienna via Amsterdam.

Lauda Air ☎ 1-800/645-3880, *www.laudaair.com*. Part of Lufthansa, flies to Vienna from Miami via Munich.

Lufthansa US & Canada ☎ 1-800/399 5838; US *www.lufthana-usa.com*; Canada *www.lufthansa-ca.com*. Flies from Toronto, Montréal, New York and other major departure points to Vienna via Munich, Frankfurt and Düsseldorf.

SwissAir – *www.swissair.com*: US ☎ 1-800/221 4750; Canada ☎ 1-800/563 5954. Daily direct flights from New York, Atlanta, Boston, Chicago, Cincinnati, Los Angeles, Miami, San Francisco and Washington DC and five times a week from Montréal to Zürich with onward connections.

United Airlines ☎ 1-800/241 6522, *www.ual.com*. Regular direct flights from New York and Washington DC to Vienna.

options by contacting discount travel agents or consolidators, who buy up blocks of tickets from the airlines and sell them at a discount. It might be possible to find cheap flights on the following **websites**: Airlines of the Web – *flyaow.com*, Priceline – *www.priceline.com*, Discount Airfares Worldwide On-Line – *www.etn.nl* and Travelocity – *www.travelocity.com*.

The **high season** for travel is summer (for most airlines and tour operators June through to mid-September), and the weeks around Christmas and New Year, when fares are roughly $1450. **Low season**, when tickets can be as little as $400, is generally from the beginning of November to mid-March (excluding Christmas and New Year). The **shoulder season**, when tickets generally cost around $800, runs from mid-March to the end of May and from mid-September to the end of October.

Flights from the USA

Prices quoted below assume midweek travel (count on $40–60 extra at weekends), exclude taxes and are subject to change. Austrian Airlines offers the most extensive service, with **nonstop daily flights** from New York, Washington DC and Chicago. At the time of writing, their mid-week Apex round-trip fares from New York or Washington range from $350 to $1860, depending on season, and from Chicago, $520 to $1900, with frequent special offers including a passport fee rebate scheme (contact the Austrian National Tourist Office for North America – ANTO – for further details, *www.anto.com*). United flies from Washington DC for $540 to $1325 and from Chicago for $590 to $1370. Lauda Air flies five times weekly from Miami to Vienna via Munich, starting at $530

DISCOUNT AGENTS, CONSOLIDATORS AND TRAVEL CLUBS
IN THE US AND CANADA

Council Travel – *www.counciltravel.com*: National Reservation Center ☎1-800/226 8624 or 617/528 2091. Other offices include: 205 E 42nd St, New York, NY 10017 ☎1-800/226 8624 or 212/822 2700; 530 Bush St, Suite 700, San Francisco, CA 94108 ☎415/421 3473; 931 Westwood Blvd, Los Angeles 90024 ☎310/208 3551; 1138 13th St, Boulder, CO 80302 ☎303/447 8101; 3301 M St NW, 2nd Floor, Washington, DC 20007 ☎202/337-6464; 1153 N Dearborn St, Chicago, IL 60610 ☎312/951 0585; 3606A Chestnut St, Philadelphia, PA 19104 ☎215/382 0343. Nationwide US organization that mostly, but by no means exclusively, specializes in student/budget travel.

New Frontiers/Nouvelles Frontières – *www.NewFrontiers.com*: branches at 6 East 46th Street, New York, NY 10017 (☎1-800/677 0720 or 212/986 6006) and 1001 Sherbrook E, Suite 720, Montréal, PQ H2L 1L3 (☎514/526 8444). Other branches in LA, San Francisco and Québec City. French discount-travel firm.

STA Travel – *www.sta-travel.com*: Branches include: 7810 Hardy Drive, Suite 109, Tempe, AZ 8528410 ☎1-800/777 0112 or 1-800/781 4040; 10 Downing St, New York, NY 10014 ☎212/627 3111; 7202 Melrose Ave, Los Angeles, CA 90046 ☎323/934 8722; 36 Geary St, San Francisco, CA 94108 ☎415/391 8407; 297 Newbury St, Boston, MA 02115 ☎617/266 6014; 429 S Dearborn St, Chicago, IL 60605 ☎312/786 9050; 1905 Walnut St, Philadelphia, PA 19103 ☎215/568 7999; 317 14th Ave SE, Minneapolis, MN 55414 ☎612/615 1800. Worldwide specialists in independent travel; also student IDs, travel insurance, car rental, rail passes, etc.

Travac, 989 6th Ave, New York NY 10018 ☎1-800/872 8800, *www.thetravelsite.com*. Consolidator and charter broker, with another office in Orlando.

Travel Avenue, 10 S Riverside, Suite 1404, Chicago, IL 60606 ☎1-800/333 3335, *www.travelavenue.com*. Full-service travel agent that offers discounts in the form of rebates.

Travel Cuts – *www.travelcuts.com*: branches include: 187 College St, Toronto, ON M5T 1P7 ☎1-800/667 2887, from US ☎416/979 2406; 180 MacEwan Student Centre, University of Calgary, Calgary, AB T2N 1N4 ☎403/282 7687; 10127a 124th Street, Edmonton, AB T5N 1P5 ☎708/488 8487; 1613 rue St Denis, Montréal, PQ H2X 3K3 ☎514/843 8511; Student Union Building, University of British Columbia, Vancouver, BC V6T 1Z ☎888/ FLY CUTS or 604/822 6890; University Centre, University of Manitoba, Winnipeg, MB R3T 2N2 ☎204/269 9530. Canadian student-travel organization.

---

although they do have special offers throughout the year.

Numerous European-based airlines – Lufthansa, KLM, Swissair, British Airways, Air France and Alitalia – fly from major US cities to Vienna with **stop-offs** at their gateway cities (Frankfurt, Amsterdam, Zürich, London, Paris and Rome, respectively) and Delta Airlines offers flights to Vienna via Paris or Munich. The airlines are fairly competitive, however, and – special offers aside – you're not likely to find much difference between their standard fares and those of Austrian airlines.

Flights from Canada

Though there are **no direct flights** from Canada to Austria, there are many competitively priced one-stop options. Flights take about eleven hours from Montréal, twelve from Toronto and fourteen from Vancouver. The best deals are usually on European carriers such as Air France, Lufthansa, KLM or Swissair, which fly from major Canadian cities to **Vienna** via Paris, Frankfurt, Amsterdam and Zürich respectively. At the time of writing, KLM offer the best value, with a special low-season fare of CDN$775 (from Toronto or Montréal) or CDN$1040 (from Vancouver). In peak season, however, you'll pay around CDN$1430 (from Toronto/Montréal) or CDN$1810 (from Vancouver). Alternatively, you can fly from Toronto or Montréal with Air Canada for around CDN$1050 (low season) or CDN$1480 (high season).

Packages and city breaks

It may be worth your while checking deals with **specialist agents**. Though specialist tours often don't include air fares, they do map your itinerary and activities, fix you up with experienced guides, and – essential if you're planning your trip around any of Austria's major music festivals – organize the purchase of opera and symphony tickets and the like.

Although we've given phone numbers of specialist operators (see box on p.9), you're better off making tour reservations through your local travel agent. An agent will make all the phone calls, sort out the details and arrange flights and insurance – all at no extra cost to you.

Rail and bus passes

If you're planning on doing a decent amount of travelling in Europe, you may want to look into getting a train pass to get you to Vienna. A regular **Eurail Pass** can span from fifteen days (US$388 for under- 26s/US$554 for "first class" or over-26s) to three months (US$1089/1558). This covers seventeen countries: Austria, Belgium, Denmark, Finland, France, Germany, Greece, Hungary, Ireland (Republic), Italy, Luxembourg, Netherlands, Norway, Portugal, Spain, Sweden and Switzerland. Probably the best value for your money is the **Eurail Flexipass**, which gives you any ten days (US$458/654) or fifteen days (US$599/862) of train travel over a two-month period in any of the seventeen Eurail Pass countries.

There are further discounts if two or more people are travelling together, and a combination train/car rental pass called the **EurailDrive Pass**. There's also a **Eurail Saverpass** and a **Saver Flexipass**, which are first-class passes, valid for betweeen two and five people who must travel together on all journeys. The cost is slightly less

than for individual first-class passes. Also available are the **Austrian Railpass**, which grants any three days' unlimited train travel in Austria in a fifteen-day period (US$102/151) with up to five extra days at US$16/22 a day; the **European East Pass**, for any five days in one month (US$205) in Austria, Czech Republic, Hungary, Poland and Slovakia with the option of a maximum of five extra days at US$23 a day. For more information on the above passes visit *www.raileurope.co.uk*. For details of train passes within Austria, see p.16.

Busabout Passes are another worthwhile option (see p.7). Although there is no busabout office in the USA or Canada, tickets can be bought at either STA or Council Travel offices or on-line at *www.busabout.com* (you pay in sterling if you buy on-line). There are two types of pass: the **consecutive pass** offers unlimited travel within a certain time limit and costs (under/over 26) US$219/249 or CDN$339/379 for two weeks; US$329/359 or CDN$489/539 for three weeks; US$429/479 or CDN$649/719 for a month; US$659/739 or CDN$989/1099 for two months; US$829/909 or CDN$1229/1339 for three months and US$979/1089 or CDN$1459/1619 for a season pass (valid from April 1–Oct 31). The **flexipass**, which allows for a certain number of days' travel within a specified amount of time, costs (under/over 26): US$349/399 or CDN$539/599 for any ten days' travel in two months; US$509/569 or CDN$759/849 for any 15 days in two months; US$649/719 or CDN$969/1079 for any 20 days in three months; US$909/1009 or CDN$1339/1499 for any 30 days in four months. Additional days cost US$39/49 or CDN$59/69.

RAIL CONTACTS IN NORTH AMERICA

CIT Tours – *www.cit-tours.com*: 15 West 44th St, 10th floor, NY 10036 ☎ 1-800/ CIT TOUR; 9501 W Devon Ave, Suite 502, Rosemont, IL 60018 ☎ 1-800/223 7987; 666 Sherbrooke St, Suite 910, Montréal H3A 1G7 ☎ 1-800/361 7799 and 80 Tiverton Court, Suite 401, Markham, ON L3 OG4 ☎ 1-800/387 0711. Specialists in travel to Italy and neighbouring countries; they are also agents for Eurail and Eurostar.

Online Travel – *www.eurorail.com*: 9501 W Devon Ave, Suite 1E, Rosemont, IL 60018 ☎ 1-800/660-5300. Eurail Pass, Europass, and individual country passes for Austria.

Rail Europe – *www.raileurope.com/us*: 226 Westchester Ave, White Plains, NY 10604, US ☎ 1-800/438 7245; Canada ☎ 1-800/361 7245. Provide Eurail, Europass and point-to-point tickets between any European destinations. They also have special deals on hotels, car hire and transatlantic flights.

ScanTours – *www.scantours*: 3439 Wade St, Los Angeles, CA 90066 ☎ 1-800/223 7226 or 310/636-4656. Stock every conceivable kind of European rail pass.

Getting there from Australia and New Zealand

There's a good selection of airlines that can get you to Vienna from Australia and New Zealand. The only direct flights are with Lauda Air from Sydney to Vienna – all other airlines include either a transfer or stopover in the carrier's home city. Given the high cost of flights in general from Australasia, a "Round the World" fare can be a good option. Several rail and bus passes are worth buying before you leave home should you intend to expand your trip into Europe.

Flights

Air fares are seasonal, with **low season** running from mid-January to the end of February and October to the end of November; **high season** is mid-May to the end of August, and December to mid-January. There is no price variation during the week. Flying time is long – between twenty and thirty hours – and can be physically and mentally taxing, so you may want to consider a **stopover** en route. Flights to Europe are generally cheaper and quicker via Asia than the USA.

Tickets purchased direct from the airlines tend to be expensive – **travel agents** offer better deals and have the latest information on special offers, such as free stopovers and fly-drive/accommodation packages. Flight Centres and STA (which offer fare reductions for ISIC card-holders and

under-26s) generally have the lowest fares. You might also want to have a look on the **internet**: www.travel.com.au and www.sydneytravel.com are two sites that have a good range of discounted fares. The information is intended to act as a general guide; be sure to shop around a bit when choosing your ticket.

Fares from all eastern Australian capitals are generally the same (with Ansett and Qantas providing a free connecting service between these cities), while from Perth and Darwin you'll pay between A$100 and A$200 less via Asia, or A$200–400 more via Canada and the US. Fares from Christchurch and Wellington are between NZ$150 and NZ$300 more than from Auckland.

From Australia, Lauda Air team up with Ansett to provide a connecting service from state capitals via Sydney to Vienna for around A$1900 low season to A$2500 in the high season. In addition, several airlines can take you to Vienna via a transfer in their Asian hubs and home cities. Of these the best deals are with Alitalia for A$1500/2600 via Bangkok and Milan, and Qantas via Singapore and London or Malaysia Airlines via Kuala Lumpur, both for A$1800/2460. Swissair, KLM, Thai Airways and Singapore Airlines all offer reasonable deals for around A$2000/2500.

From New Zealand, Lauda Air, in conjunction with Air New Zealand, have a good through-service to Vienna from Auckland, Christchurch and Wellington from around NZ$2200 low season to NZ$2800 high season. Good deals on flights to Vienna are also offered by KLM, Malaysia Airlines, Alitalia, Thai Airways and Singapore Airlines, via their Asian hubs and home cities, for around NZ$2300–3000. Alternatively, United Airlines fly to Vienna via LA from Auckland starting at NZ$2600 in the low season and rising to NZ$3100 in the high season.

If you want to fly to another European gateway and then **travel overland** to Austria by road or rail, you'll find the lowest fares are with Garuda via either Jakarta or Denpasar to Frankfurt, and Sri Lankan Airlines via Colombo to either Frankfurt,

AIRLINES IN AUSTRALIA AND NEW ZEALAND

Air New Zealand – *www.airnz.com*: Australia ☎ 13/24 76; New Zealand ☎ 0800/737 000 or 09/357 3000.
Code-shares with Lauda to provide a through service from Auckland, Wellington and Christchurch to Vienna.

Alitalia – *www.alitalia.it*: Australia ☎ 02/9244 2400; New Zealand ☎ 09/302 1452. Three flights per week from Sydney to Vienna via Bangkok and Milan (code-share with Qantas).

Ansett Australia – *www.ansett.com.au*: Australia ☎ 13/14 14 or 02/9352 6707; New Zealand ☎ 09/336 2364. Code-shares with Swiss Air and Lauda to provide a through service from Sydney, Brisbane, Melbourne, Adelaide and Perth to Vienna.

Garuda Australia ☎ 1300/365 330; New Zealand ☎ 09/366 1862 or 1800/128 510. Three flights a week from Sydney, Brisbane, Cairns, Darwin, Melbourne, Adelaide, Perth and Auckland to Amsterdam and Frankfurt with a transfer/stopover in Jakarta/Denpasar.

KLM – *www.klm.com*: Australia ☎ 1300/303 747; New Zealand ☎ 09/309 1782. Two flights a week from Sydney via either Singapore and Amsterdam or LA and Amsterdam, or from Auckland to Vienna via Singapore and Amsterdam.

Lauda Air – *www.laudaair.com*: Australia ☎ 1800/642 438 or 02/9251 6155; New Zealand ☎ 09/308 3368. Three flights a week to Vienna via Sydney from Brisbane, Melbourne, Perth and Auckland. Code-shares with Ansett and Air New Zealand.

Malaysia Airlines – *www.malaysiaair.com*: Australia ☎ 13/26 27; New Zealand ☎ 09/373 2741 or 008/657 472. Twice-weekly flights from Sydney, Brisbane, Darwin, Melbourne, Adelaide, Perth and Auckland to Vienna, with a transfer or overnight stop in Kuala Lumpur.

Qantas – *www.qantas.com.au*: Australia ☎ 13/13 13; New Zealand ☎ 09/357 8900 or 0800/808 767. Daily flights from Sydney, Melbourne, Darwin, Cairns and Brisbane, and several flights a week from Adelaide, to Vienna via London.

Singapore Airlines – *www.singaporeair.com*: Australia ☎ 13/10 11 or 02/9350 0262; New Zealand ☎ 09/303 2129 or 0800/808 909. Several flights a week from Sydney, Brisbane, Melbourne, Perth and Auckland to Vienna with a transfer in Singapore.

Sri Lankan Airlines Australia ☎ 02/9244 2234; New Zealand ☎ 09/308 3353. Three flights a week from Sydney and Auckland to London, Rome, Frankfurt, Paris and Zürich with either a transfer or an overnight stop in Colombo.

Swissair – *www.swissair.com*: Australia ☎ 02/9232 1744 or 1800/221 339; New Zealand ☎ 09/358 3216. Several flights a week from Sydney, Brisbane, Melbourne, Perth and Auckland to Vienna via Zürich. Code-shares with Ansett.

Thai Airways – *www.thaiair.com*: Australia ☎ 1300/651 960; New Zealand ☎ 09/377 3886. Several flights a week from Sydney, Brisbane, Cairns, Melbourne, Perth and Auckland to Vienna via Bangkok.

Zürich, Paris or Rome from A$1500/NZ$1900 (low season) to A$1900/NZ$2400 (high season).

If you're planning to visit Vienna as part of an extended trip, a **Round-the-World** ticket, valid for a year, can be very good value – often working out just a little more than a standard return ticket. There are a number of airline combinations to choose from that include Vienna, offering a range of stopovers: for example, the cheapest is a straightforward fare (no backtracking and side trips) from Sydney or Auckland to Singapore/Bangkok/Hong Kong, Frankfurt/Milan/Zürich, Vienna, London, New York/Toronto, LA/Vancouver and back home, which starts at A$2200/NZ$2600 during the low season, rising to A$2600/NZ$3100 in the high season. More flexible mileage-based tickets – such as the "Star Alliance 1" offered by Ansett Australia/Air New Zealand/United/Thai, starting at A$2500/NZ$2900, and "One World Explorer" by Qantas/British Airways/American Airlines/Cathay which starts at A$2600/NZ$3000 – allow side trips, backtracking and open-jaw travel.

Specialist tours

If you're interested in Austrian art and architecture or music, and prefer to have all the arrangements made for you before you leave, then

United Airlines – *www.ual.com*: Australia ☎ 13/17 77; New Zealand ☎ 09/379 3800.

Several flights a week from Sydney and Auckland to Vienna via Los Angeles.

DISCOUNT TRAVEL AGENTS IN AUSTRALIA AND NEW ZEALAND

Anywhere Travel, 345 Anzac Parade, Kingsford, Sydney ☎ 02/9663 0411, *anywhere@ozemail.com.au*. Discounted flights, as well as accommodation, tours and car rental.

Budget Travel, 16 Fort St, Auckland, plus branches around the city ☎ 09/366 0061 or 0800/808 040. Long-established agent dealing with budget airfares and accommodation packages.

Destinations Unlimited, 220 Queen St, Auckland ☎ 09/373 4033. Discount fares plus a good selection of tours and holiday packages.

Flight Centre – *www.flightcentre.com.au*: 82 Elizabeth St, Sydney, Australia ☎ 02/9235 3522, plus branches nationwide (for nearest branch ☎ 13/16 00); 350 Queen St, Auckland, New Zealand ☎ 09/358 4310, plus branches nationwide. Competitive discounts on airfares, and a wide range of package holidays and adventure tours as well as rail passes.

Northern Gateway, 22 Cavenagh St, Darwin ☎ 08/8941 1394, *oztravel@norgate.com.au*. Low-cost flights from Darwin.

STA Travel – *www.statravel.com.au*: fastfare telesales Australia ☎ 1300/360 960; 855 George St, Sydney; 256 Flinders St, Melbourne; other offices in state capitals and major universities (nearest branch ☎ 13/17 76); fastfare telesales New Zealand ☎ 09/366 6673; 10 High St, Auckland ☎ 09/309 0458, plus branches in Wellington, Christchurch, Dunedin, Palmerston

North, Hamilton and at major universities. Fare discounts for students and those under 26, as well as visas, student cards and travel insurance.

Student Uni Travel, 92 Pitt St, Sydney ☎ 02/9232 8444, *sydney@backpackers.net*; plus branches in Brisbane, Cairns, Darwin, Melbourne and Perth. Student/youth discounts and travel advice.

Thomas Cook – *www.thomascook.com.au*: direct telesales Australia ☎ 1800/801 002175; Pitt St, Sydney ☎ 02/9231 2877; 257 Collins St, Melbourne ☎ 03/9282 0222; plus branches in other state capitals (local branch ☎ 13/17 71); New Zealand office, 191 Queen St, Auckland ☎ 09/379 3920. Low-cost flights, also tours, accommodation, travellers' cheques, and bus and rail passes.

Trailfinders – *www.trailfinder.com.au*: 8 Spring St, Sydney ☎ 02/9247 7666; 91 Elizabeth St, Brisbane ☎ 07/3229 0887; Hides corner, Shield St, Cairns ☎ 07/4041 1199. Independent travel and long-haul flight specialist.

Travel.com.au, 76–80 Clarence St, Sydney ☎ 02/9249 5444 or 1800/000 447, *www.travel.com.au*. Online flight discounts.

USIT Beyond, cnr Shortland St and Jean Batten Place, Auckland ☎ 09/379 4224 or 0800/788 336; plus branches in Christchurch, Dunedin, Palmerston North, Hamilton and Wellington. Student/youth travel specialists.

---

seeking the help of a **specialist agent** is a good way to plan your trip. Unfortunately, there are few pre-packaged tours that include airfares from Australasia, but most specialist agents will be able to assist with flight arrangements as well. In turn, many of the tours we've listed (see box on p.16) can also be arranged through your local travel agent.

Bus and rail passes

If you're planning to visit Vienna as part of an extensive European trip, it's worth looking into one of a variety of **Eurail** passes, which are valid in seventeen European countries.

The **Eurail Youthpass** (for under-26s) costs A\$733/NZ\$915 for 15 consecutive days, A\$942/NZ\$1175 for 21 days, A\$1176/NZ\$1470 for one month, A\$1665/NZ\$2080 for two months and A\$2055/NZ\$2570 for three months; if you're 26 or over you'll have to buy a **first-class pass**, available in 15-day (A\$1046/NZ\$1307), 21-day (A\$1355/NZ\$1695), one-month (A\$1680/ NZ\$2100), two-month (A\$2378/NZ\$2970) and three-month (A\$2940/NZ\$3675) increments.

The **Eurail Flexipass** is good for a certain number of travel days in a two-month period and also comes in youth and first-class versions:

ten days cost A$865/1234 or NZ$1080/1542, fifteen days A$1131/1627 or NZ$1415/2033. A scaled-down version of the Flexipass, the **Europass** allows travel in France, Germany, Italy, Spain and Switzerland for (youth/first class) A$440/657 or NZ$550/821 for five days in two months, or up to A$968/1374 or NZ$1210/1717 for fifteen days in two months; there's also the option of adding adjacent "associate" countries (Austria, Hungary, Benelux, Portugal and Greece) for around A$85/NZ$110 per country (the respective cost shrinks with the number of associate countries added). There's also a **Eurail Saverpass**, **Saver Flexipass** and **Euro Saverpass**. These are first-class passes, valid for between two and five people who must travel together on all journeys. The cost is slightly less than the full first-class passes.

If you just want to explore Austria on its own, the **Austrian Railpass** allows for unlimited travel for three days in fifteen for (under/over 26) A$230/336 or NZ$289/420. Rail passes can be obtained from CIT World Travel, Flight Centres (see box p.15), or from Rail Plus – Australia: Level 3, 459 Little Collins St, Melbourne VIC 3000 ☎1300/555 003 or 03/9642 8644, *info@railplus .com.au*; New Zealand: Level 2, 6 Parnell Road, Auckland 1 ☎09/303 2484.

Busabout's hop-on hop-off bus passes cost around (youth/adult) A$359/399 or NZ$449/495 for fifteen days, A$669/749 or NZ$835/935 for one month and A$1029/1159 or NZ$1285/1449 for two months, see p.7 for more details. Bus passes are available from **Trailfinders** (see box on p.15), and **Busabout Europe**, 27 Belgrave St, Manly NSW ☎1300/301 776.

SPECIALIST AGENTS

Adventure World *www.adventureworld.com .au*: 73 Walker St, North Sydney, Australia ☎02/9956 7766 or 1300/363 055; plus branches in Adelaide, Brisbane, Melbourne and Perth; 101 Great South Rd, Remuera, Auckland, NZ ☎09/524 5118.
Vienna city packages from A$310/NZ$385 (twin share) including accommodation, city tour and concert tickets; also day tours from A$210/NZ$260 and the Vienna Woods from A$75/NZ$90. Also agents for Lauda Air and an array of international adventure companies that offer trips to Austria.

Australians Studying Abroad, 1st Floor, 970 Armadale, Victoria ☎03/9509 1955 or 1800/645 755, *www.asatravinfo.com.au*. Twenty-day all-inclusive tours delving into the art and culture of the Habsburg cities of Vienna, Prague and Budapest, for around A$6000/NZ$7690 (land only).

CIT, 263 Clarence St, Sydney ☎02/9267 1255, *www.cittravel.com.au*; plus offices in Melbourne, Brisbane, Adelaide and Perth. Hotel and tour packages, including round-trip coach tours from Vienna via Graz, Salzburg and Melk, from A$990/NZ$1230 (twin share); also arranges rail passes and car rental.

Danube Travel, 800 Glenhuntly Rd, Caulfield, Melbourne (☎03/9530 0888). Extensive range of tours and accommodation throughout Austria, from budget to first class, including Danube cruises from A$130/NZ$160 and hydrofoil trips from Vienna to Budapest for A$150/NZ$185.

European Travel Office, 122 Rosslyn St, West Melbourne ☎03/9329 8844; Suite 410/368 Sussex St, Sydney ☎02/9267 7714; 407 Great South Rd, Auckland ☎09/525 3074. Two-night accommodation and concert packages from A$300/NZ$375 (twin share); half-day Vienna city tours from A$75/NZ$90; and day boat trips on the Danube from A$150/NZ$185.

Explore Holidays, 55 Blaxland Road, Ryde NSW ☎02/9857 6200, *www.exploreholidays.com.au*. Offer three night city-stays in Vienna from A$470/NZ$585 (includes a sightseeing tour, an opera ticket and a concert ticket); Vienna hotel accommodation from A$70/NZ$90 (twin share); and car rental.

Red tape and visas

Citizens of EU countries need only a valid national identity card to enter Austria. Since Britain has no identity card, however, British citizens have to take a passport. EU citizens can stay for as long as they want, but if they're planning on staying permanently they should register with the local police. Citizens of the US, Canada, New Zealand and Australia require a passport, but no visa, and can stay up to three months.

Visa requirements do change, however, and it is always advisable to check the current situation before leaving home. A list of Austrian embassies abroad is given below; addresses of foreign embassies and consulates in Vienna are given on p.339.

Customs

Customs and duty-free restrictions vary throughout Europe, with subtle differences even within the European Union. British and Irish travellers returning home directly from another EU country do not have to make a declaration to customs at their place of entry. In other words, British and Irish citizens can effectively take back as much **duty-paid** wine or beer as they can carry, the guideline limits being 90 litres of wine (of which no more than 60 litres should be sparkling), 110 litres of beer, 800 cigarettes or 1kg of tobacco.

Residents of the US and Canada can take up to 200 cigarettes or 50 cigars and one litre of spirits (or 2.25 litres of wine, or three litres of beer) back home. **Australian** citizens must limit themselves to 200 cigarettes or 250g of tobacco and just one litre of wine or spirits, while **New Zealanders** are allowed 200 cigarettes or 250g of tobacco, 4.5 litres of beer or wine, and one litre of spirits. Again, if in doubt consult the relevant embassy.

AUSTRIAN EMBASSIES/CONSULATES ABROAD

Australia 12 Talbot St, Forrest, Canberra ACT 2603 ☎ 02/6295 1533, *www.austriaemb.org.au*. Consulates in Adelaide, Brisbane, Cairns, Melbourne, Perth & Sydney.

Canada 445 Wilbrod St, Ottawa, Ontario KIN 6M7 ☎ 613/789 1444, *www.austro.org*. Consulates in Calgary, Halifax, Montréal, Regina, Toronto, Vancouver & Winnipeg.

Ireland 15 Ailesbury Court, 93 Ailesbury Rd, Dublin 4 ☎ 01/269 4577, *austroam@iol.ie*.

New Zealand Consular General: Level 2, Willbank House, 57 Willis St, Wellington

☎ 04/499 6393. Consulate: 98 Kirtchner Road, Milford, Auckland 1 ☎ 09/489 8249.

South Africa 1109 Duncan St, Momentum Office Park, 0011 Brooklyn, Pretoria ☎ 460 3361. Consulates in Durban, Johannesburg & Cape Town.

UK 18 Belgrave Mews West, London SW1 8HU ☎ 020/7235 3731, *www.austria.org.uk*.

USA 3524 International Court NW, Washington, DC 20008 ☎ 202/895 6700, *www.austria.org*. Consulates in many US cities including Boston, Chicago, Houston, Honolulu, Los Angeles, Miami, New York & San Francisco.

Insurance

A typical travel insurance policy usually provides cover for the loss of baggage, tickets and – up to a certain limit – cash or cheques, as well as medical emergencies and cancellation or curtailment of your journey. Many companies will also tailor policies for you if you plan on going skiing, or if you want to take part in other "dangerous" sports or adventure activities.

Read the small print and benefits tables of prospective policies carefully; **coverage** can vary wildly for roughly similar premiums. Many policies can be chopped and changed to exclude coverage you don't need – for example, sickness and accident benefits can often be excluded or included at will. If you do take medical coverage, ascertain whether benefits will be paid as treatment proceeds, or only after you return home, and whether there is a 24-hour medical emergency number. When securing baggage cover, make sure that the per-article limit – typically under £500 equivalent – will cover your most valuable possession.

If you need to make a **claim**, you should keep receipts for medicines and medical treatment, and in the event you have anything stolen, you *must* obtain an official statement from the police. Few insurers will arrange on-the-spot payments in the event of a major expense; you will usually be reimbursed only after going home (see p.22 for what to do if you lose your credit cards, travellers' cheques or money). Note that debit, credit and charge cards often have certain levels of medical or other insurance included, and you may automatically get travel insurance if you use the card to pay for your trip.

US and Canadian travellers may well already be covered and so should check their insurance policy before buying anything extra. Canadian provincial health plans typically provide some

---

ROUGH GUIDES TRAVEL INSURANCE

Rough Guides now offers its own **travel insurance**, customized for our readers by a leading UK broker and backed by a Lloyds underwriter. It's available for anyone, of any nationality, travelling anywhere in the world.

There are two main Rough Guide insurance plans: **Essential**, for basic, no-frills cover, starting at £11.75 for two weeks; and **Premier** – with more generous and extensive benefits – starting at £12.50. Unlike many policies, the Rough Guides schemes are calculated by the day, so if you're travelling for 27 days rather than a month, that's all you pay for. Alternatively, you can take out annual **multi-trip insurance**, which covers you for any number of trips throughout the year (with a maximum of 60 days for any one trip), starting at £47.26 (European) and £83.99 (worldwide). If you intend to be away for the whole year, the **Adventurer** policy will cover you for 365 days from £90. Each plan can be supplemented with a "Hazardous Activities Premium" if you plan to indulge in sports considered dangerous, such as skiing, scuba-diving or trekking. Rough Guides also does good deals for older travellers, and will insure you up to any age.

For a **policy quote**, call the Rough Guides Insurance Line on UK freefone ☎ 0800/015 0906, or, if you're calling from outside Britain, on ☎ 0044/1243 621 046. Alternatively, you can get a quote or buy online at *www.roughguides.com/insurance*.

---

overseas medical coverage, although they are unlikely to pick up the full tab in the event of a mishap. Holders of official student/teacher/youth cards are entitled to accident coverage and hospital in-patient benefits. Students may also find that their student health coverage extends during the vacations and for one term beyond the date of last enrolment. Homeowners' or renters' insurance often covers theft or loss of documents, money and valuables while overseas.

Information and maps

There are branches of the **Austrian National Tourist Office in most large foreign countries** (for current addresses, see below), although many only deal with the public by telephone rather than admit personal callers – ring ahead and check before trying to visit them in person. The staff are, as a rule, very helpful, and can usually supply brochures, accommodation lists and maps, providing you're focused about your interests.

The main **tourist office** of the Vienna Tourist Board or *Wiener Tourismusverband* is behind the opera house on Albertinaplatz (daily 9am–7pm; ☎211 14-222; phone enquiries Mon–Fri 8am–4pm only; *www.info.wien.at*). The staff should be able to answer most enquiries, but it's a small office, so it's best to be specific about what you want. For more on the city's tourist offices and listings magazines, see *Introducing the City*, p.33.

Maps

The maps in this guide, together with the untold number of **free city plans** you'll pick up from tourist offices and hotels, should be sufficient to help you find your way around. For something more durable, the best maps are by Freytag & Berndt, who produce a whole variety of plans of the city, marked with bus and tram routes. The 1:20,000 spiral bound *Buchplan Wien* map is the most comprehensive. Alternatively, Falkplan produce an attractive fold-out map, with a good large-scale section of the Innere Stadt.

To get hold of either of the above **maps of Vienna** in the UK, try Stanfords (12–14 Long Acre,

---

London WC2E 9LP ☎020/7836 1321, www.stanfords.co.uk). In North America, Rand McNally should be able to help (call ☎1-800/333 0136 ext 2111 for the address of your nearest store, or for direct-mail maps; www.randmcnally.com). In Australia and New Zealand, Mapland (372 Little Bourke St,

Melbourne ☎03/9670 4383, www.mapland .com.au) is worth contacting, as is Speciality Maps (46 Albert St, Auckland ☎09/307 2217, www.ubd-online.co.nz/maps). Otherwise, you can wait until you get to Vienna, where you can visit the flagship store of Freytag & Berndt – see p.335 for details.

VIENNA AND AUSTRIA ON THE NET

Specific websites for the museums, galleries, sights, hotels and restaurants mentioned in the Guide are listed within the text at the relevant point. In addition, a few useful, quite general websites are reviewed below.

Austrian Encyclopaedia *www.aeiou.at*
Website based on the Austrian Encyclopaedia, so should give the answer to any Austrian query you have. You can navigate in English, though occasionally source material is in German only. Exhaustive links.

Austria – general information
www.tiscover.com
An excellent site for tourist information, with almost everything in English and German. Can book accommodation, including self-catering and campsites, flights and car hire online. Updated regularly so it can tell you what's happening in the next few weeks/months in Vienna.

Austrian National Tourist Board
www.anto.com and *www.austro-tourism.at*
The official tourist board websites. Not much better than looking at the brochures.

Austrian Search Engine
www.austrosearch.at
The best Austrian-specific search engine on the

Net. Not only can you get three-day weather forecasts and up-to-date Austrian news, you can join chat groups, and find links for all sorts of Austro-nonsense.

Austria Today *www.austriatoday.at*
Excellent web site for the weekly English-language newspaper, with all the latest news and listings as well as lots of useful general tourist information.

Vienna Tourist Board *www.info.wien.at*
The official Vienna tourist board's English/German website is very good indeed and leads to other useful sites. Information on everything from second-hand bookshops to late-night eating options and art exhibitions. Can also book hotel accommodation online.

Wiener Zeitung *www.wienerzeitung.at*
Website of the official Vienna city authorities newspaper. The English version gives you lots of tourist information and has plenty of useful links.

Costs, money and banks

Although Vienna is by no means a budget destination, it is not quite as expensive as people imagine. It's true to say that there are a few bargain deals to be had, and even though coffee and cake at a traditional coffeehouse will cost you dear, restaurants on the whole are moderately priced, as are rooms in the city's pensions and hotels. That said, Austria is one of the wealthiest countries in the world, and if you have the money, Vienna has plenty of luxury shops, hotels and restaurants ready to relieve you of it.

Money

Until it is superseded by the Euro in 2002, the **currency** in Austria remains the Austrian Schilling (österreichische Schilling). It is abbreviated to öS within Austria (and within this book), but is also often written as ATS or AS. Each Schilling is divided into one hundred Groschen. Coins come in the denominations öS20, öS10, öS5 and öS1, plus 50 and 10 Groschen; notes are öS5000, öS1000, öS500, öS100, öS50 and öS20.

Average costs

Accommodation will be your biggest single expense, with hostel beds going for around öS200/€14.54 (£10/US$15), and the cheapest reasonable double rooms in a pension about öS600–800/€36.34–54.50 (£30–40/US$45–60). A double in a more comfortable pension or hotel is more likely to be around öS800–1200/€54.50–87.20 (£40–60/US$60–90).

After you've paid for your own room, count on a **minimum** of £20/$30 a day, which will buy you breakfast, a take-away lunch, a budget dinner and a beer or coffee, but not much else. Eating sit-down meals twice a day, visiting museums and drinking more beer and coffee (espe-

---

THE EURO

Austria is one of twelve European Union countries who have changed over to a single currency, the euro (€). The transition period, which began on January 1, 1999, is, however, lengthy: euro notes and coins are not scheduled to be issued until January 1, 2002, with Schillings remaining in place for cash transactions, at a fixed rate of öS13.7603 to 1 euro, until they are scrapped entirely at the end of February 2002.

Even before euro cash appears in 2002, you can opt to pay in euros by credit card and you can get travellers' cheques in euros – you should not be charged commission for changing them in any of the twelve countries in the euro zone (also known as "Euroland"), nor for changing from any of the old Euroland currencies to any other (French francs to Schillings, for example).

Euro notes will be issued in denominations of 5, 10, 20, 50, 100, 200 and 500 euros, and coins in denominations of 1, 2, 5, 10, 20 and 50 cents and 1 and 2 euros.

All prices in this book are given in Schillings and the exact equivalent in euros. When the new currency takes over completely, prices are likely to be rounded off, and if decimalization in the UK was anything to go by, rounded up.

For information on the British government's current line on the euro visit *www.euro.gov.uk*; for the Irish view see *www.emuaware.forfas.ie*; and for the Austrian position go to *www.oenb.at*.

---

cially coffee) will cost you more like £40/$60 a day; if you want to go to the opera or a nightclub, then you could easily double that figure.

Tipping is expected in the more upmarket hotels, taxis and in most cafés, bars and restaurants, usually up to the nearest öS5 or öS10 depending on how much you've spent and how good the service was. In more expensive restaurants, you'll find the bill arrives with a fifteen percent service charge already tacked on to the total.

Banks and changing money

Banking hours vary, but are generally Monday to Friday 8am to 12.30pm and 1.30 or 2pm to 3 or 4pm. Banks stay open until 5.30pm on Thursdays. Outside these hours, you will have to rely on the **Wechselstube**, or exchange booths. Those with the longest hours are found at the train stations and the airport (see box below). There are also 24-hour automatic exchange machines dotted around the city centre, accepting notes of most major currencies, although commission rates will be more punitive than those charged in a bank.

Travellers' cheques and plastic money

In small pensions, restaurants and shops, you'll find that **cash** is often either the sole or the preferred method of payment. Make sure you always have a supply of cash on you, otherwise it's perfectly possible to carry your money in the form of **debit/credit cards** and withdraw money from cashpoints. Although not as convenient, **travellers' cheques** are still a good, safe option

---

Exchange Booths and Banks

Banks
(with 24hr automatic exchange machines)
Bank Austria, Stephansplatz 2.
Creditanstalt, Karntnerstrasse 7.
Die erste Bank, Graben 21.

Exchange booths
Airport (arrivals: daily 8am–11pm; departures: daily 6am–11pm).
Main Post Office, Fleischmarkt 19 (24hr).
Südbahnhof (daily: May–Oct 6.30am–10pm; Nov–April 6.30am–9pm).
Westbahnhof (daily 7am–10pm).

---

and are accepted pretty much everywhere. They're available for a small commission (usually one percent of the amount ordered) from any bank and some building societies, whether or not you have an account, and from branches of American Express and Thomas Cook. Most banks keep Austrian Schillings on hand for over-the-counter exchange, so you can bring a small supply with you.

The majority of banks in Vienna will have English-language **ATMs** (cash machines or bankomats) which accept foreign debit and credit cards. Look out for branches of Bank Austria, Creditanstalt or Die erste Bank, and make sure you have a PIN number for your card. The daily limit for taking cash out of a bankomat is öS5000/€363.36. As usual, **charge cards** such as Amex and Diners are not as widely accepted as debit/credit cards, and tend to be restricted to top-end purchases.

If you have an Australian or New Zealand key or debit card, arrange for Cirrus, Plus or Maestro withdrawal facilities to be added before you leave home. You will be charged for withdrawing cash but the rates compare favourably.

Emergencies

When you buy your **travellers' cheques**, make a note of the emergency phone number given. On your trip, keep a record of all cheque serial numbers and note which ones you spend – and report any loss or theft immediately. All being well, you should get the missing cheques reissued within a couple of days. Things can be trickier if you lose your **credit card**: your bank should be able to give you details of the number to call if this happens, but you won't be provided with a replacement card until you get home.

Assuming you know someone who is prepared to send you the money, the quickest way to have funds sent out to you in an emergency is **wiring money** (see box opposite). If you have a few days' leeway, you can simply get your bank to wire your money to an Austrian bank, a process that shouldn't take more than a couple of days. If you can last out for a week, then an **international money order**, exchangeable at any post office, is by far the cheapest way of sending money.

If you're in really dire straits, you can get in touch with your consulate in Vienna, who will usually let you make one phone call home free of charge, and will – in worst cases only – repatriate you, but will never, under any circumstances, lend money.

WIRING MONEY FROM ABROAD

Wiring money is a fast but expensive way to send and receive money abroad, and should be considered only in emergency situations. The sum wired should be available for collection in Austrian Schillings/euros from the company's local agent within a few minutes of being sent via Western Union or Moneygram; both charge on a sliding scale, so sending larger amounts of cash is better value. Thomas Cook have a much cheaper flat rate but it takes 1–2 days for the money to arrive. You should always check with your bank before travelling to see if they have reciprocal arrangements with any banks in Austria.

Agents vary country to country; in Britain, for instance, Western Union is at Going Places travel agents and some newsagents and chemists, while Moneygram is at Thomas Cook offices, Eurochange and all post offices. Rates for both are broadly similar: £12–14 to send £100, or £33–37 for £500, for example, while from the US, wiring US$500 will cost about US$40. Thomas Cook's Telegraphic Transfer service from the UK costs £15 plus one percent of the amount to be sent (with a minimum charge of £25). Thomas Cook can also credit foreign bank accounts for the same fee (2–3 days).

Western Union *www.westernunion.com*
UK: ☎ 0800/833 833
Eire: ☎ 1800/395 395
Australia: ☎ 1800/649 565
New Zealand: ☎ 09/270 0050
USA & Canada: ☎ 1-800/325 6000

Moneygram *www.moneygram.com*
UK: ☎ 00800/018 0104
Eire ☎ 00800 666 39472
Australia: ☎ 1800/230 100

New Zealand: ☎ 0800/262 263
USA & Canada: ☎ 1-800/926 9400

Thomas Cook *www.thomascook.com*
UK: ☎ 01733/318922
Eire: ☎ 01/677 1721
Australia: ☎ 02/9231/287
Canada: ☎ 1-888/8234 7328
New Zealand: ☎ 09/379 3920
USA: ☎ 1-800/287 7362

Communications and the media

The main post office (*Hauptpostamt*) in Vienna is at Fleischmarkt 19, A-1010, just off Schwedenplatz. It's open 24 hours a day, seven days a week, as are the post offices in the Westbahnhof, Südbahnhof and Franz-Josef-Bahnhof, though not the one at the airport (open Mon–Fri 7.30am–8pm). All other post offices – identified by a yellow sign saying *Postamt* – have regular opening hours (Mon–Fri 8am–noon & 2–6pm), with the main ones eschewing their lunch break and opening on Saturdays, 8am to 10am.

Air mail (*Flugpost*) between Austria and the UK usually takes three or four days, about five days to reach the US, and a week to ten days to

Australia and New Zealand. Stamps (*Briefmarken*) for postcards within the EU are obtainable from tobacconists (*Tabak*), though for anything more complicated or further afield, you'll probably have to go to a post office, where they like to weigh everything.

Poste restante (*Postlagernd*) letters can be sent to any post office, if you know the address. At the main post office (see above) go to the counter marked *Postlagernde Sendungen*. Mail should be addressed using this term rather than "poste restante"; it will be held for thirty days (remember to take your passport when going to collect it).

Telephones

Austrian **phone booths** are easy enough to spot – usually dark green with a bright yellow roof and logo – and to use, most having instructions in four languages (including English). The dialling tone is a short followed by a long pulse; the ringing tone is long and regular; engaged is short and rapid. At the time of going to press the minimum charge is öS2, but you're likely to need much more to make even a **local call**, since telephone calls are still quite expensive despite the recent deregulation.

You can make an **international call** from any phone, though it's easier to do so with a **phone card** (*Telefonkarte*) rather than from a coin-oper-

---

DIALLING CODES

To Austria
From Australia and New Zealand ☎ 0011 43
From Britain and Ireland ☎ 00 43
From North America ☎ 011 43
Note that the Vienna city code is 1 when phoning from abroad; but 0222 when phoning from elsewhere in Austria.

From Austria
Australia ☎ 0061
Ireland ☎ 00353

New Zealand ☎ 0064
North America ☎ 001
UK ☎ 0044

Information
Local directory enquiries ☎ 1611
International operator ☎ 1616

You can also view the **Vienna telephone directory** online at *www.etb.at*, and the yellow pages at *www.gelbe-seiten.at*.

---

ated phone. *Telefonkarten* are available from all post offices, tobacconists and some other shops, currently in öS50, öS100 and öS200 denominations. The other option is to go to one of the 24-hour post offices and use their **direct phone service** facility: a booth will be allocated to you from the counter marked *Ferngespräche*, which is where you pay once you've finished. The post office is also the place to go if you want to make a collect call (*Rückgespräch*).

Mobile phones work on the GSM European standard. Some Viennese are very keen on mobiles (known as a *Handy* in German), though they're nothing like as common as in London or New York. If you're taking your mobile, make sure you have made the necessary "roaming" arrangements before you leave home – which may involve paying a hefty (refundable) deposit.

The Viennese phone system is currently being overhauled, so don't worry that the **telephone numbers** within the city vary in length. One further peculiarity is those numbers which end in -0. It's not necessary to dial the final 0, which simply signals that it's a line with **direct dial extension numbers** (*Durchwahlen*). If you know the extension you want, or it's given as part of the number, then you may dial it immediately after the main number.

Email and the internet

Use of the **internet** by organizations and individuals is highly developed in Austria. However, facilities for those wishing to send or receive emails whilst away are fairly limited. Several cafés and bookshops have internet access, but **cybercafés** themselves are by no means commonplace. We've listed the more interesting or useful internet cafés on p.315. As for **websites**, they are listed throughout the text and we've also gathered together a few useful general sites on Vienna and Austria on p.20.

The media

The newspaper stands in the city centre stock a variety of **English-language newspapers**. You can usually get the European edition of the British broadsheet *The Guardian* (*www.guardian.co.uk*), printed in Frankfurt, by mid-morning the same day. Similarly, the *International Herald Tribune* (*www.iht.com*) is widely available the same day, and contains a useful distilled English version of the *Frankfurter*

Allgemeine, also available online at *www.faz.de*. Other papers tend to be a day or so old. The weekly English-language newspaper *Austria Today* is available at most news stands, and gives a fairly dull rundown of Austrian news, plus a few listings.

Heavily subsidized by the state, the **Austrian press** is for the most part conservative and pretty uninspiring. Nearly half the population reads the reactionary *Neue Kronen Zeitung* tabloid, while plenty of the rest read another right-wing tabloid, *Kurier*. Of the qualities, *Der Standard*, printed on pink paper, tends to support the Social Democrats (SPÖ) while the rather strait-laced *Die Presse* backs the conservative People's Party (ÖVP). One peculiarly Austrian phenomenon are the bags of newspapers you'll find hung from lampposts. Law-abiding Austrians take one and put their money in the slot provided.

Vienna boasts a good weekly **listings** tabloid, *Falter* (*www.falter.at*), which is lively, politicized and critical, and comes out on a Friday. Although it's entirely in German, it's easy enough to decipher the listings. The national dailies also have limited listings of what's on in Vienna. Nearly all cafés and bars, and, in particular, the traditional Viennese coffeehouses, have a wide selection of newspapers and magazines for patrons to browse through, occasionally even English-language ones.

Austrian **television** is unlikely to win any international awards for cutting-edge programming or presentation. There are just two state-run channels: ORF 1 and ORF 2, with no independent competition at all as yet. As a result, Austrians tend to tune into German channels such as ARD and ZDF for a bit of variety. Many hotels and pensions have satellite TV, bringing the joys of CNN and MTV straight to your room.

The state-run **radio** channels all feature a lot of chattering, though Ö1 (87.8/92FM) offers some decent classical music, in addition to news in English at 8am, followed shortly after by news in French. The state-run English-language Blue Danube Radio was axed in 2000 after over twenty years of service, to be replaced with FM4 (103.8FM), an anodyne soft-rock music station with hourly news and weather in English. The BBC World Service (*www.bbc.co.uk/worldservice*) broadcasts in English on 100.8FM in Vienna, though you can also receive it on short wave. Also available on short wave is Radio Austria International, which broadcasts Austrian news in English, Spanish and Russian.

Opening hours, public holidays and festivals

In general, Vienna's museums and galleries are open from Tuesday to Sunday from 10am to 6pm, though there are no hard and fast rules, so check in the margins beside each entry within the text of the Guide before setting out.

Churches in the centre of the city tend to stay open daily from 7am to 7pm or later, but many of those out in the suburbs only allow you to peep in from the foyer, except just before and after Mass. Again, if a church has set opening times, we've said so in the margins beside the text of the Guide.

Until very recently, all shops had to conform to the following **opening hours**: Monday to Friday 9am to 6pm, with late shopping on Thursdays, and Saturday 8am to noon – except on the first Saturday of the month (known as the *Langersamstag*, or "long Saturday"), when hours are 8am to 5pm. This is now more relaxed and shops – particularly in the centre – tend to open all day every Saturday, though many – mainly those in the suburbs – still stick to the old *Langersamstag* routine. The only exceptions to this rule, apart from pharmacists, are the shops in the main train stations and the airport, which are open late and at weekends. Those in search of cigarettes after hours will find cigarette machines outside most state-run tobacconists.

Cafés, bars and restaurants tend to be open for much longer. The traditional coffeehouses in particular often open as early as 7am and continue until or after 11pm, and the trendier cafés stay open until 2am and later. Formal **restaurants** tend to open at lunch and dinner, but close in between. Most places where you can drink and eat have a weekly **closing day** or *Ruhetag*.

Public holidays

On the national **public holidays** listed below, banks and shops will be closed all day. Museums and galleries will, somewhat confusingly, either be closed or open for free; for example, the vast majority are open for free on

PUBLIC HOLIDAYS	
January 1 (Neues Jahr)	**August 15** (Assumption Day/Maria Himmelfahrt)
January 6 (Epiphany/Dreikönigsfest)	
Easter Monday (Ostermontag)	**October 26** (National Day/Nationalfeiertag)
May 1 (Labour Day/Tag des Arbeit)	**November 1** (All Saints' Day/Allerheiligen)
Ascension Day (6th Thurs after Easter/Christi Himmelfahrt)	**December 8** (Immaculate Conception/Maria Empfängnis)
Whit Monday (6th Mon after Easter/Pfingstmontag)	**December 25** (Weihnachtstag)
Corpus Christi (2nd Thurs after Whitsuntide/Fronleichnam)	**December 26** (Zweite Weihnachtsfeiertag)

October 26, whereas most are closed on December 25 and 26. During the school summer holidays – July and August – you'll find Vienna quieter than usual, with many theatres and other businesses closed for all or some of the period.

Festivals

Vienna's calendar of events begins with the world-famous, schmaltzy Strauss-fest **New Year's Day Concert** (Silvesterkonzert), broadcast live around the world from the Musikverein.

The city's main cultural festival – featuring opera, music and theatre – is the **Wiener Festwochen** (*www.festwochen.or.at*), which lasts from early May until mid-June. Once that's over, there's barely any breathing space before the city's big summer music festival, **Klangbogen Wien** (*www.klangbogen.at*), begins, lasting until early September. The festival includes a two-week **Jazzfest** in late June/early July. In July and August, you can also watch **open-air opera**, recordings of which are projected onto the facade of the Rathaus.

Other one-off and popular culture events to look out for include the **Vienna Marathon** (*www.vienna-marathon.at*), which starts at Schönbrunn and finishes with a circuit of the Ring on a weekend in May. The **Donauinselfest**,

sponsored by the Social Democrats (SPÖ), is a free pop festival held on the Donauinsel on a weekend in August.

October is the trendy month to visit, with the city's film festival, the **Viennale** (*www.viennale.or.at*), taking place towards the end of the month, and the **Wien Modern** festival of contemporary classical music continuing into November.

All Saints' Day (Allerheiligen) on November 1 is taken seriously, with huge numbers of Viennese heading for the city's cemeteries, in particular the Zentralfriedhof, to pay their respects to the dead. November 11 marks the official beginning of **Fasching** (*www.ball.at*), the carnival – or more accurately, ball – season, which lasts until Ash Wednesday, though the balls don't really get going until after New Year. Towards the end of November, the city starts to get ready for Christmas (Weihnacht). The biggest of the numerous Christmas markets is the **Christkindlmarkt**, which takes place in front of the Rathaus; another one worth visiting is on Freyung. The Austrians celebrate Christmas itself on December 24. These are just the main festivals and events – in fact, such is their number throughout the year, it's hard to turn up without coinciding with at least one.

Crime and personal safety

Vienna comes across as pretty safe compared to many capital cities. The Viennese themselves are a law-abiding lot, almost obsessively so. Old ladies can be seen walking their dogs in the city's parks late at night, and no one jaywalks. That said, crime does, of course, exist in Vienna as elsewhere and is on the rise, so it's as well to take the usual precautions.

EMERGENCY PHONE NUMBERS	
Fire	☎ 122
Police	☎ 133
Ambulance	☎ 144

Large sections of the **Gürtel ring road** double as a red-light district, and as such are best avoided. The **Karlsplatz** underpass and the **Stadtpark** both have dubious reputations, as do the major train stations, in particular the **Südbahnhof**, after dark. Even so, none of these places are strictly speaking no-go areas.

Almost all problems encountered by tourists in Vienna are to do with **petty crime**. Reporting thefts to the **police** is straightforward enough,

though it takes some time to wade through the bureaucracy. The Austrian police (*Polizei*) – distinguishable by their dark green uniforms and army-style officers' caps – are armed, and are not renowned for their friendliness, especially towards people from other cultures. It's important to carry ID with you at all times, ideally your passport, or at the least a driving licence. Making photocopies of your passport and tickets is a very sensible precaution.

Travellers with disabilities

Like most western European countries, there are now regulations in force in Austria which mean that all public buildings must provide wheelchair access. As a result Vienna is becoming gradually more accessible for travellers with special needs.

Wheelchair access to **hotels** is by no means universal, however, and is more likely to be a feature of upmarket establishments than of the more inexpensive places. Access to the **public transport** system is quite good providing you plan your trip and contact the relevant train station several days in advance.

Access to **urban transport** in Vienna is patchy, with only the new U3 and U6 subway lines fully equipped with lifts, escalators and a guidance system for the blind. The old trams are not at all wheelchair-friendly (*Rollstuhlfreundlich*), but the newer ones are, and buses in Vienna "kneel" to let people on and off. For a clearer picture, phone for the English-language leaflet *Vienna for Guests with Handicaps* from the Austrian tourist board (see p.38) before you set off. This describes the level of access to U-Bahn stations, hotels and many tourist sights, and contains lots of other useful pieces of information.

CONTACTS FOR TRAVELLERS WITH DISABILITIES

AUSTRALIA

ACROD (Australian Council for Rehabilitation of the Disabled), PO Box 60, Curtin, ACT 2605 ☎ 02/6282 4333.

BRITAIN

Access Travel, 6 The Hillock, Astley, Lancashire M29 7GW ☎ 01942/888844, *www.access.co.uk*. Small tour operator that can arrange flights, transfer and accommodation.

Holiday Care, 2nd Floor, Imperial Building, Victoria Rd, Horley, Surrey RH6 9HW ☎ 01293/774535, Minicom ☎ 01293/776943, *www.holidaycare.org.uk*. Information on all aspects of travel.

RADAR, 12 City Forum, 250 City Rd, London EC1V 8AS ☎ 020/7250 3222, Minicom ☎ 020/7250 4119, *www.radar.org.uk*. A good source of advice on holidays and travel abroad.

IRELAND

Irish Wheelchair Association, Blackheath Drive, Clontarf, Dublin 3 ☎ 01/833 8241, *www.iwa.ie*. National voluntary organization working with people with disabilities with related services for holidaymakers.

NEW ZEALAND

Disabled Persons Assembly, 173–175 Victoria St, Wellington ☎ 04/801 9100.

NORTH AMERICA

Access-Able – *www.access-able.com*: an online resource for travellers with disabilities.

Directions Unlimited, 123 Green Lane, Bedford Hills, NY 10507 ☎ 1-800/533 5343 or 914/241 1700. Tour operator specializing in custom tours for people with disabilities.

Mobility International USA, 451 Broadway, Eugene, OR 97401, Voice and TDD ☎ 541/343 1284, *www.miusa.org*. Information and referral services, access guides, tours and exchange programmes. Annual membership $35 (includes quarterly newsletter).

Society for the Advancement of Travelers with Handicaps (SATH), 347 5th Ave, New York, NY 10016 ☎ 212/447 7284, *www.sath.org*. Non-profit educational organization that has actively represented travellers with disabilities since 1976.

Travel Information Service ☎ 215/456 9600. Telephone-only information and referral service.

Twin Peaks Press, Box 129, Vancouver, WA 98661 ☎ 360/694 2462 or 1-800/637 2256, *www.twinpeak.virtualave.net*. Publisher of the *Directory of Travel Agencies for the Disabled* ($19.95), listing more than 370 agencies worldwide; *Travel for the Disabled* ($19.95); the *Directory of Accessible Van Rentals* ($12.95) and *Wheelchair Vagabond* ($19.95), loaded with personal tips.

Wheels Up! ☎ 1-888/389-4335, *www.wheelsup.com*. Provides discounted airfare, tour and cruise prices for disabled travellers; also publishes a free monthly newsletter and has a comprehensive website.

The City

The City

Chapter 1

Introducing the City

For all its grandiosity, **Vienna** is a surprisingly compact city: the centre is just a kilometre across at its broadest point, and you can travel from one side of the city to the other by public transport in less than thirty minutes. Although the **Danube** is crucial to Vienna's identity, most visitors see very little of the river, whose main arm flows through the outer suburbs to the northeast of the city centre.

Orientation

Vienna's central district is the old medieval town or **Innere Stadt** (Chapter Two), literally the "inner town". Retaining much of its labyrinthine street layout, it remains the city's main commercial district, packed with shops, cafés and restaurants. The chief sight here is **Stephansdom**, Vienna's landmark cathedral and its finest Gothic edifice, standing at the district's pedestrianized centre. Tucked into the southwest corner of the Innere Stadt is the **Hofburg** (Chapter Three), the former imperial palace and seat of the Habsburgs, now home to a whole host of museums.

When the old fortifications surrounding the Innere Stadt were torn down in 1857, they were gradually replaced by a showpiece boulevard called the **Ringstrasse** (Chapter Four). It is this irregular pentagon-shaped thoroughfare that, along with the Danube Canal, encloses the Innere Stadt. Nowadays the Ringstrasse is used and abused by cars and vans as a ring road, though it's still punctuated with the most grandiose public buildings of late-imperial Vienna: the parliament, town hall, opera house and university, plus the new **MuseumsQuartier** and several other museums. One of these – the **Kunsthistorisches Museum** – houses one of the world's finest art collections, detailed in Chapter Five.

Beyond the Ringstrasse lie Vienna's seven inner suburbs or **Vorstädte** (Chapter Six), whose outer boundary is comprised of the traffic-clogged Gürtel (literally "belt") or ring road. If you're travelling on any kind of budget, you're likely to find yourself staying

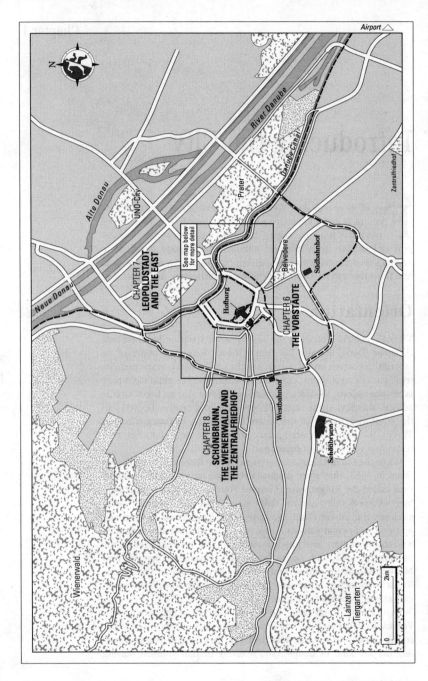

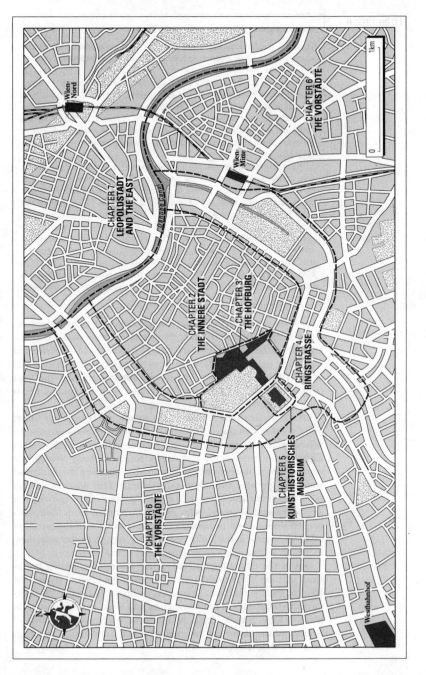

CHAPTER 6
THE VORSTÄDTE

CHAPTER 7
LEOPOLDSTADT
AND THE EAST

CHAPTER 2
THE INNERE STADT

CHAPTER 3
THE HOFBURG

CHAPTER 4
RINGSTRASSE

CHAPTER 5
KUNSTHISTORISCHES
MUSEUM

CHAPTER 6
THE VORSTÄDTE

Wien-
Nord

Wien-
Mitte

Westbahnhof

Donau Canal

0   1km

N

Vienna's postal districts and addresses

Vienna is divided into 23 **postal districts** or *Bezirke*, which spiral outwards from the first district (the Innere Stadt), in a clockwise direction, with only the odd geographical hiccup. The heart of the first district is the old town, though the Hofburg and Ringstrasse are also, strictly speaking, located within its boundaries. The city's second district (Leopoldstadt) is the old Jewish quarter, while the third to ninth districts make up the *Vorstädte* or inner suburbs that surround the old town. In 1890, Vienna's municipal boundaries were expanded to include the outer suburbs or *Vororte* – the tenth to twentieth districts – and since then three more have been added.

When writing **addresses**, the Viennese write the number of the district first, followed by the name of the street, and then the house number; most residential addresses also include an apartment number, separated from the house number by a slash. For example: 9, Löblichgasse 11/14, denotes Flat 14 at no. 11 Löblichgasse in the ninth district. We have used this system throughout the book. Sometimes you'll find addresses preceded by the postal code rather than the district, often with an "A" (for Austria) hyphenated to the beginning. However, it's easy enough to decipher the postal district from the code, for example: A-1010 Wien denotes the first district, A-1020 the second, and so on. Lastly, there are a few common **abbreviations** to be aware of, including: –str. for –strasse, –g. for –gasse, and –pl. for –platz.

somewhere out in the Vorstädte. The highlight here is the **Belvedere**, to the south of the Innere Stadt, where you can see a wealth of paintings by Austria's trio of modern artists, Egon Schiele, Gustav Klimt and Oskar Kokoschka. Those sections of the city worth visiting east of the Danube Canal are covered in **Leopoldstadt and the East** (Chapter Seven), though only the Prater, with its famous Ferris wheel and funfair, is essential viewing.

On the whole, there's little reason to venture beyond the Gürtel into the outer suburbs or *Vororte*. Exceptions are **Schönbrunn,** the **Wienerwald** – Vienna Woods – and the **Zentralfriedhof** (all Chapter Eight). Schönbrunn is the Habsburgs' former summer residence, a masterpiece of Rococo excess and an absolute must if only for the wonderful gardens. The hilly woodland paths of the Wienerwald have been a popular rural retreat for the Viennese since the days of Beethoven and Schubert, who gained inspiration from their vine-backed slopes. Both composers now lie – along with thousands of other Viennese – at the opposite end of the city, in the far southeast, in the city's fascinating Zentralfriedhof (Central Cemetery).

Out of the city (Chapter Nine), there's scope for further excursions into the Wienerwald, the old imperial spa town of Baden, the court of the Esterházys at Eisenstadt; or up the Danube to the spectacular monasteries of Klosterneuburg and Melk, to Tulln, the birthplace of Egon Schiele, or to the medieval, wine-producing town of Krems. All the above can be easily reached from Vienna within an hour by public transport.

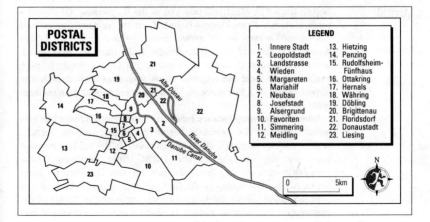

Arrival

Flying into Vienna, you'll arrive at the city's **international airport**, Flughafen Wien-Schwechat (*www.viennaairport.com*), which lies around 20km southeast of the city. The airport is clean and efficient, has a supermarket open seven days a week until late at night, and a half decent selection of bars and restaurants. It's connected to the centre by the S-Bahn line S7; **trains** leave every thirty minutes between 5am and 10pm, taking thirty minutes to reach Wien-Mitte (U-Bahn Landstrasse), where most people alight, and terminating at Wien-Nord (U-Bahn Praterstern). This is the cheapest way of getting into town, costing öS38/€2.76 one-way, or, if you plan to do a bit of travelling when you first arrive, öS19/€1.38 plus the price of a travel pass for the central zone (see p.39), which you can buy at the same time. **Buses** from the airport to the City Air Terminal bus station behind the *Hilton Hotel* (opposite Wien-Mitte/U-Bahn Landstrasse) are even more frequent, leaving every twenty minutes from 6.30am until 11.30pm, and every thirty minutes throughout the night (April–Oct only); they take around twenty minutes to reach the city centre, and cost öS70/€5.09 one way, öS130/€9.45 return. There are also hourly buses to the Südbahnhof and Westbahnhof (see below). For more information on the buses and trains to and from the airport, visit the website *www.oebb.at/regional/wien /wien4.html*. **Taxis** to the centre take twenty minutes or so and charge around öS400/€29.07.

Arriving in Vienna by train from the west, you'll end up at the **Westbahnhof**, five U-Bahn stops west of Stephansplatz in the city centre on the U3 line. Trains from the east, Italy and the Balkans terminate at the **Südbahnhof**, to the south of the city centre; you can either walk five minutes west to Südtiroler Platz U-Bahn station, or hop on tram #D, which will take you to the Ringstrasse. Of Vienna's other stations, **Franz-Josefs-Bahnhof**, in the northern suburb of Alsergrund, serves as an arrival point for services from Lower Austria and the odd train from Prague (take tram #D into town), while **Wien-Nord** (U-Bahn Praterstern), in Leopoldstadt, is used exclusively by local and regional trains, including the S-Bahn to the airport (see p.37). For more on Vienna's international train connections, see p.5.

International long-distance buses arrive at Vienna's **main bus terminal**, the City Air Terminal beside Wien-Mitte, on the eastern edge of the city centre (U-Bahn Landstrasse). In the unlikely event of your arriving on one of the **DDSG boat services** (*www .ddsg-blue-danube.at*) from further up the Danube, or from Bratislava or Budapest, you'll find yourself disembarking at the Schiffahrtszentrum by the Reichsbrücke, some way northeast of the city centre; the nearest station (U-Bahn Vorgartenstrasse) is five minutes' walk away, one block west of Mexikoplatz.

Information

The main **tourist office** of the Vienna Tourist Board or *Wiener Tourismusverband* (*www.info.wien.at*) is behind the opera house on Albertinaplatz (daily 9am–7pm; ☎211 14-222; phone enquiries Mon–Fri 8am–4pm only). There are only a few leaflets on open display, but if you have a specific enquiry the staff will happily help out. It's worth asking for the latest *Museums* leaflet, listing all the current opening times. Other leaflets include the tourist board's monthly *Programm* for opera, concert and theatre schedules, upcoming exhibitions, and the monthly goings-on at the *Bundesmuseen* (State Museums). Depending on your age, you might prefer to try the youth-oriented tourist office, *Jugendinfo*, at Babenbergerstrasse 1 (Mon–Sat noon–7pm; *www.jugendinfowien.at*), on the corner of the Ringstrasse. There are also **information desks** at the airport (daily 8.30am–9pm) and at the Westbahnhof (daily 7am–10pm).

For the most comprehensive and critical **listings**, you need the weekly tabloid *Falter* (öS28/€2.03; *www.falter.at*), which comes out on Wednesdays. Even if your German isn't great, you should be able to decipher the pull-out *Wienprogramm & Lexicon* section, which contains the week's listings. Most of the headings are self-explanatory, but it's just as well to know that Musik-E covers classical music, while Musik-U is for pop, jazz and folk, with a separate weekly calendar called *Party-Time* for clubs. A cheaper alternative is the free weekly, *Winside* (*www.winside.cc*), which comes out every Thursday, or the monthly *Wien Magazin* (öS28/€2.03; *www .wienmagazin.at*), which gives you a whole month's listings. A cheaper, trashier alternative is the weekly colour tabloid *City* (öS10/€0.72), which also has a *Wienprogramm* in its centre pages.

City transport

Vienna's city centre is best explored on foot, but for covering larger distances, you'll need to use the **public transport system**, known as the *Wiener Linien* (*www.wienerlinien.co.at*). If there's one thing every visitor would like to take home with them, it's the public transport system, which is just about one of the most efficient in the world. The trams and buses are punctual and the rapidly expanding U-Bahn (metro) is clean and very quick, and not too overpriced either.

There are maps of Vienna's public transport systems in the colour insert at the back of this book.

Tickets

A single journey ticket (*Fahrschein*), standard for all forms of public transport, costs öS19/€1.38 from machines and ticket booths (*Vorverkauf*) at U-Bahn stations, and also from tobacconists (*Tabak-Trafik*). When you enter the U-Bahn, or board a tram or bus, you must punch (*entwerten*) your ticket in one of the blue machines. You can then make one journey, during which you can change buses, trams or U-Bahn lines as many times as you like, as long as you proceed in a logical direction without any "breaks". If you don't get it together to buy a ticket before boarding a tram or bus, you can buy a ticket for öS22/€1.60 from the machines beside the driver – these need not be punched. Tickets for kids from 6 to 14 cost öS10/€0.73; under-6s travel free and under-15s travel free on Sundays, public holidays and during school holidays (you can pick up a calendar at a Wiener Linien information office); women over 60 and men over 65 can buy a two-journey ticket for öS25/€1.82.

If you're planning on making more than two journeys a day, you should invest in a **travel pass** or *Netzkarte*, which allows travel on all trams, buses, U- and S-Bahn trains within the city limits. You can buy a 24-hour ticket (öS60/€4.36) or a 72-hour ticket (öS150/€10.90) from machines and booths at all U-Bahn stations; when buying your ticket from a machine, select the central zone or *Kernzone* (*Zone 100*) which covers all of Vienna. You must punch your single *Netzkarte* at the beginning of your first journey – your 24 or 72 hours starts from that point. The much-touted Vienna Card/Wien-Karte (öS210/€15.26) gives various discounts at local attractions as well as being a 72-hour *Netzkarte* (see p.44 for more details). The *Wiener Einkaufskarte* (öS50/€3.63) is a daily travel

---

Travel information offices

There are Wiener Linien **information offices** at the following U-Bahn stations: Stephansplatz, Karlsplatz and Westbahnhof (all Mon–Fri 6.30am–6.30pm, Sat & Sun 8.30am–4pm); Floridsdorf, Spittelau (both Mon–Fri 6.30am–6.30pm); Praterstern, Philadelphiabrücke, Landstrasse and Volkstheater (all Mon–Fri 7am–6.30pm).

---

pass valid between 8am and 8pm, aimed at shoppers and therefore not available on a Sunday.

Another option is a **strip ticket** or *Streifenkarte*, which is available as a four-journey card (öS76/€5.52) or eight-journey card (öS152/€11.05). The card can be used by one or more people – simply punch one strip on the card for each person in the group. To do this you must fold the card over before inserting it in the blue machines, starting with strip 1. Even more useful is the **8-day ticket**, or *8-Tage-Karte* (öS300/€21.80), which works like the strip ticket, but is valid for eight (not necessarily consecutive) days' travel, calculated in 24-hour periods from the hour of purchase. It can be used by one person for eight days, two people for four, and so on. If you only need to go a couple of stops on the U-Bahn, tram or bus, you can buy a **four- short journey** strip ticket called a *Kurzstrecke* (öS38/€2.76).

If you're staying in Vienna longer than three days, it might be worth buying a **weekly card** or *Wochenkarte* (öS155/€11.26), available only from coded ticket machines or ticket offices at U-Bahn stations. The pass runs from 9am Monday to 9am the following Monday so there's no need to punch the ticket, and it is transferable (in other words it may be passed on to another person for them to use, but two people travelling together need two separate tickets). The **monthly ticket** or *Monatskarte* (öS560/€40.70), which runs for a calendar month, works in much the same way.

The Viennese being a law-abiding bunch, there are few **ticket inspectors**, but if you are caught without a valid ticket or pass – known by the politically incorrect term *Schwarzfahren* (black travelling) – you'll be handed an on-the-spot fine of öS560/€40.70 (plus öS22/€1.60 for a ticket).

U-Bahn

There's a map of the U-Bahn system in the colour insert at the back of this book.

Vienna's **U-Bahn**, which opened in 1978, boasts five lines (U1–4 and U6), and is by far the fastest way of getting around the city, with trains running from between 5 and 6am to between midnight and 1am (the times of the first and last trains are posted up at each station). Not all U-Bahn lines are underground: the U4 and U6 lines run partly on the old overground Stadtbahn created in the 1890s, and both lines retain some of their original stations and bridges designed by Otto Wagner. Each line is colour-coded (U1 is purple, U2 red and so on); to figure out which platform you want, look out for the name of the end station in the direction you wish to travel. The next extension planned is for the U2 line, which should stretch from Schottenring to Stadion (in the Prater) by the end of 2002.

A couple of useful words to know on the U-Bahn are Ausgang *(Exit) and* Not *(Emergency).*

Trams and buses

Vienna has one of the largest **tram** systems in the world, with more than thirty routes criss-crossing the capital. Electric trams –

Strassenbahn or *Bim* (after the noise of the bell) as they're known colloquially – were introduced in 1897 and they still sport the traditional red-and-white livery. After the U-Bahn, trams are the fastest and most efficient way of getting around, running every five to ten minutes, depending on the time of day. They're pretty punctual, though some lines don't run on weekends or late at night, so be sure to check the timetables posted at every stop (*Haltestelle*). The final destination of the tram is also indicated by a small sign above the timetable itself.

Buses (*Autobusse*) tend to ply the narrow backstreets and the outer suburbs, and despite having to battle with the traffic, are equally punctual. In the heart of the Innere Stadt, where there are no trams and only two U-Bahn stations, there are several very **useful bus services** (Mon–Sat only): #1A, which winds its way from Schottentor to Stubentor; #2A from Schwedenplatz through the Hofburg to U-Bahn Neubaugasse; and #3A from Schottenring to Schwarzenbergplatz. Bus #13A wends its way through the fourth to the eighth districts of the Vorstädte.

S-Bahn and Regionalbahn

The **S-Bahn**, or *Schnellbahn* to give it its full name, is of most use to Viennese commuters. It's also the cheapest way of getting to and from the airport, and is useful for day-trips to places like Klosterneuburg, Tulln and Krems. S-Bahn trains are less frequent than U-Bahn trains – running every fifteen to thirty minutes – and are strictly timetabled. You're even less likely to have to use the suburban railway system or **Regionalbahn**, unless you're heading out to Melk or Eisenstadt; trains leave from the mainline stations.

Taxis and Nightbuses

Taxis are plentiful and fairly reliable too, with the minimum charge around öS25/€1.82, followed by an extra öS10/€0.73 or so per kilometre or couple of minutes. You can't flag down a taxi, but you can catch a cab at one of the taxi ranks around town, or phone ☎31330, 40100 or 60160.

The only other way of getting home in the small hours is to catch one of the NightLine **night buses**, which run every thirty minutes from 12.30am to 4am; all 22 routes pass through Schwedenplatz at some point. Travel passes are not valid. If you think you might be using night buses a few times, or if you're in a group, it's probably worth buying a **four-journey ticket** or *4er-Vorteilsticket* (öS45/€3.27), which works like a strip ticket (see opposite), and can be used by up to four people.

Bicycles, cars and Fiaker

Despite the fact that **cycling** isn't very popular in Vienna, there's a fairly good network of cycle paths – over 500km in total. If you haven't brought your own, you can rent bicycles (*Fahrräder*) cheaply enough between April and October from Westbahnhof, Südbahnhof, Wien-Nord and Floridsdorf train stations for between öS120/€8.72 and öS180/€13.08 a day and can return the bikes to a different station. Bicycles can be taken on the U- and S-Bahn from Monday to Friday between 9am and 3pm and after 6.30pm, and on Saturdays and Sundays from 9am. You must buy a half-price ticket for your bike. If you're thinking of taking a day-trip out of Vienna, it's useful to know that you can rent bikes from Klosterneuburg, Tulln, Melk, Krems and Eisenstadt stations for between öS90/€6.54 and öS160/€11.62 a day, if you've travelled by train.

Cars are really not necessary for getting around Vienna. If, however, you arrive in Vienna by car and need to park, it's as well to know the **parking restrictions** in the blue zones (*Blauzonen*) – also called short-term parking zones (*Kurzparkzonen*). In general, the maximum length of stay in the first district (Altstadt or Innere Stadt) is one and a half hours (Mon–Fri 9am–7pm, Sat as indicated on sign); in the second to ninth districts (inner suburbs or Vorstädte), and in the twentieth district, you can park for up to two hours (Mon–Fri 9am–8pm, Sat as indicated on sign). At the weekend it's a free-for-all. However, check the signs before parking, as exact restrictions do vary. If there's no pay-and-display machine, you'll need to buy a parking voucher (*Parkscheine*) from a tobacconist or post office, and fill it in before displaying it. For car rental firms, see p.339.

An expensive Viennese indulgence is a ride in a soft-top horse-drawn carriage or **Fiaker**, driven by bowler-hatted, multilingual coachmen; there are *Fiaker* ranks at Stephansplatz, Heldenplatz, Michaelerplatz and Albertinaplatz. It's best to settle on the price and duration of your ride beforehand; the going rate is öS500/€36.34 for twenty minutes, or öS800/€58.14 for forty minutes, but it's worth haggling.

Boats

The main company running **boat trips** on the Danube are the DDSG or Donaudampfschiffahrtsgesellschaft (*www.ddsg-blue-danube.at*). They run two basic round trips: the so-called **Hundertwasser Tour** (mid-April to Sept) and the slightly longer **Grosse Donaurundfahrt** (May–Sept). Both depart from the Danube canal beside Schwedenplatz, and stop off halfway round at the Reichsbrücke on the Danube itself, so you can embark and disembark at either halt. A one-way ticket between the two points costs öS130/€9.45, a return costs öS180/€13.08. Children under 10 travel free; those aged 10 to 15 go half price. Vienna doesn't look at its best from the canal or the river, but whichever tour you take, you'll get to see Hundertwasser's paper incinerator (see p.250), Otto Wagner's Nussdorfer Schleusenanlage (weir and lock – see p.254), and the new

Guided tours and walks

Vienna Sightseeing Tours (*www.viennasightseeingtours.com*) run a variety of **bus tours** around the city and surrounding districts. Their standard city tour (daily 9.30am, 10.30am & 2.30pm; öS400/€29.07) takes around three and a half hours; pick up a leaflet at the tourist office or any hotel or pension. They also run a **hop-on hop-off** bus hourly (daily 9.30am–4.30pm), with running commentary in English and German; tickets cost öS250/€18.17 and are valid for two days.

Alternatively, you can save yourself the commentary by hopping on **tram #**1 or #2, which circumnavigate the Ringstrasse clockwise and anticlockwise respectively. Every Saturday (11.30am and 1.30pm) and Sunday (9.30am, 11.30am & 1.30pm) from early May to early October, you can leap aboard a 1920s tram outside the Otto-Wagner-Pavillon on Karlsplatz and go on an hour-long **tram tour**, run by Wiener Linien; tickets cost öS200/€14.54 and are available from Karlsplatz U-Bahn.

From May to October several companies run **boat trips** along the River Danube and the Danube Canal, leaving from the quayside of the latter by U-Bahn Schwedenplatz. The DDSG "Hundertwasser Tour" is one of the least expensive, lasting ninety minutes and costing öS140/€10.17. Be warned, however, that Vienna's waterfront buildings are none too beautiful.

Most appealing are the **walking tours** organized by Vienna's official tourist guides – you'll find details, such as whether the tours are in German or English, in the monthly *Wiener Spaziergänge* leaflet from the tourist office (*www.wienguide.at*). These cover a relatively small area in much greater detail, mixing historical facts with juicy anecdotes in the company of a local specialist. Subjects covered range from Jugendstil (Art Nouveau) architecture to Jewish Vienna, and the weekly Third Man tour takes you round the locations associated with the eponymous 1948 film (☎774 8901). Tours cost around öS140/€10.17 and last between one and a half and two hours. Simply turn up at the meeting point specified.

Millenniumstower (see p.218). The longer tour also takes you past the Prater (see p.208) and the Buddhist temple.

There are various other themed **evening cruises** available, ranging from the inevitable Sound of Johann Strauss tour to the unmissable Spare Ribs Fahrt. For more details pick up a leaflet or visit the DDSG website. In the summer, the company also runs a **regular boat service** to Budapest up the Danube, stopping at Tulln, Krems and Melk. For more on this, see p.276.

Museums and monuments

The selective **opening hours and prices** listed on the following page (and in the following guide chapters) are the latest available, though bear in mind that some places are prone to raising their charges dramatically from year to year. A concessionary rate is generally available for students (*Studenten*), under-18s (*Kinder*) and over-60s (*Senioren*); you'll need ID. Most museums are either closed or free

Museums and monuments

on public holidays, and those marked * in the purely selective list below are free on Friday mornings until noon. Nearly all the city's museums are also free on May 17 (International Museum Day) and October 26 (National Day).

The only discount card of any value to tourists is **The Vienna Card** (*Die Wien-Karte*), which costs öS210/€15.26 and allows free travel on the public transport system for 72 hours. In addition, you also get discounts at sights such as the Hofburg and Schönbrunn palaces, plus selected restaurants and shops. If you're in Vienna for a long weekend and intend to do quite a bit of sightseeing, then the ticket will probably pay for itself. However, the savings are less than they appear at first sight: a 72-hour *Netzkarte* costs just öS150/€10.90 and the discounts rarely amount to more than öS20/€1.45 per sight.

Akademie der bildenden Künste Tues–Sun 10am–4pm; öS50/€3.63; ☎588 16-225; see p.136.

Albertina closed until 2002, *www.albertina.at*; see p.112.

Belvedere Tues–Sun 10am–6pm; öS120/€8.72; ☎795 57-134, *www.belvedere.at*; see p.176.

***Figarohaus** (Mozart Museum) Tues–Sun 9am–6pm; öS25/€1.82; ☎513 62 94, *www.museum.vienna.at*; see p.57.

Sigmund-Freud Museum daily: July–Sept 9am–6pm; Oct–June 9am–5pm; öS60/€5.09; ☎319 1596, *www.freud-museum.at*; see p.203.

Haus der Musik daily 10am–10pm; öS110/€7.99; ☎516 4851, *www.haus-der-musik-wien.at*; see p.63.

Heeresgeschichtliches Museum (Arsenal) daily except Fri 9am–5pm; öS70/€5.09, free on the first Sun of the month; ☎79561, *www.bmlv.gv.at/hgm*; see p.188.

***Historisches Museum der Stadt Wien** Tues–Sun 9am–6pm; öS50/€3.63; ☎505 87 47-84 021, *www.museum.vienna.at*; see p.144.

Hofburg

Burgkapelle Jan–June & mid-Sept to Dec Mon–Thurs 11am–3pm, Fri 11am–1pm; öS15/€1.09; Vienna Boys' Choir mass mid-September to June Sun 9.15am; öS70–380/€5.09–27.62; ☎533 9927; see p.103.

Kaiserappartements daily 9am–4.30pm; öS80/€5.81; ☎533 7570; see p.95.

Prunksaal (Nationalbibliothek) mid-May to Oct Mon–Wed, Fri & Sat 10am–4pm, Thurs 10am–7pm, Sun 10am–1pm; Nov to mid-May Mon–Sat 10am–2pm; closed for the first three weeks of Sept; öS60/€4.36; ☎53410, *www.onb.ac.at*; see p.108.

Schatzkammer daily except Tues 10am–6pm; öS100/€7.27; ☎533 7931; see p.100.

Spanische Reitschule (Spanish Riding School); training mid-Jan to June & late Aug to mid-Dec Tues–Sat 10am–noon; öS100/€7.27; performances March–June & Sept to mid-Dec Sun 10.45am and less frequently Wed 7pm; *tickets@srs.at*; *www.spanische-reitschule.com*; öS200–900/€14.54–65.41; Lipizzaner Museum daily 9am–5pm; ☎533 7811, *www.lipizzaner.at*; öS70/€5.09; see p.107.

Jüdisches Museum daily except Sat 10am–6pm, Thurs until 9pm; öS70/€5.00; ☎535 0431, *www.jmw.at*; see p.66.

Kunsthistorisches Museum Tues–Sun 10am–6pm, Thurs until 9pm; öS100/€7.27; ☎52524, *www.khm.at*; see p.155.

Museum für angewandte Kunst (MAK) Tues 10am–midnight, Wed–Sun 10am–6pm; öS90/€6.54; ☎71136, *www.mak.at*; see p.149.

MuseumsQuartier *www.mqw.at*; see p.132.

Naturhistorisches Museum daily except Tues 9am–6.30pm, Wed 9am–9pm; öS30/€2.18; ☎52177, *www.nhm.at*; see p131.

* Otto-Wagner-Pavillon April–Oct Tues–Sun 1–4.30pm; öS25/€1.82; *www.museum.vienna.at*; see p.142.

Riesenrad daily: March & April 10am–10pm; May–Sept 9am–midnight; Oct 10am–10pm; Nov to early Jan 10am–6pm; öS50/€3.63; ☎729 5430; see p.211.

Schönbrunn *www.schoenbrunn.at*

Prunkräume daily: April–Oct 8.30am–5pm; Nov–March 8.30am–4.30pm; öS95–150/€6.90–10.90; ☎81113; see p.225.

Tiergarten (Zoo) daily: Feb 9am–5pm; March & Oct 9am–5.30pm; April 9am–6pm; May–Sept 9am–6.30pm; Nov–Jan 9am–4.30pm; öS95/€6.90; ☎877 92 94; see p.235.

Secession Tues–Sun 10am–6pm, Thurs 10am–8pm; öS60/€4.36; ☎587 5307, *www.secession.at*; see p.138.

Museums and monuments

Chapter 2

The Innere Stadt

Vienna's first district – the **Innere Stadt** (Inner City) or Altstadt (Old City) – has been the very heart of the place since the Romans founded Vindobona here on the banks of the Danube in 15 BC. It was here, too, that the Babenberg dukes built their powerbase in the twelfth century, and from 1533, the Habsburgs established the Hofburg as their primary imperial residence (covered separately in Chapter Three). Consequently, unlike the older quarters in many European cities, the Innere Stadt remained the chief place of residence for the city's aristocracy throughout the Baroque period and beyond, and its narrow, cobbled lanes remained the unlikely addresses of dukes and duchesses, princes and ambassadors. In fact, the city occupied pretty much the same space from the thirteenth century until the zig-zag fortifications, which had protected the city on two occasions against the Turks, were finally taken down in the mid-nineteenth century.

The focus of the Innere Stadt – and the one thing on all tourists' itineraries – is the city's magnificent Gothic cathedral, **Stephansdom**, whose single soaring spire also acts as a useful geographical landmark. Close by are the chief pedestrianized shopping streets of **Kärntnerstrasse**, **Graben** and **Kohlmarkt**, which get progressively more exclusive the nearer you get to the Hofburg. There's a steady ebb and flow of folk along these streets at most times of the day, but the **Kaisergruft**, the last resting place of the Habsburgs, just off Kärntnerstrasse, is the only other sight which gets clogged up with tour groups. Head off into the rest of the Innere Stadt with its baffling medieval lanes, hidden courtyards and passageways, and you'll soon lose the crowds. For although most of the city's finest Baroque churches and palaces are to be found here, the dearth of premier league sights puts many off the scent.

Stephansplatz

The geographical heart of the Innere Stadt is **Stephansplatz**, a lively, pedestrianized square overlooked by the hoary Gothic bulk of the city cathedral. The square hasn't always been so central – the first church built here lay outside the medieval city walls, and the square itself was a graveyard until 1732. Nowadays, though, it's one of the best places for watching Viennese streetlife, from the benign young slackers who lounge around on the benches by the U-Bahn, to the beleaguered folk in eighteenth-century costumes, wearily flogging tickets for classical concerts. The smell of horse dung wafts across the square from the fiakers lined up along the north wall of the cathedral.

Apart from the cathedral, the most dominant feature of the square is the **Haas Haus**, probably the singly most inappropriate building in the Innere Stadt and one which, not surprisingly, caused something of a furore when it was unveiled in 1990. The real disappointment is that the architect, Hans Hollein, is clearly gifted (his equally uncompromising jewellery stores along Graben and Kohlmarkt are minor masterpieces). Here, though, the metal-coated glass and polished stone facade lacks subtlety, and the protruding turret is a veritable carbuncle; to cap it all, the interior is an unimaginative mini-shopping centre.

Despite appearances, Haas Haus isn't in fact on Stephansplatz at all, it's on **Stock-im-Eisen-Platz**, a little-known geographical entity which covers the no-man's-land between Graben, Stephansplatz and Kärntnerstrasse. The square takes its name – literally "stick-in-iron" – from the nail-studded, sixteenth-century slice of larch tree that stands in a glass-protected niche set into the grandiose **Equitable Palace** on the corner of Kärntnerstrasse. According to Viennese tradition, apprentice locksmiths and blacksmiths would hammer a nail into the trunk for good luck. The Equitable building itself is well worth exploring: built in the 1890s and now wonderfully restored, the ornate vestibule (originally designed to be a metro entrance) is a superb example of the Ringstrasse style of the period, with lashings of marble and wrought iron, and a glass-roofed courtyard faced in majolica tiles.

In the paving between the Haas Haus and the cathedral, the groundplan of the **Chapel of St Mary Magdalene**, a charnel house which burnt to the ground in 1781, is marked out in red sandstone. Almost immediately below it is another church building, the Romanesque **Virgilkapelle**, which was discovered during the construction of the U-Bahn in the 1970s, and is now preserved in the Stephansplatz station itself. The thirteenth-century chapel – at one time the family crypt of the Chrannests, one of whom was finance minister to the Habsburgs – is little visited, though the strangeness of its location and the simple beauty of its recesses, decorated with red wheel crosses, make it an intriguing sight. If the chapel is closed, you can satisfy your curiosity by looking down from the metro's viewing platform by the information office.

Stephans-platz

The nearest U-Bahn is Stephansplatz.

The Virgilkapelle is open Tues–Sun 1–4.30pm; öS25/€1.82.

Stephansdom

The **Stephansdom** (St Stephen's Cathedral) still towers above the Innere Stadt and dominates the Viennese skyline as it has done for

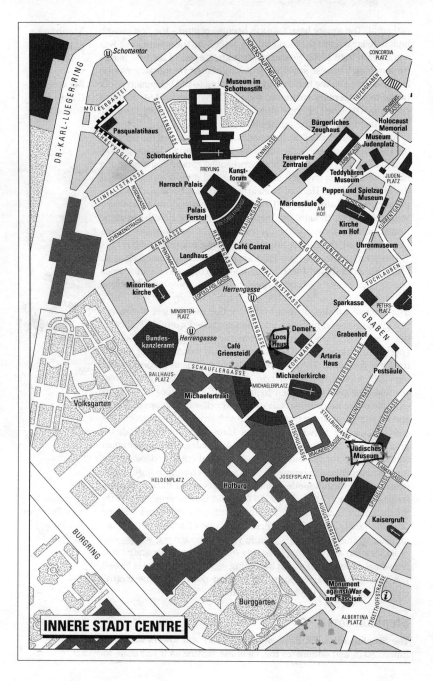

INNERE STADT CENTRE

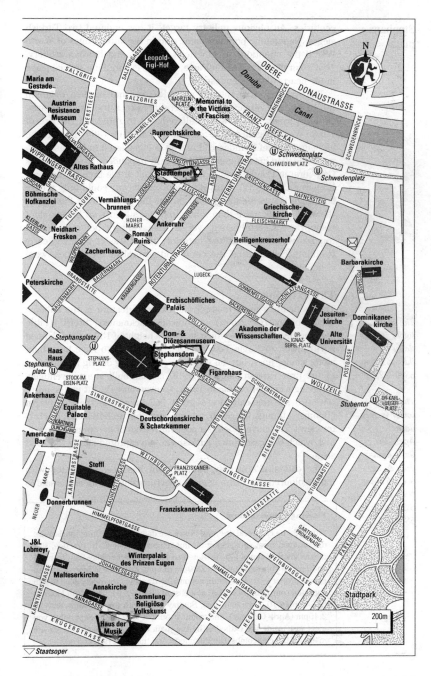

centuries. An obvious military target, it has endured two Turkish sieges, Napoleonic bombardment, and in the latter stages of World War II the attentions of American bombers and Russian artillery. That it survived at all is a miracle, and has ensured it a special place in the hearts of the Viennese.

The first church on this site was a Romanesque basilica, begun in the 1130s, but replaced after several fires by a transitional, early-Gothic variant, which was itself reduced to rubble in the fire of 1258. Work began on the current building in 1304, though the cathedral's chief founder and patron is considered to be Rudolf IV, who modelled his designs for the greatly expanded nave on St Vitus Cathedral in Prague, which was being built at the time by his rival, Emperor Charles IV. Poor old Rudolf, however, could only secure collegiate status for his church, under the bishopric of Passau. In the end, it took more than a hundred years before an independent bishopric was established, yet another century before the final touches were added to the exterior, and it wasn't until the early twentieth century that the choir and several of the chapels were completed.

The exterior

The cathedral's most magnificent **exterior** feature is the sublime south tower (*Hochturm*) – ironically nicknamed "**Steffl**" (Little Stephen) by the locals – which soars to a height of 137m. The planned north tower, or Eagle Tower (*Adlerturm*), was to have been built along similar lines, but fell victim to cost-cutting during the build-up to the first Turkish siege of 1529, its half-built stump eventually receiving a copper cupola in 1556. You can take the lift up the north tower to see the cathedral's great bell known as the **Pummerin** (Boomer), though the Steffl, a blind scramble up 343 steps, has better views. The current bell is a postwar rehash of the twenty-ton original, which was cast from a Turkish cannon captured during the 1683 siege.

The cathedral's steeply pitched **roof** has been decorated with multi-coloured tiles forming giant chevrons since 1490, and is said to

*The south
tower is open
daily
9am–5.30pm;
öS30/€2.18.*

*The north
tower is open
daily:
April–Oct
9am–6pm;
July & Aug
9am–6.30pm;
Nov–March
8.30am–5pm;
öS40/€2.91.*

Visiting Stephansdom

Although the cathedral **opening hours** are daily 6am to 10pm, tourists are discouraged from sightseeing during religious services. In practice, this means **visiting times** are restricted to Monday to Saturday 9am to noon and 1pm to 5pm and Sunday 12.30pm to 5pm. Entrance is free, though to have a proper look at anything beyond the transept, you really need to join a **guided tour** (*Domführung*) at a cost of öS40/€2.91. These run Monday to Saturday 10.30am and 3pm, Sunday 3pm, with English tours daily at 3.45pm (April–Oct only), and evening tours at 7pm (June–Sept only); you meet just inside the cathedral by the main door. Additional charges are made for the catacombs, the Pummerin and the Steffl (see above).

be modelled on a Saracen carpet; on the south side is a double-headed imperial eagle, dating from 1831, while on the north are the emblems of the City of Vienna and the Second Republic and the date 1950, when the roof was retiled.

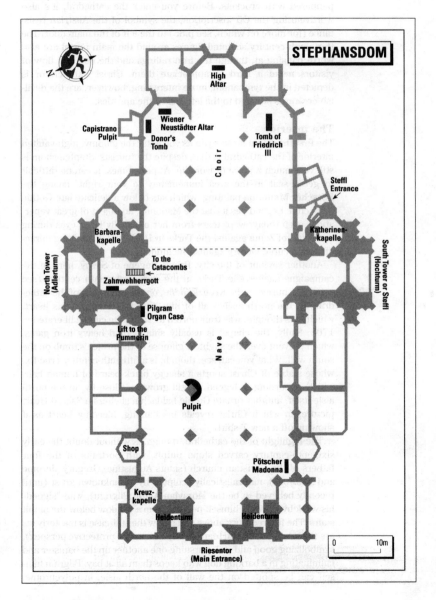

STEPHANSDOM

High Altar

Capistrano Pulpit

Wiener Neustädter Altar

Donor's Tomb

Tomb of Friedrich III

Choir

Steffl Entrance

Barbarakapelle

Katherinenkapelle

To the Catacombs

North Tower (Adlerturm)

Zahnwehherrgott

South Tower or Steffl (Hochturm)

Pilgram Organ Case

Lift to the Pummerin

Nave

Pulpit

Shop

Pötscher Madonna

Kreuzkapelle

Heidenturm

Heidenturm

Riesentor (Main Entrance)

0   10m

The main entrance to the cathedral is via the **Riesentor** (Giants' Gates), a rare survivor from the present building's twelfth-century predecessor. Flanking the Riesentor are two robust Romanesque towers, known as the **Heidentürme** (Pagans' Towers), which are peppered with crockets. Before you enter the cathedral, it's also worth noting the O5 inscription, the symbol of the Austrian resistance (for more on which, see p.85) to the left of the main door. The thirteenth-century sculpted figures around the main portal are also worth pausing at, though the iron railings and the ebb and flow of visitors make it hard to appreciate them. Christ Pantocrator is depicted in the tympanum; more interesting, however, are the devilish creatures situated to the left, below the apostles.

The interior

The first thing that strikes you as you enter the gloomy, high-vaulted interior of the cathedral is that, despite the tourists, Stephansdom is still very much a place of worship. At peak times, it can be difficult to get a seat in the area immediately to your right, facing the **Pötscher Madonna** painting, which sits below a delicate late-Gothic baldachin. Legend has it that the Madonna, an object of great veneration, even today, wept tears from her unusually large eyes during the Battle of Zenta against the Turks in 1697, and in so doing miraculously secured victory against the infidels.

Another saviour of the city, Prince Eugène of Savoy, hero of the campaigns against the Turks in the early eighteenth century (see p.181), is buried in the **Kreuzkapelle**, on the other side of the cathedral, off the north aisle – all of him, that is, except for his heart, which, it is thought, was transported to Turin, the city he liberated in 1706. Sadly, the chapel is usually shut behind heavy iron gates, which prevent even the slightest glimpse of the prince's tomb on the south wall. What you can see, though, is a fifteenth-century crucifix, whose statue of Christ sports a shaggy black beard of human hair, which, according to legend, is still growing. Close by, in the north aisle itself, another ornate Gothic baldachin shelters a Sacred Heart picture, in which Christ reveals his flaming, bleeding heart as if showing off a new T-shirt.

The highlight of the cathedral, though, is without doubt the early sixteenth-century carved stone **pulpit**, with portraits of the four fathers of the Christian church (saints Augustine, Gregory, Jerome and Ambrose), naturalistically sculpted by an unknown artist (until recently believed to be the Moravian Anton Pilgram), who "signed" his work by showing himself peering from a window below the pulpit stairs. The filigree work above and below the staircase is masterly, as are the salamanders and toads (sadly now under protective perspex), symbolizing good and evil, pursuing one another up the banister and culminating in a barking dog who keeps them all at bay. Pilgram himself can be spotted on the wall of the north aisle, in polychrome,

peeping out below one of his works, the now defunct organ case. The
organ itself originally sat above the last of the cathedral's late-Gothic
baldachins, whose lovely, lacy filigree work can be seen on the opposite side of the nave.

If you want to escape the crowds, head for the twin chapels at
either end of the transepts. Though shut off behind wrought-iron railings, the **Katharinenkapelle**, to the south, boasts a beautiful baptismal font, made in 1481; the marble base features the four apostles, the niches of the basin are decorated with the twelve disciples,
Christ and St Stephan, while the wooden lid is shaped like a church
spire and smothered with sculpted scenes. Up above, there's a wonderful ceiling boss of St Catherine with her wheel and sword, on the
end of a drooping pendant. To the north, the **Barbarakapelle** also
features hanging pendants, this time stamped with heraldic bosses.
The chapel is dedicated to all those killed in concentration camps,
and the small triangle in the crucifix below Christ's feet contains
ashes from Auschwitz. On the wall opposite, as you leave the chapel,
look out for a half-torso of Christ in suffering, known as the
Zahnwehherrgott (Our Lord of the Toothache). According to
Viennese legend, the three students who coined the nickname were
immediately struck down with toothache, which no barber-surgeon
could cure, until the young men had fallen prostrate before the statue and prayed for forgiveness.

The **choir**, beyond the transepts, is roped off, and only strictly vis-
itable on a guided tour (see box on p.50). At the far end of the
Women's Choir (to the north), however, you should just be able to
make out the winged **Wiener Neustädter Altar**, a richly gilded masterpiece of late-Gothic art which dates from the mid-fifteenth century but was only brought to the cathedral in 1883. During Easter, the
altar's wings are closed and only four rows of saints are depicted;
during Lent and Advent, the wings are opened to reveal up to 72
saints; the rest of the time you should be able to see the altar's show-
stopper: the Madonna and Child, the Birth of Christ, the Adoration of
the Magi, the Coronation of Mary and the latter's death, all sculpted
in high relief out of wood. Below the altar to the left lies the **Donor's
Tomb**, adorned with sandstone effigies of Rudolf IV and his wife,
Catherine of Bohemia (they're actually buried in the catacombs; see
p.54), which would originally have been richly gilded and peppered
with precious stones.

In the Apostles' Choir to the south stands the glorious red marble
Tomb of Emperor Friedrich III. In among the 240 statues, 32 coats
of arms and numerous scaly creatures which decorate the tomb is the
emperor's mysterious acronym composed of the vowels of the
Roman alphabet, which has prompted numerous interpretations,
ranging from the obvious *Austria Erit In Orbe Ultima* ("Austria will
be the last in the world"), to the ingenious *Aquila Electa Iovis
Omnia Vincit* ("The chosen eagle conquers all things"). Friedrich

*In Latin, the
letters "u" and
"v" are both
rendered as
"V".*

himself revealed the German version to be *Alles Erdreich Ist Österreich Untertan* ("The whole world is subject to Austria"), though
some wags put forward the more appropriate *Aller Erst Ist Österreich Verloren* ("In the first place, Austria is lost"), since Friedrich had
great difficulty keeping hold of Upper and Lower Austria and was in
fact driven out of Vienna by the Hungarian king Matthias Corvinus in
1485.

The catacombs

*The catacombs
are open for
guided tours
only: every
30min
Mon–Sat
10–11.30am &
1.30–4.30pm,
Sun
1.30–4.30pm;
öS40/€2.91.*

*The bodies of
the later
Habsburgs are
buried in the
Kaisergruft,
see p.60; their
hearts are
buried in the
Augustiner-
kirche, see
p.111.*

A stairway in the north transept leads down into the **catacombs**
(*Katakomben*), which, initially at least, are a bit disappointing, having been over-restored in the 1960s. It's here that Rudolf IV and his
wife are actually buried, along with other early Habsburg rulers, plus
sundry priests, bishops and archbishops who served in the cathedral.
Rudolf himself died aged 26, though during his seven-year reign he
managed to found both the cathedral and the university; he died in
Milan in 1365 and was carried back to Vienna sewn into a cowhide to
preserve his body. Last of all, there's a small chamber lined with
cages filled with bronze caskets containing the entrails of the later
Habsburgs.

From the bottom of the stairs you enter the damp, dimly lit
labyrinth of eighteenth-century catacombs, which were closed in
1783 after the stench became too overpowering, and have been left
more or less untouched by the city's otherwise over-zealous restor-
ers. Around 16,000 locals are buried here, their bones piled high in
over thirty rooms, and in the final chamber, there's a particularly
macabre pile left over from a medieval plague pit. You exit from the
catacombs via a secret staircase which deposits you outside the
cathedral, by the place where Mozart's body was blessed before
being buried in St Marxer Friedhof (see p.191). At the very northeastern corner of the cathedral, near the exit from the catacombs, is
the **Capistrano Pulpit**, originally the cathedral's main pulpit, placed
outside after its replacement by the present version. It was from here
that the Venetian priest, St John of Capistrano, preached his sermons
against the Turks during the fifteenth century; the extravagant sunburst and statue of St Francis trampling on a Turk are Baroque additions.

Around Stephansplatz

Badly bombed in the war, few of the buildings on Stephansplatz itself
are worthy of mention. Even those that survived the bombs lack a little something – you'd hardly suspect that the unassuming two-storey
building on the north side of Stephansplatz is in fact the seventeenth-
century **Erzbischöfliches Palais** (Archbishops' Palace). Next door is
the equally nondescript **Zwettlhof**, originally an abbey founded by
Cistercians from Zwettl in Lower Austria, but bought by Rudolf IV for
use as the cathedral priory.

The Zwettlhof now houses the **Dom- and Diözesanmuseum** on its first floor (access through the passageway at Stephansplatz 6). This is basically the dumping ground for a mishmash of the cathedral's most valuable treasures and artwork. There are, however, some arresting medieval sculptures in wood – St Dionysius (aka Denis) carrying his severed head to his place of burial (in 3D relief), St Aegydius (aka Giles) looking rather sadly at the arrow stuck through his hand – and some High Baroque, not to say high kitsch, pieces, like the shrine of the Madonna, whose cloak opens up to reveal God (forming the main part of her body) surrounded by a host of worshippers' faces. The highlight, though, is the dimly lit treasury of monstrances and macabre reliquaries, including St Leopold's hipbone, a piece of the Virgin Mary's belt and the cranium of St Stephen. Follow the signs to the "Kapelle", and you can experience the additional thrill of seeing one of Beethoven's quills.

The Dom- and Diözesanmuseum is open Tues–Sat 10am–5pm; öS70/€5.09.

Schatzkammer and Deutschordenskirche

A much more intriguing ecclesiastical treasure trove can be seen at the **Schatzkammer des Deutschen Ordens** (Treasury of the Order of Teutonic Knights), spread over five rooms on the second floor of the Deutschordenshaus; enter from Singerstrasse 7, one block south of Stephansplatz, and be sure to ask for the information sheets in English. The Teutonic Knights were one of the three main military-religious orders to emerge during the Crusades in the twelfth century and for many centuries had their base in Marienburg (in what is now Poland). When the Order split along religious lines in the sixteenth century, those still loyal to Catholicism moved their headquarters to Mergentheim in Bavaria, until they were disbanded by order of Napoleon in 1809. Thirty years later the Order was reconstituted in Vienna, where it remains active as a charitable body.

The treasury's varied collection, assembled by seven centuries of Grand Masters (*Hochmeister*), ranges from the mundane – seals, coins and crosses in room I – to the bizarre, in room II: a red coral salt-cellar tree hung with fossilized sharks' teeth, which were thought to be adders' tongues and could therefore detect poisoned food, and two "chocolate sets", one with silver cups and saucers, complete with tiger-shell spoons sporting wonky silver handles, and another in Chinoiserie style. There are other bizarre exhibits from the Kunstkammer, collected by the Grand Master Archduke Maximilian III, like the three bezoars – petrifications of ibex stomachs – to which the Persians attributed great healing powers, and an onyx pendant depicting Jonah reclining on the tongue of a diminutive whale. The Order's military past is represented by a collection of exotic arms and armour, including a wiggly sixteenth-century Sumatran sword and scabbard, and a poisoned dagger with a handle carved out of rhino horn into the shape of the Buddha, with sapphire eyes and ruby

The Schatzkammer is open May–Oct Mon, Thurs & Sun 10am–noon, Wed 3–5pm, Fri & Sat 10am–noon & 3–5pm; Nov–April closed Fri morning & Sun; öS50/€3.63.

Mozart in Vienna

Wolfgang Amadeus Mozart (1756–91) moved to Vienna in March 1781 after a summons from his employer, the irascible Archbishop of Salzburg, Count Colloredo, who was visiting his sick father in the city. Within three months Mozart had resigned from his post as court organist to the archbishop or "arch-oaf" (*Erzlimmel*) as he called him, causing a rift with his overbearing father, who was assistant *Kapellmeister* in Salzburg. The relationship was further strained when Mozart, against his father's wishes, moved in with the all-female Weber family, and grew particularly attached to one of the daughters, Constanze. In August 1782 Mozart eventually married the 19-year-old Constanze in the Stephansdom. Their union appears to have been happy, despite most biographers' misogynist attacks on Constanze as unworthy of his genius. Mozart himself hated to be parted from her, if his letters – "I kiss and squeeze you 1,095,060,437,082 times" – and the fact that he rarely left her side, are anything to go by.

After giving many concerts as conductor and pianist, Mozart turned his hand to opera, enjoying his greatest success in July 1782 with what is now his least-known operatic work, *Die Entführung aus dem Serail* (The Escape from the Harem). It was after hearing *Die Entführung* for the first time that the Emperor Josef II is alleged to have said: "Too beautiful for our ears, and an awful lot of notes, dear Mozart", to which Mozart replied "No more notes than necessary, Your Majesty!". Such tales have led to a popular belief that Mozart and Josef were constantly feuding over artistic debates: in his letters, however, Mozart's criticisms of the notoriously stingy emperor were on purely financial matters.

Mozart's next opera, *Le Nozze di Figaro* (The Marriage of Figaro), was premiered in May 1786 to a decidedly mixed reception, running for just nine performances. This was partly because its subject matter, in which a lecherous count is prevented from seducing a servant girl by an alliance

eyebrows. And in the final room, there is the most amazing table clock, smothered in a garland of silver-gilded leaves studded with garnets and turquoise.

Before you leave, be sure to pop inside the **sala terrena** (which looks like a gazebo) on the ground floor, at the bottom of the staircase, to admire the Baroque trompe l'oeil murals of flowers, birds, statues and carousing gods. After the *sala terrena*, the Order's church, the **Deutschordenskirche**, on street level, appears relatively modest. Incorporated into the Order's buildings in the fourteenth century, the church has retained its Gothic origins (despite remodelling in later centuries), is decorated with the Order's numerous coats of arms, and features a superb sixteenth-century Flemish winged altarpiece depicting the Passion. Also worth a peek is the misshapen cobbled **courtyard** to the rear, an almost pastorally peaceful spot festooned with ivy and flower boxes. Brahms spent the best part of two years here in 1863–65, but inevitably it's Mozart who gets the plaque for his brief sojourn here in the spring of 1781.

between the serving classes and his own long-suffering wife, was controversial – as a play it had already been banned in Paris and Vienna. Josef II obviously liked it, however, inviting the cast to give a special performance at his summer residence at Laxenburg. And *Figaro*'s subversive overtones went down a storm in Prague, where Mozart premiered two later operas, *Don Giovanni* and *La Clemenza di Tito* (The Clemency of Tito), both of which were written in Vienna.

Mozart's final work was his *Requiem*, which was commissioned anonymously by an "unknown messenger" in the last year of Mozart's life. Only after Mozart's death did the patron's identity became known: it was the recently widowed Count Franz Walsegg-Stuppach, who wished to pass the composition off as his own. In the end it became Mozart's own requiem, since it was still unfinished when he died during the night of December 4–5, 1791, after suffering rheumatic fever for two weeks. Few biographers have forgiven Constanze for not attending the funeral service at Stephansdom; others assert that she was too distraught to show up. She has also been criticized for having the *Requiem* completed by one of Mozart's pupils, Sussmayr, so as to get the final payment – though this seems fair enough for a widow left with two children to raise (and apparently Mozart had suggested this course of action on his deathbed).

Yet more anecdotes surround the generally accepted rivalry with the *Kapellmeister* Antonio Salieri, though this, too, has been overplayed. Salieri was exclusively an opera composer, while Mozart, at least until 1786, was known chiefly as an instrumental composer and virtuoso pianist. Some went as far as to suggest that Salieri himself poisoned Mozart, an allegation strenuously denied by Salieri on his deathbed years later, but to no avail: Alexander Pushkin dramatized it, Nicolai Rimsky-Korsakov made it into an opera, and most famously *Amadeus*, Peter Shaffer's play on the subject, was made into an Oscar-winning film by Miloš Forman. For the story of how Mozart was condemned to a pauper's grave, see p.191.

Figarohaus

The **Figarohaus**, home of Vienna's Mozart Museum, lies immediately east of the cathedral (to get there, pass through the *Durchhaus* at Stephansplatz 5a and enter at Domgasse 5). Here, on the first floor, Mozart, Constanze and their son, Karl Thomas, lived for three years, during which the composer enjoyed his greatest success. It was Mozart's swankiest accommodation in Vienna, where he even had his own billiards room and space for visitors. The composer Johann Nepomuk Hummel stayed here as Mozart's live-in pupil for two and a half years; Josef Haydn was a regular visitor, opining that Mozart was "the greatest composer that I know in person or by name".

Sadly, however, there's not a lot to see inside. Only one of the rooms retains the original decor of marble and stucco (the Camesina family, who owned the property, were stucco artists). There are none of Mozart's personal effects, no period furniture, no atmosphere, just a few facsimiles of original scores, and pictures of the composer and his circle of friends. Nevertheless, it's worth a visit, if only for the

*The Figarohaus
is open
Tues–Sun
9am–6pm;
öS25/€1.82.*

On Mozart's Trail

It's almost as difficult to avoid images of Mozart in Vienna – on chocolate boxes, on liqueur bottles, on tourist brochures, on flyers for concerts – as it is in his home town of Salzburg. For it was in Vienna that Mozart spent the last decade of his life, during which he composed almost all of his most famous works. He moved thirteen times, for a variety of reasons, not least because he never managed to secure a permanent posting, which meant that he was always on the point of leaving the city. Today the streets of the Innere Stadt are littered with plaques marking his various addresses, though in fact, only one – the Figarohaus – still stands, and is now a museum to the composer. The following is a chronological list of all his known Viennese residences:

Singerstrasse 7. On his arrival in March 1781, Mozart stayed here with the Archbishop of Salzburg in the House of the Teutonic Knights.

Petersplatz 11. In May, Mozart rented a room from the Weber family, but had to move out in early September, due to rumours about his liaison with one of the daughters, Constanze.

Graben 17. After leaving the Webers, he moved round the corner to lodge with the Arnsteins, the city's most privileged Jewish family.

Wipplingerstrasse 19. Following the success of his opera *Die Entführung aus dem Serail*, Mozart moved here in July 1782, to be joined, after their marriage in August, by Constanze.

Wipplingerstrasse 14. In December 1782, the Mozarts moved down the street to a house belonging to a wealthy, converted Jew, Baron Wetzlar, where they lived in two rooms on the fourth floor.

Kohlmarkt 7. Three months later, in February 1783, Mozart moved again, as a favour to Wetzlar, who needed the rooms. Wetzlar waived the back rent, paid for the move, and paid for the Kohlmarkt lodgings.

building's lovely courtyard, the views along Blutgasse, and the chance to hear some of Mozart's music on the headphones provided.

Kärntnerstrasse and around

As a whole the street has gone downmarket over the last century. One exception is **J. & L. Lobmeyr** at no. 26, which, as well as flogging expensive glass and crystal, also houses an informal glass museum. The assistants are quite happy for you to wander through to the back of the shop, where you'll find the stairs that lead to the second-floor balcony. The wonderful, mostly antique, exhibits here include an incredible range of chandeliers, culminating, in both senses of the word, in a copy of the 1960s chandelier which graces the New York Metropolitan Opera House. Downstairs in the shop itself, you'll see glassware sets still made to designs by Adolf Loos and Josef Hoffmann for the Wiener Werkstätte (see p.152).

The Lobmeyr shop and museum are open Mon–Fri 9am–6pm, Sat 10am–4pm.

The only other buildings of any architectural merit are no. 16, opposite the Steffl department store, which sports quasi-medieval

Judenplatz 3. In April 1783, Mozart moved into "good accommodations", where his first child, Raimund Leopold, was born (his wife's cries during labour are alluded to in the second movement of his D minor String Quartet).

Graben 29. In January 1784, the Mozarts moved to the Trattnerhof, one of the most famous addresses in all Vienna at the time, owned by the wealthy publisher, Johann Thomas von Trattner, whose second wife, Maria Theresia, was one of Mozart's first pupils.

Schulerstrasse 8. In September 1784, the Mozarts moved into the Camesina House, behind Stephansdom (now the Figarohaus; see p.57).

Landstrasse Hauptstrasse 75–77. In April 1787, the Mozarts moved out of the Innere Stadt into a garden apartment in the third district of Landstrasse – here he composed *Eine kleine Nachtmusik*.

Tuchlauben 27. In December 1787, landlord problems forced them to move to the corner of Schultergasse and Tuchlauben.

Währingerstrasse 26. In June 1788, due to financial difficulties, the Mozarts moved again. Mozart's financial crisis was partly precipitated by the Turkish threat – 1788 was known as the *Türkenjahr* – and compounded by the French Revolution.

Judenplatz 4. They kept this address from January 1789 for almost two years. It was here that their fifth child died and Constanze's illness began – an ulcerated leg with fears of infection, which brought further financial worries, as she had to move temporarily to Baden to take the cure.

Rauhensteingasse 8. Mozart's last move – his thirteenth address – took place in September 1791, when it appears that he had largely overcome his money problems. During their time here the couple's sixth child, Franz Xaver, was born, Mozart wrote *Die Zauberflöte*, *La Clemenza di Tito*, and spent his last days working on his *Requiem*. The plot is now occupied by the Steffl department store, whose ground floor contains a memorial/shop dedicated to the composer (daily 9.30am–7pm; free).

frescoes, and the **Malteserkirche** (Church of the Knights of Malta; *www.malteser.at*), directly opposite Lobmeyr. The latter is less difficult to miss thanks to its imposing Neoclassical entrance, a misleading introduction to what is basically a simple, single-nave Gothic church. Inside is a splendid Neoclassical monument to Jean de la Valette, who in 1565, as depicted in the monument's frieze, defended Malta from the Turks – two of whose moustachioed brethren hold up the Grand Master's monument. Beyond, on the corner of Annagasse, is the street's oldest secular building, the modest three-storey Palais Esterházy, now a casino. Kärntnerstrasse continues south past the Staatsoper (see p.133), across the Ringstrasse to Karlsplatz (see p.138).

The American Bar, on Kärntner Durchgang, is an architectural masterpiece from 1908 by Adolf Loos.

Neuer Markt

Kärntnerstrasse's most interesting sights lie off the street itself, most conspicuously in the **Neuer Markt** to the west, formerly the city's medieval flour market, now used as a car park. The centrepiece of the square is the Baroque Providentia fountain, better known as the **Donnerbrunnen**, after its sculptor Georg Raphael Donner. The nudi-

*The original
lead figures
can be seen in
the Unteres
Belvedere, see
p.179.*

ty of the figures perched on the edge of the fountain – they represent the four Austrian tributaries of the Danube: the Enns, March, Ybbs and Traun – was deemed too risqué by the Empress Maria Theresia, who had the lead statues removed in 1770 to be melted down and made into cannons. They were returned unharmed in 1801, and in 1873 replaced by bronze copies: the young male figure of Traun, in particular, depicted on the point of catching a fish with his trident, clearly showed rather too much buttock for contemporary tastes, hence the judiciously placed fig leaf.

The buildings which surround the square are as undistinguished as those on Kärntnerstrasse itself – and that goes, too, for the **Kapuzinerkirche**. Yet this grim-looking church is one of the premier sights in Vienna, for since 1633, its crypt – the **Kaisergruft** – has been the unlikely resting place of the Habsburgs (with just a few notable exceptions). They chose the lowly, mendicant Order of the Capuchins as a gesture of modesty; to underscore the point, an elaborate ceremony was enacted at each Habsburg funeral. As the funeral cortege approached the church, the prior would ask "Who seeks entry here?". The grand master of the court would reply "I am His Majesty the Emperor of Austria, King of Hungary". The prior would then maintain "I know him not, who seeks entry?". "I am the Emperor, Apostolic King of Hungary, King of Bohemia, Dalmatia, Croatia, Slavonia, Galicia, Lodomeria, Illyria, Jerusalem, Archduke of Austria, Grand-Prince of Transylvania, Grand Duke of Tuscany and Krakow, Duke of Lorraine, Salzburg, Styria, Carinthia and Carniola." The prior would insist "I know him not, who seeks entry here?". At this the grand master would kneel, saying "A humble sinner, who begs God's mercy" – only then would the coffin be allowed in.

Kaisergruft

*The
Kaisergruft is
open daily
9.30am–4pm;
öS40/€2.91.*

The **Kaisergruft** itself is entered from a doorway to the left of the church. While a monk relieves you of your money, notices demand

---

Meissl und Schadn

Emperor Franz-Josef was famous for eating *Tafelspitz* (boiled rump of beef) for lunch every day. His courtiers, naturally, followed suit; one of the best places to sample the dish was at the legendary **Meissl und Schadn** restaurant on Neuer Markt, which regularly offered more than 25 varieties of *Tafelspitz*. The restaurant was also the scene of imperial Vienna's most famous political **assassination**. On October 21, 1916, Prime Minister Count Karl von Stürgkh was shot dead, while enjoying his after-dinner cigar, by fellow diner Friedrich Adler. The assassin, son of the leader of the Social Democrats, Viktor Adler, was appalled by the slaughter of the war, and incensed by Stürgkh's refusal to reconvene parliament. He was sentenced to life imprisonment, but later released in an act of clemency by Emperor Karl I, and went on to outlive *Meissl und Schadn* itself, which was destroyed in the air raids of World War II.

---

a respectful *Silentium!* – but don't let them kid you, this place is a tourist attraction above all else. Inside, though the crypt is neither gloomy nor Gothic in any sense of the word, it is, nevertheless, an intriguing insight into the Habsburgs' fascination with death.

To follow the tombs in chronological order, turn right immediately as you enter the crypt, and head for the small **Founders' Vault** on the right at the far end; here you'll find Matthias and his wife, Anna, who thought up the Kaisergruft, and whose bodies were transferred here in 1633 (a decade or so after their deaths). The tombs that line the vault along which you've just walked are mostly fairly modest seventeenth-century works, though when you consider that twelve of the incumbents are children, these are clearly pretty big coffins. The exceptions are the final four monster Baroque pewter sarcophagi by the main entrance. Those of Leopold I and Josef I were both designed by Johann Lucas von Hildebrandt, the latter sporting ghoulish skulls in full armour below, and with bat wings above. Those of Karl VI and his wife are utterly "his n' hers" designs carried out by Rococo artist, **Balthasar Ferdinand Moll**: his sits on lions, with toothy skulls sporting crowns at each corner; hers sits on eagles, with women in mourning veils at each corner.

The main focus and highlight of the crypt is the nearby **Maria Theresia Vault**, almost entirely taken up with Moll's obscenely large double tomb for the empress and her husband, Franz Stephan. Over three metres high and wide, six metres long, and smothered in Rococo decorations, the imperial couple are depicted sitting up in bed, as if indignantly accusing one another of snoring. Immediately below their feet lies the simple copper coffin of their son, Josef II, to whom such pomposity was an anathema. It was he who instigated the idea of a reusable coffin, and issued a decree enforcing its use in all funerals – not surprisingly, given the Viennese obsession with elaborate send-offs, the emperor was eventually forced to back down. Several more of Maria Theresia's sixteen children lie in the shadow of their mother, in ornate Rococo coffins, as does the only non-Habsburg among the crypt's 143 coffins, Karoline Fuchs-Mollard, the empress's governess.

After the Maria Theresia Vault it's all downhill architecturally. The **Franz II Vault** contains only the fairly plain tombs of the emperor and his four wives. Ferdinand I and his wife share the **Ferdinand Vault** with 37 others, though they're all buried in niches in the wall. At the far end of the crypt is the gloomy postwar bunker of the **New Vault**, which features jazzy, concrete, zig-zag vaulting. Star corpses here include Maximilian I, Emperor of Mexico, who was assassinated in 1867, and Marie Louise, Napoleon's second wife. Their son, the Duke of Reichstadt or "L'Aiglon" (see p.232), who died of consumption at the age of 21, was also buried here until 1940, when Hitler had his remains transferred to Paris as a gesture of goodwill.

Kärntnerstrasse and around

The Habsburgs' entrails are buried in the catacombs of Stephansdom, see p.54; their hearts are in the Augustinerkirche, see p.111.

**Kärntner-
strasse and
around**

*For more on
the Empress
Elisabeth, see
p.240.*

Finally, there's the **Franz-Josef Vault**, the emperor's sarcophagus, permanently strewn with fresh flowers. Even more revered,
though, is his wife, Empress Elisabeth, who was assassinated in
1898, her tomb draped in Hungarian wreaths and colours. On the
other side of the emperor is the coffin of their eldest son, Crown
Prince Rudolf, who committed suicide in 1889 (see p.266).

The **Chapel** beyond contains the Kaisergruft's most recent arrival,
the Empress Zita, who died in 1989 in exile in Switzerland, and was
buried here with imperial pomp and circumstance. In the corner is a
bust of her dashing, bemedalled husband, the Emperor Karl I, who
was deposed in 1918, and is buried on the island of Madeira, where
he died of pneumonia in 1922.

East of Kärntnerstrasse

The Kleines
Café, *on
Franziskaner-
platz, is one of
Vienna's finest
small
Kaffeehäuser;
see p.312.*

The Kaisergruft may be the main tourist attraction off Kärntnerstrasse,
but there are a couple of other sights a short stroll east of the street.
The most obvious is **Franziskanerplatz**, a pretty little square halfway
along Weihburggasse, centred on a statue of Moses, and dominated by
the Renaissance facade of the **Franziskanerkirche**, with its distinctive
volute gable adorned with miniature obelisks. The interior, though, is
High Baroque, with a high cherub count on just about every altar and
ledge, and an incredible slab of sculpted drapery falling down in folds
from the ceiling, on the left as you walk in. The St John of Nepomuk
monument employs a similar theatrical effect – this time it's sculpted
water flowing over the side – while the high altar features a huge
Gothic Madonna set against a giant sunburst.

*The
Winterpalais
is open
Mon–Thurs
8am–4pm, Fri
8am–3.30pm;
free.*

One block south, at Himmelpfortgasse 8, is the former
Winterpalais des Prinzen Eugen (Winter Palace of Prince
Eugène), a typically mighty Baroque palace strung out along a narrow street. Designed by Fischer von Erlach and extended by
Hildebrandt, the palace now houses the Ministry of Finance; the
only part visible to members of the public is the staircase, executed in grandiose style despite the restricted space. Four writhing
Atlantes flank the stairs, and a figure of Hercules stands in the
niche above the landing; the ceiling painting of Apollo is by Louis
Dorigny. To reach the staircase, pass through the main entrance
and take the last door on the right before the Rococo courtyard. To
view the equally splendid state rooms, where the prince received
foreign dignitaries, you must make a prior appointment; ☎51433.

*The Sammlung
is open
March–Dec
Wed 9am–4pm
& Sun
9am–1pm;
öS25/€1.82.*

Another block south at Johannesgasse 8 is the **Sammlung
Religiöse Volkskunst**, a department of the Folk Art Museum, housed
in the city's former Ursuline convent (now the Academy of Music).
Among the small collection of eighteenth-century folk paintings,
travelling altars, and simple drawings illustrating the roads to heav-
en and hell, the highlight is, without doubt, the Baroque convent
apothecary, built in 1747 and still in situ, with its pots and bottles
arrayed in tall glass-fronted dressers.

One final block south is the pretty little pedestrianized street of Annagasse, lined with Baroque houses and named after its church, the **Annakirche**, an oasis of calm disturbed only by the odd snatch of muffled music coming from the nearby conservatoire. Built in the seventeenth century, the church was given a Baroque going-over in the following century by the Jesuits, who employed David Gran to paint a series of superb ceiling frescoes, and the high altar painting of the Holy Family.

Kärntner-strasse and around

Haus der Musik

Signposts on Kärntnerstrasse point east to the **Haus der Musik** (House of Music), a hugely enjoyable new attraction down Annagasse in the newly revamped headquarters of the Wiener Philharmoniker (Vienna Philharmonic; *www.wienerphilharmoniker.at*). On the first floor is a museum dedicated to this world-famous orchestra, which only allowed women to join its ranks in 1996. It comes as something of a surprise then, to find on the second floor a startling, state-of-the-art exhibition on the nature of sound, filled with high-tech installations.

The Haus der Musik is open daily 10am–10pm; öS110/€7.99; www.haus -der-musik -wien.at.

To get you into the mood, the walls of the first, bare room you enter vibrate with pre-natal synthesized sound. After a brief rundown on the biology of the ear, you enter the "laboratory of perception", where a bank of beautifully designed touch-screen computers explore human responses to frequency, volume and so on. Elsewhere on this floor, you can watch and stretch the sound waves created by your own voice, play around with pre-recorded sounds in the dimly lit "sea of voices" room, and stick your head into sound bowls to hear everyday noises from around the world.

On the third floor, the subject is more conventional, with a room on each of the big three classical composers – Haydn, Mozart and Beethoven – as well as one each dedicated to Schubert, Strauss, Mahler and Schönberg's modernist posse. The displays are still a whole lot more imaginative than all the city's other musical memorials put together. There's plenty of hands-on fun and games: you can isolate each of the parts to Mozart's *Eine kleine Nachtmusik*, have a virtual tour of musically significant parts of Vienna, and do some virtual conducting.

There's yet more musical tomfoolery upstairs in the Brain Opera, where you can create your own music on the Gesture Wall, come over all percussive at the Rhythm Tree, and feed musical chips into a sophisticated computer bank of sounds at the end.

Graben and Kohlmarkt

The prime shopping streets of **Graben** and **Kohlmarkt** retain an air of exclusivity that Kärntnerstrasse has lost. Their shops, many of which are preserved in aspic as if the Empire lives on, advertise long-defunct branches in places such as Karlsbad, Leipzig and Prag. Others still sport the "K. K." or "k.u.k" emblem – *kaiserlich und*

königlich (Imperial and Royal) – the Austrian equivalent of the "By Appointment to Her Majesty the Queen" flaunted by the shops of upper-crust London. In between these old-fashioned stores are several Art Nouveau edifices, and trendy designer jewellers produced by the doyen of modern Austrian architecture, **Hans Hollein**.

Graben

Graben – its name translates as "ditch" – was once a moat that lay outside the Roman camp. It was filled in sometime in the thirteenth century, and, like Kärntnerstrasse, was widened at the beginning of the nineteenth century, from which era most of its buildings date. The most conspicuous monument on Graben is Fischer von Erlach's **Pestsäule** (Plague Column), or Dreifaltigkeitssäule (Trinity Column) to give its full title, a towering, amorphous mass of swirling clouds, saints and cherubs, covered in a cobweb of netting to keep the pigeons off. On the south side of the column, below the kneeling Emperor Leopold I, Faith and a cherub can be seen gleefully plunging a flaming torch into the guts of an old hag (Plague). Ostensibly erected to commemorate the end of the 1679 plague, similar monuments were raised throughout the Empire on the initiative of the Jesuits, as much to celebrate deliverance from the Protestant or Turkish "plague". As such, they became symbols of the Counter-Reformation.

Designer shops

The shops at street level on Graben and neighbouring Kohlmarkt are by no means all stuck in the Habsburg era; in fact, several are minor masterpieces of twentieth-century design. First off, there's the **Knize** tailors at Graben no. 11, whose luxuriant black marble facade was designed by Adolf Loos in 1910. It's a typical example of Loos's work, which combines a love of rich materials with a strict aversion to unnecessary ornamentation. The sales room on the ground floor is tiny, but upstairs there's a much larger wood-panelled fitting room, unchanged since Loos's day. Another characteristic Loos facade can be seen at Kohlmarkt 16, designed in 1912 for the bookshop **Manz**. Despite his name (and rumours to the contrary), Loos did not design the underground toilets on Graben, which are the work of Wilhelm Beetz.

After the war, Hans Hollein, of Haas Haus infamy (see p.47), continued where Loos had left off. The first real shot across the bows of the city's dour postwar architecture was his **Retti** candle shop at Kohlmarkt 8–10, designed in the 1960s, the doorway of its smooth aluminium facade shaped like a giant keyhole. Then, in the early 1970s, he gave the **Schullin** (now Deutsch) jewellers, Graben 26, a polished marble facade spliced by a seam of mercurial gold which trickles down into the door frame. The jewellers were clearly enamoured, and commissioned Hollein to design their branch at Kohlmarkt 7 in the 1980s; this time, he chose a more subtle interplay of shapes and materials rather than a single arresting image: slender wooden columns support a gilded industrial sheet metal pediment, while portholes serve as showcases, and brass snakes as doorhandles.

The Pestsäule, and the Hildebrandt-designed **Bartolotti-Partenfeld palace** at no. 11 on the corner of Dorotheergasse, are the only survivors of the Baroque era on Graben. The two most imposing buildings on the street were designed by Otto Wagner, best known for his Jugendstil architecture: the 1895 **Ankerhaus**, at no. 10, which forms the block between Spiegelgasse and Dorotheergasse, and the much earlier **Grabenhof**, whose red marble loggia forms the most eye-catching ensemble. If you look up at the roof of the Ankerhaus, you'll see a wrought-iron and glass superstructure, originally intended as Wagner's own purpose-built studio.

The **Sparkasse** at the far end on the right, is a classic post-Napoleonic, or Biedermeier, building, both in its function, as a savings bank for the burgeoning bourgeoisie (note the busy bee symbol on the facade), and in its severe, unadorned Neoclassicism. The latter became the officially sanctioned style of the Metternich era, its lack of ornament acting as a visual symbol of the latter's repressive, reactionary politics. The cluster of naked caryatids – the Graben nymphs – at the far end of the street are an unintentional reminder of the area's one-time associations as a red-light district, which stretch back to the Josephine era. The caryatids flank the entrance to the flagship store of **Julius Meinl** (*www.meinl.com*), Vienna's equivalent of Harrod's food hall.

Peterskirche

Set back slightly from Graben, occupying a little square of its own, is the **Peterskirche**, more or less completed by Hildebrandt in 1708, and without doubt the finest Baroque church in the Innere Stadt. The confines of space within which he had to design the building mean that the twin-towered church is somewhat overwhelmed by its great green oval dome, both outside and in. Within, the dome's fresco of *The Assumption of the Virgin Mary* by Johann Michael Rottmayr is difficult to discern, but still adds immeasurably to the overall sense of theatrics, created by the lashings of ochre and gold stucco employed throughout. The High Baroque main altar and the fabulous cupola painting in the choir are the work of the Galli-Bibiena theatrical designers, a group of early eighteenth-century artists from Bologna who specialized in trompe l'oeil. The lavish gilded pulpit is, likewise, truly magnificent, but the most dramatic work of art is the silver and gold monument, designed by Lorenzo Mattielli, opposite, depicting St John of Nepomuk being thrown off Prague's Charles Bridge by some nasty-looking Czech bully boys, with Václav IV in Roman garb directing the proceedings. Also worth noting are the church's fabulously ornate pew ends, which sprout a trio of cherubic heads, and the bejewelled and fully clothed skeletons from the catacombs in Rome, which lie in glass coffins in the Michaelskapelle and the Kapelle der Heilige Familie. The latter also boasts a portrait of the founder of the Opus Dei

Places to eat and drink in the Innere Stadt are detailed on p.301.

movement, José Maria Escrivá, whose Viennese base is here in the Peterskirche.

Dorotheergasse

Of all the streets that fan out from Graben, the most rewarding is **Dorotheergasse**, home of several famous Viennese institutions. The first two face each other at the bottom of the street: the bohemian, nicotine-stained *Café Hawelka*, run by the same couple (now in their eighties) since World War II, and the ultimate stand-up sandwich bar, *Trześniewski*, opposite. Further up on the left is the *Hotel Graben*, where, from 1914 until his death in 1919, the poet Peter Altenberg (see Kaffeehäuser, p.310) was a permanent guest.

Jüdisches Museum

*The Jüdisches
Museum is
open daily
except Sat,
10am–6pm,
Thurs until
9pm; öS70/€5;
combined
ticket with
Museum
Judenplatz &
Synagogue
öS100/€7;
www.jmw.at.*

A relatively new arrival on Dorotheergasse is the city's intriguing **Jüdisches Museum** (Jewish Museum), halfway up in the Palais Eskeles at no. 11. Vienna was home to the first Jewish Museum in the world, founded in 1896 but forcibly closed by the Nazis in 1938; it wasn't until 1989 that it was finally re-established. Lavishly refurbished with money from the city council, the museum now boasts state-of-the-art premises, including a bookshop and the excellent *Teitelbaum Café*.

On the ground floor, the covered courtyard (now a lecture hall) is dominated by a giant glass cabinet of Judaica etched with quotations from the Torah and other sources, whose prophetic nature is revealed on the walls, which are peppered with photographic images from the Holocaust. On the whole, though, the curators have rejected the usual static display cabinets and newsreel photos of past atrocities. Instead, the emphasis of the museum's excellent temporary exhibitions on the first floor is on contemporary Viennese Jewish life and displays works by local Jewish artists and photographs of the current community. It's a bold and provocative approach, which succeeds in challenging the viewer's prejudices.

Special exhibitions also occupy part of the second floor, which contains the museum's permanent displays. Taking the Marxist Jewish critic Walter Benjamin's contention that "the past can only be seized as an image which flashes up at the instant when it can be recognized and is never seen again", the museum employs a series of free-standing glass panels imprinted with holograms – ranging from the knob of Theodor Herzl's walking stick, to a short clip capturing an everyday instance of anti-Semitism from 1911. These ghostly images, accompanied by judiciously selected soundbites (in German and English) on Zionism, assimilation and other key issues, pithily trace the history of Vienna's Jewry, juxtaposing the enormous achievements of the city's Jews – from Gustav Mahler to Billy Wilder – with its justified reputation as a hotbed of anti-Semitism.

*For more on
the city's Jews,
see p.78.*

Taking something of a different tack, the third floor contains the museum's *Schaudepot* or storage depot. The displays of Hanukkah candelabra and other ritual objects, located in large moveable glass cabinets, are deliberately haphazard – they constitute all that is left of the pre-1938 Jewish Museum and the community it served, and include many items literally pulled from the burnt embers of the city's synagogues, torched during *Kristallnacht* (see p.355).

Graben and Kohlmarkt

Dorotheum

Further on, beyond the Jüdisches Museum, stands the institution from which the street gets its name. The **Dorotheum** is the city's premier auction house, founded in 1707 by the Emperor Josef I as a pawnshop for the rich – the euphemism for those who had fallen on hard times was "going to visit Aunt Dorothy". Nowadays auctions take place daily, and you'll find almost anything up for sale from second-rate artworks, which go for a song, to Jugendstil furniture and minor works by the likes of Klimt and Schiele, for which you need to take out a second mortgage.

The Dorotheum is open Mon–Fri 9am–6pm; www.dorotheum .com.

Don't, however, be intimidated by the plush interior – anyone can walk in and view the goods free of charge. In the Glashof, on the ground floor, there are even fixed-priced goods for sale over the counter, everything from Hoffmann chairs to utter tat. The grandest of the showrooms is the main auction hall on the first floor with its high ceiling and second-floor balcony. There's another fixed-price shop for fine art on the second floor, along with an excellent café.

Kohlmarkt

The line of the old Roman moat continues down the narrow street of Naglergasse, but most shoppers and strollers turn left at the end of Graben up **Kohlmarkt**, site of the old wood and charcoal market. The most striking aspect of the street is the perfectly framed vista of the Michaelertor, its green dome marking the main entrance to the Hofburg from the Innere Stadt. Before you head up Kohlmarkt, though, be sure to look up at the roof of the building on the corner, whose copper cupola is topped by a splendid Hussar, once used to advertise a shop.

Even more than Graben, Kohlmarkt is the last bastion of luxury retailing, perhaps best expressed by **Demel**, a very "k.u.k." establishment, which still advertises itself as the imperial and royal confectioners. Established in 1786 as *Zuckerbäckerei* to the Habsburgs, its very famous and opulent *Kaffee-Konditorei*, dating from 1888, is at no. 14. Another Viennese institution is the **Artaria Haus**, a Jugendstil building set back from the street at no. 9, and faced in marble by Max Fabiani in 1901, the bolted slabs on the first floor anticipating Wagner's Postsparkasse (see p.153). The bookshop of the master mapmakers, Freytag & Berndt, occupies the ground floor, while Artaria & Co itself, publishers of musical tracts by the likes of Haydn, Mozart and Beethoven, is situated on the first floor.

For more on the shops of Kohlmarkt, see the box on p.64; for reviews of its eating and drinking options, see p.301.

The nearest U-Bahn is Herrengasse.

Michaelerplatz to the Mölker Bastei

Michaelerplatz, the square at the top of Kohlmarkt, is the Hofburg's backdoor, and, like nearby **Herrengasse** ("Lords' Lane") and **Minoritenplatz**, has long been a high-prestige address due to its proximity to the royal court. Once upon a time, every single house here was the town palace of some aristocratic family or another; these now serve as ministries and embassies for the most part, making this something of a lifeless quarter, especially at the weekend. Nevertheless, both Michaelerplatz and Minoritenplatz are showpiece squares, and Herrengasse is worth exploring, if only for the Palais Ferstel, which houses the famous *Café Central* and Vienna's only nineteenth-century shopping arcade, which brings you out onto the triangular square of **Freyung**, home to some of the city's finest exhibition galleries.

Michaelerplatz

The Hofburg itself is covered in detail in Chapter Three.

Michaelerplatz is dominated on one side by the exuberant arc of the neo-Baroque **Michaelertrakt**, begun in the 1720s by Fischer von Erlach's son, but only completed in the 1890s. Its curving balustrade is peppered with a lively parade of eagles, giant urns and trophies, while the gate's archways are framed by gargantuan statues of Hercules, and, at either end, fountains overburdened with yet more ungainly statuary: to the right, imperial land power; to the left, imperial naval power – though both were in short supply at the time the works were erected in 1897. The centre of the square is now occupied by a collection of archeological remains uncovered during work on the nearby U-Bahn station of Herrengasse. LED texts in several languages explain the significance of the rubble which lies exposed in a designer concrete trench (another of Hollein's works); most of what you see are heating ducts dating only from the nineteenth century – hardly heart-stopping stuff.

Much more significant is the **Loos Haus**, on the corner of Kohlmarkt and Herrengasse, which caused uproar when it was built in 1909–11 by Adolf Loos. Franz-Josef despised this "house without eyebrows" – in other words without the customary sculpted pediments which sit above the windows of most Viennese buildings. Work on the building was temporarily halted due to the protests, and only allowed to continue after Loos had acquiesced to adding bronze flower-boxes (to be filled with flora all year round). Today, it's difficult to see what all the fuss was about. The rich Cippolin marble columns that frame the main entrance look inoffensive enough, but the building's lack of ornamental dressing, particularly in the upper storeys, was shocking at the time. The original occupants, Loos's own tailors, Goldman & Salatsch, went bank-

rupt in 1925, but the current owners, Raiffeisenbank, have their
name displayed in simple gilt letters across the upper facade, just
as Loos originally instructed Goldman & Salatsch. The bank holds
regular exhibitions on the first floor of the building, so feel free to
walk in.

The next block along from the Loos Haus is taken up by the alto-
gether more conventional late nineteenth-century Palais
Herberstein, erected on the site of the **Café Griensteidl**, which was
demolished in 1897. Reconstructed and reopened on the ground
floor in 1990 to cash in on the nostalgia for *fin-de-siècle* Vienna, the
Griensteidl was, in its day, the preferred meeting place of the *Jung-
Wien* (Young Vienna) literary circle, most notably Arthur Schnitzler,
Hermann Bahr and Hugo von Hofmannsthal. The journalist, Karl
Kraus, another regular, wrote his most famous diatribe, *The
Demolished Literature*, against the "Young Vienna" circle, shortly
after the destruction of the café, suggesting that the movement
"would soon expire for lack of a foyer". Instead, the *Jung-Wien*
posse simply moved down Herrengasse to the *Café Central* (see
p.70), much to the annoyance of Kraus himself, who was a regular
there, too.

Michaelerkirche

The oldest building on Michaelerplatz, and the source of its name, is
the **Michaelerkirche**, first built in the thirteenth century, though the
Neoclassical facade, added in 1792, somewhat obscures this fact.
Inside, the church retains its plain Gothic origins, but it's the later
additions which are of more interest, in particular the *Fall of Angels*,
a Rococo cloudburst of cherubs and angels rendered in alabaster,
tumbling from the ceiling above the high altar. From November to
April you can get a closer look at this by simply walking in via the
west door; from May to October you can only do so by entering from
the *Durchgang* via the south door. After paying a small entrance fee
– depending on the time of year – (and picking up a confusing information sheet in English) you may then explore the church and the
exhibition which spreads out into the adjoining monastery.

By far the most interesting exhibits lie outside the main body of
the church, though the gilded organ – the largest Baroque organ in
Vienna – is very fine and there are regular recitals. The best place to
start is the sacristy, to the right of the chancel, alive with stucco, frescoes and inlaid cabinets. Liturgical silverware lurks beyond in the
summer sacristy, while the church's two stunning gold monstrances
are displayed in the priests' secret choir behind the main altar. To the
north of the choir lies the old sacristy, with an intriguing miniature
chest of drawers containing tiny reliquary cases. From here, you
cross a peaceful plant-filled courtyard to the wood-panelled refecto-
ry, whose cornice is richly decorated with acanthus leaves and
cherubs holding writhing scrolls.

*The church is
open May–Oct
Mon–Sat
10.30am–4.30
pm, Sun 1–5pm,
öS25/€1.82;
Nov–April
daily
dawn–dusk,
free.*

*Guided tours
of the crypt
take place
Mon–Fri 11am
& 3pm;
öS25/€1.82.*

From a doorway in the north choir aisle, you can descend into the church's suitably gloomy, labyrinthine **crypt**, which stretches the length and breadth of the building. A brief guided tour (in German) takes you past piles of paupers' bones and numerous musty coffins taken from the now defunct graveyard which once occupied Michaelerplatz, many with their lids off revealing desiccated bodies, still clothed and locked in a deathly grimace. Before you leave, be sure to check out the bizarre collection of imperial funereal crowns from the church's days as parish church to the court, displayed just off the crypt's vestibule. Finally, there's a chance to glimpse one of the church's original Romanesque north doors from 1230, discovered only recently, having been hidden for several centuries at the back of a tool shed.

Herrengasse

Herrengasse was the preferred address of the nobility from the time the Habsburgs moved into the Hofburg until the fall of the dynasty in 1918. Its name dates from the sixteenth century, when the Diet of Lower Austria (Niederösterreich) built its regional headquarters or **Landhaus**, which still stands at no. 13. As well as being a federal Land in its own right since 1922, Vienna was for centuries also the capital of Lower Austria – the region which surrounds the city – until 1986, when St Pölten became the new capital. It was here at the Landhaus

*For more on
the 1848 revo-
lution, see
p.348.*

that the Viennese revolution began on March 13, 1848. A large crowd of students, artisans and workers gathered outside the building demanding, among other things, freedom of the press and the resignation of the arch-conservative Prince Metternich. At one o'clock in the afternoon, soldiers fired into the crowd, killing several people and sparking off a mass uprising in the city. Metternich resigned and fled the city the next day, disguised, so the story goes, as a washerwoman. The Emperor Ferdinand was a later casualty, abdicating in favour of Franz-Josef, but the revolt was eventually crushed on October 31.

Opposite the Landhaus is the grandiose Italianate **Palais Ferstel**, built in the Ringstrasse style (see p.122) by Heinrich Ferstel in 1860 for the Austro-Hungarian National Bank (it also housed the Stock Exchange until 1877). More importantly, the palace has long been

*For a review
of the Café
Central, see
p.312.*

home to Vienna's most famous *Kaffeehaus*, **Café Central**, restored in 1986 primarily as a tourist attraction, though admittedly a very beautiful one. At the turn of the century, the café's distinctively decorated Gothic vaults were *the* meeting place of the city's intellectuals, harbouring not only the literary lights of the *Jung-Wien* movement, but also the first generation of Austrian Socialists: Karl Renner, Viktor Adler and Otto Bauer. The latter were occasional chess adversaries of Leon Trotsky, who whiled away several years here before World War I. At the entrance to the café is a life-size papier-mâché model of the moustachioed poet Peter Altenberg, another of the café's *fin-de-siècle* regulars.

Further up Herrengasse, past the café, is the entrance to the **Freyung Passage** – built in the 1860s as part of the Palais Ferstel – an eminently civilized, lovingly restored shopping arcade, which

Michaeler-platz to the Mölker Bastei

The Redl Affair

Without doubt the greatest scandal to hit the Habsburgs in their twilight years was the infamous affair of **Colonel Alfred Redl**, who committed suicide in the early hours of May 25, 1913. Not only had the head of counter-espionage in the imperial army been uncovered as a Russian secret agent, but he had been blackmailed into it because of his homosexuality, and had been in the pay of the Russians for the past seven years.

For some time, the Austrian military had been concerned about the leaking of classified information to the Russians. Then, early in April 1913, a letter was discovered to one "Nikon Nizetas", containing a considerable sum of money and the names and addresses of several Russian spies. It had been sent to the main post office in Vienna, but had remained unclaimed. Austrian counter-espionage decided to stake out the post office and wait for someone to pick up the incriminating letter. For six weeks, two agents sat in the building opposite waiting for a clerk in the post office to ring the bell which had been specially installed to warn them of the arrival of "Nikon Nizetas".

When the bell finally rang at 5.55pm on May 24, one agent was having a pee, and the other was in the canteen. By the time they reached the street, they had missed their man, though they managed to take down the cab number. As the two men stood around considering their next move, the self-same cab miraculously reappeared outside the post office. Not only could they now continue the chase, but they also discovered that "Nizetas" had left the felt sheath for his dagger in the back of the cab. They eventually retraced "Nizetas" to the *Hotel Klomser*, in the Palais Battyány, Bankgasse 2. The agents were shocked to find that the man who answered to "Nizetas's" description was one of their own superiors, Colonel Redl, who had just returned to the hotel. The agents handed the sheath to the concierge and waited to see if Redl would reclaim it. Caught off-guard as he left the hotel, Redl accepted the sheath from the receptionist, and then realizing what he had done, took flight. After a brief chase through the Innere Stadt, Redl gave himself up. He was handed a loaded revolver and told to go to his hotel room and do the honourable thing.

The whole affair would have been successfully hushed up – suicide among the upper echelons was very common – if it hadn't been for the locksmith who was called in to break into Redl's Prague flat. The place was decked out like a camp boudoir with pink whips on the wall and women's dresses in the cupboard. Unfortunately for the authorities, the locksmith in question was supposed to be playing football with the investigative journalist, Egon Erwin Kisch. When he told Kisch why he had been unable to turn up, Kisch immediately sent the story to a Berlin newspaper, and on May 29, the War Ministry was forced to admit the real reasons behind Redl's suicide. Redl's lover, Lieutenant Stefan Hromodka, on whom he had spent a small fortune, was sentenced to three months' hard labour (he later married, had several children and lived for another fifty years). Kisch became a popular hero overnight, with the best table in the *Café Central* reserved for him on all his visits to Vienna. The Redl affair later served as the plot for John Osborne's 1965 play *A Patriot for Me* and the subject of the 1985 film *Colonel Redl* by István Szabó.

THE INNERE STADT   71 links Herrengasse with Freyung (see below). The focus of this elegant marble passage is a glass-roofed, hexagonal atrium, with a fountain crowned by a statue of the Donaunixen (Danube Mermaid), whose trickling water echoes down the arcade.

Minoritenplatz

On the opposite side of Herrengasse, hidden away round the back of the Hofburg, is **Minoritenplatz**, a peaceful, cobbled square entirely surrounded by the Baroque former palaces of the nobility, now transformed into ministries and embassies.

*The Minoriten-
kirche belongs
to the city's
Italian com-
munity.*

At its centre is the fourteenth-century **Minoritenkirche**, whose stunted octagonal tower is one of the landmarks of the Innere Stadt (the top was knocked off by the Turks during the 1529 siege). The main entrance boasts probably the best preserved Gothic portal in Vienna, with a tripartite tympanum depicting the Crucifixion. Inside, the Gothic church is impressively lofty, but it's the tacky copy of Leonardo da Vinci's *Last Supper*, on the north wall, which steals the show – only close inspection reveals it to be a mosaic, so minuscule are the polished mosaic pieces. The work was actually commissioned in 1806 by Napoleon, who planned to substitute it for the original in Milan, taking the latter back to Paris. By the time it was finished, however, Napoleon had fallen from power and the Emperor Franz I bought it instead, though it wasn't until 1847 that the Austrians managed to bring it back to Vienna.

On the south side of the square is a magnificent palace built for the Emperor Karl VI by Hildebrandt as the Court Chancery, and now the **Bundeskanzleramt** (Federal Chancery), home of the Austrian Chancellor and the Foreign Ministry, whose main entrance opens onto Ballhausplatz. It was in this palace that Prince Metternich presided over the numerous meetings of the Congress of Vienna in 1814–15 (see opposite), and here, in the Chancellor's office, that the Austro-fascist leader, Engelbert Dollfuss, was assassinated during the abortive Nazi putsch of July 25, 1934. On that day, 154 members of the outlawed SS entered the building, and in the melee, Dollfuss was shot; his demands for a doctor and a priest fell on deaf ears, and, after two and a half hours, he died from his wounds.

Freyung

The aforementioned Freyung Passage from Herrengasse brings you out onto **Freyung** itself, a misshapen square centred on the Austria-Brunnen, unveiled in 1846 with bronze nymphs representing Austria and the key rivers in the Habsburg Empire at the time: the Danube, Po, Elbe and Vistula. In medieval times Freyung was a popular spot for public executions, and during the annual Christkindl Markt, held here in the eighteenth and nineteenth centuries, there were open-air theatre performances; the market has recently been

The Congress of Vienna

The one time that Vienna truly occupied centre stage in European history
was during the **Congress of Vienna**. Under the chairmanship of Prince
Metternich, 2 emperors, 3 kings, 11 princes, 90 ambassadors and 53 unin-
vited representatives congregated in October 1814 to try and thrash out a
balance of power following the collapse of the Napoleonic Empire. In addition to the Big Four of Austria, Prussia, Britain and Russia, there were
innumerable smaller delegations, including 32 minor German royals, with
their wives, mistresses and secretaries of state – there was even an unofficial deputation from the Jews of Frankfurt. Lord Castlereagh, Britain's
chief emissary, thought the Congress would last four weeks at the most –
in the end, it dragged on for nearly nine months. The Final Act of the
Congress wasn't signed until June 1815, long after Napoleon's escape
from Elba – "the Congress is dissolved", he announced on landing at
Cannes – and just twelve days before the final showdown of Waterloo.

The Congress has gone down in history as the largest and longest party
the city has ever seen, encapsulated in the famous quote by the Prince de
Ligne*: *"le congrès danse, mais il ne marche pas"* ("the Congress
dances, but it doesn't work"). Empress Maria Ludovica, Franz I's wife, said
the Congress cost her ten years of her life – and indeed she died within a
year of its conclusion. In order to distract the lesser participants from the
futility of the Congress, a vast programme of entertainment had to be
organized. Ironically, the Austrian Emperor Franz I, who ultimately footed
the bill, was no great party animal himself. Nevertheless, every night dinner was served in the Hofburg at forty tables; 1400 horses were required
to transport the royal guests to the palace. There were tombolas, fireworks, tournaments, ballooning, theatre performances, sleighing expeditions in the Wienerwald, concerts, including the premiere of *Fidelio* conducted by Beethoven himself, and lots of dancing. The Tsar, it was said,
danced forty nights on the trot, his amorous adventures compounding his
political rivalry with Metternich; the Russian Princess Bagration, nicknamed "the naked angel" for her habit of displaying her décolletage publicly, was voted the most beautiful; and Lord Castlereagh was deemed the
most ridiculous. He was later joined by the Duke of Wellington, who hated
the whole charade: "the hot rooms here have almost killed me," he wrote
home. At one ball in the palace's Redoutensaal, 6000 guests turned up
instead of the 3000 invited, as the imperial bouncers re-sold the tickets,
and there was a brisk trade in the uneaten food from the tables of the
Hofburg. Appropriately enough, probably the congress's most lasting con-
tribution to posterity was the popularization of the waltz.

* The prince, who was in his eighties at the time, actually coined the epi-
gram even before the congress had begun, repeating it on every possible
occasion until his death in December, brought on by a cold contracted
while waiting outside his house for his latest mistress.

re-established, and is held here on a much more modest scale in the
run-up to Christmas (see Public holidays and Festivals p.26).
Freyung also boasts three major art galleries: the **Harrach Palais**
(*www.khm.at*), adjacent to the Freyung Passage, which hosts temporary exhibitions put on by the Kunsthistorisches Museum; the
Kunstforum (*www.kunstforum-wien.at*), a major venue for

visiting exhibitions of fine art; and the **Museum im Schottenstift**
(see below).

Schottenstift

Freyung – meaning "Sanctuary" – derives its name from the
Schottenstift (Monastery of the Scots), which dominates the north
side of the square, and where fugitives could claim asylum in
medieval times. The monastery was founded in 1155 by the
Babenberg Duke Heinrich Jasomirgott, though the Benedictine
monks invited over were, most probably, Irish and not Scottish. They
were eventually expelled, after having shocked Viennese society by
"trading in furs, initiating wild dances and starting games of ball".
The monastery's glory days may be over, but its highly respected
grammar school, the Schottengymnasium, founded in 1807, remains
one of the most prestigious boys' schools in the country. Beyond the
ornate Baroque plasterwork and faux marble, the **Schottenkirche**
retains just a few reminders of its Romanesque origins in its southern choir chapel.

*The
Schottenkirche
is used by the
city's French
community.*

To view the former monastery's impressive art collection, in the
Museum im Schottenstift, you must first buy a ticket from the
Klosterladen (monastery shop) beside the church, and take the
stairs to the first floor. The walls are covered with mostly seven-
teenth- and eighteenth-century Dutch and German still lifes and landscapes. The prize exhibit, though, is the fifteenth-century winged
altarpiece, which used to reside in the Schottenkirche. Thirteen out
of the original sixteen panels survive: one side depicts scenes from
the life of the Virgin; the reverse side (originally shown only at
Easter) tells the story of the Passion. The vivid use of colour, the
plasticity of the faces, and the daring stab at perspective mark this
out as a masterpiece of late-Gothic art. Interestingly, the story is
given a local setting: the town of Krems is portrayed during the holy
family's search for an inn, while medieval Vienna forms the backdrop
for the Flight to Egypt.

*The Museum
im Schottenstift
is open
Thurs–Sat
10am–5pm,
Sun
11am–5pm;
öS50/€3.63.*

Mölker Bastei

*The nearest
U-Bahn is
Schottentor.*

The **Mölker Bastei**, one of the few remaining sections of the old zig-
zag fortifications that once surrounded the Innere Stadt, can be
found on Schreyvogelgasse, to the west of Freyung. The sloping cobbled lane should be familiar to fans of the movie *The Third Man*, for
it's in the doorway of no. 8 that Harry Lime (played by Orson Welles)
appears for the first time.

*The museum is
open
Tues–Sun
9am–12.15pm
& 1–4.30pm;
öS25/€1.82.*

High up on the Mölker Bastei itself, at no. 8, is the
Pasqualatihaus, where Beethoven lived on and off from 1804
onwards (he stayed at over thirty addresses during his thirty-five
years in Vienna). Mr Pasqualati wisely left the flat below empty so
Beethoven could make as much noise as he wanted. The composer's
apartment is now a museum (one of three museums dedicated to

Beethoven in Vienna), though as usual, there's no indication of how the place might have looked at the time he lived there. Perhaps this is just as well – according to one visitor it was "the darkest, most disorderly place imaginable . . . under the piano (I do not exaggerate) an unemptied chamber pot . . . chairs . . . covered with plates bearing the remains of last night's supper". Instead, you're left to admire Ludwig's gilded salt and pepper pots and battered tin sugar container, or sit down and listen to some of his music through headphones.

Michaeler-platz to the Mölker Bastei

For more information on Beethoven in Vienna, see p.253.

Am Hof to Hoher Markt

The area of the Innere Stadt which lies between **Am Hof** and **Hoher Markt** is where Vienna began. It was here that the Roman camp of Vindobona lay, with Hoher Markt, roughly speaking, as its main forum; later, the Babenbergs established their royal court at Am Hof, with the city's medieval Jewish ghetto close by. Few reminders of those days remain – above ground at least – although Marc-Aurel-Strasse (which commemorates the philosopher Emperor Marcus Aurelius, who died here in 180 AD), like neighbouring Wipplinger Strasse and Tuchlauben, is an old Roman road. Several of the city's most beguiling alleyways are hidden deep within this part of the Innere Stadt, as is the controversial new **Holocaust memorial** and one of the city's finest Gothic churches, **Maria am Gestade**.

Am Hof

Am Hof is the largest square in the Innere Stadt, an attractive, tranquil spot, marred only by the surface protrusions of its underground car park. The name – *Hof* means both "royal court" and "courtyard" – dates from medieval times, when this was the headquarters of the Babenbergs, who lorded it over Vienna until the Habsburgs took over the reins in 1273. Today the jousting tournaments, religious plays and public executions have long gone, and the centrepiece is now the rather forbidding, matt black **Mariensäule** (Marian Column), erected by the Emperor Ferdinand III as a thank you to the Virgin for deliverance from the Protestant Swedish forces in the Thirty Years' War. At the base of the column, blackened cherubic angels in full armour wrestle with a dragon, lion, serpent and basilisk, representing hunger, war, heresy and the plague.

Dominating the square is the **Kirche am Hof**, from whose balcony the Austrian Emperor Franz I proclaimed the end of the Holy Roman Empire in 1806, on the orders of Napoleon. The church's vast Baroque facade, topped by a host of angels, belies the fact that this is, for the most part, a fourteenth-century Gothic structure. Inside, it's quite frankly a stylistic mess, with the old Gothic Carmelite

The Kirche am Hof belongs to the city's Croat community.

**Am Hof to
Hoher Markt**

church struggling to get out from under some very crude later additions, dating from the period when the place was handed over to the Jesuits: Corinthian capitals are glued onto the main pillars, and the aisles have been turned into a series of side chapels, with stuck-on stucco porticos – only the coved and coffered ceiling of the choir works at all well. The adjoining former Jesuit seminary became the imperial war ministry, and as such was a prime target during the 1848 revolution. On October 6, the mob stormed the building, dragged out the War Minister, Count Latour, and promptly strung him up from a nearby lamppost. Three railway workers were later hanged for the offence.

Opposite the church is another architectural illusion, for behind the palatial facade of no. 7–9 is the city's **Feuerwehr Zentrale** (Central Fire Station). The engines are hidden behind the series of double doors, while above them, on the first floor, is the little-visited **Feuerwehrmuseum** (Firefighting Museum). Prize attraction is the mock-up of the *Alte Türmestube* (look-out post) in the spire of Stephansdom; from 1534 until as recently as 1956 fires in the Innere Stadt were spotted from here, by a guy with a telescope and loud hailer. You should also be able to take a look at a couple of the older fire engines on the floor below. In the basement of no. 9, you can view a few **Roman ruins**, including a re-assembled conduit made from rooftiles stamped with the logo of the 13th Legion.

Feuerwehrmuseum is open Sun & public holidays 9am–noon; free; Mon–Fri by appointment: ☎531 99. The Roman remains are open Sat & Sun 11am–1pm; öS25/€1.82.

The firemen originally kept their equipment next door at no. 10 in the former **Bürgerliches Zeughaus** (Civic Armoury), suitably decorated with a panoply, several trophies, a double-headed eagle and crowned by a spectacular cluster of figures holding up a gilded globe.

Off Am Hof

If you pass under the archway by the Kirche am Hof, and head down Schulhof, you can see the church's Gothic origins clearly in its tall lancet windows and buttresses. Watchmakers continue to ply their trade from tiny lock-ups in between the buttresses at the back of the church, while opposite stands the Baroque Obizzi Palace, home to the city's **Uhrenmuseum** (Clock Museum), ranged over three floors of Schulhof 2. Founded in 1917, this is the world's oldest museum of its kind, but sadly, it lacks the crucial information in either German or English to bring the collection alive. Nevertheless, you'll find every kind of time-measuring device, from sophisticated seventeenth-century grandfather clocks to primitive wax candles containing tiny lead balls, which drop onto a metal dish as the candle melts. Other unusual exhibits include the smallest pendulum clock in the world, which fits inside a thimble, and a wide selection of eighteenth-century *Zwiebeluhren*, literally "onion clocks", set within cases shaped like fruit, musical instruments and the like.

The Uhrenmuseum is open Tues–Sun 9am–4.30pm; öS50/€3.63; www.museum .vienna.at.

For most people, the **Puppen und Spielzeug Museum** (Doll and Toy Museum), next door on the first floor of Schulhof 4, holds more appeal, further enhanced by the building's well-preserved Baroque interior. It's an old-fashioned kind of a place, with ranks of glass cabinets and no buttons to press for younger kids. The majority of the exhibits are dolls – from Biedermeier porcelain figures to those portraying Chinese, Native American and African characteristics, which were all the rage between the wars – with just a small selection of teddies, toys and trains (for more teddies, see below). Also on show are a toy marionette stage, a Punch and Judy booth, a shadow screen and a dolls' toy shop, grocer's and house, complete with miniature Jugendstil coffee set.

Am Hof to Hoher Markt

The Puppen und Spielzeug Museum is open Tues–Sun 10am–6pm; öS60/€4.36.

Off Am Hof, a short way down Drahtgasse, another toy museum, this time the **Teddybären Museum**, holds a private collection of antique teddy bears from all over the world. As well as the cuddly variety, there are china bears, bears on carousels and one of the very earliest battery-operated bears from before World War I, whose eyes light up in a way that would give most kids nightmares.

The Teddybären Museum is open Mon–Sat 10am–6pm, Sun 2–6pm; öS45/€3.27.

Judenplatz

Taking either of the two alleyways that lead north from Schulhof brings you to **Judenplatz**, one of the prettiest little squares in Vienna, now totally dominated by a bleak concrete mausoleum designed by British sculptor Rachel Whiteread as a **Holocaust-Mahnmal** (Holocaust Memorial) and unveiled in 2000. Smothered in row upon row of concrete casts of books like an inside-out library, the bunker-like memorial deliberately jars with its surroundings; a chilling A to Z of Nazi death camps is inscribed into its low plinth.

As the name suggests, Judenplatz was originally the site of the city's medieval Jewish ghetto, dating as far back as the twelfth century, and during the building of the Holocaust memorial, excavations revealed the smoke-blackened remains of the ghetto's chief synagogue, which was burnt to the ground in 1421. The foundations, and a few modest finds, can now be viewed in the **Museum Judenplatz**, whose entrance is at no. 8. In addition, there's a short video with an English audioguide, and an interactive multimedia exhibition, both on medieval Jewish life in Vienna.

The Museum Judenplatz is open Mon–Thurs & Sun 10am–6pm, Fri 10am–2pm; öS42/€3; combined ticket with the Jüdisches Museum and the Synagogue (Stadttempel) öS100/€7.

Ironically, Judenplatz already has a much older memorial commemorating the pogrom of 1421, known as the Wiener Geserah, and clearly visible on the oldest house on the square, **Zum grossen Jordan** (The Great Jordan), at no. 2. However, in this case, the inscription, beside a sixteenth-century relief of the Baptism of Christ, celebrates the slaughter, when the Jews were driven out of Vienna. Those Jews lucky enough to escape fled to Hungary; the rest were burned at the stake, or – to avoid that fate – killed by the chief rabbi, who then committed suicide himself. The Latin inscription reads: "By baptism in the River Jordan bodies are cleansed from dis-

Jews in Vienna

Nine tenths of what the world celebrated as Viennese culture of the nineteenth century was a culture promoted, nurtured or in some cases even created by Viennese Jewry.

Stefan Zweig, *The World of Yesterday*, 1942

Most Jews have mixed feelings about Vienna: the city that nurtured the talents of Jewish geniuses such as Sigmund Freud, Gustav Mahler and Ludwig Wittgenstein also has a justifiable reputation as a hotbed of **anti-Semitism**. The city where the father of Zionism, Theodor Herzl, spent much of his adult life (see p.249) is also seen by many as the cradle of the Holocaust, where Hitler spent five years honing his hatred; where in 1986, Kurt Waldheim was elected president, despite (or more likely thanks to) rumours that he had participated in Nazi atrocities in the Balkans; and as recently as 2000, when Jörg Haider's extreme right-wing FPÖ were invited to join in a coalition government.

Jews have lived in Vienna on and off for something like a thousand years, yet like most of the diaspora, they have been tolerated only when it suited the powers that be. They have been formally **expelled** twice, firstly in 1420, when the community was accused of supporting the Czech Hussite heretics (the real incentive for the expulsion was to boost the royal coffers by appropriating the Jews' property). The following year, those that remained – around 200 of them – were burned at the stake. Apart from a few individual exceptions, Jewish resettlement only took off again at the beginning of the seventeenth century, when Ferdinand II established a walled **ghetto** east of the Danube (now Leopoldstadt; see p.206). For around fifty years Jewish life flourished in the ghetto, but as the Counter-Reformation gathered pace, there was increasing pressure from Catholics to banish the Jews altogether. Finally, in 1670, Emperor Leopold I once more expelled the community.

The city suffered financially from the expulsion, and with the Turks at the gates of the city, a small number of Jewish financiers and merchants, hastily granted the status of *Hofjuden* or "**Court Jews**", were permitted to resettle. The most famous of the Court Jews was Samuel Oppenheimer, who was appointed chief supplier to the imperial army by Leopold I in 1677. Despite the elevated status of the Court Jews, their position was pre-

ease and evil, so all secret sinfulness takes flight. Thus the flame rising furiously through the whole city in 1421 purged the terrible crimes of the Hebrew dogs. As the world was once purged by the flood, so this time it was purged by fire".

The square's Jewish associations are also recalled by the statue of the writer **Gotthold Ephraim Lessing** (1729–81), striding forward in a great trench coat. Lessing, himself a theology graduate, was a key figure in the eighteenth-century German Enlightenment, who pleaded for tolerance to be shown towards the Jews. Erected in 1935, the statue proved too much for the Nazis, who had it destroyed; after the war, the sculptor Siegfried Charoux made a new model, but it wasn't returned to its original spot until 1982.

carious, and it wasn't until Josef II's 1781 **Toleranzpatent** that they were allowed to take up posts in the civil service and other professions and to build their own synagogue. At the same time, the *Toleranzpatent* began the process of assimilation, compelling Jews to take German names and restricting the use of Yiddish and Hebrew.

After the **1848 revolution**, all official restrictions on Jews were finally abolished. At this point there were only around 2000 Jews living in Vienna. In the next sixty years, thousands arrived in the city from the Habsburg provinces of Bohemia, Moravia and Galicia, the majority of them settling, initially at least, in **Leopoldstadt**. By 1910, there were approximately 180,000 Jews in the city – almost ten percent of the total population and more than in any other German-speaking city. Though the majority of them were far from well-off, a visible minority formed a disproportionately large contingent in high-profile professions like banking, medicine, journalism and the arts. The Rothschilds were one of the richest families in the empire; virtually the entire staff on the liberal newspapers *Neue Freie Presse* and the *Wiener Tagblatt* were Jewish; the majority of the city's doctors were Jews, as were most of the **leading figures** in the Austrian Socialist Party. Other prominent Viennese Jews were the writers Arthur Schnitzler, Robert Musil, Stefan Zweig and Josef Roth; and the composers Arnold Schönberg, Alban Berg and the Strauss family.

Those Gentiles who found themselves sinking into poverty after the stock market crash of 1873 desperately needed a scapegoat. They eagerly latched onto anti-Semitism, which began to be promoted by the Christian Social Party under Karl Lueger, the city's populist mayor from 1897 to 1910. Perversely, this virulent anti-Semitism helped to save more Jews from the Nazis than in other more tolerant places, since thousands had already fled the country before the 1938 **Anschluss**. Initial humiliations instigated by the Nazis, such as making Jews clean toilets with prayer shawls, or forcing them to chew the grass of the Prater like cows, which were enjoyed by voyeuristic locals, meant that by 1941 a total of 120,000 Viennese Jews had escaped. Those that remained however, were trapped, and some 65,000 died in the **Holocaust**. Right now, the community of around 7000 – many of them immigrants from the former eastern bloc – is enjoying something of a **renaissance**, much of it centred once again in Leopoldstadt, maintaining a dozen synagogues and several schools across the city.

The most elaborate building on the square is the former **Böhmische Hofkanzlei** (Bohemian Court Chancery), designed by Fischer von Erlach and so monumental its Baroque facade continues halfway down Jordangasse. What you see on Judenplatz is, in fact, only the side of the building, whose elaborate main portal actually looks out onto Wipplingerstrasse. It was from here that the Austrians ruled over the Czechs from 1627 onwards; the building now houses the country's supreme Constitutional and Administrative courts.

Altes Rathaus

On the other side of busy Wipplingerstrasse from the Böhmische Hofkanzlei is the **Altes Rathaus** (Old Town Hall), a dour-looking

Baroque palace that served as the city's town hall until 1885 (when the huge Ringstrasse Rathaus was finished, see p.125). The main courtyard is undistinguished but for Donner's wonderful **Andromeda Brunnen** from 1741, which depicts the Greek myth in lead relief. Andromeda is sculpted in full relief, left at the mercy of a sea monster to appease the gods, and looks unfeasibly calm as Perseus, in very low relief, descends from afar on a winged horse to do away with the beast, which meanwhile spouts water noisily from its mouth into the basin below.

*The Austrian
Resistance
Museum is
open Mon, Wed
& Thurs
9am–5pm;
free.*

The Altes Rathaus now houses, among other things, the highly informative **Austrian Resistance Museum**, situated on the ground floor, with a permanent exhibition on the Austrian anti-fascist resistance, accompanied by German and English labelling throughout. The bulk of the displays covers resistance to the Nazi regime, but there's also a brief summary of the political upheavals of the interwar republic, including a detailed section on the rise of Austro-fascism in the 1930s. Despite the high level of popular support for the Nazis, the Austrian resistance remained extremely active throughout the war, as a result of which 2700 of its members were executed and thousands more were murdered by the Gestapo.

No one knows where the city's original town hall stood, but by the fourteenth century there was one located close to what is now the oldest part of the Altes Rathaus. The **Salvatorkapelle**, a Gothic chapel founded as the town hall chapel, is today hidden away at the opposite end of the courtyard from the fountain. It's a strange little building, much altered over the centuries, whose most handsome feature is its ornate Renaissance portal, flanked by richly carved columns, and visible only from Salvatorgasse.

Maria am Gestade

A more compelling ecclesiastical edifice by far is the Gothic church of **Maria am Gestade**, up Salvatorgasse, which is topped by an elaborate filigree spire prickling with crockets and pinnacles, symbolizing the Virgin's heavenly crown – a stunning sight after dark when lit from within. With its drooping, beast-infested pendants and gilded mosaics, the stone canopy of the tall, slender west facade is also worth admiring, best viewed from the steps which lead up from Tiefergraben. The unusual interior – the nave is darker and narrower than the choir and set slightly askew – is a product of the church's cramped site, lying as it does on the very edge of the old medieval town. Much of what you see, it has to be said, both inside and out, is the result of nineteenth-century over-restoration, as the church caught fire in 1809 when it was used by the Napoleonic forces as an arms depot.

In one of the side chapels, the remains of the city's little-known patron saint, **Klemens Maria Hofbauer** (1751–1820), can be seen in a gilded reliquary, set within a jazzy modern marble table beneath some rare medieval stained glass. As well as reviving the Marian cult, being a trained baker, and kick-starting Catholicism after the reforms of Josef II, Hofbauer was also made responsible for the welfare of the city's Czech community, which at its peak numbered over 100,000, and which the church has served since 1812. Incidentally, the church's name "am Gestade" means "by the riverbank", as the steep drop from the west door, which now goes down to Tiefergraben, used to be a minor tributary of the Danube, and the church was originally founded as a church for bargees.

Hoher Markt and around

It's difficult to believe that the **Hoher Markt**, now an unremarkable square surrounded by dour, postwar buildings and packed with parked cars, is Vienna's oldest square – yet this was the heart of the Roman camp, Vindobona. The **Roman ruins** of two large houses, with under-floor- and wall-heating, can now be viewed beneath the shopping arcade on the south side of the square. In medieval times, Hoher Markt became a popular spot for public humiliations, the victims being displayed in a cage (later replaced by a pillory and gallows). That particular spot is now occupied by the square's centrepiece, Fischer von Erlach's **Vermählungsbrunnen** (Marriage Fountain), depicting the marriage of Mary and Joseph by the High Priest, for which there is no Biblical evidence and few iconographical precedents. Even more remarkable is the ornate bronze baldachin and gilded sunburst, held aloft by Corinthian columns with matching rams'-head urns, under which the trio shelter.

The Roman ruins are open Tues–Sun 9am–12.15pm & 1–4.30pm; öS25/€1.82.

The real reason folk crowd into Hoher Markt, however, is to see the glorious Jugendstil **Ankeruhr**, a heavily gilded clock designed by Franz Matsch in 1914, which spans two buildings owned by Der Anker insurance company on the north side of the square. Each hour, a gilded cut-out figure, representing a key player in Vienna's history, shuffles across the dial of the clock, and at noon tour groups gather to watch the entire set of twelve figures slowly stagger across to a ten-minute medley of slightly mournful organ music (the identities of the figures, which range from Marcus Aurelius to Josef Haydn, are revealed on the clock's street level plaque). Before you leave, check out the brackets on the underside of the clock bridge, which feature Adam, Eve, the Devil and an Angel.

There are a couple of other sights worth seeking out in the streets around Hoher Markt, in particular the secular medieval **Neidhart-Fresken**, discovered in 1979 at Tuchlauben 19 during rebuilding works there. Executed around 1400, the wall paintings are patchy but jolly, some of them illustrating the stories of the *Minnesinger* (aristocratic minstrel) Neidhart von Reuenthal, others depicting a snowball fight, a ball game, dancing and general medieval merriment.

The Neidhart-Fresken are open Tues–Sun 9am–12.15pm; öS25/€1.82.

Round the corner in Brandstätte is a rather more recent architectural highlight, the **Zacherlhaus**, a residential block with business premises on the ground floor, built by the Slovene Josip Plečnik in 1905. The exterior is all grim, grey granite, relieved only by the winged figure of the Archangel Michael above the ground floor, but it's the building's lens-shaped stairwell, hidden next door to a barber's at no. 2–4 Wildpretmarkt, that makes its way into the coffee-table books and postcards. Once you've made it down the black marble corridor, and sneaked past the janitor, you can admire the weird and wonderful lamps whose twisted bronze stands topped by lighted globes punctuate each floor of the wood-panelled stairwell.

Simon Wiesenthal

The Holocaust survivor and Nazi hunter, Simon Wiesenthal, now in his 90s, remains one of the most controversial figures in Austria's postwar political scene.

Born in 1908 in Buczacz, a Yiddish-speaking *shtetl* in the Austro-Hungarian province of Galicia (later part of Poland and now Ukraine), Wiesenthal's father was a well-to-do sugar merchant, who was killed fighting for the Habsburgs on the eastern front during World War I. As a young man, Wiesenthal studied architecture in Prague, since Polish architecture faculties were closed to Jews, and in 1936 returned home to marry Cyla Müller, an old schoolmate. The newlyweds moved to Lvov, where Wiesenthal worked as an architectural engineer until the Nazi-Soviet Pact of September 1939, when the Red Army marched into town and Wiesenthal was forced to forgo his "bourgeois" profession and work in a bedding factory.

The Nazi invasion of Soviet territory in June 1941 was celebrated with an anti-Semitic pogrom led by Ukrainian auxiliaries, during which Wiesenthal was lined up in front of a firing squad. He was saved by the timely ringing of the church bells calling the faithful (including the soldiers who were about to execute him) to Mass. That night a Ukrainian friend helped him by accusing him of being a Soviet spy – this meant he was beaten up and interrogated but not killed. He was then put to work in the OAW, a forced labour railway repair works, first as a sign painter, and later as a draughtsman. He and his wife were comparatively well treated by the Nazi in charge, who even helped Cyla to escape, first to Lublin, and later to Warsaw. He also saved Wiesenthal from imminent execution in April 1943 – he was naked and lined up ready to be shot – and, in September of that year, encouraged him to go into hiding.

After concealing himself in an attic and hanging out with some partisans, Wiesenthal was eventually discovered hiding under the floorboards of a flat in June 1944. Transferred to the Gestapo headquarters in Lvov and fearing torture, he tried to commit suicide three times without success. As German troops fled from the advancing Soviets, he was sent westwards via Plaszow, Auschwitz, Gross-Rosen and Buchenwald, before ending up in Mauthausen in Austria, where he was left for dead in the "death block". On this occasion, he was saved by a Polish Kapo, who needed someone to design birthday cards for the guards. This meant that he was one of the lucky few still alive on May 5, 1945, when Mauthausen was liberated by the US Army.

Just three weeks after the liberation of Mauthausen, Wiesenthal began to work for the US War Crimes Unit, helping them track down SS officers.

Bermuda Triangle

Since the 1980s, the area around the Ruprechtskirche has been known as the "Bermuda Dreieck" or **Bermuda Triangle**; the idea being that there are so many bars in these few narrow streets that you could get lost forever. It's certainly true that there are a staggering number of designer bars, late-night drinking holes, music venues and restaurants literally piled on top of one another, particularly along Seitenstettengasse and Rabensteig, but you'd have to do some

He was soon transferred to the OSS, the American wartime intelligence group, in nearby Linz, where he was re-united with his wife, Cyla, who had also, remarkably, survived, spending the last year of the war working as a slave labourer in Germany. In 1947, frustrated with the Allies' waning interest in Nazi-hunting, Wiesenthal eventually founded the Dokumentationszentrum (Documentation Centre), for which he is best known. It was during this period that he helped track down some two thousand former Nazis, including Adolf Eichmann and other leading Nazis. In 1953, he gave up his full-time pursuit of ex-Nazis and took a job helping with the rehabilitation and re-training of refugees. In 1961, Eichmann was kidnapped in Argentina by Mossad, the Israeli secret service, and spirited away to Israel to face prosecution. Wiesenthal was invited to attend the trial, and, with Mossad denying any involvement in the kidnapping, was only too happy to give press conferences on his early role in the pursuit of Eichmann. With the publication of *I Hunted Eichmann*, Wiesenthal's fame became widespread, and he decided to move to Vienna and re-open his Dokumentationszentrum to "work against Holocaust amnesia".

In Austria, Wiesenthal is probably best known for his public feud with Bruno Kreisky, the Austrian chancellor (1970–83) and fellow Jew, which began in 1970 when Wiesenthal exposed four of Kreisky's first cabinet as ex-Nazis. Kreisky called Wiesenthal a "Jewish fascist", and accused him of being a Nazi collaborator during his time at the OAW in Lvov (see above). Legal battles between the two dragged on for years, and Wiesenthal was eventually awarded damages for slander, but Kreisky remained more popular with the public throughout the 1970s. Wiesenthal made even more enemies during the Waldheim affair (see p.359), when he refused to back the line of the World Jewish Congress (WJC) and the US government, and accuse the Austrian president of being a war criminal. Wiesenthal maintained that there wasn't enough evidence to make such claims, and would only go so far as to brand Waldheim a liar and call for his resignation on those grounds.

The 1990s saw Wiesenthal's stature rise both globally and within Austria. Poland and Austria both bestowed their highest decorations on him, and shortly before his 87th birthday, the Vienna City Council voted to make him an *Ehrenbürger* (honorary citizen). Wiesenthal himself is nearing the end of his life, but with the Dokumentationszentrum in Vienna and the establishment of the Simon Wiesenthal Center in Los Angeles (*www.wiesenthal.com*), he at least has the satisfaction of knowing that his work will continue beyond his death.

serious drinking to actually lose your way. The night-time clientele tends to be young(ish) and well turned out but not that trendy. During the day, however, the scene is pretty muted, and you're more likely to rub shoulders with tourists who've come to appreciate the area's narrow cobbled streets and the two main sights: the Ruprechtskirche, the city's oldest church, and the Stadttempel, the only synagogue to survive *Kristallnacht*.

Stadttempel (Synagogue)

The Stadttempel is open for guided tours Mon–Thurs 11.30am & 3pm; öS30/€2; combined ticket with the Jüdisches Museum and Museum Judenplatz öS100/€7.

Ironically, it was the building restrictions in force at the time the Stadttempel was built, in 1826, that enabled it to be the only synagogue (out of twenty-four) to survive *Kristallnacht* in 1938. According to the laws enacted under Josef II, synagogues had to be concealed from the street – hence you get no hint of what lies behind 2–4 Seitenstettengasse until you've gone through the security procedures (take your passport) and passed through several anterooms to the glass doors of the temple itself. Despite its hidden location, it did suffer some damage in 1938, since the area was predominantly Jewish and the surrounding buildings were torched, though it has since been lavishly restored. Designed from top to bottom by Biedermeier architect Josef Kornhäusel, it's a perfect example of the restrained architecture of the period, its top-lit, sky-blue oval dome dotted with golden stars and supported by yellow Ionic pillars which frame the surrounding two-tiered gallery. The slightly sinister presence of police with dogs and machine guns outside on Seitenstettengasse is a sad consequence of the terrorist attack on the Stadttempel which killed three people in 1983, and the continuing vandalism of Jewish property that takes place in Austria.

Ruprechtskirche and around

Round the corner from the Stadttempel on Ruprechtsplatz stands the ivy-covered **Ruprechtskirche**, its plain, stout architecture attesting to its venerable age. Originally built as long ago as the eighth century, the current building dates partly from the twelfth century, though it has been much altered and expanded since. Inside, the vivid reds and blues of the modern stained glass are a bit overwhelming, detracting from the church's uniquely intimate ambience. Mass is still said here, and the space is also frequently used for art exhibitions.

Steps lead down from beside the Ruprechtskirche to **Morzinplatz** by the Danube Canal, a notorious address during the Nazi period. On the west side of the square stood the *Hotel Metropol*, erected by a rich Jewish family to cope with the influx of visitors to the city's 1873 exhibition, but in 1938 taken over by the Gestapo, and used as their headquarters. Thousands were tortured here before the building was razed to the ground towards the end of the war. The plot is now occupied by the Leopold-Figl-Hof, named after the country's postwar Foreign Minister, who passed through the *Metropol* en route to Dachau. A **Monument to the Victims of Fascism** showing a prisoner surrounded by granite boulders from Mauthausen concentration camp was erected in front of the apartments in 1985. There's also a permanent **Memorial to the Victims in the Austrian Resistance Movement** round the back of the building, on Salztorgasse, where detainees were bundled in for interrogation.

For the duration of the war, O5, the Austrian resistance movement, had their headquarters right under the noses of the Gestapo at Ruprechtsplatz 5. Meanwhile, the tradition of anti-Nazi activities continues on nearby Rudolfsplatz, at the Dokumentationszentrum (*www.wiesenthal.com*) headed by **Simon Wiesenthal** (see box pp.82–83), which monitors ex- and neo-Nazis. Wiesenthal, himself a survivor of the Holocaust, is best known for pursuing fellow Austrian Adolf Eichmann, the SS chief who was hiding out in Argentina; Eichmann was eventually kidnapped, tried and executed by the Israelis in 1961.

Bermuda Triangle

The memorial is open Mon 2–5pm, Thurs & Fri 9am–noon & 2–5pm; free.

For full listings in the Bermuda Triangle, see p.301.

East of Rotenturmstrasse

East of Rotenturmstrasse, which stretches from Stephansplatz to Schwedenplatz, Vienna's intricate, medieval streetplan continues. It's this, more than any specific sight, that makes a wander in this quarter rewarding, though four churches, varying in styles from High Baroque to neo-Byzantine, punctuate the streets. Incidentally, the red tower that gave Rotenturmstrasse its name – it was actually a red and white chequered city gate – has long since disappeared.

Fleischmarkt and Postgasse

Fleischmarkt, the old meat market, straddles Rotenturmstrasse east as far as Postgasse. Greek merchants settled here in the eighteenth century and, following the 1781 "Toleranzpatent" (see p.79), built their own Greek Orthodox church on Griechengasse. The only inkling you get that there's a church there is from the cupola and pediment, which face onto Hafnersteig. On Fleischmarkt itself, though, there's another more imposing stripy, red-brick **Griechische Kirche**, redesigned in mock-Byzantine style in 1861 by Ringstrasse architect Theophil Hansen, its decorative castellations glistening with gilt. Opening hours are erratic, and you may not be able to get past the gloomy, arcaded vestibule – the best time to try is on a Sunday – to see the candle-lit interior, pungent with incense and richly decorated with icons, gilded frescoes and a giant iconostasis. Next door to the church, at no. 11, is the popular inn, *Griechenbeisl*, a Viennese institution for over five centuries; patronised by the Greeks, by textile merchants from Reichenberg (Liberec) in

The nearest U-Bahn is Stubentor.

Bohemia, and by the likes of Beethoven, Brahms, Schubert and Strauss – inevitably, it milks the connections.

At the end of Fleischmarkt, turn right into Postgasse and you'll come to another neo-Byzantine edifice, the Greek-Catholic **Barbarakirche**, a much lighter concoction, with a pistachio- and apricot-coloured facade. It's worth peeking inside at the pale pink and blue nave to see this Greek-Catholic church's Rococo iconostasis studded with medallion-style icons. Far more imposing, though, is the Italianate facade of the **Dominikanerkirche**, further south along Postgasse; the vast interior is an orgy of early Baroque stucco and frescoes, rebuilt from scratch in the 1630s after being damaged in the first Turkish siege.

Dr-Ignaz-Seipel-Platz and Heiligenkreuzerhof

One block west of Postgasse along Bäckerstrasse lies **Dr-Ignaz-Seipel-Platz**, named after the leader of the Christian Socials, who became the country's chancellor in 1922. Son of a cab driver, a trained priest, and, ironically, one-time professor of moral theology, Seipel was one of the most vociferous anti-Semites, who openly flirted with the idea of re-ghettoizing the Jews. Given the eventual fate of Austria's Jews, this rather attractive little square might have been better left as Universitäts Platz, since its east side is still taken up by the **Alte Universität** (Old University), founded by Rudolf IV in 1365, and thus the second oldest (after Prague) in the German-speaking world. The current barracks-like building dates from the seventeenth century when, along with many of the country's leading educational institutions, it was handed over to the Jesuits.

By the eighteenth century, the university had outgrown its original premises and a more fanciful Baroque extension – now the **Akademie der Wissenschaften** (Academy of Sciences) – was built on the opposite side of the square. The building's barrel-vaulted Freskenraum, decorated with frescoes by Franz Maulbertsch, is occasionally open to the public during the summer vacation for exhibitions (Mon–Fri 10.30am–5.30pm). Josef Haydn made his last public appearance here when he attended the premiere of his oratorio *Die Schöpfung* on his seventy-sixth birthday in 1808. It was at this concert that Haydn – commonly known, even during his lifetime, as "Papa Joe" – is alleged to have laid his hands on the kneeling Beethoven, saying "What I have started, you shall finish".

Next door to the university is the **Jesuitenkirche** (also known as the Universitätskirche), whose rigidly flat facade rises up in two giant tiers that tower over the square. Begun in 1627 at the peak of the Jesuits' power, the church smacks of the Counter-Reformation and is by far the most awesome Baroque church in Vienna. Inside, the most striking features are the gargantuan red and green barley-sugar spiral columns, the exquisitely carved inlaid pews and Andrea Pozzo's clever trompe l'oeil dome – the illusion only works from the back of the church; walk towards the altar and the "dome" is revealed as a sham.

Behind the Jesuitenkirche runs the picturesque, cobbled lane of Schönlaterngasse (Beautiful Lantern Lane); a copy of the ornate lamp, immortalized in the street's name, juts out of the wall of no. 6. Opposite, at no. 9, the **Alte Schmiede**, now home to an art gallery and literary club, houses an old smithy in the basement. Next door, at no. 7, stands the **Basilikenhaus**, where the dreaded basilisk – the half-toad, half-cock king of the serpents – was allegedly discovered in 1212 at the bottom of a well. The canny baker's apprentice, who volunteered to go down and capture the beast, took a mirror with him, and the basilisk, seeing its own reflection, turned to stone – you can view a sculpture of the creature in a niche on the facade.

At no. 5, there's a gateway into one of Vienna's hidden gems, the **Heiligenkreuzerhof**, the secret inner courtyard belonging to the Cistercian abbey of Heiligenkreuz, which lies to the southwest of Vienna. A perfectly preserved slice of eighteenth-century Vienna, the courtyard is used for a weekly craft market on Sunday mornings. To visit the courtyard's winsome Bernhardskapelle – a favourite venue for posh weddings – you must ring the bell of the *Hauswart* (caretaker) and ask permission, or phone ☎513 1891.

East of Rotenturmstrasse

The Alte Schmiede is open Mon–Fri 10am–3pm; free.

Chapter 3

The Hofburg

*His gaze wandered up high walls and he saw an island – gray,
self-contained, and armed – lying there while the city's speed
rushed blindly past it.*

Robert Musil, *A Man without Qualities*, 1930–43

Enmeshed in the southwest corner of the Innere Stadt, the
Hofburg (Court Palace) is a real hotchpotch of a place, with
no natural centre, no symmetry and no obvious main
entrance. Its name is synonymous with the Habsburgs, the dynasty
which, at one time, ruled a vast multi-national empire, stretching the
length and breadth of Europe. Nowadays, apart from the tiny proportion that has been retained as the seat of the Austrian president,
the palace has been taken over by various state organizations, museums and, even more prosaically, a conference centre.

Seven centuries of architecture lie within the sprawling complex,
much of it hidden behind anodyne, Baroque facades. Part of the reason for the palace's complicated ground-plan was the unwritten rule
among the Habsburgs that no ruler should use the rooms of his or
her predecessor. Oddly enough, the most attention-grabbing wing of
the palace, the vast Neue Burg, is a white elephant, only completed
in 1913, and never, in fact, occupied by the Habsburgs.

Despite its plummet in status, two of Vienna's most famous attractions keep the Hofburg at the top of visitors' agendas: the **Wiener
Sängerknaben** (Vienna Boys' Choir) who perform regularly in the
Burgkapelle, and the **Spanische Reitschule** (Spanish Riding School)
who trot their stuff in the Winterreitschule. The other chief sights are
the **Schatzkammer** (Imperial Treasury), with its superb collection of
crown jewels, the **Prunksaal**, Fischer von Erlach's richly decorated
Baroque library, and the dull **Kaiserappartements**, where the
Emperor Franz-Josef I (1848–1916) and his wife Elisabeth lived and
worked. The palace also boasts several excellent museums and galleries: the **Albertina**, home to one of the world's great graphics collections (open from 2002 onwards), several departments of the
Kunsthistorisches Museum, housed within the Neue Burg – the

Hofjagd- und Rüstkammer (Court Hunting and Arms Collection), the **Sammlung alter Musikinstrumente** (Collection of Early Musical Instruments) and the **Ephesosmuseum** (Ephesus Museum) – the **Museum für Völkerkunde** (Museum of Ethnology), and the **Schmetterlinghaus** (Butterfly House), part of the Burggarten.

For details on entry to the Hofburg museums see pp.92–93.

The Hofburg in history

The first fortress to be built on the site of the Hofburg was erected around 1275 by the Bohemian King Otakar II, who was also Duke of Austria. Three years later, the first of the Habsburgs, **Rudolf I** (1273–91), defeated and killed Otakar in battle, and set about expanding and strengthening the place. Rudolf's successor, Albrecht I (1291–1308), added a chapel to the palace, but it wasn't until **Ferdinand I** (1556–64) decided to make Vienna the Habsburgs' main base, that the Hofburg became established more or less permanently as the chief dynastic seat.

Although the palace was protected by the city walls until 1857, the Habsburgs left nothing to chance after **Friedrich III** (1440–93) and his family were besieged in 1462 by the angry Viennese, and later by the Hungarian King Mathias Corvinus, during which they were forced to eat the pets – and the vultures who landed on the roof – in order to survive. Subsequent generations usually quit the palace (along with the imperial treasury) long before the enemy arrived. In 1683, with the Turks at the gates of Vienna, **Leopold I** (1657–1705) left in such haste, one eye-witness reported "the doors of the palace were left wide open". The same happened in 1805 and 1809, when Napoleon and his troops passed through, and in 1848, when the court fled, leaving the revolutionaries free to convene in the Winterreitschule.

Court life at the Hofburg reached its dramatic climax under Leopold I, who built a huge wooden theatre onto the palace fortifications, its three tiers of galleries seating up to 1500 under a trompe l'oeil painting of a Baroque church vault. Here, Leopold's own musical compositions were performed, along with numerous theatrical productions, in which the emperor himself often took the lead role. Inside the palace, courtiers had to wear the elaborate dress and abide by the complex etiquette of the Spanish court, described by one former courtier as "a strange medley of Olympian revelry, of Spanish monastic severity, and the rigorous discipline of a barrack". To get away from such formalities, the emperor was as keen as the rest of the court to spend much of the year in the more informal atmosphere of the family's various country retreats.

Though the Hofburg remained the Habsburgs' official winter residence, neglect of the complex became something of a recurring pattern with subsequent generations. Even under **Karl VI** (1711–40), who was responsible for building the incredible library and riding school, the palace remained lifeless for much of the year.

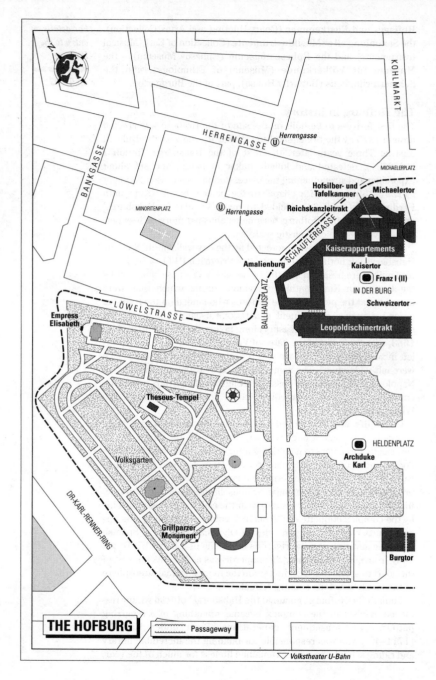

THE HOFBURG

Passageway

▽ Volkstheater U-Bahn

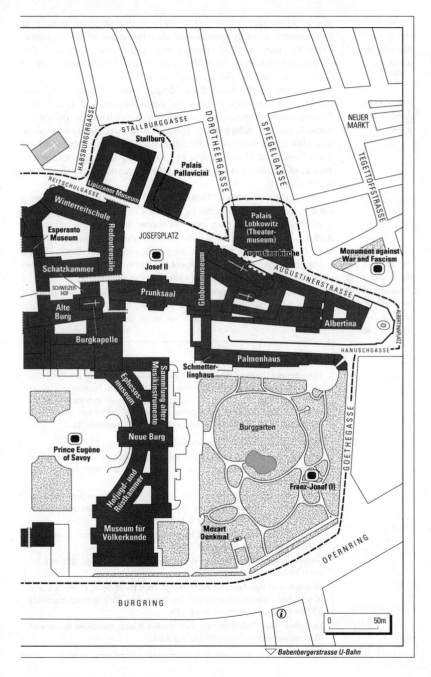

NEUER
MARKT

STALLBURGGASSE

Stallburg

**Palais
Pallavicini**

Lipizzaner Museum

HABSBURGERGASSE

DOROTHEERGASSE

SPIEGELGASSE

TEGETTOFFSTRASSE

REITSCHULGASSE

Winterreitschule

**Esperanto
Museum**

Redoutensäle

JOSEFSPLATZ

Josef II

Globenmuseum

**Palais
Lobkowitz
(Theater-
museum)**

Augustinerkirche

AUGUSTINERSTRASSE

**Monument against
War and Fascism**

Schatzkammer

SCHWEIZER
HOF

Prunksaal

**Alte
Burg**

Burgkapelle

Ephesosmuseum

Sammlung alter Musikinstrumente

**Schmetter-
linghaus**

Palmenhaus

Albertina

ALBERTINAPLATZ

HANUSCHGASSE

**Prince Eugène
of Savoy**

Neue Burg

Hofjagd und Rüstkammer

Burggarten

GOETHEGASSE

Franz-Josef (I)

**Museum für
Völkerkunde**

**Mozart
Denkmal**

OPERNRING

BURGRING

ⓘ

0   50m

▽ Babenbergerstrasse U-Bahn

THE HOFBURG

91

For more on
Maria
Theresia, see
p.230.

For more on
Josef II, see
p.104.

For more on
the Emperor
Franz-Josef I,
see p.96; for
more on
Elisabeth, see
p.240.

Maria Theresia (1740–80) preferred the summer palace at Schönbrunn, even in winter, and after the death of her husband, Franz Stephan, in 1765, stayed there more often than not. The rooms they shared in the Hofburg were turned into empty shrines, while on the rare occasions when Maria Theresia did stay here, she used rooms on the third floor, draped with funereal black silk. Under the large-scale reforms of Emperor **Josef II** (1780–90), Spanish court ceremonial was abolished, much of the palace lay unused, and the palace guard reduced to a mere ninety men, considerably fewer than today. By 1792, one English visitor found the place "much out of repair, and so abominably dirty that its appearance is (if possible) more shabby and contemptible than that of our St James's".

During the **Congress of Vienna** in 1815 (see p.73), court life came back to the Hofburg for a hectic nine-month period. Tsar Alexander II of Russia had his own suite of rooms in one wing, while the Austrian Emperor Franz I (1792–1835), as the congress's chief host, was obliged to serve dinner for forty tables of foreign dignitaries on a nightly basis. Even **Franz-Josef I** (1848–1916), whose austere personal tastes are those most visible in the imperial apartments of the Hofburg, actually preferred to stay at Schönbrunn, not least because he could drop in on his mistress for breakfast there. His unhappy wife, Elisabeth, spent as little time as possible in the

---

Hofburg Opening Times

The **opening times** of the various sights within the Hofburg are fiendishly complex; note especially that many are closed on Tuesdays. Though there's a charge for just about each attraction, most **entrance fees** are waived on May 18 and October 26; in addition, the collections in the Neue Burg are free on November 2, December 24 and December 31.

Albertina open from 2002; www.albertina.at; see p.112.

Burgkapelle guided tours Jan–June & mid-Sept to Dec Mon–Thurs 11am–3pm, Fri 11am–1pm; öS15/€1.09; Mass mid-Sept to June Sun 9.15am; see p.103.

Ephesosmuseum daily except Tues 10am–6pm; combined ticket with the Hofjagd- und Rüstkammer and the Sammlung alter Musikinstrumente öS60/€4.36; www.khm.at; see p.116.

Esperantomuseum Mon & Fri 10am–4pm, Wed 10am–6pm; closed first three weeks of Sept; free; see p.109.

Globenmuseum Mon–Wed & Fri 11am–noon, Thurs 2–3pm; öS25/€1.82; see p.109.

Hofjagd- und Rüstkammer daily except Tues 10am–6pm; combined ticket with the Ephesosmuseum and the Sammlung alter Musikinstrumente öS60/€4.36; www.khm.at; see p.114.

Hofsilber- und Tafelkammer daily 9am–4.30pm; combined ticket with Kaiserappartements öS95/€6.90; see p.99.

Hofburg (or at Schönbrunn), to escape from the strictures of court life.

After the downfall of the Habsburgs, the palace became more or less a state-run concern, though the imperial apartments and the court silver and porcelain collection are now run by a private company. Only one wing, the Leopoldischinertrakt, is retained for affairs of state, and since 1946 has been home to the Austrian federal president. Otherwise, the Hofburg is a relaxing place to wander round, mercifully free of officious types telling you to refrain from sitting on the steps and the like, and you can walk through the courtyards at any time of the day or night – there's even a bus service that runs right through the palace (see p.94).

For a virtual tour of the president's plush apartments, visit his website www .hofburg.at.

Approaching the Hofburg

The following account is divided into four main sections: In der Burg, the Alte Burg, Josefsplatz and the Neue Burg. If time is limited, the two most rewarding sights are the imperial Schatzkammer and the Nationalbibliothek's Prunksaal. The Spanish Riding School and Vienna Boys' Choir are the top tourist attractions, though getting to see either of them takes considerable forward planning, time and money, which you might be better off spending elsewhere. The tourist office leaflet, *Spanische Reitschule/Wiener Sängerknaben*, explains the intricate schedules of both institutions.

Kaiserappartements daily 9am–4.30pm; öS80/€5.81; combined ticket with Hofsilber- und Tafelkammer öS95/€6.90; see p.95.

Lipizzaner Museum daily 9am–5pm; öS70/€5.09; combined ticket with a training session at the Winterreitschule öS140/€10.17; *www.lipizzaner .at*; see p.107.

Museum für Völkerkunde daily except Tues: Jan–March 10am–6pm; April–Dec 10am–4pm; öS50/€3.63; *www.ethno-museum.ac.at*; see p.116.

Papyrussammlung Mon & Wed–Fri: Oct–June 10am–5pm; July–Sept 10am–3.45pm; öS25/€1.82; see p.111.

Prunksaal mid-May to Oct Mon–Wed, Fri & Sat 10am–4pm, Thurs 10am–7pm, Sun 10am–1pm; Nov to mid-May Mon–Sat 10am–2pm; closed first three weeks of Sept; öS60/€4.36; *www.onb.ac.at*; see p.108.

Sammlung alter Musikinstrumente daily except Tues 10am–6pm; combined ticket with the Ephesosmuseum and the Hofjagd- und Rüstkammer öS60/€4.36; *www.khm.at*; see p.115.

Schatzkammer daily except Tues 10am–6pm; öS100/€7.27; see p.100.

Schmetterlinghaus daily: April–Oct 10am–5pm; Nov–March 10am–4pm; öS70/€5.09; see p.118.

Spanische Reitschule training Tues–Sat 10am–noon; öS100/€7.27; performances Sun 10.45am & Wed 7pm; *www.spanische-reitschule.com*; see p.107.

Theatermuseum Tues & Thurs–Sun 10am–5pm, Wed 10am–8pm; öS50/€3.63; *www.theatermuseum.at*; see p.110.

With an amorphous mass like the Hofburg, it's difficult to know how to go about attacking the place. There are two main **approaches**: from the Ringstrasse (trams #1 and #2, or U-Bahn Volksoper or Babenbergerstrasse) or from Michaelerplatz in the Innere Stadt (U-Bahn Herrengasse). Bus #2a passes right through the complex, to and from the Michaelertor, through In der Burg, across Heldenplatz, underneath the Burgtor, and on to U-Bahn Neubaugasse.

In der Burg

In der Burg is the largest of the Hofburg's enclosed courtyards, and the one which sees the most human traffic – mostly tourists and passengers alighting from bus #2a. It was once a much livelier place, the venue for the daily changing of the guard under the Habsburgs, and, in the Middle Ages, the scene of tournaments, military parades and executions. The courtyard's seemingly uniform Baroque facades are the result of a century of ad hoc imperial extensions and not some grand plan. At the centre is an overblown monument to the **Emperor Franz**, dressed, appropriately enough, in a Roman toga, since as well as being (as Franz I, after 1804) the first Austrian Emperor, he was (as Franz II, until 1806) the last Holy Roman Emperor (see p.346). Erected in the 1840s, the monument was a culmination of the patriotic cult of "Franz the Good", victor over Napoleon and host of the Congress of Vienna. Franz fever took off as soon as the emperor breathed his last in 1835, when aristocratic ladies fought over the feathers from the pillow on his deathbed.

The south side of the courtyard is occupied by the vast range of the **Leopoldischinertrakt** (Leopold Wing), with its lime green pilasters. Built by, and named after, Leopold I, and later occupied by the Empress Maria Theresia, it is now part of the president's official residence and is closed to the public. Opposite, the **Reichskanzleitrakt** (State Chancellery Wing), a giant, cream-coloured, Baroque confection, was built by a combination of Hildebrandt and the Fischer von Erlachs. Taking its name from the bureaucrats of the Holy Roman Empire, who resided here until 1806, it now houses the Kaiserappartements of Franz-Josef. The two wings are joined at the west end by the **Amalienburg**, built in the sixteenth century for the Emperor Rudolf II, though he preferred Prague to Vienna. It takes its present name from Amalia, the widow of Josef I, who lived here until her death in 1742. Though essentially a Renaissance building, it sports a dinky little Baroque bell tower and weather vane, not to mention a sundial, a clock and a gilded globe which shows the current phase of the moon. Several subsequent emperors resided here, but the rooms now open to the public date from the time of the Empress Elisabeth, who died in 1898, and the Emperor Karl I (1916–18).

Kaiserappartements

Of all the sights within the Hofburg, it is the **Kaiserappartements** (Imperial Rooms) that are the most disappointing. Virtually every room is decorated in the same style – dowdy, creamy-white walls and ceilings with gilded detailing, parquet flooring and red furnishings. There aren't even any guided tours in English to bring these mundane surroundings to life, nor is there very much information or labelling in the rooms themselves. Consequently, there is something to be said for shelling out another öS40/€2.90 for an audioguide for the Kaiserappartements in English.

The Kaiserappartements are open daily 9am–4.30pm; öS80/€5.81; combined ticket with Hofsilber- und Tafelkammer öS95/€6.90.

The Kaiserappartements' current state is a legacy of their last full-time imperial occupant, the Emperor Franz-Josef, who, though a stickler for pomp and protocol at official functions, was notoriously frugal in his daily life. Despite being a field marshal, he almost invariably dressed in a simple lieutenant's uniform. His eating habits were equally spartan: a breakfast of coffee, *Semmel* (bread roll) and a slice of ham (except during Lent) was followed by a lunch of *Tafelspitz* (boiled rump). He distrusted telephones, cars and electricity, and his only concession to modern life was his use of the telegraph. For opulence, you need to see Maria Theresia's apartments at Schönbrunn (see p.225).

The ticket office and entrance are accessible through the main Kaisertor of the Reichskanzleitrakt, or from under the Michaelertor. After viewing the rooms, you exit onto Ballhausplatz, which means if you've bought a combined ticket, including entry to the Hofsilber- und Tafelkammer (see p.99), you'll have to walk back across In der Burg to the Kaisertor. Note that there are no cloakroom facilities, and that senior citizens only get discounts on Wednesdays and Thursdays.

Franz-Josef's apartments

To get to Franz-Josef's apartments, you must first climb – just as courtiers and ambassadors did – the **Kaiserstiege** (Imperial Staircase), carved in heavy white marble and punctuated with huge gilded urns. The first moderately interesting room you come to is the **Audience Chamber**, whose formulaic Neoclassical frescoes glorifying the Emperor Franz I were executed by Johann Peter Krafft, a pupil of Jacques-Louis David, and commissioned by the emperor's fourth wife, Caroline of Bavaria. Those awaiting an audience would kick their heels here until ushered forward into the adjacent **Audience Room**, where the emperor would stand twice a week behind the high desk to receive the hoi polloi – the *Audienz-Liste* from January 3, 1910 can be seen on the desk. According to court etiquette, visitors had to bow three times at the beginning and at the end of the audience, backing out of the room so as not to display their derrière to the emperor. Of the imperial portraits in the room, the most familiar – reproduced on countless postcards across the city – is the easel painting of the

In der Burg

Emperor Franz-Josef I (1848–1916)

Emperor Franz-Josef I was Europe's longest-serving monarch, and Austria's most popular. His sixty-eight year reign was the most sustained period of relative stability the country had ever known, and a stark contrast with what followed. Like his grandfather, Franz I – "Franz the Good", see p.94 – he was a legend in his own lifetime, and, thanks to the Viennese love of nostalgia, the myth continues today. As historian William Johnston wrote, "Franz-Josef I symbolized more than he achieved". His aversion to innovation was legendary, epitomized by his addiction to the Spanish Court Ceremonial. At dinner, guests could only begin to eat when the emperor did, and had to cease eating at the moment the emperor finished each course. Since Franz-Josef was a very fast eater, his guests rarely got more than a few mouthfuls. Such dinners were also very silent, as no one was permitted to speak unless spoken to by the emperor – and he was more intent on eating. On his sickbed during a particularly severe illness, though he could barely speak, he is said to have reprimanded the doctor who had been hastily summoned: "Go home and dress correctly." "Lord, this court is stuffy" remarked Edward VII, when in Vienna while Prince of Wales.

Despite the pomp and protocol which surrounded him, Franz-Josef was a simple man. When the first official census was conducted in Austria, he famously wrote down his occupation as "self-employed civil servant". Indeed, his dedication to his job was legendary: he woke at 4am (occasionally 3.30am), washed in cold water and would be at his desk by 5am. Twice a week he would give general audience to any of his citizens who wished to see him – as many as one hundred in a morning (the supplicants were, of course, vetted first). After finishing work around 5.30pm, he would tidy his desk and, towards the end of his life, be in bed by 8.30pm. He had no great love of the arts – "I go to the opera as a sacrifice to my country" he once wrote to his mistress. His only passions were hunting and mountain climbing, and his annual holiday was invariably taken in Bad Ischl, in the Salzkammergut.

Franz-Josef's personal life was something of a disaster. He was in awe of his powerful mother, the Archduchess Sophie, who arranged and then proceeded to sabotage his marriage to Elisabeth, one of his cousins (see p.240). Despite his estrangement from Elisabeth – she spent as little time as possible in his company – Franz-Josef remained dedicated to her all his life. Meanwhile, for over thirty years, he conducted an affair with the Burgtheater actress Katharina Schratt. Matters outside the bedroom were no better. His brother Maximilian was executed in Mexico in 1867, his only son Rudolf committed suicide in 1887, and his wife was assassinated in 1898.

On the morning of November 20, 1916, at the age of 86, Franz-Josef rose at 3.30am for the very last time. His last words to his valet that night were: "tomorrow morning, half past three."

octogenarian Franz-Josef, sporting his trademark bushy sideburns and slumped slightly in his chair, the year before his death.

Passing swiftly through the pale turquoise Conference Room, where the emperor used to consult his ministers, you come to the

Emperor Franz-Josef's Study. Here, the emperor used to sit at his rosewood desk, poring over official paperwork and giving each document, however trivial, his close attention before signing it, thus earning himself the nickname, "the first bureaucrat of the empire". Pride of place over the emperor's desk was always given to Franz Xavier Winterhalter's famous portrait of the Empress Elisabeth, décolletée, hair down and ready for bed, though the version you see here is, in fact, a copy. A hidden door leads into a cramped room which was occupied by the emperor's personal valets. Franz-Josef went through valets "like candles", literally wearing them out with his early morning routine.

In der Burg

The **Emperor's Bedroom** features the simple iron bedstead in which he would sleep under a camelskin cover. The delights of a modern washbasin were alien to the ascetic emperor, hence the fold-away toilet set. It was only at the insistence of Elisabeth that Franz-Josef agreed to install lavatories in the Hofburg; he himself preferred to use a bed-pan. The **Emperor's Great Salon** features Winterhalter's even more famous portrait of the empress, aged 28, again décolletée, and with jewelled stars in her hair. In the adjacent Small Salon or **Emperor's Smoking Room** hang portraits of Franz-Josef's ill-fated brother, Maximilian, Emperor of Mexico, and his wife, Charlotte, daughter of the King of the Belgians. The bust is of the Austrian naval hero, Tegethoff, who defeated the Italians at the Battle of Lissa in 1866, and was later entrusted with bringing back Maximilian's body to Vienna from Mexico, after his assassination in 1867.

Elisabeth's apartments

The empress's suite of rooms in the Amalienburg adjoins the Smoking Room, beginning with the **Empress's Drawing Room and Bedroom**. Originally kitted out for the imperial newlyweds in 1854, these rooms were used exclusively by Elisabeth after the couple's estrangement, though the empress considered the Hofburg "a prison fortress", and spent as little time as possible here. Any feminine touches there might have been have long since disappeared – in any case, the empress slept on a simple fold-away iron bed, which was removed to another room during the day.

For more on the Empress Elisabeth, see p.240.

The **Empress's Dressing Room**, formerly the imperial bedroom, is the highlight of the tour. Significantly, apart from a bust of Elisabeth as a small child, the paintings in the room are not of the imperial family – most of whom she despised – but of her beloved horses and dogs. Here you get to see some of the gymnastic equipment on which the empress exercised daily, a practice considered highly unorthodox at the time. She even had wooden rings screwed into the gilded panelling above the doorway. Elisabeth was obsessed with her beauty, whose maintenance became a full-time job as she entered her middle age. She was in the habit of rising at 5am, plunging into a cold bath – you can spy the bath through the bathroom door, reflected in the mirror – after which she would have a massage and then do some gym. Elisabeth took as long as three hours to dress, and in order to maintain the inch-perfect waistline demanded of nineteenth-century women – she boasted a 50cm waistline until the day she died – the empress would lace herself so tightly she was frequently short of breath. Her hair, which reached down to her heels, often took another three hours to prepare; washing it in cognac and egg took up an entire day.

In the **Empress's Great Salon**, it's difficult to miss Antonio Canova's life-size marble statue of Napoleon's eldest sister, Elisa, which she presented to the Emperor Franz I in 1817 in an effort to ingratiate herself. There's also a wonderfully idealized pen-and-ink portrayal of the imperial couple enjoying breakfast together – by the time depicted in the picture, they were barely speaking. In the **Empress's Small Salon**, the cult of "Sisi" – as Elisabeth is still affectionately known by the Viennese – gathers pace with an entire glass cabinet of memorabilia, including a photograph of the dress she wore when she was assassinated in Geneva in 1898. Her apotheosis occurs in the shrine-like Small Entrance Room, at the far end of the **Large Anteroom Hall**, with a serene life-size white plaster statue, sculpted posthumously by Hermann Klotz in 1906. The paintings of the numerous children of Franz-Josef's great-great-grandmother, Maria Theresia – she had sixteen in total – in the Large Anteroom itself, are by the court painter Martin van Meytens. Their jollity and frivolity come as a complete contrast to the stiff portraits in the rest of the palace.

Alexander's apartments

The next four rooms are named after the Russian Tsar who stayed in the Hofburg for the best part of a year during the Congress of Vienna in 1815. The decor, as usual, is almost identical to the rooms in the rest of the palace, and there are no reminders of Alexander's time here. Passing quickly through the Anteroom and the Red Salon, hung with Gobelin tapestries, you come to the **Dining Room**, laid out as it would have been in the time of Franz-Josef, with silver and gold cutlery placed to the right of the plate, in compliance with the Spanish Court Ceremonial, and napkins folded according to a secret court formula. The strictures of eating with the emperor are described above; Elisabeth herself detested formal dinners, and on the few occasions when she did appear, refused to touch the food.

The final room in the Kaiserappartements, the White or **Small Salon**, features portraits of the last of the Habsburgs, Emperor Karl I (1916–18), who used a couple of the rooms during his brief spell on the throne, and his wife, the Empress Zita, who outlived Karl by more than 75 years. Also on display is a terse memorial to two of the three heirs to Franz-Josef's throne who suffered untimely deaths. There's a photograph of Franz-Josef's only son, Crown Prince Rudolf, who committed suicide in 1889 (see p.266). Franz-Josef's younger brother, Karl Ludwig (1833–96), who was next in line for the throne, is not represented, though he too cut short his life by insisting on drinking the holy (and contaminated) waters of the River Jordan. The oil painting on the wall is of Karl Ludwig's son, the Archduke Franz Ferdinand, who was assassinated in Sarajevo in 1914. The painting of Rudolf's wife, Stephanie, is by Hans Makart. Conspicuous by her absence is Franz Ferdinand's morganatic wife, Sophie Chotek, who suffered the same fate as her husband, but who was snubbed by the court in death as in life. Despite the fact that a crown prince was expected to marry a princess of royal blood, Franz Ferdinand contracted a marriage of love to a mere countess, who ranked lower than over thirty archduchesses, who, however young, were entitled to walk ahead of her on ceremonial occasions. Even after her assassination, the Habsburgs refused to elevate her and vetoed her burial in the Kaisergruft.

Hofsilber- und Tafelkammer

Beyond the ticket office, on the ground floor of the Reichskanzleitrakt, are a maze of seven rooms devoted to the **Hofsilber- und Tafelkammer** (Court Silver and Porcelain Collection) – not to be confused with the Schatzkammer in the Schweizerhof, which is where the crown jewels are displayed. The latter has universal appeal (and is described on p.100), whereas the Court Silver and Porcelain Collection is something of an acquired taste. You really have to be seriously into dinner services to get the most out of it, though if you're visiting the Kaiserappartements anyway, it doesn't cost much more to get a combined ticket, and there's a fair amount of English information to help you.

The Hofsilber- und Tafelkammer is open daily. A combined ticket with the Kaiserappartements costs öS95/€6.90.

Among the numerous cake moulds, kitchen utensils, and Sèvres, Minton and Meissen porcelain, the star exhibit is the early nineteenth-century monster Milanese table centrepiece in gilded bronze, which stretches for more than thirty metres in a covered courtyard along a table strewn with classical figures and gilded bronze and crystal urns. There are a few pieces from the board service of the *Navarra* that took Maximilian to Mexico, as well as his vast Chinese-style dinner service from 1865, when he had become Emperor of Mexico. Less in-your-face are the Meissen Service from 1775, delicately and sparsely decorated with flowers, and the series of plates by the Vienna Porcelain Factory from 1803, featuring painted landscapes. The Hungarian earthenware service made for Empress Elisabeth's private dairy at Schönbrunn is more unusual. Finally, don't miss the stone jugs and salvers, with which the Emperor and Empress washed the feet of twenty-four ordinary men and women every year on Maundy Thursday – there are pictures close by depicting the event, though the Empress Elisabeth, who only had to wash the feet of the oldest woman, usually opted out altogether (which meant all the women missed out on the ceremony).

Alte Burg

The **Alte Burg** (Old Palace) lies at the very heart of the Hofburg, occupying roughly the same space as the first fortress built here in 1275, and gradually enlarged over the centuries by successive Habsburgs. A small section of the old moat, and the original drawbridge mechanism, can still be seen by the main entrance to the Alte Burg, known as the **Schweizertor** (Swiss Gate) after the Swiss mercenaries who were employed to guard it under Maria Theresia. The gateway itself, with its maroon and grey banded columns and gilded relief, is the finest in the Hofburg. It was erected in 1552 under Ferdinand I, whose innumerable kingdoms are listed in the gilded inscription above the gateway, ending with the glorious "ZC", meaning "etc". Passing through the Schweizertor, you enter the inner courtyard of the Alte Burg, or **Schweizerhof** (Swiss Courtyard), given a unified, rather dull facade by Maria Theresia's court architect, Nicolo Pacassi. The stairs on the right lead up to the Burgkapelle, where the Vienna Boys' Choir performs Mass every Sunday. Below is the entrance to the world-famous Schatzkammer, where the Habsburgs' most precious treasures reside.

Schatzkammer

The Schatzkammer is open daily except Tues 10am–6pm; öS100/€7.27.

Of all the museums in the Hofburg, the imperial **Schatzkammer** (Treasury) is far and away the most rewarding. Here you can see some of the finest medieval craftsmanship and jewellery in Europe, including the imperial regalia and relics of the Holy Roman Empire, not to mention the Habsburgs' own crown jewels, countless reliquaries and robes, goldwork and silverware. Much of it was collected by Ferdinand I for his *Kunstkammer*, and from his reign onwards, the collection became a sort of unofficial safety-deposit box for the Habsburgs. In the reign of Karl VI, the treasury was gathered together and stored on the ground floor of the Alte Burg; the iron door at the entrance is dated 1712. You can wander at will around the twenty or so rooms, though since the labelling is in German only, you should avail yourself of the free English-language portable computer guide.

Insignia and mementoes of the Habsburgs

From the fifteenth century onwards, with only a brief caesura, the Habsburgs ruled as Holy Roman Emperors. Since the imperial insignia were traditionally kept in Nuremberg, they devised their own private insignia, which are displayed in the first two rooms. However, the most striking exhibit in room 1, a plain silver-gilt orb and sceptre made in Prague in the late fourteenth century, originally formed part of the Bohemian crown jewels.

In 1804, Franz II pre-empted the dissolution of the Holy Roman Empire by two years, declaring himself Franz I, Emperor of Austria, and using the stunning golden **Crown of Rudolf II**, studded with diamonds, rubies, pearls, and, at the very top, a huge sapphire, as the Austrian imperial crown. The crown now forms the centrepiece of room 2, and, like the accompanying orb and a sceptre carved from a narwhal's tusk, it was made in Prague at the beginning of the seventeenth century. There's a bronze bust of the moody, broody Rudolf by his court architect, Adriaen de Vries, displayed here too. For Franz I's coronation as King of Hungary in 1830, he commissioned for himself a glorious gold-embroidered purple cloak, with an ermine collar and a long train, now displayed in room 3 alongside some lovely velvet hats for knights, sporting huge ostrich feathers. Room 4 contains the coronation regalia of the King of Lombardo-Venetia – territory awarded to the Habsburgs at the Congress of Vienna in 1815, and later lost by Franz-Josef in 1859 and 1866.

The sequence of rooms goes slightly awry at this point, so pass quickly through room 9, and turn left into room 5, where the mother of all cots resides: an overwrought, silver-gilt cradle with silk and velvet trimmings, made in 1811 by the City of Paris for Napoleon's son – known variously as the **Duke of Reichstadt** or "King of Rome" – by his second wife, Marie Louise, daughter of the Emperor Franz I. The poor boy must have had nightmares from the golden eagle which hovers over the cot, and it comes as no surprise that this sickly, sensitive child died of tuberculosis at the age of just 21 (see p.232). Also displayed here are mementoes of Franz-Josef's ill-fated brother, Emperor Maximilian of Mexico, including his Mexican gold sceptre and chain of state.

Passing swiftly through the baptismal robes and vessels in room 6, some of which were embroidered by Maria Theresia herself for her grandchildren, you enter room 7, which contains the remnants of the **Habsburgs' private jewellery** (most of it was spirited out of the country on the orders of Emperor Karl I in the last few weeks of World War I). There are some serious stones on display here, like the 2680-carat Colombian emerald the size of a fist, which was carved into a salt cellar in Prague in 1641 and stands centre stage, and the huge garnet, "La Bella", which forms the centre of a double-headed eagle, along with an amethyst and an opal set in enamel. Another notable treasure is the solid gold Turkish crown of the rebel King of Hungary, István Bocskai, from 1605, inlaid with pearls and precious stones. More difficult to spot are the few pieces of the Empress Elisabeth's jewellery, looking a bit upstaged among such illustrious company. Finally, before you leave, don't miss the golden rosebush presented by the Pope to Franz I's wife, a traditional papal gift on the fourth Sunday in Lent to "the most worthy person".

Room 8 contains the so-called **"inalienable heirlooms"**, two pieces collected by Ferdinand I, which the Habsburgs were very keen to hold onto: a fourth-century agate dish, stolen from Constantinople in 1204 and thought at the time to be the Holy Grail, and a 2.43m-long narwhal's tusk, which was originally believed to have come from a unicorn and therefore to be a sacred symbol of Christ.

Geistliche Schatzkammer

At this point, you come to the five rooms (I–V) devoted to the **Geistliche Schatzkammer** (Sacred Treasury), which kicks off with a long corridor of ecclesiastical robes, plus a silver-gilt, gem-encrusted miniature of the Mariensäule on Am Hof (see p.75). Elsewhere there are a bewildering number of golden goblets, crystal crosses, jade candlesticks, huge monstrances, and best of all, reliquaries. In room IV, the star reliquary is the one purporting to contain the nail that pierced the right hand of Christ, though there's also a monstrance boasting a fragment of the cross, and Saint Veronica's sweatband. One of the most macabre items is the small seventeenth-century ebony-framed glass cabinet, filled with miniature skeletons partying round the glittering red and gold tomb of Ferdinand III.

Insignia of the Holy Roman Empire

Continuing a thematic tour through the Schatzkammer entails back-tracking through the sacred treasury, followed by rooms 6 and 5, to return to room 9. Here, you'll find the **regalia of the Electoral Prince of Bohemia**, including matching gold lamé cloak, gloves and hat. Since the Holy Roman Emperor was automatically also King of Bohemia from the fourteenth century onwards, someone had to stand in for the latter during the imperial coronation. There are still more ancient royal insignia in room 10, which found their way into Habsburg hands via the Hohenstaufen dynasty. Among the most striking items have got to be the snazzy red silk stockings of William II of Normandy, and the red silk mantle worn by Roger II when he was crowned King of Sicily in the twelfth century.

The highlight of the whole collection are the **crown jewels of the Holy Roman Empire** in room 11, which were traditionally kept in Nuremberg, but were brought to Vienna in 1796 and retained by the Habsburgs after the abolition of the empire in 1806. The Nazis brought them back to Nuremberg in 1938, but the Americans made sure they were returned to the Austrians in 1945. The centrepiece is the octagonal imperial crown itself, a superb piece of Byzantine jewellery, smothered with pearls, large precious stones and enamel plaques. Legend has it that the crown was used in the coronation of Charlemagne in 800, but it now seems likely that it dates back only to that of Otto I in 962. Similarly encrusted with jewels are the eleventh-century imperial cross, the twelfth-century imperial orb, and the very venerable Purse of St Stephen, which belonged to Charlemagne himself and, so the story goes, contained earth soaked in the blood of the first Christian martyr. Also on display is the legendary **Holy Lance**, with which the Roman soldier pierced the side of Christ whilst he was on the cross. The lance, which actually dates from the eighth century, was alleged to have magic powers – whoever possessed it held the destiny of the world in their hands. It was in front of this exhibit that the young Hitler is supposed to have had a mystical revelation, which changed the course of his life (and therefore of twentieth-century history), though the story is probably apocryphal.

Room 12 is given over to the **imperial relics**, many of them donated to the treasury by Emperor Karl IV, who was a serious relic freak. What you see is a mere soupçon of the original collection – he is thought to have gathered together over two hundred relics (he apparently even stole one from the Pope). There's a tooth from John the Baptist, a bit of the tablecloth from the Last Supper, a bone from the arm of Saint Anne, a chip of wood from Christ's manger, and even a small piece of his bib.

The Burgundian Treasures

The last four rooms (13–16) of the Schatzkammer contain the substantial dowry that came into Habsburg hands in 1477, when the Emperor Maximilian I married the only daughter and heiress of the Duke of Burgundy. By so doing, Maximilian also became Grand Master of the **Order of the Golden Fleece**, the exclusive Burgundian order of chivalry founded in 1430, whose insignia are displayed here: heavy mantles embroidered with gold thread, a collar of golden links from which the "fleece" would hang, and the ram emblem, worn by the 24 knights of the order at all times. The Grand Master was responsible for replacing any collars that were lost in battle; to his financial embarrassment, Maximilian had to pay for four golden collars that vanished in hand-to-hand fighting during the Battle of Guinegate in 1479. After Maximilian, the Habsburgs became more or less hereditary sovereign Grand Masters of the Order, which still exists, albeit in a debased form, today. The final room contains an amazing collection of gold-embroidered Mass robes from the fifteenth century covered in portraits of saints.

Burgkapelle

The **Burgkapelle** (Palace Chapel), up the stairs above the entrance to the Schatzkammer, was built in the late 1440s by the Emperor Friedrich III. Despite numerous alterations over the centuries, the interior retains its Gothic vaulting, its carved ceiling pendants, and much of its fifteenth-century wooden statuary protected by richly carved baldachins. The chapel is a favourite venue for society weddings, but for the public the real point of visiting it is to hear Mass performed by the Hofmusikkapelle, made up of members of the Wiener Sängerknaben, or **Vienna Boys' Choir**, accompanied by musicians from the Staatsoper (see p.133).

Founded back in 1498 by the Emperor Maximilian I, the choir was closely linked to the imperial family, for whom they used to perform;

The Burgkapelle is open for guided tours Jan–June & mid-Sept to Dec Mon–Thurs 11am–3pm, Fri 11am–1pm; öS15/€1.09.

Alte Burg

*For more on
how to hear
the Vienna
Boys' Choir,
see p.329.*

famous Sängerknaben have included Schubert and Haydn. In 1918, the choir went under with the dynasty, but was revived in 1924 and, dressed in ludicrous sailor's uniforms and caps (fashionable in the 1920s), has since become a major Austrian export. There are, in fact, four choirs, who rotate jobs, the most important of which is to tour the world. The easiest way to hear them in Vienna is to go to Mass at the Burgkapelle on Sunday mornings (and on religious holidays) at 9.15am, mid-September to June only. They remain just about out of sight up in the organ loft for the whole of the Mass, and the only time you get a proper look at them is when they get their photos taken next to the congregation after the service.

Josefsplatz and around

Josefsplatz is without doubt one of the most imposing squares in Vienna, lined on three sides by the blank, brilliant-white Baroque facades of the Hofburg. The square started out as the churchyard of

---

Emperor Josef II (1780–90)

If any Habsburg embodied the spirit of the Enlightenment it was the **Emperor Josef II**. Born in 1741, the eldest son of the Empress Maria Theresia, Josef was groomed for his role from an early age. After the death of his father, Franz Stephan, in 1765, his mother appointed him co-regent with her, and from 1780 he ruled in his own right. Though his reforming zeal surpassed that of all his predecessors put together – it's estimated that he published 6000 decrees and 11,000 new laws – he was in many ways only continuing and furthering the work his mother had begun.

Josef's most famous reform was the 1781 **Toleranzpatent**, which allowed freedom of worship for non-Catholics, and, significantly, lifted many restrictions on Jews. In addition, he expelled the Jesuit order, and dissolved and sold off four hundred contemplative and "idle" monasteries. Though his policies incurred the wrath of the established church (including Pope Pius VI), Josef himself was a devout Catholic – his intention was to reduce the power of the church in secular life, thereby giving him and his officials a much freer hand. Other decrees had more altruistic motives: aristocratic privilege before the law was abolished, with miscreant counts made to sweep the streets as punishment in the same way as commoners had for centuries. Among his most popular measures were the opening of the royal gardens of the Prater and Augarten in Vienna to the public, and of the court opera house to non-aristocratic patrons.

Josef's decrees didn't end with the general populace. During his reign, the royal household was stripped of its former grandeur, and court ceremony virtually disappeared. One of his first acts as co-regent was to abolish the imperial birthdays and gala-days, forty of which were observed annually. He wore simple, almost bourgeois clothing, drove through the streets in a two-seater carriage and was often seen on foot with the people. On becoming regent, he handed over his personal inheritance to the state

---

the **Augustinerkirche** (now masked by the south wing of the Augustinertrakt), and later served as the training ground for the **Spanische Reitschule** (now housed to the north). It's appropriate then, that the centre of the square features an equestrian statue of the Emperor Josef II – rather surprisingly the first ever public statue of a Habsburg when it was unveiled in 1807. It's Josef who lends his name to the square, which he opened to the public by tearing down the wall that enclosed it within the Hofburg.

The facades of the north and south wings, by Nicolo Pacassi, are typically severe and unadorned, but the middle wing – which houses the **Prunksaal** of the Nationalbibliothek – is a much earlier, more exuberant work by Johann Bernhard Fischer von Erlach, completed in 1735 by his son, Josef Emanuel. The attic storey bristles with marble statuary and urns, the central sculptural group above the main entrance features Minerva, goddess of wisdom, trampling Ignorance and Hunger with her four-horse chariot; on either side Atlantes struggle to contain a cluster of scientific instruments and two giant gilded globes from tumbling onto the cobbles below.

---

treasury and demanded that his brother Leopold do the same, much to the latter's disgust. He lived for most of the time in a small outbuilding in the Augarten (see p.216), boarding up much of the Hofburg and Schönbrunn to avoid the expense of having to guard them.

Despite his policies, Josef was a despot – "everything for the people, and nothing through the people" was his catchphrase – who listened to no advice, and whose invasions of his subjects' privacy did not endear him to them. He forbade the wearing of corsets, on health grounds, the superstitious practice of ringing of church bells to ward off lightning, the dressing of saintly images in real clothes, and even the baking of honeycakes (which he considered bad for the digestion). Most famously, he banned the use of coffins, because of a shortage of wood, insisting corpses should be taken to the cemetery in reusable coffins, and buried in linen sacks to hasten decomposition, again on health grounds. In the end, he issued so many decrees that few of them could be effectively executed, and many were rescinded as soon as his reign was over.

"As a man he has the greatest merit and talent; as a prince he will have continual erections and never be satisfied. His reign will be a continual Priapism." Despite the Prince de Ligne's predictions, it was the emperor's wives who ended up dissatisfied. Though Josef clearly loved his first wife, Isabella of Parma, she had eyes only for his sister, Maria Christina. Isabella died of smallpox in 1763, having given birth to two daughters, neither of whom survived to adulthood. Josef's second marriage, to Maria Josepha of Bavaria, was no love match. "Her figure is short, thick-set, and without a vestige of charm. Her face is covered with spots and pimples. Her teeth are horrible," he confided to a friend on first setting eyes on her. He treated her abysmally, and it was a release for her when she too died of smallpox in 1767. The emperor failed to attend the funeral, never remarried, took no mistresses, and lived as a bachelor until his death of tuberculosis at the age of just 48 in 1790.

The north wing on Josefsplatz houses the **Redoutensäle**, original-ly the court theatre, but remodelled in the 1740s as a ballroom and banqueting hall. Mozart and Beethoven both conducted perfor-mances of their own works here, and the rooms became the tradi-tional venue for the annual Hofball, held in February under the Habsburgs at the high point of the *Fasching* (carnival or ball sea-son). Anthony Trollope's mother, Fanny, who attended a masked ball here in 1836 at which over four thousand were said to be present, thought "the press was almost intolerable, and the dust raised by it such as quite to destroy the beauty and effect of this very magnificent room."

Josefsplatz features heavily in the film *The Third Man* – it's here that Harry Lime is alleged to have been run over by a truck. The Baroque **Palais Pallavicini**, at no. 5, with its distinctive caryatids flanking the entrance, was used as Harry's apartment. The palace is now partially occupied by a **Dalí-Ausstellung**, a paltry exhibition of works by the Catalan surrealist – mostly bronze sculptures and book illustrations – that fill just a single corridor and room.

*The Dalí-
Ausstellung is
open daily
10am–6pm;
öS90/€6.54.*

Winterreitschule and Stallburg

Performances of the Spanische Reitschule (see opposite) take place regularly in the splendid Baroque **Winterreitschule** (Winter Riding School) on the west side of Reitschulgasse. Purpose-built by Josef Emanuel Fischer von Erlach in 1735, the 55m-long Reitsaal is sur-rounded by a two-tiered spectators' gallery (with notoriously bad sightlines) held up by 46 Composite columns. Situated at one end of the Reitsaal, the former imperial box features an equestrian portrait of the Emperor Karl VI, to which all the riders raise their hats on entering, in thanks for the wonderful arena he bequeathed them. It was in these unlikely surroundings that Austria's first democratically elected assembly met in July 1848 – the court having fled to Innsbruck – and voted to abolish serfdom.

Visiting the Winterreitschule

Access to the Winterreitschule is usually from the north side of Josefsplatz, outside which the riding school's complicated public schedule of training sessions and performances is posted up. There are one or two **performances** (*Vorführungen*) a week (usually Sun 10.45am, and less frequently Wed 7pm) from March to June and from September to mid-December, though for at least a month of the latter period, the school is usually on tour. Seats **cost** öS300–900/€21.80–65.41, and standing room is öS200/€14.54. Even at those prices, the performances are booked solid months in advance; to be sure of a place, you must **check the website** (*www.spanische-reitschule.com*) for availability and then email *tickets@srs.at* to book a seat. The alternative is to buy direct through a ticket agency in Vienna, who will charge you a heavy commission.

Spanische Reitschule

The Habsburgs' world-famous **Spanische Reitschule** (Spanish Riding School) has its origins with the Archduke Karl, brother of Maximilian II, who established several studs at Lipizza, northeast of Trieste (now the Slovene town of Lipica), in the 1570s. By cross-breeding Spanish, Arab and Berber horses, the studs created the Lipizzaner strain, which subsequently supplied the Habsburgs with all their cavalry and show horses. However, it was only properly expanded by the Spanish-bred Emperor Karl VI, who gave the riding school a permanent home in the Hofburg. After World War I, the stud was moved to Piber near Graz, though the horses are now bred at both places.

Since an imperial decree in the early nineteenth century, only silver-white stallions have been used, though when they're born Lipizzaner foals can be any shade of brown to grey, their coats turning white when they are at least 4 years old. They begin to learn the dressage steps from the age of 7, gradually progressing to the aerial exercises for which they are famous, and can live to the ripe old age of 32. The highlight of the dressage is the Kapriole, where the horse leaps into the air and tucks up all four of its legs. In deference to tradition (and with an eye to their tourist appeal) the riders wear period costume: black boots which reach above the knee, white buckskin jodhpurs, double-breasted brown jackets, white gloves and a black bicorn hat.

The Spanish Riding School is such an intrinsic part of Vienna's Habsburg heritage industry, it's difficult not to feel a certain revulsion for the whole charade. That said, to witness the Lipizzaners' equestrian ballet is an unforgettable, if faintly ridiculous, experience; certainly those with any interest in horses will feel compelled to see at least a rehearsal. As Edward Crankshaw famously remarked more than half a century ago: "The cabrioling of the pure white Lipizzaners is, by all our standards, the absolute of uselessness. The horses, fine, beautiful, and strong, are utterly divorced from all natural movement, living their lives in an atmosphere of unreality with every step laid down for them and no chance whatsoever of a moment's deviation. And so it was with the nineteenth-century Habsburgs."

From mid-February to June and from late August until late November, the school also holds **training sessions** (*Morgenarbeit;* Tues–Sat 10am–noon), which are open to the public. Seats cost öS100/€7.27 and are sold at the Josefsplatz entrance box office or from the Lipizzaner Museum (see below). If you want a good seat, it's best to queue up early; if you don't want to queue, turn up after 11am, when it's usually easy enough to get in as folk get bored.

Stallburg: Lipizzaner Museum

Sixty-five horses are kept in the **Stallburg** (stables), an arcaded Renaissance palace, on the other side of Reitschulgasse, conceived in 1559 by Ferdinand I as a private residence for his son, Maximilian. Lack of finance delayed the project, and when Maximilian became emperor, he converted the building into the imperial stables. You can glimpse the horses as they are taken over to (and brought back from)

*The Lipizzaner
Museum is
open daily
9am–5pm;
öS70/€5.09;
combined
ticket with a
training
session
öS140/€10.17;
www
.lipizzaner.at.*

the Winterreitschule for their morning exercise, but for a closer look at the nags, you need either to watch a training session (see p.107), or visit the **Lipizzaner Museum**, which is now housed in part of the Stallburg. Along with various equestrian bits (literally) and bobs, you can watch videos of the various set pieces of equestrian ballet, look at the horses snoozing in their stables through a two-way mirror, and catch a clip from the Disney film of the riding school's liberation by the US Army under General Patton in 1945.

Nationalbibliothek

Spread out across the Hofburg, the **Nationalbibliothek** (National Library; *www.onb.ac.at*) is first and foremost the country's largest working library, home to millions of books. Although the main reading room (in the Neue Burg) is open to the public, most visitors only ever see the library's Baroque Prunksaal on Josefsplatz, which, though it holds some 200,000 venerable volumes, is primarily an architectural tourist attraction. You can also see the library's assortment of papyrus, musical manuscripts, globes and maps, and its offshoots, the Esperantomuseum and Theatermuseum.

Prunksaal

*The Prunksaal
is open mid-
May to Oct
Mon–Wed, Fri
& Sat
10am–4pm,
Thurs
10am–7pm,
Sun
10am–1pm;
Nov to mid-
May Mon–Sat
10am–2pm;
closed first
three weeks of
Sept;
öS60/€4.36.*

If the Karlskirche (see p.143) is Johann Bernhard Fischer von Erlach's sacred masterpiece, then the **Prunksaal** (Grand Hall) is his most stunning secular work. The library was begun in 1723, the year of his death, and, like so many of his projects, had to be finished off by his son, Josef Emanuel. It's by far the largest Baroque library in Europe, stretching the full length of the first floor of the central wing on Josefsplatz. Access to the Prunksaal is via the monumental staircase in the southwest corner of the square.

The first thing that strikes you on entering the library is its sheer size: nearly 80m in length and 30m in height at its peak. Not an architect to be accused of understatement, Fischer von Erlach achieves his desired effect by an overdose of elements: massive marble pillars and pilasters, topped by gilded capitals, gilded wood-panelled bookcases, carved balconies accessed by spiral staircases, and from floor to ceiling, over 200,000 leather-bound books, including the 15,000-volume personal library of Prince Eugène of Savoy.

The space is divided into two quasi-transepts by a transverse oval dome, underneath which stands a statue of the Emperor Karl VI, just one of sixteen marble statues of Spanish and Austrian Habsburg rulers executed by the unlikely-named Strudel brothers, Peter and Paul. Directly above you (and Karl) is Daniel Gran's magnificent, colourful fresco, with the winged figure of Fame holding a rather misshapen pyramid. The emperor himself appears on a medallion just below Fame, flanked by Hercules and Apollo. Among the other celestial groups, there's a model of the library heading Karl's way – in case you miss it, the woman depicted as Austrian magnanimity is pointing to it. At the lowest level, Gran has painted trompe l'oeil balconies, on which groups of figures hold scholarly discussions. If you're really keen to work out what's going on, there's an inexpensive guide to the dome fresco available at the ticket desk.

Globenmuseum

There are several antique globes in the Prunksaal itself, but if that has only whetted your appetite, you can view lots more at close quarters in the two rooms of the **Globenmuseum**, situated next door on the third floor of the Augustinertrakt, the south wing on Josefsplatz. The majority of the globes date from the nineteenth century, although one of the oldest was made in 1541 by Mercator (of Projection fame) for Emperor Karl V; another particularly fine example is Eimmart's celestial globe from 1705, which is decorated with pictorial symbols representing the constellations of the zodiac.

The Globenmuseum is open Mon–Wed & Fri 11am–noon, Thurs 2–3pm; öS25/€1.82.

The museum also displays a selection of the library's **Kartensammlung** (Map Collection). Check out the upside-down map of the world from 1154, and the sixteenth-century charts, one of which features a magnificent sea dragon happily swimming in the south Atlantic, while another depicts a bevy of parrots in the *terra incognita*, now known to us as South America.

Esperantomuseum

One of the least-visited sights in the entire Hofburg complex is the **International Esperanto Museum** (Internacia Esperanto Muzeo) deep in the bowels of the palace. To get there, use the entrance under the Michaelertor, and take the elevator to the third floor; thereafter follow the signs. In addition to a library and a bookshop, there is a small historical exhibition on the language (captions are in German and Esperanto).

The Esperanto museum is open Mon & Fri 10am–4pm, Wed 10am–6pm; closed first three weeks of Sept; free.

Esperanto is an artificial language, created by the Polish Jew, Dr Ludvik Zamenhof, in 1887, as an easy-to-learn, worldwide *lingua franca*. Though it has never caught on in the way its creator originally hoped, there are an estimated 30,000 Esperanto-speakers worldwide and the argument for such a language remains powerful: translation budgets are a permanent drain on organizations such as the European Union, and opting for a language like English entails enormous political consequences. Yet although Esperanto carries less ideological baggage than English, it is still a deeply Eurocentric language for an international *lingua franca*. Its roots come almost exclusively from Latin-based Romance languages, making it plain sailing for an Italian, but virtually impenetrable at first sight for, say, an Egyptian.

The curators of the museum are, understandably, die-hard Esperantists, and will gladly enthuse about (and in) the tongue. All kinds of Esperanto texts are on display, ranging from the first book

published by Zamenhof in 1887, and translations of well-known
books, to the latest Esperanto fiction. To continue the theme of artificial and obscure tongues is a version of *Asterix* in Romansch (a lit-
tle-spoken Swiss language) and a Klingon-English dictionary (apparently *Hamlet* has recently been translated into Klingon, but that's
another story).

Palais Lobkowitz (Theatermuseum)

*The Theater
museum is
open Tues &
Thurs–Sun
10am–5pm,
Wed 10am–
8pm; öS50/
€3.63; www
.theatermuseum
.at.*

The **Theatermuseum** – not strictly speaking part of the Hofburg
complex, but part of the Nationalbibliothek's collection – is a short
distance from Josefsplatz. To get there, head up Augustinerstrasse
and take the second street on your left (Spiegelgasse). Here, on the
corner, overlooking Lobkowitzplatz, stands the splendid, silver-
white, early Baroque **Palais Lobkowitz**, originally designed by
Giovanni Tencala for Count Dietrichstein, but later acquired by the
powerful Lobkowitz family, and now home to the Theatermuseum.
The museum is worth visiting for its architecture alone, though its
recent quirky revamp has also made it much more fun to visit for
non-specialists and English-speakers.

From the main courtyard, which centres on a Hercules fountain,
you ascend a grandiose stuccoed staircase to reach the magnificent
marble-decked **Eroicasaal**, decorated with the most wonderful
trompe l'oeil ceiling fresco, on which are superimposed strikingly
colourful allegorical portraits of the arts. This former banqueting
hall, where both Haydn and Mozart gave concerts, gets its name from
Beethoven's Third Symphony, which was premiered here for the
composer's patron, Count Lobkowitz, in 1804, followed three years
later by his Fourth Symphony.

The various rooms off the Eroicasaal feature tricksy displays on
the history of Austrian theatre: in one you have to hold up a mirror
to read the text the right way round; another has a giant "swing of
thought" in the middle; to view the set designs, you open the door to
a theatre box. In the Figure-Theatre room, visitors can make up their
own puppet performance, and admire Richard Techner's finely
carved rod puppets and his Golden Shrine stage from 1912; check
the current programme for details of up-and-coming puppet shows.
In the manuscript room, you'll find copies of Richard Strauss's notes
on *Elektra*, Max Reinhardt's Hollywood diary and Mahler's farewell
note to Vienna's opera house. Look out for Picasso's costumes for
the *Three Cornered Hat* in amongst the costume display, and for
Gustav Klimt's *Nuda Veritas*, which was bequeathed to the museum
by the critic Hermann Bahr.

*The children's
section is open
Tues–Sun
10–10.30am &
2–2.30pm.*

In the basement, there's also a **children's section** where kids'
workshops are occasionally held, reached by a huge metal slide
from the ground floor. Here, too, you'll discover more puppets –
glove, rod, string and shadow – plus a paper theatre and a wonderful *Geistertheater* (ghost theatre). Lastly, for the truly dedicated,

there's an **annexe** to the museum round the corner at Hanuschgasse 3, with memorial rooms dedicated to the likes of producer and director Max Reinhardt, critic Hermann Bahr and sculptor Fritz Wotruba.

Papyrussammlung

The library's **Papyrussammlung** (Papyrus Collection) is on the second floor of the Albertina (see p.112), in a small room off the Papyrus Library. What you see is but a minuscule selection of the 100,000 or more papyri in the collection. The labelling and translations are all in German, so make sure you pick up the English leaflet available for a small sum. There are sample texts in numerous ancient tongues from Hebrew to Aramaic, many of them receipts of one sort or another or snippets of literature, with one or two quirkier items: a fourth-century BC Greek recipe for toothpaste, Arabic advice from the ninth century on how to mix up a laxative, and questions to ask the oracle from turn-of-the-millennium Greece.

Augustinerkirche

Masked by Pacassi's bland facade, the **Augustinerkirche**, to the south of Josefsplatz, is one of the oldest parts of the Hofburg, dating back as far as the 1330s. The church was originally built for the monks of the adjacent Augustinian monastery, but was gradually swallowed up by the encroaching Hofburg, which adopted it as the court parish church in 1634. It was the scene of several notable Habsburg weddings, including those of Maria Theresia and Franz Stephan, Franz-Josef and Elisabeth, Crown Prince Rudolf and Stephanie, and the proxy marriage of the Archduchess Maria Louisa to Napoleon in 1810 (his stand-in was the Archduke Karl who had defeated the French Emperor at Aspern the previous year).

Inside, the church has clearly taken a beating over the years, though it retains its lofty quadripartite Gothic vaulting. The chief attraction is Antonio Canova's Neoclassical **Christinendenkmal** in the right-hand aisle, a lavish memorial to Maria Christina, favourite daughter of Maria Theresia, erected in 1805 by her husband, Albrecht, Duke of Saxony-Teschen. A motley procession of marble mourners heads up the steps for the open door of the pyramidal tomb, while a winged spirit and a sad lion embrace on the other side, and another winged genius holds aloft the Duchess's medallion. They'd be disappointed if they ever got inside, though, for she's actually buried in the Kaisergruft. Canova's pupils were so taken with the mausoleum that they adapted the design for Canova's own mausoleum in Venice's Frari church.

Several more monumental tombs can be found in the **Georgskapelle**, a self-contained, two-aisled chapel, built in the fourteenth century to the right of the chancel (and only sporadically open – try Sundays after Mass). In the centre of the chapel lies the empty

The Theater museum annexe is open Tues–Fri 10am–noon & 1–4pm, Sat & Sun 1–4pm.

The Papyrussammlung is open Mon & Wed–Fri: July–Sept 10am–3.45pm; Oct–June 10am–5pm; öS25/€1.82.

Josefsplatz and around

marble tomb of the Emperor Leopold II, whose brief reign of less than two years ended in 1792. Balthasar Ferdinand Moll's gilded wall tomb to Count Leopold Daun, on the far wall, is significantly more extravagant, and includes a relief of the 1757 Battle of Kolín in which Daun trounced the Prussians. Also buried here is Maria Theresia's faithful physician, Gerhard van Swieten, who saw her successfully through fifteen pregnancies.

The Habsburgs' bodies are buried in the Kaisergruft, see p.60; their entrails are in the catacombs of Stephansdom, see p.54.

To get to the Georgskapelle, you must pass through the Lorettokapelle, at the far end of which lies the **Herzgrüftel** (Little Heart Crypt), where, arranged neatly on two semi-circular shelves, are 54 silver urns containing the hearts of the later Habsburgs. The two tiny grilles in the wrought-iron door are usually kept shut, so if you want to have a peek, you must sign up for one of the guided tours by phoning the monks (Mon–Fri 11am & 3pm; ☎533 70 99; free). Before you leave, take time to admire the richly gilded Rococo organ, on which Anton Bruckner composed and gave the premiere of his Mass no. 3 in F minor in 1872. The church still has a strong musical tradition, and a full orchestra accompanies Sunday morning Mass.

Albertina

At the far end of Augustinerstrasse, beyond the Augustinerkirche, the **Albertina** is a mish-mash of a building, incorporating parts of the former Augustinian monastery, the late eighteenth-century Taroucca Palace, and the southernmost bastion of the Hofburg. There are steps up to the bastion, which overlooks the back of the Staatsoper and is surmounted by a grand equestrian statue of the Archduke Albrecht, who vanquished the Italians at the Battle of Custozza, one of the few bright moments in the otherwise disastrous Austro-Prussian War of 1866.

The Albertina re-opens in 2002; for more information visit www .albertina.at.

Founded in 1768 by Albrecht, Duke of Saxony-Teschen (after whom the gallery is named), the Albertina boasts one of the largest collections of **graphic arts** in the world, with approximately 50,000 drawings, etchings and water-colours, and over a million and a half printed works. Within its catalogue, it has some 43 drawings by Raphael, 70 by Rembrandt, 145 by Dürer – more than any other gallery in the world – and 150 by Schiele, plus many more by the likes of Leonardo da Vinci, Michelangelo, Rubens, Bosch, Bruegel, Cézanne, Picasso, Matisse, Klimt and Kokoschka.

With such a vast archive, the gallery can only hope to show a tiny fraction at any one time, and in any case, graphics are notoriously sensitive to light. As a result, the Albertina only ever stages temporary exhibitions, devoted to one artist, period or theme, as well as showing a few facsimiles giving some idea of the range of the collection: whatever the exhibition, it'll be worth a look. After more than a decade of refurbishment, the Albertina is due to open once more in 2002, with newly expanded exhibition halls, an international study centre, a winter garden, and a restaurant on the terrace.

The Albertina is also home to the Nationalbibliothek's papyrus collection (see p.111), and the Filmmuseum – not, in fact, a museum, but a cinema, which shows a wide range of documentaries and full-length features drawn from its extensive archives (see p.332).

Josefsplatz and around

Neue Burg

The last wing of the Hofburg to be built – completed in 1913 – was the **Neue Burg**, a piece of pure bombast crafted in heavy neo-Renaissance style by Gottfried Semper and Karl von Hasenauer. Semper originally planned to create a vast *Kaiserforum* by enclosing Heldenplatz with another new palatial wing mirroring the Neue Burg, and by linking both wings to the nearby *Hofmuseen* via a pair of triumphal arches spanning the Ringstrasse. In the end, only the southern arc of the Neue Burg got built; the exterior was completed in 1913, but the interior was still being given the finishing touches in 1926, long after the Habsburgs had departed.

Heldenplatz (Heroes' Square) thus remains a wide, slightly meaningless, expanse, which nonetheless affords a great view across to the Rathaus and Parlament buildings on the Ringstrasse (see p.119). The square takes its name from Anton Fernkorn's two nineteenth-century equestrian statues, whose generals appear to be marshalling the surrounding parked cars into battle. The more technically remarkable of the two is the earlier one of the Archduke Karl, who defeated Napoleon at Aspern in 1809 (and then lost to him shortly afterwards) and whose horse is cleverly balanced on its hind legs. Fernkorn failed to pull off this unique trick with the statue of Prince Eugène of Savoy, and had to resort to using the horse's tail for extra stability; he died insane the following year.

The Neue Burg itself is now home to the Nationalbibliothek's main reading room, an offshoot of the Naturhistorisches Museum, and three departments of the Kunsthistorisches Museum. For the Viennese, though, it's forever etched in the memory as the scene of Hitler's victorious return to Vienna on March 15, 1938, when thousands gathered here to celebrate the Anschluss. "To say that the crowds which greeted him . . . were delirious with joy is an understatement," observed eye-witness George Clare before he fled the country. Hitler appeared on the central balcony of the Neue Burg and declared: "As Führer and Chancellor of the German nation and the German Reich I hereby announce to German history that my homeland has entered the German Reich."

To the west of Heldenplatz, the **Burgtor** cuts something of a pathetic figure as the official entrance to the Hofburg. Built into the walls in the 1820s – to commemorate the Battle of Leipzig in 1813, when the Austrians defeated Napoleon – it is the city's only surviving gateway. However, stripped of its accompanying walls, its classical lines and modest scale are at odds with everything around it. It was

Neue Burg

converted by the Austro-fascists in the 1930s to serve as Vienna's chief memorial to the fallen soldiers of World War I.

Neue Burg museums

The Neue Burg museums are open daily except Tues 10am–6pm; combined ticket öS60/€4.36; www.khm.at.

Access to the **museums** within the Neue Burg is via the main entrance. A single ticket (öS60/€4.36) covers all three departments run by the Kunsthistorisches Museum: the Hofjagd- und Rüstkammer (Court Hunting and Arms Collection), the Sammlung alter Musikinstrumente (Collection of Early Musical Instruments), and the Ephesosmuseum (Ephesus Museum). There's no English information provided for the above museums, so if you're keen, you'll need to buy a guidebook; the musical instruments collection has an audio-guide, but in German only (it does have some pleasant music, though). The Museum für Völkerkunde (Museum of Ethnology) has its own separate entrance, different opening hours and requires a separate ticket (see p.116).

Hofjagd- und Rüstkammer

The **Hofjagd- und Rüstkammer** or Waffensammlung (Weaponry Collection) boasts one of the world's finest assemblages of armour. Most items date from the fifteenth to the seventeenth century; for the arms and armour of the later imperial army, you must go to the Arsenal (see p.188). Before you get to the first room, as you mount the stairs, admire the Albanian helmet from 1460, which sports a golden goat's head, and the fourteenth-century crested funereal helmet, which, weighing 7kg, was too heavy to be used for anything except tournaments. Further up the stairs, the two dog-snout-shaped visors – devised to replace the closed helmet, in which it was extraordinarily difficult to breathe – probably came from the estate of Duke Ernst of Austria (1377–1424), who was responsible for starting the weaponry collection.

To the right of Saal I, in the first of the side galleries, there's a splendid array of **jousting equipment,** made for the knights of the Emperor Maximilian I (1493–1519). To try and minimize the death-rate among competitors, whose necks were particularly vulnerable, the helmets were attached to the armour. The High Renaissance **costume armour** in Saal III was meant only for show, its design deliberately imitating the fashionable clothes of the time: puffy sleeves, decorative bands inlaid with gilded silver, and slightly comical pleated skirts. It's difficult to imagine getting married in the wedding suit made for Albrecht of Brandenburg in 1526, with its huge pleated skirt, beetle-crusher shoes and grotesque helmet with wings and a beak.

There's some fabulous sixteenth-century **Milanese armour** crafted by Filippo Negroli in Saal IV, including numerous shields depicting heroic exploits, and a suit of armour with a cap complete with naturalistic ears and curly hair. The museum's other great weaponry freak was the manic collector Archduke Ferdinand of Tyrol

(1525–95), who ordered the bank-breaking **Adlergarnitur** (Eagle Armour) in Saal V, with its exquisite gilded garniture. Equally resplendent is the blue-gold suit of armour made for Emperor Maximilian II, with vertical gold bands in imitation of contemporary Spanish court dress; the chain of the Order of the Golden Fleece can be seen around the neck. The **gold rapier** in this room, with its gilded cast-iron hilt, was a gift to Ferdinand from his brother, Maximilian II, and is one of the finest works in the entire collection. Check out, too, the ghoulish Turkish masks in the side gallery, ordered for a jousting tournament in the 1550s.

Saal VI features some great Ottoman arms and armour – sabres, jewel-studded daggers, horse plumes and the like – taken as spoils during the sixteenth-century wars against the Turks. Yet more richly decorated suits of armour fill Saal VII, including the **Rosenblattgarnitur** (rose-petal armour) ordered by Maximilian II for the tournament held in Vienna in 1571 to celebrate his brother Karl's wedding; equally fancy suits, known as the **Flechtbandgarnitur** (interwoven armour), were created for his two sons, Rudolf and Ernst. There's more Milanese craftsmanship in Saal VIII, including a rapier whose hilt features numerous moors' heads.

Sammlung alter Musikinstrumente

If you've absolutely no interest in instruments of death, however beautifully crafted, you can skip the entire collection, and head straight for the early musical instruments. The Archduke Ferdinand of Tyrol is again responsible for many of the rare pieces, which were designed to be admired for their artistry rather than the sound they produced.

The unique set of six sixteenth-century **dragon-shaped shawms**, in Saal X, is from Ferdinand's *Kunstkammer*. Also on display are the set of miniature instruments he had made up as toys for his kids, and an ivory-backed lute from 1580, which Ferdinand himself used to play. The vertically strung **clavicytherium** in Saal XI, richly inlaid with ivory, ebony, tortoise-shell and mother-of-pearl, was also played by royalty, in this case the Emperor Leopold I, who was a musician and composer in his own right. Saal XII is loosely based around Josef Haydn, featuring instruments from his day, plus a quadruple music stand for a string quartet; the extraordinarily lifelike beeswax bust of the composer sports a wig of real human hair.

The **tortoise-shell violin**, decorated with gold and ivory, in Saal XIII, was bought by Maria Theresia for the imperial Schatzkammer, and, like many such showpieces, is totally unsuitable for playing. Also in this room is a wooden composing table made for the elderly empress after she became blind, and a set of six ornate silver and gold trumpets used in the Hofmusikkapelle until the end of the nineteenth century. If you're itching to hear what kind of sound any of these instruments make, look out for the room's reproduction clavicord, marked with a green spot, on which visitors are welcome to play. In the far corner, you'll find an early nineteenth-century **glass harmonica** of the variety invented by the American statesman Benjamin Franklin.

Next door the ornate **Marble Hall** (Saal XIV) is still occasionally used as a concert venue. Eye-catching exhibits in Saal XV include a crystal flute, and a string instrument that doubled as a walking stick, both from the time of Schubert. An aluminium violin and a "dummy keyboard" – stringless, for silent practice – can be found in Saal XVI, and in the final room there's an entire late nineteenth-century orchestra as well as a Bösendorfer grand piano designed by Theophil Hansen and given to the Emperor Franz-Josef for his wife, Elisabeth, to play. Several more Bösendorfer grands, including one by Wiener Werkstätte designer Josef Hoffmann, and an early synthesizer, round off the collection.

Ephesosmuseum

From 1866 until a ban on the export of antiquities from Turkey stopped the flow early this century, Austrian archeologists made off with a lot of first-class relics from the ancient city of Ephesus, on the coast of Asia Minor. It wasn't until 1978 that the loot was finally publicly displayed in the **Ephesosmuseum**, occupying one half of the Neue Burg's monumental staircase.

The most significant find of the lot is the impressive forty-metre-long **Parthian Frieze**, sculpted in high relief around the second century AD, shortly after the Roman victory in the Parthian Wars. The relief formed the outer walls of a pantheon in honour of the commander of the Roman forces, Lucius Verus, who was joint emperor of the Roman Empire, along with his adoptive brother, Marcus Aurelius. The adoption of the two brothers by Antoninus Pius (himself adopted by the Emperor Hadrian), is depicted at the end of the corridor on the right, followed by battle scenes from the campaign, and finally Lucius Verus's apotheosis on the far left of the corridor (he was deified on his death in 169 AD).

Other notable finds include one side of the Octagon, a burial chamber with Corinthian columns, an Amazon from the Temple of Artemis – one of the Seven Wonders of the Ancient World – and a Roman bronze copy of a classical Greek sculpture depicting an athlete cleaning sand from his hands with a scraping iron. You can also see a vast wooden model of Ephesus (and lots of text in German on the excavations), and a model of the Temple of Artemis. Finally, there's a selection of minor finds from the Sanctuary of the Great Gods on the Aegean island of Samothrace, excavated in the 1870s by Austrian archeologists.

Museum für Völkerkunde

In the section of the Neue Burg nearest the Ring, the **Museum für Völkerkunde** (Museum of Ethnology) houses a bewildering array of secular and religious artefacts from around the world. Unfortunately, large sections of the museum will continue to remain closed for renovation over the next few years as it drags itself into the twenty-first century. This is a good thing, as those galleries which have already been modernized are far more appealing than the old-style displays. The museum has a grandiose central Aula, with balconies held up by marble columns streaked like blue cheese. There's a coffee machine, and a few seats; temporary exhibitions are held in the rooms straight ahead. Much of the labelling in the museum is in German and English.

The Museum für Völkerkunde is open daily except Tues: Jan–March 10am–6pm; April–Dec 10am–4pm; öS50/€3.63; www .ethno-museum .ac.at.

It's difficult to know where to start with such a wide-ranging collection. The ground-floor galleries are badly in need of modernization and are now mostly given over to temporary exhibitions. Just three rooms currently house permanent displays, from the Far East. The centrepiece in the **China** room is a Buddhist bronze incense burner from 1660 that's nearly four metres tall. Check out, too, the funky smoky topaz sunglasses, and the leather for whipping recalcitrant women's cheeks. Items to look out for in the **Korea** room include a desiccated frog and a copy of a stunning fifth-century crown hung with gold sequins and green beans. The **Japan** section displays some superb Samurai armour, and a wonderful reed raincoat with matching rice straw boots.

The new displays upstairs kick off with artefacts from **Polynesia**, many of them brought back from Captain Cook's expeditions, and then snapped up at auction in 1806 by the Emperor Franz I – who could resist the Hawaiian firelighter shaped like a giant penis? The highlight of the Americas section is undoubtedly the stunning sixteenth-century gilded **Aztec feather headdress**, believed by many to have once belonged to Emperor Moctezuma II (Montezuma), and to be among the gifts presented to Hernán Cortés, the Spanish imperialist, on his arrival in Mexico in 1519. To try and pacify the museum's Mexican critics, who recently took to protesting outside the museum, there's a handout explaining that the headdress was originally worn by priests not royalty, and that dozens were shipped to Europe – what makes this one unique is the fact that it has survived.

Elsewhere on this floor, there's a section on **Native Americans** that comes up to date with Apache-Power T-shirts, and information on life in the USA for the country's indigenous peoples. The new **Eskimo** gallery is similarly contemporary, featuring a cramped wooden shack from Greenland, in which a family of seven lived until 1975, and some serious parkas and anoraks.

Volksgarten

The Volksgarten is open daily: April–Oct 8am–10pm; Nov–March 8am–8pm; free.

The **Volksgarten**, which forms a large triangular wedge to the northwest of Heldenplatz, was opened in 1820 on the site of the old Burgbastei (palace bastions), blown up by Napoleon's troops in 1809. Appropriately enough, given its origins, it was laid out as a formal French garden, and quickly became a favourite resort of the nobility – especially the "Aristocratic Corner", for which an entry fee

Neue Burg

had to be paid. When the rest of the fortifications were torn down in 1857, the garden was extended, and it remained an upper-crust haunt long after that.

The focal point today is the Doric **Theseus-Tempel** – a replica of the Theseion in Athens – erected in the 1820s. Originally commissioned by Napoleon to house *Theseus and the Minotaur* by Antonio Canova, it's been more or less permanently closed since the statue was transferred to the staircase of the newly opened Kunsthistorisches Museum in 1890. Plans in the 1930s by Carl Moll and Josef Hoffmann to turn the temple into a pantheon of Austria's musicians sadly came to nothing and the building remains unused for the most part. In the far northern corner of the garden, a seated statue of the **Empress Elisabeth** (1837–98) presides over a melancholic sunken garden of remembrance. The opposite corner of the Volksgarten shelters an equally imposing monument to **Franz Grillparzer** (1791–1872), the poet and playwright, seated before a marble backdrop with reliefs illustrating his plays.

Burggarten and Schmetterlinghaus

The Burggarten is open daily: April–Sept 6am–10pm; Oct–March 6am–8pm; free.

The **Burggarten**, like the Volksgarten, came into being fortuitously after Napoleon blew up the bastions around the Hofburg. Unlike the Volksgarten, however, it was landscaped in the informal English style, and retained as a private garden for the Habsburgs until 1918. It now lies hidden behind the giant Neue Burg, though its entrance off the Ringstrasse is announced grandly enough by the marble **Mozart Denkmal** by Viktor Tilgner. Unveiled on Augustinerplatz in 1896 and moved to its present site in 1953, the plinth features frolicking cherubs, two reliefs from *Don Giovanni*, as well as representations of the composer's father and sister, with whom he used to tour Europe as a *Wunderkind*.

Elsewhere, in the shrubbery, there's an equestrian statue by Balthasar Ferdinand Moll of Franz Stephan, Maria Theresia's husband, which has come down in the world since the bastion it used to adorn was blown up, and a rather downcast statue of Franz-Josef in his customary military garb. Incredibly, despite the omnipresence of the latter's image during his long reign – the emperor's portrait hung in millions of households across the empire – and the great trade in memorabilia since then, there was no public statue of Franz-Josef in Vienna until this one was erected by private individuals in 1957.

The Schmetterling-haus is open daily: April–Oct 10am–5pm; Nov–March 10am–4pm; öS70/€5.09.

On the far side of the garden is the elegant glass **Palmenhaus** (Palm House), designed by Friedrich Ohmann in Jugendstil around 1900. The left-hand section provides a suitably steamy environment for the colourful tropical butterflies and moths of the **Schmetterlinghaus** (Butterfly House), which until recently lived out in Schönbrunn. The much larger, middle section of the Palmenhaus has been converted into a very swish, palmy café (see p.313), while the right-hand section has yet to be restored.

Chapter 4

The Ringstrasse

From morning until late at night, I ran from one object of interest to another, but it was always the buildings that held my primary interest. For hours I could stand in front of the Opera, for hours I could gaze at the parliament; the whole Ring-Boulevard seemed to me like an enchantment out of The Thousand and One Nights.

Adolf Hitler, *Mein Kampf*

On Christmas Eve 1857, the Emperor Franz-Josef I announced the demolition of the zig-zag fortifications around the old town and the building of a Ringstrasse, a horse-shoe of imperial boulevards to be laid out on the former glacis (the sloping open ground between the walls and the suburbs). Vienna had been confined within its medieval walls since the last Turkish siege of 1683 – now, with the Ottoman threat receding, the Habsburgs could create a boulevard befitting an imperial capital. Twelve major public buildings were set down along its course between 1860 and 1890 – among them a court opera house and theatre, two court museums, a parliament building, a university and a town hall – all at no cost to the taxpayer. By the end of World War I, though, the Habsburgs were no more: as Edward Crankshaw wrote, "[the Ringstrasse] was designed as the crown of the Empire, but it turned out to be a tomb".

Today Vienna's Ringstrasse looks pretty much as it did in the last days of the Habsburgs, studded with key landmarks. The monumental public institutions remain the chief sights: heading anti-clockwise, they include the **Börse**, **Votivkirche**, **Rathaus**, **Burgtheater**, and **Parlament** buildings, the two monster museums – the **Naturhistorisches** and **Kunsthistorisches** (covered in Chapter Five) – and the **Staatsoper**. Countless other cultural institutions occupy prime positions on the Ring and neighbouring Karlsplatz, most notably the **Musikverein**, the city's premier concert venue, the glorious Jugendstil **Secession** building, the city's new cultural complex, the **MuseumsQuartier**, and three more excellent museums: the **Akademie der bildenden Künste**, the **Historisches Museum der**

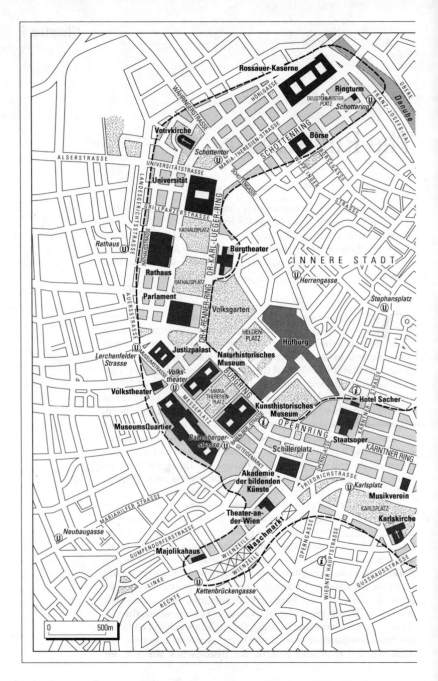

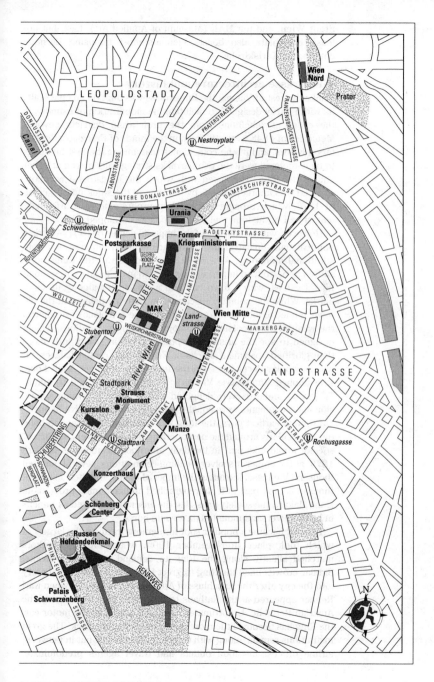

Stadt Wien, and the MAK (Museum of Applied Art). Last, but not least, Karlsplatz also boasts Vienna's most imposing Baroque church, the **Karlskirche**.

Ringstrasse architecture and history

Unlike the rest of Vienna, the Ringstrasse was built on an epic scale, its width partly designed to facilitate the mobilization of cannons in the event of rebellions from the proletarian districts beyond. Memories of 1848 were still fresh in the minds of Franz-Josef's military advisors, and it's no coincidence that among the first buildings to be completed were the two barracks strategically placed at either end of the Ring. The speed with which the Ringstrasse was constructed was unprecedented: by the time of the stock market crash of 1873, which brought the building programme to a brief halt, almost half of the total real estate had been developed.

However, within a decade of the imperial decree of 1857, Austria's political make-up had changed from an undiluted autocracy to a constitutional monarchy. As a result, the emphasis of the Ringstrasse shifted, too, from an imperial showpiece to more of an expression of liberal values, with a town hall and a parliament among its landmarks. While the nobility, ensconced in Baroque palaces in the old town, tended to look down on the Ringstrasse as a place of residence, the wealthy **bourgeoisie** were happy to snap up buildings, which, designed to ape the aristocratic *palais*, were in reality little more than glorified apartment blocks or *Zinspalais* (rented palaces). It was a popular deceit, as even the modernist architect Adolf Loos, who dubbed Ringstrasse Vienna's "Potemkinstadt", had to admit: "Viennese landlords were delighted with the idea of owning a mansion and the tenants were equally pleased to be able to live in one".

From its earliest days, the Ring was a **fashionable** place to hang out, particularly around the new opera house, where every stratum of society would take part in the daily afternoon promenade. In April 1879, at the emperor's silver wedding celebrations, several hundred thousand Viennese, including the imperial family, watched as tens of thousands took part in a choreographed and costumed procession. Hans Makart, the society artist, led the ensemble, dressed as Rubens in black velvet, and mounted on a white horse.

Later, it became a popular spot for **demonstrations**, the largest of which took place in November 1905, when 250,000 workers marched silently along the Ring to demand universal suffrage. Similar crowds lined the Ring to greet Hitler on his triumphal entry into the city after the Anschluss of April 1938 – and again when Karl Renner appeared at the Rathaus to proclaim the restoration of the Austrian Republic. Unfortunately, with the advent of the motor car, the Ring has become little more than a public racing track. The great institutions remain, along with their attendant cafés, but in between, airline offices, fast-food outlets and travel agents predominate.

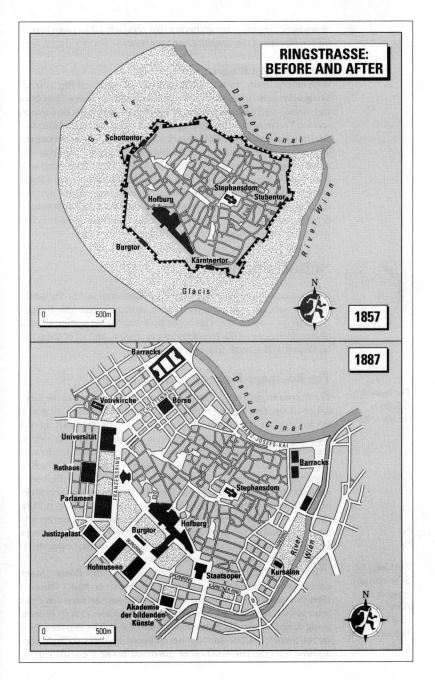

**RINGSTRASSE:
BEFORE AND AFTER**

1857

- Glacis
- Danube Canal
- Schottentor
- River Wien
- Stephansdom
- Stubentor
- Hofburg
- Burgtor
- Kärntnertor
- Glacis
- 0 — 500m
- N

1887

- Barracks
- Danube Canal
- Votivkirche
- Börse
- SCHOTTENRING
- FRANZ-JOSEFS-KAI
- Universität
- FRANZENSRING
- Rathaus
- Parlament
- Stephansdom
- Barracks
- Justizpalast
- Burgtor
- Hofburg
- PARKRING
- BURGRING
- River Wien
- Hofmuseen
- OPERNRING
- Staatsoper
- Kursalon
- KÄRNTNER RING
- Akademie der bildenden Künste
- 0 — 500m
- N

Nowadays, the only mass gathering that regularly takes place here is for the last lap of the annual Vienna marathon.

Exploring the Ringstrasse

With all the heavy traffic, the Ringstrasse is not much fun to stroll along nowadays. In addition, the boulevard's sheer size – 5km from end to end – and its uneven distribution of sights precludes exploration on foot. You're better off adopting a hit-and-run approach, making forays from the nearest U-Bahn or tram stop. The best way to circumnavigate and appreciate the scale of the Ring is by **tram**: #1 goes round in a clockwise direction; #2 runs anti-clockwise. From the trams, only Karlsplatz lies entirely hidden from view. Each section of the Ring is **individually named** (eg Schottenring, Dr-Karl-Lueger-Ring, etc); the following account works **anti-clockwise** from the Ring's most northerly point, at Schottenring U-Bahn, to the final segment of Stubenring, where the boulevard once more rejoins the Danube Canal.

Schottenring

If you take the tram along any part of the Ring, it should be the northernmost section, **Schottenring**, which stretches from the Danube Canal to the Votivkirche. This is the least interesting portion to walk along, since none of the buildings can be visited, and all of them can be viewed well enough from the tram window.

The Rossauer-Kaserne and the Börse

The nearest U-Bahn is Schottenring.

The **Ringturm**, erected in 1955 at the very northern apex of the Ring, is one of the few high-rise buildings in central Vienna, acting as a marker (or so its architects like to think) for the start of the Ringstrasse. A more distinguished building, on the opposite side of the Ring, is the **Rossauer-Kaserne**, a fanciful, red-brick barracks (currently used by the police), built in the late 1860s. One of the first constructions on the Ring, occupying three blocks, it formed a strategic and architectural pendant to the former imperial barracks on Stubenring, where the Postsparkasse now stands (see p.153). Only the crenellated central block, with its mock-Gothic turrets and machicolations, is actually visible from the Ring, across **Deustchmeisterplatz**, which features a giant militaristic monument, topped by a flag-wielding bronze soldier.

The Café Schottenring *opposite the* Börse *is a classic Ringstrasse Kaffeehaus; see p.313.*

The key public building on Schottenring is the **Börse** (Stock Exchange), designed in the 1870s by the Danish architect Theophil Hansen, one of the pioneers of the historicist architecture that characterizes the Ringstrasse. In his design of the Börse, exactly halfway along Schottenring, Hansen chose to ape the Italian Renaissance – viz the arches, rooftop battlements and corner towers – a style popularized with the construction of the opera house a decade earlier.

The main hall was partially destroyed by fire in 1956, so you're not missing anything by viewing the building from the tram, though it's not clear from the building's solid exterior that much of its vast ground plan is in fact taken up with a large central, open courtyard.

Schottenring

Votivkirche

The first public building on the Ringstrasse – begun in 1854 even before the emperor had ordered the demolition of the city ramparts – was the **Votivkirche**, a monumental church built by the Vienna-born architect Heinrich Ferstel in the style of the great Gothic cathedrals of Cologne and Chartres. Erected opposite the spot where a Hungarian tailor, János Libényi, had tried to stab the Emperor Franz-Josef the previous year – he was thwarted only by the emperor's collar and cap – the church was to be "a monument of patriotism and of devotion of the people to the Imperial House". Forever associated with the old order – the church and crown – the Votivkirche differed from the later Ringstrasse buildings, which derived much of their inspiration from the liberal ideology of the newly ascendant middle class.

The nearest U-Bahn is Schottentor.

For all its size, there is something spiritually lacking in the Votivkirche. Built partly to serve the large influx of soldiers to the capital following the 1848 revolution, the church has no natural parishioners, and the interior, badly damaged in World War II, is gloomy, and remains underused and little visited. The one monument worth a look is the sixteenth-century marble tomb of Count Salm, who commanded Vienna during the Turkish siege of 1529.

Rathausplatz

Rathausplatz is the Ringstrasse's showpiece square, framed by no fewer than four monumental public buildings – the Rathaus, the Burgtheater, Parlament and the Universität – all completed in the 1880s. The architectural style of each building was carefully chosen to allude to its function: Flemish Gothic for the Rathaus, conjuring up municipal wealth and independence; hybrid Baroque for the Burgtheater, recalling the era in which theatre first flourished in Vienna; Neoclassicism for the Parliament building, in honour of the birthplace of democracy, Ancient Greece; and Italian Renaissance for the University, that bastion of secular scholarship.

Rathaus

The most imposing building of the four is the cathedralesque **Rathaus** (City Hall) – strictly speaking the Neues Rathaus – a powerful symbol of the city's late nineteenth-century political clout. Designed by the German architect Friedrich Schmidt in imitation of Brussels' Gothic *Hôtel de Ville*, the Rathaus opened for business in

Rathausplatz

1884, though one can only feel sympathy for the city bureaucrats who had to work in its gloomy neo-Gothic chambers before the advent of electricity. The central tower, which soars to a height of over 100m, is topped by a copper statue of a medieval knight in full armour, known affectionately as the *Rathausmann*; you can inspect a replica of him at close quarters in the Rathauspark below.

You're free to walk through the town hall's seven courtyards, but to get a look at the ornate interior, home to the *Bürgermeister* (mayor) and the *Gemeinderat* (city council), you must join a 45-minute guided tour (in German). Concerts are occasionally held in the main Arkadenhof, and in July and August, free opera and classical concerts are beamed onto a giant screen on the town hall's main facade. Restaurants set up stalls selling food and beer, though these are as nothing compared to the number of stalls which fill the Rathauspark in the month leading up to Christmas, when the famous **Christkindlmarkt** takes place (mid-Nov to Christmas; *www.christkindlmarkt.at*). During this period, the area in front of the Rathaus is crowded with stalls selling candy, decorations, traditional wooden toys, and just about every kitsch Christmas present you can think of. Families come to admire the luminous tree decorations, play on the rides, and participate in the workshops for kids within the town hall, while even more folk flock here after work to drink hot *Glühwein* and *Punsch* to ward off the cold. For the New Year, the area in front of the Rathaus is turned into a giant outdoor ice-skating rink (daily noon–11pm).

Free guided tours of the Rathaus take place Mon, Wed & Fri at 1pm if there is no city council session; call ☎525 50 to confirm, and assemble at the information office in the Schmidthalle.

Burgtheater

The Burgtheater is open July & Aug for guided tours (in German) Tues, Thurs & Fri 9am & 3pm, Sat 3pm, Sun 11am & 3pm; öS50/€3.63.

Directly opposite the Rathaus, the **Burgtheater** (*www.burgtheater .at*) seems modest by comparison – until you realize that the sole function of the theatre's two vast wings is to house monumental staircases leading to the grand boxes. In practical terms, though, the design by Gottfried Semper and Karl Hasenauer was none too successful. Less than a decade after the opening night in 1888 the theatre had to close in order to revamp the acoustics, which were dreadful, and to modify the seating, some of which allowed no view of the stage at all. The auditorium was badly gutted by fire during the liberation of Vienna in April 1945, and has since been totally modernized. Thankfully, the staircase wings survived, and still boast their sumptuous decor, including ceiling paintings by Franz Matsch and Gustav Klimt.

When the Burgtheater opened, it was, of course, known as the k.k. Hofburgtheater (Imperial and Royal Palace Theatre), as the lettering on the facade still proclaims. The royals had their own entrance, so they could slip in from the Hofburg. Nowadays, the theatre devotes itself solely to spoken drama, but the original Burgtheater, which stood on Michaelerplatz in the Innere Stadt, also functioned as the chief ballet and opera house. It was there that Mozart's *Die*

Karl Lueger (1844–1910)

Karl Lueger, mayor from 1897 to 1910, is by far the most famous of Vienna's *Bürgermeister* – the section of the Ring that crosses Rathausplatz is named after him, and his statue occupies a prime site at the beginning of Stubenring. Brought up by his widowed mother, who ran a tobacco shop, Karl made it to the city's most prestigious private school, the Theresianum, as a day scholar, subsequently becoming a lawyer before entering politics as a left-wing Democrat in 1870.

His elegant appearance, impeccable manners and skillful oratory earned him the nickname "*der schöne Karl*" (handsome Karl), but his reputation will always be clouded by the **anti-Semitic rhetoric** he adopted during the 1880s. In 1890, he made a speech in the Reichsrat suggesting that the city's Jews should be put on a ship, sent out to sea and sunk. By 1893, he had formed the **Christian Social Party** (Christlichsoziale Partei), whose blend of municipal socialism, Catholicism and anti-Semitism proved irresistible to the Viennese petite bourgeoisie, in which Lueger had his roots. However, his election as mayor in 1895 was followed by two years of deadlock as the Emperor Franz-Josef refused to ratify his taking office, wary of his popularity and his crude anti-Semitism. Once in power, Lueger toned down his anti-Semitism, resorting to it when he needed to maintain his popular appeal, and dropping it when he needed the co-operation of the city's wealthy Jewish financiers – hence his catchphrase, "*Wer a Jud is bestimm' i*" ("I decide who is a Jew").

In his thirteen years as mayor, Lueger succeeded in laying the foundations for the municipal socialism that was greatly extended by the Social Democratic Workers' Party (SDAP) in the 1920s. He was responsible for much of the infrastructure the Viennese enjoy today: he piped in water from Styria, built gas works, established a green belt around the city, made provisions for cheap burials, built schools and old people's homes, enlarged the parks and electrified the tram and subway network. His funeral in 1910 was the largest the city had ever seen, with over 200,000 lining the streets, among them one of Lueger's biggest fans, the young, out-of-work artist, Adolf Hitler.

Entführung aus dem Serail, *Figaro* and *Così fan tutte* were premiered, as well as Gluck's *Orfeo*, *Alceste* and *Paris and Helen*, and Beethoven's *Second Piano Concerto* and his *First Symphony*. It was also where the Emperor Franz-Josef first clapped eyes on the actress Katharina Schratt, who was to be his mistress for more than forty years.

Universität

The **Universität** (University; *www.univie.ac.at*) – strictly speaking the Neue Universität – is the most unassuming of the four public buildings on Rathausplatz. It's also the one which had to campaign longest to secure a prominent Ringstrasse site, owing to its radical past. Vienna's students had been among the most enthusiastic supporters of the 1848 revolution, forming their own Academic Legion, manning the barricades and dying in their hundreds. Finally in 1873,

The Café Landtmann *by the Burgtheater has been a favourite with the city's politicians, actors and professors – Sigmund Freud was a regular – for over a century;* see p.313.

Heinrich Ferstel was commissioned to design new premises for the Law and Philosophy faculties in the ubiquitous neo-Renaissance style. More famously, in 1894, the painter Gustav Klimt was commissioned, along with Franz Matsch, to paint three murals for the university's Aula (Great Hall).

Sadly, it's no longer possible to view these paintings, which caused possibly the biggest scandal in the university's history. Klimt and Matsch had already completed murals for the Burgtheater (1886–88) and the Kunsthistorisches Museum (1891), and the university no doubt expected more of the same. However, by the time the first picture, *Philosophy*, was unveiled in March 1900, Klimt had broken with Vienna's main independent artists' association and helped found the rebellious Secession (see p.138) – more importantly, he had moved a long way from the university's original proposal for a painting to illustrate the triumph of light over darkness. It was this, as much as anything else, which caused 87 professors to sign a petition of protest. The painting's tangled mass of naked, confused humanity – "a victory of darkness over all" in the words of one critic – was certainly not what the Ministry of Culture and Education had had in mind.

The scandal drew 34,000 onlookers to see the painting in just two months. Unperturbed, Klimt exhibited the second of the murals, *Medicine*, the following year, its naked and diseased figures provoking further abuse. Questions were asked in parliament, where the artist was accused of "pornography" and "perverted excess". Eventually in 1905, having completed the last, but by no means least controversial, of the trio, *Jurisprudence*, Klimt returned his fee and claimed back the paintings. The industrialist August Lederer immediately bought *Philosophy*, while the artist Kolo Moser, co-founder of the Secession, purchased the other two in 1911. All three were placed in Schloss Immendorf in the Sazlkammergut for safe-keeping during World War II, but were destroyed in a fire started by retreating SS troops on May 5, 1945.

Parlament

On the south side of Rathausplatz stands the Neoclassical **Parlament** (Parliament; *www.parlament.gv.at*), one of five major Ringstrasse buildings by the Danish architect, Theophil Hansen. From street level, it's difficult to see past the giant Corinthian portico and its accompanying wings and pavilions. Stand back, though, and it becomes clear that the huge main body of the building – home to the Bundesrat (Federal Council) and Nationalrat (National Council) of the Austrian parliament – is mostly hidden behind the projecting facade.

When it came to the building's **sculptural decoration**, there wasn't much of an indigenous democratic tradition to draw on. The main pediment frieze shows the Emperor Franz-Josef I granting the seventeen peoples of the empire a deeply undemocratic constitution, but for the most part, Hansen plumped for classical antiquity, with Roman horse-tamers and seated historians punctuating the two ramps. Between the ramps stands a gargantuan statue of Athene, goddess of wisdom, sporting a natty gilded plume in her helmet and presiding over a fountain served by four writhing mermen, representing the Danube, Inn, Elbe and Moldau. The attic of the main building, meanwhile, is peppered with 76 classical statues, 66 reliefs and four bronze chariot groups – these are best viewed from the sides of the building, where you'll find porticos held up by caryatids modelled on the Erechtheion on the Acropolis.

The Austrian parliament has had a chequered history since it moved into its new premises in 1883. Initially, it served as the Reichsrat (Imperial Council) for the Austrian half of the empire, a body deadlocked by nationalist factions of Croats, Czechs, Poles, Romanians, Slovenes and Germans. The nadir came in 1897 when the Polish Count Kasimir Badeni attempted to introduce his language ordinances, which would put Czech on an equal footing with German in the Czech Lands. Conservatives and German-Nationals organized an "Obstruction Concert", with whistles, sleigh bells, harmonicas, cowbells, gongs, toy trumpets, hunting horns and snare drums. During the din, one member delivered a twelve-hour filibuster which ended at 8.45am the following morning. Following the Badeni debacle, the Emperor bypassed parliament and ruled through the bureaucracy, until the introduction of universal male suffrage in 1907. Parliament was again prorogued shortly before World War I and didn't re-convene until after Franz-Josef's death.

On November 12, 1918, the Reichsrat held its last session, during which the Austrian republic – known officially as Deutsch-Österreich (German-Austria) – was declared from the ramps before parliament. The Babenberg colours of the new Austria, red-white-red, were hoisted on the tall masts either side of Athene; also present were the Pan-German nationalist students with their black-red-gold banners, and the Communist-dominated 41st battalion of the *Volkswehr* known as the Rote Garde (Red Guard). The latter tore up the Pan-German banners, and also removed the white from the Austrian banners, leaving red rags flying. Shots were fired, the Rote Garde tried to storm the parliament building; two people were killed and 45 injured. Five months later, there were more revolutionary rumblings as a posse of Communists, spurred on by the Soviet republics in Bavaria and Hungary, broke in and set fire to the parliament building. In the street fighting that followed, five policemen and a woman were killed.

On the Ides of March, 1934, democracy was put on hold indefinitely as the Austro-fascists ordered police to block the entrance to the building to prevent parliamentary members from assembling. On

Rathausplatz

There are free guided tours (in German), provided there's no parliamentary session taking place: mid-Sept to June Mon–Thurs 11am and 3pm, Fri 11am, 1, 2 & 3pm; July to mid-Sept Mon–Fri 9, 10 & 11am and 1, 2 & 3pm.

seizing power, one of the Austro-fascists' first acts was to remove the **Monument of the Republic**, erected to the south of the parliament building after World War I, and featuring the busts of the Socialist politicians: Jakob Reumann, Viktor Adler and Ferdinand Hanusch. Strangely, the monument wasn't destroyed, but simply put into storage (rather like Austrian democracy itself), and returned to its rightful place after World War II.

Justizpalast

The nearest U-Bahns are Volkstheater and Lerchenfelder Strasse.

Set back slightly from the Ring, behind the Monument of the Republic, lies the **Justizpalast**, an impressive neo-Renaissance monster of a building that holds a special place in Austrian history. On July 15, 1927, the day after three right-wing activists were acquitted of murdering a Socialist man and boy, a spontaneous demonstration of several thousand workers descended on and set fire to the Justizpalast. Chaos ensued, with mounted, armed police charging the crowd, and police reinforcements shooting live ammunition, leaving eighty-odd people dead, and up to one thousand wounded. The Socialists promptly called a general strike, which was deftly crushed by the heavily armed *Heimwehr*, the right-wing militia, who acted as strike breakers, and civil war was put off for a few more years.

Burgring

On the other side of **Burgring** from the Hofburg stand the two so-called *Hofmuseen* (court museums), which were opened to the public in the late nineteenth century. The **Kunsthistorisches Museum** (History of Art Museum), which houses one of the world's top art collections, is covered in detail in Chapter Five; the **Naturhistorisches Museum** (Natural History Museum) is described below. Designed in pompous neo-Renaissance style, with giant copper-domed cupolas and colossal wings, they are both the work of Karl Hasenauer, and as such, virtual mirror images of each other. The overall plan was thought up by the great Dresden architect, Gottfried Semper, who envisaged a monumental *Kaiserforum*, linking the museums to the Neue Burg via a pair of triumphal arches spanning the Ringstrasse. The project was interrupted by World War I, and then binned altogether after the fall of the Habsburgs.

The Kunsthistorisches Museum is covered in Chapter Five.

Today, the museums remain cut off from the Hofburg by the traffic roaring round the Ring. They stare blankly at one another across **Maria-Theresien-Platz**, a formal garden, peppered with topiary and centred on a gargantuan monument to the Empress Maria Theresia who presides over four of her generals (on horseback), and three of her advisers, plus her doctor (standing). If you stand between the two big museums with your back to the Hofburg, you will find yourself confronted with the **MuseumsQuartier**, Vienna's new cultural complex, due to open as this book goes to print, and described in a little more detail in the box on p.132. Housed in the former Messepalast (Trade Fair Palace), originally the imperial stables, built in the eighteenth century by Johann Bernhard Fischer von Erlach, the MuseumsQuartier hopes to do for Vienna what the Tate Modern has done for London.

Burgring

Naturhistorisches Museum

In many ways very little has changed at the **Naturhistorisches Museum** (*www.nhm.at*) since it opened in 1889. Whereas most European cities have tried to pep up their natural history collections with automated dinosaurs, ecological concerns and the like, the hard sell has passed Vienna by. The display cabinets are over a century old, as is the exclusively German labelling – places as distant as Illyria (the eastern Adriatic coast) and Galicia (part of present-day Poland and Ukraine) are still described as part of Austria – the dim panes of glass are almost pre-industrial, and the stuffed animals have all succumbed to a uniform, musty, grey hue. It's really only as a museum of museums that the Naturhistorisches continues to be of any interest – though, of course, it goes without saying that the building itself is a visual feast.

The Naturhistorisches Museum is open daily except Tues 9am–6.30pm Wed until 9pm; öS30/€2.18. The nearest U-Bahn is Volkstheater.

The ground floor (or Parterre as it's called) kicks off with five rooms of minerals (I–V) in the east wing, among them some impressive slabs of green malachite, a giant fluorescent red ammonite and a huge chunk of transparent quartz. Polished marble tiles are accompanied by the names of buildings within the old Empire which feature the materials. The penultimate room (IV) contains various objects made from precious and semi-precious stones – perhaps the most interesting section for the non-specialist – including an ostrich made with 761 precious stones and 2102 diamonds, given as a (morning-after) wedding gift by Maria Theresia to Franz Stephan. The final room contains several meteorites which fell on the Empire in the late nineteenth century, and Franz Stephan's very own orrery.

The paleontology section is currently under wraps, with the exception of room X – a huge hall decorated with caryatids struggling with weird, evolutionary beasts – where you can find the skeleton of a diplodocus and various fossils. The prehistoric section begins in room XI with the **Venus of Willendorf**, by far the most famous exhibit in the entire museum. This tiny fertility symbol – a stout, limestone figure with drooping breasts – stands just a few centimetres high, but is something like 25,000 years old, and as such is an object of some fascination.

The west wing includes finds from the prehistoric Beaker folk and various implements, jewellery and arms from Iron Age burial tombs at Hallstatt in the Salzkammergut. There's some impressive Thracian

Burgring

MuseumsQuartier

The Messepalast's vast complex of old stables was earmarked to become the new **MuseumsQuartier** (*www.mqw.at*) way back in the 1980s. However, the architects, Ortner & Ortner, who won the commission in 1990, ran into numerous problems over their designs, in particular their plan to erect a 56-metre-high library tower (*Leseturm*). The tower was eventually rejected as an inappropriate eyesore, as a result of which the Sammlung Essl, Austria's largest private collection of modern art, has now been exiled to Klosterneuburg (see p.273), and a scaled-down version of Ortner & Ortner's plans were finally completed in 2001. The most popular attraction in the MuseumsQuartier is likely to be the **Leopold Museum** (*www.leopoldmuseum.org*), containing the world's biggest collection of works by **Egon Schiele**, as well as paintings by Klimt and Kokoschka. These works were collected by Rudolf Leopold, an opthalmologist (now in his seventies), who began collecting Schiele's works in the late 1940s. By the early 1990s, Leopold had amassed an unrivalled collection, but was deeply in debt, so, after much negotiation, the government baled him out and established a public museum for the works.

Also based in the MuseumsQuartier is the city's chief permanent collection of modern art, the **Museum moderner Kunst**, previously on show at the Palais Liechtenstein and the 20er Haus. Here, you should get to see a reasonable sprinkling of early twentieth-century works by the likes of Picasso, Miró, Magritte, Kupka, Klee, Kandinsky and Kirchner, a smattering of Pop Art and a fair cross-section of pieces by the Wiener Aktionismus group, Austria's very own violent performance-art movement. In addition, you'll find several other museums and galleries here, including the **Kunsthalle** (*www.kunsthallewien.at*), which stages contemporary art exhibitions, as well as smaller concerns such as the **Kinder Museum** (Children's Museum), and the state-sponsored **Tabakmuseum** (Tobacco Museum). To service the needs of the MuseumQuartier's visitors, numerous restaurants and bars will stay open until the early hours.

silver jewellery, a reconstructed funereal chariot from the Iron Age, and a staggering collection of human skulls. The Kindersaal, beyond, is the museum's one concession to modernization, though this tired playroom, built in the 1970s, isn't going to impress kids brought up on interactive, hands-on displays.

Zoology occupies the top floor, with the exception of the first room (XXI), which is a lecture hall and contains a panopticon, plus two 3D viewfinders, through which you can take a peek at natural wonders of the world (including bits of the museum itself). The zoology displays progress from starfish, corals and sea shells in the east wing, through butterflies, spiders and frogs, to a bevy of bears, big cats and monkeys in the west. Some may find the pickled fish and lizards, the jars of snakes and reptiles, and the dissected frog, more than they can stomach, but young kids will undoubtedly enjoy it. There's a little light, historical relief in room XXIX, where you can see two stuffed eagles caught by Crown Prince Rudolf, just nine days before his suicide.

Around Oper

The human congestion around **Oper** – the opera house – makes this the busiest section of the Ringstrasse. It's here that the shoppers of Kärntnerstrasse cross the Ring, or rather descend into the Opernpassage, which stretches south as far as Karlsplatz (see p.138). In the late nineteenth century, this crossroads became known as the "Sirk Ecke", after the then fashionable *Sirk Café* on the corner of Kärntnerstrasse and Kärntner Ring. The latter, which runs down to Schwarzenberg Platz, quickly became the Viennese Corso, where, according to one French visitor, "every branch of society from the great world, to the *demi-monde*, to the 'quarter world', as well as the world of diplomacy and the court" promenaded in the afternoon. Nowadays most people prefer to stroll along Kärntnerstrasse rather than battle with the roaring Ringstrasse traffic.

The nearest U-Bahn is Karlsplatz.

Staatsoper

That the **Staatsoper** (State Opera House; *www.wiener-staatsoper .at*) was the first public building to be completed on the Ringstrasse – opening in May 1869 with a performance of Mozart's *Don Giovanni* – is an indication of its importance in Viennese society. Designed in heavy Italian Renaissance style – even the Austrians deferred to Italy as the home of opera – it has a suitably grandiose exterior, with a fine loggia beneath which the audience could draw up in in their carriages. However, compared with the other monumental edifices on the Ringstrasse the opera house sits low. This was the most common criticism of the building when it was completed, and when the Emperor Franz-Josef was heard to concur with his aides on this issue, one of the architects, Eduard van der Nüll, hanged himself. Van der Nüll's grief-stricken friend and collaborator on the project, August Siccardsburg, died two months later of a heart attack; neither architect lived to witness the first night. Thereafter Franz-Josef always chose the safe riposte "*Es war sehr schön, es hat mir sehr gefreut*" ("It was very beautiful, I enjoyed it very much") whenever he was asked his official opinion.

Schedules for guided tours (in English) are listed beneath the arcade on the east side of the building; öS60/€4.36.

The Staatsoper has always had a special place in the hearts of the Viennese, besotted with their musical heritage, so it was a particularly cruel blow when the building caught fire during an air raid in March 12, 1945. The main auditorium was rebuilt in a much plainer style, and is now pretty undistinguished. Shortly after the withdrawal of the Allied Powers and the declaration of independence in November 1955, the building reopened with a performance of Beethoven's *Fidelio*. Prestigious past directors include Gustav Mahler (see p.134), Richard Strauss, Herbert von Karajan and Claudio Abbado, though each one had notoriously difficult relation-

Around Oper

For more on
how to obtain
tickets for the
opera, see
p.329

ships with the opera house. It still receives massive state subsidy, and hundreds of cheap *Stehplätze* (standing room tickets) are sold each day on a first-come-first-served basis.

Behind Oper

Vienna's top three hotels – the *Sacher*, the *Bristol* and the *Imperial* – are all within a stone's throw of the opera house. The most famous of the trio, directly behind the Staatsoper, is the **Hotel Sacher**, built in the 1870s on the site of the old Kärntnertor Theater, where Beethoven's *Ninth Symphony* premiered in 1824. Founded by Eduard Sacher, the hotel became the aristocrats' favourite knocking shop, particularly after 1892 when it was run by Eduard's widow, the legendary, cigar-smoking Anna Sacher, until her death in 1930. Without doubt, the most famous incident that took place here was when the Archduke Franz Ferdinand's younger brother, the flam-

---

Gustav Mahler (1860–1911)

Mahler's symphonies are now firmly established in the concert repertoire, but it wasn't that long ago that his music was only rarely performed. In his lifetime Mahler was much better known as a conductor. Born to a Jewish family in provincial Bohemia, he studied at the **Vienna Conservatory**, before spending the best part of a decade as a jobbing Kapellmeister at various provincial theatres in the Prussian and Habsburg empires. At the age of just 28, the ambitious Mahler got his big break when he landed the job at the Royal Hungarian Opera in Budapest. Ten years later, in 1897, following a judicious (and entirely mercenary) conversion to Roman Catholicism, he reached his "final goal" and became director of the **Hofoper**, Vienna's imperial opera house (now the Staatsoper).

Mahler's ten years in charge of the Oper (including a couple as chief conductor of the Vienna Philharmonic as well), were stormy to say the least. He instituted a totally new regime in the house, banning claques (opera stars' paid supporters), insisting that the lights of the auditorium be dimmed during performances, and allowing latecomers entry only after the overture or between acts. In his behaviour towards performers he was also something of a tyrant, hiring and firing with abandon and earning himself the nickname of *Korporal vom Tag* (Duty Corporal) for his demanding work schedules and his bluntness. "Is music meant to be so serious?" the emperor is alleged to have said when hearing of these innovations, "I thought it was meant to make people happy".

The music critics were evenly divided, many praising his painstaking attention to detail, others lambasting him for constantly reworking other composers' scores. Needless to say, the anti-Semitic press had a field day, subjecting Mahler to racist jibes, objecting to his "Jew-boy antics on the podium", and caricaturing his eccentric appearance. The gossip columnists were also kept busy, especially when in 1902, Mahler married **Alma Schindler**, the strikingly beautiful step-daughter of Carl Moll, the Secession artist, and, at 22, a woman almost half his age. Mahler's views

---

boyant Archduke Otto, appeared in the hotel lobby naked except for his sword and the Order of the Golden Fleece around his neck. The *Sacher's* continuing popularity, though, rests on its famous *Sachertorte* invented by Eduard's father, Franz, who was Prince Metternich's chef. *Sachertorte* is, of course, available all over Vienna, but the *Sacher* claims that no one else has the true recipe.

The Philipphof, a typically ornate Ringstrasse-style building which was home to the exclusive Jockey Club, originally stood to the north of the *Sacher*. However, during the air raid of March 12, 1945, the building received two direct hits, killing several hundred people sheltering in the basement. The lot remained vacant until the 1980s, when the city council commissioned Alfred Hrdlicka to erect a **Monument against War and Fascism** – a controversial move given the site's history and its extreme prominence. Hrdlicka's final design makes no direct mention of the Holocaust, but includes instead a crouching Jew

Around Oper

For more on Vienna's cakes and cafés, see p.310.

---

on marriage were rigidly bourgeois: she was to give up her music, despite the fact that she was a fledgling composer in her own right. "You must become 'what I need' if we are to be happy together, ie my wife, not my colleague," he wrote to her. Not surprisingly, the marriage was to prove an extremely difficult one for both parties.

Ten years at the helm of the Oper took its toll: "Other theatre directors look after themselves and wear out the theatre. I look after the theatre and wear out myself," he wrote to a friend. Towards the end of 1907, Mahler pinned a farewell note to the opera-house notice board, saying "I meant well, I aimed high ... In the heat of the moment, neither you nor I have been spared wounds, or errors". The previous summer, at the Mahlers' private villa by the Wörthersee in Carinthia, their elder daughter, Maria (Putzi), had died of scarlet fever, and Mahler himself had been diagnosed as having a heart valve defect. It was time to move on. By signing up with the **New York Metropolitan Opera**, Mahler simultaneously doubled his income and drastically reduced his workload. However, the increased travelling and the strain it put his marriage and health under proved too much.

By 1910, Alma was more or less openly conducting an affair with the modernist architect Walter Gropius, and Mahler, in desperation, travelled all the way to Holland to consult Freud. Mahler blamed himself (probably rightly so) for selfishness, and attempted to make amends, showering Alma with affection and encouraging her to compose again. As it turned out, though, Mahler didn't have long to live. In New York he was diagnosed as having subacute bacterial endocarditis, and the family travelled back to Vienna for the last time. Crowds gathered outside the sanatorium, the press issued daily bulletins from the bedside of "der Mahler". He died during a thunderstorm (just like Beethoven), and his last words are alleged to have been "Mozart!". According to his wishes, his tombstone in **Grinzinger Friedhof**, designed by Josef Hoffmann, has nothing but "Mahler" written on it. "Any who come to look for me will know who I was", he explained, "and the rest do not need to know".

Around Oper

scrubbing the pavement, recalling the days following the Anschluss, when some of the city's Jews were forced to clean up anti-Nazi slogans with scrubbing brushes dipped in acid. Many Jews, however, have found the image degrading, among them Simon Wiesenthal, who successfully campaigned for a proper Holocaust memorial to be erected in Vienna, which can now be seen in Judenplatz (see p.77).

The Albertina (see p.112) is currently housed in the Akademiehof, to the east of the Akademie der bildenden Künste, on Makartgasse.

Akademie der bildenden Künste

Set back from the Ring, the **Akademie der bildenden Künste** (Academy of Fine Arts) occupies an imposing neo-Renaissance building by Theophil Hansen on Schillerplatz, to the southwest of the Staatsoper. The Academy itself was founded in 1692, and its main purpose continues to be teaching, but the school also houses a small, much-overlooked study collection. To see the paintings, follow the signs to the **Gemäldegalerie**: turn right after the porter's lodge, up four flights of stairs to the first floor, then right again to the end of the corridor. The **Aula** – straight ahead as you pass through the main entrance – is also worth a glimpse, both for its decor and for the regular wacky student installations.

The permanent collection is open Tues–Sun 10am–4pm; öS50/€3.63.

The Academy's collection is tiny, and extremely patchy, compared with the Kunsthistorisches Museum. Nevertheless, it does have one or two superb works, and one star attraction: *The Last Judgement* triptych by **Hieronymus Bosch** (c.1450–1516), the only Bosch triptych outside Spain. The action in the left panel, *Paradise*, is a taster for the central panel, the *Last Judgement* itself, most of which is taken up with strange half-animal devil figures busy torturing sinners in imaginatively horrible ways; the right panel, *Hell*, looks even less fun. Overall, the possibility of salvation seems painfully slim, with only a lucky few having made it to the small corner of the painting given over to heaven.

Displayed in the same room as the Bosch are two works by Lucas Cranach the Elder: *Lucretia*, a classic Cranach nude, and his moralistic–erotic *Ill-Matched Couple*. The Academy's Italian works are fairly disappointing, with the exception of a Botticelli rondel of the Madonna and Child, and Titian's *Tarquin and Lucretia*, a late work replete with loose brushwork and brooding, autumnal colours. In the same room as the last two, look out for Murillo's sentimental *Two Boys Playing Dice*.

It's Flemish and Dutch paintings that make up the core of the Academy's collection, however, with an early Rembrandt portrait of a young woman in a black dress, a self-portrait by Van Dyck aged just fourteen, preparatory studies for the Jesuit Church frescoes in Antwerp (and lots of nudes) by Rubens, plus works by Jordaens, Ruisdael, Hoogstraten and David Teniers the Younger. After Bosch, though, the other outstanding masterpiece is the *Family Group in a Courtyard* by **Pieter de Hooch** (1629–84), with its sublime tranquillity and clever play on perspective.

Hitler in Vienna

Although he was born and grew up in Upper Austria, **Adolf Hitler** (1890–1945) spent five-and-a-half formative years in Vienna. He arrived in the city aged just seventeen, hoping to enrol at the Academy of Fine Arts. However, though he passed the entrance exam, his portfolio, mostly architectural sketches of Linz, was rejected as "inadequate". Saying nothing about his failure to his family, he stayed in Vienna for a whole year, living fairly comfortably off his father's inheritance and, following the death of his mother, his orphan's pension. In September 1908, Hitler tried once more to get into the Academy: this time he failed the entrance exam. These two rejections hit hard, and still rankled with Hitler two years on, as he wrote to a friend, "Do you know – without any arrogance – I still believe that the world lost a great deal by my not being able to go to the academy and learn the craft of painting. Or did fate reserve me to some other purpose?"

Very little is known about the rest of Hitler's time in Vienna, though he spent a good three years in a men's hostel in the eastern district of Brigittenau, abutting Leopoldstadt, where he sold his mediocre paintings mostly to Jewish frame dealers. (As the saying goes, some of his best friends were Jewish, though Hitler never allowed anyone to get too close.) The evidence is scanty, but Hitler appears to have worked for brief periods as a snow shoveller at the Westbahnhof, and as a painter and decorator at the Kunsthistorisches Museum – he even auditioned for a part in the chorus at the Theater-an-der-Wien, but was rejected when he couldn't produce the right clothes for the part.

Though there is no proof to back up the rumour that Hitler contracted syphilis from a Jewish whore while in the city, it is possible that he may have contracted some minor sexually transmitted ailment, hence his obsession with syphilis and prostitution – both of which he rails against at length in *Mein Kampf*. Other accounts portray Hitler as some kind of proto-hippy, with beard and long hair, practising yoga and tripping on mescaline. Again, there's no concrete evidence, though Hitler certainly experienced a period of homelessness in the winter of 1909, after which he became increasingly unkempt, wearing his beard and hair long.

For much of his stay in Vienna, Hitler was a draft evader – something he neglects to mention in *Mein Kampf* – since he should have signed up in 1909. By the end of 1912 he was liable to a year in prison and a large fine; it was this which eventually led him to flee to Germany in 1913. After a 25-year gap, Hitler returned to Vienna under rather different circumstances in March 1938, following the Anschluss. He stayed at the *Hotel Imperial* on the Ringstrasse, gave a speech to the multitude from the Neue Burg on Heldenplatz, and within twenty-four hours, was on a plane back to Germany.

Also on display are several Venetian views by Guardí, Biedermeier paintings by Waldmüller (who taught at the Academy), and a much-reproduced portrait of Maria Theresia by her official court painter, Martin van Meytens. In the final room, there's a brief selection of twentieth-century Austrian art, including works by Friedensrich Hundertwasser, Fritz Wotruba and Herbert Boeckl.

Karlsplatz

*The nearest
U-Bahn is
Karlsplatz.*

Overlooked by the city's most awesome Baroque church, several key
Ringstrasse institutions, the gilded Secession building and Otto
Wagner's wonderful Art Nouveau pavilions, **Karlsplatz** should be
one of Vienna's showpiece squares. Instead, the western half is little
more than a vast traffic interchange, with pedestrians relegated to a
set of seedy subways that stretch north as far as Oper. There has
never been any grand, overall plan at Karlsplatz – the Naschmarkt
was held here until the 1890s, and when it moved to the nearby
Wienzeile, the heart was ripped out of the square. The city council
provided a site for the Secession, but the avenue that should have
connected it with the Karlskirche never materialized. As a result, it's
actually impossible to stand back and admire the Secession building
without seriously endangering your life. The most recent abomination, Adolf Krischanitz's mustard yellow and blue pre-fab Kunsthalle,
is set to reach the end of its shelf life and should be removed in 2001
when the MuseumsQuartier opens (see p.132).

Secession

*The Secession
building is
open
Tues–Sun
10am–6pm,
Thurs until
8pm;
öS60/€4.36.*

In 1898, Joseph Maria Olbrich completed one of the most original
Jugendstil works of art in Vienna, the headquarters for the art movement known as the **Secession** (*www.secession.at*). The dome of
gilded bronze laurel leaves is obviously the most startling feature –
the Viennese dubbed it the "golden cabbage" – though all the building's decorative details are unusual. On the side, three wise owls suddenly emerge from the rendering, while the main entrance is adorned
with a trio of gorgons, a pair of salamanders and copious gilded
foliage; above is the group's credo, "For every age its art; for art its
freedom", replaced after being removed by the Nazis. Don't miss the
tortoises at the feet of the ornamental bowls, Georg Klimt's bronze
doors with snake handles, and Arthur Strasser's bronze statue of an
overweight Mark Anthony on a chariot drawn by panthers (originally displayed at the group's fourth exhibition in 1899).

*Klimt and his
followers used
to meet at the
nearby* Café
Museum, *see
p.313.*

The main hall upstairs stages provocative contemporary art installations, while downstairs in the basement Gustav Klimt's **Beethoven
Frieze** is on permanent display. The frieze was intended to last only
for the duration of the fourteenth exhibition held in 1902 – in the end
it was preserved, but not shown to the public again until 1986. The
centrepiece of the exhibition was a heroic nude statue of Beethoven
by the German sculptor Max Klinger (now in the entrance of
Leipzig's Neues Gewandhaus, with an incomplete copy in Vienna's
Historisches Museum der Stadt Wien). For the opening of the exhibition, Gustav Mahler conducted his own orchestration of the fourth
movement of Beethoven's *Ninth Symphony*. Auguste Rodin deemed
Klimt's frieze "tragic and divine", but most visitors were appalled by

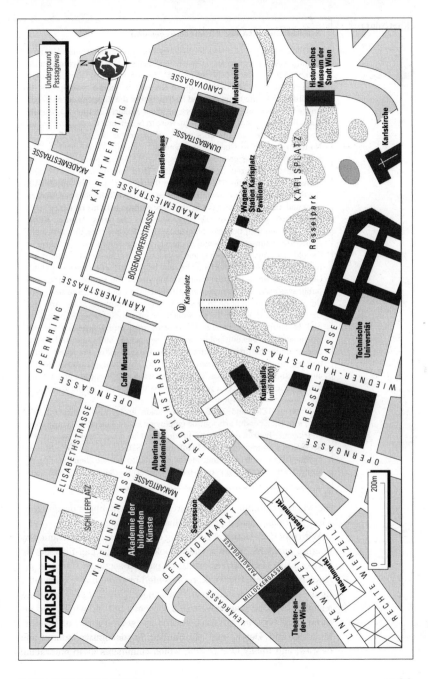

KARLSPLATZ

Undergraound
·········· Passageway

N

AKADEMIESTRASSE

KÄRNTNER RING

AKADEMIESTRASSE

CANOVAGASSE

Musikverein

DUMBASTRASSE

Künstlerhaus

Historisches Museum der Stadt Wien

KARLSPLATZ

Karlskirche

Wagner's Station Karlsplatz Pavilions

BÖSENDORFERSTRASSE

Resselpark

KÄRNTNERSTRASSE

OPERNRING

Karlsplatz

RESSELGASSE

WIEDNER-HAUPTSTRASSE

Technische Universität

Café Museum

FRIEDRICHSTRASSE

OPERNGASSE

Kunsthalle (until 2000)

OPERNGASSE

ELISABETHSTRASSE

SCHILLERPLATZ

MAKARTIGASSE

Albertina im Akademiehof

NIBELUNGENGASSE

Akademie der bildenden Künste

Secession

GETREIDEMARKT

Naschmarkt

Naschmarkt

PAPAGENOGASSE

MILLÖCKERGASSE

LINKE WIENZEILE

Theater-an-der-Wien

LEHARGASSE

RECHTE WIENZEILE

0   200m

A Brief Guide to the Viennese Secession

In 1897, a number of artists broke away from the Künstlerhaus, Austria's leading independent artists' association, and set up their own organization, which they named the **Secession**. The second half of the nineteenth century had seen the ossification of the arts in Vienna, exemplified in architecture by the heavy-handed historicism of the Ringstrasse, and epitomized in painting by the flattery of Hans Makart (1840–84). Broadly speaking, the aims of the new group were to regenerate the arts in Vienna, and to promote "art for art's sake", in particular the latest style, Art Nouveau, known in German as Jugendstil (literally "Youth-style"). "We want to declare war on sterile routine, on rigid Byzantinism, on all forms of bad taste," declared the critic Hermann Bahr, one of the literary champions of the movement. The other major thrust, which sat less happily with the Secession's other commitments, was to strip off the mask of historicism and, as Otto Wagner put it, "to show modern man his true face".

The first president of the Secession was the artist **Gustav Klimt** (1862–1918), who became the group's driving force over the next eight years. Klimt himself had begun his career as a promising young master of the old ideology. In the movement's striking, purpose-built headquarters, in full view of the Künstlerhaus, he now helped put on a series of exhibitions of new work. Initially, the reception among the Viennese critics and public was good; the emperor himself visited the exhibition, and several of the Secessionists went on to receive faculty appointments at the Arts and Crafts School. However, the movement ran into trouble when Klimt exhibited *Medicine* here, part of his controversial mural intended for the University. The ensuing public scandal (see p.128) and the mixed reception given to the group's fourteenth exhibition in 1902, for which Klimt painted the *Beethoven Frieze* (see p.138), eventually prompted Klimt, along with a number of his followers, to leave the Secession and retreat from public life for several years, before returning to the public arena with the Kunstschau exhibitions (see p.148).

Between 1898 and 1903, the Secession group also published *Ver Sacrum*, a successful arts journal employing lavish Jugendstil typography and layout. Instrumental in its production and design were two of the Secession's co-founders, **Josef Hoffmann** (1870–1955) and **Kolo Moser** (1868–1918). Hoffmann and Moser went on to pursue their interest in applied art, forming the craft-based Wiener Werkstätte in 1902 (see

the whole exhibition, with its bare concrete chambers designed by Josef Hoffmann, and it proved a financial disaster.

With much of the mural consisting of huge blank spaces framed by floating maidens, Klimt's frieze looks strangely half-finished. In between the blank spaces are three painted sections: *Longing for Happiness*, where the weak, represented by three naked emaciated figures, appeal to a knight in golden armour; *Hostile Forces* features a slightly comical giant ape, with a serpent's tail and wings, and his three daughters, the gorgons, backed up by the figures of Disease, Madness and Death, and surrounded by decorative sperm and ovaries; and finally *Ode to Joy*, which culminates in an embracing p.152), and eventually leaving the Secession in 1905 along with Klimt. All three later worked together to organize the Kunstschau exhibitions of 1908 and 1909 (see p.148), which marked a fundamental shift in the art scene. The decorative art of the Secession was left behind in favour of Expressionism, and the two leading artists to emerge from the Kunstschau were Oskar Kokoschka and Egon Schiele. Unlike Klimt, Hoffmann was strongly influenced by the more elongated, geometric style of Scotland's Charles Rennie Mackintosh, and later became one of Vienna's most intriguing early modernists, both in his architectural work and in his applied art (his villas on the Hohe Warte and in Hietzing are described on p.251 and p.239).

Though only a peripheral character in the Secessionist organization, the architect **Otto Wagner** (1841–1918) was a seminal figure in the Viennese art world throughout the period – as Hermann Bahr wrote, "without Wagner, there would be no Secession, no Klimt group, no applied art". Wagner not only completed more buildings than any other Secession architect, he also designed the entire Stadtbahn system from 1894 to 1901, including all the stations and bridges, many of which are extant on the U4 and U6 metro lines. As such, he remains the most high-profile exponent of the Secession style, though his works in fact range from nine-teenth-century historicism to twentieth-century modernism. He began his career as a Ringstrasse architect, and had become something of an establishment figure by the time he joined the Secession in 1899. In the decade that followed he executed some of his finest work, initially opting for ornate curvilinear motifs derived from nature, but later moving towards more rectilinear, abstract forms. Wagner's shift towards minimalism and his enthusiastic adoption of new materials such as concrete and alumini-um – best seen in his Postsparkasse (see p.153) – make him a key figure in the emergence of modernism.

Last, but not least, it's worth mentioning **Adolf Loos** (1870–1933), who published two articles in *Ver Sacrum*, one of which was a stinging attack on Ringstrasse architecture. Loos's relationship with the Secession was brief, however, and in 1908 he published a thinly veiled criticism of the movement in an article entitled *Ornament is Crime*. As an architect, Loos went on to design some of Europe's first, truly modernist buildings, most notably the Loos Haus (see p.68) and his series of villas in Hietzing (see p.239).

couple, offering, in Schiller's words, "this kiss to all the world". There's an excellent leaflet in English available (from the ticket desk), which explains in greater detail the symbolism behind the frieze; also on display are Klimt's preparatory sketches.

Resselpark

The central, traffic-free section of Karlsplatz is the leafy **Resselpark**, named for Josef Ressel, the Czech inventor of the screw propellor. Despite thinking up the device some ten years before John Ericsson, Ressel was prevented from experimenting with it by the Habsburg bureaucracy, and was thus confined to relative historical obscurity.

Karlsplatz

Ressel's statue stands close to that of another hapless innovator, the tailor Josef Madersperger, who invented a sewing machine in 1815, but died penniless because no Austrian would market it. Johannes Brahms, who died in 1897 at Karlgasse 4, now a part of the nearby Technische Universität, is also represented.

Resselpark is chiefly remarkable, however, for Otto Wagner's duo of Jugendstil entrance pavilions for the now defunct **Station Karlsplatz**, erected in 1899. Wagner broke with his usual design here, partly in deference to the presence of the nearby Karlskirche, adding gold trimmings and a sunflower motif. The green, wrought-iron framework, which was a feature of all his Stadtbahn stations, forms an essential part of the overall design, framing a series of thin marble slabs and creating a lovely, curving, central canopy. Today, one of the pavilions is put into use as a café during the summer months, while the other holds exhibition space for the Historisches Museum der Stadt Wien; both have retained some of their original interior decor.

The exhibition pavilion is open April–Oct Tues–Sun 1–4.30pm; öS25/€1.82.

From the terrace between the pavilions, you can also admire two key institutions on the north side of Karlsplatz, both executed in Ringstrasse style. The neo-Baroque **Künstlerhaus** (*www.k-haus.at*) was built in 1881 as the exhibition hall of Austria's leading artists' association (from which the Secession group split in 1897); its diminutive extension was converted into a mid-scale theatre in the 1970s. Next door stands the **Musikverein**, Vienna's number one concert hall, designed by the ubiquitous Theophil Hansen in the 1860s. The classical terracotta exterior apes the opera house with its front loggia, but you really need to attend a concert in the Grosser Saal to appreciate the unbeatable acoustics and the sumptuous decor with its parade of gilded caryatids. Home to the world-famous *Wiener Philharmoniker* (Vienna Philharmonic; *www.wienerphilharmoniker.at*), the Musikverein's most prestigious event is the annual schmaltzy New Year's Day concert, a tradition started under the Nazis in 1939, and one which is now transmitted live around the world to an estimated 1.3 billion viewers (it's also beamed live onto a large screen on the front of the Rathaus).

The concert hall itself also has a rich musical history as the place where the composer Arnold Schönberg and his followers unleashed atonal music – Schönberg preferred to call it "the emancipation of dissonance" – on an unsuspecting and unready Viennese public. The worst disturbance took place on March 31, 1913, at a concert conducted by Schönberg, during which two of Alban Berg's *Altenberg Lieder*, songs based on the *bon mots* scribbled on the back of postcards by poet Peter Altenberg, were premiered. Programmes were used as missiles, blows were exchanged and the concert had to be abandoned after an ambulance was sent for. Schönberg, of all people, later complained that Berg's *Altenberg Lieder* were "so brief as to exclude the possibility of extended thematic development". Berg was mortified and the *Lieder* remained unheard and unpublished until seventeen years after his death in 1935.

Karlsplatz

Those keen on Schönberg should visit the Arnold Schönberg Center; see p.148.

Karlskirche

Rising majestically above everything around it, the **Karlskirche** is, without doubt, the city's finest Baroque church. A huge Italianate dome with a Neoclassical portico, flanked by two giant pillars modelled on Trajan's Column, and, just for good measure, a couple of hefty Baroque side towers, it's an eclectic and rather self-conscious mixture of styles, built to impress. Even surrounded by the mess that is now Karlsplatz, the church is an awesome sight – particularly at night when it is bathed in blue light and reflected in the lake – and must have been even more so when there was nothing between it and the Hofburg except the open space of the glacis.

The story goes that the Emperor Karl VI vowed to build a church during the plague of 1713. Architect Johann Bernhard Fischer von Erlach won the competition to design the building; his son, Johann Michael, completed the job in 1737. The church is actually dedicated to the sixteenth-century saint, Carlo Borromeo, who was canonized for his ministrations during the famine and plague in Milan. However, the fact that the emperor and saint shared the same name no doubt played a part in Karl VI's choice, conveniently glorifying both of them at the same time. The Karlskirche's dual nature – votive and imperial – is nowhere more evident than with the columns, imperial symbols, whose reliefs, rather than portraying the Emperor Trajan's campaigns (as on the originals), illustrate the life of Borromeo. As if to emphasize the point, the columns are topped by giant gilded Habsburg eagles, and, above the lanterns, the imperial crown.

Thanks to the windows and lantern in the oval dome, the interior is surprisingly sparse and light, allowing a much better appreciation of Johann Michael Rottmayr's vast fresco than you get of the artist's work in the Peterskirche (see p.65). The subject is the apotheosis of

The Karlskirche is open Mon–Sat 9–11.30am & 1–5pm, Sun 1–5pm; öS40/€2.90.

Carlo Borromeo, along with a bit of Counter-Reformation Luther-bashing – note the angel setting fire to the German's bible. Everything else in the church finds it rather hard to compete with the sublime beauty of the dome, though Fischer von Erlach's sunburst above the main altar is definitely worth a closer look. Interwoven with the golden rays are stucco clouds and cherubs accompanying Saint Carlo as he ascends into heaven.

Historisches Museum der Stadt Wien

The museum is open Tues–Sun 9am–6pm; öS50/€3.63.

Housed in an unprepossessing modernist block to the side of the Karlskirche, the **Historisches Museum der Stadt Wien** (Historical Museum of the City of Vienna) is foolishly overlooked by many visitors. The permanent collection may be uneven, but it does contain, among other things, a pretty good *fin-de-siècle* section, which alone more than justifies a visit: there are paintings by Gustav Klimt, Egon Schiele, Carl Moll and Richard Gerstl, an interior by Adolf Loos, and several cabinets of Wiener Werkstätte pieces. Excellent temporary exhibitions are held on the ground floor.

The first floor

The permanent display begins on the first floor where you can view a smattering of spoils from the city's two Turkish sieges in 1529 and 1683: a vast red silk banner, Turkish horse plumes sporting crescent moons, several swash-buckling sabres, and an ornate tent lantern. The museum also owns a welter of paintings, including minor works by the key artists of the **Baroque** period. There are several representative works – though no masterpieces – by the three artists whose frescoes adorn so many churches in the former empire: Paul Troger, Johann Michael Rottmayr and Franz Anton Maulbertsch. Before you head upstairs be sure to take a look at the model of Vienna, which shows the city shortly before the old zig-zag fortifications were torn down in 1857.

See p.123 for a map of Vienna in 1857.

The second floor

To continue viewing the exhibits chronologically, ignore the tempting *fin-de-siècle* stuff ahead and to your right at the top of the stairs, and instead turn left into the section devoted to the **Biedermeier** era (1815–48), which marked a return to simple, bourgeois values, after the excesses of the Baroque period. There's an entire room decorated in "Pompeii style" from a now demolished old town palace where, in the early nineteenth century, the wealthy Geymüller family entertained a coterie of artists. Among the guests was the Austrian poet and playwright Franz Grillparzer, whose musty living quarters are lovingly preserved further on. Surrounding Grillparzer's room are more than enough mawkish Biedermeier paintings for most people, epitomized by Ferdinand Georg Waldmüller's sentimental depictions of rural folk and flattering portraits of the bourgeoisie.

Moving on through the modest collection of 1848 revolutionary memorabilia, you come to two sultry portraits of society ladies from thirty years later by Hans Makart. In his day Makart was lionized by the Viennese, but his works have not worn well, and his art has since been eclipsed by his more famous pupil, **Gustav Klimt**. Several of Klimt's works can be found towards the end of the late nineteenth-century section, including his *Pallas Athene* from 1898, marking his first extensive use of gold, which was to become a hallmark of his work. Max Kurzweil's portrait of a *Woman in Yellow*, lounging luxuriantly on a sofa, is a classic *fin-de-siècle* painting, as is Josef Engelhart's emblematic *Im Sophiensaal*, which captures perfectly the loose sexuality of café life. Don't miss, too, the wonderful mother-of-pearl studded chair, designed by Otto Wagner, and presented to Karl Lueger on his sixtieth birthday.

The centrepiece of this section, though, is another model of Vienna, this time from after the construction of the great Ringstrasse buildings of the late nineteenth century, accompanied by before and after photos. To the side is an entire living/dining room designed in 1903 by the modernist architect **Adolf Loos** for his first marital home on nearby Bösendorferstrasse. Despite his diatribes against ornament of any kind, Loos loved rich materials – marble, mahogany and brass – and created for himself a typically plush interior. Close by Loos's room is the copy of Max Klinger's nude statue of Beethoven, which formed the centrepiece of the Secession exhibition of 1902 (see p.138), albeit without its coloured marble drapery and seat.

Beyond Loos's room are various works of art from Vienna's artistic golden age. There are several glass cabinets – including one designed by Kolo Moser – stuffed with Wiener Werkstätte produce, but it's the collection of works by **Egon Schiele** which really stand out. A typically distraught study of sunflowers from 1909 and the harrowing *Blind Mother II* hang beside a fondly painted view of the artist's bedroom in Neulengbach, a clear homage to Van Gogh, executed shortly before his brief imprisonment on a charge of "displaying an erotic drawing in a room open to children". The characteristically angular portraits of the art critic and collector Arthur Roessler and his wife Ida – loyal friends and patrons throughout Schiele's life – are among the artist's earliest commissioned portrait oils. Also of note are Richard Gerstl's nervous self-portrait from 1905 and his portrait of Arnold Schönberg, with whose wife Gerstl had a disastrous affair. Schönberg's own portrayal of fellow composer, Alban Berg, hangs close by.

For more on the Wiener Werkstätte, see p.152.

Naschmarkt

The River Wien, which used to wend its way across Karlsplatz, was, by all accounts, an unsavoury stretch of water: "this black and vilely-smelling ditch is a foul blot upon the beauty and neatness of this

The market is
open Mon–Sat
9am–6pm.

There are
some great
cafés on either
side of the
Naschmarkt;
see p.313.

lovely city, and must certainly produce a miasma extremely prejudicial to health," noted Anthony Trollope's mother, Fanny, in the early nineteenth century. So it was no doubt with some relief that it was eventually paved over in the 1890s, allowing the **Naschmarkt** to move from the square to its present site over the old course of the river, the Wienzeile. The market is now the city's premier source of fruit and vegetables, and is one of the few places where you get a real sense of the city's multicultural make-up: Turkish, Arab, Slav and Chinese stallholders vie for customers all the way to the Kettenbrückengasse metro station. It's a great place to eat some food on the hoof, and on Saturdays, the market extends even further west as the weekly flea market joins in.

The Linke and Rechte Wienzeile, which run parallel to each other on either side of the market, now function as a six-lane motorway. There are, however, a couple of sights along the Linke Wienzeile which make a stroll through the market doubly rewarding. First off, at no.6, there's the **Theater-an-der-Wien**, which opened in 1801 under the directorship of Emanuel Schikaneder, depicted as the feathered bird-catcher Papageno from Mozart's *Die Zauberflöte* (Magic Flute) above the main portico. Schikaneder wrote the libretto for the opera and was instrumental in supporting Beethoven, putting the theatre at his disposal, and even allowing him to live there on and off. Beethoven's opera *Fidelio* premiered here on November 20, 1805, exactly a week after the French had marched into Vienna. Under such extreme conditions – French soldiers made up much of the audience – it's hardly surprising that the opera flopped, running for just three performances. The theatre is also intimately connected with many other Austrian classics: Franz Grillparzer's *Ahnfrau*, almost all of Johann Nestroy's farces, Johann Strauss's *Die Fledermaus* and Franz Lehár's *Die lustige Witwe*, were all first performed here. After World War II, while the Staatsoper was being repaired, the theatre once more staged operas, though it now concentrates on musicals.

A good 500m further west on the same side are two of Otto Wagner's most appealing Secession buildings from 1899, the apartment blocks of **Linke Wienzeile 38** and **40**, next to each other overlooking the market. Wagner's ultimate aim was to transform the Wienzeile – which leads eventually to Schönbrunn – into a new Ringstrasse, though stylistically both buildings signal a break with the Ringstrasse style. Eschewing any pretensions to resemble a palace, the separation between the commercial ground floor and the residential apartments above is deliberately emphasized. The right-hand building (no. 38) is richly embossed with gold palm leaves and medallions – the latter designed by Kolo Moser – and even features an elaborate top-floor loggia with Art Nouveau swags, urns and a couple of figures. The left-hand building (no. 40) is more unusual, its pollution-resistant cladding of majolica tiles giving rise to the nickname, **Majolikahaus**. To contemporary eyes, the facade looks highly decorative, but what mattered to the Viennese was that – as with the Looshaus – there was virtually no sculptural decoration, and no mouldings or pediments above the windows. Instead, Wagner weaves an elaborate floral motif – a giant, spreading rose tree or a vine of sunflowers – on the tiles themselves.

From Schwarzenberg Platz to Stubenring

The last stretch of the Ringstrasse – Schubertring, Parkring and Stubenring respectively – runs more or less in a straight line from Schwarzenberg Platz to the Donaukanal (Danube Canal). With fewer landmark buildings than the rest of the Ringstrasse, it does, however, boast the city's most congenial central green space, **Stadtpark**, Vienna's superb applied arts museum, the **MAK**, and Otto Wagner's seminal exercise in modernism, the **Postsparkasse**.

Schwarzenberg Platz

Faced with the din of cars and trams whizzing across its cobbles, it's difficult to believe that the large, rectangular, traffic intersection of **Schwarzenberg Platz** was once a fashionable address. The aristocracy, though they owned up to a third of the property on the Ring, usually turned their noses up at actually living there – with Schwarzenberg Platz they made an exception. The square became the nobility's own personal enclave, centred on an equestrian statue of one of their own, Prince Karl von Schwarzenberg, a member of one of the most powerful Austrian families, commander-in-chief at the Battle of Leipzig in 1813.

At the southern end of the square, dramatically floodlit at night and spurting water high into the air, stands the **Hochstrahlbrunnen** (High Jet Fountain), erected in 1873 as a celebration of the city's nascent modern water supply system. Once the focal point of the square, it is now thoroughly upstaged by the bombastic **Russen Heldendenkmal** (Russian Heroes' Monument), which rises up behind the jet of water. A giant curving colonnade acts as the backdrop to the central column, crowned by the Unknown (Soviet) Soldier in heroic stance, flag aloft, sporting a gilded shield and helmet; on the red granite plinth are the names of the fallen and a quote from Stalin (after whom the square was briefly renamed in 1945). For the Viennese, though, it's more a grim reminder of the brutality of the liberators and the privations suffered by those in the city's postwar Russian zones. No doubt aware of their unpopularity, the Soviets made sure that a clause ensuring the proper upkeep of the monument was written into the 1955 Austrian State Treaty.

**From
Schwarzen-
berg Platz to
Stubenring**

*For a review
of the Hotel im
Palais
Schwarzenberg,
see p.297.*

*The Café
Schwarzenberg
is one of the
smartest
Ringstrasse
cafés; see
p.313.*

*The Arnold
Schönberg
Center is open
Mon–Fri
10am–5pm;
öS70/€5.09.*

Before the erection of the Soviet war memorial, the backdrop to the fountain was the **Palais Schwarzenberg**, Lucas von Hildebrandt's grandiose Baroque palace, built for Count Mansfeld-Fondi in 1704 and now hidden behind foliage. It was bought by the Schwarzenbergs who employed Hildebrandt's arch rival, Fischer von Erlach, to further embellish it in 1716. A bomb lopped off the central dome in World War II, and destroyed most of the frescoes by Daniel Gran, but the palace is otherwise well preserved. The Schwarzenbergs still live here, though they've turned the best rooms into a hotel and restaurant, and rented out one of the outbuildings to the Swiss Embassy. Sadly, the palace and its extensive gardens are closed except to hotel and restaurant guests, or embassy staff.

More accessible, though rather more specialist, is the **Arnold Schönberg Center** (*www.schoenberg.at*), situated in the Palais Fanto, to the east of the Soviet war memorial, on the corner of Zaunergasse and Daffingerstrasse. The centre holds vast archives, puts on talks, concerts and temporary exhibitions about the composer, which are held on the second floor of the building (the entrance is on Zaunergasse). Schönberg is considered the father of atonal music, and was the leading figure in what has become known as the Second Viennese School. He was an accomplished artist, too, and one or two of his drawings are usually on display as part of the exhibitions – most people find that his artwork is a lot easier on the eye than his atonal works are on the ear. There's also a reconstruction of Schönberg's study in Los Angeles (to which he fled in the 1930s), containing original furniture and objects, many of which he himself designed from recycled materials. And whatever you do, don't forget to ask about Schönberg's greatest invention: chess for four players.

Konzerthaus

*The nearest
U-Bahn is
Stadtpark.*

The most illustrious concert venue in Vienna after the Musikverein (see p.142) is the **Konzerthaus**, east of Schwarzenbergplatz on Lothringerstrasse, home to the *Wiener Symphoniker* (Vienna Symphony Orchestra), three concert halls, the Akademietheater and a studio theatre. Built in late Secession style in 1913 by the great Austrian theatre-building firm, Helmer and Fellner, it boasts a lovely, illuminated wrought-iron and glass canopy, surmounted by octagons and a half-moon gable.

Shortly before the Konzerthaus was built, Klimt and his followers, who had left the Secession in 1905 (see p.140), staged their own exhibition, **Kunstschau Wien 1908**, on this very site. Josef Hoffmann designed the pavilion and formal garden as a sort of stripped-down summer house, Oskar Kokoschka designed the poster, the Wiener Werkstätte took part and the centrepiece was a retrospective of Klimt's work hung in a room designed by Kolo Moser. The show was an outstanding success, and even before the exhibition closed, the Austrian state had purchased Klimt's *The Kiss* (now in the Belvedere, see p.176).

The next year, with Klimt's blessing, Egon Schiele exhibited his work for the first time at the **Kunstschau Wien 1909**, but the scandal which Kilmt dreaded never materialized. Instead, it came from the Kunstschau's garden theatre, where Kokoschka's brutal, sexually aggressive play, *Murderer, Hope of Women*, was premiered. Some imperial army soldiers from Bosnia in the audience took exception to the play and started a riot. The Archduke Franz Ferdinand, reading the newspaper reports the next day, memorably opined, "every bone in that young man's body should be broken". Though Kokoschka avoided that particular fate, his art school stipend was withdrawn at the instigation of the Ministry of Culture.

From
Schwarzen-
berg Platz to
Stubenring

Stadtpark

Straddling the canalized River Wien much as the glacis once did, the **Stadtpark** is the largest of the Ringstrasse parks. Opened in 1862 as the city council's first public park, it's best known for Edmund Hellmer's eye-catching, over-the-top **Strauss Monument** from 1925, with its statue of the "Waltz King", Johann Strauss Junior, violin in hand. Gilded from head to toe and dramatically floodlit at night, the composer stands framed by a stone arch of naked, swirling naiads. Tour groups turn up at regular intervals to admire the monument, while the benches close by are a favourite spot for Vienna's elderly population. Vienna's younger generation also like to hang out here, too, smoking, drinking on the grass, and selling dope; the authorities occasionally move the scene on a few hundred metres or so, but without any great enthusiasm.

*For more on
the Strauss
family, see
p.214.*

Several other artistic types are honoured with statues in this park, but none deserves much attention. You're better off heading for the much diminished River Wien itself, where the **Wienflussportal** – a series of rather wonderful Jugendstil pavilions and quaysides – was constructed in 1905 by Friedrich Ohmann, nicely complementing Otto Wagner's adjacent Stadtbahn station, which survives as Stadtpark U-Bahn. The other architectural landmark is the **Kursalon**, built in neo-Renaissance style at the same time as the park, daubed in soft *Kaisergelb* (imperial yellow) and still a prime venue for waltzing. Another possible focus for your wanderings is the **Münze** (Mint), built in the 1830s on the eastern edge of the Stadtpark, and the place where the country's Groschen and Schillings will be produced until 2002. Somewhat surprisingly, the Mint puts on excellent temporary exhibitions, often with only a very vague numismatic bent.

MAK

North of the Stadtpark, the **Österreichisches Museum für angewandte Kunst** (Austrian Museum of Applied Art) – better known simply as the **MAK** (*www.mak.at*) – is one of the most enjoyable

From Schwarzen-berg Platz to Stubenring

The MAK is open Tues 10am–midnight, Wed–Sun 10am–6pm; öS90/E6.54. The nearest U-Bahn is Stubentor.

The MAK *Café is open Tues–Sun 10am–midnight; see p.313.*

museums in Vienna. The highlights of its superlative, highly eclectic selection of *objets d'art*, stretching from the Romanesque period to the twentieth century, are Klimt's *Stoclet Frieze* and the unrivalled collection of Wiener Werkstätte products. But what really sets it apart is the museum's interior design; the MAK gave some of Austria's leading designers free rein to create a unique series of rooms.

The MAK was founded as a Museum of Art and Industry in the 1860s by Rudolf Eitelberger, who was inspired by a visit to what is now London's Victoria and Albert Museum. Designed by Heinrich Ferstel in a richly decorative neo-Renaissance style in 1872, the building was later extended to house the Arts and Crafts School (now the Academy of Applied Arts), where Kokoschka and Klimt both trained. At the turn of the century the school became a stronghold of the Secession movement, handing out faculty positions to Josef Hoffmann and Kolo Moser, and promoting the work of the Wiener Werkstätte. At the ticket office in the beautiful, glass-roofed court-yard, with its double-decker loggia, you'll be given a plan of the museum in German and English. On the wall of each room there's a slightly pretentious, bilingual introduction by the designer, and a leaflet in English cataloguing and explaining each exhibit. Temporary exhibitions are held, for the most part, in the museum's Ausstellungshalle, whose main entrance is on Weiskirchnerstrasse.

Romanesque to Rococo

To follow the collection chronologically, you should begin with the **Romanik, Gotik, Renaissance** room, on the ground floor where the minimalist display cabinets are beautifully offset by deep cobalt-blue walls. The designers have deliberately restricted the number of items on show, allowing you to pay detailed attention to each exhibit, though inevitably you also end up with a slightly staccato history of the applied arts. Aside from a few pieces of beautifully inlaid six-teenth-century furniture and some very early thirteenth-century canonical garments, most of the exhibits are items of Italian six-teenth-century majolica, decorated with richly coloured mythologi-cal scenes and grotesque faces.

The main focus of the next-door room – **Barock, Rokoko, Klassizismus** – is a room within a room. Acquired by the museum in 1912, the mid-eighteenth-century Porcelain Room was removed piece by piece from the Palais Dubsky in Brno and reassembled here. It derives its name from the ceramics that have been used to decorate everything right down to the wall panelling, candelabra, chandeliers and table-tops. Outside the Porcelain Room exhibits include two huge eighteenth-century maple and walnut marquetry panels, an unusually large section of Chinese wallpaper from the same period, portraying an idealized landscape, and a pair of pink, gilded double doors salvaged from the Palais Paar in the Innere Stadt in 1938.

Renaissance to Art Deco and the Orient

As you cross the courtyard to the next set of rooms, the designers begin to impose themselves more emphatically. **Barock, Rokoko** consists of two long, central glass cabinets displaying Bohemian, Silesian and Venetian glass, with examples of Italian, French and Flemish lacework set against a black background all along the walls. The **Empire, Biedermeier** room is much quirkier. A parade of early nineteenth-century Viennese chairs, arranged as if for a game of musical chairs, occupies the central space, while, up above, the cornice is broken by fast-moving, polemical, multi-lingual LED text on the social history of the era. To take it all in, sit down on the aluminium version of one of the Biedermeier sofas on display.

The museum's *pièce de résistance*, though, in terms of design, comes in the **Historismus, Jugendstil** room. Two parallel shadow screens, running the length of the room, create a corridor down which you can stroll, while admiring the changing geometry of chair design over the last hundred years in silhouette. If you want a 3D look at the chairs, you can simply go round the back of the screens. The exhibits include modernist designs by the likes of Josef Hoffmann, Otto Wagner and Adolf Loos, and, of course, the bentwood Thonet chair that became a cheap, classic design which sold by the million all around the world.

The final ground-floor room is devoted to tiles and carpets from the **Orient**, laid on the walls and floors, creating a mosque-like atmosphere. The carpets, mostly from the sixteenth and seventeenth centuries, were avidly collected by the Habsburgs. Star turn is the world's only surviving sixteenth-century silk Egyptian Mamluke carpet, spread out on the floor to the left as you enter.

The twentieth century

Three rooms on the first floor are given over to the permanent collection. One room is devoted to the **Wiener Werkstätte** (see overleaf), whose archives were donated to the museum in 1955. The range and scope of the WW is staggering, and just about every field in which they were active is represented here, from jewellery and metalwork, primarily by Peche and Hoffmann, to the WW's prolific fashion off-shoot. One of the finest works is Kolo Moser's wood-inlaid writing-desk, which includes a retractable armchair that can be slotted into place to make the whole thing appear like a chest of drawers.

The **Jugendstil, Art Deco** room is dominated by Gustav Klimt's working designs for his *Stoclet Frieze*, a series of mosaics commissioned in 1904 for the dining room of the Palais Stoclet in Brussels. Predominantly gold, with Byzantine and Egyptian overtones, the frieze marks the climax of Klimt's highly ornamental phase (the finished product was inlaid with semi-precious stones). The tree of life is the central motif, the birds of prey in its branches symbolizing

Wiener Werkstätte

After the Secession, probably the most important Austrian art movement was the **Wiener Werkstätte** (Vienna Workshop), founded in 1903 by the architect Josef Hoffmann, the designer Kolo Moser and the rich Jewish textile merchant, Fritz Waerndorfer. Hoffmann and Moser, both founder members of the Secession, were initially inspired by William Morris and the English Arts and Crafts Movement. As with Morris & Co, the idea was to grant designers and craftsmen equal status – all Wiener Werkstätte produce bears the WW monogram, and the name of both the artist and craftsman. The other parallel with Morris & Co was the sheer range and breadth of the WW, whose work encompassed furniture, glassware, metalwork, porcelain, fashion, children's toys, postcards and even wrapping paper.

Artistically, the WW drew on a wide range of talents, including the likes of Oskar Kokoschka, Egon Schiele and Gustav Klimt. However, the strongest influences on Hoffmann and Moser were the Glaswegians Charles Rennie Mackintosh and his wife, Margaret Macdonald, who exhibited at the Secession in 1900 – their rectilinear, geometrical style became the hallmark of the WW in their first decade. In 1907, the WW made a big splash in Vienna with the opening of the legendary *Cabaret Fledermaus* on Kärntnerstrasse, which they had designed from the toilets to the cutlery. However, despite winning numerous international prizes, and opening shops as far afield as New York and Zürich, the WW proved less successful financially. Unlike Morris & Co or Bauhaus, their works were not meant for mass production, and they remained attached to the old-fashioned idea of the single, unrepeatable object, designed for rich patrons, the majority of whom recoiled from such avant-garde designs. Though from 1915 onwards, Dagobert Peche's softer, more decoratively playful style, dubbed *spitzbarok* (spiky Baroque), significantly widened the appeal of the WW, the company eventually folded in 1932.

The most complete WW work – the 1905 Palais Stoclet designed by Hoffmann (in collaboration with Klimt) – is actually in Brussels, but the room devoted to the WW in the MAK is the next best thing. There are also exhibits in the Historisches Museum der Stadt Wien (see p.144) and in the Lobmeyr glass shop (see p.58).

death, and the figures beneath it representing paradise. Close by the Klimt hangs a frieze by Margaret Macdonald, executed for Fritz Waerndorfer, and clearly inspired by Klimt's own *Beethoven Frieze*. Also on show is furniture by the likes of Otto Wagner and Kolo Moser, Charles Rennie Mackintosh, and an amazing selection of Bohemian glass – from the Lötz factory's iridescent, plant-like Art Nouveau vases to monochrome, geometric bowls from Haida (Nový Bor) – displayed in a glass cabinet suspended from the ceiling. A staircase leads up to **Gegenwartskunst,** an entire room of contemporary art.

More recent work is also displayed in the adjacent **20. Jahrhundert, Architektur, Design** room. Among the more bizarre exhibits are a monochrome room installation by Jasper Morrison, architectural models by the Austrian deconstructionists Coop Himmelblau, and a wonderful cardboard armchair by Frank O. Gehry.

Studiensammlung

If you've got the time and energy, head off down to the museum's **Studiensammlung** (Study Collection), hidden away in the basement. The rooms here are as crowded as those in the permanent collection are sparse. The first room, **Ostasien**, displays a whole variety of stuff from the Far East, from wood, stone and bronze Buddhas to Chinese ceramic beasts, nephrite vases, porcelain bowls, rhino-horn beakers, and wooden boxes inlaid with mother-of-pearl. Top marks, though, go to the two rooms devoted to **Möbel** (Furniture), for the staggering pile of furniture stacked right to the ceiling. In a truly democratic display, painted chests from the fifteenth century share space with bean bags, De Stijl chairs, classic Wiener Werkstätte works and a Dutch cardboard sleeping box for the homeless.

The two **Keramik, Glas** rooms boast a collection ranging from Meissen porcelain figures to Jugendstil and Wiener Werkstätte produce; the glass, which kicks off with medieval stained-glass windows, ends with another incredible display of Jugendstil and Art Nouveau glassware similar to that in the permanent collection, with works from Gallé, Tiffany and Lobmeyr as well as from several Bohemian factories. In the **Metall** room, a watering can from Wolverhampton sits happily among gold goblets, silver chalices, Art Nouveau candelabra and a collection of teapots. The **Textil** rooms hold ecclesiastical robes, dating from medieval times to the twentieth century, the majority displayed in giant pull-out cases. Finally, there's a partial reconstruction of the utopian **Frankfurter Küche**, a fitted kitchen designed in 1926 by Margarete Schütte-Lihotsky, and replete with funky aluminium pull-out drawers.

Postsparkasse and around

The final segment of the Ringstrasse, from Stubentor to Urania, was the last to be laid out, erected mostly in the decade before World War I. The two biggest public buildings built here were the new Kriegsministerium (War Ministry) and the central office of the **Postsparkasse** (Postal Savings Bank). The latter was a state-funded attempt to counteract the perceived threat of Jewish capital, in particular that of the Rothschilds. With this duo in place, the Ringstrasse had, in many ways, come full circle: it had begun with a barracks and a church – the Votivkirche – in the 1850s; it was to end with another reassertion of the army and Catholicism.

*The
Postsparkasse
is open
Mon–Fri
8am–3pm,
Thurs until
5.30pm.*

Despite the reactionary politics behind the Postsparkasse, the design with which Otto Wagner won the competition for its construction was strikingly modern. The building is by no means entirely devoid of ornament – this is, after all, a prime Ringstrasse site – for a start, there's a pergola hung with laurel wreaths on the roof, flanked by two winged Victories. The rest of the building, though, looks something like a giant safety deposit box, its otherwise smooth facade studded with aluminium rivets, used to hold the thin grey marble slabs in place. Aluminium – a new and expensive material – is also used for the delicate glazed canopy over the entrance, and, most famously, for the heating cowls, which rise up into the main banking hall like giant curling tongs. Sadly, some of the interior furnishings have been carelessly modified, but the curving glass ceiling and the thick glass tiles in the floor survive intact. There's also a model of the building and regular exhibitions on modern architecture on display in the main banking hall.

You can still see the Emperor Franz-Josef's ceramic bust *in situ* above the main staircase, though moves by the Christian Socials to have the bust of the Postsparkasse's founder, government bureaucrat **Georg Coch** (1842–90), placed in the new building were foiled, allegedly by high-placed Jewish opposition. The anti-semitic mayor Karl Lueger (see p.127) stepped into the breach and got the square named after Coch, and – with Wagner's consent – placed Coch's bust on a plinth in the centre.

The Archduke Franz Ferdinand remained unimpressed by Wagner's architecture, and made sure the competition for the **Kriegsministerium**, situated opposite the Postsparkasse, was won by Ludwig Baumann's conservative neo-Baroque entry. Completed in 1912, it's a thoroughly intimidating building, smacking of reactionary, bombastic militarism, personified by the equestrian figure of Marshal Josef Radetzky, scourge of the 1848 revolution in northern Italy, which stands in front of the main entrance. Grim busts of the empire's soldiers keep watch from the keystones above the ground-floor windows, while armed cherubs and a vast military panoply guarded by a giant double-headed eagle with wings outstretched look down from the pediment. The building now houses various governmental departments.

Stubenring ends at the Danube Canal, beside which stands Max Fabiani's **Urania** building, built in the shape of an unorthodox ship in 1910. Conceived as an adult education centre, it remains a multipurpose institution, which houses a cinema, a puppet theatre, a planetarium and an observatory.

The Urania observatory is open Wed, Fri & Sat 8pm, Sun 11am; April–July & Sept also 9pm; closed Aug to mid-Sept; www.urania-sternwarte.at.

Chapter 5

Kunsthistorisches Museum

In a city somewhat overloaded with museums, the **Kunsthistorisches Museum** (Art History Museum; *www.khm.at*) stands head and shoulders above the rest. Thanks to the wealth and artistic pretensions of successive Habsburg rulers, it contains not only the fourth largest collection of paintings in the world, but also Egyptian, Greek and Roman antiquities, plus sundry more recent *objets d'art*. So numerous are the exhibits that several of the museum's departments are now housed in the Neue Burg wing of the Hofburg (see p.113).

The vast majority of the art collection is comprised of sixteenth- and seventeenth-century masters. Most people come to see the collection of **Bruegels** – the largest in the world – which forms part of a superlative early Netherlandish and Flemish section. Thanks to the Habsburgs' territorial acquisitions, the museum is also loaded with **Venetian** works by the likes of **Tintoretto**, **Veronese** and **Titian**, and a goodly selection of **Velázquez** portraits. In addition, there are numerous paintings by **Rembrandt**, **Cranach** and **Dürer**, and whole rooms devoted to **van Dyck** and **Rubens**. Lastly, don't miss the unrivalled collection of Mannerist works from the court of Rudolf II, especially the surrealist court painter, **Giuseppe Arcimboldo**.

One of the glories of the Kunsthistorisches Museum is, of course, the **building** itself, especially the main foyer and staircase, which is sumptuously decorated, from the monochrome marble floor to the richly stuccoed dome. Don't overlook Canova's *Theseus and the Minotaur*, which greets you on the main staircase, and note the lunettes, spandrel and intercolumnar murals on the first-floor balcony, which illustrate the history of art from ancient Egypt to Florence. Hans Makart was commissioned to undertake the work, but only managed to complete the lunettes before his death from syphilis in 1884. The spandrel and intercolumnar murals were completed, very much in Makart's classical style, by the youthful trio of Franz Matsch, Ernst Klimt and his more famous brother Gustav; diagrams point out which mural was painted by which artist.

The
Kunsthistor-
isches museum
is open
Tues–Sun
10am–6pm;
öS100/€7.27.
The picture
gallery is also
open Thurs
until 9pm.

Visiting the museum

The admission fee to the Kunsthistorisches Museum includes entry to the museum's temporary exhibitions; the museum is free on public holidays. Even if you spend the whole day here, you'll be pushed to see everything, so it's best to concentrate on just one or two areas. You'll also be extremely hungry, since the only place to eat is the pricey **café** in the upper foyer. You are, however, allowed to nip out for a picnic (or a cigarette break), as long as you inform the museum staff.

The painting titles are all in German; in our account they're given the English names by which they're usually known. There are information sheets in each room of the Gemäldegalerie (see below), though these often go walkabout. **Guided tours** of the museum in English set off daily at 3pm and cost öS30/€2.18. If you come on Thursday evenings to the Gemäldegalerie, you should be treated to some live music too.

The Gemäldegalerie

The **Gemäldegalerie** (Picture Gallery), on the first floor, has around 800 paintings on display at any one time, a mere tenth of the museum's total catalogue. It's easy to become overwhelmed by the sheer volume of art, which dates mainly from the sixteenth and seventeenth centuries. Unlike most big galleries the Kunsthistorisches makes no attempt to cover a broad span of art history – the collection has changed very little since the Habsburgs bequeathed it. Consequently, British and French artists, and the early Italian Renaissance, are all under-represented, and the collection stops at the late eighteenth century.

The paintings are arranged in parallel rooms around two courtyards: the Italians, plus a few French and Spanish, lie to one side; the Germans, Dutch and Flemish to the other. The larger rooms which face onto the courtyards sport Roman numerals (I–XV), while the smaller outer rooms use the standard form (1–24), though the latter are often unmarked. It would be difficult to concoct a more confusing numerical system, but at least both wings are laid out (vaguely) chronologically. The account below starts, for want of a better place, with the Bruegels and continues in an anti-clockwise direction to Vermeer; then it switches back to Titian and ends with Canaletto. However you plan your itinerary, be sure to avail yourself of one of the great assets of the Gemäldegalerie, the comfy sofas in the larger rooms.

Bruegel and his contemporaries

Before you get to the Bruegel room you must pass through room IX, which contains works by the likes of **Pieter Aertsen** (c.1508–75), a contemporary of Bruegel's who also worked in the

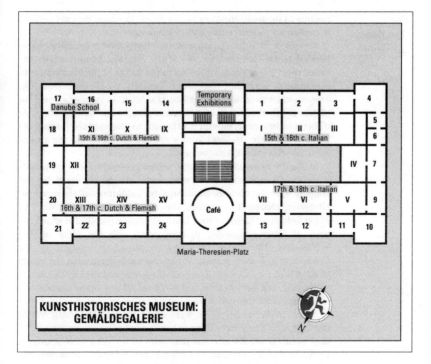

17
16
Danube School
15
14
Temporary Exhibitions
1
2
3
4

18
XI
15th & 16th c. Dutch & Flemish
X
IX
5
I
II
III
15th & 16th c. Italian
6

19
XII
IV
7

20
XIII
16th & 17th c. Dutch & Flemish
XIV
XV
Café
17th & 18th c. Italian
VII
VI
V
9

21
22
23
24
13
12
11
10

Maria-Theresien-Platz

KUNSTHISTORISCHES MUSEUM: GEMÄLDEGALERIE

N

---

peasant genre. *Vanity – Still Life* is typical of his style: the detailed still life of the feast being prepared by Martha upstages her sister Mary at the feet of Jesus, portrayed in the background. **Frans Floris** (1516–70), a painter more famous in his day than Bruegel ever was, contributes a gruesome *Last Judgement*, while **Lucas van Valckenborch**'s (1535–97) months of the year (only five of them survive) are modelled on Bruegel's, which you'll see in the next room.

The great thing about the museum's works by **Pieter Bruegel the Elder** (c.1525–69), in room X, is the breadth and range of the collection, from innovative interpretations of religious stories to allegorical peasant scenes. Though well connected in court circles in Antwerp and, later, Brussels, Bruegel excelled in these country scenes, earning himself the soubriquet "Peasant Bruegel" – the story goes that he used to disguise himself in order to move freely among the peasantry. A classic example of the genre is his *Children's Games*, an incredibly detailed picture with more than 230 children playing 90 different games. Perhaps the most beguiling of all Bruegel's works within the peasant genre is the cycle of seasons, commissioned by a rich Flemish banker. Three (out of six) hang in this room: *The Gloomy Day*, *The Return of the Herd* and, the most famous of them all, *Hunters in the Snow*, in which Bruegel perfectly captures a monochrome wintry landscape.

Several of Bruegel's peasant works clearly have a somewhat high-handed moral message, too, as in the *Peasant Dance*, where the locals revel irreverently, oblivious to the image of the Madonna concealed in the top right-hand corner. Similarly, the *Peasant Wedding* comes over less as a religious occasion than as another excuse for gluttony. Others, such as *The Peasant and the Bird-Thief*, are more difficult to interpret, though it's thought to illustrate the inscrutable Flemish proverb: "He who knows where the nest is, has the knowledge; he who robs it, has the nest."

In *The Procession to Calvary*, we are confronted with a typically vigorous Bruegelian crowd, who seem utterly unmoved by the tragedy quietly and inconspicuously unfolding in their midst. Gruesome characters, revealing the influence of Bosch, inhabit *The Fight between Carnival and Lent*, a complex painting in which the orgy of Shrove Tuesday is contrasted with the piety of Ash Wednesday. *The Tower of Babel* (inspired, it's thought, by the Colosseum in Rome) is more straightforward, illustrating the vanity of King Nimrod – the detail on both the tower and the city below it is staggering, but get too near and you'll set off one of the alarms.

Bruegel lived through a particularly turbulent period in the history of the Netherlands, which were under Spanish Habsburg rule at the time, and many have tried to read veiled allusions to contemporary political events into his paintings (the troops accompanying Christ in *The Procession to Calvary* are Austrian). However, the most oft-quoted example, *The Massacre of the Innocents*, was, in fact, painted prior to the appointment of the Duke of Alba, and therefore cannot refer to the duke's Council of Blood, during which 12,000 were executed, despite what some art historians might say.

Early Netherlandish painting

Works by the generation of Flemish painters who preceded Bruegel are displayed in the adjoining rooms 14 and 15. **Jan van Eyck** (c.1390–1441), by far the most famous, is represented by two extremely precise portrait heads. There's a similar realism in **Hugo van der Goes's** (1440–82) diptych, *The Fall of Man and the Lamentation of Christ*; the story here is given a misogynist twist by the portrayal of the serpent with a woman's head. The triptych by **Hans Memling** (1440–94) is altogether more Italian in form, with its carefully balanced symmetry and rich architectural framing.

The three panels that make up *Altarpiece with the Crucifixion and Two Donors* by Memling's teacher, **Rogier van der Weyden** (c.1400–64), are cleverly unified by the undulating landscape that continues across all three frames. Uniquely, the two donors, positioned to the right of the cross in the main scene, and the holy figures, are given almost equal importance. Meanwhile, **Gerhard**

David's (d.1523) *St Michael's Altar* features the saint serenely smothering seven very nasty apocalyptic beasties with his red velvet cloak. Also in this room is the museum's one and only work by **Hieronymus Bosch** (c.1450–1516), *Christ Carrying the Cross*, a canvas packed with a crowd of typically grotesque onlookers.

Dürer, Cranach and Holbein

If you continue with the smaller rooms, you come to the excellent German collection, in particular the so-called "Danube School", a loose title used to group together various sixteenth-century German-speaking painters inspired by the landscape of the Danube. Room 16 shelters a colourful *Adoration of the Trinity* by **Albrecht Dürer** (1471–1528). Amid his gilded throng are the donor, Matthäus Landauer (lower row, to the left), his son-in-law (lower row, to the right) and, with his feet firmly on the ground, Dürer himself (bottom right). The frame (a modern copy of the original) bears closer inspection, too, with those not heading for heaven being chained up and devoured by the devil. Dürer also appears, somewhat incongruously dressed in black, in the centre of his *Martyrdom of the Ten Thousand*; amid scenes of mass murder, he strolls, deep in conversation, with his recently deceased friend, the humanist Conrad Celtes.

Room 17 contains more Dürer, including his portrait of Maximilian I, from the year of the latter's death; the emperor holds a pomegranate, symbol of wealth and power. A prime example of the Danube School of painting is *The Crucifixion* by **Lucas Cranach the Elder** (1472–1553), one of his earliest works, with its gory depiction of Christ, spattered with, and vomiting up, blood, set against a rugged Danubian landscape. Cranach went on to become court painter to the Elector of Saxony, after which his style became more circumspect. In *Judith with the head of Holofernes*, the Biblical heroine is depicted as an elegant Saxon lady, while his *Stag Hunt of Elector Frederick the Wise*, in which numerous stags are driven into the water so the royals can pick them off with crossbows, is almost playful, with little sense of the subsequent bloody slaughter. His son, Lucas Cranach the Younger (1515–86), contributes an equally jolly scene of slaughter in *Stag Hunt of the Elector John Frederick*, which hangs close by. Also in room 17 are several melodramatic religious paintings by **Albrecht Altdorfer** (c.1480–1538), another artist of the Danube School, who reveals his penchant for the pornographic in the incestuous *Lot and his Daughters*.

The large collection of works in room 18 by **Hans Holbein the Younger** (1497–1543), who was almost a generation younger than Cranach and Dürer, date from his period as court painter to the English King Henry VIII. One of his first royal commissions was a portrait of *Jane Seymour*, lady-in-waiting to Henry VIII's second wife, Anne Boleyn, who, after the latter's execution, became his third wife (she died giving birth to Henry's one and only son, the future Edward VI). The portrait of Emperor Karl V with his Ulm Mastiff, by Austrian artist **Jakob Seisenegger** (1505–67), helped popularize the full-length portrait among the European nobility, and was undoubtedly the model for Titian's more famous portrait of the emperor, which hangs in the Prado in Madrid.

Spranger, Arcimboldo and Van Dyck

In room 19, you enter the court of Rudolf II (1576–1612), the deeply melancholic emperor who shut himself up in Prague Castle surrounded by astrologers, alchemists and artists. It is Rudolf, whose portrait by **Hans von Aachen** (c.1551–1615) hangs in the room, we have to thank for the Bruegels and Dürers in the museum. Rudolf particularly enjoyed the works of Mannerist artists like **Bartholomäus Spranger** (1546–1611), who pandered to the emperor's penchant for depictions of erotic, mythological dream-worlds as in his *Venus and Mars warned by Mercury*. One of Rudolf's favourite court artists was **Giuseppe Arcimboldo** (1527–93), whose "composite heads" – surrealist, often disturbing, profile portraits created out of inanimate objects – so tickled the emperor that he had portraits made of every member of his entourage, right down to the cook. Among the four in the Kunsthistorisches, all of which are allegorical, are *Water*, in which the whole head is made of sea creatures, and *Fire*, where it's a hotchpotch of burning faggots, an oil lamp and various firearms.

Room 19 also contains several works by the son of "Peasant Bruegel", **Jan Brueghel the Elder** (1568–1625), whose detailed still lifes of flowers were highly prized, his luminous paintwork earning him the nickname "Velvet Brueghel". One of his most famous, non-flowery paintings is his reverential *Adoration of the Kings*, a beautifully detailed work that's a firm favourite on Christmas cards. **Anthony van Dyck** (1599–1641) predominates in the adjacent room (XII): some pieces, like *The Apostles Philip and Simon*, date from the time when van Dyck was working closely with Rubens, hence the characteristic, "ruffled" brushstrokes; others – mostly portraits – date from after van Dyck's appointment as court painter to the English King Charles I.

Rubens

Thanks to the Habsburgs' long-term control of the southern Netherlands, the Kunsthistorisches boasts one of the largest collections of paintings by **Peter Paul Rubens** (1577–1640) in existence, spread over three rooms (rooms 20, XIII & XIV). As is clear from his self-confident self-portrait at the age of sixty-two, in room XIII, Rubens was a highly successful artist, who received so many commissions that he was able to set up a studio and employ a group of collaborators (among them van Dyck and Jordaens). Rubens would supply the preliminary sketches – witness the sketches for giant high-altar paintings commissioned by the Jesuits in room XIV, and the end result, in the same room.

Perhaps the best-known of all the Rubens works is *The Fur*, in room XIII, a frank, erotic testament to the artist's second wife, Hélène Fourment, who was thirty-seven years his junior. Rubens was clearly taken with his sixteen-year-old wife, who appears as an angel, saint or deity, in two other late works: the *Ildefonso Altar* and the *Meeting near Nördlingen*. The loose brushwork and painterly style in these two bear comparison with Titian's late work in room I, and Rubens pays tribute to the Italian in his *The Worship of Venus*, a veritable chubby cherub-fest set in a classical landscape.

Rembrandt, Vermeer and the Brits

Rubens' Baroque excess is a million miles from the sparse, simple portraits by **Rembrandt van Rijn** (1606–69), several of which hang in room XV. There's a sympathetic early portrait of his mother, the year before she died, depicted in all the fragility and dignity of old age, and a dream-like later study of his son, Titus, reading. There are also three self-portraits from the 1650s, when, as the art critics love to point out, Rembrandt was beginning to experience financial difficulties. Whether you choose to read worry into Rembrandt's face or not, these are three superb studies of the human face.

Next door, in room 24, is the museum's one and only painting by **Jan Vermeer**, *Allegory of the Art of Painting*, considered by many to be one of his finest. The bright light from the onlooker's left, the yellow, blue and grey, the simple poses, are all classic Vermeer trademarks, though the symbolic meaning, and even the title, of the work have provoked fierce debate. Close by are the museum's only **British paintings**: a gentle, honey-hued *Suffolk Landscape* by Thomas Gainsborough, a portrait of painstaking realism by Joseph Wright, an unfinished portrait of a young woman by Joshua Reynolds, and a portrait by Henry Raeburn.

Titian and the Venetians

Over in the west wing, the museum boasts an impressive selection of Venetian paintings, especially works by **Titian** (c.1488–1576), which span all sixty years of his artistic life. Very early works like *The Gypsy Madonna* in room I reveal Titian's debt to Giovanni Bellini, in whose studio he spent his apprenticeship. The colours are richer, the contours softer, but the essentially static composition is reminiscent of Bellini's own *Young Woman with a Mirror* (see p.162). The largest canvas in room I is Titian's *Ecce Homo* from his middle, Baroque period, in which, amid all the action and colour, Christ is relegated to the top left-hand corner.

In *Girl in a Fur* and the portrait of Benedetto Varchi, Titian shows himself equally capable of sparing use of colour, allowing the sitter's individual features maximum effect. By contrast, Titian's very last portrait, of the art dealer Jacopo Strada, whom the painter disliked, is full of incidental detail, colour and movement. Towards the end of his life, Titian achieved a freedom of technique in his own personal works (as opposed to those produced for commission by his studio), in which "he used his fingers more than his brush" according to fellow painter Palma il Giovane. His masterpiece of this period is the *Nymph and Shepherd*, painted without a commission, using an autumnal palette and very loose brushwork.

A fragment of an altarpiece by Antonello da Messina, who is credited with introducing oil painting to northern Italy, hangs in the adjacent room 1, along with *Young Woman with a Mirror* and *Presentation of Christ in the Temple*, both by **Giovanni Bellini** (1460–1516), and a sculptural *St Sebastian* by Bellini's brother-in-law, **Andrea Mantegna** (c.1430–1506). Next door, in room 2, the subject matter of the *Three Philosophers* – in which the left-hand section of the painting appears to have gone missing – is almost as mysterious as its painter, **Giorgone**. All we know about him is that he was tall, handsome and died young (possibly of the plague); as for the painting, no one's sure if it depicts the Magi, the three stages of man's life or some other subject. Giorgone's sensuous portrait, *Laura* – fur and naked breasts are a recurring theme in the gallery – is one of his few works to be certified and dated on the back.

Colourful, carefully constructed, monumental canvases by **Paolo Veronese** (1528–88) fill the walls of room II – the *Anointing of David* is a classic example, with the subject matter subordinated to the overall effect. In room III, there are several impressive portraits by **Tintoretto** (1518–94), and a voluptuous *Susanna and the Elders*, full of contrasts of light and shade, old age and youthfulness, clothed and naked. However, it's the horizontal panels, depicting scenes from the Old and New Testaments and intended for use on furniture, which draw your attention, not least for their refreshing immediacy and improvised brushstrokes.

Raphael, Bronzino and Caravaggio

In room 3, the scene shifts across northern Italy to the Mannerist school of Emilia. **Antonio Correggio** (c.1489–1534) puts his bid in for the gallery's most erotic painting with *Jupiter and Io*, in which the latter is brought to the verge of ecstasy by Jupiter in the form of a cloud. *Self-portrait in a Convex Mirror* by **Parmigianino** (1503–40) was just the sort of tricksy art that appealed to Rudolf II, in whose collection it appeared in 1608. In room 4, the masterly *Madonna in the Meadow* is a study in Renaissance harmony and proportion, painted by **Raphael** (1483–1520) at the tender age of

22. Further on, in room 7, there's a typically icy *Holy Family* by **Agnolo Bronzino** (1503–72).

Caravaggio (1571–1610), several of whose works hang in room V, was nothing if not controversial. His chief artistic sin, in the eyes of the establishment, was his refusal to idealize his Biblical characters, frequently using street urchins as his models, as in his *David with the Head of Goliath*; he also painted his self-portrait as the severed head of Goliath. He may have managed to outrage more than a few of his religious patrons, but his works had a profound effect on artists like Rubens and Bruegel, both of whom at one time or another owned the *Madonna of the Rosary*.

Velázquez, Bellotto and Canaletto

If the Italians start to get you down – and there is a lot of less-than-fantastic seventeenth-century art out there – head for the Spanish in rooms 9 and 10. Here you can see Alonso Sánchez Coëllo's portrait of Don Carlos, Philip II's mentally and physically handicapped son, who was incarcerated by his father some four years later, and died shortly afterwards. Another portrait by Coëllo depicts Elisabeth of Valois, Philip II's third wife, whom he married despite the fact that she was already betrothed to Don Carlos – events familiar to those who know the plot of Verdi's opera *Don Carlos*.

The museum's smattering of works by **Diego Velázquez** (1599–1660), most of them gifts from the Spanish Habsburgs to the Austrian side of the family, include a portrait of Queen Maria-Anna of Spain, whose hairdo is twice the size of her face, and two of Charles II of Spain, though neither is as grotesque as the early portrait of Charles by Juan Carreño de Miranda – it's scary to think that he probably looked even worse in real life. The most famous works are those of the Infanta Margarita Teresa, who was betrothed to her uncle, the future Emperor Leopold I, from the age of three.

Lastly, you might want to take a look at the large eighteenth-century views of Vienna in room VII, commissioned by the court from **Bernardo Bellotto**, to see how little the view from the Upper Belvedere has changed over the centuries. The Viennese insisted on calling Bellotto "Canaletto", though he was in fact the latter's nephew and pupil. For real **Canalettos**, you must go next door, to room 13, where his much smaller, picture-postcard views of Venice hang alongside works by his compatriot, Francesco Guardi.

The ground-floor galleries

The ground floor is laid out entirely chronologically using only Roman numerals: it kicks off with the Egyptian and Near Eastern Collection (I–VIII), passes through Greek and Roman Antiquities

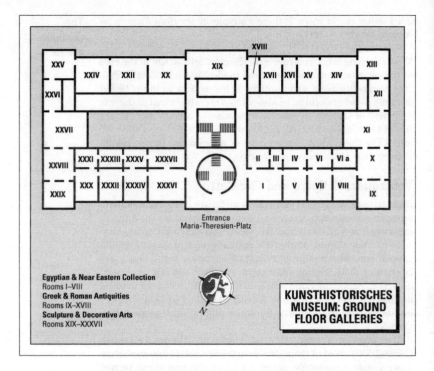

Egyptian & Near Eastern Collection
Rooms I–VIII
Greek & Roman Antiquities
Rooms IX–XVIII
Sculpture & Decorative Arts
Rooms XIX–XXXVII

KUNSTHISTORISCHES
MUSEUM: GROUND
FLOOR GALLERIES

Entrance
Maria-Theresien-Platz

(IX–XVIII) and heads off into Sculpture and Decorative Arts (XIX–XXXVII). The Coin Cabinet has been closed for renovations for what seems like an eternity now and shows no immediate signs of reopening.

Egyptian and Near Eastern Collection

Immediately to the right as you enter the museum are the purpose-built galleries of the **Egyptian and Near Eastern Collection**, which sport appropriately hieroglyphic decorations. Pink granite papyrus-stalk columns from around 1410 BC are even incorporated into the construction of room I, which is devoted to the **Egyptian death cult**. The entrance to the room is guarded by two statues of the fearsome, lion-headed goddess, Sekhmet; the museum owns just four out of the six hundred which once formed a colossal monument to the deity erected at Thebes by Amenophis III.

In the room itself, there's only one actual mummy, wrapped in papyrus leaves, but there are numerous wooden inner coffins in the shape of mummies, smothered with polychrome symbols and hiero-glyphs. Below the mummy cases are the tiny canopic jars, used for storing the entrails removed during mummification, with lids carved in the shape of animal deities. Elsewhere, there are cabinets full of *shabti* figurines, in wood, stone and pottery, which were placed in the tomb in order to perform any task the gods might require (there had to be at least 365 in each tomb, plus 36 overseers). Another display cabinet to make for, in room III, contains the mummies of various animals, including cats, falcons, snakes, crocodiles and a bull's head, alongside figurines evincing the strength of Egyptian animal cults.

The Kunsthistorisches owns some superb examples of **Egyptian sculpture**, beginning in room V with an unusual depiction of a lion tucking into a bull, and Isis, sporting cow's horns, a solar disc and a vulture headdress, breast-feeding Horus as a child. Horus appears in his adult, falcon-headed form in a rather wonderful duo in room VII, seated alongside King Horemheb, who was the power behind the throne of Tutankhamun. Also in this room is a winsome blue pottery hippo, whose body is tatooed with papyrus leaves, lotus flowers and a bird, pictorial elements from its natural swamp habitat. Room VIII contains one of the collection's most prized possessions, the so-called **Reserve Head** from around 2450 BC, a smooth, stylized head carved in limestone, which exudes an extraordinary serenity. Excavated by an Austrian archeological team at the beginnging of the last century at Giza, it is thought to be a surrogate head for the immortal *ka* or cosmic double which the Egyptians believed was born with every person.

In the smaller side room IV, notice the cabinet of heart scarabs, that were placed upon the chests of mummies, bearing a spell that implored the deceased's heart not to bear witness against him or her during the Judgement of Osiris. The statuette of the woman servant making bread, in room VI, would also have been placed inside the tomb to provide the *ka* with food in the after-life. The miniature wooden pleasure boat – known as a "solar boat" by archeologists – was thought to provide the *ka* with a method of transport through eternity. Don't miss the prehistoric fertility symbols in this room – small men with inordinately large erections and rotund women showing off their labia – not to mention the penis fragments. Last, but not least, room VIA contains the complete *mastaba* or **Tomb Chamber of Kaninisut** from Giza. Hieroglyphs and relief cartoons decorate the cramped chamber where the *ka*-priest, in charge of tending to the deceased in the after-life, would offer food, burn incense and sprinkle water.

Greek and Roman Antiquities

The **Greek and Roman Antiquities** begin in room X, though one of the most prominent statues here – the **Youth of Magdalensberg** – is in fact a sixteenth-century bronze copy of the Roman original, something that was only discovered in 1983 when research was being conducted into the methods used in the casting. The vigorous high relief

The ground-
floor
galleries

on the **Amazonian Sarcophagus**, also in room X, from the fourth century BC, depicts the struggle between the Greek heroes and the mythical women warriors.

At the centre of the large, arcaded room XI, is the magnificent fourth-century AD **Theseus Mosaic**, discovered in a Roman villa near Salzburg. Theseus and the Minotaur are depicted in the middle of a complex geometric labyrinth, out of which the hero escapes with the help of the red thread given to him by Ariadne, who is pictured abandoned to the right. The extraordinarily busy **Lion-Hunt Sarcophagus**, from the late third century AD, has two of its main characters' heads uncarved – proof that funerary art was often produced before actually being commissioned.

*There are
more Greek
antiquities
from Ephesus
in the Neue
Hofburg, see
p.116.*

Those in search of **Greek vases** need look no further than room XIV, which contains an excellent selection, from early Geometric vases from the eighth century BC to the sophisticated black- and red-figure vases of the Classical period. Among the many onyx cameos in the adjoining room XV is one of the finest in the world, the seventeenth-century **Gemma Augusta**, which is surprisingly large at 19cm in height. The upper scene depicts the Emperor Augustus in the guise of Jupiter, seated on a bench alongside Roma, with the emperor's star sign, Capricorn, floating between them; the lower scene shows the Romans' victory over the Dalmatians under Tiberius. Also in this room is the oldest Latin Edict of Senate in existence, dating from 186 BC, forbidding Bacchic orgies.

The last three small rooms (XVI–XVIII) contain **gold work**, much of which, strictly speaking, post-dates the collapse of the Roman Empire. The chain of honour with 52 pendants is an excellent example of early Germanic gold, its centrepiece a bead of smoky topaz, mounted with two tiny pouncing panthers. The most impressive haul is the treasure from Nagyszentmiklós (Sînicolaul Mare) in Romania, twenty-three pure gold vessels, weighing a total of 20kg, with runic inscriptions that continue to fox the experts.

Sculpture and Decorative Arts

The **Sculpture and Decorative Arts** collection occupies more than half of the ground floor galleries. It's a patchy collection, with some real gems, and a lot of objects of great craftsmanship, but dubious artistic taste. Most of the exhibits were collected or specially commissioned for the various *Kunstkammern* (Chambers of Marvels), which became *de rigueur* among German-speaking rulers during the Renaissance – the most avid collectors were the Archduke Ferdinand II of Tirol (died 1595) and the Emperor Rudolf II (1576–1612). The latter took the whole thing very seriously indeed, even going so far as to incarcerate the Augsburg clockmaker, Georg Roll, when the celestial globe he made for him broke down, while the one supplied to his brother, the Archduke Ernst, continued to work.

Room XIX contains objects made from precious and semi-precious stones, and sets the tone – slightly vulgar, exquisitely executed kitsch – of much of the collection. A prime example is the gold vase holding tulips made from agate, jasper, chalcedony and rock crystal, or the gold chain, inset with rubies and made up of forty-nine portraits of the Habsburgs carved in shell. Most of the exhibits have no function, but the rock-crystal dragon-lions were something of a party piece: liquid poured into their tails would gush into a shell through nozzles in the beast's breasts.

In the seventeenth century, highly complex **ivory sculptures** became all the rage with royalty. It's difficult to look at ivory *objets d'art* without thinking of the unnecessary slaughter of elephants, and all the more so when the subject matter is also one of bloodshed, and the work itself so grotesquely cloying as in the example in room XX, depicting Leopold I and Josef I gazing fondly into each other's eyes, while the vanquished Turks make a muddled mess below. Also on display is the heavy gold breakfast service of Maria Theresia, and the matching toilet set of her husband, Franz Stephan – over seventy pieces in total – which were donated to the collection after the death of the empress.

In room XXV you can see an elaborate ebony and ivory piggy bank, peppered with gilded figures, which belonged to the Archduke Ferdinand II of Tirol. The ostrich led by a Moor in this room is a typical *Kunstkammer* object, with its combination of exotic natural materials, such as coral, and human craftsmanship, exemplified by the silver-gilt ostrich. Probably the most famous exhibit in the entire collection is Benvenuto Cellini's **Saliera**, in room XXVII, a slightly ludicrous sixteenth-century salt cellar, in which the gold figures of Neptune, holding a phallic trident, and Earth, squeezing her own nipple, appear to be engaged in some sort of erotic see-saw.

Room XXVIII contains a typical hotchpotch of exhibits, ranging from a striking six-winged sixteenth-century altarpiece, comprised of 156 panels, to a dubious trio of pearwood cherubs, playing with one another's private parts, and a richly carved backgammon set, featuring erotic scenes on each of the counters. Moving swiftly on, you'll find some remarkable miniature mining scenes carved out of tiny rocks, and some exquisitely beautiful astrological and scientific instruments, including one of the aforementioned celestial globes by Georg Roll. Unfortunately, the gold and silver automata in room XXXV can't be put through their paces, nor is there much ticking from the clocks and watches in room XXXVII.

Chapter 6

The Vorstädte

O nce the Turks were beaten back from the city gates in 1683, Vienna could, at last, spread itself safely beyond the confines of the medieval town walls. A horseshoe of districts, known as the Vorstädte (Inner Suburbs), quickly grew up and engulfed the villages around the old town, beyond the glacis (the sloping open ground outside the city walls). In 1704, the great military leader, Prince Eugène of Savoy, ordered the construction of a second, outer line of fortifications or Linienwall, to protect the new suburbs. Later, the Linienwall became the municipal boundary, where, in a Habsburg custom going back to the Middle Ages, every person entering the city had to undergo a thorough search, and pay a consumer's tax on goods purchased outside the city.

As the city spread still further out into the *Vororte* or rural parishes, the *Linienwall* was finally demolished in 1890, and became what's known today as the **Gürtel** – literally "belt" – a thunderous ring road, which has the added indignity of doubling as the city's redlight district. The seven districts of the Vorstädte – the third to the ninth – are neatly confined between the Ringstrasse and the Gürtel. They have remained residential for the most part, though each one is cut through with a busy commercial thoroughfare, the largest of which is the city's main shopping drag, **Mariahilferstrasse**, which divides the sixth and seventh districts. Sights in the Vorstädte are widely dispersed, so it pays to be selective – a *Netzkarte* and a grasp of the transport system are essential (see p.39). Our account goes round in a clockwise direction, beginning with the third district and finishing with the ninth.

For more on the postal districts of Vienna, see p.36.

The one sight in the Vorstädte that no visitor should miss is the **Belvedere**, in the third district, with its formal gardens and twin-set of Baroque palaces, which house some wonderful works of art, including the city's finest collection of paintings by Gustav Klimt. Two other sights that positively heave with visitors in summer are the **Hundertwasserhaus**, also in the third district, and the **Freud Museum** in the ninth. The former is a wacky piece of council housing by an old hippy, and, as such, is some kind of must, since opinion is so divided on the building. As for Freud's apartment, there's really not much to see, yet it remains the pilgrim's choice. There are, of course, other reasons to explore the Vorstädte, among them a visit to the **Arsenal**, worth a stop for its fine quasi-Moorish architecture even if you're not particularly keen on military paraphernalia.

Landstrasse

Landstrasse – Vienna's third district – lies to the east and southeast of the Innere Stadt, framed by the Danube Canal (Donaukanal) to the east, and to the west by Prinz-Eugen-Strasse and Arsenalstrasse. By far the largest of the Vorstädte, it's a predominantly working-class area, with a high immigrant population, mostly refugees from the former eastern bloc and Yugoslavia. The one exception is the diplomatic quarter around the **Belvedere**, where Prince Eugène of Savoy's summer palaces house a feast of fine art from medieval times to the early twentieth century. Just south of the Gürtel lies the city's **Arsenal**, home to the **Heeresgeschichtliches Museum** built to glorify the Imperial Army in the nineteenth century.

Other sights are more widely dispersed. The **Hundertwasserhaus**, an idiosyncratic housing development in the nub of land to the north of the district, is now one of Vienna's top tourist attractions, something which cannot be said for the nearby modernist **Wittgensteinhaus**, designed by the famous philosopher. An incredible number of diehard fans make it out to the **St Marxer Friedhof**, where Mozart is thought to be buried – no one is quite sure where his bones actually lie. Finally, for tram-lovers, the **Strassenbahnmuseum** beckons in the far southeast of the district.

To get to Hundert-wasserhaus, take tram #N to Hetzgasse from Schwedenplatz U-Bahn.

Hundertwasserhaus and KunstHausWien

In 1983, the ageing hippy artist Friedensreich Hundertwasser (see p.173) was commissioned to redesign some council housing on the corner of Löwengasse and Kegelgasse, in an unassuming residential area of Landstrasse. Following his philosophy that "the straight line is godless", he transformed the dour apartment block into **Hundertwasserhaus**, a higgledy-piggledy, kitsch, childlike jumble of brightly coloured textures that caught the popular imagination, while enraging the architectural establishment. It certainly runs the gamut

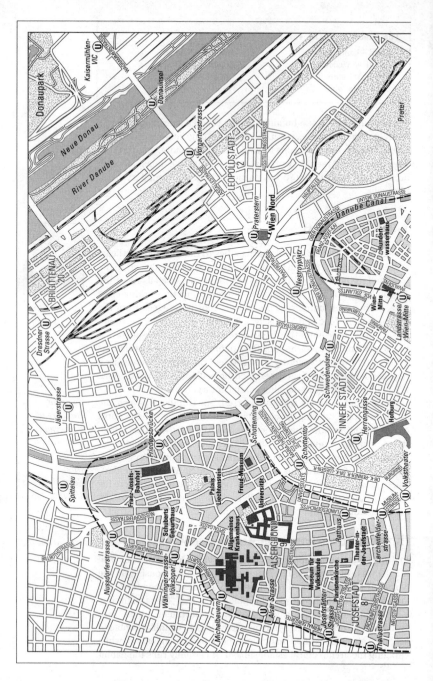

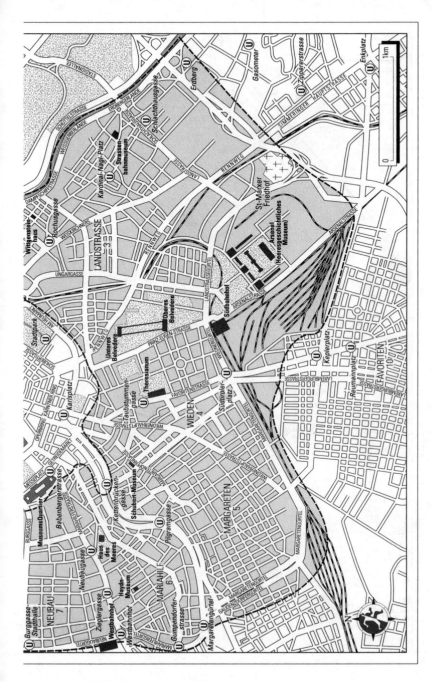

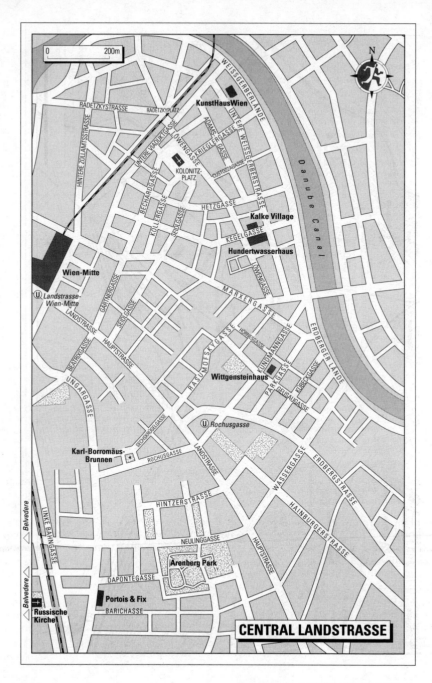

CENTRAL LANDSTRASSE

of styles and consists of a frenzy of oriel windows, loggias, ceramic pillars, glass embellishments, a gilded onion dome, roof gardens and even a slice of the pre-1983 building.

Understandably, the residents were none too happy when hordes of pilgrims began ringing on their doorbells, asking to be shown round, so Hundertwasser obliged with an even tackier shopping arcade opposite, called **Kalke Village**, providing a café (with a stream running along the bar) and information centre to draw the crowds away from the apartments (which are closed to the public), while simultaneously increasing the sales outlets for his artwork. Here, you can get the full Hundertwasser experience, the most disconcerting aspect of which is his penchant for uneven floors.

KunstHausWien

KunstHausWien (*www.kunsthauswien.com*), housed in a former Thonet furniture factory, four blocks north up Untere Weissgerberstrasse, is another of Hundertwasser's Gaudi-esque conversions, though it has been less successful at attracting visitors; it features another shop and café, and a gallery devoted to Hundertwasser's own paintings. The gallery also hosts temporary exhibitions (another öS95/€6.90; combined ticket öS150/€10.90) by other headline-grabbing contemporary artists. It's worth noting that admission is half-price all day on Mondays.

The KunstHausWien is open daily 10am–7pm; öS95/€6.90; Mon half-price.

Friedensreich Hundertwasser (1928–2000)

Born in Vienna, under the name Friedrich Stowasser, **Friedensreich Hundertwasser** was brought up singlehandedly by his Jewish mother, who wisely enrolled him into the Hitler Youth shortly after the Anschluss, thus saving both their lives. Having spent just three months training as an artist at the Akademie der bildenden Künste, Hundertwasser left formal education for good in 1948 and shortly afterwards adopted his new nom de plume. He first made it as an artist in the 1950s, using distinctive coiling forms to produce "kaleidoscopic landscapes", reminiscent of Gustav Klimt, with a dash of Paul Klee. In the late 1960s, at the height of the hippy era, he achieved even greater notoriety for his speeches given in the nude, one of which was his architecture boycott manifesto *Los von Loos* (Down with Loos), in which he attacked the establishment in the form of modernism.

In many ways, Hundertwasser anticipated the current, widely accepted critique of modernism – that its emphasis on machine-like, undecorated flat surfaces was dehumanizing and alienating – stressing green issues and arguing for architectural variety. However, as an unrepentant hippy, experienced self-publicist and shrewd businessman, he has made no small number of enemies along the way, not least among contemporary Viennese architects, who feel his forays into their art form – his "painted boxes" – have been crass, irreverent and populist. As one critic put it, his wavy lines and individually designed windows are akin to "a nineteenth-century quack flogging his bottles of coloured horsepiss as a miracle cure for all diseases."

Two floors of the KunstHausWien are devoted to Hundertwasser's art and life, though devotees will be disappointed to discover the gallery floors are entirely flat. It's certainly easy to mock Hundertwasser's *bons mots*, which are scattered throughout the gallery, not to mention inventions such as his Water Purification Plant, and his colourful, childlike paintings are not everyone's cup of tea. The second-floor gallery offers more varied food for thought, from Hundertwasser's campaign to retain old-style Austrian number plates to his politically correct designs for various national flags. You can watch a video of Hundertwasser sailing his converted Sicilian salt trader, *Regentag*, painting in the nude and eating soup. Also displayed here are models of some of his architectural projects, such as the rubbish incineration plant in the north of Vienna, described on p.250.

Wittgensteinhaus to Portois & Fix

One sure way to lose the crowds is to head four blocks south to Kundmanngasse 19 and the **Wittgensteinhaus**, a grey, concrete-rendered house built in the modernist spirit of Adolf Loos, the very architect Hundertwasser spoke out against in 1968. It's a one-off design, executed in the late 1920s by the philosopher Ludwig Wittgenstein – as rigorous in his architecture as in his philosophical thinking, advocating an austere functionalism – with the help of the architect Paul Engelmann. The house was commissioned by Wittgenstein's sister, Gretl, herself a leading light among the Viennese intelligentsia and a personal friend of Freud's. Gretl no doubt saw the funny side of making Klimt's highly decorous portrait of her the focal point of the house's implacably minimalist interior. The building now belongs to the Bulgarian embassy – hence the bronze statues of the Slav saints, Cyril and Methodius, in the garden – and is open during the exhibitions regularly held there; phone ☎713 3164 to check if it's open.

The Wittgenstein- haus is open Mon–Fri 9am–5pm; the nearest U-Bahn is Rochusgasse.

To the west, on the other side of Landstrasser Hauptstrasse, two blocks up Rochusgasse, is the little-known and rather unusual **Karl-Borromäus-Brunnen**, erected in 1909 by the sculptor Josef Engelhart, one of the founders of the Secession (see p.140), and the Slovene architect, Josip Plečnik. Set within its own little sunken square, whose entrances are flanked by flower pots sporting rams' and eagles' heads, the fountain is one of the hidden gems of Landstrasse. Centring on a plain triangular obelisk, it is shaped like a three-leaved clover, and covered with salamanders, bog-eyed frogs and reptiles of various kinds. Rings of cherubs holding hands dance beneath the leaves, while above, three groups of diminutive, free-standing figures tell the story of the saint, to whom the Karlskirche is also dedicated (see p.143).

Another arresting sight in the vicinity is the **Portois & Fix** building, reached by going one block west of the fountain, and then south on Ungargasse to no. 59–61. Designed by Max Fabiani in 1900, this Jugendstil building copies Otto Wagner's innovative use of tiling for the facade of his Majolikahaus (see p.146). Instead of Wagner's more conventional floral pattern, however, Fabiani creates a strikingly modern, abstract, dappled effect with his tiles in various shades of lime green and brown, topped by a decorative, wrought-iron balustrade.

Along Rennweg

"East of Rennweg, the Orient begins" is one of Prince Metternich's much-quoted aphorisms, though he clearly meant a bit further along the road than his own house at no. 27 (now the Italian embassy), where he lived until forced to flee the city in 1848. **Rennweg** begins at Schwarzenbergplatz and runs for several kilometres through Landstrasse towards Hungary, but the section close to the Belvedere has always had a certain cachet. Nowadays, the streets immediately to the north are more desirable, dotted with embassies, among them the German, British and Russian legations. The last two are provided with their own churches, a red-brick Anglican one and an onion-domed Orthodox one, both on Jaurèsgasse.

Rennweg itself is now too busy with traffic to be truly fashionable, but when **Otto Wagner** built himself a "town house" here in 1891, at no. 3, it was clearly still des res. Now known as the Palais Hoyos and occupied by the Yugoslav embassy, this early Wagner work is very much in the Ringstrasse style (see p.122), with its elaborate wrought-iron balconies, but you can discern hints of his later work in touches such as the projecting cornice and the very fine reliefwork in the upper floor. Wagner also designed the much less ornate houses on either side, including no. 5, where Gustav Mahler lived from 1898 to 1907.

Just up from Wagner's trio, towards Schwarzenbergplatz, is the **Gardekirche**, originally completed by Maria Theresia's court architect, Nicolo Pacassi, in 1763, but refaced in a rather dour, Neoclassical style just six years later. The Rococo interior, however, was left alone, and still retains its richly gilded stucco work, ribbed dome, bull's eye windows and lantern. Built as the chapel of the imperial hospital, it was handed over to the Polish Guards in 1782. The Gardekirche stands directly opposite the entrance to the Belvedere, but the great green dome which features so prominently in the view from the top of the Belvedere, is, in fact, the **Salesianerkirche**, further up on the south side of Rennweg. Along with its neighbouring convent, it was founded by Amelia Wilhelmina, widow of Josef I, in 1716, as her own private residence and as a college for daughters of the nobility (it's now the Botanisches Institut). Josef Emanuel Fischer von Erlach assisted in designing the exterior, which has more spatial interplay than the Gardekirche; the interior is less interesting, however.

Gardekirche serves the city's Polish community.

Ludwig Wittgenstein

Whatever can be said can be said clearly, and that of which one cannot speak, one must remain silent about.

Tractatus Logico-Philosophicus

With such pithy aphorisms, **Ludwig Wittgenstein** (1889–1951) – who published only one complete text in his entire lifetime – made his name as one of the world's greatest philosophers. The youngest of a large, wealthy, cultured family in Vienna, Ludwig was raised a Catholic like his mother, though his father, a leading industrialist, was a Protestant convert of Jewish descent. Sceptical from an early age, Ludwig rejected his comfortable upbringing, reportedly never wearing a tie after the age of 23, and dispersing the fortune he inherited from his father to struggling writers such as Rainer Maria Rilke and Georg Trakl.

Like all the Wittgenstein children (three of whom committed suicide), Ludwig was educated at home, entering the Gymnasium in Linz at the age of fourteen (Adolf Hitler, almost the same age as Wittgenstein, was a fellow pupil). From 1906 to 1908, he studied mechanical engineering in Berlin, completing his research in Manchester. From there, his interests shifted to mathematics and eventually to philosophy, which he studied at Cambridge under Bertrand Russell, who took a shine to the eccentric young Austrian, considering him a genius, "passionate, profound, intense and domineering". From 1913, Wittgenstein lived in a hut in Norway for two years, meditating and writing a series of notes on logic, which he put forward as his degree, only to be turned down when he refused to add a preface and references. During World War I, in between winning several medals for bravery, and being taken prisoner on the Italian front, he completed his *Tractatus Logico-Philosophicus*, seventy pages of musings on a wide range of subjects, including logic, ethics, religion, science, mathematics, mysticism, and, of course, linguistics.

After the war, Wittgenstein inherited still more of his father's fortune, this time handing it over to his brothers and sisters. He trained as a

The Belvedere

Forget the Hofburg or even Schönbrunn – the **Belvedere** (*www.belvedere.at*), to the south of Rennweg, is the finest palace complex in the whole of Vienna, at least from the outside. Two magnificent Baroque mansions, designed in the early eighteenth century by Lukas von Hildebrandt, face each other across a sloping formal garden, commanding a superb view over central Vienna. The man for whom all this was built was **Prince Eugène of Savoy**, Austria's greatest military leader, whose campaigns against the Turks enabled the city, at last, to expand beyond the walls of the old town. Today, the loftier of the two palaces, the Oberes Belvedere, houses one of the most popular art galleries in Vienna, with an unrivalled collection of paintings by Gustav Klimt plus a few choice works by contemporaries such as Egon Schiele and Oskar Kokoschka.

teacher, writing a spelling dictionary for schools, and working in several villages south of Vienna. Prone to pulling a pupil's hair if he or she failed to understand algebra, he wasn't greatly liked by the locals, and eventually returned to Vienna to design a house for his sister, Gretl (see p.174). During this time, he fell in love with a Swiss friend of his sister's called Marguerite, who refused his marriage proposal. In 1927, Wittgenstein became part of the **Vienna Circle**, a group of philosophers, scientists and mathematicians, including Karl Popper, Kurt Gödel, Rudolf Carnap and Moritz Schlick, who rejected traditional philosophy and espoused instead logical positivism. The Circle had chosen *Tractatus* as their working text, but their interpretation of it as an anti-metaphysical tract infuriated Wittgenstein, who preferred to dwell on its ethical and mystical aspects.

He was persuaded to return to Cambridge in 1929, putting forward *Tractatus* as his PhD, and consoling his examiners – among them Russell – with the remark, "Don't worry, I know you'll never understand it". He became a legend in his own lifetime: scruffily dressed, discussing philosophy with his chambermaid, devouring American pulp fiction, delivering lectures without notes, gesticulating violently and cursing himself at his own stupidity or maintaining long silences. Such was his ambivalence towards the smug, unnatural world of academia, and his conviction that philosophy precludes improvement, that he frequently tried to dissuade his students from continuing with the subject. He succeeded in persuading his lover, a promising young mathematician called Francis Skinner, to give up his studies and become a factory mechanic. After Skinner died of polio in 1941, Wittgenstein gave up his post, considering it intolerable to be teaching philosophy in time of war. He took a job as a porter at London's Guy's Hospital, and later worked researching wound shock. In 1946, he fell in love with another undergraduate, a medic forty years his junior called Ben Richards, with whom he stayed until his death from prostate cancer in 1951. He is buried in Cambridge.

Prince Eugène himself was a great patron of the arts, but he left no direct heirs, and after his death in 1736, a distant cousin, Anna Victoria, inherited the estate, and sold off the prince's possessions. The statues from Herculaneum were bought by the court of Dresden; nearly two hundred paintings were purchased by the King of Sardinia, head of the house of Savoy; the menagerie fell into disrepair; but the Emperor Karl VI succeeded in buying the prince's personal library, which now resides in the Prunksaal of the Nationalbibliothek (see p.108). Finally in 1752, the Belvedere itself was snapped up by the Empress Maria Theresia, who decided to house the Habsburgs' own court art collection here, and who opened the palace gardens to the public in 1779.

The imperial art collection eventually moved into the purpose-built Kunsthistorisches Museum in the 1890s. In 1903, the Unteres Belvedere became home to the new Moderne Galerie (later to become the Österreichisches Galerie), while the Oberes Belvedere was taken

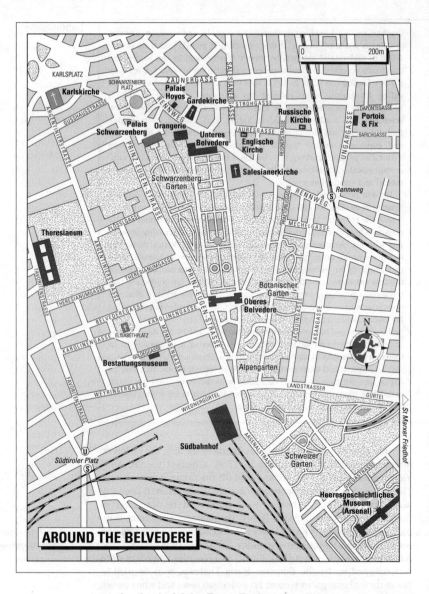

AROUND THE BELVEDERE

over by the **Archduke Franz Ferdinand** until his assassination in
Sarajevo in 1914. He stayed here only occasionally, preferring to
reside at his Bohemian castle of Konopiště, near Prague, since his wife
was snubbed by the Habsburgs (see p.99). Thanks to the patronage of
the Emperor Franz-Josef's daughter, the Archduchess Valerie, the ail-

ing composer, **Anton Bruckner**, was granted the ground-floor flat in the gatehouse of the Oberes Belvedere in July 1895 and spent the remaining sixteen months of his life here.

After World War I, both palaces were used as state art galleries (as they are today), though under the Austro-fascists (1934–38), Chancellor Kurt Schuschnigg also chose to reside here, before he was interned by the Nazis following the Anschluss. In 1955, the Austrian State Treaty, or Staatsvertrag, was formally signed by the Allied Powers, in the Marmorsaal of the Oberes Belvedere. Fifteen years later, the superpower Stategic Arms Limitation Talks (SALT) were officially opened in the same room by the then Foreign Minister, Kurt Waldheim.

Unteres Belvedere

Completed in 1716 at the very bottom of the formal gardens, the **Unteres Belvedere** (Lower Belvedere) is a relatively simple garden palace, built for Prince Eugène's personal use, rather than for affairs of state or entertainment. Inside, however, it actually preserves more of its lavish original decor than the Oberes Belvedere, and for that reason alone it's worth exploring the **Barock-Museum** now installed in its rooms.

To get to the Unteres Belvedere, take tram #71 one stop from Schwarzenbergplatz – or just walk.

The museum possesses a representative sample of works by all the leading Austrian painters of the late seventeenth and eighteenth centuries, including Daniel Gran, Franz Anton Maulbertsch, Johann Georg Platzer, Johann Michael Rottmayr, Johann Martin Schmidt and Paul Troger. The highlight of the palace, though, is the richly decorated **Marmorsaal** (Marble Hall), which extends over two floors at the central axis of the building. The whole hall is a hymn to Prince Eugène's military prowess, white stucco trophies and reliefs contrasting with the rich red marbling. Extra depth is given to the walls through trompe l'oeil niches and balconies, and to the ceiling by illusory moulding, leading up to Martino Altomonte's fresco featuring Prince Eugène himself enjoying his apotheosis in the guise of Apollo. At ground level, you can admire the original lead statues from the Donnerbrunnen on Neuermarkt (see p.59), sculpted by Georg Raphael Donner (1693–1741).

There are more works by Donner in the adjoining room, once the prince's bedroom, decorated with yet more illusory painting and Altomonte frescoes. The adjacent room contains Jacques-Louis David's famous heroic equestrian portrait, *Napoleon on the St Bernhard Pass*. At the far end of the wing lies the **Groteskensaal**, with a "grotesque" decor of birds and beasts, and fanciful floral murals. The inspiration for this style of painting, very fashionable in its day, came from ancient Roman wall decoration, discovered during excavations of underground rooms. The rooms became known as "grottos" and the style of decor was dubbed "grotesque". Displayed here is a series of bizarre, hyper-realist "character heads", carved by the eccentric sculptor Franz Xaver Messerschmidt (1732–83), each depicting a different grimace. Next comes the **Marmorgalerie**, a richly stuccoed white and red reception room built by Prince Eugène to house his trio of classical statues from Herculaneum. These, now in Dresden, provided the inspiration for the Neoclassical sculptures by Domenico Parodi, which stand in niches along the walls.

By far the most mind-blowing room, though, is the adjacent **Goldkabinett**, a cabinet of mirrors, dating from Maria Theresia's reign, dotted with oriental vases and adorned with yet more "grotesques" painted onto a vast expanse of gaudy, 23-carat gold panelling. Dominating this small room is *Apotheosis of Prince Eugène*, an explosion of marble by the Dresden court sculptor, Balthasar Permoser, in which a tangle of figures struggles to stay on the plinth. The prince is depicted in full armour, trampling on the enemy, while attempting modestly to muffle the horn of Fame.

A secret door in the Goldkabinett leads to a toilet; if the place isn't too crowded, the attendant might let you use it.

The Goldkabinett marks the end of the Barock-Museum, but there are further artistic treasures in the former **Orangerie**, down the steps from the palace. Converted into stables by Maria Theresia, the orangery now houses the **Museum mittelalterlicher Kunst** (Museum of Medieval Art). The sculptures and paintings here range from the twelfth to the sixteenth centuries, though the greater part dates from the fifteenth. One of the most remarkable altarpieces is the high-relief crucifixion scene from Znaim (Znojmo) in South Moravia from 1450. The collection of paintings by the fifteenth-century Tyrolean artist Michael Pacher are also worth noting, representing, as they do, the transition between the more static, one-dimensional art of the Gothic period and the love of perspective that heralds the Renaissance. The same is true of the seven large-scale works by Rueland Frueauf the Elder, who, like Pacher, spent much of his career in Salzburg. The gallery also boasts two panels by the artist responsible for the altarpiece now housed in the Museum im Schottenstift (see p.74).

The gardens

The formal **gardens** of the Belvedere are laid out on a wide slope, punctuated with box hedges, fountains, waterfalls and statuary, and centred on a grand vista culminating in the magnificent Oberes Belvedere itself. Prince Eugène began buying up land for the gardens way back in 1693, employing Dominique Girard to use the skills he learnt at Versailles to create the perfect Baroque landscape. In the prince's day, the gardens would have been much more lavishly laid out, and the schematic arrangement of the sculptures far more com-

---

Prince Eugène of Savoy (1663–1736)

The Austrians have never enjoyed the greatest of military reputations, so it comes as little surprise that their most revered military figure is, in fact, a Frenchman, **Prince Eugène of Savoy**. His first taste of military warfare came at the age of twenty, when he offered his services to the Emperor Leopold I, partly to avenge his brother, Louis Julius, who had recently died fighting the Turks. Eugène immediately fought in the front line against the 1683 Turkish siege of Vienna, earning himself a pair of golden spurs for his bravery. Subsequently, he was given command of a regiment by Leopold; by thirty, he was a field marshal. His victory over the Turks at Zenta in 1697 helped win back Hungary for the Habsburgs, and he was made president of the Imperial War Council. His capture of Belgrade in 1718 was the single most important act in making western Europe safe from the Ottomans. In between times, he even fought against his fellow countryman, Louis XIV, in the Spanish Wars of Succession (1701–14), assisting the Duke of Marlborough in the victories at Blenheim, Oudenarde and Malplaquet. Meanwhile, back in Vienna, he became one of the greatest patrons of the arts the city has ever known, building fabulous Baroque palaces, and amassing a huge library, art collection and menagerie.

If the prince's military achievements and artistic endeavours are well documented, very little is known about his childhood or his later personal life. There are no memoirs, and nothing written about him by anyone who was close to him. Born in Paris into a leading aristocratic family, Eugène was brought up in the most extraordinary circumstances. His mother, the Countess of Soissons, was not only one of Louis XIV's mistresses, but also a wild party animal, with a penchant for intrigue and black magic. She was eventually exiled from France in 1680, on suspicion of having poisoned her husband, and of plotting to kill the king himself. Whether the infant Eugène participated in the transvestite orgies conducted in his childhood home, will never be known for sure. He remained unmarried all his life, and there is no mention of him ever having taken a mistress. Again, whether this was due to his own sexual preference, his troubled relationship with his mother, or his notoriously unprepossessing appearance, remains a mystery. Certainly, the Duchess of Orléans' description of him as a boy is far from flattering: "It is true that his eyes are not ugly, but his nose ruins his face; he has two large teeth which are visible all the time. He is always dirty and has lanky hair which he never curls . . . and an upper lip so narrow that he cannot close his mouth." As a result of the child's physical deficiencies, Louis XIV decided he should be brought up for the church rather than follow a military career. Given his mother's reputation, it's hardly surprising that Eugène was denied admission into the French army by the king in 1683, though Louis lived to rue his decision when the prince went on to humiliate him on the battlefield on several occasions.

---

plex: the lower section was put aside as the domain of the elements, while the upper section belonged to the gods. Today, this elaborate allegorical scheme only partially survives.

The central axis, flanked by statues of the Eight Muses, leads up to the **Lower Cascade**, a giant shell held up by tritons and sea-nymphs. On either side of the central axis are sunken bosquets, or hedge gardens, two circular and two square, with statues of Pluto and Proserpina from the Underworld. The balustrades, which line the steps either side of the cascade, are peppered with putti representing the seasons, and, beyond, the first of the sphinxes for which the Belvedere is famous. Fearsome beasts spurt water over the crest of the **Upper Cascade**, from where the water flows over a set of steps. The upper section of the garden was meant to represent Olympus, but the statues of the Greek gods were replaced in the nineteenth century by yet more sphinxes.

The main entrance lies to the south of the Oberes Belvedere, on Landstrasser Gürtel, its wonderful wrought-iron gateway flanked by standing lions clasping the Savoy coat of arms. The prince himself was a keen gardener, bringing rare and exotic plants and trees from all over the world to his garden. He also established a **menagerie**, situated to the east of the Oberes Belvedere (the ground plan of radial paths is all that survives), and an **aviary** (originally facing the orangery but now converted into apartments), where he kept numerous species of rare birds, and his favourite pet eagle that he himself fed by hand every day.

To the east of the main entrance on Landstrasser Gürtel is the small **Alpengarten** (Alpine Garden), founded in 1793. It's a small, walled garden, packed with heathers, shrubs and hardy alpine flowers that stick close to the rockery to escape the chilling winds. To the north of the Alpengarten lies the university's **Botanischer Garten** (Botanical Garden), founded in 1754, and as large again as the formal gardens in the Belvedere. The overall layout is more like an English park, with a woodier section popular with red squirrels, sloping down to another pseudo-alpine shrubbery near the Mechelgasse entrance.

The Alpengarten is open April–July daily 10am–6pm; öS40/€2.91.

The Botanischer Garten is open Easter–Oct daily 9am–one hour before dusk; free.

Oberes Belvedere

Completed in 1724, the **Oberes Belvedere** (Upper Belvedere) is at least twice as big and twice as grand as the Unteres Belvedere. Its unusual roofline, like a succession of green tents, seems deliberately to echo the camps erected by the Turks during the siege of Vienna; others have even interpreted the domed octagonal pavilions as quasi-mosques. The whole building was purpose-built for the lavish masked balls, receptions and firework displays organized by the prince. Guests would pull up in their coaches underneath the central *sala terrena*, thickly adorned with white stucco, its four columns decorated with military trophies and held up by writhing Atlantes.

To get to the Oberes Belvedere, take tram #D from the Ringstrasse.

Originally an open arcade, the *sala terrena* was glassed in during the nineteenth century and now serves as the ticket office and entrance area of the museum. To the right is the trompe l'oeil frescoed **Gartensaal**, the first in a series of ground-floor rooms occasionally used for temporary exhibitions; to the left lies the bookshop and the café. The permanent galleries, displaying nineteenth- and twentieth-century art, are located on the first and second floors. The exact position of the paintings on the first floor changes from year to year, and you may find a handful of the paintings described below are on tour elsewhere.

If you're here for the Klimts and Schieles, then head straight upstairs to the **Marmorsaal**, a lighter and loftier concoction than the one in the Unteres Belvedere; it was here that the Austrian State Treaty of 1955 was signed, guaranteeing the withdrawal of foreign troops in return for Austria's neutrality. The permanent collection usually begins in the room to the right of the Marmorsaal where you should be able to pick out the *Plain at Auvers* painted by **Vincent van Gogh** a month before his suicide in 1890. Alongside it hangs *Rack Railway on the Kahlenberg*, painted by fellow depressive Richard Gerstl in a similar, though slightly less intense, style; **Egon Schiele**'s *Interior 1907* also pays homage to the Dutch genius. Auguste Rodin's bust of Mahler, and a small terracotta study for the Victor Hugo Monument, in which the author is overwhelmed by allegorical figures from his own imagination, are also found in this room.

Gustav Klimt

The gallery's works by **Gustav Klimt** (1862–1918) are displayed along with works by his contemporaries, Kolo Moser, Carl Moll and Max Kurzweil. Klimt's ethereal, slightly aloof *Portrait of Sonja Knips*, from 1898, marked his breakthrough as an independent artist, and was the first of several portrait commissions of the wives of the city's wealthy Jewish businessmen. Two later examples are the *Portrait of Fritza Riedler*, from 1906, in which Klimt's love of ornamentation comes to the fore, and the *Portrait of Adele Bloch-Bauer I*, painted at the height of his "golden phase" in 1908, with the subject almost engulfed in gilded Mycenaean spirals and Egyptian eyes, or as one critic put it, "mehr Blech als Bloch" ("more rubbish than Bloch").

The culmination of Klimt's golden age is his monumental work, *The Kiss*, displayed behind a protective glass shield, and depicting Klimt himself embracing his long-term mistress, Emilie Flöge. Klimt's use of gilding – derived partly from his father, who was an engraver – proved extremely popular, and the painting was bought for the Austrian state during the Kunstschau of 1908 (see p.148), a rare seal of official approval for an artist whose work was mostly frowned upon by the establishment. Another of Klimt's famous works is *Judith I*, an early gold work from 1901, with the Jewish murderess (modelled by Adele Bloch-Bauer) depicted in sexual ecstasy having beheaded Holofernes. Note that the original is far smaller than many reproductions, and therefore easy to miss.

The gallery also owns eight landscapes on square canvases usually arranged in two neat rows on one wall. Every summer Klimt spent his vacations at the Flöge family house on the Attersee in the Salzkammergut. As a way of relaxing, he liked to paint landscapes alfresco straight onto canvas, without preliminary sketches. Like Monet, he often used to row out into the middle of the lake and set up his easel on board, finishing the works off after the holidays in his Vienna studio. The results are rich, almost flat, one-dimensional tapestries of colour – some almost pointillist – which are easy on the eye and which sold extremely well in the salons (and still do).

During Klimt's late period, he dispensed with gold, and became more influenced by Japanese art and the primary colours of Fauvists such as Matisse. The results can be seen in the doll-like *Portrait of Adele Bloch-Bauer II*, painted in 1912, just four years after the gilded version in the previous room. Klimt regularly worked on several canvases at once, often painting his models in the nude before clothing them, as is clearly demonstrated in *The Bride*, discovered unfinished in his studio at his death.

From one of the rooms dedicated to Klimt's work, you can look down into the richly gilded, octagonal **Schlosskapelle**, designed by Hildebrandt to extend over two floors, looking pretty much today as it would have in Eugène's day.

Egon Schiele and his contemporaries

Klimt actively supported younger artists like **Egon Schiele** (1890–1918), introducing them to his patrons, allowing them to exhibit in shows he organized, and even, in the case of Schiele, passing on his young models after he'd finished with them. Such was the case with the seventeen-year-old Wally Neuzil, with whom Schiele enjoyed a four-year affair. *Death and the Maiden* is a disturbingly dispassionate farewell portrait to Wally, painted in 1915, the year they split up. In it, Wally clings to Schiele, depicted in deathly, detached decay. The gallery also owns one of Schiele's most famous, erotic oil paintings, *The Embrace*, a double nude portrait of the artist and his model. (One artist who had a profound influence on both Schiele and Kokoschka was the Belgian sculptor **George Minne**, whose emaciated *Kneeling Boy*, sculpted in marble in the 1890s, is usually displayed here.)

Schiele went on to marry Edith Harms, who came from a respectable middle-class family, in the same year. *The Artist's Wife* was bought by this very gallery, though only after the director had got Schiele to repaint Edith's tartan skirt, which he felt was too "proletarian". Edith's pregnancy in spring 1918 was the inspiration for *The Family*, Schiele's last great painting, which remained unfinished at the time of his death from the influenza epidemic that had claimed Edith's life just three days earlier (and Klimt's eight months before that). Schiele is the father figure, the child is Schiele's nephew, Toni, but Edith had reservations about posing nude, and is clearly not the model for the mother. Though melancholic, the painting is positively upbeat compared with the harrowing *Mother with Two Children* from 1915, with its skeletal mother, and two mannequin-like children.

Among the collection of Schiele portraits commissioned by the sitters is one of Eduard Kosmak, who was an amateur hypnotist, which may explain his somewhat intense stare. Often displayed alongside Schiele's works is **Richard Gerstl**'s manic *Laughing Self-Portrait* from 1908, a deeply disturbing image given that its subject was, in fact, in a deep depression at the time – his lover, Mathilde, whose portrait also hangs here, had gone back to her husband, the composer Arnold Schönberg. Gerstl committed suicide the very same year at the age of just 28.

Oskar Kokoschka and others

The gallery's works by **Oskar Kokoschka** (1886–1980) mostly date from his first ten creative years when he lived in Vienna. After 1915, Kokoschka only occasionally returned, usually staying with his mother, an affectionate portrait of whom hangs in the first room entirely devoted to his work, which comes straight after the Schiele rooms. Kokoschka's portraits contrast sharply with those of Schiele. "A person is not a *still* life" Kokoschka insisted, and he encouraged his sitters to move about and talk, so as to make his portrayals more animated. Among the portraits here is one of fellow artist, Carl Moll, who was stepfather to Alma Mahler (widow of the composer) with whom Kokoschka had a brief, passionate affair. Moll committed suicide in 1945 when the Russians liberated Vienna, along with his daughter, Marie, and her husband.

Other works by Kokoschka, owned by the gallery, include his primeval *Tiger-Lion*, painted in London Zoo, and *Still Life with Lamb and Hyacinth* from 1910, painted in the kitchen of the art collector Dr Oskar Reichel, who had commissioned him to paint a portrait of his son. A smattering of other artists' works finishes off the early twentieth-century section, among them a characteristically dark, intense work by Emil Nolde, a Cubist offering from Fernand Léger and Max Oppenheimer's evocative *Klingier Quartet*.

Historicism, Realism and Impressionism

The rooms in the west wing, on the other side of the Marmorsaal, are given over to more turn-of-the-century paintings. In the first room, it's difficult not to be somewhat taken aback by the gargantuan *Judgement of Paris* by Max Klinger, surrounded by an incredible 3D-frame, within which a bored Paris is confronted by a boldly naked goddess, while the two others get ready to strip in the wings. Giovanni Segantini's *Evil Mothers* is a misogynist piece of anti-abortion propaganda, donated by the Secession to the gallery shortly after its foundation in 1903. Two sculptures – Auguste Rodin's *Eve* and Auguste Renoir's *Victorious Venus* – also diplayed in this room, continue the feminine theme. The next two rooms are crowded with further works by French Impressionists, among them Edouard Manet, Claude Monet and Camille Corot.

Less well known, and less well thought of now, is the Austrian artist **Hans Makart** (1840–84), to whom the westernmost room is devoted. Makart was a high society favourite who was in great demand during his lifetime, but his work has suffered partly because of the materials he used, which have caused his paintings to lose much of their original vitality. He also had the posthumous misfortune of being one of Hitler's favourite artists. One wall is almost entirely taken up with Makart's gigantic, triumphant flesh-fest of *Bacchus and Ariadne*; on the opposite wall in long vertical panels are four of the *Five Senses*, featuring typically sensuous Makart nudes.

In the adjacent room, you can admire more work by Makart, whose fame eclipsed several of his more innovative contemporaries, among them **Anton Romako** (1832–89), so much so that the latter's death was rumoured to be a suicide. Compared with Makart's studied flattery, it's easy to see why Romako's uncomfortably perceptive psychological portraits were less popular – consider how far removed from official portraiture Romako's portrait of the Empress Elisabeth is, with its gloomy palette and its emphasis on Sisi's defensive body language. Romako's most famous work, *Tegetthoff at the Naval Battle of Lissa*, hangs in the final room, and again reveals his unconventional approach; there's no hint of heroics, but simply manic fear and foreboding in the expressions of the crew.

Biedermeier, Classicism and Romanticism

If you thought the previous section was patchy, then the top floor galleries are positive deserts. Nevertheless, there are one or two fine works, such as **Angelika Kaufmann**'s relaxed *Portrait of Lord John Simpson*, executed during her lengthy sojourn in England. More rigidly Neoclassical is Gérard's portrait of the fabulously rich Fries family, who are deliberately posing like some sort of modern Holy Family. After wading through some uninspiring Italian and Italianate landscapes by minor Austrian artists, you should at least pause at Scheffer von Leonhardshoff's *The Dead Saint Cecilia*, a remarkable Raphaelite religious pastiche, which was a personal favourite of Franz I.

If you feel like you haven't quite got to grips with Biedermeier art, the final few rooms are your big chance. There are copious genre paintings, portraits and landscapes by the chief exponent of Biedermeier, **Ferdinand Georg Waldmüller**, and his successful col-

leagues Friedrich von Amerling and Peter Fendi – Fendi's *Eviction*
and *Girl in Front of a Lottery* have a certain contemporary appeal.
Of more general interest, however, are Rudolf von Alt's view of the
Stephansdom from 1832, and *Still Life with Flowers*, by Delacroix,
whose loose brushwork comes as something of a relief.

Südbahnhof and around

Vienna lost all its wonderful nineteenth-century railway stations in
World War II, and the Südbahnhof, on the other side of the
Landstrasser Gürtel from the Belvedere, is a typically grim post-war
building. It is, in fact, two stations rolled into one: Südbahnhof (Ost),
platforms 1 to 9, and Südbahnhof proper (platforms 11–19), each of
which has separate arrivals and departures timetables. Trains from
the former eastern bloc tend to arrive here, a fact which has given the
area something of a seedy reputation.

From the Südbahnhof, Prinz-Eugen-Strasse runs north along the
side of the Belvedere to Schwarzenbergplatz. En route it passes the
innocuous-looking Kammer für Arbeiter und Angestellte (Chamber of
Workers and Employees), at no. 20–22. Before World War II, this was
the site of the Palais Rothschild, where **Adolf Eichmann** set up the
Nazis' euphemistically named "Central Office for Jewish Emigration",
which oversaw the "final solution". At his trial, Eichmann remem-
bered his days there as "the happiest and most successful of my life".
Round the corner, on Theresianumgasse 16–18, another former
Rothschild palace served as the headquarters of the Nazi SD, the security service of the SS. Both palaces were destroyed in World War II.

West of Prinz-Eugen-Strasse lies **Wieden** – Vienna's fourth district
– which is worth a mention for the **Theresianum**, on
Favoritenstrasse. Originally built in the early seventeenth century by
the Habsburgs, and known as the Favorita, it was the chief imperial
summer residence before Schönbrunn was completed; Leopold I,
Josef I and, most famously, Karl VI all died here. The latter expired
unexpectedly, leaving no male heir, after having eaten a "pot of
mushrooms which changed the course of history" as Voltaire put it.
The Empress Maria Theresia, who succeeded Karl, turned the palace
over to the Jesuits, and it eventually became the most prestigious
school in the country. Nowadays the school shares its premises with
a college for diplomats and civil servants and the state radio and television company Österreichischer Rundfunk (ÖRF), and its performance space, the Radiokulturhaus.

*The
Theresianum is
not open to the
public.*

Bestattungsmuseum
The only sight as such in Wieden is the **Bestattungsmuseum**
(Undertakers' Museum), run by the state funeral company, at
Goldeggasse 19. Since the guided tours are in German only, this is
really only for those who share the strong, morbid fascination with
death for which the Viennese remain famous. The custom of magnif-

Landstrasse

The Bestattungs-museum is open Mon–Fri noon–3pm for guided tours by appointment only; ring ☎501 95-4227.

icent funerals – known as having a "beautiful corpse" or *schöne Leich* – is one to which many Viennese still aspire (only 18 percent opt for cremation).

Inside the museum, you can admire the elaborate costumes of undertakers over the years, their banners, équipage and so on, and learn about some of the more bizarre rituals associated with Viennese funerals. Dead Habsburgs, for instance, used to have their faces smashed in, to make them appear more humble in the eyes of God, and it was common practice to install a bell inside the coffin, which the deceased could ring in case they came back to life. There are some wonderful examples of funereal merchandising: matches, photo albums, toy cars, and, best of all, undertakers' cigarettes, with the motto *Rauchen sichert Arbeitsplätze* ("Smoking guarantees work"). The *pièce de résistance*, though, is the reuseable coffin instigated by Josef II (see p.105).

Arsenal and the Heeresgeschichtliches Museum

A short distance south of the Südbahnhof, down Arsenalstrasse, lies the city's former **Arsenal**, a huge complex of barracks and munitions factories, built on strategic heights above the city in the wake of the 1848 revolution. At the same time, the Emperor Franz-Josef I ordered the construction of the city's first purpose-built museum, the **Heeresgeschichtliches Museum** (Museum of Military History; *www.bmlv.gv.at/hgm*), designed to glorify the Imperial Army. All Vienna's leading architects were invited to compete for the commission, and the winning design, a wonderful red-brick edifice, adorned with light-brick crosses and machiolated crenellations, was completed by the Ringstrasse architect Theophil Hansen, in neo-Byzantine style in 1856.

The museum is open daily except Fri 9am–5pm; öS70/€5.09; free on the first Sun of the month.

The ticket office and cloakroom of this vast museum are in the vaulted foyer or **Feldherrnhalle** (Hall of the Generals), which is crowded with life-size marble statues of pre-1848 Austrian military leaders. Pick up the museum's excellent free audioguide (in English) and head upstairs to the **Ruhmshalle** (Hall of Fame), on the first floor, a huge domed hall of polished marble, decorated with worthy frescoes depicting Austrian military victories over the centuries. It's a heady mixture of architectural styles, gilded and arcaded rather like a Byzantine church or Moorish palace.

From the Thirty Years' War to the Austro-Prussian War

The museum kicks off with the **Thirty Years' War** (1618–48), to the left as you reach the top of the stairs, and tells the story of the rise of the musketeer over the pikeman – there's an informative video showing how hellish it was to try and fire a musket. Beyond hang twelve huge battle paintings by the Dutch artist Pieter Snayers portraying the decisive encounters of the war.

The rich pickings to be had during the **Turkish Wars** proved a useful incentive to the imperial troops fighting the Ottomans, and a fine selection of trophies is displayed here. Among the most impressive is the Great Seal of Mustafa Pasha, which the Grand Vizier wore round his neck as a symbol of his absolute authority, and which fell into the hands of **Prince Eugène of Savoy** at the Battle of Zenta in 1697. Other bits and bobs relating to Prince Eugène include his minuscule vest, his marshal's baton and the pall and cortège decorations from his magnificent state funeral.

For more on Prince Eugène of Savoy, see p.181.

The end room contains the vast tent of the Grand Vizier, Damad Ali-Pasha, which Prince Eugène later used on hunting trips. The Grand Vizier was killed at the Battle of Peterwardein in 1716, in which Prince Eugène triumphed over an Ottoman army more than twice the size of his. Also displayed here is the "Mortar of Belgrade", a shot from which hit the Turkish powder magazine during the siege of 1717, killing 3000 Ottoman soldiers in one go and considerably aiding Prince Eugène's victory

To continue chronologically, you need to retrace your steps and walk to the far end room of the east wing, where you'll find a French hot air balloon captured by the Habsburgs in 1796. Most of the items displayed here relate to the **Napoleonic Wars**: Field-Marshal Radetzky's hat, map bag and sword, Prince Karl von Schwarzenberg's hat, sword and medals, and Napoleon's Russian greycoat, thought to have been worn during his exile on Elba. The room closer to the Ruhmshalle is filled with splendid early nineteenth-century military uniforms, and concludes with paintings of the disastrous **Austro-Prussian War**, which ended in the Habsburgs' defeat at Könniggrätz in 1866.

The road to World War I

A large section of the ground-floor west wing is taken up with the glorious **uniforms of the Imperial Army**, and those belonging to their opponents. At the beginning of the twentieth century, the Habsburgs could at least boast that they had the best-dressed army in Europe – while the other superpowers were donning various dull khakis as camouflage, their pristine white and cream won the prize for the most elegant uniform at the 1900 Paris Exhibition. The uniforms were at their most resplendent during the ball season, and certainly had the right effect on many female guests, as Anthony Trollope's mother, visiting in 1836, swooned: "I really know nothing at once so gorgeous and picturesque as the uniform of the Hungarian noble bodyguard, with their splendid silver accoutrements, their spotted furs, uncut, hanging at their backs, and their mustard-yellow Morocco boots. The rich and beautiful skins which they all carry, apparently in the very shape in which they came off the animal, give the most striking air of primitive and almost barbarous magnificence." The Imperial Army also clung to other outdated practices, such as the code of honour, which meant that an officer's challenge to a duel had to be obliged (a practice only discontinued in 1911). Officers were automatically accepted at court, and like the aristocracy, used the familiar *du* with one another.

By far the most famous exhibits in this wing, though, relate to the **Archduke Franz Ferdinand**, in particular the splendid Gräf & Stift convertible in which the archduke and his wife, Sophie, were shot dead on June 28, 1914, by the Bosnian Serb terrorist, Gavrilo Princip. The car still has a bullet hole in it, but even more macabre is the archduke's reverentially preserved bloodstained light-blue tunic and unblemished, slightly comical hat with green feathers (the ceremonial uniform of an Austrian Cavalry General), and the chaise-longue on which he expired.

The final room of the wing is devoted to **World War I**, and includes video footage of the Habsburgs' various (mostly disastrous) campaigns. The room itself is dominated by a massive 38cm Howitzer, designed by Ferdinand Porsche, which had a range of 15km. Overlooking the gun is Albin Egger Lienz's chilling *To the Unknown Soldier*, whose repetitive image of advancing infantry perfectly captures the mechanical slaughter of modern warfare.

Republic and Dictatorship
Beyond the café in the east wing of the ground floor lies **Republic and Dictatorship**, an excellent new section that takes you through the heady, violent interwar years that ended with the Anschluss in 1938. There are lots of period posters from both sides of the political spectrum, and plenty of fascinating interwar video footage. You can view the couch on which Dollfuss died during the abortive Nazi coup of 1934 (see p.72), a bust of his successor Kurt Schuschnigg, by Anna Mahler, the composer's daughter, who was a committed Austro-fascist. Amonst the Nazi memorabilia is the bust of Hitler that used to stand in the museum's Ruhmshalle during the Nazi period.

Naval Power
The last room in the east wing is concerned with Austria's **Naval Power**, not something normally associated with a land-locked country, though, of course, under the Habsburgs, the empire had access to the Adriatic. Amid the model ships, figureheads and nauticalia, there's a model of the U-27 submarine, commanded by Austria's most famous naval captain, Georg Ritter von Trapp of *Sound of Music* fame. Among the more suprising material is the video of the Austrian navy's involvement in the Boxer Rebellion, and the section on the Austrian Arctic expedition (1872–74), which discovered and named Franz Josef Land, an archipelago in the Barents Sea.

If you're keen on tanks, don't miss the **Panzergarten**, with its international parade of tanks from Soviet T34s to American Centurions.

St Marxer Friedhof

In the 1780s, the Emperor Josef II closed all the inner-city cemeteries, and decreed that all burials, for health reasons, should take place outside the city walls. The first of these out-of-town graveyards was the **St Marxer Friedhof** (St Mark's Cemetery), founded in 1784 near the Landstrasser Gürtel, closed down in 1874, and also known as the Biedermeier cemetery since its corpses date mostly from that era. The main reason tourists trek out here is because it was here, on a rainy night in December 1791, that Mozart was given a pauper's burial in an unmarked mass grave with no one present but the gravediggers.

The cemetery is open daily: April & Oct 7am–5pm; May & Sept 7am–6pm; June–Aug 7am–7pm; Nov–March 7am–dusk; four stops on tram #18 from Südbahnhof, or five stops from Schwarzenberg Platz on tram #71.

Though to contemporary minds the bare facts of Mozart's final journey seem a particularly cruel end for someone considered by many to have been the greatest composer ever, the reality is less tragic. In the immediate period after Josef II's reforms mass burials were the rule; only the very wealthy could afford to have a family vault, and the tending of individual graves was virtually unknown. Funeral services took place in churches (Mozart's in the Stephansdom), and it was not customary for mourners to accompany the funeral cortège to cemeteries. In fact, bodies were only allowed to be taken to the cemetery after nightfall, where they were left in the mortuary overnight for burial the next day.

By the mid-nineteenth century, the Viennese had adopted the lavish tastes for funerals and monuments for which they remain famous to this day, and it was in this context that it became a scandal that no one knew where Mozart was buried. In 1844, his wife Constanze returned to try to locate the grave, but to little avail as graves were usually emptied every eight years and the bones removed to make way for more corpses. The most that Constanze discovered was that he had most likely been buried three or four rows down from the cemetery's central monumental cross. In 1859, the **Mozartgrab** was raised around this area, featuring a mourning angel and a pillar, broken in half to symbolize his untimely death.

Nowadays, the St Marxer Friedhof gives little indication of the bleak and forbidding place it must have been in Mozart's day, having been tidied up in the early part of the twentieth century and planted with a rather lovely selection of trees. To get to the Mozartgrab, head up the main avenue and bear left; you'll also find the graves of several other eighteenth-century artists here (a plan at the entrance to the cemetery locates the most famous graves).

Strassenbahnmuseum

Occupying three brick-built sheds in the eastern corner of Landstrasse, the **Strassenbahnmuseum** (Tram Museum), on Ludwig-Koessler-Platz, houses examples of just about every type of rolling stock that has trundled over the tramlines of Vienna, with a

The Strassenbahnmuseum is open May–Sept Sat & Sun 9am–4pm; öS20/€1.45; the nearest U-Bahn is Schlachthausgasse.

few buses thrown in for good measure. The vast majority of the trams sport the familiar municipal red livery, with the exception of the wartime exhibits, the horse-drawn trams from the 1870s, and the wonderful steam tram (still working). Children will be disappointed not to be able to climb on any of the exhibits, although the model tram railway in the ticket office might just mollify them. You can also take a ride on a 1920s tram known as the Oldtimer-Tramway: there are **sightseeing tours** every weekend between May and September (Sat & Sun 9.30am & 1.30pm; 1hr; öS200/€14.54). Trams leave from beside the Otto Wagner pavilions on Karlsplatz; tickets are available from Karlsplatz U-Bahn.

Mariahilf, Neubau and Josefstadt

Mariahilf and Neubau – Vienna's sixth and seventh districts – lie on either side of Mariahilferstrasse, the city's busy, mainstream shopping street, which stretches for more than 2km from the Kunsthistorisches Museum in the east to the Westbahnhof in the west. A few minor tourist sights are scattered across both districts, but the only area which actually merits a stroll is the narrow network of eighteenth- and early nineteenth-century streets in Neubau known as **Spittelberg**, the liveliest spot in the entire Vorstädte after dark. You might also find yourself wandering up Burggasse or Neustiftgasse, further north, in search of some of the area's numerous restaurants, cafés and pubs. The eighth district, **Josefstadt**, to the north, is a slightly more homogenous residential area, created in the eighteenth century. It, too, has its sprinkling of sights; it's also popular with students, owing to its proximity to the university.

For details of the cafés, pubs and restaurants of the three districts, see p.301.

On and off Mariahilferstrasse

Unlike most Western capitals, Vienna has relatively few big department stores, but those it does have are almost exclusively to be found on **Mariahilferstrasse**. Most of the stores are small Austrian affairs, with the obvious exceptions being the multinational Virgin Megastore, C&A, and Gerngross, now simply a roof under which various franchises compete for custom.

Take the U-Bahn to Neubaugasse to get to the Strasse der Sieger.

As you stroll along Mariahilferstrasse, you may well come across the Strasse der Sieger or "Avenue of Champions", which begins at the **Generali-Center**, at no. 77, one of Vienna's few indoor shopping malls. The Strasse der Sieger is a series of footprints, handprints and signatures in the pavement, belonging to the country's fifty most famous sports stars, and "as significant for sports fans as Hollywood's 'Walk of Fame' is for film enthusiasts", as the promotional blurb rather hopefully describes it. The first half – among them Arnold Schwarzenegger and Franz Klammer – are inside the shopping precinct; the next twenty-five – starring Thomas Muster, Niki

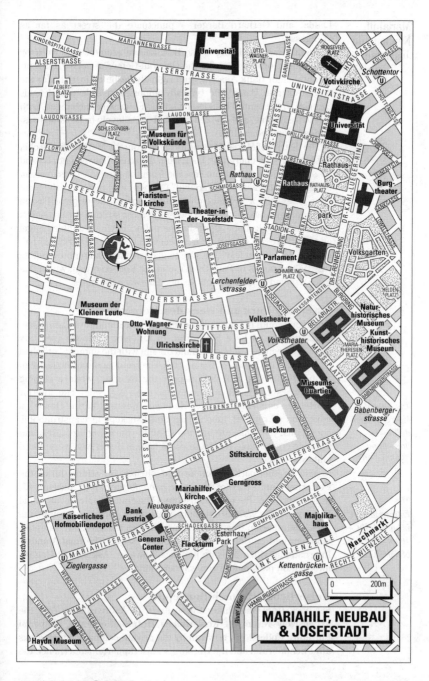

MARIAHILF, NEUBAU
& JOSEFSTADT

Lauda, and Gerhard Berger – punctuate the street as far as Webgasse.

Slightly more edifying is the little-known architectural work by Adolf Loos, located opposite the Generali-Center at no. 70, currently a branch of **Bank Austria**, but originally designed in 1914 for the Anglo-Austrian Bank. The typically imposing marble portal leads through to the central banking hall, which is largely unchanged, with lots more marble, a glass-tiled roof and some lovely brass lamps suspended from the ceiling.

The district of Mariahilf takes its name from the **Mariahilferkirche**, the big Baroque church set back from the street between no. 55 and 57 and providing a welcome escape from the rampant consumerism outside. The miraculous "Mariahilf" (Mary's help) picture in the main altar is actually a seventeenth-century copy of the original Passau Madonna by Lucas Cranach. One of the most striking furnishings is the Schutzengelgruppe, opposite the pulpit, in which a gilded angel and child are set against an iridescent blue and gold curtained baldachin. Before you leave, be sure to glance up and admire the ceiling frescoes by pupils of Paul Troger, and the Rococo organ, which features a gilded filigree clock suspended between the pipes.

Esterházy-Park and Haus des Meeres

One block south of Mariahilferstrasse lies the diminutive **Esterházy-Park**, dominated by a Flackturm, or anti-aircraft tower (see box opposite), which is daubed around the rim with the gnomic "smashed into pieces (in the still of the night)". The hand- and foot-holds of an artificial climbing wall now pepper the exterior, while a sloping green glass excrescence has appeared on one side. The interior houses the eminently missable **Haus des Meeres** (Marine House), a collection of reptiles, amphibians and fish kept in claustrophobic conditions; the tanks are just too small for these big creatures, and the only conceivable reason to come here is if you have very bored children in tow.

The Haus des Meeres is open daily 9am–6pm; öS95/€6.90.

Also in the park is an air-raid shelter, in which lurks the **Foltermuseum** (Torture Museum; *www.folter.at*) or Museum für mittelalterliche Rechtsgeschischte (Museum of Medieval Legal History). With various tableaux illustrating tortures through the ages, the museum treads a fine line between using torture as entertainment and putting across a serious message. The final Amnesty International video pulls no punches, however. Ask for the English information pack before you wander round.

The Foltermuseum is open daily 10am–6pm öS85/€6.18

Kaiserliches Hofmobiliendepot

Set back from Mariahilferstrasse itself, at Andreasgasse 7, is the expensively revamped **Kaiserliches Hofmobiliendepot** (Imperial Furniture Collection), now run by the private company which looks after Schönbrunn and the Hofburg's Kaiserappartements (hence the

Flacktürme

Vienna's six unsightly **Flacktürme** (anti-aircraft towers), built during World War II, are one of the few visible legacies of the Nazi period. Positioned in three sets of two across the city, these tall, concrete monstrosities form a triangle with the Stephansdom at the centre: two in the Augarten (see p.216), two in Arenberg Park in Landstrasse, one in the Stifskaserne courtyard, on the other side of Mariahilferstrasse, and one in Esterházy-Park. The towers were used both as observation posts to light up the sky and as anti-aircraft gun posts; in addition, they were capable of housing up to 30,000 troops and could become completely self-sufficient in an emergency, with their own underground field hospital, munitions factory, water and power supply and even air filters in case of a poison-gas attack. The Flacktürme were built to last for thousands of years, and after the war, the Nazis planned to clad the towers in marble and make them into victory monuments. Many Viennese view them with acute embarrassment; others argue that they serve as a useful and indelible reminder of that period. The real reason for their survival, though, is that, with walls of reinforced concrete up to 5m thick, they would be very costly and difficult to demolish. The only Flackturm that has been put to good use is the one in Esterházy-Park.

high admission charge). Yet despite its uninviting title, this is a surprisingly interesting museum – something like a cross between a junk warehouse and an applied arts study collection.

Established by Maria Theresia in 1747, the Hofmobiliendepot basically supplied all the furniture needed by the Habsburgs for their various palaces, which, as a rule, were only furnished when members of the family stayed there. It was also a dumping ground for those items of furniture which had gone out of fashion. After 1918, the depot found itself with over 650,000 items, and no imperial family to serve, so it became a museum. The first room, **Das Erbe** (The Heritage), gives you some idea of the sheer scale of the collection, with its forests of candelabra and coatstands, not to mention the bevy of Biedermeier spittoons.

The Hofmobiliendepot is open daily 9am–5pm; oS90/€6.54.

The **Habsburgersaal** panders to imperial nostalgia with Crown Prince Rudolf's ebony high-chair, scallop-shell cot, and, later on, funeral crown, while Maximilian of Mexico's serpent-wrapped walking stick and vastly oversized sombrero have to be seen to be believed. What follows is a whole series of reconstructed **period interiors** ranging from one of Prince Eugène's wonderful chinoiserie rooms to the aforementioned Rudolf's Turkish boudoir, draped with carpets snapped up on his oriental version of the Grand Tour in 1881. One of the most arresting interiors is that of Maria Ludovica d'Este, third wife of Franz I, who had very expensive (and outrageous) tastes. Here, you get to see her penchant for South American-themed murals, featuring genocidal acts by Spanish invaders; downstairs in the foyer, her vogueish Egyptian cabinet from the Hofburg is worth a peek.

The museum is planning to expand its twentieth-century collection, on the top floor, which is currently pretty sparse, with just a few minor minimalist pieces by the likes of Josef Hoffmann and Adolf Loos to get excited about. More fun for the moment is the **Hygienemöbel** (Sanitary Furniture), which displays imperial commodes, bed-pans and more spittoons through the ages. Before you head back down the stairs, however, make sure you take a look inside the **Wappensaal**, a library from a swanky villa in Mödling, its ceiling smothered in imperial coats-of-arms, originally designed in the 1880s to glorify the Habsburgs, but later modified to give it a more Pan-German character.

Haydn-Museum

*The Haydn-
Museum is
open
Tues–Sun
9am–12.15pm
& 1–4.30pm;
öS25/€1.82;
the nearest U-
Bahn is
Zieglergasse.*

For dedicated museum fans, there may be some compensation in the form of the **Haydn-Museum**, at Haydngasse 19, two blocks south of Mariahilferstrasse. Josef Haydn (1732–1809) spent much of his life in the service of the Esterházy family at their seats in Eisenstadt (see p.269) and Esterháza (now in Hungary), but with the death of his chief patron, Prince Nikolaus Esterházy, in 1790, the composer was free at last to settle permanently in Vienna. He bought this single-storey house in 1793, adding an extra floor in which he lived until his death in 1809. Here he wrote, among other works, his great oratorio, *Die Schöpfung* ("The Creation") and spent the last few months of his life sitting at home, silently handing visitors a specially printed calling card, which began with a quote from one of his own texts, "Gone is all my strength...". At the time of his death, Vienna was occupied by Napoleonic troops, but such was his renown, that – so the story goes – Napoleon himself ordered a guard of honour to be stationed outside his house, and a French Hussars officer came and sang an aria from *Die Schöpfung* at his deathbed. Sadly, none of the original fittings survive from Hadyn's day, and you'll learn little about the composer's life from this formulaic museum. The house also contains an equally unenlightening memorial room dedicated to the composer **Johannes Brahms** (1833–97), who lived near Karlsplatz.

Spittelberg

*For details of
the area's
cafés, pubs
and restaurants, see
p.301.*

Few areas in the Vorstädte have retained their original eighteenth- or early nineteenth-century appearance – the exception is the half dozen parallel narrow cobbled streets between Siebensterngasse and Burggasse known as the **Spittelberg** quarter. Traditionally a working-class and artisan quarter, it also doubled as the red-light district, conveniently backing onto two sets of barracks, full of sex-starved soldiers. Bypassed by the late nineteenth-century, the area was saved from demolition in the 1970s, its Baroque and Biedermeier houses carefully restored – and inevitably gentrified – and many of the streets pedestrianized.

It's a pleasant place to wander on any day of the week, but there's a small **craft market** on Saturdays along and around Spittelberggasse during the summer, which makes the stroll even more enjoyable. This functions daily during Easter and in the month leading up to Christmas, when the streets are heaving with folk drinking *Glühwein* and *Punsch*. Spittelberg also boasts one of the densest concentrations of bars, cafés and restaurants in the Vorstädte, not so much throbbing as gently swaying until the early hours. There's a sort of spill-over onto nearby Sankt-Ulrichs-Platz, a small, sloping square to the northwest, pedestrianized and dominated by the Baroque **Ulrichskirche**, where Christoph Willibald Gluck was married, Schubert's requiem was celebrated and Strauss the Younger was christened.

Those with an interest in the work of Otto Wagner should stroll a couple of blocks west up Neustiftgass to the **Otto Wagner-Wohnung**, on the first floor of Döblergasse 4. This was Wagner's town apartment and studio until his death in 1918. Both Döblergasse 4, and the next-door corner apartment block of Neustiftgasse 40 were designed by Wagner himself in 1912, and the only decoration on their austere facades are the bands of indigo-blue glass tiles and the sparing use of aluminium – it's the closest Wagner, better known for his Jugendstil works, ever came to the kind of austere functionalism later championed by the modernists. Inside, the blue patterning and aluminium theme are continued to great effect, while within the flat itself, though few of the original fittings have survived, there are plans to return the walls to their original colour, and recreate some feeling of how it was in Wagner's day.

A little further up Neustiftgasse, at no. 89–91, is the little-visited **Museum der kleinen Leute** (Museum of the Man in the Street), a private collection of bygone bric-a-brac from thimbles to old imperial uniforms, displayed in a couple of tiny rooms. The eccentric curator is only too happy to play you his 78 collection, let you leaf through photo albums, and serve you sweet white coffee.

Josefstadt

Josefstadt – Vienna's eighth district – was laid out in the early eighteenth century and named after the Emperor Josef I (1705–11). Almost immediately, the Piarists were given a large slice of the land for their monastery, the Maria-Treu Kloster, which now forms a pleasant Baroque ensemble, centred on a cobbled square with its own Marian column, three-quarters of the way along Piaristengasse. Overlooking the square is the splendid convex Baroque facade, tall pediment and twin towers of the monastery church, better known as the **Piaristenkirche**, originally designed by Hildebrandt, but only completed in 1753. The light interior is a glorious slice of High Baroque, full of playful oval shapes and faded frescoes by the youthful Franz Anton Maultbertsch, though you can barely get a glimpse

Mariahilf, Neubau and Josefstadt

The nearest U-Bahn is Volkstheater.

The Otto Wagner-Wohnung is open by appointment only; ☎ *523 2233; free.*

The Museum der kleinen Leute is open Tues–Fri 4–7pm, Sat & Sun 1–6pm; free.

Tram #J runs along Josefstädter Strasse.

of it outside of services. It was on the church's still extant nine-teenth-century organ that the young Anton Bruckner was examined, after which one of the judges exclaimed: "He should have been testing us!"

Close by the monastery, on the other side of Piaristengasse, facing Josefstädter Strasse, is the **Theater-in-der-Josefstadt**, founded in 1788 as a variety theatre, but remodelled in Neoclasscial style by Josef Kornhäusel, and reopened in 1822 with a premiere of Beethoven's *Consecration of the House* overture, conducted by the composer himself. Between the wars, the theatre was under the direction of Max Reinhardt, the great theatrical innovator who helped found the Salzburg Festival, staged incredible large-scale productions, and eventually fled to Hollywood in the 1930s. Today, the theatre has returned to its light-entertainment roots, staging comedies, melodramas and farce.

*The Museum
für Volkskunde
is open
Tues–Sun
10am–5pm;
öS50/€3.63;
tram #5 from
Josefstädter
Strasse U-
Bahn.*

Three blocks north of the theatre, in Hildebrandt's Baroque Palais Schönborn on Laudongasse, is the **Österreichisches Museum für Volkskunde** (Austrian Museum of Folk Art), a collection that seems out of place in such an urban setting. The museum, founded in 1894, has been sensitively modernized and there's enough variety to keep you entertained for an hour or so, with exhibits ranging from grass raincoats and magnificent Tirolean wardrobes to an incredible lime-wood shrine to Emperor Karl I.

Alsergrund

Alsergrund – Vienna's large, roughly triangular ninth district – is dominated by its medical institutions and associations. A vast swathe of land is taken up with the **Allgemeines Krankenhaus** or AKH (General Hospital), established by Josef II in 1784. The following year, Josef founded the **Josephinum**, an academy for training military surgeons, next door. Since then, various university science faculties have relocated here, and the area remains popular with doctors and medical students, as it has been since **Freud**'s day – his museum is now Alsergrund's chief tourist attraction. Alsergrund also boasts one of the few aristocratic summer palaces to survive into the modern era, the **Palais Liechtenstein**, home to Vienna's premier modern art museum until the collection was relocated to the MuseumsQuartier (see p.132).

Allgemeines Krankenhaus

*To get to the
Allgemeines
Krankenhaus,
take tram #43
or #44 two
stops up
Alserstrasse.*

The **Allgemeines Krankenhaus** (General Hospital) was one of the most modern medical institutions in the world when it was founded in 1784 to replace the Grossarmenhaus (Great Poor House). Vienna was the "medical Mecca" of the empire, and from its foundation, the overriding philosophy of the Allgemeines Krankenhaus

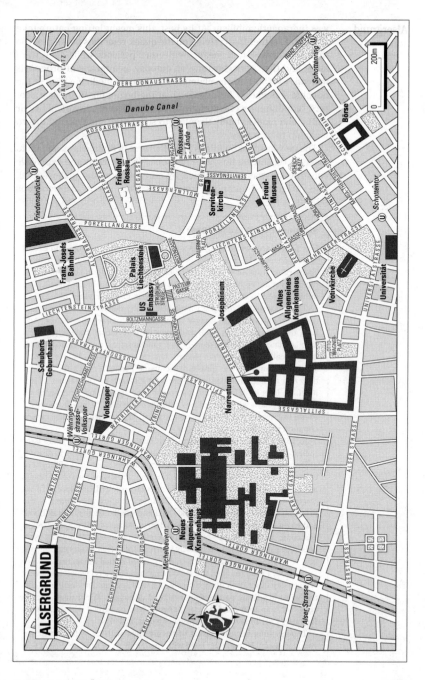

ALSERGRUND

GAUSSPLATZ

OBERE DONAUSTRASSE

Danube Canal

ROSSAUERSTRASSE

Friedensbrücke

Friedhof Rossau

Börse

Schottenring

FRANZ-JOSEFS-KAI

Rossauer Lände

HAHN-GASSE

PRAMERGASSE

GRÜNENTORGASSE

MÜLLNERGASSE

SEEGASSE

GLASERGASSE

SERVITENGASSE

SCHLICK PLATZ

BERGGASSE

Serviten-kirche

Freud-Museum

PORZELLANGASSE

Schottentor

LIECHTENSTEINSTRASSE

ALSERBACHSTRASSE

BAUERNFELD-PLATZ

PORZELLANGASSE

Franz-Josefs Bahnhof

Palais Liechtenstein

US Embassy

STRUDLHOF-STIEGE

PASTEUR-GASSE

Josephinum

WASAGASSE

THURNGASSE

BERGGASSE

WÄHRINGERSTRASSE

UNIVERSITÄTSSTRASSE

Votivkirche

Universität

Altes Allgemeines Krankenhaus

BOLTZMANNGASSE

NUSSDORFERSTRASSE

SPITALGASSE

SENSENGASSE

OTTO-WAGNER-PLATZ

Schuberts Geburtshaus

Narrenturm

SPITALGASSE

SECHSSCHIMMELGASSE

WÄHRINGERSTRASSE

SEVERINGASSE

Volksoper

Währinger-strasse Volksoper

WÄHRINGER GÜRTEL

WÄHRINGER GÜRTEL

GENTZGASSE

SCHULGASSE

STAUDGASSE

Michelbeuern

Neues Allgemeines Krankenhaus

LAZARETTGASSE

ALSER STRASSE

WÄHRINGER GÜRTEL

SCHÖPFENAUER STRASSE

KREUZGASSE

Alser Strasse

ALSERSTRASSE

N

0   200m

Alsergrund was therapeutic nihilism. At its best, this meant letting nature take its course, rather than relying on the quack remedies popular at the time. At its worst, it meant neglecting patients while they were alive, and then concentrating on autopsy as a means of prognosis instead. By 1850, it was claimed that the only medicine used at the hospital was cherry brandy. Even at the beginning of the last century, conditions were dire, with nurses forced to work 24-hour shifts, and paid so badly they had to sell coffee and demand tips to make up their wages.

The new hospital buildings lie to the west of Spitalgasse, and go to make up the largest hospital in Europe. Their lengthy and expensive construction was accompanied by corruption at the highest level. The original buildings, known as the **Altes Allgemeines**

Sigmund Freud (1856–1939)

Few people are so intimately associated with one place as **Sigmund Freud** is with Vienna. He may have been born to a Jewish wool merchant in Freiberg in Moravia in 1856, and died in 1939 in exile in London, but in the intervening eighty-three years, he spent most of his life in Vienna. The family moved to the capital when Freud was just four years old, and in 1873 he entered the university's medical faculty determined to be a scientist. He took three years longer than usual to complete his degree, and then decided to switch tack and train as a medic at the Allgemeines Krankenhaus. In 1887 Freud began practising as a neuropathologist, experimenting with cocaine, electro-therapy and hypnosis, before eventually coming up with the "pressure technique", using a couch for the first time and asking questions, while pressing his hand on the patient's forehead. He later switched to the method of "free association", during which the patient says whatever comes into their mind. "The aim is modest," Freud said when describing his new science: "to turn neurotic misery into common unhappiness."

In 1896, Freud coined the term "psychoanalysis", and four years later published the book which established his originality, *The Interpretation of Dreams*. In it, Freud argued that "all dreams represent the fulfillment of wishes", and that these wishes are often (but not always) sexual. Freud's impact on twentieth-century thought has been profound, and several of his discoveries – the death wish, the Oedipus complex, transference, the Freudian slip, penis envy, the oral, anal and phallic stages of childhood, and so on – have become common parlance. (Much of this popularization has come at the expense of Freud's original meaning – "Freudian symbols", for example, used exclusively by Freud for dream interpretation, are now widely used simply as a day-to-day form of sexual innuendo.)

In 1902, Freud founded the Psychoanalytical Society, which met every Wednesday evening in his apartment, his wife serving *Guglhupf* and coffee, while academic papers were read and discussed. Freud ruled his disciples with an iron hand, ejecting anyone who disagreed with him, most famously Carl Jung, the Swiss psychoanalyst, in 1913.

Though Jung accused Freud of having slept with his wife's attractive younger sister, Minna, who lived with the family in Berggasse, Freud was

---

Krankenhaus, lie to the east of Spitalgasse and are now occupied by university departments. The courtyards and the various bars within the complex spill over with students, especially in the summer. The prime motive for exploring the old hospital's spacious courtyards, however, is to visit the **Museum of Pathological Anatomy** in the former lunatic asylum of the Narrenturm (see below). The scandal-ridden modern hospital, or Neues Allgemeines Krankenhaus, lies to the northwest, on the other side of Spitalgasse, but there's little reason to head this way – unless, that is, you're ill.

Alsergrund

Narrenturm

The circular **Narrenturm** (Fools' Tower; *www.pathomus.or.at*) is an unprepossessing building, that looks something like a converted

The Narrenturm is open Wed 3–6pm, Thurs 8–11am & first Sat of the month 10am–1pm; free.

in fact a disappointingly conventional Viennese paterfamilias. "What a terrible man! I am sure he has never been unfaithful to his wife. It is quite abnormal and scandalous," reported one of his fans, the French poet Countess Anna de Noailles, after meeting him. He was happily married all his life to Martha Bernays, a good Jewish *Hausfrau*, who gave birth to and brought up six healthy children. He saw patients without appointment daily from three to four in the afternoon, using the proceeds to buy the (occasionally erotic) antiquities that filled his study; afterwards he would write until as late as three in the morning. Every afternoon, he would walk the entire circuit of the Ringstrasse at a brisk pace; every Saturday evening he played the card game Tarock, every Sunday in summer, the family would dress up in traditional Austrian peasant gear, right down to their leather underpants, and go mushroom picking in the Wienerwald.

In 1923, he was diagnosed as having cancer of the jaw (he was an inveterate cigar-smoker) and given just five years to live. A year later, aged 68, he was granted the freedom of Vienna, two years earlier than was the custom. As he joked to a friend, they clearly thought he was going to die. In the end, he lived another sixteen years in some considerable pain, taking only aspirin, undergoing thirty-three operations, and having his mouth scraped daily to accommodate an ill-fitting prosthesis.

Shortly after the Anschluss in March 1938, the SS raided Freud's flat. Martha, ever the accommodating host, asked them to put their rifles in the umbrella stand and to be seated. The Freuds' passports were subsequently confiscated and their money (öS6000) taken from the family safe. Freud dryly commented that *he'd* never been paid so much for a single visit. Before being allowed to leave the country, he was forced to sign a document to the effect that he had been treated with respect and allowed "to live and work in full freedom" after the Anschluss. This he did, but he asked to be allowed to add the following sentence "I can heartily recommend the Gestapo to anyone."

Only through the efforts of his friends was Freud able to escape to Britain on June 3, 1938. Four of his sisters were not allowed to join him and died in the Holocaust. Finally, just over a year after having arrived in London, Freud's doctor fulfilled their eleven-year-old pact, and, when the pain became too much, gave him a lethal dose of morphine.

gasometer, situated in a scruffy, neglected courtyard of the Altes Allgemeines Krankenhaus. It was built in 1784 as a lunatic asylum with five floors, each housing 28 cells which feed off a circular corridor; its nickname was the "Guglhupf", after the popular, circular cake. Despite its forbidding, prison-like design and slit windows, conditions were exceptionally humane for the period. It fell into disuse in 1866, and now houses the **Pathologisch-anatomische Bundesmuseum** (Federal Museum of Pathological Anatomy). Locating the Narrenturm can be tricky as there are several entrances to the Altes Allgemeines Krankenhaus – on Garnisongasse, Spitalgasse and, most conveniently, Alserstrasse – and whichever you choose, you'll need to consult the map inside each of the gateways in order to find your way to courtyard no. 13.

The museum is popular with medical students, and it certainly helps to have a strong stomach. The ground-floor cells contain a mock-up of Dr Robert Koch's 1882 discovery of the bacillus that causes tuberculosis, an apothecary from 1820, a section on artificial limbs, a mortuary slab, wax models of TB sufferers and the odd piece of anatomy preserved in formaldehyde. If you're already feeling queasy, don't, whatever you do, venture upstairs where the cells and corridors are filled with yet more examples of abnormalities and deformities preserved in formaldehyde from autopsies conducted around a hundred years ago.

Josephinum

The Josephinum is open Mon–Fri 9am–3pm; öS20/€1.45; take any tram two stops up Währinger Strasse from Schottentor U-Bahn.

Founded in 1785 to the northeast of the Allgemeines Krankenhaus, the **Josephinum** is housed in an austere silver-grey palace, set back from Währinger Strasse behind a set of imposing wrought-iron railings. Having observed the primitive techniques used by army surgeons at first hand during his military campaigns, the Emperor Josef II decided to set up an Institute for Military Surgery. The institute was closed in 1872, and the building now houses the Pharmacological Institute for Medicine and History of Medicine Institute instead – plus a museum run by the latter, known as the Museum des Institutes für Geschichte der Medizin.

Aside from the leech cups, amputation saws, dental instruments and the odd pickled stomach, the chief attraction of the institute's museum is its remarkable collection of anatomical wax models, or Wachspräparate Sammlung, commissioned by Josef II from a group of Florentine sculptors in 1780. The models are serene life-size human figures, for the most part, presented as if partially dissected, revealing the body's nerves, muscles and veins in full gory technicolour. Equally beautiful are the original display cases, fashioned from rosewood and fitted with huge, bobbly, hand-blown panes of Venetian glass. There's also a model of the Allgemeines Krankenhaus and the Narrenturm as they would have appeared in 1784, just for good measure.

Sigmund-Freud Museum

Sigmund Freud moved to the second floor of Berggasse 19 in 1891 and stayed here until June 3, 1938, when, unwillingly, he and his family fled to London. His apartment, now the **Sigmund-Freud Museum** (*www.freud-museum.at*), is a place of pilgrimage, though he himself took almost all his possessions – bar his library, which he sold – with him into exile (where they can still be seen in London's Freud Museum). His hat, coat and walking stick are still here, and there's home movie footage from the 1930s, but the only room with any original decor – and consequently any atmosphere – is the waiting room, which contains the odd oriental rug, a cabinet of antiquities, and some burgundy-upholstered furniture, sent back from London by his daughter Anna after the war. The rest of the flat is taken up with a couple of rooms of photographs, a few works of Freud-inspired art, a library, with a CD-Rom on Freud, and a shop. There's a file available with English translations of the museum's captions, or an audioguide in English (for an extra öS20/€1.45).

The Sigmund-Freud Museum is open daily: July–Sept 9am–6pm; Oct–June 9am–5pm; öS60/€5.09.

Servitenkirche and Friedhof Rossau

If you're heading from Freud's apartment to the Palais Liechtenstein (see p.204), it's worth taking a slight detour to visit the **Servitenkirche**, an early Baroque gem of a church up Servitengasse, designed in the mid-seventeenth century by Carlo Carnevale, and the only church in the Vorstädte to survive the 1683 Turkish siege. Its oval-shaped nave, the first to be built in Vienna, was a powerful influence on the layout of the Peterskirche and Karlskirche. You can only peek through the exquisite wrought-iron railings, but that's enough to get a feel for the cherub-infested, stucco-encrusted interior, which features an exuberant gilded pulpit by Balthasar Moll. To the side of the entrance are two side chapels worth noting, especially the one to the north, with its stucco relief of St John of Nepomuk taking confession from the Bohemian queen, and its very own grotto of the Virgin Mary.

A couple of blocks to the north, at Seegasse 9–11, is Vienna's oldest surviving Jewish cemetery, **Friedhof Rossau**, with gravestones dating back to 1540. In disuse now for two centuries, today it remains hidden from the street behind a supremely ugly modern old people's home, which occupies the site of the former Jewish Hospital and Old People's Home, demolished in 1972. It's possible to visit the cemetery at any reasonable time by simply walking through the foyer to the back of the building, where the graves that survived the Nazi desecration shelter under tall, mature trees. One of the most famous people to have been buried here was Samuel Oppenheimer (1630–1703), the first of the Court Jews to be allowed to settle in Vienna after the 1670 expulsion (see p78). He supplied the Habsburg army for its war with France, and organized the logistics of the defence of Vienna in 1683. When he died, however, the Habsburgs refused to honour their debts to his heirs, causing the family to go bankrupt, which in turn caused a major European financial crisis. His protégé, Samson Wertheimer (1658–1724), who became chief administrator of financial affairs to three successive Habsburg emperors, is also buried here.

From the Palais Liechtenstein to Schuberts Geburthaus

At the turn of the seventeenth century, when the enormously wealthy Liechtenstein family commissioned Domenico Martinelli to build a summer palace, Alsergrund was still a rural idyll. Now hemmed in by nineteenth-century apartment blocks, the Baroque **Palais Liechtenstein** comes as something of a surprise, hidden away down the backstreet of Fürstengasse. It's built on a giant scale, with an imposing entrance hall, two grandiose marble staircases and frescoes by the likes of Johann Micheal Rottmayr and Andrea Pozzo. The family used to display their own vast art collection here (since removed to Vaduz, Liechtenstein), followed some years later by Vienna's Museum moderner Kunst (Museum of Modern Art). In 2001, that collection was rehoused in the MuseumsQuartier (see p.132), and it remains to be seen what lies in store for this suburban summer palace.

If you've just passed the Palais Liechtenstein, you might as well take a stroll up the **Strudlhofstiege**, an imaginative set of Jugenstil steps designed in 1910 by Theodor Jäger, that link Pasteurgasse with Strudlhofgasse above it. They may not have the fame nor the setting of Rome's Spanish Steps, but they are a beguiling vignette of *fin-de-siècle* Vienna, and provided the inspiration for a long novel of the same name written in 1951 by Heimito von Doderer, which is dear to the hearts of many Viennese.

Schuberts Geburthaus

Schuberts Geburthaus is open Tues–Sun 9am–12.15pm & 1–4.30pm; öS25/€1.82; take tram #38 or #39 five stops from U-Bahn Schottentor.

Further north still, at Nussdorfer Strasse 54, is **Schuberts Geburthaus**, the unassuming, two-storey house where the composer was born in 1797. Inside, the charming courtyard has been lovingly restored, with wooden balconies festooned with geranium flower boxes. As so often with Vienna's musical memorials, however, there has been no attempt to reconstruct Schubert's family home, which would have consisted of just one room and a kitchen (the latter survives). In any case, Schubert would have had very little recollection of the place as the family moved down the road, to Säulengasse 3, when he was four years old. So, beyond admiring the composer's broken spectacles and his half-brother's piano, there's little to do here but listen to the excerpts from his music on the headphones provided. However, fans of **Adalbert Stifter**, the writer and artist from the Böhmerwald who slit his throat in 1868 rather than suffer

Franz Schubert

Of all the composers associated with Vienna, **Franz Schubert** (1797–1828) fulfils more Romantic criteria than most. He died of syphilis at the age of just 31 (younger even than Mozart), he really was penniless (unlike Mozart, who was just careless with his money), and never lived to hear any of his symphonies performed (the first one wasn't published until fifty years after his death). The picture would be complete had he died while writing his Eighth (Unfinished) Symphony – in fact, he abandoned it before he died, and went on, instead, to complete a Ninth Symphony.

Schubert was born the eleventh child of an impoverished teacher. At the age of nine or ten, he was sent to study with the organist at the local church on Marktgasse, where he had been baptized. He went on to become the church organist, and composed his first mass for the church at the age of seventeen. In between times, he served as a chorister at the Burgkapelle, where he studied under Antonio Salieri, Mozart's famous court rival, before working as an assistant teacher at his father's school for three years. At the end of this period, he became a freelance musician, thanks to financial help from his friends, and spent two summers as music tutor for the Esterházy family (see p.269).

His intensely lyrical chamber music, fragile songs and melodic piano works were popular among the Viennese bourgeoisie, and he performed at numerous informal social gatherings, which became known as "Schubertiaden". In his personal life, he was fairly dissolute; a heavy drinker, who frequented "revolutionary" circles, he remained unmarried all his life, his sexual appetite confined to prostitutes. Towards the end of his short life, he fulfilled a lifetime's ambition and met up with his hero Beethoven, though there are no reliable details of the encounter. He was one of the torchbearers at the great composer's funeral, and was buried, according to his wishes, three graves away from him in Währinger Friedhof the following year (he now lies with Beethoven in the Zentralfriedhof, see p.257).

---

cancer of the liver, fare a little better than those on Schubert's trail. Although Stifter had nothing whatsoever to do with Schubert, several rooms in the museum have been given over to his idyllic Biedermeier landscapes, and for an extra öS10/€0.73, you can view them at your leisure.

Schubert's brother's house – 4, Kettenbrückengasse 6 (Tues–Sun 1–4.30pm; öS25/€1.82), near the Naschmarkt – the *Sterbezimmer* in which the composer died, has been made into a similarly unenthralling museum for the truly dedicated.

Chapter 7

Leopoldstadt and the east

L eopoldstadt – the city's second district – is separated from the centre of Vienna by the Danube Canal, and, along with the district of Brigittenau, forms a misshapen island bordered to the east by the main arm of the Danube. For the most part, it's a drab and uninteresting residential suburb, only redeemed by the Prater, the vast city park, with its funfair, ferris wheel, woods and numerous recreational facilities. Leopoldstadt also boasts a long history as the city's foremost Jewish quarter, though few traces of the old community remain. More recently, the area has been settled by a wave of immigrants from Turkey and the Balkans. It's also still something of a red-light district, with a sprinkling of strip joints and sex shops in the backstreets between Taborstrasse and Praterstrasse.

Jewish Leopoldstadt

In Leopoldstadt, where the humbler Jews mostly congregate, there was suddenly an endless concourse of new, strange figures – men in long gabardines, tiny circular caps of silk or velvet on their heads, and corkscrew curls meandering down the sides of the face; women with wigs and ancient finery, blooming young Esthers and Susannahs ambling along with downcast eyes. Along the quays of the Danube Canal there was an endless procession of these – a new edition of Hebrew fugitives mourning by the waters. Rabbis in every costume and of every degree of holiness were scattered amongst them all.

Wolf von Schierbrand,
an American journalist stationed in Vienna in the late nineteenth century.

It was probably Leopoldstadt's physical separateness that persuaded the Emperor Ferdinand II to choose the area in 1624 as a site to establish a walled Jewish ghetto. For around fifty years the Jewish quarter flourished, the financial acumen and clout of its wealthiest burghers happily used by the Habsburgs to fund the Thirty Years' War. At the end of the 1660s the population peaked at around 3000 or 4000, but as the Counter-Reformation gathered pace, there were

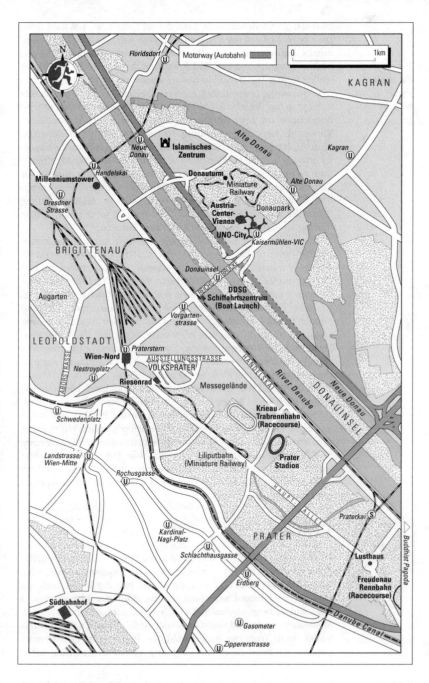

Motorway (Autobahn)

0   1km

N

Floridsdorf

KAGRAN

Neue
Donau

Islamisches
Zentrum

Kagran

Alte Donau

Millenniumstower

Handelskai

Donauturm

Alte Donau

Dresdner
Strasse

Miniature
Railway

Austria-
Center-
Vienna

Donaupark

BRIGITTENAU

UNO-City

Kaisermühlen-VIC

Augarten

Donauinsel

DDSG
Schiffahrtszentrum
(Boat Launch)

LEOPOLDSTADT

Vorgarten-
strasse

Praterstern

Wien-Nord

AUSSTELLUNGSSTRASSE

Nestroyplatz

VOLKSPRATER

Riesenrad

Messegelände

River Danube

DONAUINSEL

Neue Donau

Schwedenplatz

Krieau
Trabrennbahn
(Racecourse)

Landstrasse/
Wien-Mitte

Rochusgasse

Liliputbahn
(Miniature Railway)

Prater
Stadion

Kardinal-
Nagl-Platz

HAUPT ALLEE

Praterkai

Buddhist Pagoda

Schlachthausgasse

PRATER

Lusthaus

Erdberg

Freudenau
Rennbahn
(Racecourse)

Südbahnhof

Danube Canal

Gasometer

Zippererstrasse

*For more on
the plight of
Vienna's Jews,
see p.78.*

increasingly vociferous calls from devout Catholics – not least from the city council and the Emperor's Spanish wife – to banish the community entirely. In 1670, the Emperor Leopold I bowed to the zealots' pressure and expelled Jews from the city on the charges of spying for the Turks and blasphemy against the Virgin Mary.

Fortuitously, Leopoldstadt enjoyed a second period of Jewish settlement in the decades following the 1848 revolution, when official restrictions on Jews within the empire were finally abolished. Thousands took the opportunity to leave the *shtetls* of Bohemia, Moravia, Hungary and Galicia and migrated to the capital, the majority arriving by train at Wien-Nord or the now defunct Nordwestbahn, and settling, initially at least, in the surrounding district of Leopoldstadt, where housing conditions were poor and rents cheap. The Strauss family, Sigmund Freud, Gustav Mahler, Arthur Schnitzler and Theodor Herzl all lived here at some point, before moving up in the world to the city's richer suburbs.

This time around, Leopoldstadt was only ever an unofficial Jewish quarter – even at their numerical peak, in 1910, the district's 60,000 Jews only constituted a third of the population – though the area had the appearance of an old walled ghetto, partly owing to the high proportion of orthodox Hasidic Jews, with their distinctive dress. With the richer Jewish families moving out at the earliest opportunity, and poorer families constantly arriving to fill their place, the area remained trapped in a cycle of poverty, attracting the underprivileged ranks of Viennese society. By the beginning of the twentieth century the area was notorious as a hotbed of prostitution, much to the delight of the city's numerous anti-Semites.

During World War II, the Nazis turned Leopoldstadt back into the official ghetto, and forced the city's remaining Jews into its confines. The deportations to the camps began in earnest in 1941 and by the end of the following year the ghetto's Jewish population was reduced to a few thousand, most of whom were married to gentiles. A mere 500 Jews returned to Vienna after the war, but with more recent Jewish immigration from the former eastern bloc, these numbers have increased to around 7000, many of whom have chosen to settle once more in Leopoldstadt.

Prater

Of all the places in Leopoldstadt, it is the **Prater** – derived from the Spanish *prado* (plain) – which draws the biggest crowds. This large, flat tract of land, taking up almost half the island, includes vast acres of mixed woodland, sports stadiums, racecourses, a miniature railway, allotments, a trade fair centre, a planetarium, an amusement park, and, most famously of all, Vienna's giant Ferris wheel. Aside from the Wienerwald, the Prater is by far the most popular weekend destination for any Viennese searching for a

---

Visiting the Prater

The Prater is vast, and its backbone is the chestnut-lined **Hauptallee** which runs dead straight for 5km, from the Ferris wheel and tacky Volksprater in the northwest, to the woodier section around the Lusthaus to the southeast.

The easiest way of **approaching the Prater** is from the northwest, from Wien-Nord station (U-Bahn Praterstern), which is the terminus for **trams** #5 and #O, and a stop on tram #21, which terminates at S-Bahn Praterkai. Alternatively, tram #N from U-Bahn Schwedenplatz has its terminus right by the Hauptallee, a third of the way down from the Ferris wheel. Halfway down, **bus #80B** (hourly) and **#83A** cross the Hauptallee en route to and from U-Bahn Schlachthausgasse. Finally, bus #77A (every 30min) from the same U-Bahn will take you all the way to or from the Lusthaus, even travelling some of the way down the Hauptallee itself.

Getting around the Prater, you can walk, jog, rollerblade, cycle, take a Fiaker, or rent one of the **pedal carriages**, which seat two adults (plus two kids if you wish). Another possibility is to buy a one-way ticket on the miniature railway or **Liliputbahn**, which will get you almost halfway down the Hauptallee.

---

breath of fresh air, a stroll in the woods, a jog in the park, or a spot of rollerblading.

Traditionally a royal hunting preserve, the Prater was opened to the public in 1766 by Josef II, and soon became a popular spot for Viennese society. As the eighteenth-century Irish opera singer, Michael Kelly, noted: "There are innumerable cabarets, frequented by people of all ranks in the evening, who immediately after dinner proceed thither to regale themselves with their favourite dish, fried chicken, cold ham and sausages; white beer and Hoffner wines by way of dessert; and stay there until a late hour: dancing, music, and every description of merriment prevail; and every evening, when not professionally engaged, I was sure to be in the midst of it." In 1791, Mozart broke off work to go and watch François Blanchard go up in a hot-air balloon, with the Archduke Franz himself cutting the rope.

Throughout the nineteenth century, the Prater continued to be *the* place to be seen, particularly on the long, central Hauptallee. On Sundays, the latter was the scene of the *Praterfahrt*, when, as one observer put it, "the newest shape in carriages, the last 'sweet thing in bonnets', the most correct cut of coat *à la Anglais*, is to be seen, walking, riding, or driving up and down." On Easter Sunday, May 1 and other special occasions, something like half the population of the city would turn up for the *Praterfahrt*. As one historian put it: "Everyone in Vienna joined in... if they could call a carriage their own or anything else on wheels with a nag to pull it. If not, they walked. Vienna had no more glamorous sight to offer, nor any which united all classes in this way."

In 1873, the Prater was the venue for the empire's Weltausstellung or **World Trade Fair**, bringing unprecedented numbers of tourists to

Vienna. Some 50,000 exhibitors from 40 countries set up displays in the exhibition's rotunda, topped by a huge cupola 108m in diameter (the rotunda burned down in 1938). Unfortunately, just eight days after the emperor opened the fair on May 1, the Vienna stock exchange collapsed and what had been touted as a celebration of the empire's thriving liberal economy became a charade. In July, to further dampen the mood, a cholera epidemic broke out in the city, claiming 3000 victims. By November, seven million admissions were recorded – thirteen million fewer than expected – and the fair was forced to close.

In 1890, the First of May *Praterfahrt* was appropriated by the Socialist leader Viktor Adler, who helped organize the first **May Day Parade** of workers down the Hauptallee, though he himself was in prison on the day itself. There was panic among the ruling classes; "soldiers are standing by, the doors of the houses are being closed, in people's apartments food supplies are prepared as though for an impending siege, the shops are deserted, women and children dare not go out into the street," reported the *Neue Freie Presse*. Even so, thousands took part, marching four abreast, carrying red flags and singing, and the demonstration passed off peacefully. The May Day Parade quickly became a permanent fixture in the city's calendar of celebrations.

Volksprater

The Volksprater is open Easter–Oct daily 8am–midnight; the nearest U-Bahn is Praterstern.

The easiest point of access from the city centre – and by far the busiest section of the Prater – is the northwest end, where you'll find the park's permanent funfair, known as the **Volksprater**. (It's also known as the *Wurstelprater*, not for the sausages sold in abundance here, but for the Punch-like character of Hanswurst, whose puppet booths were once a common sight.) Tourists flock to the Volksprater for the Riesenrad, but the Viennese come here for the other **rides**, a strange mixture ranging from high-tech helter-skelters and white-knuckle affairs to more traditional fairground rides like ghost trains, dodgems and strength contests judging participants from *Weichling* (weakling), through *Fräulein* (girly) to *Weltmeister* (world champion). The fair has an impressive range of bad-taste attractions, too, including a tawdry "Sex-Museum" and a "Jack the Ripper" dark ride, with mock graves of the victims on the outside. For the kids, there are bouncy castles, horse rides and even a rather sad sleigh carousel pulled by real ponies.

The atmosphere is generally fairly relaxed during the day, though it can get a little bit more charged at night. If you get lost, you should be able to orientate yourself by one of the two open areas, Rondeau and Calafattiplatz, the latter named after the man who set up the first carousel in the Prater in 1840. The easiest point of reference of all is, of course, the Riesenrad. Sadly, there are no longer over fifty restaurants and pubs to choose from as there were a hundred years ago, but if you're peckish, there's no shortage of Würst stands, plus a few more appetizing options, such as the famous *Schweizer Haus* (see p.321), whose roast pig is legendary.

Prater

Riesenrad

Taking a ride on the **Riesenrad** (Giant Wheel) is one of those things you simply have to do if you go to Vienna; it's also a must for fans of the film *The Third Man*, as the place in front of which Orson Welles does his famous "cuckoo clock" speech. Built in 1898 for the Emperor Franz-Josef I's golden jubilee celebrations, the Riesenrad was designed by the British military engineer Walter Basset, who had constructed similar Ferris wheels in Blackpool and Paris (both long since demolished). The cute little red gondolas were destroyed during World War II, and only half were replaced after 1945 in deference to the Riesenrad's old age. Acrophobes can reassure themselves with the fact that the gondolas, which hold up to twelve people standing, are entirely enclosed, though they do tend to wobble around a bit, and reach a height of over 65m. You should also be prepared for the fact that the wheel doesn't so much spin as stagger slowly round, as each gondola fills up with passengers; once you've done a complete circuit, you've had your twenty-minute ride.

The Riesenrad is open April 10am–10pm; May–Sept 9am–midnight; Oct 10am–10pm; Nov to early Jan 10am–6pm; öS45/€3.27.

Prater Museum and Planetarium

If you've no interest in the amusements at the Volksprater, you're probably best off heading instead for the nearby **Prater Museum**, which records the golden age of the funfair. Old photographs of the likes of Semona, the fiery Amazonian snake charmer, and Liliputstadt, an entire miniature city inhabited by dwarves, give you something of the nineteenth-century flavour. Also displayed here are some of the characters from Hanswurst, various antique slot machines (some of which you can play on) and a model of the 1873 *Weltausstellung*. The museum is housed in one room of the **Planetarium** (closed Aug to mid-Sept; *www.planetarium-wien.at*; öS50/€2.91), which was founded by the German optician Carl Zeiss in 1927, and puts on a varied programme, with commentary nearly always in German. Pick up one of the leaflets to find out the latest listings.

The Prater Museum is open Tues–Fri 9am–12.15pm & 1–4.30pm, Sat & Sun 2–6.30pm; öS25/€1.82.

Beyond the Volksprater

The quickest method of escape from the Volksprater is by the miniature railway, known as the **Liliputbahn**, which runs from near the Riesenrad over to the main stadium, a return trip of around 4km. The engines are mostly diesel, but some steam trains run in the summer. There are three stations: Praterstern by the Ferris wheel, the midpoint station Rotunde, named after the now defunct exhibition hall of the 1873 *Weltausstellung*, and Stadion. En route, you pass the Hockey-Stadion and Bowling-Halle to the south, the ugly, expansive

The Liliputbahn runs April to mid-Oct daily 10am–11pm; öS20/€1.45 one-way; öS35/€2.54 return.

Messegelände (trade fair grounds) and the Krieau Trabrennbahn (trotting-racecourse), to the north.

Prater Stadion

Beyond the Trabrennbahn lies the **Prater Stadion** (aka the Wiener or Ernst-Happel-Stadion). Opened in July 1931 with the International Workers' Olympics, the stadium's playing field was transformed into a giant stage, on which 4000 musicians, actors and gymnasts re-enacted the struggle of Labour over Capital from the Middle Ages to the present day. As a grand finale, the giant gilt idol representing capitalism was toppled, thousands of youths dressed in white marched forward carrying red flags and the crowd sang the *Internationale*. The show was repeated four times that year before a total audience of 260,000, and proved the cultural highpoint of inter-war "Red Vienna" (see p.353).

The stadium itself – the largest in Austria, holding just over 60,000 spectators – was given a face-lift in the 1980s, including the addition of a technically remarkable roof; invisible from the outside, it's a self-supporting light steel structure that hangs gracefully over the terraces. Despite this, the stadium remains underused, hosting no regular soccer matches, only the odd European or international match, plus sporadic large-scale pop concerts. On the north side of the stadium by sector B, along Meiereistrasse, is the **Fussballmuseum**, which traces the history of Austrian soccer, whose golden days were back in the early 1930s before the Austro-fascists took over.

*The Fussball-
museum is
open Tues–Fri
9am–12.15pm
& 1–4.30pm,
Sat & Sun
2–6.30pm;
öS25/€1.82.*

Beyond the Stadion

Notwithstanding the Autobahn and the railway line that cut across the southeastern half of the Prater, the woods beyond the Stadion are among the most peaceful sections of the entire park, perfect for a picnic. If you've no provisions, walk to the far end of the Hauptallee where you'll find the **Lusthaus** restaurant, a pretty octagonal building, remodelled from a hunting lodge into a pleasure palace by Isidor Canevale in 1783. Entirely surrounded by water in those days, it served as the centrepiece for a mass picnic laid on for 20,000 soldiers on the first anniversary of the 1813 Battle of Leipzig, during the Congress of Vienna. It now forms the island of a roundabout, but preserves its original frescoed interior, and is still a popular spot for lunch, as is the more rustic *Altes Jägerhaus*, opposite.

*For details of
the* Lusthaus
and Altes
Jägerhaus, *see
p.320.*

To the southeast of the *Lusthaus* lies the **Freudenau Rennbahn**, a lovingly restored racecourse from the late nineteenth century. The racing season traditionally opens on Easter Sunday and reaches its apogee during the annual Derby, organized by the Austrian Jockey Club since 1868, the year it was founded. Held on a Sunday in June, the Derby used to be attended almost unfailingly by the emperor himself, with various aristocrats often among the riders, and the wealthy young Viennese crowd dressed to the nines.

Central Leopoldstadt

Though Leopoldstadt's days as a flourishing Jewish quarter are a distant memory, the pockets of kosher shops on Hollandstrasse and Tempelgasse, and the Jewish school on Castellezgasse, are evidence of the area's modest Jewish renaissance. The surviving wing of the district's largest synagogue, the neo-Byzantine **Leopoldstädter Tempel**, on Tempelgasse, gives a vague idea of the building's former glory; there's a mosaic from the missing central section on the facade of the Desider Friedmann building on the corner of Ferdinandstrasse and Tempelgasse. Elsewhere, at Kleine Sperlgasse 2a and Malzgasse 7, plaques record two of the locations used by the Nazis to round up the city's Jews for deportation to the camps. Otherwise, there's really very little to see in contemporary

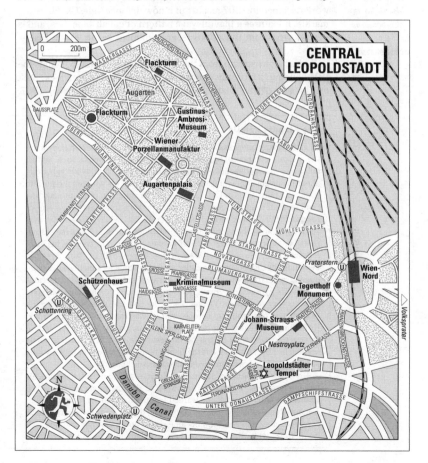

Leopoldstadt, beyond the **Johann Strauss-Museum**, and, perhaps, the collection of sculptures in the **Gustinus Ambrosi-Museum**. And if Meissen porcelain is your thing, the Augarten **Porzellan-manufaktur** will not disappoint.

The Danube Canal

The **Danube Canal** (Donaukanal), which separates Leopoldstadt from the old town, is the narrowest of the four arms of the River Danube. As the channel nearest to the city, this was the first section of the Danube to be regulated, as far back as 1598. Despite its human proportions, its banks are by no means pretty, having been an easy target for bombs during World War II. The only building of note is Otto Wagner's dinky **Schützenhaus** (literally "defence tower"), on the embankment below Obere Donaustrasse, a late work designed in 1907 as part of a now defunct weir. Clad in white marble, it features a playful wave pattern of cobalt-blue tiles, and is best viewed from the opposite embankment below Franz-Josefs-Kai.

*The nearest
U-Bahn for the
Schützenhaus
is
Schottenring.*

Further downstream from the Schützenhaus, at no. 95, stands the IBM building, a typically unimaginative corporate office block, built on the site of the Diana Rooms, where, on February 15, 1867,

---

The Strauss Family

Of all the many tunes associated with Vienna, perhaps the best known are the waltzes composed by the Strausses. Born in Vienna to a Jewish innkeeper in Leopoldstadt, Johann Strauss the Elder (1804–49) kept quiet about his origins, though it was the Nazis themselves who felt the need to falsify the parish register of Vienna's Stephansdom, in order to make the Strauss family appear as true Aryans (a similar leniency was shown towards Hitler's much-loved composer Franz Léhar, whose wife was Jewish). Strauss began his career serenading diners in Viennese restaurants, along with the likes of Josef Lanner, who was to become his chief musical rival. However, it was in the dance hall of Zum Sperl in Leopoldstadt that Strauss the Elder made his name as a band leader, conducting a mixture of dances, orchestral phantasies and more serious music. His gypsy-like features, and wild, vigorous conducting style soon became very popular in Vienna. Later, he and his orchestra achieved a modicum of fame touring Europe, and he was eventually appointed k.k. Hofballmusikdirektor (Imperial-Royal Director of Music for Balls). Strauss's touring took its toll on domestic life, and he created a public scandal in 1842, when he left the family home and moved in with a young seamstress, who bore him several illegitimate children.

His eldest son, Johann Strauss the Younger (1825–99), followed in his father's footsteps, writing his first waltz at the age of six, though much against the latter's wishes (he wanted him to be a banker). It was, in fact, Johann's long-suffering mother, Anna, who directed her sons into musical careers. Father and son soon became rivals, both musically and political-ly. In 1848, while the Elder was busy conducting his famous *Radetzky*

Johann Strauss the Younger first performed the city's most famous signature tune, *An der schönen, blauen Donau*, known to the English-speaking world simply as *The Blue Danube*. A plaque by the building's entrance records the fact. What it doesn't tell you, however, is that the waltz was originally scored for male chorus, not orchestra, complete with ludicrous lyrics, and wasn't at all well received after its inept first performance. Only when Strauss took it to Paris, and performed it with an orchestra, did it become a stratospheric success.

Praterstrasse: Johann-Strauss-Museum

Johann Strauss the Younger lived on nearby **Praterstrasse**, once a majestic boulevard, peppered with Yiddish theatres, leading to the Prater, now just a busy, wide street with little to recommend it. At the far end of Praterstrasse, nearest the Prater, stands the splendid **Tegetthoff Monument**, a tall rostral column, complete with frolicking sea horses and topped by a statue of Wilhelm von Tegetthoff himself, celebrating the rear admiral's 1866 naval victory over the Italians at the Battle of Lissa.

Fans of the "Waltz King", however, should head for the **Johann-Strauss-Museum** on the first floor of no. 54, where the composer

The Strauss-Museum is open Tues–Sun 9am–12.15pm & 1–4.30pm; öS25/€1.82; the nearest U-Bahn is Nestroyplatz.

March, the signature tune of the *ancien régime*, the Younger was composing stirring tunes such as the *Revolution March* and the *Song of the Barricades*. Fourteen years after his father's death, Strauss the Younger was appointed k.k. Hofballmusikdirektor in 1863, rapidly surpassing even his father's enormous fame. He was one of the world's first international celebrities, feted on both sides of the Atlantic. On one memorable occasion in Boston in the US, he conducted *The Blue Danube* with 20,000 singers, an orchestra of over 1000 and 20 assistant conductors, to an audience of more than 100,000. Johann's operetta, *Die Fledermaus*, written to take Viennese minds off the economic crash of 1873, was another huge success – by the end of the decade, it was playing in some 170 theatres.

Despite his success, Johann, a difficult character like his father, was something of an outsider. He was also constantly irked by his lack of acclaim among serious musical critics, and his several attempts at straight opera flopped. Again like his father, he too caused a scandal, divorcing his second wife, Lili, in order to marry his mistress Adele. As the Vatican would not annul his marriage, he was forced to convert to Lutheranism and become a citizen of Saxony, though he continued to live in Vienna until his death in 1899.

As for the remaining Strauss sons, Johann's two younger brothers, Josef – "the romantic-looking, chaotically pale" Strauss as he was dubbed by one Viennese critic – and Eduard, were also musicians (again against their absent father's wishes). Josef was a successful composer in his own right, but died at the age of forty-three, while Eduard became k.k. Hofballmusikdirektor after Johann in 1872 and was left in charge of the Strauss orchestra.

lived from 1863 until the death of his first wife, the singer Jetty Treffz, in 1878. In contrast to most of the city's musical museums, some attempt has been made here to recreate a period interior; one room, decorated with ceiling panels of cherubs, contains his grand piano, house organ and standing desk at which he used to compose. There's also a fascinating collection of ephemera from the balls of the day, with various gimmicky dance cards – one laid out in the form of a staircase – and quirky ball pendants, which were kept as a sort of memento of the evening.

Kriminalmuseum

*The Kriminal-
museum is
open
Tues–Sun
10am–5pm;
öS60/€4.36.*

Leopoldstadt's most popular museum is the **Kriminalmuseum** (Museum of Crime), a prurient overview of Vienna's most gruesome crimes, at Grosse Sperlgasse 24. In between the voyeuristic photos of autopsies, there are some interesting sections on the city's social and political history, though with labelling in German only, these are lost on most foreign visitors. To cap it all, there's a fairly gratuitous section on flagellation, while the biggest criminals of the lot – the Nazis – get only the very briefest of mentions. All in all, it's worth giving this museum a wide berth. A much more edifying museum on the same subject is the Foltermuseum (Torture Museum), described on p.194.

Augarten

*To get to the
Augarten, take
tram #31 two
stops from U-
Bahn
Schottenring.*

The **Augarten**, in the north of Leopoldstadt, is one of Vienna's oldest parks, laid out in formal French style in 1650, and opened to the public in 1775 by Josef II. Sadly, it's come down in the world since its fashionable halcyon days when Mozart gave morning concerts here, and, a century later, Strauss the Younger championed Wagner's overtures. Old-age pensioners are the park's main visitors now, and the melancholic air is further compounded by the forbidding presence of not one, but two World War II Flacktürme (see p.195). These sinister concrete hulks put the dampeners on the formal section of the park; the only way to escape them is to head off into the woody network of chesnut-lined paths to the north, home to numerous very tame red squirrels.

*The Gustinus-
Ambrosi-
Museum is
open
Tues–Sun
10am–5pm;
öS60/€4.36;
take tram #5
from U-Bahn
Praterstern.*

Hidden in this dense section of the park, by the eastern boundary, is the intriguing **Gustinus-Ambrosi-Museum**, a little-visited offshoot of the Österreichisches Galerie, which runs the Belvedere (the same ticket is valid for both). It's devoted to the prolific Austrian sculptor, Gustinus Ambrosi (1893–1975), whose larger works are clearly influenced by Auguste Rodin. However, Ambrosi is at his best with his bronze portrait heads, of which there are plenty here, his subjects drawn mainly from the artistic and political circles of the inter-war period. Note the emaciated Otto Wagner the year before his death, a suitably overblown Nietzsche, and a youthful Mussolini (with hair).

On the ruins of the Alte Favorita, Leopold I's summer palace, which was burnt to the ground by the Turks in 1683, Josef II erected a long, low-lying garden pavilion. From 1782, the pavilion's restaurant was the venue of the fashionable musical matinées conducted by the likes of Mozart and Beethoven; the building now serves as the headquarters of the **Wiener Porzellanmanufaktur** (*www.augarten.at*), founded in 1718, eight years after Meissen. The factory's famous "flower and figure" porcelain is exhibited in the Hofsilber- und Tafelkammer in the Hofburg (see p.99), though temporary exhibitions are also staged in the showroom foyer. The factory's current offerings – from gaudy Rococo to more subtle designs by the likes of Josef Hoffmann – are sold in the adjacent shop.

Central Leopoldstadt

The Porzellanmanufaktur is open Mon–Fri 9am–6pm, Sat 9.30am–noon; free.

The **Augartenpalais**, to the east of the Porzellanmanufaktur, was designed by Johann Bernhard Fischer von Erlach at the end of the seventeenth century, and bought by the Emperor Josef II in 1780. Unfortunately, you can't get a good look at the building, as it's now the boarding school of the Wiener Sängerknaben (Vienna Boys' Choir), for more on which see p.103. Those boys whose voices have broken are housed in the **Kaiser-Josef-Stöckl**, a pavilion hidden behind the palace, designed by Isidor Canevale in 1781 for Josef II, who preferred the Augarten above all his other residences.

The Augartenpalais is closed to the public.

Donauinsel and Kaisermühlen

In the second half of the nineteenth century, the main course of the River Danube was straightened to allow larger vessels to dock. A parallel channel, the slow-flowing Neue Donau, was cut in the 1970s, thus creating a long, thin, artificial island, officially known as the **Donauinsel**, though dubbed variously Spaghetti Island or Copa Cagrana (after the end station on the nearby U-Bahn line). The original course of the Danube, to the east of the Neue Donau, was simultaneously dammed to create the semi-circular nub of land known as **Kaisermühlen**, home to Vienna's UNO-City and the accompanying Donaupark. Neither deserves to top your itinerary, but each provides an interesting insight into modern Viennese life.

Donauinsel

To be perfectly honest, the **Donauinsel** – measuring 20km by just 200m – is pretty bleak, a situation not helped by the views over to the unsightly east bank. Nevertheless, the Viennese flock to the beaches here in the summer, when the island's numerous bars, discos and food stalls, centred around the Donauinsel U-Bahn station, open for custom. Joggers, skateboarders and cyclists also use the island, and every June it becomes the focus for the *Donauinselfest*, an open-air rock festival with fireworks organized by the Social Democrat Party (SPÖ). To the north, there's a huge watersports complex, Aquadrom,

There are two U-Bahn stations on the Donauinsel: Donauinsel in the centre, and Neue Donau, to the north.

with a 200m-long water slide, boat rental, windsurfing and the like. To the south, there are fixed barbecue spots, and a nudist beach (FKK).

Vienna International Centre and the Donaupark

*The nearest U-
Bahn is
Kaisermühlen-
Vienna
International
Centre.*

Since 1979, the **Vienna International Centre** (*www.unis.unvienna.org*) – known as VIC to its inmates, and UNO-City to the mapmakers – has been the United Nations' number-three base, after New York and Geneva. The idea for this was first mooted by the then UN Secretary General, Kurt Waldheim, and its construction nearly bankrupted the country. The UN functionaries, until then housed in the Hofburg, were none too happy either. Today, the VIC is home to, among other bureaucracies, the International Atomic Energy Authority, the Commission for Infectious Diseases, and the ever-busy High Commission for Refugees (UNHCR).

Of the 4000 folk employed here, only a third are Austrians, but the place is clearly an important source of income for the city, and has ensured Vienna a bit part on the international stage. The adjacent conference centre – the imaginatively named Austria Center Vienna – completed in 1987 at a cost of millions, has proved less of a money-spinner. However, whatever the financial benefits, UNO-City is not a beautiful place to visit. Within earshot of a roaring Autobahn, cordoned off with wire fencing, and bristling with armed police and

*There are
guided tours of
the VIC
Mon–Fri 11am
& 2pm;
öS50/€3.63.*

CCTV cameras, the whole place is intimidating and, essentially, ugly. The six Y-shaped, glass-fronted high-rise offices soar to a height of 110m, and radiate from a central block like a three-legged man on the run. The interior is generously sprinkled with works of art by contemporary Austrian artists, and you can sign up for a guided tour should you so wish; tours start from Checkpoint One (remember to take your passport).

It's with a certain amount of relief that you descend from the VIC to the adjacent **Donaupark**, laid out on an old rubbish dump in 1964 as part of the Vienna International Garden Show. The most pleasant section is around the artificial lake, Irissee, and in the rose garden and walled Chinese garden beyond. An added incentive for kids is the miniature railway, the **Kleinbahn**, which wends its way around the

*The
Donauturm is
open daily
April–Sept
9.30am–
midnight;
Oct–March
10am–10pm;
öS65/€4.72.*

park (round-trip öS40/€2.91). Overlooking the park is the futuristic **Donauturm** (Danube Tower; *www.donauturm.at*), which reaches a height of 252m. For a not insignificant sum, you can take the lift to the viewing platform, and for even more money, you can eat in one of the tower's two revolving restaurants. Clearly visible to the west, by the Danube, is Vienna's latest skyscraper, the **Millenniumstower**, a shiny double cylinder designed by Peichl, Podrecca & Weber that's 202m tall.

Chapter 8

Schönbrunn, the Wienerwald and the Zentralfriedhof

Vienna's outer suburbs or Vororte have little to recommend them for the most part. Until 1890, they lay beyond the city limits of the Gürtel, and since then have been ruthlessly built over in order to properly accommodate the city's population.

There are, of course, exceptions, the prime one being **Schönbrunn**, the Habsburgs' former summer residence to the west of the city centre, which is one of Vienna's most popular tourist sights after the Hofburg. The palace boasts some of the best Rococo interiors in central Europe, while the surrounding **Schlosspark** is home to the **Tiergarten**, Vienna's zoo, and the **Palmenhaus** (Palm House). To the west of the neighbouring villa district of **Hietzing** is the much wilder parkland of the **Lainzer Tiergarten**, a former royal hunting ground that's now a haven for wildlife.

The rest of the suburbs have a scattering of interesting museums and sights that call for a targeted approach, relying on the tram system to get you around. Vienna is very lucky to have the **Wienerwald** (Vienna Woods) on its doorstep, and a trip up to one of its forested hills is rewarded with glorious views over the entire city. Finally, there's the **Zentralfriedhof**, Vienna's truly awesome Central Cemetery, with a population almost twice that of the city itself, and featuring the graves of the likes of Beethoven, Schubert, Brahms, Schönberg and the Strauss family.

Schönbrunn

Compared with the hotchpotch that is the Hofburg, the Habsburgs' summer residence of **Schönbrunn** (*www.schoenbrunn.at*) is everything an imperial palace should be: grandiose, symmetrical and thor-

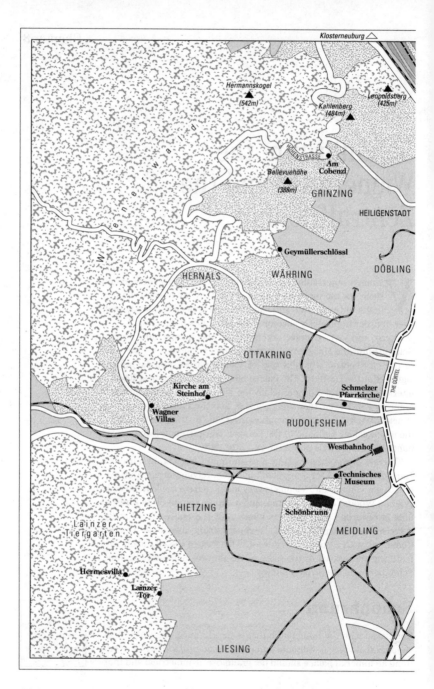

Hermannskogel
(542m)

Leopoldsberg
(425m)

Kahlenberg
(484m)

Am
Cobenzl

HÖHENSTRASSE

Bellevuehöhe
(388m)

GRINZING

HEILIGENSTADT

Geymüllerschlössl

WÄHRING

DÖBLING

HERNALS

ÖTTAKRING

Kirche am
Steinhof

Schmelzer
Pfarrkirche

THE GÜRTEL

Wagner
Villas

RUDOLFSHEIM

Westbahnhof

Technisches
Museum

HIETZING

Schönbrunn

MEIDLING

Lainzer
Tiergarten

Hermesvilla

Lainzer
Tor

LIESING

Wiener Wald

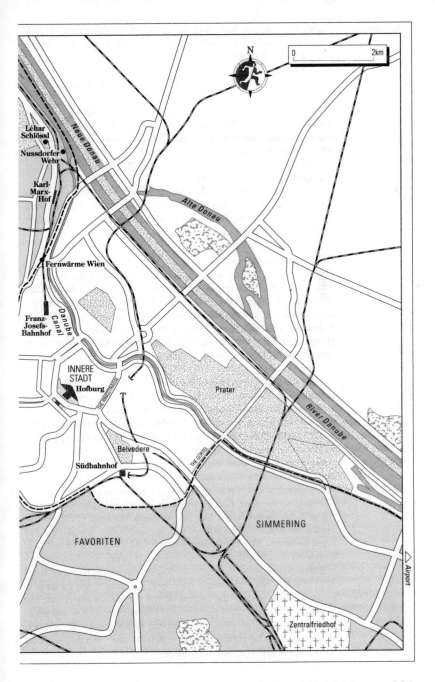

Schönbrunn

oughly intimidating. Built over the course of the eighteenth century, it contains nearly 1500 rooms, and, in its day, would have housed more than 1000 servants. However, while the sheer scale of the place is undeniably impressive, the building itself is something of an acquired taste, its plain facade painted a rather sickly mustard yellow.

The riches are inside, with its superb array of Baroque and Rococo **Prunkräume** (State Rooms), dating from the time of the Empress Maria Theresia, the first of the Habsburgs to make Schönbrunn the official imperial summer residence. There's also a fine collection of imperial carriages in the outbuilding of the **Wagenburg**, plus temporary exhibitions in the **Orangerie**.

In the **Schlosspark**, you'll find the **Tiergarten** (Zoo), far more uplifting than most inner-city zoos, and close by, the **Palmenhaus**. Last, but not least, there's the whole of the magnificent Schlosspark, and its follies, to explore.

Schönbrunn in history

Compared with the Hofburg, Schönbrunn has a short Habsburg history. It only came into imperial ownership in 1569, when **Maximilian II** (1564–76) bought the property – then known as Katterburg – close to what is now the Meidlinger Tor, as a hunting retreat. His son **Matthias** (1612–19) had the place rebuilt after marauding Hungarians laid it to waste in 1605, and it was he who discovered the natural spring, from which the name Schönbrunn (Beautiful Spring) derives.

After the Habsburgs themselves had destroyed the place in anticipation of the Turks in 1683, **Leopold I** (1657–1705) commissioned a new summer palace for his son and heir from Johann Bernhard Fischer von Erlach. The latter's initial plans envisaged a structure to rival Versailles, perched on top of the hill and approached by a series of grandiose terraces. In the end, a much more modest building was agreed upon, and work began in 1696. Enough was built to allow **Josef I** (1705–11) to occupy the central section, but construction was stymied by the War of the Spanish Succession (1701–14).

Josef I's successor, Karl VI, was only interested in pheasant-shooting at Schönbrunn, and it was left to **Maria Theresia** (1740–80) to create the palace and gardens that we see today. Employing her court architect, Nicolo Pacassi, she added an extra floor to the main palace, to accommodate her ever increasing family, and had the interior transformed into a sumptuous Rococo residence. Her son, **Josef II** (1780–90), an enthusiastic gardener, rearranged the gardens in classical style, adding the largest of the garden's monuments, the Gloriette triumphal arch, and growing his own tea, coffee and sugar which he took great pleasure in serving to his guests. He did not, however, share his mother's love of Schönbrunn, and had much of the palace boarded up to save money.

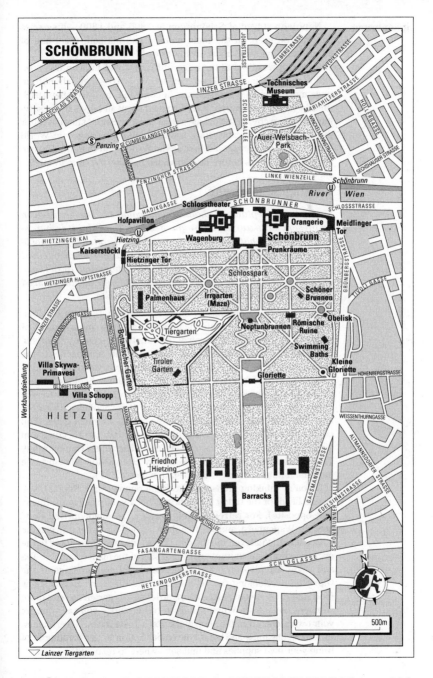

SCHÖNBRUNN

Technisches Museum

Auer-Welsbach-Park

Penzing

Schönbrunn
Wien

River

Schlosstheater SCHÖNBRUNNER

Hofpavillon

Hietzing

Wagenburg

Orangerie

Schönbrunn

Meidlinger Tor

Prunkräume

Kaiserstöckl

Hietzinger Tor

Schlosspark

Palmenhaus

Irrgarten (Maze)

Schöner Brunnen

Tiergarten

Neptunbrunnen

Römische Ruine

Obelisk

Villa Skywa-Primavesi

Tiroler Garten

Swimming Baths

Kleine Gloriette

Villa Schopp

Gloriette

Botanischer Garten

HIETZING

Werkbundsiedlung

Friedhof Hietzing

Barracks

N

0   500m

Lainzer Tiergarten

Napoleon stayed at Schönbrunn in 1805 and 1809 – his eagles can still be seen on the main gates – and his son, the Duke of Reichstadt, lived out most of his brief life here, too (see p.232). However, it wasn't until the reign of **Franz-Josef I** – who was born within the palace in 1830 and died here in 1916 – that Schönbrunn once more occupied centre stage in court life. In November 1918, the last of the Habsburgs, **Karl I**, signed away all hopes of preserving the monarchy, in the palace's Blue Chinese Salon, and thereafter the entire place became state property. Badly damaged in World War II, Schönbrunn served first as the Soviet, and then the British, army headquarters before being handed back to the state in 1947.

Visiting Schönbrunn

Surely this receptacle of abominations could not have existed in its present state during the reign of Maria Theresia. It is impossible to believe that one whose days may be counted by the noble and beautiful works with which she adorned her empire, could have passed to her imperial creation at Schönbrunn within reach of this black and noxious stream, and suffered its unhallowed waters to flow between the wind and her regality.

The comments by Anthony Trollope's mother in 1838 on the foul-smelling River Wien, which flowed past the main gates of Schönbrunn, were not atypical of nineteenth-century tourists. Though the river no longer stinks like it once did, approaches to the palace now suffer from a different kind of plague: the roar of traffic from the nearby Linke Wienzeile and Schönbrunner Schloss Strasse. Consequently, the best way to **get there** is to head straight for the Meidlinger Tor on Grünbergstrasse from U-Bahn Schönbrunn, rather than struggle along the multi-lane freeway to the main gates. You could also continue one stop further on the U-Bahn to Hietzing, and dive into the park via the Hietzinger Tor on Hietzinger Hauptstrasse. This enables you to peek at the nearby Hofpavillon Hietzing, the imperial family's private U-Bahn station (see p.237).

If you're thinking of visiting the Prunkräume (State Rooms), you should head for the **ticket office** first to book your place in the queue (see opposite). For **refreshments**, there's a reasonably priced *Beisl* near the Wagenburg, and a coffee shop beyond the ticket office in the palace itself. Whatever you do, don't be hoodwinked into going to the overpriced café–restaurant on the east side of the main courtyard. Tea and cakes are also on offer in the wonderful surroundings of the Gloriette, overlooking the Schlosspark, and there are usually a few food stalls in the main palace courtyard. The Tiergarten has still more eating options, from Würst stands to restaurants – you can even fix your own picnic from the shop in the zoo's Tirolerhaus. Nevertheless, by far the cheapest and most convenient option in fine weather is to bring your own supplies and find somewhere to relax in the park.

Prunkräume

Compared to the sterility of the Hofburg's state apartments, Schönbrunn's **Prunkräume** (State Rooms) are a positive visual feast. That said, not every room is worthy of close attention, so don't feel bad about walking briskly through some of them. Visits to the Prunkräume are carefully choreographed. First, you must make your way to the ticket office on the ground floor of the east wing. Here, you'll be allocated a visiting time; if the palace is busy, you may well have to wait several hours, in which case you should head off into the gardens, or visit one of Schönbrunn's other sights.

The Prunkräume are open daily: April–Oct 8.30am–5pm; Nov–March until 4.30pm.

There's a choice of two tours: the "Imperial Tour" (öS95/€6.90), which takes in 22 state rooms, and the "Grand Tour" (öS125/€9.08), which includes all 40 rooms open to the public. Even if you're no great fan of period interiors, it seems pointless to go on the "Imperial Tour", since it skips some of the palace's most magnificent Rococo delights. For both tours, you are given a hand-held audioguide in English, lasting 35 and 50 minutes respectively; for the "Grand Tour", you also get the option of paying extra for an hour-long tour with a guide (öS150/€10.90). The disadvantage of following a tour guide is that they give you the same, short space of time in each room, whether it's worth pausing in or not.

Emperor Franz-Josef I and Empress Elisabeth's apartments

Whichever tour you're on, the entrance is via the **Blauerstiege** (Blue Staircase) on the ground floor of the west wing. If you're on the "Imperial Tour", you'll miss the nine private apartments of Franz-Josef – no great loss, as anyone who's been to the Hofburg will tell you – entering at Elisabeth's Salon (see p.228).

For more on the Emperor Franz-Josef I, see p.96.

Visitors on the "Grand Tour", meanwhile, pass through the Guard Room into the **Billiard Room**, where, in Franz-Josef's day, those wishing for an audience with the emperor were made to wait. While kicking their heels, they could admire the paintings, but sadly weren't invited actually to play billiards. Audiences with the emperor were given in the **Nussbaumzimmer** (Walnut Room) next door, named after the wood used for the chairs and gilded Rococo panelling; even the chandelier is carved from wood (painted over with pure gold). A nasty brown hue lines the walls of the emperor's gloomy **Study**, where Franz-Josef spent much of the day stood over his desk, pedantically reading and signing thousands of official documents; on the wall is a portrait of the Empress Elisabeth at sixteen, when she was betrothed to Franz-Josef. Next is the widower's **Bedroom**, with the simple iron bed on which the emperor died on November 21, 1916, at the age of 86. Beside it stands Franz Matsch's reverential rendition of the scene.

Passing through several tiny rooms, where the emperor did his ablutions, you come to the imperial couple's **Bedroom**, decorated in time for their nuptials in 1854 with matching blue Lyon silk upholstery, and twin rosewood beds. Elisabeth managed to avoid consummating the marriage for the first two nights. The story goes that at family breakfast on the first morning, Elisabeth's crabby mother-in-law, the formidable Archduchess Sophie, asked her how well her son

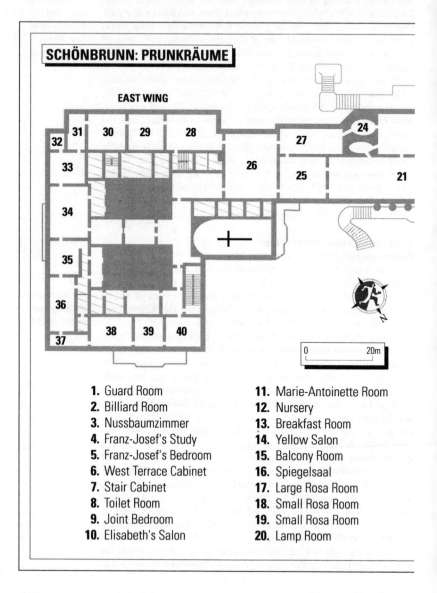

SCHÖNBRUNN: PRUNKRÄUME

EAST WING

1. Guard Room
2. Billiard Room
3. Nussbaumzimmer
4. Franz-Josef's Study
5. Franz-Josef's Bedroom
6. West Terrace Cabinet
7. Stair Cabinet
8. Toilet Room
9. Joint Bedroom
10. Elisabeth's Salon
11. Marie-Antoinette Room
12. Nursery
13. Breakfast Room
14. Yellow Salon
15. Balcony Room
16. Spiegelsaal
17. Large Rosa Room
18. Small Rosa Room
19. Small Rosa Room
20. Lamp Room

had performed in bed, at which the young bride broke down and wept. Though the empress dutifully produced a son and heir (Rudolf, who later committed suicide, see p.266), within five years she had fled the marital bed entirely, apart from a brief reconciliation in 1867, so it's unlikely Elisabeth spent many nights here.

Schönbrunn

Rooms Closed to the Public

21. Great Gallery	**31.** Porcelain Room
22. Little Gallery	**32.** Miniatures Room
23. Round Chinese Cabinet	**33.** Millions Room
24. Oval Chinese Cabinet	**34.** Gobelin Hall
25. Carousel Room	**35.** Memorial Room
26. Ceremonial Hall	**36.** Red Salon
27. Rössel Room	**37.** East Terrace Cabinet
28. Blue Chinese Salon	**38.** Maria Theresia's Bedroom
29. Vieux-Laque Room	**39.** Franz Karl's Study
30. Napoleon Room	**40.** Franz Karl's Salon

Schönbrunn

For more on the Empress Elisabeth, see p.240.

The Empress Elisabeth's personal apartments, which begin with her **Salon**, smack even less of her personality than those in the Hofburg – hardly surprising since she spent so little time here. The decor, in fact, mostly dates from the time of the Empress **Maria Theresia**, a century or so earlier, and the walls of the next three rooms – the Marie Antoinette Room, the Nursery and the Yellow Salon – are lined with portraits of the empress's numerous offspring. Her father, Karl VI, failed to produce a male heir, leaving Maria Theresia with an uphill struggle to convince the rest of Europe she was "man" enough for the job. She herself was determined to produce a good cropful of heirs – after the birth of her fourth child, she was heard to comment "I wish I were already in the sixth month of a new pregnancy". Out of her sixteen children, nine survived to adulthood.

Two of her sons went on to become emperors, Josef II and Leopold II, but the most famous of the lot was her youngest daughter, **Marie Antoinette**, who married Louis XVI and followed him to the guillotine in 1793. Under her portrait in the Nursery, to the right of the door to the Empress Zita's private bathroom, is the only piece of furniture sent back to Vienna by the French after her execution. Off the Empire-style Yellow Salon lies the intimate **Breakfast Room**, a frothy Rococo concoction decorated with gilded cartouches containing floral silk embroidered by Maria Theresia and her daughters.

The state apartments

The first of the more elaborate state apartments is the **Spiegelsaal** (Mirror Hall), where, in 1762, the precocious seven-year-old Mozart performed a duet with his older sister Nannerl, in the presence of the Empress Maria Theresia and family, and famously "sprang on the lap of the empress, put his arms round her neck and vigorously kissed her", according to his father. From here you enter the **Large Rosa Room**, named for the idealized landscapes executed by the Polish court painter Josef Rosa in the 1760s, set into gilded frames on the walls.

The **Great Gallery** is, without doubt, the most splendid of all the rooms so far, a vast long hall, heavy with gilded stucco embellishments, lined with fluted pilasters sporting acanthus capitals and originally lit by over 4000 candles. Of the three ceiling frescoes by Guglielmo Guglielmi glorifying the Habsburgs, the last – depicting Austria's military prowess – was, ironically enough, destroyed by bomb damage in World War II, and is therefore a copy. Naturally, the hall was used for banquets during the Congress of Vienna in 1815, and it was here, in 1961, that J. F. Kennedy and Nikita Krushchev held their historic détente meeting.

It's worth venturing from here into the **Little Gallery**, which lies through the three arches to the south of the Great Gallery, to take a peek at the two chinoiserie rooms – one round, one oval – to either side. The parquet flooring is sublime, but it's the oriental lacquer panels set into the wainscoting, and the numerous pieces of blue-and-white Chinese porcelain, that give the rooms their names. Of the two, the **Round Chinese Cabinet** is the most renowned, as this was where Maria Theresia used to hold her secret meetings with, among others, her chief adviser, Prince Kaunitz, whose apartments were linked to the room by a spiral staircase hidden behind one of the doors in the panelling. Another quirky feature of the room was the table designed to rise up through the floor, laden with food and drink, allowing the empress to dine without the need of servants, who might otherwise eavesdrop on matters of state. Kaunitz himself was particularly fond of food, and his table manners were legendary; on one memorable occasion, he "treated the company with the cleaning of his gums, a nauseous operation which lasted a prodigious long time and was accompanied with all manner of noises."

At the far end of the Great Gallery, you must pass through the **Carousel Room**, which gets its name from the painting of the special ladies' tournament held in the Winter Reitschule in 1743 (the sleighs used can be viewed in the Wagenburg). The final room for those on the "Imperial Tour" is the **Ceremonial Hall**, displaying five large paintings by pupils of the court painter, Martin van Meytens. The majority are concerned with recording the elaborate festivities which accompanied the wedding of Maria Theresia's eldest son, Josef II, to Isabella of Parma, in 1760. The magnifying glass, over one section of the painting of the wedding's opera performance, helps you pick out Mozart and his father from the crowd, though the family didn't, in fact, arrive in Vienna until two years after the event.

It was in the beautiful surroundings of the **Blue Chinese Salon**, on November 11, 1918, that the last Habsburg Emperor Karl I signed the document renouncing "all participation in the affairs of state". (He refused formally to abdicate or to renounce his claim to the throne, and made two unsuccessful attempts to regain the Hungarian half of his title in 1921, before dying in exile on Madeira the following year). As the name suggests, the room is another chinoiserie affair – all the rage in the eighteenth century – lined with yellow wallpaper, hand-painted on rice paper, and inset with serene scenes of Chinese life on a deep blue background.

The audience rooms

The lightness of the Blue Chinese Room is in complete contrast to the oppressively opulent **Vieux-Laque Room**, with its black and gold lacquer panels, exquisite parquetry and walnut wainscoting. During his two sojourns at Schönbrunn, Napoleon is thought to have slept in the neighbouring walnut-panelled **Napoleon Room**, lined with Brussels tapestries depicting the Austrian army in Italy. It was also

Empress Maria Theresia (1740–80)

In 1740, the Emperor Karl VI died suddenly, leaving no male heir. That the emperor's daughter, **Maria Theresia**, was able to ascend the throne was thanks to the Pragmatic Sanction of 1713 passed by her father granting her the right of inheritance. But as she herself put it, "I found myself without money, without credit, without an army, without experience and knowledge, even without counsel, because all my ministers were wholly occupied in trying to discover which way the cat was going to jump". Despite this inauspicious beginning, she surprised her male entourage by surviving against the odds, no thanks to her husband, Franz Stephan, who was good at fencing, hunting, shooting and womanizing, but unfortunately not much else.

Throughout Europe she was known as the "Virgin Empress", though with sixteen children to her name, she clearly wasn't in the literal sense. She was, however, out of step with the promiscuity of the period. Jesuit-educated and deeply pious, she insisted, much to her husband's discomfort, that they share a marital bed (this was by no means the usual custom). It was partly her husband's extra-marital activities that prompted her to set up the **Chastity Commission** in the autumn of 1747. Its commissioners were empowered to search houses, and to arrest any man found entertaining an opera singer, dancer or any other woman of presumed loose morals; offending ladies could be locked up in a convent or banished from the realm. Though in the end the commission fizzled out after just six months, it caused a certain amount of havoc – several acting troupes fell foul of the commission, as did Casanova himself, and one of the most celebrated sopranos of the day, Santini, who was escorted to the Venetian border.

here that Maria Theresia is thought to have given birth to her brood, and that Napoleon's son by the Archduchess Maria Louisa died in 1832, aged just 21 (see p.232).

Despite its name, only three items in the remarkable **Porcelain Room**, designed by Isabella of Parma, are actually genuine Meissen porcelain: the chandeliers, the clock and the wall bracket. The rest of the decor is carved from wood and painted over in blue and white to appear like porcelain. The delicate ink drawings set into the walls are signed works by Empress Maria Theresia's daughters, copied from French originals.

The most precious of all the rooms in Schönbrunn is the **Millions Room**, so called because it's estimated that Maria Theresia paid over a million silver florins to have it decorated. Unfortunately the most priceless items in the room – the miniature seventeenth-century Persian watercolours of life in the Moghul court – are somewhat overwhelmed by the surrounding, richly gilded cartouches set into the Caribbean rosewood panelling. Just off the Millions Room is the handy little breakfast room, known as the **Miniatures Room**, containing more works by the talented archduchesses. Next door in the **Gobelin Hall** are yet more Brussels tapestries, not only deco-

Like her son, Josef II (see p.104), Maria Theresia was a keen reformer, establishing one of the best education systems in Europe at the time, with compulsory education for both sexes. However, she was no liberal, holding notoriously rabid anti-Semitic views. Though Vienna had barely 500 Jews, the empress considered them to be an abomination, eventually expelling them all from the city in 1777, stating: "I know no worse public plague than this people, with their swindling, usury, and money-making, bringing people to beggary, practising all evil transactions which an honest man abhors; they are therefore to be kept away from here and avoided as far as possible." Normally, she would only communicate with them from behind a screen, though she happily used their money to help build Schönbrunn, and made an exception of the baptized Jew Josef von Sonnenfels, who was one of her chief advisors.

Though Maria Theresia acquired a fun-loving reputation early in her reign, playing cards and dancing until all hours, her demeanour changed after the unexpected death of her husband on August 18, 1765. Thereafter she went into perpetual mourning, cutting her hair short, and wearing no jewellery or make-up. For the next thirty years, she is supposed to have heard Mass every day in the Kaisergruft at the foot of the sepulchre containing her dead husband, spending every 18th of the month and the whole of August in silent prayer. On Franz Stephan's death, she immediately appointed Josef co-regent, and pretty much left him to take over the day-to-day running of the state. In her old age, she grew so large she found it hard to walk and rarely left Schönbrunn at all. She had difficulty breathing, and would keep the windows at the palace constantly open, though the wind and rain which came in gave her terrible rheumatism, and prevented her from writing the sackful of letters she usually winged off to her children.

rating the walls but also upholstering the six chairs, which depict the twelve months. Tapestries were a status symbol, partly because they were so labour-intensive, and therefore very expensive; the central tapestry in this room took eight people twelve years to complete.

The **Memorial Room** is dedicated to Napoleon's son, known as "L'Aiglon" (The Little Eagle), who was kept a virtual prisoner in Schönbrunn, the stuffed skylark on the table among his few companions. Passing quickly through the Red Salon, and the East Terrace Cabinet, with its trompe l'oeil fresco of cherubs "in an azure firmament", as the brochure puts it, you reach **Maria Theresia's Bedroom**. The empress never actually slept in the red velvet and gold-embroidered four-poster bed, which was brought here from the Hofburg. Instead, the room was used exclusively for levées – a kind of official breakfast-in-bed – during her frequent pregnancies. This was also the modest little room in which Franz-Josef was born in 1830.

The last two rooms of the "Grand Tour" are those used by the **Archduke Franz Karl** (Franz-Josef's epileptic father) and his wife, the Archduchess Sophie, decked out in the usual red-damask and white panelling, and stuffed full of Habsburg portraits, including several by Martin van Meytens. The only items of note are the miniatures in Franz Karl's Study, to the right of the window, by Maria Christina – Maria Theresia's favourite daughter who was also the lover of Josef II's wife, Isabella of Parma. After Isabella's death from smallpox, Maria Christina went on to marry Albrecht of Saxony-Tetschen, with whom she helped found the Albertina (see p.112).

The Berglzimmer are open for special exhibitions or by appointment; phone ☎811 13.

Berglzimmer

The **Berglzimmer**, on the ground floor of the palace's east wing, are only occasionally open to the public during special exhibitions, though if you're really keen to see them, you can phone and make an appointment. They consist of four, relatively informal, though highly decorated rooms, dating from the reign of Maria Theresia, all of which look out onto the Schlosspark. The colourful floor-to-ceiling frescoes feature an abundance of exotic flora, fauna and trompe l'oeil trelliswork, and are the work of the Bohemian painter, Johann Wenzel Bergl, after whom the rooms are now named. Don't miss the wonderful gilded Baroque stove in the shape of a tree trunk, with birds and animals frolicking on it.

L'Aiglon

When Napoleon's only son was born in 1811 to his second wife, Archduchess Maria Louisa, daughter of Franz I, he was destined to inherit a vast empire. Just four years later, in a futile gesture shortly after Waterloo, Napoleon abdicated and proclaimed his infant son Emperor of France in his place, saying: "I would rather my son were strangled than see him brought up as an Austrian prince in Vienna". It was, however, too late for Napoleon to have any say in the destiny of **L'Aiglon** or the "Little Eagle", as his son, Franz Karl Josef, was known. Maria Louisa had already returned to Vienna with Franz Karl during Napoleon's exile to Elba, and went on to marry a dashing cavalry officer called Count Neipperg, who was granted the Duchy of Parma.

Franz Karl, or "der kleine Napoleon", as the Viennese dubbed him, was left, orphaned, in Schönbrunn and given precisely the Habsburg aristocratic upbringing his father had dreaded. Abandoned by his parents, the little boy enjoyed a privileged, but lonely childhood: his language of instruction was switched to German, all reminders of his past life, including toys, were removed. As Napoleon's son, he had been declared King of Rome, but under the Habsburgs, who had no use for him at all, he was given the title Duke of Reichstadt, a duchy that didn't in fact exist.

Franz Karl's health deteriorated badly from 1830 onwards, and by the winter of the following year he was seriously ill. He was prevented from moving to a drier climate, or even to the Habsburgs' favourite spa of Bad Ischl. He died at the age of 21 in the same room his father had slept in during his stay at Schönbrunn. Rumour had it that he had been poisoned by Prince Metternich, who saw him as a political embarrassment; others alleged that he had overindulged in sex; tuberculosis seems the most likely cause.

The outbuildings

With two exceptions (the Orangerie and the Wagenburg), the majority of the yellowy outbuildings that radiate from the main palace at Schönbrunn are closed to the public. A few, like the small Baroque **Schlosskapelle** in the ground floor east wing close to the ticket office, have limited opening hours (Sun 8–11am). The ornate **Schlosstheater**, built in 1747 by Pacassi on the west side of the main courtyard, is open only occasionally for summer performances by the Kammeroper (*www.austriaculture.net/vienotheropera1615 .html*) or the Marionettentheater (*www.marionettentheater.at*); pick up a leaflet in the main ticket office.

The vast **Orangerie**, to the east of the palace, is used for temporary exhibitions, usually on an appropriately imperial theme, for which there is an additional charge. Aside from this, by far the most rewarding of the outbuildings is the **Wagenburg**, housed in the former winter riding school to the west of the palace.

Wagenburg

The main exhibition space of the **Wagenburg** is crowded with nineteenth-century carriages, which are of limited interest to the non-specialist. The best thing to do is pass quickly to the far end of the hall, where, below the gallery, there's an odd assortment of carriages and sleighs used to transport the imperial offspring. The most poignant is the phaeton designed for Napoleon's son, "L'Aiglon" (The Little Eagle), with mudguards in the shape of eagles' wings; the bees that decorate the sides of the carriage were the Bonaparte family symbol.

The Wagenburg is open April–Oct daily 9am–6pm; Nov–March Tues–Sun 10am–4pm; öS60/€4.36.

The highlights of the collection, though, lie beyond the gallery, where you'll find the Baroque and Rococo carriages of the Habsburgs. The most outrageous is the enormously long **coronation carriage of Franz Stephan**, Maria Theresia's husband, dripping with gold-plating, and fitted with windows of Venetian glass. The painted panels were added in time for the coronation of Josef II as Holy Roman Emperor in 1764. The whole thing weighs an incredible 4000kg, every kilo of it taken to pieces and transported on several occasions for coronations in Budapest, Frankfurt and Milan. Check out the wonderful horses' harnesses, too, embroidered in red velvet and gold, and the horses' plumes of ostrich feathers.

The equally ornate carriage opposite, painted entirely in black, was used during oath fealty ceremonies for the new emperor, which coincided with periods of official mourning for the previous incumbent. The relatively modest **red-leather litter,** which stands close by, studded with over 11,000 gold-plated nails and buckles, is also worth a look. Originally built for long-distance travelling, to be carried by horses or mules, it was used, after 1705, solely for transporting the Archduke of Austria's hat from Klosterneuburg to Vienna and back for oath fealty ceremonies.

The richly carved, gold-plated carousel or **racing sleigh of Maria Theresia** is the sole survivor of a whole set built in the shape of giant scallops for the special ladies' tournament held in the Winter Reitschule in 1743; note the sleigh bells on the horses' mane decoration. Sleighs were frequently used during *Fasching* for rides in the parks and on the *glacis* outside the city walls. The wheels, on hand in case there was no snow, would be removed and the sleighs pulled by horses, steered by drivers who sat in the back seats and controlled the reins over the heads of the seated ladies.

The gallery is the place to head for if you've a yen to see the Empress Elisabeth's horsewhip, with a photo of her husband set into the ivory handle, or the hoof of the horse used by the Emperor Franz-Josef I during his coronation as King of Hungary in 1867.

Schlosspark

The park is open daily 6am–dusk; free.

Even if you've no interest at all in visiting the interior of Schönbrunn, it's worth coming out here to enjoy the glorious **Schlosspark**, concealed behind the palace. Like the Belvedere, the park is laid out across a sloping site ideal for the vistas and terraces beloved of Baroque landscape gardeners. Yet despite the formal French style of the gardens, originally executed in 1705 by Jean Trehet to Fischer von Erlach's design, there are also plenty of winding paths in the woods on the slopes to give a hint of wildness, the result of modifications made under Josef II's co-regency by Adriaen van Steckhoven and later Ferdinand Hetzendorf von Hohenberg. The latter was also responsible for the park's numerous architectural follies and features. Thanks to Josef II (see p.104), the Schlosspark was opened to the public as long ago as 1779.

The lower park

The lower section of the Schlosspark is laid out in the formal French style, with closely cropped trees and yew hedges forming an intricate network of gravel paths. If you're approaching from the palace, however, the first thing that strikes you is the central axis of the **parterre**, decorated with carefully regimented flower beds, leading to the Neptunbrunnen and, beyond, to the triumphal colonnaded arch of the Gloriette. Along the edges are just some of the park's tally of stone statues, more of which lie concealed in the lower section of the park.

The theatrical **Neptunbrunnen** (Neptune Fountain) itself, erected in 1781 at the foot of the hill rising up to the Gloriette, is by no means upstaged by its grand setting. In it, the eponymous sea god presides over a vast array of wild sea creatures and writhing Tritons and Naiads attempting to break in their sea-horses. Kneeling below Neptune, Thetis pleads with the sea god for calm seas to speed her son Achilles to Troy.

Hidden among the foliage to the east of the Neptunbrunnen are some of Hetzendorf's architectural follies. Particularly fine are the

Römische Ruine (Roman Ruins), designed to tickle the imperial fancy of the Habsburgs. The idea was that these were the remains of some Corinthian palace – they were, in fact, taken from the Schloss Neugebäude (see p.261) – whose fallen stones now provide a watery retreat for a couple of river gods. The ruins were built as a stage set for open-air concerts and theatre, a tradition that continues to this day, in August and September (contact the tourist office or Kammeroper for information). Close by the ruins is the outlet of the original **Schöner Brunnen**, a small grotto pavilion in which the nymph, Egeria, dispenses mineral water from a stone pitcher into a giant scallop basin.

Further east still stands an **Obelisk**, smothered in hieroglyphs glorifying the Habsburgs, topped by an eagle and an orb, and supported at the base by four, originally gilded, long-suffering turtles. Below the obelisk is a giant cascade of grottos, and a pond inhabited by yet more river gods. Up the hill, past Schönbrunn's municipal swimming baths, stands the **Kleine Gloriette** hidden among the trees. The imperial family used to breakfast here in fine weather, but despite its name, it's nothing like its larger namesake, and not worth bothering with. The real reason to explore this heavily wooded part of the park is to look for **woodpeckers**: Great Spotted and Green Woodpeckers are the most common, though you may be lucky and spot a Middle Spotted or Grey-headed Woodpecker.

The Gloriette

If you do nothing else in the Schlosspark, you should make the effort to climb up the zig-zag paths from the parterre to admire the triumphal **Gloriette**, and, of course, the view. Designed in Neoclassical style by Hetzendorf to celebrate the victory of the Habsburgs over the Prussians at the 1757 Battle of Kolín, the Gloriette stands at the focal point of the entire park, where Fischer von Erlach originally intended to build Schönbrunn itself. One eighteenth-century visitor found the whole thing a bit *de trop*, describing it as a "long portico-kind of building, as ugly as possible". It's certainly an overblown affair, its central arch flanked by open colonnades of almost equal stature, and surmounted by trophies and an enormous eagle, wings outstretched; yet more colossal trophies, guarded by lions, stand at either end of the colonnades. The central trio of arches have recently been enclosed to form a swanky café, from which – if you can get a window table – you can enjoy the view down to the palace. Alternatively, you can climb to the top of the colonnades and take in the scene from there.

The Gloriette café is open daily 9am to dusk.

Tiergarten

A substantial segment of the palace gardens is taken up by the **Tiergarten** (Zoo; *www.tiergarten.at*), which, originating in the royal menagerie founded by Franz Stephan back in 1752, is the

Schönbrunn

The zoo is open daily: Feb 9am–5pm; March & Oct 9am–5.30pm; April 9am–6pm; May–Sept 9am–6.30pm; Nov–Jan 9am–4.30pm; öS95/€6.90.

world's oldest zoo. Here, the imperial couple would breakfast among the animals, in the octagonal pavilion designed for them by Jean-Nicholas Jadot, and decorated with frescoes by Guglielmi depicting Ovid's *Metamorphoses*. The pavilion has miraculously survived to this day – and is now a very good restaurant – along with several of the original Baroque animal houses, making this one of the most aesthetically pleasing zoos any captive animal could hope for.

There are three **entrances** to the Tiergarten: the main entrance closest to Hietzing; the Neptunbrunnen entrance; and the Tirolergarten entrance up in the woods to the south.

Once inside, you'll find all the usual attractions – elephants, tigers, lions, giraffes, zebras, penguins, camels, monkeys – plus a few less common inhabitants such as beavers, wolves, polar bears and giant tortoises. Kids can get a bit closer to the more benign animals at the *Streichelzoo* (literally "stroking zoo"), but the nicest feature of the zoo, by far, is the **Tirolergarten**, on whose woody slopes perches a wonderfully large timber-framed farmhouse from the Tyrol. The original Tirolergarten was the dreamchild of the Archduke Johann, younger brother of Franz II, who was fond of the Alps, and commissioned two Tyrolean houses and an alpine garden, in which the imperial family could dispense with the formalities of court life and "get back to nature". Sheep, cows and horses occupy the lower floors of the farm, while upstairs there's an exhibition on the history of the building. If you're short of provisions, or just a glutton, check out the traditional Tyrolese soup, bread, cheese and cold meats in the farmhouse kitchen/shop.

Palmenhaus and the Botanischer Garten

The Palmenhaus is open daily: May–Sept 9.30am–6pm; Oct–April until 5pm; öS45/€3.28.

While its claim to be the largest greenhouse in the world, when it opened in 1882, may well be suspect, the Schönbrunn **Palmenhaus** is certainly one of the most handsome, with its gracefully undulating wrought-iron frame. Inside, three climate-controlled rooms each have a glorious canopy of palm trees and lots of rhododendrons, lilies, hydrangeas and begonias to provide a splash of colour below. Schönbrunn also boasts a new hedge maze or **Irrgarten** (daily: April–Sept 9am–5.30pm; Oct 9am–4.30pm), close by the Neptunbrunnen, and a small **Botanischer Garten** of its own, established by Franz Stephan to the west of the Tiergarten, tucked away between the zoo and Maxingstrasse, and a beautiful place in which to escape from the crowds.

Hietzing

With the imperial family in residence at Schönbrunn for much of the summer, the neighbouring quarter of **Hietzing** – now Vienna's thirteenth district – had become a very fashionable suburb by the nineteenth century. Over the years, it has remained a favourite with

Vienna's wealthier denizens, and today boasts some of the city's finest villas, ranging from the Biedermeier summer residences beloved of the nobility, to the Jugendstil and modernist villas favoured by the more successful artists and businessmen of late-imperial Vienna. If you've a passing interest in architecture, you should check out the several villas within easy walking distance of Schönbrunn. The incumbents of the local cemetery also reflect the area's cachet, and include the likes of Gustav Klimt and Otto Wagner. In the far west of the district is the **Lainzer Tiergarten**, the former imperial hunting ground that is now a vast woody retreat for the hoi polloi.

Hofpavillon Hietzing

One sight in Hietzing which you shouldn't miss is the newly restored **Hofpavillon Hietzing**, a one-off, Jugendstil pavilion built on the initiative of Otto Wagner in 1899 for the exclusive use of the imperial family and guests whenever they took the Stadtbahn (as the U-Bahn was then known). On the palace side of the gleaming white pavilion, Wagner provided a graceful wrought-iron canopy topped with miniature gilded crowns, underneath which the imperial carriage could shelter. At the centre of the building's rectangular groundplan is an octagonal waiting room, where, "in order to shorten the seconds spent waiting by the monarch with the sight of a work of art", Wagner commissioned a painting by Carl Moll, giving an eagle's-eye-view of Vienna's Stadtbahn system. Wagner tried further to ingratiate himself with the Emperor Franz-Josef by decorating the interior with patterns formed out of the Empress Elisabeth's favourite plant, the split-leaved philodendron. Despite all Wagner's best efforts, however, the pavilion was used precisely twice by the emperor, who had a pathological distrust of all things modern. Now looking well preserved, if a little forlorn, beside the three-lane highway of Schönbrunner Schloss Strasse, the pavilion houses a small photographic exhibition of Wagner's other works (see p.142), and of the ornate *Kaiserzug* (imperial train) which the emperor used for his rides on the subway system.

The Hofpavillon is open Tues–Sun 1–4.30pm; öS25/€1.82; the nearest U-Bahn is Hietzing.

Hietzinger Hauptstrasse

On the whole, Hietzing is just a sleepy little suburb now, with little to remind the visitor of the social whirl that was a feature of the place in the nineteenth century. The *Café Dommayer*, on the corner of **Hietzinger Hauptstrasse**, is one of the few social institutions of the period to have survived (see p.315). It was here that Johann Strauss gave his first public concert in 1844, with a programme that included six of his own waltzes and one of his father's. Round the corner from the café, the enormous *Parkhotel Schönbrunn* (see p.298), built in 1907 for the emperor's personal guests, is another Hietzing landmark that's still going strong; the Kaiserstöckl, opposite, once the Foreign Minister's summer residence, is now the local post office.

Friedhof Hietzing

The **Friedhof Hietzing** can be a confusing place: not least because although it backs on to Schönbrunn's Schlosspark, the one and only entrance to the cemetery is on Maxingstrasse. And once you're inside, despite the map by the main gates, and the smallness of the graveyard, it's actually quite difficult to locate the tombs you want to see. Still, with perseverence, you should be able to find your way to Otto Wagner's rather pompous tomb from the early 1890s, designed by the architect himself, with some gloriously exuberant ironwork, but disappointingly devoid of even a hint of the Jugendstil motifs that became his later trademarks. Plans for a sarcophagus designed by Josef Hoffmann over Gustav Klimt's grave were never carried out, and a simple slab with gold lettering is all that marks the artist's resting place. Other notables buried here include Klimt's friend, the artist Kolo Moser; the Austro-fascist leader Engelbert Dollfuss, murdered by the Nazis in 1934; Franz Grillparzer, Austria's greatest nineteenth-century playwright; Katharina Schratt, the Emperor Franz-Josef's mistress; and Alban Berg, the composer, who died in 1935 after an insect sting led to septicemia.

The cemetery is open daily: March, April, Sept & Oct 8am–5pm; May–Aug until 6pm; Nov–Feb 9am–4pm; ten minutes' walk or two stops on bus #56B, #58B or #156B from Hietzing U-Bahn.

Hietzing's villas

A short stroll down Gloriettegasse immediately to the west of the Schlosspark gives a fair indication of the variety of architecture in Hietzing's villa-encrusted backstreets. Only fans of the international modern movement need continue their explorations further west to the Werkbundsiedlung; the rest can take tram #60 or #61 back to Hietzing U-Bahn, or continue west to the Lainzer Tiergarten.

Gloriettegasse

Your first port of call should be the modest Biedermeier villa at Gloriettegasse 9, with its delicate window pediments of necking swans, where Franz-Josef's mistress, the Burgtheater actress **Katharina Schratt**, used to live. It was procured for Ms Schratt by the emperor himself, so that he could pop in for breakfast at around 7am, to enjoy a bit of intimacy before continuing with his paperwork. "Do not get up too early tomorrow morning, I beg of you," he would write to her, "Allow me to come and sit on your bed. You know that nothing gives me greater pleasure." Afterwards they would go for a stroll in Schönbrunn, where onlookers would applaud the happy couple, who would regularly feed the remains of their imperial breakfast to the bears in the Tiergarten.

Turning right down Wattmanngasse to no. 29, brings you to an interesting terraced apartment block embellished by Ernst Lichtblau in 1914 with bands of majolica between the windows, depicting various quasi-medieval figures holding fruits and flowers. Back on Gloriettegasse, at no. 21, stands the **Villa Schopp**, a wonderful Jugendstil house designed in 1902 by Friedrich Ohmann, set back from the street behind curvaceous wrought-iron railings, and flanked by hefty gateposts topped by big, black-capped lamps. The house itself is in need of attention, but the stucco swags and floral flourishes on the facade are still impressive.

On the opposite side of the street, again set within its own grounds, is one of the most unusual of all Hietzing's villas, the **Villa Skywa-Primavesi**, at Gloriettegasse 14–16. Built in 1913–15 by Josef Hoffmann for the wealthy patrons of the Wiener Werkstätte, this is an almost obscenely large private house, designed in Neoclassical vein, with fluted pillars and huge triangular pediments. Nude miniatures perch on shelves at the tops of the pillars, while two larger figures recline in the pediments. Unfortunately, from the street, there's no way of seeing the bizarre, modern Teetempelchen (Little Tea Temple) Hoffmann built in the garden, complete with pergola and pond.

Adolf Loos and the Werkbundsiedlung

"Loos swept clear the path before us. It was a Homeric cleansing: precise, philosophical, logical. He has influenced the architectural destiny of us all," Le Corbusier effused in the 1930s. The building authorities were less enthusiastic in 1912 when planning permission was sought for Adolf Loos's first Hietzing commission, **Haus Scheu**, at Larochegasse 3, on the other side of Lainzer Strasse from Gloriettegasse. As with the infamous Loos Haus in the old town (see p.68), the architect's almost religious aversion to ornament provoked a hostile reaction, as did the building's asymmetry, caused by the series of west-facing terraces that give the house its "stepped" look. Loos completed four other houses in Hietzing alone – Villa Strasser, Kupelwiesergasse 28; Villa Rufer, Schliessmanngasse 11; Haus Steiner, St-Veit-Gasse 10; and the Wagonhaus (covered-wagon house), Haus Horner, at Nothartgasse 7, with its barrel-shaped roof – though they're widely dispersed across the district. The main frustration, however, when visiting Loos's houses is that it was in his use of the open-plan, and of in-built furniture, that Loos truly excelled – neither of which skills can be appreciated from his ornament-free exteriors.

A better bet for those in search of Bauhaus-style inspiration is to head for the **Werkbundsiedlung**, a model housing estate of seventy houses, situated towards the west end of Veitingergasse. It was laid out between 1930 and 1932 by the Socialist city council for an exhibition of the Wiener Werkbund, an association for the advancement of industrial design, inspired by a similar housing estate exhibition held at Stuttgart in 1927. Josef Frank was in overall control, inviting an international posse of modernists, including Adolf Loos and Josef Hoffmann, to take part. The emphasis was not on technical innova-

The Werkbundsiedlung is a short walk up Jagdschlossgasse from the terminus for trams #61 and #62.

Empress Elisabeth (1837–98)

The **Empress Elisabeth** was born into the eccentric Wittelsbach dynasty that produced the likes of "Mad" King Ludwig II of Bavaria, one of Elisabeth's cousins. She enjoyed a carefree, sheltered upbringing, only to find herself engaged to the Habsburg Emperor Franz-Josef I – another cousin – at the age of just fifteen, after an entirely public, two-day courtship. Franz-Josef was undoubtedly devoted to his new bride, but he was also in thrall to his mother, the Archduchess Sophie, who was a control freak obsessed with court ceremonial. She prevented Elisabeth from fulfilling her role either as empress or mother to her children, by hand-picking her ladies-in-waiting, and having the children removed from her care as soon as they were born. Later, Elisabeth advised her daughter, "marriage is an absurd institution. At the age of fifteen you are sold, you make a vow you do not understand, and you regret for thirty years or more that you cannot break it."

By 1860, having dutifully produced a male heir, Elisabeth developed a pathological aversion to the Viennese court, abandoning her children and husband and fleeing to Madeira for six months. She spent much of the rest of her lonely life travelling around Europe, under the pseudonym of Countess Hohenembs. She criss-crossed the continent, never staying in one place for long, and went on interminable cruises – she had an anchor tattooed on her shoulder – alarming her companions by asking to be tied down on deck during storms. She sought solace in fencing, hiking, riding – she was reckoned to be one of the finest horsewomen in Europe – and in the preservation of her beauty. When her cousin, King Ludwig, and then her only son Rudolf, committed suicide within a few years of each other, she became convinced that she too was mentally unstable. From then on, she dressed only in black, and carried a black fan that she used to hide the wrinkles that were beginning to appear on her face. As she herself put it "When we cannot be happy in the way that we desire there is nothing for it but to fall in love with our sorrows."

The similarities between Elisabeth's life and that of Princess Diana are difficult to ignore. Her marriage to Franz-Josef was the wedding of the century. The Emperor was marrying a virginal, "fairytale princess", whom he hardly knew, and, despite public appearances, the marriage was a dis-

tion, but on creating cheap, single-family houses using minimal space, Frank's "planned randomness" offering a more human alternative to the big housing projects of Red Vienna (see p.251). Fortunately, many of the houses are still owned by the council and were renovated in the 1980s, so the whole estate looks in pretty good shape. The most surprising thing about the whole project is how small the houses are, with miniature roads to match. Within the estate, at Woinovichgasse 32 (designed by Frank himself) there's a small documentation centre with information on the estate.

Egon Schiele in Hietzing

In 1912, the painter **Egon Schiele** rented a studio at Hietzinger Hauptstrasse 101, and, in between canvases, began flirting with the two respectable middle-class girls, Adele and Edith Harms, who lived aster. The issue of Franz-Josef and Elisabeth, like that of Charles and Diana, divided folk then, as it does historians and biographers now. Either Franz-Josef was a boorish, unimaginative prig, who visited brothels during their honeymoon, or Elisabeth was a frigid, neurotic, narcissistic brat, obsessed with her looks.

Like Diana, Elisabeth – or Sisi as she was and still is affectionately known – won over people's hearts with her beauty. Yet at the time many Viennese resented her frequent absences from the capital, and were appalled at her pro-Hungarian sentiments. She was fluent in Hungarian – she even wrote letters to the rest of the family in Hungarian – and was instrumental in the political compromise with Hungary in 1867. After a brief reconciliation between the imperial couple, which resulted in the birth of Marie Valerie, the only child Elisabeth was ever close to, Sisi and Franz-Josef remained irrevocably estranged. She even encouraged Franz-Josef to get a mistress, introducing him to the actress Katharina Schratt, "very much as a woman might put flowers into a room she felt to be dreary", as Rebecca West put it.

By 1897, Elisabeth's health began to deteriorate rapidly – a condition partly brought on by her anorexia – to the extent that she could barely walk. Despite her poor health, and her obsession with madness and death, few would have predicted her final demise. On September 10, 1898, the empress was assassinated by an Italian anarchist, Luigi Lucheni, on Lake Geneva. A local newspaper had unwisely announced the arrival of the empress, who was attempting to travel incognito. As she was about to board a steamer to go to tea with Baroness Rothschild, Lucheni rushed up and stabbed her in the heart with a sharpened file. Like the empress, Lucheni had also been wandering aimlessly around Europe, in his case looking for someone famous to kill. He was fixed on assassinating the Duke of Orléans, but when he failed to turn up in Geneva as planned, resolved to attack the Austrian empress instead. Naturally enough, thousands turned out for Sisi's funeral in Vienna; however unpopular she may have been, few would have wished her such a violent end. Over the years, her martyrdom has ensured that the myth and mystery around her life remain as compelling as ever.

opposite at no. 114. Edith and Schiele were ultimately married in 1915, and were expecting their first child when they were both killed in 1918 by the influenza that swept Europe following World War I, and which claimed more fatalities in Austria than had the war itself. Edith died first at their new studio flat at Wattmanngasse 6; Schiele succumbed three days later at his mother-in-law's house. Schiele is buried in the nearby **Friedhof Ober-St-Veit**, beneath a tombstone sculpted by the Hungarian Benjamin Ferenczy, commissioned by Schiele's friends on the tenth anniversary of his death.

To get to the Friedhof Ober-St-Veit, take bus #54B or #55B from Ober-St-Veit U-Bahn.

Lainzer Tiergarten

In the far west of Hietzing lies the former imperial hunting reserve of **Lainzer Tiergarten**, enclosed within a 25km-long wall by the

Emperor Josef II. Since 1923, however, the reserve has been the wildest of Vienna's public parks. With virtually no traffic allowed within the park boundaries, and no formal gardens at all, this is the place to head for in the summer if you want to leave the urban sprawl far behind. It may not boast the views of Wienerwald, but you're more likely to spot wildlife here, including wild boar, woodpeckers, wolves and, most easily, red squirrels and deer; in addition, the famous Lipizzaner horses of the Spanische Reitschule spend their summer holidays in the park.

The Lainzer Tor is open daily 8am–dusk; free; tram #60 or #61 from Hietzing U-Bahn to Hofwiesengasse, then fifteen minutes' walk or bus #60B down Hermesstrasse.

The park's chief sight, the **Hermesvilla** (see below), is just ten minutes' walk from the main gates of Lainzer Tor, at the end of Hermesstrasse. Unlike the rest of the park, this section of the Lainzer Tiergarten is open all year round. Those with more energy might aim for the **Huburtuswarte**, an 18m-high lookout tower at the top of Kaltbrundlberg (508m), beyond the Hermesvilla in the centre of the park. **Refreshments** are available in the Hermesvilla restaurant, and also from the *Rohrhaus* and the *Hirschgstemm*, both of which are signposted (with approximate walking times) from the Hermesvilla. Note that the St-Veiter Tor and the Adolfstor entrances, to the north of Lainzer Tor, are only open on Sundays and public holidays.

Hermesvilla

The Hermesvilla is open Tues–Sun: April–Sept 10am–6pm; Oct–March 9am–4.30pm; öS50/€3.63.

In 1882, in an effort to ingratiate himself with his estranged wife, the Emperor Franz-Josef decided to build Elisabeth an informal new residence, which she named **Hermesvilla** after her favourite Greek deity, the god of travel. Karl Hasenauer was employed to design the building, and Gustav Klimt and Hans Makart among those commissioned to decorate the interior; there was even a purpose-built exercise room in which the empress could indulge in her daily gymnastics. In the end, though, the villa failed to entice Elisabeth back to Vienna, and she stayed there only very occasionally. The house is now used to host exhibitions put on by the Historisches Museum der Stadt Wien. Even if the particular show doesn't grab you, the well-preserved interior is rewarding in itself, though there's little general information on the Hermesvilla's imperial days, nor anything specific on the Empress Elisabeth herself.

Less of a villa and more of a mini-chateau, the Hermesvilla is a rather sickly mixture of Renaissance and Baroque, surrounded by outbuildings linked by a wonderful parade of wrought-iron colonnades. Inside, the decor has that heavy, slightly sterile, strangely unweathered look common to Historicist architecture. Downstairs, the **Dining Hall** serves up rich helpings of marble and stucco, but the best stuff is preserved upstairs. Elisabeth's **Gym** is suitably decorated in Pompeiian style, with muscle men and lusty satyrs engaging in feats of strength. The **Empress's Bedroom** is smothered floor-to-ceiling in one of Makart's sumptuous trompe l'oeil frescoes depicting Elisabeth's favourite Shakespearean text, *A Midsummer Night's*

Dream, with Titania and Oberon in a chariot pulled by leopards. The
four-poster bed, with its oppressive double-headed eagle over the
headboard, would guarantee a disturbed night's sleep even in a
more balanced individual than Elisabeth. The central chamber, the so-
called **Kirchensaal**, is similarly overwrought, with gilded wood-pan-
elling and a shallow oval dome.

Further afield

The sights in this section are widely dispersed across the great
swathe of suburbs which stretch away north of Hietzing to the
Wienerwald. The first of the bunch, the **Technisches Museum**, is
within easy walking distance of Schönbrunn, but the others require
careful route-planning on the Viennese transport system. Of these,
the most rewarding destination is the **Kirche am Steinhof**, Otto
Wagner's Jugendstil masterpiece, high up on Baumgartner Höhe.
Two more **Wagner villas** can be admired in the leafy surroundings of
neighbouring Hütteldorf. There's a more brutalist piece of early
modern architecture, the **Schmelzer Pfarrkirche**, by the spiritual
godfather of post-modernism, Josip Plečnik, in the otherwise dour
suburb of Ottakring. Further north still, in Pötzleinsdorf, the city's
premier collection of Biedermeier furniture is housed in the peaceful
Geymüllerschlössl.

Technisches Museum

The **Technisches Museum** (*www.tmw.ac.at*), on the opposite side
of Auer-Welsbach-Park from the main gates of Schönbrunn, was
conceived in the last decade of Habsburg rule, and opened in 1918.
Having been closed for many years, the museum has recently
undergone a massive transformation and emerged as a truly innovative, hands-on museum, with just about enough English information to enable non-German speakers to enjoy the exhibits. Leave
yourself at least half a day to do the museum justice, and relax in
the knowledge that the café on the ground floor is relatively good
and inexpensive.

The museum's main entrance is down in the basement, where
you'll also find the **Concepts and Consequences** section, which
should teach you some basic scientific concepts from gravity to elec-
tromagnetics, while entertaining you at the same time – don't miss
the fog chamber at the far end. Also on this level is the interactive
Phenomena and Experiments gallery, where you can play at ani-
mation and doodle with a giant spirograph. Upstairs is the hangar-
like Main Hall, with an early aeroplane and a satellite suspended
above it. The **Heavy Industry** gallery, to one side, has a model of the
giant steelworks set up by the Nazis in Linz, where the Basic Oxygen
method of steel production first took place in 1952. The **Energy**

*The
Technisches
Museum is
open Mon–Wed,
Fri & Sat
10am–6pm,
Thurs
9am–8pm, Sun
10am–6pm;
öS120/€8.72;
the nearest U-
Bahn is
Schönbrunn or
you can take
tram #52 or
#58 from the
Westbahnhof.*

gallery on the other side is a lot more fun, however, especially the giant, wind-up energy contraption by the entrance.

At the time of going to press, few of the upstairs galleries had been fully refurbished, although the temporary exhibitions on the first floor are definitely worth investigating. The **Musical Instruments** section is a good place to go for a breather, as you can sit down at one of the listening stations and hear some organ, piano or harpsichord music. Those with small kids should head for the **Mini-TMW**, where 3–6-year-olds can romp around and have fun. The **Transport** section on the second floor is deservedly popular, boasting vintage cars by Porsche, Benz and Graf & Stift, plus a whole load of old bicycles, motorbikes, model ships, trams and trains. Look out, too, for the Austrian lighthouse from the Dalmatian coast, and the small section from Sisi's (see p.240) personal railway carriage.

Vienna's **IMAX cinema** (*www.imax-wien.at*) stands next door to the Technisches Museum, and has daily showings of the usual less-than-brilliant IMAX films, specially shot to show off the 180-degree projection system; tickets currently start at a hefty öS115/€8.36 for a forty-minute long film.

Kirche am Steinhof

Despite its limited opening hours, anyone with even a passing interest in Jugendstil architecture should make the effort to visit the **Kirche am Steinhof**, completed in 1907 by Otto Wagner as a chapel for the city's main psychiatric hospital. The church occupies a fantastic site on the commanding heights of the Baumgartner Höhe, looming over the hospital's grid-plan terraces below. In designing the building, Wagner clearly had the Karlskirche (see p.143) in the forefront of his mind: like the latter, the church is topped by a giant copper dome and lantern, both of which were originally gilded, and features two belfries capped with copper statues of seated saints; only Fischer von Erlach's columns are missing. Elements familiar from Wagner's other buildings are also evident, not least the marble veneer fixed onto the facade with copper bolts.

The Kirche am Steinhof is open for guided tours only Sat 3pm; öS40/€2.91; bus #47A from Unter-St-Veit U-Bahn.

Inside, the church is deliberately organized on a north–south axis, rather than the usual east–west configuration, in order to allow more light to stream through the glorious mosaic windows, designed by Kolo Moser. Hygiene and safety were obviously a major concern: continuously running holy water in the fonts, no sharp edges to the pews, a raked floor to improve sightlines and facilitate cleaning, and special doors flanking the altar to allow hospital staff rapid access to the patients in emergencies. The interior decor is light and simple, focused very much on the main altar with its eye-catching, cage-like gilt baldachin, against a backdrop mosaic featuring Christ at the top of a Hollywood-style staircase crowded with sundry saints. Sadly, the church is little used nowadays; it's too cold for services during the winter, and even in summer there are few takers among the patients.

Further afield

The guided tour – more of a static monologue really – is in German only, and is less than inspiring, so you're probably best off arriving at around 3.30pm, since it's only after the talk that you're allowed a brief wander around. Bear in mind, however, that bus #47A runs only every fifteen minutes, and it's another good ten-minute hike up the hill through the hospital grounds to the church itself.

Two Wagner villas

If you're fired with enthusiasm for Wagner's works, it's worth heading to the woody suburb of Hütteldorf, where two contrasting villas, built at either end of his career, stand side by side on Hüttelbergstrasse. **Villa Wagner I**, at no. 26, is an early work from 1888, designed in the style of a luxurious Palladian villa as the architect's very own out-of-town summer house. It's a grandiose building, typical of Wagner's Ringstrasse style (see p.122), with a central Ionic portico, flanked by two Doric pergolas. Badly damaged in World War II, the building was set to be destroyed by the council until, in 1968, a band of Austrian hippy artists, including Friedensreich Hundertwasser and Ernst Fuchs, protested by occupying the building. Fuchs, a purveyor of "fantasy-realism" from the *Judge Dredd* school of painting, eventually bought the property in 1972, and, since going into tax exile in Monaco, has turned it into the self-aggrandizing **Ernst-Fuchs-Privatmuseum**. Sadly, Wagner devotees come out of it worse off than Fuchs fans. The latter can lap up his lurid nudes and admire the rock 'n' roll decor; those hoping to see Wagner's work have to content themselves with the ceilings, and the left-hand pergola, which retains its vegetal, Jugendstil windows added in 1900. The psychedelic touches on the exterior, such as the multi-coloured cornice, are by Fuchs, though the wrought-ironwork is original. Fuchs is, naturally, responsible for the huge fertility goddess with decorated mammaries that fronts the building, and has also added his very own Gaudi-, not to say gaudy, style Nymphaeum fountain house in the garden.

To get to Wagner's villas, take tram #49 to its terminus, after which it's a ten-minute walk beside the Halterbach stream.

The Ernst-Fuchs-Privatmuseum is open by appointment Mon–Fri 10am–4pm; öS120/€8.72; phone ☎914 85 75-14.

Providing a perfect contrast to its neighbour is the cube-shaped **Villa Wagner II**, at no. 28, into which Wagner moved in 1913. It was to be his last work, and, with its austere, ornament-free facade, and its use of reinforced concrete and aluminium, conforms to his later conversion to rationalism and modernism. The exterior decoration is limited to a distinctive band of indigo-blue glass tiles alternating with aluminium bolts. Above the building's two entrances are the only other, gratuitous, decoration: the glass mosaic over the front door depicting Athene sporting her Gorgon's head shield, and the series of colourful, mythological mosaics, which also feature under the side portico.

The Villa Wagner II is closed to the public.

Schmelzer Pfarrkirche

Don't be put off by the brutal, concrete classicism of its exterior: the **Schmelzer Pfarrkirche**, designed by the Slovene architect Josip Plečnik on Herbststrasse in 1913, is one of Vienna's hidden suburban gems. As the city's first-ever concrete church, it caused huge controversy, provoking the Archduke Franz Ferdinand to pronounce it a ridiculous mixture "of a temple to Venus, a Russian bath, and a stable or hayloft". Despite such confusion, the main body of the church is surprisingly light and modern, while Otto Holub's Jugendstil high altar is simply outstanding. A dove flanked by two angels, all in aluminium low-relief, are framed against a semi-circular golden sunburst, in turn set off against a luxuriant gold and purple wall mosaic featuring the seven levitating attributes of the Holy Spirit, from *Frömigheit* (Piety) to *Gotesfurcht* (Fear of God).

To get to the Schmelzer Pfarrkirche, take tram #9 from Schweglerstrasse U-Bahn.

The church's *pièce de résistance*, however, is the concrete **crypt**, which you enter from stairs either side of the main altar; in order to see anything, you need to feed the light-meter with öS10. Several Jugendstil masterpieces brighten this gloomy underworld, with its low ceiling and trio of grottoes. On either side of the altar, murals feature Klimt-like celestial creatures: *Rachel Weeping for her Dead Children*, and *The Creation of Water*. Even more magical is the marble font, capped by a golden lid frothing with fish, out of which a heavenly figure rises up brandishing a cross.

Geymüllerschlössl

In the first decade of the early nineteenth century, the wealthy banker Johann Heinrich von Geymüller had a luxury summer house – known today as the **Geymüllerschlössl** (*www.mak.at*) – built in the sleepy village (now suburb) of Pötzleinsdorf. The Geymüllers were an archetypal wealthy Biedermeier family, *parvenu* business folk with bourgeois, artistic pretensions. Their house, so it was said, contained five grand pianos, one for each daughter; Franz Schubert and Franz Grillparzer were frequent visitors. It was at the Geymüllers' that Grillparzer fell in love with Katharina Fröhlich, a singer with "immense eyes, bottomless, really unfathomable"; they were engaged for a number of years, but in the end never married. Schubert, meanwhile, set one of Grillparzer's poems to music for a female quartet and alto solo, the serenade *Zögernd leise*, which was performed in the Geymüllers' garden one night as a surprise birthday treat for a friend of the family. Oddly, the house itself is no standard Biedermeier residence, but is, in fact, an exotic mixture of Gothic and Moorish elements executed by an unknown architect. It has the appeal of a garden folly, and the colour – white walls and green shutters – of an Italianate villa.

The Geymüllerschlössl museum is open March–Nov Thurs–Sun 10am–5pm; öS30/€2.18; take tram #41 to its terminus from Volksoper U-Bahn.

This building, so rich in Biedermeier associations, provides the best possible venue for the MAK's collection of **early nineteenth-**

century furniture, and its temporary Biedermeier exhibitions, which are staged on the ground floor. A beautiful cantilever staircase leads up to the suite of first-floor rooms, which house the **collection of clocks** bequeathed, along with the house in 1965, by Dr Franz Sobek, former director of the Austrian National Printing Works. The clocks – fascinating though they are – are a side-show to the overall effect of the painstakingly restored **Biedermeier decor**. Though the term evokes a certain dull conventionality, the artistry of the period (1815–48) connects with contemporary tastes thanks to its subtle, almost minimalist, approach, and its emphasis on inlaid detail, sparing use of gilding, smooth, polished surfaces and trompe l'oeil. The most startling room is the **Salon mit Panoramatapete**, a drawing room equipped with period furniture made from ebony and gold and upholstered in deep blue, and dominated by the panoramic murals of idealized, Oriental landscapes.

Given that the Geymüllerschlössl is something of a trek, it might be worth bringing a picnic to have in the house's extensive gardens; alternatively, you could pop across the road into the local *Heuriger*. Those with children might consider combining a trip out here with a visit to the nearby **Pötzleinsdorfer Schlosspark**, by the tram terminus, which has a big playground, red squirrel-infested woods, and a small farm with hens, goats, sheep and guinea fowl.

Further afield

The MAK is described on p.149.

For more on the district's Heurigen, see p.321.

Döbling and the Wienerwald

Over the last century, **Döbling**, once a little village to the north of Vienna's *Linienwall*, has gradually been subsumed into the city, and now gives its name to the vast nineteenth district which stretches right up into the **Wienerwald** or Vienna Woods. Though built-up in parts, the district is still peppered with vineyards and the remnants of old villages, making it a unique mixture of city and countryside. Tourists and locals alike flock here in the summer to drink the local wine in one of the district's numerous *Heurigen*, or to get some fresh air during a walk in the hills. Nearer town, there are a couple of places of pilgrimage devoted to Beethoven, which draw a fair sprinkling of tourists, as does Vienna's most famous housing estate, which remains a symbol of both the success and failure of inter-war "Red Vienna".

Oberdöbling

Döbling used to be, in fact, two separate villages: Unterdöbling and **Oberdöbling**. These lay just outside the *Linienwall* (now Gürtel), and were popular summer retreats for the wealthier denizens of Vienna in the days when they were surrounded by fields, gardens and vineyards. Nowadays, the two villages are mostly built-up, and only dedicated Beethoven fans will get much out of the district's chief sight, the **Eroicahaus**. If you're here at the weekend, however, it's worth paying a visit to the nearby **Villa Wertheimstein**, a rambling, *fin-de-siècle* house that once attracted the city's literati to its door.

Eroicahaus

*The
Eroicahaus is
open
Tues–Sun
9am–12.15pm
& 1–4.30pm;
öS25/€1.82;
take tram #37
to
Pokornygasse.*

In the summer of 1803, Beethoven took lodgings in a single-storey vintner's house – today's **Eroicahaus**, at Döblinger Hauptstrasse 92. Surrounded by gardens and vineyards, with a view across to Heiligenstadt, he grappled with the "heroic" concepts that would crystalize in his *Third Symphony*, the single most significant work of his entire life. Broadly speaking, until the emergence of this work, Beethoven was composing within the eighteenth-century tradition; with the *Third Symphony* Beethoven entered the age of Romantic complexity.

The inspiration for the piece was clearly Napoleon, whom Beethoven hoped would liberate Europe from "bigotry, police control and Habsburg-worship", as one biographer put it. He intended to dedicate the work to Napoleon, but, shortly after completing it, received news that the former First Consul had crowned himself Emperor. Beethoven flew into a rage, tore up the dedication, and renamed the symphony *Eroica*. In 1809, when Napoleon's artillery shelled Vienna, Beethoven hid under his kitchen table with a towel over his head, though this was probably less as a result of cowardice than in order to protect his poor hearing, which must have suffered terribly from the noise.

The rooms in which Beethoven lodged have been preserved, though the building's upper storey is a later addition. Despite the fact that the museum itself contains none of the composer's personal effects, you can get some idea of how the area looked in Beethoven's day from the contemporaneous maps and watercolours. All in all, notwithstanding the opportunity to listen to the *Eroica*, Beethoven fans would be better off visiting the composer's other memorial house in Heiligenstadt (see p.252).

Villa Wertheimstein

Just up the street from the Eroicahaus, at the end of a driveway, is a much more enjoyable house-museum, the **Villa Wertheimstein**, which doubles as the local museum or Döblinger Bezirksmuseum. Built in the 1830s by the silk manufacturer and patron of the arts Rudolf Arthaber, it was bought in 1870 by the wealthy Jewish financier Leopold von Wertheimstein, who was manager of the Vienna branch of the Rothschild bank. While the latter spent most of his time in the family's town house, his young wife, Josephine, stayed at the Döbling villa, presiding over one of the most celebrated *salons* in Vienna, along with her only daughter, Franziska. The pianist Artur Rubinstein played there on more than one occasion, while more frequent visitors included the artist Hans Makart, the philosopher Franz

*The Döblinger
Bezirks-
museum is
open Sat
3.30–6pm, Sun
10am–noon;
closed July &
Aug; free.*

Theodor Herzl (1860–1904)

Along with fascism, psychoanalysis and atonal music, Vienna can also be said to be the birthplace of **Zionism**. The idea of a Jewish state in Palestine emerged slowly from the mid-nineteenth century onwards, and was eventually coined as a term in 1893 by Nathan Birnbaum. However, it wasn't until **Theodor Herzl** published his seminal *Der Judenstaat* (The Jewish State) in 1896, that the movement really took off. Herzl spent his childhood in Budapest, but lived in the Austrian capital on and off for much of his adult life. He was buried in the Jewish cemetery in Döbling until after World War II when he was disinterred and reburied in Jerusalem. Yet despite his beatification by the modern state of Israel, it's not at all clear what Herzl would have thought about his current place of rest.

His family, though Jewish residents of Budapest, were thoroughly assimilated, politically liberal and culturally German. While at Vienna's university studying law, Herzl himself was something of a dandy, "dark, slim, always elegantly clothed", according to one contemporary. His true ambition was to be a playwright, or at a push, "a member of the Prussian nobility". Having failed on both counts, he became, instead, Paris correspondent of the *Neue Freie Presse*. Herzl had experienced anti-Semitism in Vienna, but nothing prepared him for the bigotry aroused during the trial of the Jewish army officer, Alfred Dreyfus, in 1893–94. During this period, Herzl toyed with the idea of challenging Vienna's leading anti-Semites to a duel; his other, equally mad-cap scheme, was to lead the Jews of Vienna into the Stephansdom for a mass conversion to Roman Catholicism, with the approval of the Pope.

Ironically enough, it was a performance of Wagner's *Tannhäuser* – in which the hero follows his heart rather than his head and returns to his spiritual homeland – that spurred Herzl into thinking about the creation of a new Jewish state, a utopian vision he later outlined in his most famous political pamphlet, *Der Judenstaat*, in 1896. Yet Herzl's new state was more of a liberal utopia than a specifically Jewish one. The principal inducement for his fellow Jews was to be the new state's seven-hour day (one less than the Socialist International promised to deliver); to drive the point home the flag was to feature seven gold stars. Yet he was no revolutionary, decrying "That a highly conservative people, like the Jews, have always been driven into the ranks of revolutionaries, is the most lamentable feature in the tragedy of our race."

Initially, he proposed that the European powers grant the Jews sovereignty over a slice of their colonial territories. He tried, but failed to elicit the support of the likes of the Rothschilds; he even approached the Tsar, the Pope, the German Kaiser and finally the Sultan, from whom he hoped to secure Palestine. Failing that, Herzl, unlike most of his followers, was prepared to accept a portion of Argentina or some central African colony. Despite his rejection by most wealthy, assimilated Jews, and by the Orthodox Jewry, Herzl's movement flourished, especially among the ghettos of Eastern Europe. At the first World Zionist Congress in Basel in 1897, Herzl was hailed "King of the Jews", and by the time of his death in 1904, the Zionist bank in London boasted 135,000 shareholders, the largest number financing any enterprise in the world.

Brentano, the poets Eduard Bauernfeld and Ferdinand Saar, and the writer Hugo Hoffmannsthal. When Franziska died in 1907, the villa and its contents were bequeathed to the city. The rooms given over to the local museum contain few surprises, but the three final rooms retain their hotchpotch decor from the *salon*'s heyday, and contain, among other things, commemorative rooms for the two poets.

Heiligenstadt

Heiligenstadt is typical of Vienna's outlying suburbs, a combination of barracks-like housing and remnants of the old wine-making village. The latter became a fashionable spa retreat for the Viennese from 1784 onwards, thanks to the discovery of a curative mineral spring. Nowadays, the easiest way to get there is on the U-Bahn, from which you get one of the best views there is of Friedensreich Hundertwasser's funky **Fernwärme Wien**, his colourfully decorated paper incineration plant, which provides electricity for the surrounding district. Architecturally, it is, as one critic caustically dubbed it, merely "a painted shed", though it's certainly a lot more visually entertaining than most industrial plants, looking something like a psychedelic mosque.

For more on Hundertwasser, see p.173.

Karl-Marx-Hof

If there is one housing complex that has come to symbolize the inter-war municipal socialism of "Red Vienna", it is the **Karl-Marx-Hof**, the kilometre-long, peach-and-salmon-coloured "people's palace", whose distinctive giant archways greet you as you exit from Heiligenstadt U-Bahn. Though right-wing critics charged that these housing complexes were built as fortresses by the socialists to protect their workers in case of civil war, their fragility was proved on February 12, 1934, when the World War I artillery of the Austro-fascist government reduced much of the Karl-Marx-Hof to rubble in a few hours. It took another four days for the government forces to flush the last defenders out, however. This is only the most famous of the battles of the civil war, which was fought just as keenly and bloodily in numerous other working-class housing estates in Vienna and other Austrian cities. Shortly after the battle, Edward VIII visited Vienna as Prince of Wales, and endeared himself to the Viennese socialists by asking to be taken to see the Karl-Marx-Hof – it would be difficult to think of a more unlikely political sympathizer.

The nearest U-Bahn is Heiligenstadt.

Hohe Warte

In the first decade of this century, the architect Josef Hoffmann built five houses in the fashionable **Hohe Warte**, the high ground above the village church of Heiligenstadt. Hoffmann, a pupil of Otto Wagner, was one of the founders of the Secession (see p.138) and later of the Wiener Werkstätte (see p.152), but his architec-

To get to the Hohe Warte, take tram #37 to its terminus.

tural style, with its pared-down classicism and minimal decoration, is very much his own. The best-preserved of the houses is the ivy-strewn **Villa Spitzer**, Steinfeldgasse 4, an idiosyncratic mixture of the classical and the medieval, completed in 1902. The **Villa Ast** (now the Saudi Arabian embassy), at no. 2, completed nearly a decade later at the height of Hoffmann's classical period, provides an interesting contrast. Earliest of the villas, the **Villa Moser-Moll I**, a couple of semi-detached houses built for his fellow Secession artists, Kolo Moser and Carl Moll, at no. 6 and no. 8 respectively, features decorative half-timbering similar to that of the Villa

---

Red Vienna

The bloody history and colourful, monumental exterior of Karl-Marx-Hof have made it a potent symbol of **Red Vienna**, the city's Austromarxist experiment in municipal socialism (1919–33). While other European socialist parties attempted piecemeal reforms, the Social Democratic Workers' Party (SDAP) developed a comprehensive proletarian counter-culture which was intended to serve as an alternative to both bourgeois culture and the Bolshevik experiment in Russia. Cheap tickets to the theatre and opera were provided for the workers, and workers' symphony concerts were held under the baton of one of Schönberg's pupils, Anton Webern. Perhaps the most powerful display of working-class/SDAP power took place during the International Worker Olympics in 1931, when 100,000 people marched through the city to take part in a mass festival held in the Prater Stadium (see p.208), watched by countless more thousands.

Though one cannot but be impressed by the ambition and scope of the SDAP's social and cultural programme, a large section of the working class remained untouched by either initiative. Throughout, the SDAP remained controlled and led by an oligarchy of party elite, who held a patronizing and deeply paternalistic view of the rank and file, by and large fulfilling a passive role in the whole process. The real achievements and failures of Red Vienna have become lost in the myths of time, but its legacy remains highly visible in the huge housing complexes that punctuate Vienna's outer suburbs. These workers' enclaves – purpose-built with communal laundries, bath-houses, kindergartens, libraries, meeting rooms, co-operative shops and health clinics – were designed to help create the "neue Menschen" of the Socialist future. They may have failed in that lofty aim, but they continue to provide cheap and well-maintained housing for a populace who had, until then, been crowded into unsanitary tenements within the *Vorstädte*.

Karl-Marx-Hof may be the most famous of the Red Vienna housing complexes, but it is by no means the largest. Sandleiten-Hof and Friedrich-Engels-Hof are both larger; other biggies include Karl-Seitz-Hof and Raben-Hof. Though all are imposing, none are architecturally innovative, eschewing the modernist, avant-garde aesthetic of the inter-war era for a more traditional monumental architecture. If you're interested, there are guided tours organized by the city council, or you can visit them off your own bat. After Karl-Marx-Hof, the most impressive are Reumann-Hof, 5, Margaretengürtel (tram #6 or #8) and Raben-Hof, 3, Rabengasse (Kardinal-Nagl-Platz U-Bahn).

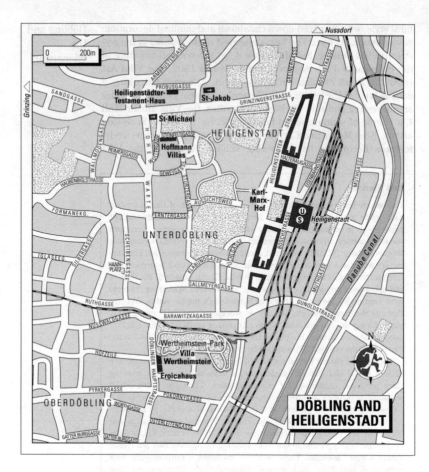

Spitzer. Carl Moll was, of course, the step-father of Alma Mahler-Werfel (née Schindler), and it was to no. 8 that the composer Gustav Mahler went a-courting in the winter of 1901–02 (see box, pp.135-135).

Heiligenstädter-Testament-Haus

Beethoven moved out to the **Heiligenstädter-Testament-Haus**, Probusgasse 6, in 1802 on the advice of his doctor, who hoped the country air would improve his hearing. It was here he wrote his "Heiligenstadt Testament" – a facsimile of which is at the museum – addressed but never sent to his brothers. In it he apologizes for appearing "unfriendly, peevish, or even misanthropic", talks honestly about his deafness: "a sense which in me should be more perfectly developed than in other people", and the pain and embarrassment it brought him: "I was on the point of putting an end to my life – the only thing that held me back was my art". It reads like a will, though it was more of a confession, the cathartic soliloquy of someone who had reached rock bottom.

After the onset of his deafness, Beethoven kept a Conversation Book and a pencil with him at all times. He would offer the book and pencil to whoever he was trying to communicate with, though he

---

Ludwig van Beethoven (1770–1827)

Born in 1770 in Bonn, **Ludwig van Beethoven** came to Vienna in 1787, but remained for just a few months owing to his mother's illness. Her death, and his father's subsequent death from alcoholism in 1792, freed Beethoven to return to the Austrian capital, where he lived until his own demise in 1827. Like Mozart, who was fourteen years his senior, he was taught by his father, a singer in the Hofkapelle, and played piano in public at a very early age (though his father used to pretend he was two years younger than he actually was). Again like Mozart, Beethoven was a virtuoso pianist, yet their techniques couldn't have been more different: Mozart gliding over the keys with smooth fluency, Beethoven raising his hands above his head, and smashing the keys with such force that he regularly broke the strings. Unlike both Haydn and Mozart, Beethoven was never a slave to the aristocracy, but an independent artist, whose patrons clubbed together to pay him an annuity just to keep him in Vienna, and prevent him having to take up the post of *Kapellmeister* at Westphalia which was offered him in 1809.

Though recognized as a genius by Viennese high society, he was also regarded as something of a freak: unprepossessing, scruffily dressed, reeking of body odour and swearing like a trooper. Despite such shortcomings, he was clearly attractive to women, and was, in his own words, "generally involved in one entanglement or the other". However, while the names of the women he was involved with are well known, no one can be sure that his love was ever consummated or even fully reciprocated. The objects of his affections were almost invariably young, beautiful, educated, aristocratic, and occasionally even married – in other words, unobtainable. One theory put forward as to why Beethoven never married is that he had syphilis, hence why he frequently changed doctors, and talked in his letters of "a malady which I cannot change and which brings me gradually nearer to death" – some suggest it may even have been the cause of his deafness.

In 1815, Beethoven's brother, Karl, died at the age of just forty-one. Beethoven then made the fateful decision to adopt his nephew, also named Karl, no doubt hoping that Karl would be the son he never had. After a long drawn-out custody battle with his sister-in-law, Beethoven succeeded in removing the boy from his mother in 1820, only to send him to boarding school. Beethoven proved totally unsuitable as a father, and Karl's misery reached such a pitch that in 1826, the fifteen-year-old tried unsuccessfully to shoot himself. He was immediately removed from Beethoven's care, at which the composer fell into despair, eventually dying of pneumonia in March 1827. His funeral, in contrast to Mozart's, attracted a crowd of 20,000 to the Trinity Church of the Minorites on Alserstrasse, with Austria's chief poet, Franz Grillparzer, composing the funeral oration. Beethoven was buried in Währinger Friedhof, but now rests in the Zentralfriedhof (see p.257).

---

*The house is
open Tues–Sun
9am–12.15pm
& 1–4.30pm;
öS25/€1.82;
bus #38A to
Armbruster-
gasse from U-
Bahn
Heiligenstadt,
or a short walk
from tram
#37 terminus.*

himself rarely wrote in them, simply bellowing his replies to his companions. By the time of his death in 1827 there were 400 "conversations", 136 of which have survived (and are kept in the Royal Library in Berlin). Despite his personal distress, while resident at Probusgasse Beethoven completed his joyful *Second Symphony*, "brought home right from the meadows of Heiligenstadt, so full is it of summer air and summer flowers" – a keen antidote to the simplistic theory of trying to fit the works to the composer's mood and life.

Beethoven changed addresses more times even than Mozart (see p.58), and spent a further four summers at various locations in Heiligenstadt. The house in Probusgasse is one of the best preserved of all Beethoven's many residences, and probably the most rewarding of the city's three memorial museums to the composer. Confusingly, there are, in fact, two museums situated here. The official municipal one, on the far side of the shady, cobbled courtyard, occupies the rooms rented by Beethoven, and contains a lock of the composer's hair, his death mask, and the original doorhandle and lock from the Schwarzspanierhaus (now demolished), in which he died in 1827.

*The Beethoven
Ausstellung is
open Tues,
Thurs & Sat
10am–noon &
1–4.30pm;
öS10/€0.73; at
other times,
enquire at
no.5.*

On the opposite side of the courtyard is the rival **Beethoven Ausstellung**, run by the elderly lady who lives at no. 5, on behalf of the Beethoven Society. There's more of an attempt at a bit of period atmosphere here, and an information sheet in English detailing the exhibits. However, there's still little to get excited about, beyond a few woodcuts by turn-of-the-century artist Carl Moll.

Nussdorf and Grinzing

*Nussdorf is
accessible on
tram #D.*

Nussdorf has less going for it than Heiligenstadt, though devotees of Otto Wagner might be persuaded to take a trip out here to see the architect's monumental **Nussdorfer Wehr- und Schleusenanlage** (weir and lock), completed in 1898 as part of Wagner's regulation of the Danube Canal. The most distinctive feature of the design are the pylons topped by a pair of fine bronze lions. Nussdorf's other claim to fame is that from 1932 the composer Franz Lehár lived in the small Baroque palace at Hackofergasse 18, previously home to the musical maestro Emanuel Schikaneder. The building, known as the **Lehár Schlössl**, is now a memorial museum, open to groups only, though it's always worth trying to arrange a private visit; phone ☎318 54 16.

Further inland, up the slopes towards the Wienerwald, is the village of **Grinzing**, by far the most famous of the wine-making districts, whose *Heurigen* are mobbed by tour groups throughout the summer. To find a more authentic *Heuriger*, you're better off in any of the less well-known neighbouring districts, but fans of the composer Gustav Mahler might consider a trip to **Grinzinger Friedhof**. The composer was buried here in 1911, having converted to

Catholicism earlier in his career in order to make himself more acceptable to the anti-Semitic Viennese establishment that ran the opera house. His modernist tombstone, designed by Josef Hoffmann, was commissioned by his widow, Alma Mahler-Werfel, who lies close by. Other notable corpses include the one-armed pianist Paul Wittgenstein (brother of philosopher Ludwig), and the writer Heimito von Doderer.

Döbling and the Wienerwald

Wienerwald

The forested hills of the **Wienerwald** (Vienna Woods) stretch from the northern tip of the city limits to the foothills of the Alps, away to the southwest. The peaks you can see to the north and west of Vienna are an uplifting sight – few other capitals can boast such an impressive green belt on their doorstep. In the eighteenth century, the wealthier folk used to move out into the villages on the vine-clad slopes of the Wienerwald for the duration of the summer. With the arrival of public transport, even those without such means could just hop on a tram to the end of the line, and enjoy a day in the country-side. Even today, the Wienerwald remains a popular weekend jaunt, and throughout the summer, the wine-gardens of the local *Heurigen* are filled not only with tour groups, pumped on the Wienerwald nostalgia industry, but also the Viennese themselves, who come here to sample the new wine.

The Grinzinger Friedhof is open daily: May–Aug 7am–7pm; March, April, Sept & Oct until 6pm; Nov–Feb 8am–5pm; tram #38 terminus is close by.

For more on the district's numerous Heurigen, see p.321.

Approaching the Wienerwald

There are several ways of **approaching the Wienerwald**. Tram #38 deposits you in the centre of Grinzing. If you walk up Cobenzlgasse, turn right up Krapfenwaldgasse and then go straight on at the crossroads, up Mukenthalerweg, you'll find yourself on the right path to Kahlenberg (see p.256). To avoid the worst of the crowds and the traffic, though, it's probably better to start walking from the terminus of tram #D in Nussdorf, following Beethovengang past the Beethoven memorial, then going up Kahlenberger Strasse. Either way, it's a good 3km uphill to Kahlenberg itself. The shortest, stiffest climb is from Kahlenbergerdorf S-Bahn station up Nasen Weg, a kilometre-long path of tight switchbacks that takes you to the top of Leopoldsberg.

For more on the Wienerwald, see Chapter Nine, "Out of the City".

The lower reaches of the Wienerwald are no longer the rural idyll they once were, partly owing to the winding corniche, known as the Höhenstrasse, which was built in the 1930s, allowing traffic access to both Kahlenberg and Leopoldsberg. Bus #38A from Heiligenstadt U-Bahn will take you all the way to Kahlenberg, Cobenzl and (less frequently) Leopoldsberg. If you want to lose the traffic altogether, the best plan is to take the bus to one of the above places, and start walking from there. If you haven't got it together to bring your own picnic, all the above have several restaurants and cafés.

Döbling and the Wienerwald

Kahlenberg, Leopoldsberg and around

One of the most popular places from which to admire the view over Vienna is **Kahlenberg** (484m), the higher of the two hills that rise to the north of Vienna, close by the Danube. There's a café, with a magnificent terrace and a viewing platform, but the whole place is literally mobbed at the weekend. According to tradition, this was where the papal legate, Marco d'Aviano, and the Polish king, Jan Sobieski, celebrated mass in 1683, before Sobieski led the Polish army down the mountain to relieve the city from the Turks. The Baroque Josefskirche, in which the event is supposed to have taken place, is now run by the Poles, and the church's Sobieski Chapel is a Polish national shrine. The most striking thing about the plain interior is the hundreds of rosaries, pendants and lucky Madonna and Child talismans, which hang on the walls from floor to ceiling.

Tradition notwithstanding, it has been proved fairly conclusively that the aforementioned mass actually took place on the neighbouring peak of **Leopoldsberg** (425m), just over 1km by road east of Kahlenberg. To confuse matters further, the two hills swopped names after the Leopoldskirche was built on what is now Leopoldsberg in 1693. This is certainly a more beguiling spot in which to relax and enjoy the view. There's a much more pleasant courtyard and café, shaded by pine trees, and a more dramatic view from the restored ramparts, originally built by the Babenbergs in 1135. The main lookout point doubles as a memorial for the Austrian POWs who were finally allowed home from the Soviet Union in the 1950s. The church itself is also better looking than the one on Kahlenberg, and has a historical display of prints and documents relating to the Turkish siege.

If you're planning a longer walk in the woods, it probably makes more sense to get off bus #38A in the big car park at **Am Cobenzl**, which gives better access to some of the other peaks in this part of the Wienerwald. Cobenzl itself offers a variety of eating and drinking options, from the posh *Schlossrestaurant Cobenzl* to the more modest *Café Cobenzl*, both of which enjoy extensive views over Vienna. If you've got children with you, be sure to check out the wild boar penned up round the back of the *Schlossrestaurant*. A nicer spot for something to drink or eat is the *Oktogon*, a modern octagonal café, off the road, five minutes' walk to the west at Am Himmel. Behind the café is a newly planted musical tree circle that's worth a quick look. From Cobenzl, it's around 3km via Bei der Kreuzeiche and Jägerkreuz to the lookout tower on **Hermannskogel** (542m). Alternatively, you can enjoy the view while walking downhill from Am Himmel or Am Cobenzl via the **Bellevuehöhe** (388m), where there's a plaque, erected in 1977 to commemorate Freud's discovery of the secret of dreams. At the bottom of the hill, you can catch bus #39A to Oberdöbling.

Zentralfriedhof

In a city where some people still keep a separate savings account in order to ensure an appropriately lavish funeral, it comes as little surprise that the **Zentralfriedhof** (Central Cemetery) is one of the biggest cemeteries in Europe. Larger than the entire Innere Stadt, and with a much greater population – 2.5 million – than the whole city, it's so big it even has its own bus service to help mourners get about. It was opened in 1874, at the height of Viennese funereal fetishism, when having *eine schöne Leich* ("a beautiful corpse") was something to aspire to. Today, it's still very much a working graveyard, and is particularly busy on Sundays and on religious holidays, most notably All Saints' Day (November 1), when up to a million Viennese make the trip out here and virtually every grave is left with a candle burning in remembrance.

The cemetery is open daily: May–Aug 7am–7pm; March, April, Sept & Oct until 6pm; Nov–Feb 8am–5pm.

Visiting the cemetery

The quickest way to **reach the Zentralfriedhof** is on tram #71 or #72 from Simmering U-Bahn. Take note, however, that the cemetery has three separate tram stops on Simmeringer Hauptstrasse: the 1. Tor, the first stop, deposits you outside the old Jewish section; the

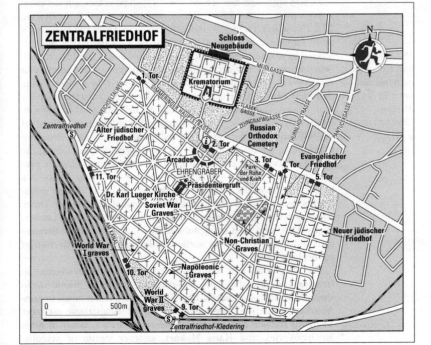

second stop, the 2. **Tor**, serves the main entrance; the third stop (and the terminus for tram #72) is the 3. **Tor**, close to the entrance to the Protestant section, and within easy walking distance of the new Jewish section. In addition to the tram stops on Simmeringer Hauptstrasse, there are two S-Bahn stations along the southwest wall of the cemetery: Zentralfriedhof, a short walk from the 11. Tor and 12. Tor, and Zentralfriedhof-Kledering by the 9. Tor. Both stations are on the S7 line to the airport, which calls at Wien-Nord, Wien-Mitte and Rennweg. The Rundkurs bus does a circuit of the grave-yard every thirty minutes. There's an **information centre** (Mon–Fri 8am–2pm) in the building to the right of the 2. Tor, where you can buy a guide with a plan (in English) to the cemetery.

The Ehrengräber

Passing through the monumental Jugendstil main gates (2. Tor), designed by Max Hegele in 1905, you come to a semi-circular sweep of red-brick arcades, which, though a little uncared-for, contains some very elaborate tombs. The most extraordinary is in the first alcove on the left: a mock-up mine entrance guarded by lantern-wielding dwarves commemorating the Austrian mining magnate Zang.

As you approach the central church, you pass through the main area of the so-called **Ehrengräber** (Tombs of Honour). In Gruppe 32A, to the left, facing the main avenue, you'll find the cemetery's most famous musicians. Centrestage is a memorial to Mozart, topped by a woman trying to stop a load of books from falling off. Behind him, at a respectful distance, lie the graves of **Ludwig van Beethoven**, emblazoned with a busy gilded bee, and **Franz Schubert**, whose bust is about to receive the posthumous honour that eluded him during his lifetime in the shape of a garland. Beethoven and Schubert were disinterred from Währinger Friedhof in 1889, and reburied here – and fellow composer Anton Bruckner managed to get his hands on both composers' corpses during the operation, before being physically restrained by the officials present. Another composer reburied nearby is Maria Theresia's favourite, **Christoph Willibald Gluck**, who died in 1779 after refusing his doctor's orders that he drink no alcohol after dinner. Other composers to look out for include **Johannes Brahms**, Josef Lanner, Hugo Wolf, who died of syphilis in 1903, and the entire **Strauss** clan; Johann Jr's tomb, in particular, features a fine collection of musical cherubs.

The Ehrengräber on the opposite side of the main avenue, in Gruppe 14A, are the more eye-catching tombs of *fin-de-siècle* Vienna's wealthier denizens. Few of the names mean much to non-Austrians, with the possible exception of Ringstrasse architect **Theophil Hansen** and artists Emil Jakob Schindler, father of Alma Mahler-Werfel, and **Hans Makart**, another victim of syphilis.

Mozart is, in fact, buried in an unmarked grave in St-Marxer Friedhof (see p.191).

Continuing towards the church, you come to a sort of sunken round-about surrounded by shrubs; this is the illustrious **Präsidentergruft**, containing the remains of the presidents of the Second Republic, only one of whom, **Dr Karl Renner**, has any great claim to fame, as the first postwar president.

Zentralfried-hof

To the right of the presidents, in Gruppe 14C, are several other notable politicians, including the former chancellors Julius Raab and Leopold Figl; the architect **Josef Hoffmann** is also buried here. To the left of the presidents, in Gruppe 32C, you'll find more intriguing incumbents like the sculptor **Fritz Wotruba**, who lies under a self-designed tombstone. He also provided the highly appropriate cuboid tombstone for the atonal composer **Arnold Schönberg**, who died in Los Angeles in 1951. Adjacent to Schönberg, and more universally mourned by the Viennese, is **Bruno Kreisky**, the populist Austrian chancellor (1970–83). Nearby lie the graves of the writer **Franz Werfel**, the composer **Alexander Zemlinsky**, Schönberg's mentor, who died in exile in the USA in 1942, and the architect **Adolf Loos**, whose tomb is a typically ornament-free block of stone. Loos designed a similarly minimalist tombstone for his friend, the poet **Peter Altenberg**, who is buried in Gruppe O, by the wall to the left of the main gates. Those on the search for Austria's most famous pop star, Hans Hölzel – better known as "Falco", the man responsible for the hit *Rock me Amadeus* – will find him buried in Gruppe 40.

Dr Karl Lueger-Kirche and beyond

The focal point of the cemetery is the gargantuan Friedhofskirche or **Dr Karl Lueger-Kirche**, completed by Max Hegele, a pupil of Otto Wagner, in 1910. Initially at least, this domed church resembles Wagner's Jugendstil Kirche am Steinhof (see p.244), but on closer inspection, it's clear that Hegele has taken a more austere Neoclassical approach. There are guided tours of the church on the first Sunday of the month after Mass (9.45am). The chief vault in the church is that of the anti-Semitic city mayor, Karl Lueger (see p.127).

The church is open Mon–Sat 11am–3pm; free.

Few tourists venture further than the Ehrengräber and the Friedhofskirche, but there are plenty of other points of interest, if you've got the legs for it. Directly behind the church a large **Soviet war cemetery** contains the graves of those who fell during the 1945 liberation of Vienna, centred on a statue of two Red Army soldiers, flags downcast, with patriotic quotes from Stalin around the plinth. Continuing down the central avenue, you come to Anton Hanak's despairing memorial to those who fell in **World War I**; behind it, in Gruppe 91, is a semi-circular green field, its soft turf studded with small graves. To the southeast, in Gruppe 88, are the graves of Napoleonic troops who died during the 1809 French occupation of Vienna, the majority inscribed with the words "Français non identifié". Over 7000 Austrians who died fighting in the Nazi Wehrmacht in **World War II** are commemorated by a field of black crosses to the southwest in Gruppe 97.

Those who died fighting for the freedom of their country from 1934 to 1945 have their own memorial – a big heroic bronze man accompanied by two mourning women – at the giant intersection to the southeast of the Lueger-Kirche. Nearby are the uniform graves of those who died in the riot outside the Justitzpalast on July 15, 1927 (see p.130), and a memorial to war victims from the Czechoslovak section of the Austrian Communist Party. To the east, in Gruppe 28, the victims of the civil war of February 1934 (see p.354), those who died under the Austro-fascists, and martyrs of the Spanish Civil War, have their own memorial. Further east still, the **Social Democrats** have their own Ehrengräber featuring their early leaders, among them Otto Bauer, Viktor Adler, and the latter's brother, Friedrich Adler, who assassinated the prime minister Count Karl von Stürgkh in 1916 (see p.60). Opposite, the casualties of the 1848 revolution are commemorated by a simple obelisk.

Several non-Catholic denominations share the Zentralfriedhof: there's an **Evangelischer Friedhof** (Protestant Cemetery), accessible from 4. Tor, a growing Islamic section in Gruppe 26 and 36, and a small Russian Orthodox section around the onion-domed church in Gruppe 21, to the left of the main gates. In Gruppe 23, you'll also find the **Park der Ruhe und Kraft** (Park of Peace and Strength), a laudable attempt to address the spiritual needs of those who don't subscribe to an organized religion, with five symbolic areas to wander through, ranging from a stone circle to a labyrinth.

By far the largest non-Catholic sections, however, are the two Jewish cemeteries. The **Alter jüdischer Friedhof** (Old Jewish Cemetery), founded in 1863 and accessible from 1. Tor, was desecrated by the Nazis on Kristallnacht, though some 60,000 graves are still standing, and work has recently been undertaken to stop the place from falling into rack and ruin. Among those buried here are the Viennese branch of the Rothschild family and the playwright Arthur Schnitzler. The **Neuer jüdischer Friedhof** (New Jewish Cemetery), accessible from 5. Tor, on the other side of the Zentralfriedhof, was inaugurated in 1917, and, despite being damaged during Kristallnacht, still functions today. The sheer size of these two graveyards is a testament to the pre-war magnitude of Vienna's Jewish community – testament also to the several generations systematically wiped out in the Holocaust.

If you need a bite to eat, head for the Schloss Concordia, *opposite the main gates (2. Tor).*

The Krematorium and the Friedhof der Namenlosen

For the terminally obsessed, the city's **Krematorium** is but a short stroll from the main gates (2. Tor) of the Zentralfriedhof; take the underpass to the other side of Simmeringer Hauptstrasse, and walk in a northwesterly direction. The Roman Catholic church forbids cremation, which was championed by the anti-clerical Social Democrats between the wars as a secular alternative. The Viennese have never been entirely convinced by this ecologically sound form of burial, however, and less than twenty percent opt for it even today. Nevertheless, the central complex of buildings is worth checking out, a startling work designed in the early 1920s by Clemens Holzmeister. The central courtyard, with its arcade of Gothic lancet arches, is the most impressive section, along with the zig-zag roofline of the crematorium itself, all smothered in smooth grey, rendered concrete. The crenellated perimeter walls of the crematorium date back to the **Schloss Neugebäude**, built as a magnificent Mannerist palace by the Emperor Maximilian II. What remains of the palace can be seen at the far end of the Garden of Rest, behind the crematorium building. There are plans afoot to reconstruct the building, though by the looks of the place, there's some way to go yet.

Last, and probably least, is the **Friedhof der Namenlosen** (Cemetery of the Nameless Ones), to the east of the Zentralfriedhof at Alberner Hafen, containing the graves of the poor souls fished out of the Danube each year. Some of the corpses are later identified (and are therefore no longer "nameless"), but the majority are not, and the overriding feeling is one of melancholy. To get there, you have to study the timetable of bus #6A very carefully; it leaves from the terminus of tram #71, but only occasionally makes it as far as the cemetery.

Zentralfried- hof

The Krematorium is open the same hours as the Zentralfriedhof.

Chapter 9

Out of the City

Thanks to Austria's efficient public transport system, day-trips from Vienna are easy; the elegant spa town of **Baden** even has its own tram link with the capital. Though no longer the fashionable holiday retreat it once was, the town is still a good base from which to make a brief foray into the neighbouring Wienerwald (Vienna Woods). Another possible day-trip is to **Eisenstadt**, a sleepy provincial town near the Hungarian border that's associated with the

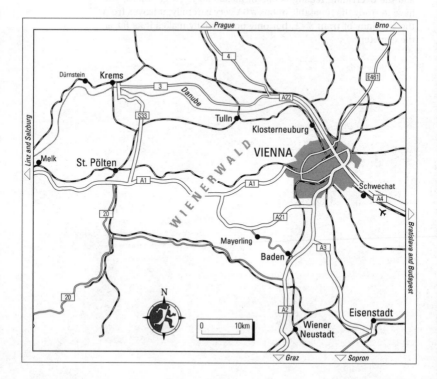

composer Josef Haydn, who worked for the Esterházy family most of his life, and is now buried in his very own mausoleum.

Heading up the River Danube is another popular way of day-tripping from the capital. The first place of interest is the glorious monastery of **Klosterneuburg**, barely beyond the northern limits of the city. Slightly further afield is the town of **Tulln**, birthplace of the artist Egon Schiele, and one of the stops for boats heading upriver from Vienna (see p.276). Of all Austrian towns on the Danube, though, there are few as beguiling as **Krems**, with its medieval counterpart, Stein. Beyond lies the **Wachau**, a tortuously winding stretch of the Danube where vine-bearing, ruin-encrusted hills roll down to the river on both sides. Marking the upstream end of the Wachau is **Melk**, arguably Austria's finest monastery, a stunning Baroque confection that towers over the town and river below.

Baden bei Wien

Just 25km south of Vienna, the spa town of **BADEN** is an easy daytrip from the capital, accessible either by train or via its very own slow-stopping tram link. This compact little town, peppered with attractive Neoclassical buildings, in varying shades of magnolia and ochre, comes across as deeply provincial, a haven of peace for its elderly spa patients. But back in the eighteenth and nineteenth centuries, Baden was *the* most fashionable spa town in the Habsburg Empire, the favourite summer holiday retreat of none other than the Emperor Franz II (1792–1835). Baden's distinctive uniform Biedermeier appearance is largely the result of a building frenzy – much of it under the direction of the architect Josef Kornhäusel – prompted by the devastating fire of 1812. A swim in Baden's hot thermal baths is still highly recommended and, as the town lies on the very edge of the Wienerwald, the walking and picnicking possibilities are a further enticement.

The Town

The small, triangular **Hauptplatz**, at the centre of Baden's pedestrian zone, gives you an idea of the modest scale of the place. Almost dwarfing the surrounding buildings, including Kornhäusel's Neoclassical **Rathaus** from 1815, is the central plague column erected a hundred years earlier, and crowned with a gilded sunburst. Even the last of the Holy Roman Emperors, Franz II, chose an unassuming three-storey building – now the **Kaiserhaus**, on the east side of the square – as his summer residence. The last of the Habsburgs, Emperor Karl I, also stayed here, during World War I, when Baden became the Austrian Army headquarters. (Baden later reached its nadir in the 1950s, when it was used as the Soviet Army headquarters.)

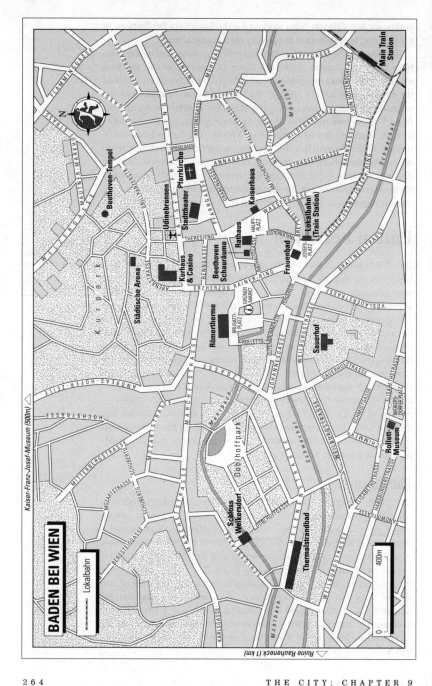

BADEN BEI WIEN

Lokalbahn

Kaiser-Franz-Josef-Museum (500m)

Main Train Station

Ruine Rauheneck (1 km)

400m

0

From 1804, Baden became a favourite retreat of Beethoven's, too; he made a total of fifteen visits, staying at various addresses, one of which, at nearby Rathausgasse 10, has been turned into the **Beethoven Schauräume**. In the 1820s, the composer was well known around the spa as the local eccentric. As one friend recalls, "his hair was coarse and bristly . . . and when he put his hand through it, it remained standing in all directions which often looked comical". He even got himself arrested in the nearby town of Wiener Neustadt, after a local had been so frightened by his dishevelled appearance that she called the police. On being arrested, the composer said "I am Beethoven", to which the constable replied "You are a tramp, Beethoven doesn't look like that". Later that night the town's musical director was finally called out to identify him, and the mayor sent him back to Baden in the state coach.

Woefully, the three small rooms Beethoven rented contain no mementoes of the composer's three sojourns here (there's even a section about later, lesser-known Badenites, including Katharina

Baden bei Wien

The Beethoven Schauräume is open Tues–Fri 4–6pm, Sat & Sun 9–11am & 4–6pm; öS20/€1.45.

S&M in Baden

The staid spa town of Baden is the unlikely setting for *Venus im Pelze* (Venus in Furs), an account of sexual slavery written by **Count Leopold von Sacher-Masoch (1836–95)**. The son of the chief of police in Lemberg (Lvov), the count was allegedly influenced as a child by the brutality of the prisons. As an adult, he became professor of history at Graz University, and wrote several historical and folkloric novels. His renown today, however, rests on his affair in the 1860s with "Baroness Bogdanoff" (real name Fanny Pistor), to whom the count willingly signed away his freedom – becoming her manservant, taking the name of Gregor, and embarking upon "a liaison, marked materially by a prodigality in which furs and foreign travel were to be conspicuous". She agreed to wear furs "as often as possible, especially when in a cruel mood", while he agreed to "comply unreservedly with every one of her desires and commands". After six months of slavery, the two parted company, but the affair had inspired the count to write *Venus im Pelze*, which was published in 1870. In 1873, the count married Aurore Rümelin, who changed her name to Wanda in honour of the book's heroine. "Gregor" and Wanda became involved in a weird *ménage à trois* with a fake Polish countess, Anna von Kottowitz, who turned out to be a chemist's assistant.

We have the count to thank for the term "sado-masochism", though he himself never coined the phrase. That was left to one of Freud's early mentors, Richard von Krafft-Ebing (1840–1902), who first used the term – with reference to Sacher-Masoch's numerous writings on the S&M theme – in his *Psychopathia Sexualis*, published in Latin in 1886 (and later translated into seven languages), about which the Emperor Franz-Josef I once quipped, "it's about time someone brought out a decent book on Latin grammar". The same year, Sacher-Masoch split from Wanda, and the following year he married his children's governess. He died in 1895, depressed by the decline of his reputation and by Krafft-Ebing's use of his name to designate a sexual perversion.

Schratt and Max Reinhardt, to pad things out). It was in these rooms that Beethoven wrote parts of his *Missa Solemnis* in 1821, and, two years later, finished his *Ninth Symphony*, though he had to get a friend to persuade the landlord to take him back on the promise of good conduct. The landlord agreed on condition that Beethoven pay for a set of new shutters (the previous set, on which Beethoven had made financial and musical calculations, had been sold by the landlord for a piece of gold).

Kurpark

In fine weather, concerts take place in the bandstand May–Sept Tues–Sun 4.30pm.

The focus of Baden the spa, as opposed to Baden the town, is the ochre-coloured Kurhaus (now a casino) and summer theatre (Städtische Arena) north of Hauptplatz by the **Kurpark**, which is laid out on the steep slopes of the Wienerwald. This is by far the nicest bit of Baden and the place to head for if you're intent on a spot of walking or picnicking, as the park's network of paths can quickly transport you high above the town. In its lowest reaches, closest to the town, the park is formally arranged around a bandstand and the **Udinebrunnen**, an eye-catching fountain featuring a

---

The Mayerling Tragedy

Mystery still surrounds the motives behind the suspected double suicide of **Crown Prince Rudolf** (1858–89), eldest son of the Emperor Franz-Josef I and heir to the throne, and his half-Greek, seventeen-year-old mistress, Baroness Maria Vetsera. The tragedy took place in the early hours of the morning on January 29, 1889, at Rudolf's hunting lodge at Mayerling, 15km northwest of Baden. Subject of a ballet, several films and countless books, the event has captured the popular imagination for over a hundred years. Even though Franz-Josef had the entire lodge demolished shortly after the incident, and a Carmelite nunnery erected in its place, folk still flock to the site, and as recently as 1988, an Austrian businessman confessed to having stolen Maria's coffin after becoming obsessed with Mayerling.

Numerous theories continue to be put forward as to why Rudolf chose to take his life. The Viennese, who love to sentimentalize the tragedy, tend to claim it was all for love, yet Rudolf was a notoriously fickle womanizer, and Maria Vetsera was just one in a long line of pretty mistresses. The plot thickens when we discover that the previous summer, Rudolf had proposed a suicide pact to another of his mistresses, Mizzi Caspar, but was turned down. On the very night before his suicide, Rudolf spent the evening with Mizzi, before leaving to meet Maria at Mayerling. It's true that his marriage to Princess Stephanie of Belgium – arranged by his father for political reasons – was a dismal failure, but it wasn't enough to drive him to suicide, and certainly didn't prevent him from keeping bachelor digs at the Hofburg where he could receive his numerous mistresses. One plausible theory is that, at the beginning of 1887, he contracted a venereal disease which he believed to be incurable. Worse still, it's thought that he had infected Stephanie, causing her to become infertile (having failed to provide a male heir to the throne).

gilded water sprite emerging from a vast rockery replete with oversized frogs, serpents, fish and the sprite's giant stepfather. Higher up the park, various monuments emerge from the foliage: statues of Johann Strauss and his chief rival Josef Lanner, a temple to Mozart and, biggest of the bunch, the vine-garlanded **Beethoven-Tempel**, a Neoclassical rotunda from 1927, sporting some dubious underlit 1920s' frescoes, but the best of all views across the spa.

For a more physically taxing walk, follow the signs to the offbeat **Kaiser-Franz-Josef-Museum**, roughly half an hour from the bandstand, in a northwesterly direction. Although it advertises itself as a museum of folk art and craftwork, the collection is a lot more eclectic than you might imagine. The reconstructed smithy is par for the course, but the mousetrap from the room in which Albrecht von Waldstein was murdered in 1634 is rather more unusual. In addition, there's a whole collection of arms and uniforms from the seventeenth to the twentieth century, banknotes, Habsburg memorabilia, a paper theatre, cake moulds, two penny farthings, and more.

The Kaiser-Franz-Josef-Museum is open April–Oct Tues–Sun 1–7pm; öS30/€2.18

Others contend that it was a political act, born of frustration with his lack of any part in the decision-making process of government. Franz-Josef allowed his son very little real power, and, in any case, disagreed with him on most issues. Rudolf, who was never close to his father, tended to mix with liberals opposed to his father's ministers' policies, and even wrote anonymous, critical articles to the liberal *Neues Wiener Tagblatt*. There were even rumours at the time that Rudolf had been assassinated by his political opponents, a version of events upheld by the Empress Zita as recently as 1982. Another possible explanation is that Rudolf, having written to the Pope to seek an annulment of his marriage, had been snubbed by the pontiff, who had returned the petition directly to Franz-Josef. We do know that on January 26, 1889, Rudolf and his father had a fierce argument – what it was about we shall never know.

Four days later, Rudolf and Maria's bodies were discovered by Rudolf's hunting partner, Count Hoyos, who had got no answer when he called in at Mayerling. The first official version of events was that Rudolf had died of apoplexy, but after the post-mortem it was admitted that he had shot himself. As suicides were denied a Christian burial, the pathologists in charge were wise enough to suggest that "the act was committed in a moment of psychological unbalance", thus allowing the Catholic authorities an escape clause. Rudolf's request to be buried in the nearby village of Alland alongside his mistress was denied, and he was buried in the Kaisergruft amid much pomp and circumstance. Maria Vetsera's presence at Mayerling was never acknowledged by the Habsburgs, though rumours abounded. Some 36 hours after the incident, her fully clothed corpse, in the first stages of rigor mortis, was wedged upright in a carriage between her two uncles, transported to Heiligenkreuz and secretly buried in the cemetery there.

The Rollett-Museum and Doblhoffpark

An even more bizarre collection of exhibits fills the **Rollett-Museum**, ten minutes' walk southwest of Hauptplatz on Weikersdorfer Platz. It's worth coming out here for the building alone, designed in extravagant neo-Renaissance style in 1905 as the town hall for Weikersdorf, only to become redundant seven years later when Weikersdorf was subsumed into Baden. The most fascinating section of the collection within is the array of skulls, busts, brains and death masks – plus a wax model of Marie Antoinette's hand, and a plaster cast of Goethe's – amassed by Franz-Josef Gall (1758–1828), the founder of phrenology, a pseudo-science which claimed a person's talents or criminal traits could be traced to areas of the brain. The rest of the museum is a hotchpotch: some crystals, an Egyptian sarcophagus and a cabinet of curios from the world tour of local nineteenth-century bigwig Josef von Doblhoff.

If you'd prefer something less mentally taxing, head for the vast hot thermal **open-air swimming pool complex**, which hides behind the 1920s facade of the *Thermalstrandbad* on Helenenstrasse, or the ultra-modern, stylish indoor pool, *Römertherme* (*www.roemertherme.at*), on Brusattiplatz, which is open daily until 10pm. After your dip, you can relax in the nearby **Doblhoffpark**, a lovely mix of formal gardens and English park, with a large rosarium, a pergola and a huge, bushy plane tree at the centre. To the north is the sixteenth-century **Schloss Weikersdorf**, seat of the Doblhoff family from 1741 until 1966 (it's now a hotel, but you should be able to sneak a look at the arcaded courtyard). Finally, if you've time to spare, check out the contemporary art in the low-slung Neoclassical **Frauenbad** (Tues–Sun 10am–noon & 3–7pm) on Josefplatz.

Practicalities

The quickest way to **get to Baden** is by train or S-Bahn from Vienna's Südbahnhof (every 30min; 20min) to Baden's main train station, ten minutes' walk southeast of the town centre. You could also jump on the special Lokalbahn trams – distinguishable from Vienna's other trams by their Prussian blue and cream livery – which run from the section of the Ringstrasse by the Staatsoper to Josefsplatz (every 15min; 1hr 10min). Baden's **tourist office** is attractively ensconced in the Leopoldsbad, a magnolia-coloured Biedermeier building on Brusattiplatz. The *Café Central*, on Hauptplatz, is a big traditional *Kaffeehaus*, and a great place for watching life go by. For lunch, *Café Damals*, Rathausgasse 3 (closed Sat eve & Sun), offers reasonably priced **food**, but if the weather's fine, you're best off packing a picnic and heading off into the woods. For something more substantial, the homely *Gasthaus zum Reichsapfel*, just east of the Pfarrkirche, down Spiegelgasse, offers a range of beers, traditional pub fare and good veggie options; the *Amterl*, at the top of Hauptplatz (closed Sun), serves up nicely presented dishes, and has tables on the street.

Eisenstadt

Some 50km southeast of Vienna, on the edge of a ridge of hills that slopes down gently to the Hungarian plain, **EISENSTADT** is known, above all, for its associations with the composer **Josef Haydn**, who was in the employ of the local bigwigs, the Esterházys, for most of his adult life. Haydn may be the main draw nowadays, but the town also has a well-preserved Jewish ghetto and an excellent Jewish museum. It also possesses a rather unusual history, having been Hungarian for much of its history, only becoming the capital of Burgenland by default in 1921, when the province changed hands from Hungary to Austria – all but for the old regional capital, Sopron (Ödenburg), which remained in Hungary.

The Town

For a provincial capital – albeit of Austria's smallest Land – Eisenstadt is a tiny little place, with a population of just 11,000 and an old town made up of just three streets. **Domplatz**, the southern-most of the three, is open to traffic and used primarily as the local bus station; its fifteenth-century Domkirche was only given cathedral

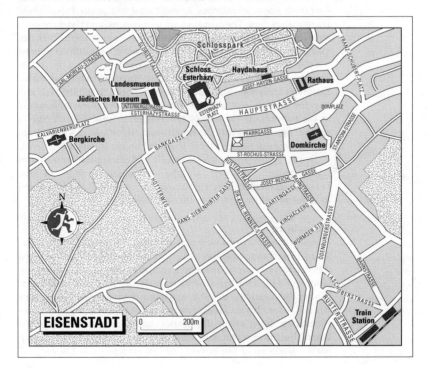

status in 1960 and, apart from its gilded pulpit and organ, is nothing special. **Hauptstrasse**, the pedestrianized main street, is prettier, particularly the Rathaus, with its shapely Baroque gables, three oriel windows and lively folk paintings of the seven virtues.

Schloss Esterházy

Nothing in the town's modest little houses prepares you for the sheer scale of the **Schloss Esterházy**, which presides over Esterházy-Platz, at the western end of Hauptstrasse. The Schloss was originally built as a medieval fortress with bulky corner towers, later received a Baroque conversion, and was finally redesigned in Neoclassical style (though you can't actually see the fancy, colonnaded north facade overlooking the gardens). The result is a strange, slightly heavy building, a sort of oversized French chateau, daubed in a fresh coat of imperial ochre-yellow paint with smart green shutters to match. Most of the rooms are now used as offices by the provincial government, but a few are open for hour-long guided tours; these are usually in German, so ask for the English notes from the ticket office.

Hourly guided tours May–Oct Tues–Sun 9am–5pm; Nov–April Tues–Fri 9am–5pm; öS50/€3.63; www.schloss-esterhazy.at.

To be perfectly frank, the only room worth seeing is the one which kicks off the tour, the **Haydnsaal**, its coved ceiling smothered with over thirty colourful frescoes, its walls lined with painted roundels of Hungarian heroes. The acoustics are tremendous, and Haydn himself conducted numerous performances of his own music here. If you can catch a live concert, do (May–Oct weekly; *www.haydnfestival.at*) – it'll also save you having to endure the second half of the guided tour. This takes you round the **Esterházy-Museum**, which contains Esterházy treasures, and traces the history of the family, who still own the Schloss, and who remain one of the wealthiest landowners in the country. At the end of this endurance test, you emerge in another fine concert hall, the **Empiresaal**, which takes its name from the Neoclassical pastel greens, blues and brown trompe l'oeil decor.

To get to the shady greenery of the **Schlosspark**, head down Glorietteallee; as well as the Neoclassical folly of the Leopoldinentempel, there's a vast orangery, currently being restored to its former glory, and set to house a café.

Unterberg

A hundred metres or so west of the Schloss lies the old Jewish quarter of **Unterberg**, established as a walled ghetto back in medieval times, and for centuries home to a comparatively large Jewish population. All 446 of the town's Jews were deported to the camps shortly after the Anschluss in 1938, and today there are just two families left in Eisenstadt, though Unterberg has since been repopulated. The remarkable thing about the district, however, is that despite the human destruction that was wrought on the community, the ghetto itself – made up of five streets and two cemeteries to the north of

Esterházystrasse – remains more or less physically intact. As you enter the ghetto's main street of Unterbergstrasse, you can even see one of the two stone piers, between which a chain was placed on the Jewish Sabbath (a practice that was continued right up until 1938).

Österreichisches Jüdisches Museum

Further up Unterbergstrasse on the right, at no. 6, is the **Österreichisches Jüdisches Museum** (Austrian Jewish Museum), in the house that once belonged to Samson Wertheimer (1658–1724). Wertheimer was chief administrator of financial affairs to three successive Habsburg emperors, became the first rabbi of Eisenstadt, and was eventually appointed *Landesrabbiner* (Chief Rabbi) of the Hungarian Jewry in 1693 by the Emperor Karl VI.

The Jüdisches Museum is open May–Oct Tues–Sun 10am–5pm; öS50/€3.63.

The museum stages temporary exhibitions on the ground floor, while the **permanent exhibition** on the first floor is a fairly standard rundown on Judaism, with a few models of Vienna's now demolished synagogues and of Eisenstadt's old ghetto. Captions are exclusively in German, with the only English-language information in the museum's over-priced catalogue.

On the first floor is the **Wertheimer'sche Schul**, Wertheimer's private synagogue, built in the early eighteenth century, but whose current trompe l'oeil decor dates from the early nineteenth. It was one of the few in the Third Reich to survive Kristallnacht, perhaps because by then Eisenstadt had already been cleared of Jews, and was used in the decade after World War II by Jewish soldiers of the Red Army.

Burgenländisches Landesmuseum

Another wealthy Jewish burgher's former home – the rather attractive house with the corner oriel at the junction of Unterbergstrasse and Museumgasse – has been converted into the **Landesmuseum**. As usual, there's no information in English, but the building itself is a lovely, rambling mansion, with a plant-filled rooftop loggia, and, in the cellar, a whole series of impressive Roman mosaics, the largest of which features Bellerophon killing the hybrid monster Chimera. The local history section on the first floor is particularly strong on the territorial dispute after World War I, with propaganda posters from the period depicting such subjects as Death in a Hungarian costume playing the fiddle over Ödenburg. Finally, you shouldn't miss Franz Liszt's plushly furnished *Blauer Salon*, transferred here in its entirety from the Schottenhof of Vienna, where the Hungarian composer stayed on and off from 1869 to 1886.

The Landesmuseum is open Tues–Sun 9am–noon & 1–5pm; öS30/€2.18.

Haydn's Eisenstadt

The house that Haydn bought in Eisenstadt, where he kept chickens, two horses and probably a cow, is now the **Haydnhaus**, on Josef-Haydn-Gasse. This was the composer's home, on and off, from 1766

The Haydnhaus is open Easter–Oct daily 9am–noon & 1–5pm; öS20/€1.45.

to 1788, but there's no attempt to recreate his abode in any way. With no information at all in English (unless you buy the pricey catalogue) and only a few battered sections of one of the composer's own organs to look at, this is one for all but the most fanatical to skip.

A better way of paying your respects to Haydn is to head for the squat Baroque **Bergkirche**, which, as its name suggests, is located on raised ground 500m west of the Schloss, on the other side of

The Bergkirche is open April–Oct daily 9am–noon & 1–5pm; öS25/€1.82.

Josef Haydn (1732–1809)

Of the big three classical composers, **Josef Haydn** is seen as coming a poor third to Mozart and Beethoven, despite the fact that his music is in many ways just as radical as theirs. Part of the problem undoubtedly lies in the ordinariness of both Haydn's character and his life – during his lifetime he acquired the nickname "Papa Joe" for his generally amiable personality (notwithstanding his boorish behaviour towards his wife).

Haydn was born in 1732 to a master wheelwright in the Lower Austrian village of Rohrau. His father, who played the harp, recognized his son's musical talents, and at the age of eight, Josef joined the choir of the Stephansdom in Vienna, where he was a pupil for the next nine years. At this point, in 1749, Haydn's voice broke and he was kicked out of the choir, his little brother Michael becoming the new star pupil. Haydn then endured a difficult poverty-stricken decade as a freelance musician, which ended with his appointment in 1758 as music director for Count von Morzin, a rich Bohemian nobleman. Two years later Haydn made the biggest mistake of his life, as he later saw it, and married Maria Keller, the daughter of a hairdresser, with whom he could neither get on nor conceive children. She showed virtually no interest in his work, and is alleged to have used his manuscripts as pastry-linings and curl papers.

More auspiciously, in 1761, Haydn was appointed assistant *Kapellmeister* to the Esterházy family at Eisenstadt. Haydn's patron, Prince Paul Anton Esterházy, was a keen music lover – he even published his own songbook, *Harmonia Celestis* – but he died the following year. Luckily, he was succeeded by Prince Nikolaus (Miklós) "the Ostentatious", another music fan and a lavish entertainer. After a visit to Versailles in 1764, Prince Nikolaus decided to establish his own version of the French chateau on the other side of the Neusiedler See from Eisenstadt. Although equipped with a theatre, opera house and a marionette theatre, the palace – named Esterháza (Fertöd) – was intended only as a summer residence. In the end, however, it became a more or less permanent home for Prince Nikolaus and for Haydn, now the family's chief *Kapellmeister*, who was, in any case, glad of the chance to escape his wife and sleep with his mistress, the young Italian mezzo-soprano, Luigia Polzelli.

In 1790, Prince Nikolaus died; his successor, Anton, was less interested in music (and had less money). The family's court orchestra was disbanded, but as a sign of the family's respect for his loyalty, the Esterházys continued to pay Haydn's salary and allowed him to keep his title. He immediately moved to Vienna, embarked on two long tours of England, and enjoyed late, but great acclaim, letting his hair down and earning himself a great deal of money at the same time. His final years were plagued by illness and he died during the second occupation of Vienna in 1809 (see p.347).

Unterberg. The church interior is a trompe l'oeil fantasy in pinks and greys, but the reason most folk come here is to visit the purpose-built **Haydn-Mausoleum**, erected by the Esterházys at the west end of the church in 1932 in order to receive Haydn's decapitated corpse. At the time, his head was still in Vienna's Gesellschaft der Musikfreunde, to which it had been bequeathed in 1895, having been stolen by one of Haydn's friends, a keen phrenologist, shortly after the composer's burial in 1809. Finally, in 1954, Haydn's head was reunited with his body, and the whole of Haydn now lies in the marble tomb mourned over by four lounging cherubs.

The Bergkirche's other star attraction (covered by the same ticket) is the **Kalvarienberg**, accessible from the eastern exterior of the church. Here, steps lead up to a small chapel, beside which a turnstile lets you into a labyrinth of mini-chapels begun in 1701, depicting the story of the Passion in theatrical tableaux of full-size statues. First, you enter a subterranean grotto, then you wind your way round the outside up to the Crucifixion tableau on top of the church (great views over Burgenland), and finally back down to the Entombment on the other side.

Practicalities

The fastest and most direct **trains** from Vienna to Eisenstadt leave from the suburban station of Wien-Meidling (U-Bahn Meidling Philadelphiabrücke); the journey takes just over an hour, with trains leaving hourly during the week, less frequently at weekends. You could also catch one of the trains from Vienna's Südbahnhof, which run hourly throughout the week, but this entails changing at Neusiedl am See.

Eisenstadt's **train station** is just ten minutes' walk southeast of the town centre, and you'll find the **tourist office** (May–Oct daily 9am–5pm; Nov–April Mon–Fri 9am–noon & 2–5pm; ☎02682/67390, *www.tiscover.com/eisenstadt*) in the east wing of the Schloss. A nice place to **eat and drink** alfresco, and enjoy a view of the Schloss, is the smart, but reasonably priced *Esterházy Café*, directly opposite in the former stables and winter riding school, on Esterházy-Platz. Alternatively, *Silberfuchs*, near the Bergkirche on Kalvarienbergplatz, offers a good range of Austrian dishes and daily specials for around öS75/€5.45. Another good bet is the *Burgenländische Gasthausbrauerei*, Pfarrgasse 22, where you can wash down your food with the new micro-brew, Haydnbräu.

Klosterneuburg

Just north of the city limits, hidden from the capital by the hills of the Wienerwald, the village of **KLOSTERNEUBURG** is one of the quickest and easiest day-trips from Vienna. Its chief attraction is its impos-

Klosterneuburg

ing Augustinian monastery, the oldest and richest in Austria, whose Baroque domes and neo-Gothic spires soar above the right bank of the Danube. Klosterneuburg also has a spanking-new private modern art museum hidden in its peripheral streets and filled with postwar Austrian art.

The Monastery

The **Stift Klosterneuburg** (*www.stift-klosterneuburg.at*) was founded in the twelfth century by the Babenberg Duke Leopold III, who, so the story goes, vowed to build an abbey on the spot where he found his wife's veil, which had been carried off by the wind from a nearby castle. Leopold himself was canonized in 1485, and later became the patron saint of Austria, making Klosterneuburg a popular place of pilgrimage. Having withstood the Turkish siege of 1683, the monastery enjoyed a second golden age under the Emperor Karl VI (1711–40), who planned a vast imperial palace here, along the lines of the Escorial in Spain. The project was never fully realized, but the one wing that was completed gives some idea of Karl's grandiose plans.

Guided monastery tours in German only; minimum 5 people, Mon–Sat hourly 9–11am & 1.30–4.30pm, Sun 11am & 1.30–4.30pm; Nov–March no 9am tour; öS70/€5.09.

The tour starts with the **Stiftskirche**, which still hints at its origins as a Romanesque basilica, despite over-zealous nineteenth-century restoration. Neo-Gothic finials and other details obscure the west front, but the south door, with its blind arcading, is still much as it would have been in the Babenbergs' day. Inside, the church is a riot of seventeenth-century early Baroque, replete with frescoes and mountains of stuccowork. The most impressive craftsmanship is in the chancel: the richly gilded choirstalls, exuberant high altar, and, above all, Johann Michael Rottmayr's *Assumption*, without doubt the pick of the frescoes.

To the north of the church are the **medieval cloisters**, built in the late thirteenth century. The central courtyard is encroached upon in the southwest corner by the little L-shaped Freisingerkapelle, containing the episcopal tomb of its namesake, who died in 1410. More intriguing is the polygonal wellhouse, which juts out into the courtyard from the eastern cloister, and boasts some fine tracery over the portal; the highlight is the magnificent, giant bronze candelabra, crafted in Verona in the twelfth century.

The monastery's most outstanding treasure by far, though, is the **Verduner Altar**, in the Leopoldskapelle to the east of the cloisters. This stunning winged altar, completed in 1181 by Nikolaus of Verdun, is made up of over fifty gilded enamel plaques, depicting Biblical scenes from both testaments. Sadly, you can't get close enough to appreciate the detail, but the overall effect is dazzling. The top half of St Leopold is buried in the Wiener Werkstätte casket underneath the altar; his legs are beneath the nearby wrought-iron grille.

You can get some idea of the Spanish-bred Emperor Karl VI's big plans for Klosterneuburg from the **Residenztrakt**, to the east of the

Kafka in Kierling

While you're in the vicinity, you might be interested to know that the Prague-born writer Franz Kafka died of tuberculosis in Sanatorium Hoffmann (now converted into flats), in the nearby village of **Kierling** on June 3, 1924, at the age of forty. Die-hard devotees can catch a bus from outside the train station to Hauptstrasse 187, and visit the place in which he spent the last few weeks of his life, correcting proofs of his collection of short stories, later published as *The Hunger Artist*. The **Kafka-Gedenkraum**, on the second floor, is not, in fact, the very one in which he died, as that overlooked the garden and is currently occupied. To gain entry to the Gedenkraum, you must retrieve the key from flat D along the corridor. Inside, there are photos of Dora Dyment, who nursed him in his sickness, and whom he intended to marry, and of the old sanatorium, plus lots of books about (and by) Kafka.

The Kafka-Gedenkraum is open Mon–Sat 8am–noon & 1–5pm; free.

medieval buildings. Plans were drawn up in 1730 for a vast imperial edifice, enclosing four inner courtyards, in deliberate imitation of El Escorial in Spain, which the Habsburgs had recently lost to the Bourbons. The building was to sprout numerous domes, which were to be capped by crowns, each one representing one of the Habsburg lands. In the end, the money ran out even before the completion of the first courtyard, and the roof sports just two domes, one capped with the imperial crown, the other with the archducal hat of Lower Austria. The showpiece of the Baroque wing is the **Marmorsaal** (Marble Hall), with its giant oval dome, supported by coupled composite columns, and decorated with frescoes by Daniel Gran glorifying the Habsburg dynasty.

After the tour, it's worth taking a stroll round the outlying monastic buildings, particularly those surrounding the **Leopoldhof**, a secluded little cobbled courtyard to the northwest of the monastery church, with an attractive, late-Gothic oriel window on one side. The main courtyard, Stiftsplatz, to the south of the church, centres on a lovely Gothic **Lichtssäule** (Lighted Column), once a common sight in Austrian towns, now a rare surviving example.

Sammlung Essl

Klosterneuburg is also home to Austria's largest private art collection, the **Sammlung Essl** (*www.sammlung-essl.at*), which is displayed in a purpose-built gallery down by the Danube, to the south of the monastery. Featuring just about every renowned postwar Austrian artist, the collection has been accumulated over the last fifty years by Karlheinz and Agnes Essl, inheritors of the bauMax chain of DIY stores, which has its corporate headquarters in Klosterneuburg. Originally destined for the new MuseumsQuartier in the heart of Vienna (see p.132), the collection found itself without a home after Ortner & Ortner's competition-winning entry for the complex ran into controversy in the mid-1990s, and was eventually scaled down.

The gallery is open Tues–Sun 10am–7pm, Wed until 9pm; öS80/€5.81.

**Klosterneu-
burg**

The Essls responded by opening their own museum in a sort of concrete, Modernist factory designed by Heinz Tesar.

The big white rooms on the first floor display a sort of overview of the collection, which is characterized by large abstract canvases, but ranges from Surrealist works by Maria Lassnig and "kaleidoscopic landscapes" by Friedrich Hundertwasser to works by the leading lights of Aktionismus, Vienna's very own extremely violent version of 1960s performance art. In addition to the Austrian art, there are works by international contemporary artists such as Britain's Sean Scully and the American Nam June Paik. Half the gallery space is given over to temporary exhibitions drawn from the collection. On the second floor, you'll find the Grosser Saal, with its distinctive floating, curved ceiling, and a café and bookshop, the latter currently the only place where you can get any information in English about the collection.

Practicalities

The easiest way to get to Klosterneuburg is on S-Bahn line S40. If you already have a travelcard (see p.39), show it when buying your ticket. Trains depart from Franz-Josefs Bahnhof every half-hour, taking just eight minutes to get to Klosterneuburg-Weidling (for the Sammlung Essl), and twelve minutes to get to Klosterneuburg-Kierling (for the monastery). To reach the Sammlung Essl, walk under the railway tracks and turn left, following the signs to the gallery. For the monastery, which is clearly visible from the train station, head up Hundskehle, and then take the steps to your left. To get to the monastery from the gallery, cross back over the railway tracks and head up Leopoldstrasse. You'll find a **tourist office** (summer daily 9am–7pm; winter Mon–Fri 9am–noon; ☎02243/32038, *www.klosterneuburg.net*) in the train station.

To visit the monastery, you must sign up for a **guided tour**. The ticket office is right by the entrance to the monastery at Rathausplatz 20. If you're peckish, or have time to kill before your tour departs, it's worth checking out the *Stiftscafé* (daily 9am–6pm), next door, which offers reasonable **food**, and a chance to sample the local **wine**.

Boats up the Danube

On Saturdays and Sundays, from mid-May to October, the Donaudampfschiffahrtsgesellschaft (DDSG; *www.ddsg-blue-danube.at*) run a daily boat up the Danube from Vienna to Dürnstein. The boat leaves from Vienna's Reichsbrücke at 8.45am, calling at Tulln at 11.20am and Krems at 1.55pm. The DDSG boat from Dürnstein calls in at Krems on the way back downstream at 4.50pm, reaching Tulln at 6.45pm, and arriving two hours later in Vienna. These times were correct when going to print, however, you should check with the local tourist office before setting out. Note that a boat launch in German is a *Schiffsstation*.

The upper floor of the pricier *Stiftskeller* restaurant, next door, is open all day, though the *Keller* itself is only open in the evenings. A much more congenial place to have an evening meal, though, is the *Römerhof*, up the Stadtplatz, at the beginning of Kierlinger Strasse, which offers a range of beers on tap, all the usual pub snacks and a range of *Spätzle* dishes.

Tulln

Another easy day-trip, slightly further up the river, is to the little town of **TULLN**, situated in the fertile Danube plain roughly 25km northwest of Vienna. The town has an ancient history, beginning its life as the Roman naval fort of Comagena, but its main claim to fame today is as the birthplace of the painter Egon Schiele (1890–1918), who was born above Tulln's main train station, where his father was stationmaster.

The Town

On the hundredth anniversary of the artist's birth, Tulln finally honoured its most famous son by opening an **Egon-Schiele-Museum** in the town's former prison by the banks of the River Danube. Before touring the museum, be sure to pick up the free booklet in English from the ticket desk. The ground floor is filled with reproductions of Schiele's works and photographs from his brief life. One of the original cells has been transformed to represent the Neulengbach prison cell in which Schiele was incarcerated for 24 days in 1912. He was charged with displaying erotic drawings in a room open to children, and sentenced to three days in prison (by a judge who was himself a collector of pornography); since he had already served more than that in the course of his remand, he was immediately released. On the walls are reproductions of the watercolours he executed while imprisoned here, mostly angst-ridden self-portraits and interiors of his tiny cell.

The Egon-Schiele-Museum is open Tues–Sun 9am–noon & 2–6pm; öS40/€2.90.

The museum's modest collection of Schiele originals is displayed on the first floor. There's a goodly selection of pencil sketches, among them numerous nudes, a ghostly *Madonna and Child* in chalk and an early oil painting from 1908 of *Trieste Harbour*, a favourite destination of the artist, who, owing to his father's occupation, benefitted from cheap train tickets. In the attic, you'll find one of the artist's sketchbooks and the energetic *Ruined Mill at Mühling*, painted in oil in 1916, when Schiele was employed as a clerk in a POW camp for Russian officers.

The Tullner Museen are open Wed–Fri 3–6pm, Sat 2–6pm, Sun 10am–6pm; öS30/€2.18.

The town's other museum, the **Tullner Museen**, housed in the former Minorite (Franciscan) monastery, three blocks west down Albrechtsgasse, is, despite its stylish modern premises, a bit of a disappointment. The main courtyard, sporting an elegant glass roof,

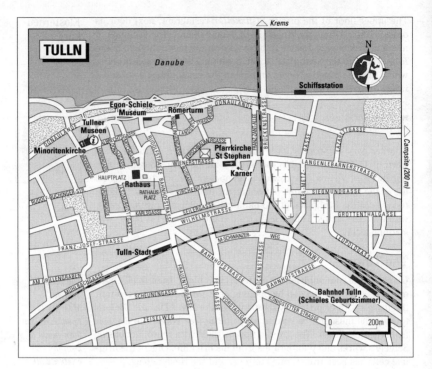

houses the town's collection of historic fire engines, from the horse-drawn carts of the eighteenth century to the diesel monsters of the 1970s. Other displays tell the story of the town's uneventful history, while the basement is given over to the less-than-impressive archeological finds dug up during the renovation of the cloisters.

You're better off taking a quick peek inside the adjacent Baroque **Minoritenkirche**, which has been lovingly restored and is positively gleaming with white Rococo stuccowork and colourful frescoes depicting, among other things, St John of Nepomuk being thrown to his death off Prague's Charles Bridge (also featured in gold relief on the pulpit). Be sure to peek through the glass door at the church's sacristy, with its cabinets of exquisite inlaid wood and Rococo ceiling decoration. At the west end of the church, is the brick-built Loretokapelle, a mock-up of Mary's house in Nazareth, complete with obligatory Black Madonna and Child, surrounded by silver clouds, gold sunbeams and cherubs.

The town's most impressive Roman remain, built under the Emperor Diocletian (284–305 AD), is the bulky **Römerturm**, an old bastion later used to store the town's precious salt supplies (and sometimes still referred to as the Salzturm), located on the riverfront beyond the Schiele Museum. Also worth a once-over is the **Pfarrkirche St Stephan**, two blocks east of the main square of Hauptplatz. Underneath this bulky Baroque church, the original Romanesque basilica can still be seen at ground level. Particularly fine is the west portal, which boasts thirteenth-century mug shots of the apostles. Best of all, though, is the old charnel house (*Karner*) to the east of the church, one of the best preserved Romanesque buildings in Austria, dating back to 1250. The hexagonal rib vaulting looks clumsily restored, but the series of weird and wonderful animals and beasts that decorate the walls, above the blind arcading, are fantastic, as are the devilish characters with outsized ears and noses that accompany them.

If you've time to kill while waiting for the train back to Vienna, you may as well visit **Egon Schieles Geburtszimmer**, occupying two rooms on the first floor of the main train station (Bahnhof Tulln), which has changed very little since Schiele's childhood. However, there's not a great deal to see beyond a reconstruction of the bedroom in which the artist was born in 1890, and a small model railway – understandably, trains were a major feature of Schiele's childhood, and a few of his early drawings of trains are reproduced here.

The Geburtszimmer is open June–Sept Tues–Sun 10am–noon & 3–5pm; öS20/€1.45.

Practicalities

Fast Regionalbahn **trains** run from Vienna's Franz-Josefs Bahnhof to Bahnhof Tulln, the main station, some fifteen minutes' walk southeast of the town centre (hourly; 25min). S40 S-Bahn trains take 45 minutes, but depart more frequently and terminate at Tulln-Stadt, less than five minutes' walk south of the centre. Tulln's **tourist office** (May–Oct Mon–Fri 9am–noon & 2–6pm, Sat & Sun 1–6pm; Nov–April Mon–Fri 9am–noon; ☎02272/65836, *www.tulln.at*), on the east side of Minoritenplatz, will furnish you with a free map and any other information you might need.

The best places for no-nonsense Austrian **food** are the *Albrechtsstuben*, Albrechtsgasse 24, east of Minoritenplatz, and the down-to-earth *Ratsstüberl*, Hauptplatz 19 (closed Sun), with tables looking over the main square. If you're looking for food on a Sunday, the only place you're likely to find open is the *Lime* restaurant, on Hauptplatz, which offers crêpes and baguettes as well as the usual fare.

Krems an der Donau

Some 75km northwest of Vienna, **KREMS** sits prettily on the terraced, vine-clad slopes of the left bank of the Danube. Site of a twelfth-century Babenberg mint, in the course of the thirteenth century Krems became a wealthy provincial wine-growing town. The architectural fruits of this boom period, which lasted until the

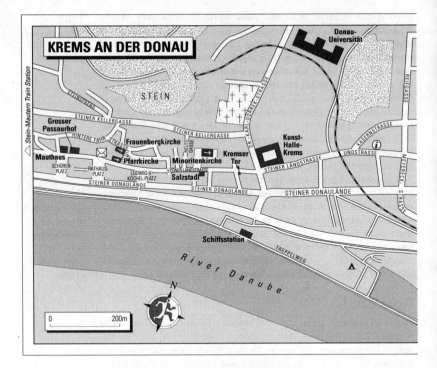

seventeenth century, are clearly visible in the narrow streets of the Altstadt. Devastation in the Thirty Years' War, a shift in the trade routes, and a wane in traffic on the Danube led to a decline in building work during the Baroque period. Krems remains an important Danube port, but the foundation of a post-graduate university and a swanky new arts centre have added a much-needed dose of youthful culture to what is essentially a sedate, prosperous town.

Krems town

Present-day Krems is actually made up of three previously separate settlements: Krems, Und and Stein, giving rise to the side-splitting local joke, "Krems Und Stein sind drei Städte" ("Krems and Stein are three towns"). Most people tend to restrict their wandering to Krems proper, though it's worth taking the time to explore Stein, too, since, in many ways, it's Stein which has most successfully retained its medieval character.

Krems's main thoroughfare, **Landstrasse**, three blocks north of the train station, is a busy, pedestrianized shopping street studded with old buildings. The finest of these is the **Bürgerspitalskirche**,

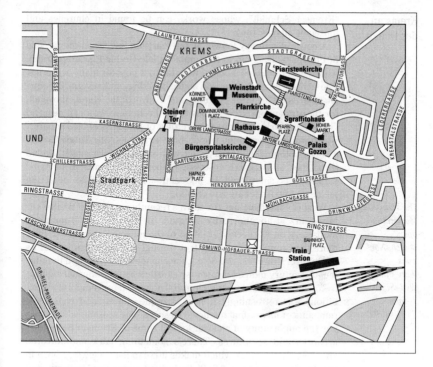

originally built in 1470 on the site of the old Jewish ghetto as the town's hospital chapel. Over the doorway is the A.E.I.O.U. motto of the Emperor Friedrich III (see p.53), while inside the little church boasts some wonderful lierne vaulting. On the opposite side of the street stands the sixteenth-century **Rathaus**, whose Renaissance origins are only visible in the corner oriel window facing onto Kirchengasse. Further west along the main street, at Obere Landstrasse 10, it's worth peeping into the exquisite arcaded courtyard of **Fellnerhof**, which features Tuscan columns from 1618.

To the north of Landstrasse, the hilly cobbled streets and squares successfully preserve their late-medieval character. The largest of the squares, Pfarrplatz, is dominated by the **Pfarrkirche**, originally a late-Romanesque church, enlarged at the end of the seventeenth century – you can see this most clearly in the tower. The interior is a perfect example of High Baroque drama, with trompe l'oeil masonry and gold covering just about everything, including the entire pulpit and the high altar: an explosion of gilded saints and cherubs set against the background of an enormous sunburst. The ceiling frescoes are by local-born Baroque artist Johann Martin Schmidt, known as

Krems an der Donau

"Kremser Schmidt", whose works can be found in churches and museums all over town.

A covered stairway known as the Piaristen Stiege, on the far side of Pfarrplatz, leads up to the imposing late-Gothic **Piaristenkirche**, whose tower doubled as the town's lookout post for many centuries. The church boasts some fine stellar vaulting, and several Baroque altarpieces by Kremser Schmidt, but it's worth the climb, above all, for the stupendous view across town. From here, you can descend via **Hoher Markt**, perhaps the prettiest of Krems's cobbled squares, which slopes down to the wonderfully scruffy-looking **Palais Gozzo**, a honey-coloured medieval palace with a ground-floor loggia. Round the corner, at Margarethenstrasse 5, the **Sgraffitohaus**, as its name suggests, is smothered in sixteenth-century sgraffito depicting medieval folk frolicking and feasting.

The Weinstadt Museum is open March–Nov Tues 9am–6pm, Wed–Sun 1–6pm; öS40/€2.91.

West of Pfarrplatz lies the town's recently overhauled **Weinstadt Museum**, atmospherically located in the former Dominican monastery on Körnermarkt. Most of the museum amounts to little more than a mildly diverting trot through Krems's history and its viticulture. However, you do get the chance to look around the thirteenth-century monastery, whose cloisters feature unusual zig-zag, trefoil arcading, and whose church – now used for temporary exhibitions – is refreshingly free of Baroque clutter, and boasts the remnants of its original medieval frescoes. The museum also allows you the opportunity of a closer look at some of **Kremser Schmidt**'s artworks and sculptures. There's something dark and tortured about Schmidt's work which makes it compulsive viewing. Born in nearby Grafenwörth in 1718, he trained under local artisans and set up his own workshop in Krems, eschewing the cosmopolitan art scene of the capital; it's this attachment to provincial roots that sets his work apart from the more academic painters of the Austrian Baroque.

Landstrasse, and the old medieval town of Krems, officially terminate at the strangely hybrid **Steiner Tor**, a monstrously belfried fifteenth-century town gate, flanked by two cone-capped bastions. Appropriately enough, the district of **Und** links Krems, in the east, with Stein, to the west. There's no reason to pause in Und, unless you wish to visit the town's tourist office (see opposite), housed in the former Capuchin monastery. And if you're keen to sample some of the region's wines, you can sign up for a wine-tasting tour of the monastery's cellars.

Stein

It's the **Kremsor Tor**, ten minutes' walk west of the Steinertor, that, confusingly, signals the beginning of Stein. As you approach the gateway, it's difficult to miss the **Kunst-Halle-Krems** (*www .kunsthalle.at*), the town's vast new arts venue, which hosts major modern art exhibitions, stages shows in the nearby Minoritenkirche

(see below) and puts on a whole series of events on Friday and
Saturday evenings.

Stein is much quieter than Krems, and really does feel like a separate town, its narrow main street, **Steiner Landstrasse**, a sequence
of crumbling old Renaissance facades with beautiful, often arcaded,
courtyards, and every 100m or so, a small cobbled square that faces
onto the Danube. The first church you come to is the impressive thirteenth-century shell of the **Minoritenkirche**, whose high vaulted,
late-Romanesque interior was used as a tobacco warehouse, and
which now stages exhibitions organized by the Kunst-Halle-Krems.
At the southern end of Minoritenplatz the two sixteenth-century
Salzstädls (salt barns) sport distinctive red and white quoins, characteristic of many of Stein's old buildings.

*The Kunst-
Halle-Krems is
open daily
10am–6pm;
entrance fee
varies.*

Further along Landstrasse, the Pfarrhof stands out owing to its
rich Rococo stuccowork, followed shortly afterwards by the Gothic
Pfarrkirche which sports a classic Baroque onion dome and some
finely carved choirstalls, but is otherwise fairly undistinguished.
Steps round the east end of the church climb sharply to the fourteenth-century **Frauenbergkirche**, now a chapel to Austrian war
dead. From here, you get a great view across Stein and the Danube
to the onion domes of the hilltop monastery of Göttweig to the
south. It's worth continuing a little further along Steiner
Landstrasse to appreciate Stein's two other winsome squares,
Rathausplatz and Schürerplatz, and its remarkable parade of
Renaissance houses: in particular, the **Grosser Passauerhof**, with
its half-moon battlements, and the **Mauthaus**, which boasts faded
trompe l'oeil frescoes.

Kremser Schmidt lived in the prettily gabled Baroque house
close by the squat **Linzer Tor**, which marks the western limit of the
old town of Stein. If you're heading back to Krems, the backstreet
of Hintere Fahrstrasse provides an alternative to Steiner
Landstrasse.

Practicalities

Trains to Krems leave from Vienna's Franz-Josefs Bahnhof (hourly;
1hr 10min). The town's **tourist office** is situated in the former Und
monastery, halfway between Krems and Stein at Undstrasse 6
(May–Oct Mon–Fri 9am–6pm, Sat 10am–noon & 1–6pm, Sun
10am–2pm; Nov–April Mon–Fri 8.30am–noon & 1.30–5pm;
☎02732/85620, *www.tiscover.com/krems*). Without doubt, one
of the best places to **eat** is at *Jell*, Hoher Markt 8–9 (closed Sat & Sun
lunch & Mon), a seriously *gemütlich* rustic place, with imaginatively prepared food, and excellent wine from their own nearby vineyards. Alternatively, the sushi sets and bento boxes at the stylish,
minimalist *Soho*, Obere Landstrasse 36, make for a pleasant change
from Austrian cuisine.

*For details of
boats to Krems,
see p.276.*

Melk

Strategically situated at the western entrance to the Wachau, some 40km upstream from Krems, the town of **MELK** boasts by far the most spectacular Baroque monastery in Austria. Dramatically perched on a high granite bluff overlooking the Danube, the palatial mustard-yellow abbey dominates the landscape from whichever direction you approach, dwarfing the town into insignificance. Initially a Roman border post and later a tenth-century Babenberg fortress, the site was handed to the Benedictines in 1089. Very little of the medieval structure survives, and what draws in a staggering half a million tourists a year is the flamboyant Baroque pile built in the first half of the eighteenth century.

Stift Melk

Melk's early renown was based on its medieval scholarship (discussed in some detail in Umberto Eco's monastic detective story *The Name of the Rose*) and its possession of some very valuable relics, including the body of the Irish missionary St Koloman, who was revered for his powers of healing. The original abbey was gut-

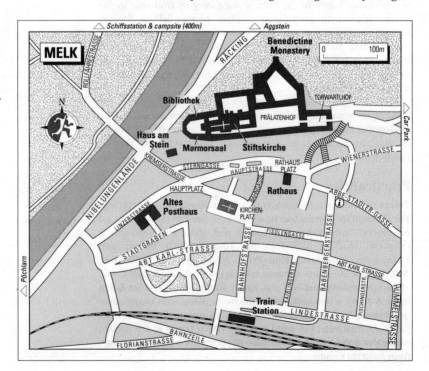

ted by fire during the Turkish invasion of 1683, and lay in ruins until Melk's ambitious abbot Bertold Dietmayr commissioned local architect Jakob Prandtauer to design a brand-new showpiece **monastery**. The project was so overblown that Dietmayr faced a rebellion by his own monks, dismayed by the affront to their asceticism, and the abbot had to prove that the monastery could afford the work before building could recommence. The abbey continues to function today, and its monastery school, containing some 700 boys and girls, remains one of Austria's most prestigious academic institutions.

Access to the monastery is via the main gates to the east. You can walk through several of the courtyards and peek at the abbey church without paying, but to see inside the monastery, you must buy a ticket from the monastery's information point on the south side of the Torwartlhof (the first courtyard).

The Kaisergang, Marmorsaal and Bibliothek

The **Kaisergang**, at the top of the Kaiserstiege, is a vast gallery – over 190m in length – designed to provide access to the 88 imperial chambers, some of which now house the abbey museum. Unfortunately, the abbey's most precious trio of treasures are kept in the treasury and only come out on display on October 13 (St Koloman's Day): the Melker Kreuz, a fourteenth-century cross containing a piece of Christ's cross, studded with aquamarines, pearls and gems; the eleventh-century portable altar of Swanhild, portraying the life of Christ in walrus horn; and a thirteenth-century reliquary of the lower jaw and tooth of St Koloman. Nevertheless, the museum owns a good crop of medieval reliquaries on permanent display, including a striking example that once contained St Agnes's head. Another work of art that you can be sure of seeing is the medieval monastery's winged altarpiece from around 1502 by Jörg Breu the Elder, one of the "Danube School" of artists, that included Lucas Cranach the Elder and Albrecht Dürer. The altar panels tell the story of Christ, employing the exaggerated facial expressions that were one of the hallmarks of the Danube School.

The rest of the abbey museum, which is basically a propaganda exercise by the monastery and its school, can be happily passed over in order to reach the two rooms by Prandtauer that make a visit to Melk worth the effort. The first is the red and grey **Marmorsaal** (Marble Hall), featuring Paul Troger's superb fresco depicting the Enlightenment. Troger specialized in fresco paintings, and his masterly handling of perspective makes the ceiling appear much higher than it really is. Despite its name, the only furnishings in the hall made from real marble are the doorframes. To get to Prandtauer's **Bibliothek** (Library), you must first take a stroll outside across the curvaceous terrace, from whose balcony you can admire the town below and the Danube in the distance. The library's ancient tomes –

Melk

The monastery is open daily: mid-April to mid-Nov daily 9am–6pm; mid-Nov to mid-April guided tours only 11am & 2pm; öS100/€7.27; öS30/€2.18 extra with a guided tour; www .stiftmelk.at.

rebound in matching eighteenth-century leather and gold leaf – are stacked up to the ceiling in beautifully carved shelves of aspen, walnut and oak. Despite having never been restored, Troger's colourful fresco – a cherub-infested allegory on Faith – has kept its original hue, thanks to the library's lack of lighting and heating. From the library, you descend a cantilevered spiral staircase to the Stiftskirche.

Stiftskirche

The **Stiftskirche**, designed by Jakob Prandtauer in 1702 and completed in 1738 after his death, occupies centre stage at Melk, dominating the monastery complex with its fanciful symmetrical towers and octagonal dome. From the balconies above the side altars to the acanthus leaf-capitals of the church's fluted pilasters, the red stucco interior literally drips with gold paint. The Galli da Bibiena family of Italian theatrical designers are responsible for the stunning all-gold pulpit, and the design of the awesome high altar with its gilded papal crown suspended above the church's patron saints, Peter and Paul. The airy frescoes and side-altar paintings are mostly by Johann Michael Rottmayr, who, along with Troger, was responsible for importing High Baroque art to Austria from Italy.

It's impossible not to notice the grisly reliquaries in the church's side altars, some of them featuring skeletons reposing in glittering garments. The most hallowed bones, those of St Koloman (presumably not including his jaw) are hidden away from the public gaze inside the sarcophagus in the north transept. Beyond this lies the entrance to the **Babenbergergruft**, where the remains of Babenberg rulers were traditionally thought to have been buried. In 1969, however, the remains were exhumed and examined, after which it was concluded that only Adalbert (1018–55), Ernst (1055–75) and possibly Heinrich I (994–1018) were actually interred here.

The Altstadt

Melk's **Altstadt** is hardly much bigger than the monastery, and, inevitably, with such enormous numbers of tourists passing through, it does suffer from overcrowding in the summer. However, there are a few good-looking houses that repay a stroll around the town. Pretty painted shutters adorn the chemist's, next door to the Rathaus, and there are a couple of dinky turrets on the old bakery at the corner of Sterngasse, but the single most attractive building is the **Altes Posthaus**, built in 1792 at Linzerstrasse 3–5. The facade features stucco reliefs of horses' heads, agricultural tools, an eagle holding a post horn in its beak and so on, while the roof balustrade is peppered with urns spouting golden cacti, and, as its centrepiece, a double-headed crowned eagle. For a glimpse of old Melk that few tourists get to see, seek out the vine-covered **Haus am Stein**, set back in its own courtyard behind Kremser Strasse.

Fast **trains** from Vienna's Westbahnhof take an hour to get to Melk, but only a few actually stop there, as is obvious by the thunderous noise of through-trains that regularly shakes the town. The more frequent slower service stretches the journey time from Vienna to two hours, unless you take the fast train to St Pölten and change there, in which case you should be able to cut it down to an hour and ten minutes. Melk's **train station** is at the head of Bahnhofstrasse, which leads directly into the Altstadt.

The **tourist office** is on Abbe-Stadler-Gasse (April–Oct Mon–Sat 9am–7pm, Sun 10am–2pm; Nov–March Mon–Fri 9am–noon & 1–4pm; ☎02752/52307, *www.tiscover.com/melk*). The plush *Hotel Stadt Melk*, Hauptplatz 1, has the town's finest **restaurant**; other places to eat include *Gasthaus Melkerstüberl*, which is a good local for lunch, with a three-course Tagesmenü for öS100/€7.27, slightly off the tourist track at Wienerstrasse 7, or the family-run *Madar* café–restaurant (closed Wed) on Rathausplatz.

Listings

Chapter 10

Accommodation

As you might expect, Vienna has some of the most opulent, historic **hotels** in Europe, with mesospheric prices to match. However, reasonably priced, central accommodation can be found, especially in the numerous **pensions**. These are not necessarily inferior in quality or price to hotels – in fact some are a whole lot better. The distinction is purely technical: pensions occupy one or more floors, but not the whole, of a building; to be a hotel, the entire block must be occupied.

Vienna also has plenty of **hostel** space in official HI and independent hostels, although these can be booked up months in advance, so try to ring ahead or email and make a reservation before you leave. Inveterate **campers** have a wide choice of peripheral sites.

The **high season** for accommodation in Vienna is from April to October, and for the two weeks over Christmas and New Year (during which there is sometimes a surcharge). Bear in mind also that it can be difficult to find a room on spec during the week running up to Lent, when *Fasching* reaches its climax (see p.331). That said, some hotels drop their rates in July and August, as the opera house and the theatres are all on vacation during this period. (The room price should, by law, be displayed in your room.) If you're arriving during the peak season, it's best to plan ahead in order to guarantee yourself a room (we've given telephone numbers and, where possible, websites or email

addresses). If you arrive without a booking, any of the **tourist offices** mentioned on p.38 can make a reservation for you, for which they charge around öS40/€2.91.

Hotels and pensions

Hotels and pensions in Vienna tend to adhere to the standards of efficiency, modernity and cleanliness you'd expect in Austria. It's perfectly possible to stay right in the **Innere Stadt** without breaking an arm and a leg, although the cheapest places tend to be in the districts beyond the Ringstrasse. This is no bad thing, as areas like **Neubau** and **Josefstadt** have a wider choice of restaurants and bars than the central tourist zone.

Breakfast is included in the price at most of the hotels and pensions, though what it actually amounts to can differ enormously. "Continental breakfast" means coffee and a couple of rolls; "full continental breakfast" means you should get a bit of choice, perhaps cold meats and cheeses, and if you're really lucky a hot egg-based snack; and "buffet" means you can gorge yourself on as much cereal, muesli, eggs, bread, rolls, cheese and meats as you can eat.

Before you commit yourself, it's always worthwhile having a look at the room as **natural light** is in short supply in some buildings in Vienna. Many old blocks of flats retain their beautiful antique **lifts**, some of which are so

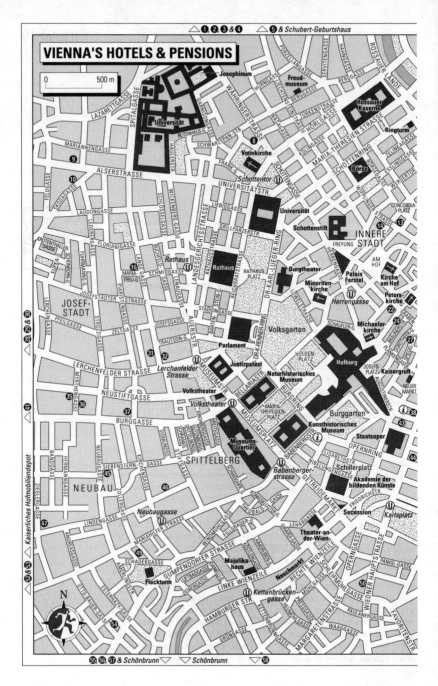

VIENNA'S HOTELS & PENSIONS

△ ❶, ❷, ❸ & ❹   △ ❺ & Schubert-Geburtshaus

0 — 500 m

Josephinum
Freud-
museum
Rossauer
Kaserne
Ringturm
Universität
Börse
Votivkirche
Schottentor
Universität
Schottenstift
INNERE
STADT
FREYUNG
Rathaus
Rathaus
Burgtheater
Palais
Ferstel
Kirche
am Hof
Peters-
kirche
AM
HOF
Minoriten-
kirche
Herrengasse
Michaeler-
kirche
Volksgarten
JOSEF-
STADT
Parlament
Justizpalast
HELDEN-
PLATZ
Hofburg
JOSEFS-
PLATZ Kaisergruft
Naturhistorisches
Museum
Lerchenfelder
Strasse
Volkstheater
Volkstheater
MARIA-
THERESIEN-
PLATZ
Burggarten
Burggarten
SPITTELBERG
Kunsthistorisches
Museum
Staatsoper
Museums-
Quartier
Babenberger-
strasse
Schillerplatz
Akademie der
bildenden Künste
NEUBAU
Neubaugasse
Secession
Karlsplatz
Theater-an-
der-Wien
Majolika
haus
Neschmarkt
Flackturm
Kettenbrücken-
gasse
N
△ ❺❺, ❺❻, ❺❼ & Schönbrunn▽   ▽ Schönbrunn   ▽❺❽

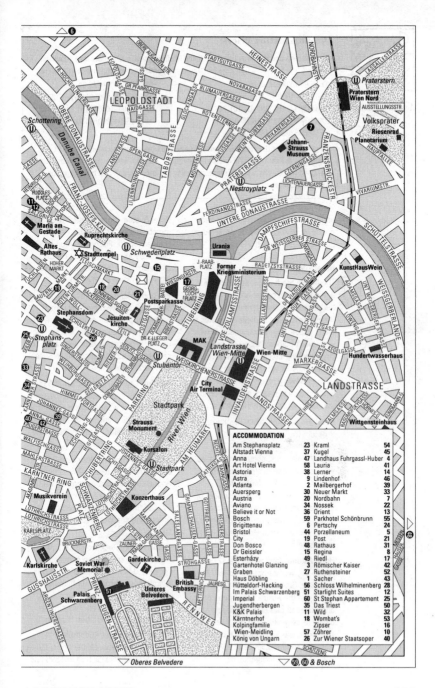

ACCOMMODATION

Am Stephansplatz	23	Kraml	54
Altstadt Vienna	37	Kugel	45
Anna	47	Landhaus Fuhrgassl-Huber	4
Art Hotel Vienna	58	Lauria	41
Astoria	38	Lerner	14
Astra	9	Lindenhof	46
Atlanta	2	Mailbergerhof	39
Auersperg	30	Neuer Markt	33
Austria	20	Nordbahn	7
Aviano	34	Nossek	22
Believe it or Not	36	Orient	13
Bosch	59	Parkhotel Schönbrunn	55
Brittenau	6	Pertschy	24
Bristol	44	Porzellaneum	5
City	19	Post	21
Don Bosco	48	Rathaus	31
Dr Geissler	15	Regina	8
Esterházy	49	Riedl	17
Gartenhotel Glanzing	3	Römischer Kaiser	42
Graben	27	Ruthensteiner	52
Haus Döbling	1	Sacher	43
Hütteldorf-Hacking	56	Schloss Wilhelminenberg	28
Im Palais Schwarzenberg	51	Starlight Suites	12
Imperial	60	St Stephan Appartement	25
Jugendherbergen	35	Das Triest	50
K&K Palais	11	Wild	32
Kärntnerhof	18	Wombat's	53
Kolpingfamilie		Zipser	16
Wien-Meidling	57	Zöhrer	10
König von Ungarn	26	Zur Wiener Staatsoper	40

Accommodation

ancient they carry passengers up and not down, and can only be operated by placing an öS1 coin in the slot.

Innere Stadt

The **Innere Stadt** is Vienna's old town and commercial centre, and is therefore the place where everyone wants to stay. Prices reflect this and there is a surfeit of bland upper-range hotels (many of which we haven't bothered listing below), and a corresponding dearth of inexpensive places (most of which we *have* listed). As all the following hotels and pensions are in the city's first district, we have omitted the district code before the address.

Hotel am Stephansplatz, Stephansplatz 9 ☎534 05, *www.nethotels.com /am-stephansplatz*; U-Bahn Stephansplatz. Just about as central as you can get, with lots of rooms (for öS2000/€145.35 a double and upwards) overlooking the west door of the Stephansdom. The decor is pretty dated, but perfectly comfortable and spacious, and all rooms are en suite, with cable/satellite TV. ⑨

Hotel Astoria, Kärntnerstrasse 32–34 ☎515 77, *www.austria-trend.at*; U-Bahn Karlsplatz. Grandiose, turn-of-the-century flagship of the Austria Trend hotel chain, and preferred pad of visiting opera stars owing to its proximity to the Staatsoper. The rooms are fully modernized and start at around öS2500/€181.68. The entrance is on Fürichgasse. ⑨

Hotel Austria, Wolfengasse 3 ☎515 23, *members.eunet.at/hotelaus*; U-Bahn Schwedenplatz. Plush family-run hotel, pleasantly located in a quiet cul-de-sac off Fleischmarkt, with some cheap rooms without en-suite facilities. ④

Pension Aviano, Marco d'Avianogasse 1 ☎512 83 30, *www.pertschy.com*; U-Bahn Karlsplatz. Part of the Pertschy pension chain, squeezed onto the top floor of a building just off Kärntnerstrasse. Low ceilings, but roomy rooms, all en suite, with TV and fluffy, floral decor. ⑤

Pension City, Bauernmarkt 10 ☎533 95 21; U-Bahn Stephansplatz. On the second floor of a wonderful late nineteenth-century building and run by a friendly woman proprietor. Tastefully decorated rooms, all en suite. ④

Pension Dr Geissler, Postgasse 14 ☎533 28 03; U-Bahn Schwedenplatz. Anonymous modern pension on the eighth floor; all rooms with cable/satellite TV, and those with shared facilities are among the cheapest in the Innere Stadt. ②

Graben Hotel, Dorotheergasse 3 ☎512 15 31, *www.kremslehner.hotels.or.at /graben*; U-Bahn Stephansplatz. The foyer is suitably lugubrious, with heavy velvet drapery, but all the rooms are modernized and smart, with en-suite shower and toilet, and the location is great. ⑦

K & K Palais Hotel, Rudolfsplatz 11 ☎533 13 53, *www.kkhotels.com*; U-Bahn Schwedenplatz. Built in 1890 and once the town house of Franz-Josef's mistress Katharina Schratt, the *K & K* retains an appropriately imperial ambience in the lobby. The rooms have been modernized, and are fully en suite, with prices starting at around öS2500/€181.68. ⑨.

Hotel Kärntnerhof, Grashofgasse 4 ☎512 19 23, *www.karntnerhof.com*; U-Bahn Schwedenplatz/Stephansplatz. Located in a cul-de-sac off Köllnerhofgasse, with pleasant, characterful rooms. Make sure you see your room first, however, as some can be a bit dingy. ⑨.

Hotel König von Ungarn, Schulerstrasse 10 ☎515 84, *www.kvu.at*; U-Bahn Stephansplatz. Tastefully modernized hotel with a remarkable wooden-panelled, covered courtyard bar/lounge. Pleasantly decorated rooms for under öS2500/€181.68 equipped throughout with air-conditioning, TV and en-suite facilities. ⑨.

Pension Lerner, Wipplingerstrasse 23 ☎533 52 19, *www.pensionlerner.com*;

U-Bahn Schottentor/Herrengasse. Small pension with just seven bright, simple rooms with shower, toilet, TV, plus nice high ceilings and fans. Big buffet breakfasts served until 11am. ③.

Hotel Mailbergerhof, 1, Annagasse 7 ☎512 06 41; U-Bahn Karlsplatz/Stephansplatz. Converted Baroque palace on a delightfully discreet, narrow side street off Kärntnerstrasse, with attractively furnished rooms for just over öS2000/€145.35. The hotel is smart, but the ambience is relaxed, and the staff are supremely efficient and friendly. ⑨.

Pension Neuer Markt, Seilergasse 9 ☎512 23 16; U-Bahn Stephansplatz. Very popular central pension on the second floor of a lovely old patrician building. Rooms are clean, comfortable and modern, those without shower or en-suite toilet are a relative bargain – only a few have views over Neuermarkt. ③.

Pension Nossek, Graben 17 ☎533 70 41, *pensions.nossek@faxvia.net*; U-Bahn

Accommodation

Vienna's Big Three

Vienna specializes in big **luxury hotels**, but three big Ringstrasse piles stand head and shoulders above the others for their heavy late nineteenth-century decor and their historical associations. At the end of World War II, the Americans took over the *Bristol*, the Russians occupied the *Imperial*, while the British holed up in the *Sacher*.

Hotel Bristol, Kärntner Ring 1 ☎515 16, *www.westin.com/bristol*; U-Bahn Karlsplatz. The least remarkable of the four from the outside, but a feast of marble inside, with barley-sugar columns in the *Korso* restaurant, and opulent repro decor in all the rooms (doubles start at öS5000/€363.36; suites can cost up to eight times that). ⑨.

Hotel Imperial, Kärntner Ring 16 ☎501 10, *www.luxurycollection.com/imperial*; U-Bahn Karlsplatz. Incredibly lavish converted palace, built for the Duke of Würtemberg, and later the "favourite hostelry of crowned heads, their heirs-apparent, and ambassadors" according to one observer in 1877. Hitler stayed

here on his return to the city in 1938, and it's still the first choice for visiting heads of government. Doubles start at a mere öS6000/€436.04; suites reach the stratospheric heights of öS45,000/€3270.28. ⑨.

Hotel Sacher, Philharmonikerstrasse 4 ☎514 56, *www.sacher.com*; U-Bahn Karlsplatz. The most famous of the lot, not only because of its legendary *Sachertorte*, but also because this was where the aristocratic playboys used to hang out in the imperial days. A heavy, wood-panelled, red velvet approach to the decor and a stiflingly formal attitude to hospitality. Double rooms range between öS4000/€290.69 and öS9000/€654.06. ⑨.

Accommodation

Stephansplatz. Large family-run pension on three floors of an old building on the pedestrianised Graben, with en-suite doubles of varying sizes, and some real bargain singles with shared facilities. It's popular so book in advance. ⑤.

Hotel Orient, Tiefer Graben 30 ☎533 73 07; U-Bahn Herrengasse. Vienna's equivalent of a Tokyo "love hotel", with rooms rented by the hour and per night. Couples come for the mind-boggling exotic decor, and the wide range of themed rooms from inexpensive to more than öS2000/€145.35. ③–⑨.

Pension Pertschy, Habsburgergasse 5 ☎534 49, www.pertschy.com; U-Bahn Stephansplatz. Flagship of the Pertschy pension chain, with rooms off a series of plant-strewn balconies looking onto a lovely old courtyard. The rooms have lots of character, high ceilings, tasteful furnishings and TV. ⑤.

Hotel Post, Fleischmarkt 24 ☎515 83, www.hotel-post-wien.at; U-Bahn Schwedenplatz. Civilized, central hotel with over a hundred mostly large, old rooms with modern furnishings. The ones without shower and toilet are the real bargain. ③.

Pension Riedl, Georg-Coch-Platz 3 ☎512 79 19; U-Bahn Schwedenplatz/Wien Mitte. Bright, cheerful pension on the fourth floor of a wonderful fin-de-siècle building overlooking the Postsparkasse. The rooms are small, though most have shower and toilet, and you get breakfast in bed. Closed mid-Jan to mid-Feb. ③.

Hotel Römischer Kaiser, Annagasse 16 ☎512 77 51, www.bestwestern-ce.com/roemischerkaiser; U-Bahn Karlsplatz. Turn-of-the-century hotel, now run by the Best Western chain, on a delightfully narrow side street off Kärntnerstrasse. New furnishings are successfully combined with the originals, though some rooms feature plainer modern decor; facilities are en suite throughout. ⑧.

St Stephan Appartement-Pension, Spiegelgasse 1 ☎512 29 90; U-Bahn Stephansplatz. Incredible location in the Braun building overlooking Graben. A beautiful antique lift takes you up to the fourth floor, where there are just six doubles, with creaky parquet flooring and furnishings in keeping with the period. All have TV, shower, toilet, fridge and cooking facilities, and some have views out on to the Graben and Stephansdom. No breakfast. ⑤.

Starlight Suites, Salzgries 12 ☎535 92 22, www.starlighthotel.co.at; U-Bahn Schwedenplatz. Totally modernized apartments for around öS2000/€145.35, in a centrally located but quiet backstreet, not far from the Bermuda Triangle. Buffet breakfast is provided as there are no kitchen facilities. Two other branches exist at Renngasse 13 and on Am Heumarkt, both a stone's throw from the Ring. ⑨.

Hotel zur Wiener Staatsoper, Krugerstrasse 11 ☎513 12 74, www.zurwienerstaatsoper.at; U-Bahn Karlsplatz. Flamboyant late nineteenth-century facade and foyer, but much plainer rooms inside. All rooms are en suite and have TVs, and the location, just off Kärntnerstrasse, is pretty good for the price. ⑥.

Landstrasse, Wieden and Margareten

Parts of **Landstrasse** (3rd district) are eminently avoidable, with the exception of the area around the Belvedere. **Wieden** (4th district) and **Margareten** (5th district) are quieter, residential districts, to the south of Karlsplatz and convenient for the Naschmarkt.

Art Hotel Vienna (aka Golden Tulip Hotel), 5, Brandmayergasse 7–9 ☎554 51 08, www.thearthotelvienna.at; tram #6 or #18 from U-Bahn Margaretengürtel. Margareten hotel with a penchant for wacky modern art and designer furnishings. All rooms are en suite. ⑤.

Pension Bosch, 3, Keilgasse 13 ☎798 61 79; S-Bahn Rennweg or tram #0. Friendly pension in a quiet residential backstreet near the Südbahnhof, behind the Belvedere, an easy tram ride into town. The thirteen rooms have lots of character, and the cheapest ones have shared facilities. ②.

Hotel im Palais Schwarzenberg, 3, Schwarzenbergplatz 9 ☎798 45 15, *www.palais-schwarzenberg.com*; tram #D. Hidden behind the Soviet War Memorial, this is *the* hotel to go for if money's no object – doubles start at öS3600/€261.62 – a Baroque palace designed by Hildebrandt and Fischer von Erlach, with period furnishings courtesy of, among others, Rubens, Meissen and Gobelins. ⑨.

Das Triest, 4, Wiedner Hauptstrasse 12 ☎589 18, *www.designhotels.com*; U-Bahn Karlsplatz. Vienna's only truly hip designer hotel is hidden away in a nondescript building a short stroll from Karlsplatz. The super-smooth, minimalist interior comes courtesy of Terence Conran, and is quirky in an understated way. Rooms, which start at around öS3000/€218.02, are immaculate, and those on the top floor have great views across the city skyline. ⑨.

Mariahilf, Neubau and Josefstadt

The 6th, 7th and 8th districts are home to some of Vienna's liveliest bars and choicest restaurants, and therefore ideal areas in which to be based. **Neubau** includes the lively Spittelberg area, while **Josefstadt** is more studenty.

Altstadt Vienna, 7, Kirchengasse 41 ☎526 33 99, *www.altstadt.at*; U-Bahn Volkstheater. A cut above most other pensions, with laid-back, well-informed staff, a relaxing lounge and full-on buffet breakfast. Tastefully decorated en-suite rooms with high ceilings and a great location, near Spittelberg, and within easy walking distance of the U-Bahn and Ring. ⑥.

Pension Anna, 7, Zieglergasse 18 ☎523 01 60, *pension.anna@chello.at*; U-Bahn Zieglergasse. First-floor pension run by a friendly couple. The startling light-blue decor doesn't extend into the fourteen bedrooms, all of which have en-suite shower and toilet. ④.

Pension Astra, 8, Alserstrasse 32 ☎402 43 54, *hotelpensionastra@aon.at*; U-Bahn Alserstrasse. Mid-sized pension on the mezzanine of an old patrician building. Friendly staff and a range of modernized rooms from simple doubles without toilet to roomy apartments. ②.

Pension Esterházy, 6, Nelkengasse 3 ☎587 51 59; U-Bahn Neubaugasse. Basic rooms with shared facilities, close to Mariahilferstrasse. There's no reception as such (it's run by the elderly lady on the floor below), and no breakfast, but it's clean and just about the cheapest place to stay short of a hostel. ①.

Pension Kraml, 6, Brauergasse 5 ☎587 8588; U-Bahn Zieglergasse/Neubaugasse. Probably the friendliest and most reliable of the cheap pensions in the quiet streets off Mariahilferstrasse. Smart, clean, modern rooms, some with en-suite facilities. ②.

Hotel Kugel, 7, Siebensterngasse 43 ☎523 33 55, *www.hotelkugel.at*; U-Bahn Neubaugasse. Good location within spitting distance of Spittelberg's numerous restaurants and bars. Plain but clean rooms, some with shared facilities, some en suite; continental breakfast is served in the *gemütlich* peasant-style breakfast room. ②.

Pension Lindenhof, 7, Lindengasse 4 ☎523 04 98; U-Bahn Neubaugasse. On the first floor of a lugubrious turn-of-the-century building at the Spittelberg end of this long street. Lovely, up-only lift (öS1), plant-strewn communal area and appealing rooms (some of which are en suite), with creaky parquet flooring. ②.

Hotel Rathaus, 8, Lange Gasse 13 ☎406 01 23, *www.nethotels.com /rathaus*; U-Bahn Lerchenfelder Strasse. Clean, comfortable and quiet hotel in an old patrician building a few blocks west of the Rathaus, with some cheap singles without en-suite bathroom. ④.

Pension Wild, 8, Lange Gasse 10 ☎406 51 74, *www.pension-wild.com*; U-Bahn Lerchenfelder Strasse. Friendly, laid-back pension, a short walk from the Ring in a student district behind the university, and especially popular with backpackers and gay travellers. Booking essential. ②.

Accommodation

Accommodation

Pension Zipser, 8, Lange Gasse 49
☎404 540, *www.notehotels.com/zipser;*
U-Bahn Rathaus. Well-equipped, modern
pension, offering a buffet breakfast – a
reliable choice, just a short walk from
the Ring behind the Rathaus. ④.

Alsergrund

Separated from the rest of the *Vorstädte* by
the giant city hospital, the 9th district has a
life of its own, with a good selection of
trendy cafés, bars and restaurants, and frequent tram connections to the centre.

Hotel Atlanta, 9, Währinger Strasse 33
☎405 12 30, *www.icnet.at/hotelatlanta;*
tram #37, #38, #40, #41 or #42. Plush
Alsergrund hotel within easy walking distance of the district's best bars and restaurants. All rooms are en suite with cable TV.
Prices drop significantly in low season. ⑦.

Hotel Regina, 9, Rooseveltplatz 15
☎404 46,
www.kremslehner.hotels.or.at/regina; U-
Bahn Schottentor. Huge Ringstrasse hotel
next door to the Votivkirche, with gloriously heavy Viennese decor in the public
areas and in some of the rooms. ⑦.

Leopoldstadt

Separated from the Innere Stadt by the
Danube Canal, **Leopoldstadt**, Vienna's
2nd district, is quiet and slightly dowdy,
and seldom visited by tourists. Yet the
area lies just a couple of tram stops from
the central district and the greenery of the
Prater. The backstreets near Wien-Nord
train station double as a red-light district,
but the atmosphere is rarely intimidating.

Hotel Nordbahn, 2, Praterstrasse 72 ☎211
30, *www.hotel-nordbahn.at;* U-Bahn
Nestroyplatz/Praterstern. If you want to stay
in the second district, then the birthplace of
Max Steiner, composer of film music to
Gone with the Wind and *Casablanca*, is
probably your best bet. It's now a large,
pleasantly modernized hotel with shower,
toilet and TV in all rooms. ⑤.

The suburbs

Gartenhotel Glanzing, 19, Glanzinggasse
23 ☎470 42 72,
www.gartenhotel-glanzing.at; tram #41.
Classic inter-war modernist villa in the
northern suburbs with amazing views over
Vienna from some rooms. TVs and en-
suite bathrooms throughout, lovely shady
garden, plus sauna and solarium. ⑦.

Landhaus Fuhrgassl-Huber, 19,
Rathstrasse 24 ☎440 30 33; bus #35A
from U-Bahn Nussdorferstrasse. A real
gemütlich country hotel right out in the
wine villages at the foot of the
Wienerwald. Not easy to get to by public
transport. ⑥.

Parkhotel Schönbrunn, 13, Hietzinger
Hauptstrasse 10–20 ☎878 04
www.austria-trend.at; U-Bahn Hietzing.
Vienna's largest hotel (nearly 400 rooms
for öS2500/€181.68), built in 1907 right
by Schönbrunn to house the imperial
guests. Lots of over-the-top touches from
those days, plus mod cons like an
indoor pool and sauna. ⑨.

Schloss Wilhelminenberg, 16,
Savoyenstrasse 2 ☎485 85 03,
www.austria-trend.at; bus #146B or
#46B from S-Bahn Ottakring or tram #J
terminus. Impressive Neoclassical pile,
with incredible views over Vienna. Not a
good idea if you want to sample the
nightlife, but otherwise a palatial place to
hole up in. There's a cheaper hostel
alternative next door (see opposite). ⑥.

Hostels, student halls, private rooms and camping

Vienna's official **Hostelling International**
Jugendherbergen (youth hostels) are efficient, clean, and, occasionally, even
friendly. However, with just one exception, they are all a long way from the
centre. Most of the beds are in segregat-
ed dorms, but some do have bunk-bed
doubles and many have en-suite facilities. Prices vary, but are usually around
öS200/€14.54 a night including a simple continental breakfast. Nowadays, you
can join Hostelling International on the
spot at any of the hostels listed below (if
you're already a YHA member, you're
automatically in the HI). Last, but by no
means least, you should make an

advance reservation as soon as you know when you might be arriving, as places occasionally get booked out in advance; at the very least, you should ring before turning up on spec.

The biggest practical drawback to the official hostels is that they throw you out each day at the ungodly hour of 9am in order to clean, and won't let you back in until 3 or 4pm. There are also **curfews**, though some hostels have 24hr receptions and will give you a night key on request. The lure of the **independent hostel**, then, is that while the prices are much the same as the HI hostels, the atmosphere is a bit less institutional, there's generally no curfew, and either no lockout or a more generous one allowing a longer lie-in. However, the places do tend to be a bit more run-down and ramshackle.

From July to September, there are singles and doubles, plus a few triples and quads, available in *Studentenheime* or **student halls** of residence. The rooms rarely have much character, and kitchen facilities are not always available, but the location is usually fairly central and you definitely get more privacy than in a hostel. Prices tend to be a little higher (and breakfast is often not included), but there's no curfew, no lockout, and no limit to how long you wish to stay.

The city's tourist offices (see p.38) have a very limited number of **private rooms** (few of them very central) for upwards of öS300/€21.80 per person per night (with a minimum of three nights' stay). The Mittwohnzentrale, 8, Laudongasse 7 (☎402 60 61; Mon–Fri 10am–2pm & 3–6pm) charges slightly less and can arrange longer-term accommodation. Another agency to try is the nearby youth travel specialist, ÖKISTA, 9, Türkenstrasse 8 (☎401 48; Mon–Fri 9.30am–4pm).

Finally, Vienna's **campsites** are all quite far out from the centre, on the perimeters of the city, and so for committed campers only. Pitches cost around öS40–60/€2.91–4.36, plus a fee of around öS60–80/€4.36–5.81 per person.

Official HI hostels

Jugendgästehaus Brigittenau, 20, Friedrich-Engels-Platz 24 ☎332 82 94, *oejhv-wien-jgh-brigittenau@oejhv.or.at*; tram #N from U-Bahn Schwedenplatz or Dresdner Strasse. Huge modern hostel in a dour working-class suburb with dorms and en-suite bunk-bed doubles. 1am curfew, but 24hr reception.

Jugendgästehaus Hütteldorf-Hacking, 13, Schlossberggasse 8 ☎877 0263, *jgh@wigast.com*; S- and U-Bahn Hütteldorf. A 220-bed dorm-only hostel way out in the sticks, but convenient for those who wish to explore the wilds of the Lainzer Tiergarten and Schönbrunn. 11.45pm curfew, but night key available for a small fee.

Kolpingfamilie Wien-Meidling, 12, Bendlgasse 10–12 ☎813 5487; U-Bahn Niederhofstrasse. Modern hostel easily reached by U-Bahn from the centre. Beds in the big dorms go for as little as öS130/€9.45 (without breakfast). Curfew midnight; 24hr reception.

Jugendherbergen Myrthengasse/Neustiftgasse, 7, Myrthengasse 7/Neustiftgasse 85 ☎523 63 16, *oejhv-wien-jgh-neustiftg.@oejhv.or.at*; bus #48A or 10min walk from U-Bahn Volkstheater. The most central of all the official hostels, with 200-plus dorm beds divided between two addresses round the corner from each other. Book well in advance and go to the Myrthengasse reception on arrival. Curfew 1am.

Schlossherberge am Wilhelminenberg, 16, Savoyenstrasse 2 ☎45 85 03-700; bus #146B or #46B from U-Bahn Ottakring or tram #J terminus. Slightly pricier dorm beds or doubles in a beautiful location next to a Neoclassical mansion in the Vienna Woods, but not a great base from which to sample the nightlife. 11.45pm curfew, or a late-entry pass.

Independent hostels

Believe It or Not, 7, Myrthengasse 10 ☎526 46 58; bus #48A or 10min walk from U-Bahn Volkstheater. Friendly,

Accommodation

Accommodation

cheap crash pad opposite the HI hostel (see p.299), with no breakfast provided, but kitchen facilities available. No curfew.

Lauria, 7, Kaiserstrasse 77 ☎ 522 25 55; U-Bahn Burggasse-Stadthalle. The *Lauria* is more of a budget hotel, with a hostel ambience. Clean doubles, triples and quads, dorm beds on the third floor, and a communal kitchen. 24hr reception.

Hostel Ruthensteiner, 15, Robert-Hamerling-Gasse 24 ☎ 893 4202, *hostel.ruthensteiner@telecom.at*; U-Bahn Westbahnhof. Excellent hostel with a nice courtyard to hang out in, within easy walking distance of the Westbahnhof, and with dorm beds, doubles and triples (discounts for HI members). No curfew. Open all year.

Turmherberge "Don Bosco", 3, Lechnerstrasse 12 ☎ 713 14 94; U-Bahn Kardinal-Nagl-Platz. Don't go with high expectations, but these are probably the cheapest beds in town (öS80/€5.81 without breakfast). Situated in a church tower in the back end of Landstrasse. Curfew 11.45pm. Open March–Nov.

Wombat's, 15, Grangasse 6 ☎ 897 2336, *wombats@chello.at*; U-Bahn Westbahnhof. Plain dorm beds and bunk-bed doubles, but a party atmosphere at this friendly, laid-back hostel, within easy walking distance of Westbahnhof. 24hr reception.

Hostel Zöhrer, 8, Skodagasse 26 ☎ 406 07 30, *info@zoehrer.com*; U-Bahn Josefstädter Strasse or trams #5 and #33. Small private hostel located in the inner suburbs with dorms and bunk-bed doubles. No curfew, no lock-out. Open all year.

Student rooms

Auersperg, 8, Auerspergstrasse 9 ☎ 406 25 40; U-Bahn Lerchenfelder Strasse. Excellent central location, just off the Ring. Singles and doubles with or without shower and toilet.

Haus Döbling, 19, Gymnasiumstrasse 85 ☎ 34 76 31; tram #38. Huge place with singles and doubles. Prices vary very

slightly according to whether you want "hotel service" or not.

Porzellaneum, 9, Porzellangasse 30 ☎ 317 72 82; tram #D. Functional singles, doubles and quads for öS175/€12.72 per head, popular with backpackers. No breakfast, but showers, courtyard, and lounge with TV.

Campsites

Camping Klosterneuburg, Donaupark ☎ 02243/527 27; S-Bahn Klosterneuburg-Kierling. Squeezed between the town centre and the Danube, just outside the city limits, this is a busy site, with very fast transport connections to Vienna. Open Feb–Nov.

Camping Neue Donau, 22, Am Kaisermühlendamm 119 ☎ 202 40 10, *west2@vie.at*; S-Bahn Lobau or bus #91A from U-Bahn Kaisermühlen-VIC. Not a first choice, as it's squeezed between the *Autobahn* and the railway lines on the east bank of the Danube. Open mid-May to mid-Sept.

Camping Rodaun, 23, An der Au 2 ☎ 888 41 54; tram #60 from U-Bahn Hietzing to its terminus, then 5 min walk. Nice location by a stream on the southwestern outskirts of Vienna, near the Wienerwald. Open mid-March to mid-Nov.

Campingplatz Schloss Laxenburg, Münchendorfer Strasse ☎ 02236/713 33; bus from Wien-Mitte, or train (R61) from Südbahnhof to Laxenburg-Biedermannsdorf, followed by a 1.5km walk. Nice location, just outside Vienna, with adjacent outdoor pool and the huge grounds of Laxenburg to explore, but inconvenient without your own transport. Open April–Oct.

Wien West, 14, Hüttelbergstrasse 80 ☎ 914 23 14; bus #151 from U-Bahn Hütteldorf or a 15 min walk from tram #49 terminus. In the plush, far western suburbs of Vienna, close to the Wienerwald; with four-person bungalows to rent between April and October (öS400/€29.07). Closed Feb.

Chapter 11

Cafés and Restaurants

Like nowhere else in Austria, Vienna has a huge variety of places to eat and drink, most of them taking great care over the preparation and presentation of their food. You can snack on a toasted baguette, stuff yourself with hearty Austrian fare or try one of the capital's numerous ethnic restaurants, mostly Chinese and Italian, but also ranging from Balkan to South Indian. And aside from the most exclusive restaurants prices are very reasonable – and fairly uniform, with Innere Stadt places just that bit more expensive – whether you eat in a traditional Kaffeehaus, a studenty café, a *Beisl* or a pizzeria.

For visitors the most difficult job is trying to find somewhere half decent in the immediate vicinity of the popular areas of Stephansplatz, the Hofburg, Karlsplatz and the Belvedere. The **Spittelberg** district (see p.196) has the highest concentration of good cafés and restaurants, and there are further options dispersed more widely throughout the surrounding district of **Neubau**, and in neighbouring **Josefstadt**.

The listings in this chapter are split into four main sections: **cheap eats** such as self-service chains and stand-up buffets, where you can snack on as much or as little as you like, more often than not on the hoof; **cafés**, which usually offer lunches as well as coffee, cakes and snacks; **restaurants**, which include *Beisln*, the Viennese version of the local pub where you can either order a meal or simply go to drink beer

or wine; and lastly Vienna's innumerable **Heurigen**, or wine taverns, mostly located in the wine-growing suburbs, though there are some in the centre of town. These come into their own in the summer, when a night out at one is just about obligatory. Although the primary reason to go to a *Heuriger* is to drink the local wine, there's usually plenty of traditional Viennese food on offer too.

Viennese cuisine

Viennese cuisine is more varied than your average German-speaking city, reflecting the multi-ethnic origins of the old empire. However, fundamentally, it most closely resembles the cuisine of Bohemia, whence the majority of Vienna's inhabitants (and certainly its cooks) once came. In other words, it's hearty stuff, with a heavy meat quotient – usually pork (*Schwein*), veal (*Kalb*) or beef (*Rind*) – accompanied by dumplings or potatoes and cabbage.

One culinary highpoint is **soup** (*Suppe*), served mainly at lunchtimes, and the starting point of most menus. Common soups include *Frittatensuppe*, a clear soup containing small strips of pancake, *Leberknödelsuppe*, a clear beef broth with liver dumplings, *Gulaschsuppe*, a much more substantial, paprika-rich beef-and-vegetable soup, the sweet smelling *Knoblauchsuppe* or garlic soup, and *Serbische Bohnensuppe* (Serbian bean soup), a

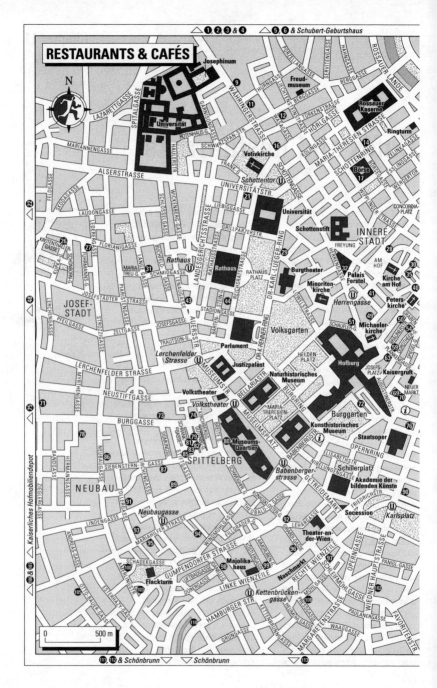

RESTAURANTS & CAFÉS

N

Josephinum

Universität

Freud-museum

Rossauer Kaserne

Ringturm

Votivkirche

Börse

Schottentor

Universität

Schottenstift

INNERE STADT

FREYUNG

Rathaus

Rathaus

Burgtheater

Palais Ferstel

Kirche am Hof

Minoriten-kirche

Peters-kirche

Herrengasse

JOSEF-STADT

Michaeler-kirche

Volksgarten

Parlament

Justizpalast

Hofburg

Kaisergruft

Lerchenfelder Straße

Naturhistorisches Museum

HELDEN-PLATZ

Burggarten

Volkstheater

Volkstheater

Kunsthistorisches Museum

Staatsoper

NEUBAU

Museums-Quartier

SPITTELBERG

Babenberger-straße

Akademie der bildenden Künste

Neubaugasse

Secession

Karlsplatz

Theater-an-der-Wien

Majolika-haus

Naschmarkt

Flackturm

Kettenbrücken-gasse

0   500 m

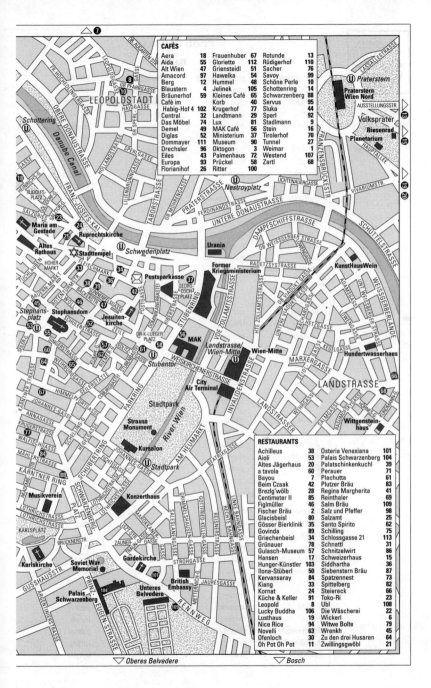

Cafés and restaurants

FOOD GLOSSARY

Basics

Abendessen	supper/dinner	*Mittagessen*	lunch
Auflauf	omelette	*Nachspeise*	dessert
Beilagen	side dishes	*Nockerl* or *Spätzle*	pasta noodles
Brot	bread	*Öl*	oil
Butter	butter	*Pfeffer*	pepper
Ei	egg	*Reis*	rice
Frühstuck	breakfast	*Salat*	salad
Gabel	fork	*Salz*	salt
Gebäck	pastries	*Semmel*	bread roll
Glas	glass	*Senf*	mustard
Hauptgericht	main course	*Suppe*	soup
Honig	honey	*Tasse*	cup
Käse	cheese	*Teller*	plate
Knödel	dumplings	*Topfen*	quark
Kren	horseradish	*Vorspeise*	starter
Löffel	spoon	*Zucker*	sugar
Messer	knife		

Vegetables *(Gemüse)*

Blaukraut	red cabbage	*Kohl*	cabbage
Bohnen	beans	*Kohlsprossen*	brussel sprouts
Champignons	button mushrooms	*Lauch*	leek
		Maiskolben	corn on the cob
Erbsen	peas	*Paprika*	green or red peppers
Erdäpfel	potatoes		
Fisolen	green beans	*Paradeiser*	tomatoes
G'röste	fried grated potatoes	*Pilze*	mushrooms
		Pommes Frites	chips/French fries
Gurke	gherkin/ cucumber	*rote Rübe*	beetroot
		Sauerkraut	pickled cabbage
Karfiol	cauliflower	*Spargel*	asparagus
Karotten	carrots	*Spinat*	spinach
Knoblauch	garlic	*Zwiebeln*	onions

Meat *(Fleisch)* **and Poultry** *(Geflügel)*

Eisbein	pig's trotters	*Kuttelfleck*	tripe
Ente	duck	*Lamm*	lamb
Fasan	pheasant	*Leber*	liver
Gans	goose	*Nieren*	kidneys
Hackfleisch	mincemeat	*Pute*	turkey
Hammelfleisch	mutton	*Rindfleisch*	beef
Hase	hare	*Rippen*	ribs
Hirn	brains	*Schinken*	ham
Hirsch	venison	*Schweinefleisch*	pork
Huhn	chicken	*Speck*	bacon
Innereien	innards	*Taube*	pigeon
Kalbfleisch	veal	*Truthahn*	turkey
Knocken	bones	*Zunge*	tongue

Fish (Fisch)

Aal	eel	*Matjes*	herring
Forelle	trout	*Meeresfrüchte*	seafood
Hecht	pike	*Muscheln*	mussels
Hummer	lobster	*Scholle*	plaice
Karpfen	carp	*Seezunge*	sole
Krabben	prawns	*Thunfisch*	tuna
Krebs	crab	*Tintenfisch*	squid
Lachs	salmon	*Zander*	pike-perch
Makrele	mackerel		

Common terms

Am Spiess	on the spit	*Gefüllt*	stuffed
Blau	rare	*Gegrillt*	grilled
Eingelegte	pickled	*Gekocht*	cooked
Frisch	fresh	*Hausgemacht*	home-made
Gebacken	fried in bread-crumbs	*Heiss*	hot
Gebraten	roasted	*Kalt*	cold
Gedämpft	steamed	*Räucher*	smoked

Fruit (Obst)

Ananas	pineapple	*Kirschen*	cherries
Apfel	apple	*Marillen*	apricots
Banane	banana	*Pfirsiche*	peaches
Birne	pear	*Pflaumen*	plums
Brombeeren	blackberries	*Ribisel*	redcurrants
Erdbeeren	strawberries	*Rosinen*	raisins
Grapefruit	grapefruit	*Trauben*	grapes
Heidelbeeren	bilberries	*Zwetschken*	plums
Himbeeren	raspberries		

Desserts (Nachtischen)

Baiser	meringue	*Mohr im Hemd*	chocolate
Bienenstich	honey and		steamed
	almond tart		pudding with
Buchtelm	sweet dumplings		ice cream
Käsekuchen	cheesecake	*Palatschinken*	pancakes

Austrian specialities

Backhendl	chicken fried in	*Powidl*	plum sauce
	bread-crumbs	*Schinken-*	ham with
Bauernschmaus	platter of pork and ham	*fleckerln*	noodles
Beuschel	chopped lung	*Stelze*	leg of veal or pork
Debreziner	paprika-spiced sausage	*Tafelspitz*	boiled beef
Grammelknödel	pork dumplings	*Wiener Schnitzel*	breaded veal
Kasspätzln	pasta noodles with	*Zwiebelrostbraten*	slices of roast beef
	cheese		topped with fried
Kümmelbraten	roasted with caraway		onions
	seeds		

For a glossary of **coffee** and **cakes** see p.311

Cafés and restaurants

Cafés and restaurants

spicy affair that makes a good lunchtime meal on its own.

Be sure to ask for some of the country's delicious **bread** (*Brot*) to go with it, and remember to count how many pieces you eat, as you'll be charged for each one at the end. Austrian bread comes in a bewildering variety of loaves, though the standard loaf or *Hausbrot* is a mixture of wheat and rye flour.

The capital's most famous **main dish** is, of course, *Wiener Schnitzel*, traditionally deep-fried breaded veal, but also made from chicken or pork, normally accompanied by *Erdäpfelsalat*, a potato salad in a watery sweet dill dressing. The Emperor Franz-Josef's favourite dish (and that of many of his subjects) was *Tafelspitz*, thick slices of boiled beef, usually served with *G'röste* (grated fried potato or rosti). Another popular meat dish is *Backhendl*, a young chicken, breaded and deep-fried, and for the adventurous, there's the likes of *Beuschel* (veal lung stew) to chew on.

On a healthier note, look out for *Eierschwammerl*, chanterelle mushrooms that appear in various guises on menus in the late summer and autumn. The prevalence of *Gulasch* (goulash) is a Hungarian legacy, while the Italians make their presence known with dishes featuring *Nockerl*, the Austrians' heavy version of pasta noodles; *Schinkenfleckerl*, flecks of ham baked in pasta, is especially popular. *Knödel* (dumplings) are ubiquitous, and are more like English dumplings than the bread-like Czech version.

You'll find **fish** featured on most menus, the most common being trout (*Forelle*), pike (*Hecht*), carp (*Karpfen*) and pike-perch (*Fogosch*). **Game** (*Wild*) is popular throughout the year, but especially in autumn when the bulk of the hunting takes place. Many restaurants offer a special game menu in the second half of October. The most common dishes are venison (*Hirsch*), chamois (*Gems*) and roe deer (*Reh*), and sometimes *Wildschwein* (wild boar) crops up.

Seasonal menus are also worth looking out for in May, when dishes featuring freshly harvested asparagus (*Spargel*) appear almost everywhere, and in November, when the period around St Martin's Day (November 11) is marked by the serving of roast goose (*Gans*).

Obviously in a country with such a famously sweet tooth, there's no shortage of rich **desserts** (*Mehlspeisen*) on most menus. Apart from the ubiquitous *Apfelstrudel*, *Palatschinken* (pancakes), filled with jam and/or curd cheese, are a regular feature. Look out, too, for *Marillenknödel*, sweet apricot dumplings, and the politically incorrect *Mohr im Hemd* – literally "Moor in a shirt" – a chocolate pudding with hot chocolate sauce and whipped cream.

In the last decade or so, there has been something of a culinary reaction to the traditional protein-heavy national food. This *Neu Wiener Küche*, as it's known, is the Viennese version of *nouvelle cuisine*, using fresh produce to come up with a new, slightly Mediterranean bent on traditional dishes. It has had a widespread influence not only in the top-class restaurants, but also in some of the more modern cafés, and even in the odd traditional Kaffeehaus.

Lastly, it's as well to remember that the *Mittagessen* or midday meal is traditionally considered the main meal of the day. The *Nachtmahl* or evening supper

---

A little-known fact: Vienna is the home of the **bagel** and the **croissant**; the former is, of course, of Jewish origin, but is said to have been popularized here after a Jewish baker presented one to Jan Sobieski after the lifting of the 1683 siege of Vienna; the croissant also arose from this historical period, its shape said to represent the half-crescent moon on the Turkish flags (Maria Theresia's daughter, Marie Antoinette, is responsible for exporting the croissant to France when she married the future Louis XVI).

Drinks *(Getränke)*			
Apfelsaft	apple juice	*Mineralwasser*	mineral water
Bier	beer	*Obstler*	fruit schnapps
Flasche	bottle	*Orangensaft*	orange juice
Gespritzer	white wine with	*Roséwein*	rosé
	soda	*Rotwein*	red wine
Glühwein	mulled wine	*Sauermilch*	sour milk
Grog	hot water with	*Schnapps*	spirit
	rum and sugar	*Sekt*	sparkling wine
Kaffee	coffee	*Sturm*	new wine
Kakao	cocoa	*Tee*	tea
Kir	white wine with	*Traubensaft*	grape juice
	blackcurrant	*Trocken*	dry
Korn	rye spirit	*Wasser*	water
Kräutertee	herbal tea	*Weisswein*	white wine
Milch	milk	*Zitronentee*	tea with lemon

Cafés and restaurants

would normally be simply a cold meal eaten at home. Obviously not everyone follows this pattern, and restaurants, in particular, consider the evening slot just as important as the lunchtime one.

Alcohol

Austrians tend to drink a lot more beer than wine, though in Vienna it's **wine** (*Wein*) that holds a special place in the capital's history and geography. It's a place literally surrounded by vineyards, many of which lie within the city boundaries – there are even suggestions that the city's name is itself derived from the word "wine".

The best place to try the local stuff is, of course, in a *Heuriger* or wine tavern (see p.321). Wine is drunk by the *Viertel* (a 25cl mug) or the *Achterl* (a 12.5cl glass). The majority of wine produced in Austria is white, the dry, fruity *Grüner Veltliner* being the most popular. Most red wine hails from Burgenland, where *Blaufränkisch* is the ubiquitous grape type, producing a characteristically peppery wine with lots of blackcurrant flavour. Burgenland is also famous, of course, for the great anti-freeze scandal of 1985, when several local wine growers were convicted of adulterating their wine.

It's common practice to water down your white wine with soda water by ordering a *Gespritzer*. Look out, too, for *Sturm*, the half-fermented young wine which hits the streets and bars in autumn, and be sure to try out a mug of *Glühwein* or mulled wine, available at Christmas markets all over the city in late November and December.

Most Austrian **beer** (*Bier*) is a high-quality brew of the light, continental-lager or pilsner type. The locals defer to the Czechs when it comes to **beer** and you should be able to find Bohemian *Budvar* and *Pilsner Urquell* in quite a few bars and restaurants. The most common Austrian beers are the local-brewed *Gold Fassl* from the suburb of Ottakring, and *Gösser*, from Styria. Those with a keen interest in beer should check out the following micro-breweries: *Siebenstern Bräu*, 7, Siebensterngasse 19 (see p.320) and *Fischer Bräu*, 19, Billrothstrasse 17 (see p.321).

Beer is generally drunk by the half litre or *Krügerl*, but you can also ask for a third of a litre or *Seidl*, an eighth of a litre or *Pfiff*, and occasionally a *Mass* or litre jug. Draught beer is *Bier vom Fass*, and you can occasionally get *dunkel* (dark) as opposed to *hell* (light) beer, or ask for it *schnitt* (literally "cut"), half dark-half light. Bottled *Weissbier* (wheat beer) is worth trying: it's extremely fizzy, and you must pour it very slowly to avoid creating a vast head.

Cafés and restaurants

Austrians are also extraordinarily fond of **spirits**, particularly *Schnapps*, made in a variety of delicate fruit flavours, and occasionally known as *Brand*.

Cheap eats

The most obvious snack in Vienna is, of course, a *Wurst* or **hot dog** – *Hasse* in the local dialect – from one of the ubiquitous *Würstelstand* around town. There are numerous varieties available: the *Bratwurst* (fried sausage) or *Burenwurst* (boiled sausage) are the most common, but you could also try a *Debreziner*, a spicy Hungarian sausage, a *Currywurst*, which speaks for itself, or a *Tirolerwurst*, a smoked variety. To accompany your sausage, you usually get a roll and some *Senf* (mustard), which can be either *scharf* (hot) or *süss* (sweet).

For something a bit healthier, there are a number of **take-away stands** that sell grilled *Maiskolben* (corn-on-the-cob), roasted *Maroni* (chestnuts), *Bratkartoffeln* (roast potatoes) and *Kartoffelpuffer* (potato puffs), depending on the season. *Anker*, the largest bakery chain in the country, with branches right across Vienna, produces excellent bread, rolls and pastries, and serves coffee too.

The best place to grab a quick bite and eat cheaply at the same time, however, is the **Naschmarkt**, Vienna's premier fruit and vegetable market (Mon–Sat), where you can feast on seafood, kebabs, felafel, burek, noodles and much more besides, or, if you prefer, assemble a king-sized picnic.

As well as the student *Mensa* (see opposite), there are plenty of other self-service places, such as *Rosenberger*, Mayserdergasse 2 (U-Bahn Karlsplatz), and *Naschmarkt*, Schottengasse 1 (U-Bahn Schottentor), with branches all over the city. More specialized, but equally reliable self-service chains include the fish and seafoody *Nordsee*, Kärntnerstrasse 25 (U-Bahn Stephansplatz), the Middle Eastern *Levante*, Wollzeile 19 (U-Bahn Stephansplatz), and the *Schnitzelhaus*, Krugerstrasse 6 (U-Bahn Karlsplatz), again, each with numerous other branches. At all these places you'll get fast and efficient service and filling snacks, but they are not places to idle away several hours.

Bizi, 1, Rotenturmstrasse 4; U-Bahn Stephansplatz. Just off Stephansplatz, and a reliable, functional filling station. Devise your own pizza toppings, assemble your own salad, or choose one of the main dishes and/or roasted vegetables. Take-away or sit-down. Daily 11am–midnight.

Breakfast

Most Viennese rise so early that they don't really bother with anything other than a gulp of coffee or tea and a bread roll. As a result, the whole concept of *Frühstuck* or **breakfast** is alien to the Viennese. At most hotels and pensions, however, breakfast is included in the price of the room, and will consist of anything from tea or coffee and a roll to an all-you-can-eat buffet with muesli, rolls and bread, cheese, cold meats, boiled eggs, yoghurt and fruit. If breakfast is not included – or you simply get up too late – there are plenty of places where you can get a proper sit-down breakfast. Most traditional *Kaffeehäuser* will offer croissant, egg-based dishes and coffee. And some of the city's trendier cafés offer more substantial brunches, especially on Sundays. A selection, described in greater detail later in this chapter, is given below:

Berg; see p.315. Breakfast/brunch daily from 10am.

Europa; see p.314. Breakfast buffet Sat & Sun from 9am.

Palmenhaus; see p.313. Brunch daily from 10am.

Santo Spirito; see p.318. Brunch daily from 11am.

Stein; see p.315. Breakfast Mon–Sat from 7am, Sun from 9am.

Mensen

If you're on a tight budget, then it's worth considering using one of the city's numerous university canteens or **Mensen**, which are open to the general public (you get an extra discount with student ID). It might not be cordon bleu, but the food is generally perfectly decent, traditional Viennese fare, and you usually get a couple of courses for under – öS50/3.63 euros, about half what you'd pay in a restaurant.

Cafés and restaurants

Arthur Grimm, 1, Kurrentgasse 10, *www.grimm.at;* U-Bahn Stephansplatz. Top-quality specialist bakery just off Judenplatz, where you can also order bread for special diets. Mon–Sat 8am–6pm.

Julius Meinl, 1, Am Graben 19; *www.meinl.com;* U-Bahn Stephansplatz. The flagship store has an excellent stand-up buffet at the rear of the ground floor, where you can eat traditional hot dishes and lighter snacks, and a seafood bar upstairs. Mon–Sat 8am–5pm.

Trześniewski, 1, Dorotheegasse 1; U-Bahn Stephansplatz. (Branches at 6, Mariahilferstrasse 95; U-Bahn Neubaugasse, and elsewhere in the suburbs). Minimalist sandwich bar that's a veritable Viennese institution, serving mouth-watering slices of rye bread (*Brötchen*) topped with fishy, eggy and meaty spreads – wash it all down with a *Pfiff.* Stand-up tables and a few seats. Mon–Fri 8.30am–7.30pm, Sat 9am–5pm.

Wild, 1, Neuer Markt 16; U-Bahn Stephansplatz. Very upmarket, long-established deli with a stand-up buffet; full meals or snacks washed down with alcohol. Mon–Fri 8.30am–6.30pm, Sat 8.30am–1pm.

Wrenkh Natürlich, 1, Rauhensteingasse 12; U-Bahn Stephansplatz, A small weekday-only snack bar round the back of the Steffl department store on Kärntnerstrasse, run by the veggie restaurant of the same name. Mon–Fri 11am–7pm.

Zanoni & Zanoni, 1, Lugeck 7; U-Bahn Stephansplatz. Primarily an ice-cream parlour or *gelateria* – though also a *pasticceria* – and one of the few that's open all year round. Daily 7.30am–midnight.

Zum schwarzen Kameel, 1, Bognergasse 5; U-Bahn Herrengasse. A terribly smart, convivial deli that's yet another Viennese institution, with stand-up tables only. Mon–Sat 8.30am–10.30pm.

Afro-Asiatisches Institut, 9, Türkenstrasse 3; U-Bahn Schottentor. Vienna's most multi-ethnic clientele, but not great for veggies; situated on the ground floor through the archway. Mon–Fri 11.30am–2.30pm.

Katholische Hochschulgemeinde, 1, Ebendorferstrasse 8. Two choices of set menu (occasionally veggie). Mon–Fri 11.30am–2pm. Closed Easter & Aug to mid-Sept.

Musikakademie, 1, Johannesgasse 8. Small central, musical *Mensa* with a pleasant summer courtyard; good for breakfast, but not great for veggies. Mon–Fri 7.30am–3pm.

Neues Instituts Gebäude, 1, Universitätsstrasse 7; U-Bahn Schottentor. This is the main university *Mensa*; take the dumb-waiter lift to floor 6 and then walk up another flight of stairs – nice view over to the Votivkirche. Mon–Fri 11am–2pm.

Technische Universität, 4, Wiedner Hauptstrasse 8–10; U-Bahn Karlsplatz. Big *Mensa* on the first floor (follow the yellow B signs) of the building behind the main university block on Karlsplatz, with regular veggie options. Mon–Fri 11am–2.30pm.

Wirtschaftsuniversität, 9, Augasse 2–6; U-Bahn Spittelau. Unusually this *Mensa* is open for breakfast as well as lunch; some veggie options. Mon–Thurs 7.30am–7.30pm, Fri 7.30am–6.30pm. July & Aug closes 3.30pm.

Cafés and restaurants

Kaffeehäuser (cafés)

*You have troubles of one sort or another –
to the COFFEEHOUSE!
She can't come to you for some reason
no matter how plausible –
to the COFFEEHOUSE!
You have holes in your shoes –
the COFFEEHOUSE!
You have a salary of 400 crowns and
spend 500 –
THE COFFEEHOUSE!
You are frugal and permit yourself noth-
ing –
THE COFFEEHOUSE!
You find no woman who suits you –
THE COFFEEHOUSE!
You are SPIRITUALLY on the threshold of
suicide –
THE COFFEEHOUSE!
You hate and disdain people and yet
cannot do without them –
THE COFFEEHOUSE!
Nobody extends you any more credit
anywhere –
THE COFFEEHOUSE!*

> The Coffeehouse
> Peter Altenberg (1859–1919)

Paris may have more of them, but
Vienna is the spiritual home of the café
or Kaffeehaus. Legend has it that coffee
was first introduced to Vienna by a certain Georg Franz Kolschitzky, an Austrian
spy who regularly penetrated the Turkish
camp during the siege of 1683. When
the siege was finally lifted, Kolschitzky
was asked what he wanted in return for
his services. He requested to be given
the "camel fodder" – in actual fact sacks
of coffee beans – left behind by the
hastily departed Turks, and went on to
open the first coffeehouse in Vienna the
same year.

Whatever the truth of this story, by
the late nineteenth century the
Kaffeehaus had become the city's most
important social institution. It was
described by writer Stefan Zweig as "a
sort of democratic club to which admission costs the small price of a cup of
coffee. Upon payment of this mite, every
guest can sit for hours on end, discuss,
write, play cards, receive his mail, and

above all, can go through an unlimited
number of newspapers and magazines".
The Kaffeehaus became an informal
office for its *Stammgäste* or regulars,
where they could work, relax and receive
clients in warmth and comfort. At certain
cafés, the head waiter or *Herr Ober*
could direct each customer to a certain
table or *Stammtisch* depending on what
subject he (or less frequently she)
wished to debate.

The Viennese coffeehouse is no
longer what it once was, not least
because much of its most loyal clientele
was to be found among the city's Jewish
intellectuals, who either fled or perished
in the Holocaust. Nevertheless, there is
still something unique about the institution even today. While the rest of the
world queues up for fast food, the
Viennese Kaffeehaus implores you to
slow down, or, as the sign in one such
café says, "sorry, we do not cater for
people in a hurry". For the price of a
small coffee, you can still sit for as long
as you like without being asked to move
on or buy another drink. Understandably,
then, the price of this first drink is astro-
nomical and will regularly set you back
around öS35/€2.54.

The meal most closely associated
with the Kaffeehaus at the beginning of
the last century was the *Jause* or afternoon snack eaten around 3pm, consisting of coffee and a pastry. This explains
why even those Kaffeehäuser that don't
serve hot meals will always have at least
a selection of cakes. Nowadays, cafés
tend to make more fuss over the midday
meal, and some will put aside a number
of tables for those customers who wish
to eat. The food is generally traditional
Austrian fare, inexpensive and tasty.

As well as the traditional Kaffeehaus
– the smoky type, with a wide range of
newspapers to read, and a waiter in a
tuxedo – there's also the Kaffee-
Konditorei, where the coffee is a mere
side-show to the establishment's cakes
and pastries (see box opposite). We've
listed both the above café types under
"Traditional". In the last decade or so,
there's been something of a café revival,

with new, modern variants on the old Kaffeehaus appearing, particularly in the Vorstädte or inner suburbs. These places generally eschew the tuxedoes, heavy Viennese cooking and *Torten*, and consequently attract a younger crowd. We've listed them under "**Szene**", the German term for a trendy hangout.

COFFEE AND CAKES

Coffee

On average, the Austrians drink almost twice as much coffee as beer (over a pint a day per head of the population). When ordering a coffee, few Viennese ever actually ask for a straight coffee, or *Kaffee*. Once you've selected the type of coffee you want, you may be asked whether you want it *kleiner* (small) or *grosser* (large). The varieties of coffee are legion, but whatever you order, if you're in a traditional Kaffeehaus, it will come on a little silver tray, accompanied by a glass of water.

Brauner Black coffee with a small amount of milk.

Cappuccino Austrian version of a cappuccino, with whipped cream

Einspänner A small black coffee, served in a tall glass and topped with whipped cream (*Schlagobers*).

Eiskaffee Iced coffee with ice cream and whipped cream.

Fiaker A coffee with a shot of rum and whipped cream.

Kaffee Crème Coffee served with a little jug of milk.

Konsul Black coffee with a spot of cream.

Kurz Viennese version of an espresso.

Mazagran Coffee served with an ice cube and laced with rum, drunk in one gulp.

Mélange (pronounced like the French) Equal measures of frothed milk and coffee – in other words more of a cappuccino than an Austrian *Cappuccino*.

Milch Kaffee Large hot, frothy, milky coffee.

Pharisäer Coffee in a glass topped with whipped cream, served with a small glass of rum on the side.

Schwarzer or *Mokka* Small or large black coffee.

Türkische Coffee grains and sugar boiled up together in individual copper pots to create a strong, sweet brew.

Verlängerten Slightly weaker than normal coffee, served with optional milk.

Cakes

Many cafés will have *Torten* piled high in a display cabinet, in which case you can simply point to the one that takes your fancy. The best cafés still bake their own cakes, and all can be served with a helping of *Schlagobers*. The following are some of the more common choices:

Apfelstrudel Apple and raisins wrapped in pastry and sprinkled with icing sugar.

Dobostorte A rich Hungarian cake made up of alternate layers of biscuit sponge and chocolate cream.

Esterházytorte Several layers of cream and sponge coated in white icing with a feather design on top.

Guglhupf Freud's favourite, at its most basic a simple sponge cake baked in a fluted ring mould and cut into slices.

Linzertorte Essentially a jam tart made with almond pastry.

Mohnstrudel A bread-like pudding rather like an Apfelstrudel, but with a poppy seed and raisin filling.

Sachertorte The most famous of the Viennese cakes – and in some ways the least interesting – a chocolate sponge cake coated in chocolate, most often with a layer of apricot jam beneath the chocolate coating.

Topfenstrudel Like an *Apfelstrudel*, but with a sweet curd cheese filling.

Cafés and restaurants

Lastly, some cafés have what is known as a *Schanigarten* – named after the assistant waiter or *Schani*, whose job it is to set out the tables and chairs – don't get too excited, however, as this is rarely much of a garden, simply a few tables alfresco.

Innere Stadt

Traditional

Aida, 1, Stock-im-Eisen-Platz 2; 1, Bognergasse 3; 1, Rotenturmstrasse 24; both U-Bahn Stephansplatz (plus many other branches). The largest Viennese Konditorei chain serving a staggering selection of calorific cakes and coffee in rather dodgy decor. Varied hours but usually Mon–Sat 7am–8pm, Sun 9am–8pm.

Alt Wien, 1, Bäckerstrasse 9; U-Bahn Stephansplatz. Bohemian Kaffeehaus with *Beisl* decor, posters on nicotine-stained walls, and a dark, smoky atmosphere even on the sunniest day. Daily 10am–2am.

Bräunerhof, 1, Stallburggasse 2; U-Bahn Herrengasse. A real Kaffeehaus atmosphere: nicotine-coloured walls, slightly snooty tuxedoed waiters and decent food, too. Live music on the weekend from 3 to 6pm. Mon–Fri 7.30am–8.30pm, Sat 7.30am–6.30pm, Sun 10am–6.30pm.

Central, 1, Herrengasse 14; *www.ferstel.at*; U-Bahn Herrengasse. The most famous of all Viennese cafés, resurrected in the 1980s and still the most architecturally interesting (see p.70). Trotsky was once a regular. Piano music from 4 to 7pm. Mon–Sat 8am–8pm, Sun 10am–6.30pm.

Demel, 1, Kohlmarkt 14; *www.demel.at*; U-Bahn Herrengasse. The king of the Kaffee-Konditorei – and one of the priciest. The cake display is a work of art, as is the interior. Daily 10am–7pm.

Diglas, 1, Wollzeile 10; *www.diglas.at*; U-Bahn Stephansplatz. Smoky old Kaffeehaus – once Franz Lehár's favourite haunt – with burgundy upholstery and piles of cakes and papers to choose from. Daily 7am–midnight.

Frauenhuber, 1, Himmelpfortgasse 6; U-Bahn Stephansplatz. One of the oldest Kaffeehäuser in Vienna – Beethoven was a regular – with vaulted ceiling, deep burgundy upholstery and an excellent menu. Mon–Sat 8am–11.30pm.

Griensteidl, 1, Michaelerplatz 2; U-Bahn Herrengasse. After a hundred-year caesura, the literary *Griensteidl* has been resurrected (at least in name) – it's perfectly OK, but not what it was in 1897 (see p.69). Daily 8am–11.30pm.

Hawelka, 1, Dorotheergasse 6; U-Bahn Stephansplatz. Small, smoky bohemian café run by the same couple since it opened shortly after World War II; you may have to fight for a table. Mon & Wed–Sat 8am–2am, Sun 4pm–2am.

Korb, 1, Brandstätte 9; U-Bahn Stephansplatz. Traditional, endearingly worn 1950s' style Kaffeehaus tucked away in the backstreets of the Innere Stadt; rather suprisingly you can play skittles in the basement. Mon–Sat 8am–midnight, Sun noon–9pm.

Krugerhof, 1, Krugerstrasse 8; U-Bahn Karlsplatz. A classic Kaffeehaus just off Kärntnerstrasse, with old upholstery, coat-stands, newspapers, billiards, food and comfy booths. Mon–Fri 7am–10pm, Sat 7am–4pm.

Tirolerhof, Tegetthoffstrasse/Fürichgasse; U-Bahn Karlsplatz. A real, peaceful, old-fashioned Kaffeehaus, with classic decor and ambience, conveniently situated just behind the opera house. Mon–Sat 7am–9pm, Sun 9am–8pm.

Szene

Aera, 1, Gonzagagasse 11; U-Bahn Schwedenplatz. Relaxing café upstairs serving tasty food to a mixed crowd of smart and trendy, above a dimly lit cellar downstairs where live bands perform. Daily 10am–2am.

Kleines Café, 1, Franziskanerplatz 3; U-Bahn Stephansplatz. Cosy little café, one of the first of the cross-overs between the new and the traditional Kaffeehaus, designed by the Viennese architect

Hermann Czech in the 1970s. Mon–Sat 10am–2am, Sun 1pm–2am.

Ringstrasse
Traditional

Eiles, 8, Josefstädter Strasse 2; U-Bahn Rathaus. Very traditional Kaffeehaus set back from the Ringstrasse, behind the Rathaus. The decor dates from the 1930s when the café was the meeting point for the Nazis who assassinated the Austro-fascist leader, Englebert Dollfuss. Mon–Fri 7am–10pm, Sat & Sun 8am–10pm.

Landtmann, 1, Dr-Karl-Lueger-Ring 4; *www.landtmann.at*; U-Bahn Herrengasse/Schottentor. One of the poshest of the Kaffeehäuser – and a favourite with Freud – with impeccably attired waiters, and a high quota of politicians and Burgtheater actors. Daily 8am–midnight.

Ministerium, 1, Georg-Coch-Platz 4; U-Bahn Stubentor. Not quite a classic Kaffeehaus – the streaked yellow paint-work puts paid to that – but the lunchtime cooking is excellent and it's popular with local civil servants. Mon–Fri 7am–11pm.

Museum, 1, Friedrichstrasse 6; U-Bahn Karlsplatz. Adolf Loos designed this L-shaped café way back in 1899 and it was a favourite haunt of Klimt, Kokoschka and Schiele, among others. It's changed a lot since then, but remains endearingly well worn, very smoky and still popular with art students. Daily 8am–midnight.

Prückel, 1, Stubenring 24; U-Bahn Stubentor. The *Prückel* has lost its ornate interior, but the dowdy 1950s' refurbishment looks appealingly dated now, and still draws in lots of elderly shoppers and dog-owners from the nearby Stadtpark. Daily 9am–10pm. Piano music Mon, Wed & Fri 7–10pm.

Sacher, 1, Philharmonikerstrasse 4; *www.sacher.com*; U-Bahn Karlsplatz. For all its fame (see p.135), the *Sacher* is a bit of a let-down. The decor is imperial red and gold, but the *Sachertorte* over-

rated – practically the only folk who come here nowadays are tourists. Daily 6.30am–11.30pm. Piano music Mon–Sat 4.30–6.30pm.

Schottenring, 1, Schottenring; U-Bahn Schottentor/Schottenring. Situated on the corner of Börsegasse, this L-shaped Kaffeehaus, with its high stuccoed ceiling, is an oasis of calm on the Ringstrasse. Mon–Fri 6.30am–11pm, Sat & Sun 8am–9pm. Live piano daily 3.30–6.30pm.

Schwarzenberg, 1, Kärntner Ring 17; U-Bahn Karlsplatz. Opulent café with rich marble, ceramic and wood-panelled decor, plus huge mirrors and a great cake cabinet. Live piano music Wed & Fri 7–9pm, Sat & Sun 5–7pm. Mon–Fri & Sun 7am–midnight, Sat 9am–midnight.

Sluka, 1, Rathausplatz 8; *www.sluka.co.at*; U-Bahn Rathaus. Lovely little Kaffee-Konditorei tucked under the arches by the Rathaus. White wood gilded panelling, mirrors and chandeliers – a Ringstrasse classic. Mon–Fri 8am–7pm, Sat 8am–5.30pm.

Szene

MAK Café, 1, Stubenring 5; U-Bahn Stubentor. Not strictly speaking a traditional Kaffeehaus, but it does have a wonderfully high coffered ceiling. This is a trendy hangout, as you might expect from the MAK (see p.149). The food is pricey, with a Mediterranean edge. Tues–Sun 10am–2am.

Palmenhaus, 1, Burggarten; U-Bahn Karlsplatz. Stylish modern café set amidst the palms of the greenhouse in the Burggarten. Breakfasts are great. The inexpensive, daily menu specializes in grilled fish and meats, and there are even DJ nights occasionally. A wonderful treat after visiting the Hofburg. Daily 10am–2am.

Landstrasse and Wieden
Traditional

Café im Habig-Hof 4, Wiedner Hauptstrasse 15; U-Bahn Taubstummengasse/Karlsplatz. A new

Cafés and restaurants

Cafés and restaurants

old-style Kaffeehaus, housed in a former imperial-era hatmakers, a short stroll south of Karlsplatz. The place retains lots of the old fittings and some great gilded stucco on the ceiling. Mon–Sat 11am–midnight.

Zartl, 3, Rasumofskygasse 7; tram #N. An unusual find in these parts, a real local corner Kaffeehaus, with cream and green decor, billiards, booths and lots of ice-cream sundaes. Mon–Fri 8am–midnight, Sat & Sun 9am–6pm; June–Aug Mon–Fri only.

Szene

Im KunstHausWien, 3, Weissgerberlände 14; www.kunsthauswien.com; tram #N. Round the corner from the Hundertwasserhaus (see p.169), a wonky, colourful, foliage-strewn café designed by the man himself. Daily 10am–midnight.

Mariahilf, Neubau and Josefstadt
Traditional

Amacord, 5, Rechte Wienzeile 15; U-Bahn Karlsplatz. Laid-back Kaffeehaus by the Naschmarkt, with trendy (occasionally live) music playing, lots of newspapers and inexpensive food on the menu. Daily 10am–2am.

Drechsler, 6, Linke Wienzeile 22; U-Bahn Kettenbrückengasse. Another laid-back, scruffy Kaffeehaus by the Naschmarkt, popular with the younger generation of Viennese, especially clubbers attracted by the early opening hours. Mon–Fri 3am–8pm, Sat 3am–6pm.

Florianihof, 8, Florianigasse 45; www.florianihof.at; U-Bahn Josefstädter Strasse. Pared-down old Kaffeehaus that has retained one or two Jugendstil touches, and yet has a light and airy, modern feel. Mon–Fri 8am–midnight, Sat & Sun 10am–midnight.

Hummel, 8, Albertgasse 27; U-Bahn Josefstädter Strasse. Bustling local Kaffeehaus, doing a brisk lunchtime trade, with tables looking out on the nearby square. Mon–Sat 7am–2am, Sun 8am–2am.

Jelinek, 6, Otto-Bauer-Gasse 5; U-Bahn Webgasse. Family-run Kaffeehaus tucked away in the backstreets south of Mariahilferstrasse, this is a rare survivor, still serving an exclusively local clientele. Mon–Fri 8am–8pm.

Ritter, 6, Mariahilferstrasse 73; U-Bahn Neubaugasse. Vast, high-ceilinged V-shaped café popular with veteran card players and shoppers. Daily 7.30am–11.30pm.

Rüdigerhof, 5, Hamburger Strasse 20; U-Bahn Kettenbrückengasse. Wonderful Jugendstil building on the outside, 1950s kitsch on the inside. Food is cheap and filling, but the riverside terrace is marred by the nearby busy road. Mon–Fri & Sun 10am–2am, Sat noon–2am.

Savoy, 6, Linke Wienzeile 36; U-Bahn Kettenbrückengasse. Wonderfully scruffy, but ornate *fin-de-siècle* decor, packed with bohemian bargain-hunters during the Saturday flea market. Mon–Fri 5pm–2am, Sat 9am–2am.

Servus, 6, Mariahilferstrasse 57–59; U-Bahn Neubaugasse. Smart traditional Kaffeehaus, with red and white decor, that's busy with shoppers at lunchtime. Mon–Sat 10am–midnight.

Sperl, 6, Gumpendorfer Strasse 11; U-Bahn Karlsplatz/Babenbergerstrasse. One of the classics of the Kaffeehaus scene, just off Mariahilferstrasse, L-shaped, with billiard tables and a hint of elegant, bohemian shabbiness. Mon–Sat 7am–11pm, Sun 3–11pm (July & Aug closed Sun).

Westend, 7, Mariahilferstrasse 128; U-Bahn Westbahnhof. Conveniently located directly opposite Westbahnhof, this traditional Kaffeehaus – once frequented by Hitler – is the best possible introduction to Vienna for those who've just arrived by train. Daily 7am–11pm.

Szene

Europa, 7, Zollergasse 8; U-Bahn Neubaugasse. Lively, spacious café that attracts a trendy crowd, who love the posey window booths. Food is a tasty mixture of Viennese and Italian. DJ nights in the back room. Daily 9am–5am.

Lux, 7, Spittelberggasse 6; U-Bahn Volkstheater. Pared-down modern version of a Kaffeehaus, with a friendly bistro feel and an eclectic menu featuring tofu-based dishes, pizzas and pancakes. Daily 10.30am–2am.

Das Möbel, 7, Burggasse 10; U-Bahn Volkstheater. Café-bar on the edge of Spittelberg, packed with minimalist furniture (which you can buy), a youngish crowd, weird toilets and reasonable sustenance on offer. Daily noon–1am.

Tunnel, 8, Florianigasse 39; U-Bahn Josefstädter Strasse. Popular clean-living student café with good food, filling breakfasts until 11am; live music in the basement of an evening. Daily 9am–2am.

Alsergrund

Traditional

Stadlmann, 9, Währinger Strasse 26; U-Bahn Schottentor. Sepia-coloured Kaffeehaus, with unrenovated red velvet alcoves, brass chandeliers and mirrors. Mon–Thurs 8am–10pm, Fri 8am–9pm; closed Aug.

Weimar, 9, Währinger Strasse 68; tram #40, #41 or #42. L-shaped Kaffeehaus with a high ceiling, chandeliers, tuxedoed waiters and snug booths. Good-value öS85/€6.18 lunchtime menu. Mon–Thurs 8am–midnight, Fri & Sat 8am–4am, Sun 10am–midnight. Live piano daily 7.30–11.30pm.

Szene

Berg, 9, Berggasse 8; U-Bahn Schottentor. Relaxed modern mixed gay/straight café with an attractive assortment of chairs and great *Neu Wiener Küche*. Daily 10am–1am.

Blaustern, 9, Döblinger Gürtel 2; U-Bahn Nussdorfer Strasse. Popular, long-established neighbourhood Kaffeehaus, in the middle of the Gürtel, that's been given a designer makeover. Daily 9am–2am.

Stein, 9, Währingerstrasse 6; *www.café-stein.com*; U-Bahn Schottentor. Posey, studenty designer café, on the corner of Kolingasse, with minimalist decor, funky music, trendy loos, online facilities, baguettes, veggie food and breakfasts served until 8pm. Mon–Sat 7am–1am, Sun 9am–1am.

Leopoldstadt

Traditional

Rotunde, 2, Ausstellungstrasse/Mölkereistrasse; tram #21. Real neighbourhood Kaffeehaus, deeply untrendy but a great escape from the nearby Volksprater, two stops from Praterstern. Mon–Sat 7.30am–midnight, Sun 8am–8pm.

Szene

Schöne Perle, 2, Grosser Pfarrgasse/Leopoldgasse; bus 5A/tram #21. Magnolia minimalism is the order of the day at this light and airy café, which offers cheap and tasty food and bar billards. Daily 11am–2am.

The suburbs

Traditional

Dommayer, 13, Dommayergasse 1; U-Bahn Hietzing. Historic Kaffeehaus where Johann Strauss Junior made his premiere. Tuxedoed waiters, comfy alcoves, occasional live music and lots of coffee and

Cafés and restaurants

Internet cafés

You can go online at convivial cafés such as *Café Stein* (see above) and *Das Möbel*, but if you just want to send or receive an email, or do a bit of surfing (and don't want to pay for it), head for one of the branches of the bookshop *Amadeus*, which offer **free internet access**: fourth floor of *Steffl* department store, 1, Kärntnerstrase 19, and in the basement of their flagship store at Mariahilferstrasse 99; *www.amadeusbuch.co.at*.

Cafés and restaurants

Restaurant Prices

Each restaurant listed below has been given one of the following price categories:

Inexpensive: under öS150/€10.90   **Moderate:** öS150–250/€10.90–18.17

Expensive: over öS250/€18.17

These categories are based on the prices for the majority of the main courses on the menu. They do not include starters, puddings, drinks or a tip.

cakes. A good rest stop after a hard day at Schönbrunn. Daily 7am–midnight.
Gloriette, 13, Schönbrunn Schlosspark; U-Bahn Hietzing/Schönbrunn. Smart café in a giant garden folly overlooking Schönbrunn from the hill in the Schlosspark. A good twenty-minute walk from the U-Bahn. Daily 9am to dusk.

Szene

Oktogon, 19, Am Himmel; bus #38A from U-Bahn Heiligenstadt. Smart modern octagonal café–restaurant that makes a perfect lunch halt whilst out in the Wienerwald. Mon–Sat noon–10pm, Sun 11am–10pm.

Restaurants

Although you can, of course, eat lunch or dinner at most of the cafés listed earlier, the **restaurants** reviewed below are, on the whole, the sort of place you can happily spend all afternoon or evening in. Phone numbers have been given only for those restaurants where it's advisable to **book a table**.

We've given each restaurant a price category (see above), which reflects the cost of the majority of **main course** dishes on the menu. These are only a guideline: obviously if you choose the most expensive item on the menu, you're going to exceed our estimate; equally, if you choose the cheapest item on the menu, you'll probably end up eating for much less. Don't forget, however, that we have not included the price of starters or puddings, since the main dish alone is often filling enough, nor the price of any drinks.

Tipping is usually done in a *Beisl* by simply rounding up to the nearest öS10, so when the waiter gives you a bill for,

say öS134, you say öS140 as you hand over the cash (few *Beisln* take plastic). In restaurants, add fifteen percent to the bill unless it's already been done for you. To keep the price of meals to a minimum, look for the set *Tagesmenu* (especially at lunchtime), which usually gives you two courses for under öS100/€7.27.

Lastly, a quick word on the **Beisl** (Yiddish for "little house"), the city's chief traditional eating and drinking establishment. A *Beisl* is a sort of unpretentious wood-panelled pub, where you're expected to share a table with other customers. The best are still family-run and as much about drinking (beer usually) and socializing, as they are about eating hearty Austrian home cooking. A number are included in the selection below.

Innere Stadt

a Tavola, 1, Weihburggasse 3–5 ☎512 79 55; U-Bahn Stephansplatz. Designer Italian *osteria* with a stylish, cave-like interior and some excellent innovative cuisine. Daily 11.30am–3pm & 6–10pm. Moderate.

Achilleus, 1, Köllnerhofgasse 3; U-Bahn Schwedenplatz. Strangely Austrian-looking, but excellent Greek restaurant. Daily 11.30am–3pm & 5.30pm–12.30am. Moderate.

Aioli, 1, Stephansplatz 12 ☎532 0373; U-Bahn Stephansplatz. Large, loud, and extremely popular Mediterranean restaurant on the third floor of the Haas Haus, overlooking the Stephansdom. Daily 10am–1am. Moderate.

Beim Czaak, 1, Postgasse 15; U-Bahn Schwedenplatz. Lovely dark-green wood panelling and low-lighting gives this well-established *Beisl* a cosy, but smart feel. Mon–Fri 8.30am–midnight, Sat 11am–midnight. Inexpensive.

Brezlg'wölb, 1, Ledererhof 9; U-Bahn Herrengasse. Wonderful candle-lit cave-like restaurant with deliberately olde worlde decor. Hidden in a cobbled street off Drahtgasse, it serves the usual Austrian favourites at knock-down prices. Daily 11.30am–1am. Inexpensive.

Figlmüller, 1, Wollzeile 5; U-Bahn Stephansplatz. Branch at 19, Grinzinger Strasse 55; tram #38. It's in every tourist guide to the city there is, but this is still *the* place to eat *Wiener Schnitzel*, with a traditional potato salad, washed down with wine (there's no beer). Daily 11am–10.30pm. Moderate.

Gösser Bierklinik, 1, Steindlgasse 4; U-Bahn Stephansplatz. Ancient inn with wooden booths for drinking, and a more formal backroom restaurant serving traditional Austrian food. Mon–Sat 10am–midnight. Moderate.

Griechenbeisl, 1, Fleischmarkt 11 ☎533 19 41; U-Bahn Schwedenplatz. Possibly the most ancient of all Vienna's inns (see p.85), frequented by the likes of Beethoven, Schubert and Brahms, something which it predictably milks in order to draw in the tourists. Daily 11am–11.30pm. Moderate.

Gulasch-Museum, 1, Schulerstrasse 20; U-Bahn Stubentor. Not a museum at all, just a *Beisl* specializing in goulash. Mon–Fri 9am–midnight, Sat & Sun 10am–midnight. Inexpensive.

Hansen, 1, Wipplingerstrasse 34 ☎532 0542; U-Bahn Schottentor. Attractive, smart restaurant located in the flower and gardening shop in the basement of the city's splendid stock exchange. Mon–Fri 9am–8pm, Sat 9am–5pm. Moderate.

Ilona-Stüberl, 1, Bräunerstrasse 2; U-Bahn Stephansplatz. Gypsy-music-free Hungarian restaurant with lashings of goulash on offer. Mon–Sat noon–3pm & 6–11pm. Inexpensive–moderate.

Kervansaray, 1, Mahlerstrasse 9 ☎512 8843; U-Bahn Karlsplatz. This is the city's top fish and seafood restaurant, which specializes in lobster (*Hummer*), though a few meat dishes are also served up. On the ground floor, in the *Hummerbar*, there's a slightly cheaper array of dishes available. Mon–Sat noon–midnight, Sun 6pm–midnight. Expensive.

Kiang, 1, Rotgasse 8; U-Bahn Schwedenplatz. Branches at 3, Landstrasser Haupstrasse 50; U-Bahn Rochusgasse; 6, Joanelligasse 3; U-Bahn Kettenbrückengasse; and 8, Lederergasse 14; tram #5 or bus #13A. Vienna's best-known designer Chinese noodles restaurant (with a sushi bar attached), decked out in loud primary colours with huge fish-bowl windows. The food is freshly prepared right in front of your nose. Mon–Sat 11.30am–3pm & 6–11.30pm. Inexpensive–moderate.

Kornat, 1, Marc-Aurel-Strasse 8; U-Bahn Schwedenplatz. Small Croatian restaurant specializing in grilled salt-water fish and seafood dishes – go for the daily specials. Mon–Sat 11.30am–3pm & 6pm–midnight. Inexpensive.

Novelli, 1, Bräunerstrasse 11 ☎513 42 00; U-Bahn Stephansplatz. Elegant new Italian restaurant, with a popular, posey bar, and top-notch modern Italian cuisine at above average prices. Mon–Sat noon–3pm & 6–11pm. Expensive.

Ofenloch, 1 Kurrentgasse 8; U-Bahn Stephansplatz. Upmarket *Beisl*, just off Judenplatz, with wood-panelled booths and a cosy, *gemütlich* atmosphere. Daily 10am–midnight. Moderate.

Palatschinkenkuchl, 1, Köllnerhofgasse 4; U-Bahn Schwedenplatz. Informal restaurant popular with kids and adults alike for its savoury and sweet pancakes and milkshakes. Mon–Sat 10am–midnight, Sun 5pm–midnight. Inexpensive.

Plachutta, 1, Wollzeile 38 ☎512 15 77, *www.plachutta.at*; U-Bahn Stubentor. Branch at 19, Heiligenstädter Strasse 179. Smart green decor and pristine service at this traditional family-run Viennese restaurant, specializing in

Cafés and restaurants

Cafés and restaurants

Tafelspitz. Daily 11.30am–midnight. Moderate.

Regina Margherita, 1, Wallnerstrasse 4 ☎ 533 08 12; U-Bahn Herrengasse. Smart, bustling Neapolitan pizza and pasta joint in the inner court of the Palais Esterházy. Pizzas are cooked in a stupendous lava oven, and you can eat alfresco in the summer. Mon–Sat noon–3pm, 6pm–midnight. Moderate.

Reinthaler, 1, Gluckgasse 5; U-bahn Karlsplatz. Dive down the steps to this genuine, no-nonsense busy Viennese *Beisl*. No concessions to modern cooking and certainly none to veggies. Mon–Fri 9am–11pm. Inexpensive.

Salzamt, 1, Ruprechtsplatz 1; *www.salzamt.at* ; U-Bahn Schwedenplatz. Typical of Vienna's popular modern *Beisln*: minimalist decor and excellent *Neu Wiener Küche*. Tables outside in the summer. Daily 6pm–2am. Moderate.

Santo Spirito, 1, Kumpfgasse 7; U-Bahn Stephansplatz. Bohemian basement bistro which plays exceptionally loud classical music, does great Sunday brunches and tapas, and attracts a mixed gay/straight crowd. Mon–Thurs & Sun 11am–2am, Fri & Sat 11am–3am. Moderate.

Siddhartha, 1, Fleischmarkt 16 ☎ 513 11 97; U-Bahn Schwedenplatz. Strangely normal decor for this Buddhist vegetarian restaurant that has a cheap weekday lunch menu. Daily 11.30am–11pm. Inexpensive.

yum!!!

Toko-Ri, 1, Salztorgasse 4; U-Bahn Schwedenplatz. Branch at 2, Franz Hochedlingergasse 2; tram #31. Possibly the freshest and finest sushi outlet in the whole of Vienna. And for sushi, the prices are a relative bargain. Daily 10.30am–midnight. Moderate.

Wrenkh, 1, Bauernmarkt 10 ☎ 533 15 26; U-Bahn Stephansplatz. Branch at 15, Hollergasse 9; U-Bahn Schönbrunn/Meidling-Haupstrasse. The fashionable modern decor and cool ambience are a cut above the average vegetarian restaurant. The food is OK, too, though not always as imaginative as it sounds. Mon–Sat 11am–1am. Moderate.

Zu den drei Husaren, 1 Weihburggasse 4 ☎ 512 10 92; U-Bahn Stephansplatz. Although only opened in 1933, this place plays heavily on nostalgia for the days of the empire, with a menu packed full of Austro-Hungarian specialities. Daily noon–3pm & 6pm–1am. Expensive.

Ringstrasse

Glacisbeisl, 7, Messeplatz 1; U-Bahn Volkstheater. Hidden in the entrails of the MuseumsQuartier, it remains to be seen how the place fares now that it's part of a whole new cultural complex. Daily 10am–midnight. Inexpensive.

Palais Schwarzenberg, 3, Schwarzenbergplatz 9 ☎ 798 45 15-600; tram #D. Idyllic setting in the glorious Baroque palace hidden behind the Soviet war memorial (see p.148), with

---

Vegetarians

Vegetarianism has not caught on in a big way in Vienna – and there are remarkably few vegetarian restaurants. The key phrases are *Ich bin vegeterianisch(e)* ("I'm vegetarian") and *Ist das ohne Fleisch?* (literally "Is that without meat?"). There are a few traditional vegetarian dishes on most *Beisl* and Kaffeehaus menus: *Gebackener Emmenthaler* (or some other kind of cheese), which is breaded and deep-fried; *Knödel mit Ei* (dumplings with scrambled egg); *Spinatnockerl* (spinach pasta). The following are the best of Vienna's small number of exclusively vegetarian restaurants:

Govinda; see opposite.
Nice Rice; see opposite.

Siddharta; see above.
Wrenkh; see above.

views across the private gardens; call to reserve a terrace table. Daily noon–2.30pm & 6–10.30pm. Expensive.

Zwillingsgwölb, 1, Universitätsstrasse 5; U-Bahn Schottentor. Popular, unpretentious, smoky student *Beisl*, just down from the university. Mon–Fri 9am–1am. Inexpensive.

Landstrasse

Osteria Venexiana, 3, Rennweg 11/corner of Marokkanergasse; tram #71. Genuinely delicious Venetian menu in this small, attractive restaurant, just round the corner from the Unteres Belvedere. Mon–Sat 10am–11pm, Sun 6–11pm. Inexpensive.

Salm Bräu, 3, Rennweg 8. Conveniently located beer hall, which brews its own beer, and serves filling pub food, right outside the Unteres Belvedere. Daily 11am–midnight. Inexpensive.

Steiereck, 3, Rasumofskygasse 2 ☎713 3168; tram #N to Löwengasse. The *Steiereck* is considered by many Viennese to be the best restaurant in the city (if not the entire country). It serves up international and Austrian dishes with an emphasis on Styrian cuisine, has an impressive wine list, superb cheeses, and a bargain set brunch for around öS100/€7.27. Mon–Fri noon–3pm & 7pm–midnight. Expensive.

Mariahilf and around Naschmarkt

Hunger-Künstler, 6, Gumpfendorferstrasse 48 ☎587 9210; U-Bahn Kettenbrückengasse. Candle-lit but unpretentious Mariahilf restaurant serving Vorarlberg specialities and plenty of veggie options. Daily 11am–2am.

Nice Rice, 6, Mariahilferstrasse 45; U-Bahn Neubaugasse. Small vegetarian place, down a passageway off Mariahilferstrasse, serving a range of inexpensive rice dishes. Mon–Sat 9am–midnight. Inexpensive.

Salz und Pfeffer, 6, Joanelligasse 8; U-Bahn Kettenbrückengasse. This place's chief virtue is the fact that it serves

hearty Viennese fare all night. Daily 6pm–8am. Inexpensive.

Schlossgasse 21, 5, Schlossgasse 21; www.cuadro.at; tram #62 or bus #13A. Local nouveau *Beisl* just south of Naschmarkt, popular with the professionals of Margareten. Good-value eclectic, multi-ethnic menu. Daily 6pm–2am. Inexpensive.

Ubl, 4, Pressgasse 26; U-Bahn Kettenbrückengasse. Lovely, long-established *Beisl* near the Naschmarkt serving inexpensive, traditional food, plus a few Italian dishes. Daily noon–2.30pm & 6pm–midnight. Inexpensive.

Neubau/Josefstadt

Centimeter II, 7, Siebensterngasse 18; U-Bahn Volkstheater/Neubaugasse. Lively, popular Spittelberg hang-out, with a mixed crowd, very cheap, filling food, and lots of beers on tap. Mon–Fri 10am–2am, Sat 11am–2am, Sun 11am–midnight. Inexpensive.

Govinda, 7, Lindengasse 2a; U-Bahn Neubaugasse. Hindu arts and crafts shop that serves a few simple vegetarian dishes at lunchtime. Mon–Fri 10am–6.30pm, Sat 10am–2pm. Inexpensive.

Grünauer, 7, Hermanngasse 32 ☎526 40 80; tram #49. Tiny local *Beisl* in the backstreets of Neubau, that takes its traditional Viennese cooking and wine cellar seriously. Mon 6pm–midnight, Tues–Fri 11.30am–3pm & 6pm–midnight. Inexpensive.

Küche & Keller, 7, Zollergasse 14 ☎523 24 80; U-Bahn Neubaugasse. Elegant and excellent Viennese cooking, and a friendly atmosphere. Mon–Sat 6pm–midnight. Moderate.

Lucky Buddha, 7, Kaiserstrasse 13; U-Bahn Westbahnhof. Despite its unpretentious decor, this is one of the best Chinese restaurants in the city, serving excellent dim sum. Daily 11.30am–2.30pm & 5.30–midnight. Inexpensive.

Perauer, 7, Zieglergasse 54; tram#49. A sort of pared-down *Beisl* with smart new

Cafés and restaurants

There are branches of Kiang (see p.317) in Landstrasse, Josefstadt and Mariahilf

Cafés and restaurants

See p.316 for an explanation of the price categories we've used in the restaurant reviews

There's a branch of Toko-Ri in Leopoldstadt (see p.318).

wood furnishings and a lighter touch with the country's traditional peasant fare. Mon–Fri 11am–3pm & 6pm–midnight, Sat 6pm–midnight. Moderate.

Plutzer Bräu, 7, Schrankgasse 2; U-Bahn Volkstheater. Spacious designer beer bar in Spittelberg, good for a quiet lunch, or a much more boisterous evening drink. Regularly shows live TV sports. Daily 11.30am–2am. Inexpensive.

Schilling, 7, Burggasse 103; tram #5 or bus #48A. A modish crowd frequent this nouveau stripped-down *Beisl* on the corner of Halbgasse; the food is traditional but imaginatively presented and freshly prepared. Daily 11am–1am. Inexpensive.

Schnattl, 8, Lange Gasse 40 ☎405 3400; U-Bahn Rathaus. Innovative, *Neu wiener Küche* cooked with a Styrian bent by Herr Schnattl himself; call to reserve a table in the courtyard. Mon–Fri 11.30am–2.30pm & 6pm–midnight, Sat 6pm–midnight. Moderate.

Schnitzelwirt, 7, Neubaugasse 52; tram #49. Aside from Figlmüller (see p.317), this is the place to eat Wiener Schnitzel – they're just as humongous, and cheaper, too. Mon–Sat 10am–11pm. Inexpensive.

Siebenstern Bräu, 7, Siebensterngasse 19; tram #49. Popular modern microbrewery, serving solid Viennese pub food, with lots of pan-fried dishes served with dark rye bread. Tues–Sat 10am–1am, Mon & Sun 10am–midnight. Inexpensive.

Spatzennest, 7, Ulrichsplatz 1; bus #13A or #48A. Much treasured, down-to-earth local Viennese *Beisl*, just off Burggasse. Sun–Thurs 10am–midnight. Inexpensive.

Spittelberg, 7, Spittelberggasse 12; U-Bahn Volkstheater. A chic Spittelberg brasserie with some veggie options and delicious crepes for dessert. Daily 6pm–midnight. Inexpensive-moderate.

Die Wäscherei, 8, Albertgasse/Laudongasse; U-Bahn Josefstädter Strasse. Funky, arty little bar with an imaginative menu, lots of veggie

choice and great beers on offer. Daily 5pm–2am. Inexpensive.

Witwe Bolte, 7, Gutenberggasse 13; U-Bahn Volkstheater. Long-established *Wiener Beisl* in the charming backstreets of Spittelberg, famous for having been visited by Josef II incognito in the eighteenth century. Lovely summer garden. Daily noon–midnight. Inexpensive.

Alsergrund

Oh Pot Oh Pot, 1, Währinger Strasse 22; U-Bahn Schottentor. Cheap pots of spicy, vaguely South American stews, plus good-value specials such as paella. Mon–Sat 11am–midnight. Inexpensive.

Stomach, 9, Seegasse 26; tram #D. A Styrian Beisl, with a lovely cobbled courtyard, specializing in creative beef dishes, but also offering enough *Neu Wiener Küche* for veggies. Wed–Sat 4pm–midnight, Sun 10am–10pm. Moderate.

Wickerl, 9, Porzellangasse 24; tram #D. Good popular neighbourhood *Beisl* serving cheap classic Viennese fillers, plus live TV sports. Mon–Fri 8am–midnight. Inexpensive.

Leopoldstadt

Altes Jägerhaus, 2, Aspernallee, Prater; bus #77A. Lively *Beisl* at the far end of the Hauptallee serving typical hearty fare washed down with Budvar beer. April–Sept daily 9am–11pm; Oct–March Wed–Sun 9am–11pm. Inexpensive.

Bayou, 2, Leopoldgasse 51 ☎214 77 52, www.bayou.at; tram #N or #21. Simple *Beisl* serving some of the hottest dishes in town, Creole gumbo stews, for the most part. Daily 6pm–midnight. Moderate.

Leopold, 2, Grosser Pfarrgasse 11; tram #N or #21. Chic modern designer *Beisl*, with high ceiling, pine furniture, imaginative *Neu Wiener Küche*; a real oasis in central Leopoldstadt. Daily Mon–Sat 6pm–2am, Sun 10am–1am. Moderate.

Lusthaus, 2, Hauptallee, Prater ☎728 95 65; bus #77A. Eighteenth-century rotunda at the far end of Hauptallee that makes a perfect food halt while exploring the Prater. May–Sept Mon, Tues, Thurs & Fri noon–11pm, Sat & Sun noon–6pm; shorter hours in winter. Moderate.

Schweizerhaus, 2, Strasse des 1 Mai 116; U-Bahn Praterstern. Czech-owned restaurant in the Prater; known for its draught beer and Czech specialities such as tripe soup and grilled pigs' trotters (*Stelzen*). March–Oct daily 10am–midnight. Inexpensive.

The suburbs

Fischer Bräu, 19, Billrothstrasse 17; U-Bahn Nussdorferstrasse. Very civilized micro-brewery pub, which produces a great, lemony, misty beer. Lots of tasty snacks and more substantial pub fare to be consumed in the bare boards interior or the shady courtyard. A short walk from the U-Bahn, but worth the trek. Mon–Sat 4pm–1am, Sun 11am–1am. Inexpensive.

Heurigen

Heurigen are the wine taverns found predominantly in the former villages of the city's outer suburbs, to the north and west of the centre on the slopes of the

Wienerwald. The word *heurig* means "this year's", as it was here that the vintner would encourage tastings in order to try and sell a few bottles of his (exclusively white) wine. As an institution they are as old as the city itself, but came into their own during the Biedermeier period (1815–48). In the good old days people used to bring their own picnics to consume, sat on wooden benches in the vintner's garden while drinking the wine, but nowadays, most *Heurigen* provide a self-service buffet of traditional Viennese fare.

According to the Emperor Josef II's 1784 law, real *Heurigen* are only permitted to open for 300 days in any one year (usually March to November), and may only sell wine and food produced on the premises. If the *Heuriger* is open, the custom is to display a *Buschen* or bunch of evergreen boughs over the entrance and a sign telling you it's *ausg'stekt* (hung out). Those that still abide by the strict *Heurigen* laws generally have a sign saying *Buschenschank*, though it has to be said that some have now got themselves restaurant licences in order to open all year round.

Traditionally a visit to a *Heuriger* is accompanied by *Schrammelmusik*,

Cafés and restaurants

There's a branch of Wrenkh (see p.318) near Schönbrunn, and a branch of Plachutta (see p.318) in Heiligenstadt.

Selected Heurigen

Grinzing is the most famous of Vienna's *Heuriger* village-suburbs, and consequently the most touristy. There are numerous *Heurigen* on the main street of Sandgasse, but to avoid the worst of the crowds head further up Cobenzlgasse. Next most popular are the nearby areas of **Heiligenstadt** and **Nussdorf**. Less touristy alternatives include Sievering and Neustift am Walde. Another option is to cross over the Danube and head for the village of Stammersdorf, and its immediate neighbour Strebersdorf. The single recommendations below are meant as a sort of starting point for each district.

Grinzing
Weingut am Riesenberg, 19, Oberer Riesenbergweg 15; bus #38A, tram #38 end terminus.

Heiligenstadt
Mayer am Pfarrplatz, 19, Pfarrplatz 2; bus #38A from U-Bahn Heiligenstadt.

Neustift am Walde
Schreiberhaus, 19, Rathstrasse 54; bus #35A from U-Bahn Nussdorfer Strasse.

Nussdorf
Schübel-Auer, 19, Kahlenberger Strasse 22; tram #D to the end terminus.

Sievering
Haslinger, 19, Agnesgasse; bus #39A from U-Bahn Heiligenstadt to the end stop.

Stammersdorf
Wieninger, 21, Stammersdorfer Strasse 78; tram #31 to the end terminus.

Cafés and restaurants

sentimental fiddle, guitar and accordion music, though today such music only features at the more touristy ventures. In addition to the *Heurigen* in the outer suburbs, there is a handful of wine taverns known as *Stadtheurigen* located closer to the centre of town, usually in the cellars of the city's monasteries. These are not real *Heurigen* at all, but are still great places to drink wine and eat the local cuisine.

In the listings below, only *Stadtheurigen* are specifically detailed; for the suburb; there are a few listings in the box on p.321. The opening times of most *Heurigen* are unpredictable (most don't open until mid-afternoon), but part of the fun is to simply set off to one of the districts and take pot luck. A display board at the centre of each village lists those *Heurigen* that are open.

Stadtheurigen

Augustinerkeller, 1, Augustinerstrasse 1; U-Bahn Karlsplatz. Vast array of green and black striped booths in the cellars underneath the Albertina. Fast service and hearty Viennese food; a tad touristy, but fun – prices are cheaper in the day. *Schrammelmusik* from 6.30pm. Mon–Fri & Sun 11am–midnight, Sat 11am–1am. Inexpensive–moderate.

Esterházykeller, 1, Haarhof 1; U-Bahn Herrengasse. Snug, brick-vaulted wine cellar with very cheap wine and a limited range of hot and cold snacks. Situated off Naglergasse. Mon–Fri 11am–11pm, Sat & Sun 4–11pm. Inexpensive.

Göttweiger Stiftskeller, 1, Spiegelgasse 9; U-Bahn Stephansplatz. Ground-floor monastic wine cellars that feel more like a family *Beisl*. Utterly traditional food and a mixed clientele – very popular, especially at lunchtime. Mon–Fri 8am–11pm. Inexpensive.

Melker Stiftskeller, 1, Schottengasse 3; U-Bahn Schottentor. Vast, high-ceilinged wine cellar owned by the famous Melk monks, serving traditional grub. Mon–Sat 5pm–midnight. Moderate.

Wein-Comptoir, 1, Bäckerstrasse 6; U-Bahn Stephansplatz. Beautiful wood-panelled *Beisl* on several levels with bottles stacked up on the walls. Mon–Sat 5pm–2am. Moderate.

Zwölf-Apostelkeller, 1, Sonnenfelsgasse 3; U-Bahn Stephansplatz. An attractive seventeenth-century building with bars housed in three levels of cellars. *The* place to drink wine, but often difficult to find a space; cold buffet only. Daily 4.30pm–midnight. Inexpensive–moderate.

Chapter 12

Bars, clubs and live venues

Surveys have shown that the vast majority of the Viennese are safely tucked up in bed by as early as 10pm. Meanwhile, however, a hard core stay up until early in the morning – in fact it's quite possible to keep drinking round the clock.

Vienna's late-night **bars** are concentrated in three main areas, the most famous of which is the so-called *Bermuda Dreieck* or **Bermuda Triangle**, which focuses on Rabensteig, Seitenstetten-gasse, Ruprechtsplatz and the streets around. The emergence of the Triangle in the 1980s helped kick-start Vienna's nightlife out of its stupor, though the area has become a victim of its own success. That said, such is the variety packed into these few streets that you're bound to find somewhere that appeals.

Other areas worth exploring are the **Naschmarkt**, where late-night licences abound, and Neubau, in particular the **Spittelberg** area – the narrow streets between Burggasse and Siebensterngasse, behind Messepalast – which has the highest concentration of late-night drinking holes, many of which double as restaurants and cafés. In the warmer weather, it's also worth checking out the courtyards of the **Altes Allgemeines Krankenhaus**, off Alserstrasse, which now belong to the university – and of course, there are the outdoor bars on the Copa Cagrana on the Donauinsel (see p.217).

Vienna's **club** scene is very small indeed for a city of 1.5 million. Dance culture, such as one would find in, say, London, is restricted to just a few venues. Aside from discos, the majority of Vienna's clubs are, in fact, bars, which either occasionally, or regularly, have live bands, or, more often than not, resident DJs spinning discs (both danceable and non-danceable), while the punters simply chill out and drink. As it's so difficult to differentiate between what's a bar, what's a club and what's a live venue, we've simply organized the listings by area. To find out what's on at Vienna's clubs, check out the *Party* section in the weekly listings tabloid *Falter* (see p.38) or visit the website *www.club.at.*

Drink prices are relatively high – bars in the Bermuda Triangle tend to charge öS40/€2.91 and upwards for a *Krügerl* (half-litre) – but in those clubs where there is an admission charge, it's rarely more than öS100/€7.27. Live acts and concerts cost from öS150/€10.90 upwards. As for how to get home in the wee small hours, there are details on the city's nightbuses on p.41. Nightbuses leave from Schwedenplatz and usually do a circuit of the Ring before heading off to their destination – pick up a leaflet from the tourist office or one of the transport offices (see p.39).

The nearest U-Bahn to the Bermuda Triangle is Schwedenplatz.

Bars, clubs
and live
venues

The Bermuda Triangle

First Floor, 1, Seitenstettengasse 1. As
the name suggests, an upstairs bar, with
a vast array of aquariums and packed
with a more sophisticated crowd than
your average BT hangout. Daily
8pm–3am.

Jazzland, 1, Franz-Josefs-Kai 29 ☎533
25 75, *www.jazzland.at*. Vienna's main
trad-jazz venue, just below the
Ruprechtskirche. Mon–Sat 7pm–2am.

Krah Krah, 1, Rabensteig 8. Crowded bar
known for its excellent selection of
draught and bottled beers; decent

snacks also on offer, and occasional live
music. Mon–Sat 11am–2am, Sun
11am–1am.

Roter Engel, 1, Rabensteig 5;
www.roterengel.at. Stylish café-bar
designed by deconstructionist mob, Coop
Himmelblau, in 1979. Live music most
nights; sets at 9.30pm (Fri & Sat at midnight, too). Daily 5pm–4am.

The rest of the Innere Stadt

American Bar (Kärntner Bar), 1, Kärntner
Durchgang; U-Bahn Stephensplatz. Small,

dark late-night bar off Kärntnerstrasse with surprisingly rich interior by Adolf Loos. Shame about the strip club next door. Daily noon–4am.

Flanagan's, 1, Schwarzenbergerstrasse 1–3; U-Bahn Karlsplatz. The most central, and probably the best of Vienna's rash of Irish pubs, with Guinness and Kilkenny, Irish/British food and big-screen sports. Daily 1pm–late.

Flex, 1, Donaukanal/Augartenbrücke; www.flex.at; U-Bahn Schottenring. Serious dance-music bar by the canal, overlooking Wagner's Schützenhaus and attracting the city's best DJs and a very young crowd. Daily 8pm–4am.

Havana, 1, Mahlerstrasse 11 ☎513 20 75; U-Bahn Karlsplatz. General Latin American/Caribbean-themed mayhem for salsa fiends every night from 8pm, just off Kärntnerstrasse. Daily 8pm–late.

Porgy & Bess, 1, Riemergasse 11; www.porgy.or.at; U-Bahn Stubentor. A converted porn cinema provides the new home for this, Vienna's top jazz venue, attracting serious jazz acts from all over the world.

Wunder-Bar, Schönlanterngasse 8; U-Bahn Schwedenplatz. Hermann Czech-designed bar from the 1970s that has a postmodern feel; an older crowd tends to sink into the brown leather seats. Daily 4pm–2am.

Ringstrasse

Guess Club, 1, Kärntnerstrasse 44; U-Bahn Karlsplatz; branch at 6, Kaunitzgasse 3; www.guessclub.com; U-Bahn Kettenbrückengasse. Very preciously posey bar to the south of the Ring, decked out in retro cream upholstery, attracting a like-minded crowd. Mon–Thurs 5pm–2am, Fri & Sat 5pm–4am, Sun 5pm–midnight.

Meierei, 3, Am Heumarkt 2a; www.sunshine.at; U-Bahn Stadtpark. Staid Stadtpark café by day, but throbbing, sweaty DJ nights take place more or less every Fri & Sat, and occasionally on other days. 10pm–4am.

Roxy, 4, Operngasse 24; U-Bahn Karlsplatz. Conveniently central nightclub with an eclectic mix of DJ tunes, located underneath Wagner's Karlsplatz pavilions. Mon–Sat 10pm–4am.

Volksgarten, 1, Burgring 1; www.volksgarten.at; U-Bahn Volkstheater. Situated in the park of the same name, Vienna's longest-running club and a firm favourite with the dance crowd; the outdoor dance floor is a summertime treat, as is the *Pavillon* garden café upstairs. May–Sept daily 10pm–5am.

Margarethen, Wieden and Mariahilf

Celeste, 5, Hamburgerstrasse 18 ☎586 53 14; U-Bahn Kettenbrückengasse. Live venue just south of Naschmarkt, with a mixed programme from jazz to flamenco. Gigs start at around 8pm.

Freihaus, 4, Margarethenstrasse 11; U-Bahn Taubstummengasse/Karlplatz. Large and lively L-shaped bar that gave its name to the surrounding Freihaus Viertel of bars and galleries. Mon–Sat 5.30pm–2am, Sun 10am–2am.

Jenseits, 6, Nelkengasse 3; U-Bahn Neubaugasse. Previously a cruisey gay bar, now a popular late-night DJ spot, which is literally bursting at the seams some nights. Mon–Sat 9pm–4am.

Nachtasyl, 6, Stumpergasse 53; U-Bahn Westbahnhof. Darkened beer hall managed by an expatriate Czech, with an eclectic mix of live music and DJs on offer nightly. Daily 8pm–4am.

Radiokulturhaus, 4, Argentinierstrasse 30a ☎50 17; U-Bahn Taubstummengasse. Austrian radio's Funkhaus, just west of the Belvedere, stages regular gigs ranging from classical and cabaret to jazz and world music. Gigs start at around 8pm.

Titanic, 6, Theobaldgasse 11; U-Bahn Babenbergerstrasse. Primarily a Latin American club, Titanic also heaves to the tune of hip-hop, house, soul, funk, just about anything, depending on the night. Daily 10pm–4am.

Bars, clubs and live venues

Bars, clubs and live venues

LATE-NIGHT CAFÉS, PUBS AND RESTAURANTS

Check out the following cafés, pubs and restaurants, all of which are open until at least 2am several nights a week; they're all reviewed in the previous chapter.

INNERE STADT
Aera, 1, Gonzagagasse 11 (see p.312)
Alt Wien, 1, Bäckerstrasse 9 (see p.312)
Hawelka, 1, Dorotheergasse 6 (see p.312)
Kleines Café, 1, Franziskanerplatz 3 (see p.312)
MAK Café, 1, Stubenring 5 (see p.313)
Palmenhaus, 1, Burggarten (see p.313)
Salzamt, 1, Ruprechtsplatz 1 (see p.318)
Santo Spirito, 1, Kumpfgasse 7 (see p.318)
Wein-Comptoir, 1, Bäckerstrasse 6 (see p.322)

NASCHMARKT TO JOSEFSTADT
Amacord, 5, Rechte Wienzeile 15 (see p.314)
Centimeter II, Siebensterngasse 18 (see p.319)
Drechsler, 6, Linke Wienzeile 22 (see p.314)
Europa, 7, Zollergasse 8 (see p.314)
Hummel, 8, Albertgasse 27 (see p.314)
Hunger-Künstler, 6, Gumpfendorferstrasse 48 (see p.319)

Lux, 7, Spittelberggasse 6 (see p.315)
Plutzer Bräu, 7, Schrankgasse 2 (see p.320)
Rüdigerhof, 5, Hamburger Strasse 20 (see p.314)
Savoy, 6, Linke Wienzeile 36 (see p.314)
Schlossgasse 21, 5, Schlossgasse 21 (see p.319)
Tunnel, 8, Florianigasse 39 (see p.315).
Die Wäscherei, 8, Albertgasse/ Laudongasse (see p.320)

ALSERGRUND
Blaustern, 9, Döblinger Gürtel 2 (see p.315)
Fischerbräu, 19, Billrothstrasse 17 (see p.321)
Weimar, 9, Währinger Strasse 68 (see p.315)

LEOPOLDSTADT
Leopold, 2, Grosser Pfarrgasse 11 (see p.320)
Schöne Perle, 2, Grosser Pfarrgasse/ Leopoldgasse (see p.315)

Neubau and Josefstadt

B72, 8, Stadtbahnbögen 72, Hernalser Gürtel ☎ 409 21 28; U-Bahn Alserstrasse. Dark, designer club underneath the U-Bahn arches – features a mixture of DJs and live indie bands. Daily 9pm–4am.

Blue Box, 7, Richtergasse 8. Café with resident DJs and a good snack menu, including excellent brunch buffet. Live music from 8pm. Mon 6pm–2am, Tues–Thurs & Sun 10am–2am, Fri & Sat 10am–4am.

Chelsea, 8, U-Bahnbögen 29–31, Lerchenfelder Gürtel; U-Bahn Thaliastrasse. Favourite venue with up-and-coming Brit guitar bands; situated underneath the U-Bahn. Mon–Sat 7pm–4am, Sun 4pm–4am.

Donau, 7, Karl-Schweighofer-Gasse 10; U-Bahn Volkstheater. Chill-out sounds from the in-house DJs, and strange projections on the walls. Daily 9pm–4am.

Miles Smiles, 8, Lange Gasse 51; U-Bahn Rathaus. Helps if you're a devotee of the trumpeter, though this mellow café does have the occasional live jazz act. Daily 8pm–2am, Fri & Sat until 4am.

Rhiz, 8, Stadtbahnbögen 37–38, Lerchenfelder Gürtel; www.rhiz.org; U-Bahn Lerchenfelder Strasse. A modish cross between a bar, a café and a club, with several DJs spinning everything from dance to trance. Daily 6pm–4am.

Schulz, 7, Siebernsterngasse 31; tram #49. Cool designer minimalist bar on the corner of Kirchengasse that sits next door to a bar of similar ilk run by the KPÖ. Mon–Sat 9am–2am, Sun 5pm–2am.

Tunnel, 8, Florianigasse 39 ☎405 34 65; tram #5. Large, clean-living student establishment with café upstairs and frequent live bands down in the cellar. Daily 9am–2am.

Alsergrund

w.u.k., 9, Währinger Strasse 59; *www.wuk.at*; tram #40, #41 or #42. Formerly squatted old red-brick school, now legitimate arts venue with a great café and a wide programme of events, including live music and DJ nights; check the *Falter* listings. Daily 11am–2am.

The suburbs

Arena, 3, Baumgasse 80; U-Bahn Erdberg. It's a long trek out to this former slaughterhouse on the corner of Französengraben, but there's a real variety of stuff that goes on here – all-night raves, outdoor concerts, open-air cinema – so check the listings before setting out. Daily 4pm–2am.

Szene Wien, 11, Hauffgasse 26 ☎749 33 41; U-Bahn Enkplatz. Regularly good live music venue, with a café serving great food. It's run by a radical bunch from Simmering and is now much easier to get to thanks to the new U-Bahn, but phone ahead to check it's happening. Daily 8pm–late.

U4, 12, Schönbrunnerstrasse 222; *www.u4club.com*; U-Bahn Meidling-Hauptstrasse. Dark, cavernous disco, mostly rock/indie, with frequent gigs; a mecca of the alternative crowd. Gay/lesbian night Thursday. Daily 10pm–4am.

Bars, clubs
and live
venues

Chapter 13

The Arts

Rock, pop and jazz venues are covered in the previous chapter.

Vienna prides itself on its musical associations, and classical music and opera, in particular, are heavily subsidized by the Austrian state. The chief cultural festival – featuring opera, music and theatre – is the **Wiener Festwochen** (*www.festwochen.or.at*), which lasts from early May until mid-June. In July and August, when the Vienna Philharmonic go on tour, the **Klangbogen** (Summer Music Festival) pulls in guest orchestras and more opera. The city's film festival or **Viennale** and the **Wien Modern** festival of contemporary classical music both take place towards the end of October, but by far the busiest time of the year is **Fasching**, Vienna's ball season.

To find out **what's on**, pick up the tourist board's free monthly listings booklet *Programm*, which gives the programmes of the big opera and concert houses and theatres, plus a day-by-day concert guide, ball calendar and details of the current art exhibitions. The weekly listings tabloid *Falter* also lists classical concerts under its *Musik-E* section.

Tickets

Ticket **prices** vary enormously in Vienna: the Staatsoper is a case in point, with seats ranging from öS70/€5.09 to öS3500/€254.35. For some events – most notably the Vienna Boys' Choir and the New Year's Day Concert – it's not so much the price as the availability that's a problem. However, the big state venues offer cheap *Stehplätze* on the day of the performance (see box below), and some offer unsold tickets at a discount to students, around an hour or thirty minutes before the show starts.

The cheapest way of **buying tickets** is to go to the venue's own box office. With the big four state theatres – Staatsoper, Volksoper, Burgtheater and Akademietheater – you can either buy direct or from their shared central box office, the *Bundestheaterkassen*, not far from the Staatsoper at 1, Hanuschgasse 3 (☎51444-2960; Mon–Fri 8am–6pm, Sat & Sun 9am–noon; *www.oebthv.gv.at*; U-Bahn Karlsplatz). There's also a ticket booth next to the Staatsoper (daily 10am–7pm), which

---

Stehplätze

Vienna may be an expensive place, but its top opera houses and concert halls are open to even the poorest music student thanks to the system of *Stehplätze* or **standing-room tickets** which can cost as little as öS30/€2.18 each. *Stehplätze* are limited to one per person and usually go on sale one hour before the performance (for very popular concerts, you may find that tickets go on sale somewhat earlier, so check first). It's standard practice, once you've got into the auditorium, to tie a scarf to the railings to reserve your standing place.

Waltz and Schmaltz

It's easy enough to hear a bit of classic Strauss or light Mozart at any time of the year in Vienna. The **Vienna Walzer Orchestra** (☎512 62 65) performs Strauss and the like decked out in Biedermeier costume every week, either at the Börse, on Wipplingerstrasse, Palais Eschenbach, on Eschenbachgasse, or in the Palais Ferstel on Freyung. Meanwhile, the **Johann Strauss Capelle** (☎718 96 66), also kitted out in period costume, sing and dance their hearts out at similar venues. Finally, if you yearn to hear schmaltzy Viennese songs sung live in a more informal setting, check out **Café Schmid Hansl**, 18, Schulgasse 31 (☎406 36 58; tram #40 or #41 from U-Bahn Volksoper; Tues–Sat 8pm–4am).

---

sells tickets for all venues, and occasionally has half-price tickets for musicals and for other events.

Opera and classical music

Vienna has a musical pedigree second to none. Josef Haydn, Wolfgang Mozart and Ludwig Beethoven spent much of their time here, as did local-born Franz Schubert. Johannes Brahms and Anton Bruckner followed in their wake, and coincided with the great waltz fever generated by the Strauss family and Josef Lanner. In the early twentieth century, the Vienna opera house was under the baton of Gustav Mahler, while its concert halls resounded to the atonal music of Arnold Schönberg, Anton Webern and Alban Berg.

Though Vienna hasn't produced any world-class composers for some time, it does still boast one of Europe's top opera houses in the **Staatsoper**, served by one of its finest orchestras, the **Wiener Philharmoniker** (*www .wienerphilharmoniker.at*). The orchestra's New Year's Day Concert (Silvesterkonzert) in the Musikverein is broadcast across the globe; to obtain tickets you must contact the box office on January 2 for the following year's concert (☎505 81 90; *www.musikverein-wien.at*). If you don't have a ticket, don't despair, not only is the concert broadcast live on Austrian TV, it's also relayed live on an enormous screen in front of the Rathaus at midday and again at 5pm. When the big state theatres are closed in July and August, opera and classical music con-

certs captured on film are also shown for free every evening outside the Rathaus.

The most famous musical institution in the city is, of course, the **Wiener Sängerknaben** (*www.wsk.at*), or Vienna Boys' Choir, which performs Mass at the Burgkapelle in the Hofburg every Sunday from mid-September to June at 9.15am. Tickets for the Mass (öS70–380/€5.09–27.62) are sold out weeks in advance, though some are held over each week and go on sale on Fridays (11am–1pm & 3–5pm). To book in advance write to Hofmusikkapelle, Hofburg, A-1010 Wien, Austria, stating which Sunday Mass you wish to attend, and you will be sent back a reservation slip to take to the box office on arrival in Vienna. The other option is to settle for one of the free *Stehplätze*, which are distributed before Mass; get there for 8.30am to be sure of a place (although some people leave early having got bored). Be warned, however, that most of the choir remain out of sight up in the organ loft for the whole of Mass.

Mostly opera and operetta

Kammeroper, 1, Fleischmarkt 24 ☎513 60 72, *http://members.magnet.at /wienerkammeroper*; U-Bahn Schwedenplatz. Vienna's smallest opera house is a Jugendstil theatre hidden in the backstreets of the Innere Stadt. Works vary – anything from Rossini to Britten – and so does the quality. In July and August, when the theatre is closed, the Kammeroper stages open-air Mozart

The Arts

operas in the Roman ruins in Schönbrunn's Schlosspark (see p.234).

Staatsoper, 1, Opernring 2 ☎ 514 44-2250, *www.wiener-staatsoper.at*; U-Bahn Karlsplatz. Vienna's largest opera house (see also p.133) stages around forty operas a season played in rep. It's a conservative place, but attracts the top names, and has the benefit of the Wiener Philharmoniker in the pit. Ticket prices range from öS70/€5.09 to öS2500/€181.68, but with over 500 *Stehplätze* (öS50/€3.63) going on sale every night, an hour before the curtain goes up, it is one of the most accessible opera houses in the world. Closed July & Aug.

Volksoper, 9, Währinger Strasse 78 ☎ 514 44-3670, *www.volksoper.at*; U-Bahn Volksoper or tram #40, #41 or #42. Vienna's number two opera house, which specializes in operetta, but also puts on more adventurous opera productions; 70 or so *Stehplätze* a night.

Mostly classical music

Bösendorfer Saal, 4, Graf Starhemberg-Gasse 14 ☎ 504 66 51; U-Bahn Taubstummengasse. Chamber music concerts performed using Bösendorfer pianos, and held in a hall with excellent acoustics, belonging to the famous Austrian piano manufacturers.

Konzerthaus, 3, Lothringerstrasse 20 ☎ 712 12 11; *www.konzerthaus.at*; U-Bahn Karlsplatz. Early twentieth-century concert hall designed by Viennese duo Helmer & Fellner. Three separate halls: the Grosser Saal, Mozart-Saal and Schubert-Saal. The programme here tends to be a bit more adventurous and varied than the Musikverein's.

Musikverein, 1, Bösendorferstrasse 12 ☎ 505 81 90; *www.musikverein-wien.at*; U-Bahn Karlsplatz. Two ornate concert halls in one building, gilded from top to bottom inside. The larger of the two, the Grosser Saal, has the best acoustics in the country, and is the unofficial home of the Wiener Philharmoniker, while the smaller hall, the Brahms-Saal, is used

mainly for chamber concerts; *Stehplätze* available for the Grosser Saal.

Theatre

Obviously for the non-German speaker, most of Vienna's **theatres** and satirical **cabarets** have limited appeal. However, there are a couple of English-speaking theatre groups, a few theatres that specialize in musicals, several puppet theatres, where language is less of a problem, and the Burgtheater, whose interior alone is worth the price of a ticket.

Straight theatres

Akademietheater, 3, Lisztstrasse 1 ☎ 514 44-4410; *www.burgtheater.at*; U-Bahn Karlsplatz. Number two to the Burgtheater, using the same pool of actors, but specializing in more contemporary drama.

Burgtheater, 1, Dr-Karl-Lueger-Ring 2 ☎ 514 44-4140; *www.burgtheater.at*; U-Bahn Herrengasse. Vienna's most prestigious theatrical stage puts on serious drama in rep. The foyer and staircases are spectacular; the auditorium was modernized after bomb damage in 1945. Tickets cost from öS50/€3.63 to öS600/€43.60, with 150 *Stehplätze* (öS25/€1.82) going on sale every night, an hour before the curtain goes up. Closed in July & Aug.

Theater-in-der-Josefstadt, 8, Josefstädter Strasse 24–26 ☎ 427 00-300; U-Bahn Rathaus or tram #J. Beautiful early nineteenth-century theatre that puts on a variety of serious German-language drama from classics to contemporary.

Volkstheater, 7, Neustiftgasse 1 ☎ 523 27 76; *www.volkstheater.at*; U-Bahn Volkstheater. Late nineteenth-century theatre designed by Helmer & Fellner, with a groovy bar to hang out in. Modern plays and classics and even the odd operetta.

English-speaking theatres

International Theatre, 9, Porzellangasse 8 ☎ 319 62 72; tram #D. Local-based ex-pat (mostly American) venue; situated

Fasching

Though clearly analogous with Mardi Gras and Carnival, Vienna's **Fasching** lasts much longer, with the first balls taking place on November 11, and continuing – mostly on Saturdays and Sundays – until Ash Wednesday the following year. Traditionally the most famous ball is the *Kaiserball*, held in the Hofburg and in days gone by presided over by the emperor himself. Its place at the top of the hierarchy is now challenged by the *Opernball*, held on the Thursday before Ash Wednesday in the Staatsoper, and pictured in many a tourist brochure, with the débutantes parading all in white. The other 300 or so balls are a hotchpotch held by various associations – everything from the gay and lesbian *Regenbogenball* to the *Ball der Burgenländischen Kroaten* – in Vienna's top hotels and palaces; those followed by the word *Gschnas* are masked. To find out what's on in Fasching, pick up a *Wiener Ballkalender* (*www.ball.at*) from the tourist office in the months leading up to and during Fasching. If you're worried about your dancing ability, there are numerous dance classes held during the season; ask the tourist board for details.

---

on the corner of Müllnergasse and Porzellangasse; closed in August.

Vienna's English Theatre, 8, Josefsgasse 12 ☎ 402 12 60; *www.englishtheatre.at*; U-Bahn Lerchenfelderstrasse. Larger, professionally run venue, serviced by companies flown in from abroad (mostly London).

Mostly musicals

Raimund Theater, 6, Wallgasse 18 ☎ 599 77-27; U-Bahn Westbahnhof. Late nineteenth-century theatre, which puts on Broadway musicals and other popular productions.

Theater an der Wien, 6, Linke Wienzeile 6 ☎ 588 30; U-Bahn Karlsplatz/Kettenbrückengasse. Historic early nineteenth-century theatre (see p.146), specializing in German-language musicals.

Puppet theatre

Lilarum Figurentheater, 3, Göllnergasse 8 ☎ 710 26 66; U-Bahn Kardinal-Nagl-Platz. Puppet theatre out in Landstrasse, with several performances a day. Wed & Fri–Sun and during school holidays.

Märchenbühne der Apfelbaum, 7, Kirchengasse 41 ☎ 523 1729-20. Puppet theatre specializing in classic fairy tales, so even without any German you can at least follow the plot. Sat & Sun.

Schönbrunner Schlossmarionettentheater, 13, Schloss Schönbrunn, Hofratsktrakt ☎ 817 32 47; *www.marionettentheater.at*. String puppet theatre in Schönbrunn specializing in over-long Mozart operas – try and catch a different show if you can. Performances Wed–Sun.

Cinema

Austrian **cinema** is not really up there with the greats, and unless your German is up to scratch, you're best off sticking to British and American films. One film that's fun to see, and is shown here every weekend at the *Burg-Kino* (see p.332), is **The Third Man** – (*Der Dritte Mann*) – made in 1949, set amidst the rubble of postwar Vienna and starring Orson Welles.

The best place to check out the week's cinema **listings** is either *Der Standard* or *Falter*, the city's weekly tabloid. *OF* means it's in the original without subtitles, *Omengu* means it's in the original with English subtitles, *OmU* means it's in the original with German subtitles, but should not be confused with *OmÜ*, which means it's in the original, but has a live voice-over German translation. And finally, *dF* means it's dubbed into German.

Cinema **tickets** cost around öS100/€7.27; Monday (*Kino-Montag*) is

The Arts

cheap ticket day. In July and August, you can watch **open-air films** in the Augarten (see p.216) and outside the Rathaus (see p.125).

Artis International, 1, Schultergasse/Jordangasse; U-Bahn Stephansplatz. Central multiplex cinema showing films in English in six different salons.

Bellaria, 7, Museumsstrasse 3; U-Bahn Volkstheater. Old Neubau cinema that specializes in German and Austrian black-and-white movies.

Breitenseer Lichtspiele, 14, Breitenseer Strasse 21; U-Bahn Hütteldorfer Strasse. Vienna's oldest cinema, which opened in 1909, is still going strong, with much the same fittings. Wed–Sun only.

Burg, 1, Opernring 19; U-Bahn Babenbergerstrasse. Two-screen cinema on the Ringstrasse that shows films in the original, without subtitles. *The Third Man* has a regular spot (Fri 10.50pm & Sun 2.15pm).

English Cinema Haydn, 6, Mariahilferstrasse 57; U-Bahn Neubaugasse. As the name suggests, this is a cinema that shows the latest films in English without subtitles.

Filmhaus Stöbergasse, 5, Stöbergasse 11–15; bus #12A or #14A. Art-house cinema south of the Naschmarkt that shows films from all over the world in their original language.

Filmmuseum, 1, Augustinerstrasse 1; U-Bahn Karlsplatz. Vienna's main art-house cinema, on the ground floor of the Albertina, with a very esoteric programme, all in the original, generally without subtitles. Closed July & Aug.

Imax Filmtheater, 14, Mariahilferstrasse 212; www.imax-wien.at; U-Bahn Schönbrunn or tram #52 or #58. Specially made forty-minute films to show off the 400-square-metre wrap-round screen's awesome scope.

Stadtkino, 3, Schwarzenbergplatz 7; U-Bahn Karlsplatz. Arthouse cinema with disabled access and only a short distance from the Innere Stadt. Closed Aug.

Visual arts

In addition to its vast permanent collections of art (detailed in the main text of the guide), Vienna has a large number of galleries that host temporary exhibitions. To check out the latest shows and opening times, consult the tourist board's free monthly booklet *Programm*.

Architektur Zentrum Wien, 7, Museumsquartier, Museumsplatz 1; www.azw.at; U-Bahn Volkstheater. In the courtyard of the vast Messespalast complex, and specializing in contemporary architectural exhibitions. Daily 10am–7pm.

Generali Foundation, 4, Wiedner Hauptstrasse 15; www.gfound.or.at; U-Bahn Karlsplatz. Funky modern space owned by the eponymous insurance company and hidden away a short stroll south of Karlsplatz, serving up interesting contemporary sculpture and mixed media work. Tues–Sun 11am–6pm, Thurs 11am–8pm.

Kunstforum, 1, Freyung 8; www.kunstforum.at; U-Bahn Herrengasse. Major venue for visiting foreign exhibitions of big-name contemporary art exhibitions sponsored by Bank Austria. Daily 10am–7pm, Wed until 9pm.

Kunsthalle Wien, 7, Museumsplatz 1; www.kunsthallewien.at; U-Bahn Volkstheater/Babenberger Strasse. The city's official space for big contemporary art exhibitions has moved from Krischanitz's yellow box in Karlsplatz to the new MuseumsQuartier. Daily 10am–6pm, Thurs until 10pm.

KunstHausWien, 3, Untere Weissgerberstrasse 13; www.kunsthauswien.com; tram #N. Friedensreich Hundertwasser's gallery, with a permanent show of his works and visiting exhibitions of fellow exhibitionists (see p.173). Daily 10am–7pm.

Künstlerhaus, 1, Karlsplatz 5; www.k-haus.at; U-Bahn Karlsplatz. Artists' Society next door to the Musikverein that puts on major retrospectives in painting, sculpture and photography. Daily 10am–6pm, Thurs until 9pm.

Palais Harrach, 1, Freyung 3; *www.khm.at;* U-Bahn Herrengasse. Temporary space used by the Kunsthistorisches Museum for its special exhibitions. Daily 10am–6pm.

Secession, 1, Friedrichstrasse 12; *www.secession.at;* U-Bahn Karlsplatz. The famous Jugendstil exhibition space, with Klimt's *Beethoven Frieze* in the basement (see p.140), continues to host provocative modern art shows and installations. Tues–Sun 10am–6pm, Thurs 10am–8pm.

The Arts

Chapter 14

Shopping

Few people come to Vienna exclusively to shop, though window shopping along **Kärntnerstrasse**, **Graben** and **Kohlmarkt** can be fun. In the backstreets of the **Innere Stadt**, you'll also find numerous excellent bookstalls and little antique shops clustered around the Dorotheum (see opposite). The streets of **Neubau**, to the north of Mariahilferstrasse, are also good for browsing, and of course, the city boasts a great Saturday flea market. For a capital, Vienna has very few large supermarkets, with just the small Billa stores scattered across the city. **Mariahilferstrasse** remains the main shopping drag for department stores and mainstream shops. Those Viennese with cars head off to **Shopping-Center-Süd** (SCS), Austria's biggest shopping complex, some way south of the city limits at Vösendorf. The easiest way to get there on public transport is on the Lokalbahn to Baden, which departs

from the tram stop opposite the Staatsoper.

Arts, crafts and antiques

There's a whole cluster of antique shops (*Antiquitäten*) in the streets around the Dorotheum (see opposite), though there are few bargains to be had. Shops specialising in Art Nouveau and early twentieth-century gear can be found in the Spittelberg area, off Siebensterngasse. For bric-a-brac, second-hand goods (*Altwaren*), and possibly a bargain or two, head for the flea market by the Naschmarkt, where you'll have to haggle.

Adil Besim, 1, Graben 30; *www .adil-besim.co.at*; U-Bahn Stephansplatz. The king of Vienna's carpet shops, in business since 1946, selling kilims, rugs and tapestries at serious prices.

Augarten, 1, Stock-im-Eisen-Platz 3–4; *www.augarten.at*; U-Bahn Stephansplatz.

Opening times

Shopping hours in Vienna are strictly controlled by the state. Until very recently, all shops had to conform to the following opening hours: Monday to Friday 8 or 9am to 5 or 6pm, with late shopping on Thursdays 7.30pm, and Saturday 8am to noon – except on the first Saturday of the month (known as *Langersamstag*, or "long Saturday"), when shops are open 8am to 5pm. Shops are now allowed to open all day on every Saturday, but many shops outside the centre still stick to the old *Langersamstag* routine. No shops may stay open any later on weekdays, or at all on Sundays, except those at the main railway stations, or a few selling food. In the city centre and the main suburban shopping streets, most shops have no weekday lunch break or *Mittagssperre*, but in the quieter streets and the sleepier suburbs, this custom is still followed, usually between noon and 2pm.

Vienna's very own hand-painted china manufacturers have an outlet here, though you can also visit and buy direct (including some seconds) from the factory (see p.216).

Dorotheum, 1, Dorotheergasse 17, *www.dorotheum.com*; U-bahn Stephansplatz. "Aunt Dorothy's", as it's known, is one of the world's leading auction houses, with daily sales and a fixed-price shop; there's even a café for posing in (see p.67).

J. & L. Lobmeyr, 1, Kärntnerstrasse 26; *www.lobmeyr.at*; U-Bahn Stephansplatz. Famous glass manufacturers, and a lovely shop, with a museum on the top floor (see p.58). You can buy glass designed by Adolf Loos and Josef Hoffmann as well as more modern pieces.

MAK-Shop, 1, Weiskirchnerstrasse 3, *www.mak.at*; U-Bahn Stubentor. Museum shop selling wacky modern furniture and accoutrements by the designers of the School of Applied Arts. Open late on Thurs until 9pm.

Thonet, 9, Berggasse 31; *www.thonet.com*; tram #D. Furniture company, famed for its bentwood chairs, and still producing Adolf Loos and Wiener Werkstätte designs.

Woka, 1, Singerstrasse 16; *www.woklamps.com*; U-Bahn Stephansplatz. Shop selling reproduction lamps and the like, designed by Adolf Loos and other Wiener Werkstätte artists.

Bookshops

Though Vienna has a staggering number of bookshops (*Buchhandlungen*), most of them in the Innere Stadt, only a handful are English-language. Nevertheless, many of the stores below stock a wide choice of English-language volumes. Be warned, however, that the Austrians slap tax on books and prices are consequently much higher than elsewhere in Europe.

Amadeus, 6, Mariahilferstrasse 99; *www.amadeus.at*; U-Bahn Neubaugasse; another branch in Steffl (see p.336). Vienna's biggest bookstore, with a well-

stocked English section, lots of media on sale, a music department and free internet access.

British Bookshop, 1, Weihburggasse 24–26; *www.britishbookshop.at*; U-Bahn Stephansplatz. A fair selection of novels and biographies in English, with half the shop given over to EFL teaching materials.

Freytag & Berndt, 1, Kohlmarkt 9; *www.freytagberndt.at*; U-Bahn Stephansplatz. Flagship store of Austria's most prestigious map-makers, with loads of maps, as well as guides on Vienna and the rest of the world in English, including a large selection of Rough Guides.

Morawa, 1, Wollzeile 11; *www.morawa.at*; U-Bahn Stubentor. Huge bookshop stretching right back to Bäckerstrasse; the English section is on the first floor, guides and a huge choice of English magazines and newspapers are at the back.

Prachner, 1, Kärntnerstrasse 30; *www.prachner.at*; U-Bahn Stephansplatz. Bookish place with shelves stacked high. Great architecture section and a selective English section with guides on Vienna, novels and some history.

Sallmayer'sche Buchhandlung, 1, Neuer Markt 6; U-Bahn Stephansplatz. Great art and photography sections, lots on hobbies – anything from trains to Barbie dolls – plus a selection of Red Army watches.

Satyr-Filmwelt, 1, Vorlaufstrasse 9–13; U-Bahn Schwedenplatz. Loads of books in German, French and (mostly) English on movies and music. Good selection of art-house videos and posters and CD soundtracks, too.

Shakespeare & Co, 1, Sterngasse 2; U-Bahn Schwedenplatz. Floor-to-ceiling English-language bookstore, with friendly staff and a great selection of novels, art books and magazines.

Clothes

Vienna has all the usual designer label stores you'd find in most European capi-

Shopping

Shopping

tals. The shops listed below concentrate on retro clothes shops and clubbing gear. There are also a few places listed where you can buy *Tracht*, the traditional Alpine costume of *Dirndl* dresses and blouses for women and *Walker* (jackets) or *Loden* (capes) for men, which is still alarmingly popular throughout the country.

Absolut Hödl, 1, Tuchlauben 27; U-Bahn Stephansplatz. Great 1960s retro and repro for men and women.

Derby Handschuhe, 1, Plankengasse 5; U-Bahn Stephansplatz. A veritable quality glove-fest in suede and leather.

Helford Jersey, 1, Franz-Josefs-Kai 19; U-Bahn Schwedenplatz. Model cars, baseball caps, Vienna T-shirts, and reasonably priced *Trachten* clothes for the kids.

Lanz, 1, Kärntnerstrasse 10; U-Bahn Stephansplatz. The full Austrian *Trachten* monty – *Dirndl*, *Lederhosen*, *Walkjanker* – at a price.

Rag, 1, Sterngasse 4; U-Bahn Schwedenplatz. Baggy trousers and other slack accoutrements for the skateboarding posse.

Tostmann, 1, Schottengasse 3a; *www.tostmann.at*; U-Bahn Schottentor. The place to fix yourself up head to toe in *Tracht*.

Wow, 7, Neustiftgasse 23; U-Bahn Volkstheater. Lots of 1960s and 1970s retro gear for women, including some serious platforms.

Department stores

Vienna is still the land of the small shop, and has remarkably few department stores. The main two are listed below.

Gerngross, 7, Mariahilferstrasse 38–48; U-Bahn Neubaugasse. Vienna's largest department store with everything from toys to clothes. Good sushi bar on the top floor.

Steffl, 1, Kärntnerstrasse 19; U-Bahn Stephansplatz. Classic department store

– the only one in the Innere Stadt – with perfume and jewellery and a memorial to Mozart (who died in a building on the same site) on the ground floor, free internet access and a café in a branch of the Amadeus bookstore (see p.335) on the fourth floor.

Food and wine

For cheap fruit and veg, you really have to go to the Naschmarkt (see box opposite). With such small supermarkets, the gap is filled, in part, by the city's flash, quality delis.

Altmann & Kühne, 1, Graben 30; *www.feinspitz.com/ak*; U-Bahn Stephansplatz. The swishest chocolate shop in the city.

Anker, 15, Westbahnhof; U-Bahn Westbahnhof (plus hundreds of branches across Vienna). The largest bakery chain in the country, producing excellent bread, rolls and pastries; most branches also serve coffee.

Arthur Grimm, 1, Kurrentgasse 10; *www.grimm.at*; U-Bahn Stephansplatz. Most bakeries in Vienna are wonderful, but Grimm's is particularly wonderful, with a vast range of fresh bread and pastries. Serves coffee, too.

Billa, 1, Singerstrasse 6; *www.billa.at*; U-Bahn Stephansplatz. The most central of the ubiquitous supermarket chain, with a very groovy trolley escalator to take you into the basement. Handy for gathering picnic fodder.

Bobby's Supermarket, 4, Schliefmühlgasse 5; U-Bahn Karlsplatz/Taubstummengasse. All those things from home you think you need, from Cadbury's chocolate to Coleman's mustard and Marmite/Vegemite.

Böhle, 1, Wollzeile 30; U-Bahn Stubentor. Top-notch Austrian deli with a huge range of beer, wine, vinegar, fruit and salads, plus a daily take-away menu.

Demmer's Teehaus, 1, Mölkerbastei 5; *www.demmer.at*; U-Bahn Herrengasse.

Tea addicts' paradise, with Indian and Chinese teas sold loose, and a café upstairs.

Julius Meinl, 1, Am Graben 19; www.meinl.com; U-Bahn Stephansplatz. The flagship store has an incredible choice of luxury goodies to eat and drink on two floors.

Sacher, 1, Philharmoniker Strasse 4; www.sacher.com; U-Bahn Karlsplatz. The only place to get the authentic *Sachertorte* (see p.311), sold in a variety of sizes, smartly boxed for export.

Schönbichler, 1, Wollzeile 4; www.schoenbichler.at; U-Bahn Stephansplatz. Amazing selection of over 100 teas, plus china teapots, coffee, brandies, Kirsch and a staggering collection of malt whiskies.

Unger & Klein, 1, Gölsdorfgasse 2; U-Bahn Schwedenplatz/Schottenring. Trendy Eichinger oder Knecht-designed wine shop where you can buy a glass to drink or a bottle to take away.

Wein & Co, 6, Linke Wienzeile 2, www.weinco.at; U-Bahn Karlsplatz. Big wine emporium and deli, situated near the Naschmarkt, where you can eat, quaff or simply buy to take-away. Open Mon–Sat 9am–midnight.

Wild, 1, Neuer Markt 16; U-Bahn Stephansplatz. Very upmarket, long-established deli with a stand-up buffet and sales counter.

Willi Dungl, 1, Schottengasse 9; www.willidungl.com; U-Bahn Schottentor. Organic fruit, veg and other foodstuffs are available at this store run by the eponymous health supremo.

Zum Schwarzen Kameel, 1, Bognergasse 5; U-Bahn Herrengasse. Terribly smart deli that's yet another Viennese institution, eat-in or take-away food and lots of very fancy wine too.

Shopping

Markets

Antikmarkt, 1, Am Hof; U-Bahn Herrengasse. Bargain-free art and antique market. March–Christmas Eve Fri & Sat.

Brunnenmarkt, 16, Brunnengasse; U-Bahn Thaliastrasse. Fruit and veg market that stretches like a kilometre along Brunnengasse. Mon–Sat.

Christkindlmarkt, 1, Rathausplatz; U-Bahn Rathaus or tram #1 or #2. The Christmas market held in front of the Rathaus, selling gifts and food, is the biggest, though there are smaller ones in Spittelberg, Freyung and outside the Mariahilferkirche. Daily late Nov–Christmas Eve.

Flöhmarkt, 6 & 7, Linke & Rechte Wienzeile; U-Bahn Kettenbrückengasse. Vienna's Saturday morning flea market is fascinating and worth checking out just for the vibe. Eastern Europeans flock to it to sell off everything from old rags to old riches. Sat only.

Freyung, 1, Freyung; U-Bahn Schottentor/Herrengasse. Organic fruit, veg and other edibles, plus a fair few arts and crafts stalls. First and third Sat of the month.

Kunstmarkt, 1, Heiligenkreuzhof; U-Bahn Schwedenplatz. Tiny, low-key art and crafts market held in a picturesque monastic courtyard. April–Sept first Sat & Sun of the month; also on the four weekends before Christmas.

Naschmarkt, 6 & 7, Linke & Rechte Wienzeile; U-Bahn Karlsplatz/Kettenbrückengasse. Vienna's most exotic fruit and veg market, with Turkish, Balkan, Chinese, Middle Eastern and Austrian produce, take-away stalls plus clothes and sundries. On Saturday mornings, there's a Flöhmarkt (flea market) extension west of Kettenbrückengasse U-Bahn. Mon–Sat.

Spittelberg, 7, Spittelberggasse; U-bahn Volkstheater. Artsy, craftsy market in the narrow streets of the Spittelberg area. April–June, Sept & Oct every third weekend of the month; Aug & Dec daily.

Shopping

Music

Arcadia, 1, Kärntnerstrasse 40; U-Bahn Karlsplatz. Bookshop beneath the arcades of the Staatsoper and full of things to do with opera. A great place to mug up on the plot before you go and see a show.

Audio Center, 1, Judenplatz 9; U-Bahn Stephansplatz. The best selection of jazz CDs and records in the city (plus some world music), and lots of info on the local jazz scene.

Black Market, 1, Gonzagagasse 9; www.blackmarket.at; U-Bahn Schwedenplatz. Record store that's Vienna's unofficial dance music HQ – the bar is something of a clubbers' hang-out.

Gramola, 1, Graben 16; www.gramola.at; U-Bahn Stephansplatz. Excellent selection of cheap classical CDs in this tiny stuccoed store.

Virgin Megastore, 6, Mariahilferstrasse 37; U-Bahn Babenbergerstrasse. Vienna – and Austria's – biggest music store, with a vast collection of rock, pop, folk, soul, roots, rave and classical; plenty of listening posts too.

Toys and accessories

Hobby-Sommer, 7, Neubaugasse 26; U-Bahn Neubaugasse. Model railways from around the world, and models of the Airfix variety.

Huber & Lerner, 1, Kohlmarkt 7; U-Bahn Herrengasse/Stephansplatz. Former imperial stationers, this is the place to get your bespoke headed notepaper (at a price).

Piatnik, 7, Kandlgasse/Kaiserstrasse; www.piatnik.com; U-Bahn Burggasse-Stadthalle. Famous Austrian firm that makes playing cards and also sells Zippo lighters, pipes, kids' toys and board games.

Rudolf Waniek, 1, Hohermarkt/Tuchlauben; U-Bahn Schwedenplatz. Former court suppliers of glassware and metalware: peddle salt cellars, decanters, coffee-making machines and quality domestic utensils.

Spielzeugschachtel, 1, Rauhensteingasse 5; U-Bahn Stephansplatz. The 'Toy Box' contains a feast of jigsaws, games, wooden toys and children's books.

Stahlwaren, 7, Siebensterngasse 39; tram #49. Amazing selection of pricey knives, scissors, daggers and swords by top manufacturers.

Chapter 15

Directory

Airlines Air France, 1, Kärntnerstrasse 49 ☎514 19, *www.airfrance.fr*; Alitalia, 1, Kärntner Ring 2 ☎505 1707, *www.alitalia.it*; Austrian Airlines, 1, Kärntner Ring 18 ☎ 517 89, *www.aua.com*; British Airways, 1, Kärntner Ring 10 ☎505 7691, *www.britishairways.com*; Canadian Airlines, 1, Krugerstrasse 4 ☎515 55-40, *www.cdnair.ca*; Delta, 1, Kärntner Ring 17 ☎512 66 46, *www.delta-air.com*; Lauda Air, 1, Opernring 6 ☎514 77, *www.laudaair.com*; Qantas, 1, Opernring 1 ☎587 77 71, *www.qantas.com.au*; TWA, 1, Opernring 1 ☎586 68 68, *www.twa.com*. The nearest U-Bahn for all the above airlines is Karlsplatz.

American Express, 1, Kärntnerstrasse 21–23 ☎515 4077, *www.americanexpress.com*; U-Bahn Stephansplatz.

Car rental All the major car rental companies have an office at the airport, and a downtown pick-up/drop-off point and office. Avis, 1, Opernring 5; *www.avis.com*; U-Bahn Karlsplatz. Europcar, 3, Erdbergstrasse 202; *www.europcar.com*; U-Bahn Erdbergstrasse. Hertz, 1, Kärntner Ring 17; *www.hertz.com*; U-Bahn Karlsplatz.

Children Children are generally neither seen nor heard in Vienna. You won't see too many of them in the cafés and restaurants around town; hotels and pensions tend to be slightly more accommodating. The obvious attractions for children are the Tiergarten (zoo), for which see p.235, and the Schmetterlinghaus (Butterfly House), see p.118. The Prater (see p.208) can also be fun, and most children love to ride on the trams. Museums that might appeal to small kids include the Strassenbahnmuseum (Tram Museum) described on p.191, the Puppen und Spielzeug Museum (Doll and Toy Museum), on p.77, and the Kinder Museum in the new MuseumsQuartier (see p.132); older kids might get more from the Technisches Museum (see p.243), the militaria at the Heeresgeschichtliches Museum (see p.188), the Haus der Musik (see p.63) or even the Theatermuseum (see p.110).

Electricity 220 Volts; standard round two-pin plugs are used. Equip yourself with an adapter/transformer before leaving home if you want to use your hairdryer, laptop, etc. while travelling.

Embassies and Consulates
Australia, 4, Mattiellistrasse 2–4 ☎512 85 80.
Canada, 1, Laurenzerberg 2 ☎531 38 30.
Czech Republic, 14, Penzinger Strasse 11–13 ☎894 12 00.
Germany, 3, Metternichgasse 3 ☎711 54.
Hungary, 1, Bankgasse 4–6 ☎533 26 31.
Ireland, 3, Hilton Centre, Landstrasse Hauptstrasse 2 ☎715 42 46.
Italy, 3, Rennweg 27 ☎712 51 21.
New Zealand, 19, Springsiedelgasse 28 ☎318 85 05.
Slovakia, 19, Armbrustergasse 24 ☎318 90 55.

Directory

Slovenia, 1, Niebelungengasse 13 ☎586 13 04.
South Africa, 19, Sandgasse 33 ☎320 64 93.
UK, 3, Jauresgasse 12 ☎71 61 30.
USA, 9, Bolzmanngasse 16 ☎313 39.

Horse-racing From September to June trotting races take place in the Prater at the Krieau Trabrennbahn, 2, Nordportalstrasse 274 (tram #N to its terminus); flat racing takes place every other weekend from March to November at the Freudenau Rennbahn, 2, Rennbahnstrasse 65 (bus #77A from U-Bahn Schlachthausgasse).

Hospital Allgemeines Krankenhaus, 9, Währinger Gürtel 18–20; U-Bahn Michelbeuern-AKH.

Language Schools Cultura Wien, 1, Bauernmarkt 18/4 ☎533 24 93, *www.culturawien.at*; U-Bahn Schwedenplatz. Universität Wien, 1, Ebendorferstrasse 10/4 ☎405 12 54, *www.univie.ac.at/wihok*; U-Bahn Schottenring.

Laundry (*Wäscherei*) 8, Josefstädter Strasse 59; tram #J (Mon–Fri 7.30am–7.30pm).

Left luggage The train stations have coin-operated lockers (*Schliessfächer*) costing from öS30–60/€2.18–4.36 for 24 hours, and a left-luggage counter (*Gepäckaufbewahrung*) costing between öS30–60/€2.18–4.36 per item per 24 hours.

Libraries American International School Secondary Library, 19, Salmannsdorfer Strasse 47; *www.ais.at*; bus #35A from U-Bahn Nussdorfer Strasse. British Council, 1, Schenkenstrasse 4; *www.britishcouncil.at*; U-Bahn Herrengasse.

Lost Property Zentrales Fundamt, 9, Wasagasse 22 (Mon–Fri 8am–noon); if lost on public transport phone ☎79 09 43-500; lost on Austrian Railways phone ☎58 00 35-656.

Religious services Anglican, 3, Jaurèsgasse 12; Baptist, 6, Mollardgasse 35; Buddhist, 1, Fleischmarkt 16; Inter-denominational, 1, Dorotheergasse 16; Islamic, 21, Am Hubertusdamm 17–19; Jewish Liberal, 2, Haidgasse 1; Jewish Orthodox, 1, Seitenstettengasse 4; Methodist, 15, Sechshauser Strasse 56; Roman Catholic, 9, Votivkirche, Schottentor.

Soccer (*Fussball*) Vienna's top soccer team, SK Rapid (*www.skrapid.at*), play at the Gerhard Hanappi Stadion on Keisslergasse in Hütteldorf (U-Bahn Hütteldorf); FK Austria (*www.fk-austria.at*), their main rivals, play at the Franz Horr Stadion on Fischofgasse in Favoriten (tram #67 two stops from U-Bahn Reumannplatz); big international games are played at the Prater (aka Wiener) Stadion in the Prater (U-Bahn Praterstern).

Swimming (*Schwimmen*) Amalienbad, 10, Reumannplatz 23 (U-Bahn Reumannplatz), has a wonderful Art Deco interior, particularly the sauna; Jörgerbad, 17, Jörgerstrasse 42–44 (tram #43) is also very beautiful inside. Krapfenwaldbad, 19, Krapfenwaldlgasse 65–73 (bus #38A) is an outdoor pool up in the foothills of the Wienerwald (May–Sept) with great views, so too the Schafbergbad, 18, Josef-Redl-Gasse 2 (bus #42B).

Time Austria is normally one hour ahead of the UK and Ireland, six hours ahead of Eastern Standard Time and nine hours ahead of Pacific Standard Time. Austrian Summer Time lasts from late March to late October.

Part 4

Contexts

A History of Vienna

The Romans

People have lived in the area of modern-day Vienna for many thousands of years, due to its geographical position at the point where the ancient trade route or amber route crossed the Danube. Following on from early Bronze and Iron Age settlements, a Celtic tribe known as the Boii occupied the hills above Vienna, probably from as early as 500 BC, but were driven from the area in around 50 BC by the short-lived Dacian kingdom. Vienna was then swallowed up by the neighbouring Celtic kingdom of Noricum.

In 15 BC the **Romans**, under the Emperor Augustus, advanced into Noricum as far as the Danube and the area was absorbed into the Roman province of Pannonia. For the next four centuries, the river was used as a natural military border or *limes* by the Romans, further strengthened by a series of forts along its banks. The main Roman camp along this stretch of the Danube was at Carnuntum, to the east, with Vienna – or **Vindobona** as it was then called – as a subsidiary fort.

The Roman Forum is thought to have been somewhere around the Hoher Markt (see p.81) in today's Innere Stadt. In the first century AD, Vindobona became the base for the 10th legion, whose job it was to fend off attacks from the neighbouring Germanic tribes to the north and east, particularly the Marcomanni and the Quadi. These two tribes crashed through the Danubian frontier in 169 AD only to be beaten back by the

Emperor Marcus Aurelius, who died in Vindobona in 180 AD.

The Babenbergs

The Romans finally abandoned Vindobona to the **Huns** in 433 AD, and the city, like the rest of Europe, entered the **Dark Ages**. However, it's interesting to note that even at this early stage in its history, during the great migrations that followed the collapse of Roman power, the area of modern-day Vienna stood on one of the main ethnic crossroads of Europe: pressed from the east by first the Huns, later the Avars, from the north and south by the Slavs, and from the west by Germanic tribes.

The coronation of **Charlemagne** as Holy Roman Emperor in 800 marked the end of the Dark Ages in Europe. Parts of modern-day Austria, meanwhile, became a military colony – referred to by nineteenth-century historians as the "Ostmark" – of Charlemagne's Frankish Empire. With the collapse of the empire in 888, it was the Saxon king, Otto the Great, who succeeded in subduing the German lands. His successor, Otto II, went on to hand the "Ostmark" to the **Babenberg dynasty** in 976, whose job it was to protect the empire's eastern frontiers, once more formed by the Danube. The Babenberg dynasty ruled the territory for the next 270 years, first as margraves and later as dukes.

In their search for some kind of official birthday for their country, many Austrian scholars have latched on to the first known mention of the name Ostarrîchi, which appears in a Latin parchment from around 996. However, throughout the Middle Ages, the region was mostly referred to either simply as *provincia orientalis* or else named after its first ruler, the **Margrave Leopold I** (976–94). To begin with, the Babenberg Margravate was confined to a small stretch of the Danube centred most probably on Melk, but gradually it expanded eastwards as far as the River Leitha and northwards as far as the River Thaya. Successive Babenbergs founded a number of monasteries in the region, in particular Leopold III (1095–1136), who was later canonized for his good works and became the country's patron saint.

In 1156, during the reign of **Heinrich II Jasomirgott** (1141–77), the Babenbergs' Margravate was at last elevated to a Duchy, with its new capital at Vienna and the ducal palace situated in Am Hof (see p.75). However, in 1246 the Babenberg male line came to an end with the death of Duke Friedrich II (1230–46) on the battlefield. The dispute over who should rule over the Duchy of Austria and Styria, as it was now known, dragged on for the next thirty years. In 1251, the future Bohemian king, **Otakar II**, took up residence in Vienna and claimed the duchy for himself, shoring up his claim by marrying Friedrich II's widow.

The early Habsburgs

While Otakar was laying claim to the Babenbergs' inheritance, he was also putting himself forward as a candidate for the throne of the Holy Roman Empire. In the end, though, the throne was handed in 1273 to **Rudolf of Habsburg**, a little-known count whose ancestral home was the castle of Habichtsburg (hence Habsburg) above the River Reuss in modern-day Switzerland. In 1278 Otakar was defeated (and killed) by Rudolf's forces at the **Battle of Marchfeld**, to the east of Vienna, allowing Rudolf to lay claim to the Duchy of Austria. The Viennese, who had backed Otakar, were less than pleased about the outcome of the battle, and weren't easily placated by Rudolf's son, Albrecht, who had been given the duchy by his father.

The Habsburgs, though, were here to stay, their dynasty destined to rule over Austria for the next 640 years. Initially, however, Vienna only sporadically served as the dynastic capital. **Rudolf IV** (1356–65) was one of the few to treat it as such, founding the university and laying the foundation stone of what is now the Stephansdom, before dying at the age of just 26. Rudolf's endeavours earned him the nickname "The Founder", but he failed in securing a bishopric for Vienna.

For that the city had to wait until the reign of **Friedrich III** (1440–93). Despite numerous setbacks – he was besieged in the Hofburg by one of his own family in 1462 and briefly lost control of Vienna to the Hungarian King Matthias Corvinus in 1485 – it was Friedrich who was responsible for consolidating the Habsburgs' power base. In 1452, he became the last Holy Roman Emperor to be crowned in Rome, and the following year elevated the family's dukedom to an archdukedom. The Holy Roman Empire, famously dismissed by Matthias Corvinus as "neither holy, Roman, nor an empire", was something of a fantasy, whose emperor, theoretically at least, ruled over all the German-speaking lands. Though the reality was somewhat different, the Habsburgs persisted with their imperial pretensions, passing the title down the male line, until its eventual dissolution in 1806 (see p.347).

In the meantime, the Habsburgs continued to add to their dynastic inheritance through a series of judicious marriages by **Maximilian II** (1564–76) and his offspring, prompting the oft-quoted maxim, adapted from Ovid: "let others wage war; you, happy Austria, marry." By the time the Emperor Karl V came to the throne in 1519, the Habsburgs ruled over an empire on which, it was said, the sun never set, with lands stretching from its Spanish possessions in South America to Vienna itself – bolstered in 1526 by the addition of the kingdoms of Bohemia and Hungary. Vienna remained just one of several imperial residences, its development constantly hampered by the threat posed by the Ottoman army of Süleyman the Magnificent who had been advancing steadily westwards across Europe.

The Turkish sieges

In 1526, the Turks scored a decisive victory at the **Battle of Mohács** against the Hungarians, and began to advance into Habsburg territory. In the summer of 1529 they captured Budapest, and by September the Sultan's vast army were camped outside Vienna, the "city of the golden apple" as they called it. Although it is the later siege of 1683 (see opposite) that captured the imagination of historians, the **1529 siege** was a much closer-run thing. The Ottoman Empire was at its zenith and Vienna was defended only by a small garrison under Count Salm. However, having shelled the city and killed some 1500 Viennese, the Turks suddenly withdrew – whether because of bad weather or some other reason, no one knows – back to Hungary in October. It seems almost as if Vienna simply wasn't worth the effort, despite the fact that the city was there for the taking.

In a defiant gesture, **Ferdinand I** (1521–64) subsequently established Vienna as his permanent base, building the zig-zag fortifications that

CONTEXTS

were to surround the city for the next 300 years or more. With the retreat of the Turks, Ferdinand's troubles were by no means over, however, for **Lutheranism** was spreading at an alarming rate among the German-speaking lands. By the middle of the century it's estimated that Vienna was eighty percent Protestant. To combat this new plague, Ferdinand called in the fiercely proselytizing Jesuits in 1556. Nevertheless, the new creed flourished under the relatively liberal reign of **Maximilian II** (1564–76), and it was only after Rudolf II (1576–1612) moved the capital to Prague, leaving the Archduke Ernst in charge of Vienna, that the tide began to turn due to the repressive measures introduced.

By the outbreak of the **Thirty Years' War** in 1618, Vienna was well on the way to becoming a Catholic city again, thanks partly to the Jesuits' stranglehold on the education system. By the time of the Peace of Westphalia in 1648, Vienna, which had emerged from the war relatively unscathed, was firmly under the grip of the Counter-Reformation, and those Viennese who would not renounce their Protestantism were forced to go into exile.

The siege of 1683

The fact that the city managed to survive the **1683 siege** was no thanks to its emperor, **Leopold I** (1658–1705), a profligate, bigoted man whose reign marked the beginning of the **Baroque era** in Vienna. Under Leopold, a whole new wing of the Hofburg was built, but the emperor is best-known for his operatic extravaganzas – he himself was a keen composer – in particular the four-hour long equestrian ballet he staged (see p.89), just one of some four hundred theatrical events put on during his reign.

While Leopold was busy working out ways of spending more of the state's coffers, the priest Abraham à Santa Clara was busy preaching against such indulgences, not to mention against the Protestant, the Jew and the Turk – "an Epicurean piece of excrement" as he put it in one of his fiery sermons. In 1679, a plague claimed the lives of an estimated 70,000 Viennese, and four years later, Vienna was to face the worst crisis in its history as the town was forced to endure its second siege by the Ottoman army. Naturally enough, at the approach of the Turks, Leopold, and anyone else who had the money, fled to the safety of Linz and Passau.

If anything, Vienna had more chance of surviving the siege of 1683 than it had in 1529. The Turks were no longer at the zenith of their power and the city was properly fortified this time – in addition, there was a relief force on its way, albeit rather slowly. Nevertheless, the city was still confronted with an army of over 200,000, made up of 100,000 infantry, 50,000 cavalry, plus a harem of over 1500 concubines guarded by 700 black eunuchs, a contingent of clowns, and numerous poets trained in bawdy songs. The Viennese, protected by a garrison of just 10,000 men, were understandably ready to make peace with the Grand Vizier, **Kara Mustafa**.

The Grand Vizier's fatal flaw was over-confidence. Convinced that the city was his for the taking, and loath to share the booty among his army (which he would have to do if he took the city by force), he orchestrated a two-month siege of Vienna. By September, however, a relief force of Poles, under their king, **Jan Sobieski**, and sundry German troops under the Duke of Lorraine, finally came to the aid of the city. On September 12, the papal legate Marco d'Aviano conducted a mass on the hills above the city and though outnumbered, the imperial forces managed to rout the Turks, in the process capturing 20,000 buffaloes, bullocks, camels and mules, 10,000 sheep, corn and flour, sugar, oil and most famously, coffee (see p.310). Diamonds, rubies, sapphires and pearls, silver and gold, and "the most beautiful sable furs in the world", belonging to Kara Mustafa, fell into the grateful hands of King Sobieski. The Grand Vizier was discovered to have decapitated his favourite wife and his pet ostrich, rather than have them fall into the hands of the infidels, and, as was the custom in humiliating cases of defeat, he effected his own execution by allowing an emissary to strangle him with a silken cord in Belgrade on Christmas Day later that year.

The eighteenth century

Following the siege of 1683, Vienna could finally establish itself as the Habsburgs' permanent *Residenzstadt* or *Kaiserstadt*. Over the following years, Baroque art and architecture really took off, as extensive rebuilding of damaged churches, monasteries and palaces took place within the Innere Stadt. The Viennese aristocracy could also now at last build in the suburbs without fear of attack. Most famously the palace of Schönbrunn began to evolve, while Prince Eugène of Savoy (see p.18), who took command of the imperial forces and drove the Turks out of Hungary, built the Belvedere.

In keeping with the spirit of the age, the **Emperor Karl VI** (1711–40) proved as spendthrift as his father Leopold, adding the magnificent Prunksaal library and the Winterreitschule to the Hofburg, and erecting Vienna's finest Baroque church, the Karlskirche (see p.143). The one area in which Karl VI singularly failed was in producing a male heir to the throne. In the end, the emperor had to accept the fact that his eldest daughter, Maria Theresia, was going to have to take over when he died. In an attempt to smooth her accession, Karl introduced the so-called Pragmatic Sanction in 1713, which allowed for female succession, and got all the states nominally within the Holy Roman Empire to promise to recognize his daughter's right to the Habsburgs' hereditary lands. Naturally enough, everyone agreed with the emperor while he was alive, and as soon as he died immediately went back on their word.

Maria Theresia (1740–80)

So it was that **Maria Theresia** (see p.230) found herself forced to fight the **War of the Austrian Succession** (1740–48) as soon as she took over from her father. For a while, she was even forced to hand over the imperial title to Karl of Bavaria in an attempt to pacify him, though it was eventually regained and handed to her husband, Franz Stephan of Lorraine (she herself, as a woman, could not become Holy Roman Emperor). At the end of the war in 1748, Maria Theresia was forced to cede Silesia to Prussia, and despite an attempt to win it back during the **Seven Years' War** (1756–63), it remained, for the most part, in Prussian hands.

On the domestic front, Maria Theresia's reign signalled the beginning of the **era of reform**, influenced by the ideas of the Enlightenment. To push through her reforms the empress created a formidable centralized bureaucracy, taking power away from the provincial Diets. When the pope abolished the Jesuit order in 1773, Maria Theresia took the opportunity of introducing a state education system. In 1776 she abolished torture, and passed de facto abolition of the death penalty (though hard labour usually killed the convict within a year in any case). Despite her

reforms, it would be wrong to get the impression that the empress was some free-thinking democrat. She believed wholeheartedly in absolutism, and, as a devout Catholic, ensured Catholic supremacy within the empire with yet more anti-Protestant edicts.

Josef II (1780–90)

With the death of her husband in 1765, Maria Theresia appointed her eldest son, Josef, as co-regent. But it wasn't until after the empress's death in 1780 that Josef's reforming zeal could come into its own (see p.104). His most significant edict was the 1781 **Toleranzpatent**, which allowed freedom of worship to Lutherans, Calvinists and the Greek Orthodox. Like his mother, he was himself a devout Catholic, but was even more determined to curtail church – and particularly papal – power. To this end, he dissolved four hundred contemplative or "idle" monasteries, and, as many saw it, was bent on "nationalizing" the church.

Under Josef II all religious processions (previously a daily occurrence on the streets of Vienna) were banned except the annual Corpus Christi procession. Pope Pius VI was so concerned he came to Vienna in person in 1782 to try to change the emperor's mind, but to no avail. With the best of intentions, Josef interfered in every aspect of his citizens' lives, causing widespread resentment. For – again like his mother – despite his enlightened policies, Josef was still very much the despot. He was, above all, responsible for creating the Habsburgs' secret police force, which was to become so infamous in the nineteenth century.

The Napoleonic era

The Emperor Leopold II, who unenthusiastically succeeded Josef II in 1790, died suddenly of a stroke after a reign of less than two years. As a result, Leopold's eldest son became the **Emperor Franz II** (1792–1835). No great military man – his troops had been fighting the French for two years before he bothered to show himself at the front line – Franz was an unlikely candidate to become one of Napoleon's great adversaries.

In 1797, during his first Italian campaign, **Napoleon** succeeded in humiliating the Habsburg forces at Mantua, and was within a hundred miles of Vienna when the Habsburg emperor sued for peace. It was a scenario that was repeated again in 1800 when Napoleon's forces were once more marching on Vienna. By 1803, the Habsburgs had lost the Netherlands plus several territories in northern Italy to the French. Napoleon then added insult to injury by declaring himself emperor the following year, with the clear intention of re-establishing the Holy Roman Empire under French hegemony. In retaliation, Franz declared himself Emperor Franz I of Austria (a hitherto non-existent title), though the gesture looked more like an admission of defeat, since Franz was already Holy Roman Emperor.

The 1805 occupation of Vienna

In 1805, in alliance with Russia and Britain, Austria decided to take on Napoleon again, only to suffer a crushing defeat at Ulm. Unable to stop the advance of the *Grande Armée*, the allies decided to regroup further east, leaving Napoleon free to march on Vienna, where he arrived on November 13, 1805. The imperial family had already taken flight to Hungary carrying the contents of the Hofburg with them. Though there was no fighting, having 34,000 French troops billeted in the city put an enormous strain on the place and supplies quickly ran short. The French stayed on until January 12, 1806, having exacted taxes, war reparations and appropriated many works of art, including four hundred paintings from the Belvedere. Four days later, Franz returned to Vienna amid much rejoicing, though in political terms there was little to rejoice about. During the French occupation, the Allies had lost the Battle of Austerlitz to Napoleon, and concluded the **Treaty of Pressburg**, leaving the Habsburgs without their Italian possessions, the Tyrol and the Vorarlberg. Further humiliation followed in 1806 when Napoleon established the Confederation of the Rhine and Franz was forced to call it a day by relinquishing his title of Holy Roman Emperor.

The 1809 occupation of Vienna

For the next few years, there was no hope of the Austrians exacting any revenge. But in the spring of 1809, with Napoleon encountering problems fighting Wellington in Spain, the Austrians decided to seize the moment to reopen hostilities. Although they were once more defeated at Ratisbon, the Austrian forces under the emperor's brother, the Archduke Karl, managed to regroup

to the east of Vienna. Once more Napoleon was free to march on Vienna. As usual, the imperial family had taken flight to Hungary, but this time the city tried to defend itself. Napoleon reached the outskirts of the city on May 10, 1809 and sent two emissaries to negotiate. They were promptly lynched by the Viennese; the French bombardment started the following evening. It was an uneven battle – "our batteries shot off a few shots; they were ineffective" as one eye-witness stated; the French, for their part, fired some 1600 shells, and killed 23 civilians. The next day the city capitulated, its 16,000-strong garrison no match for the 100,000 French troops.

Despite taking Vienna, Napoleon's *Grande Armée* went on to suffer its first major defeat ten days later at the **Battle of Aspern**, just east of Vienna, at the hands of Archduke Karl. However, Karl failed to press home his advantage, and Napoleon succeeded in holding on to Vienna, going on to defeat the Austrians decisively six weeks later at the **Battle of Wagram**, when the Austrians threw in the towel. The city was forced to celebrate the new emperor's birthday on August 13, and in the peace, signed on October 14, the Austrians were forced to give up Galicia and Croatia. Two days later Napoleon left Vienna, and on October 29, the French held a farewell ball. Towards the end of the following month, the Emperor Franz crept back incognito into the Hofburg.

Clemenz Metternich became the chief minister of Austria, and began to pursue a policy of rapprochement. His greatest coup in this direction was getting Napoleon to marry the Emperor Franz's eighteen-year-old daughter, Marie Louise, in March 1810 (see p.111). By 1813, with the tide turning against Napoleon, Metternich even managed to persuade his reluctant emperor to join the latest anti-French grand alliance.

The 1815 Congress of Vienna

Vienna missed out on the rest of the Napoleonic wars, but it was centre stage when it came to the peace. Following the defeat of Napoleon at Leipzig and his exile to Elba, the victorious powers met for the **Congress of Vienna** in the autumn of 1814. If nothing else, the congress was a great social success (see p.73), or as one participant famously put it, *"le congrès danse, mais il ne marche pas"*. The most public celebration took place on the anniversary of the Battle of Leipzig, when some 20,000 war veterans were wined and dined al fresco in the Prater (see p.208). All of Vienna was agog at the spectacle, but by New Year, most of the foreigners had outstayed their welcome. The congress was costing the emperor a fortune that even he could not afford, forcing him to raise taxes, while many of the participants were living on credit notes. Nevertheless, it dragged on until after Napoleon escaped from Elba, finally winding itself up in May 1815, just twelve days before the Battle of Waterloo.

Despite the shenanigans, the congress did, in fact, manage fairly successfully to establish a status quo in Europe. Many of the borders agreed upon in Vienna were to endure for over a century. In the peace deal, Austria won back much of North Italy and Galicia, Croatia, Salzburg, the Tyrol and the Vorarlberg, but on Metternich's advice, claims over the Netherlands and other far-flung territories that would be hard to defend, were relinquished. The congress also pledged itself to further regular meetings between the heads of the victorious states – meetings at which it was agreed that in order to maintain international peace, they would combine to suppress any further revolutionary uprisings within Europe.

Biedermeier Vienna

Following the congress, Vienna enjoyed more than thirty years of peace and stability, a period known retrospectively as the *Vormärz* – literally "pre-March", because it preceded the March 1848 revolution. The same stretch of time is also known throughout the German-speaking lands as the **Biedermeier era** (for more on the origin of the term, see p.371). In later years, the Viennese would look back on this period through rose-tinted spectacles as a time of introspective domesticity, played out to the tunes of Johann Strauss the Elder and the melodies of Franz Schubert.

As ever, there is more than a grain of truth in the myth, as there is in the counter-myth that this was one of the most oppressive regimes in the history of the Habsburgs. The man most closely associated with the conservative and reactionary politics of the Biedermeier era was Metternich. Under him, and his "poodle" – the chief-of-police Count Josef Sedlnitzky – the vast machinery of the Josephine civil service which had been designed to help push through reforms, was now used to thwart any further change. Censorship

and the activities of the secret police and its informers did so much to stifle intellectual life that by 1848 the playwright Franz Grillparzer reflected miserably, "despotism has destroyed my life, at least my literary life".

With the death of the Emperor Franz I in 1835, the Habsburgs faced something of a crisis, as the heir to the throne, Ferdinand I – a victim of Habsburg in-breeding – was, in the vocabulary of the day, an "imbecile", nicknamed *Nandl der Trottel* ("Ferdy the Dotty"). He was, in fact, nothing of the sort: he could be perfectly coherent, but suffered badly from epilepsy, which affected his short-term memory. To combat the latter's deficiencies, a Regency Council was established, with Ferdinand as chair – or in his absence his brother the Archduke Ludwig – and his brother Franz Karl, Count Kolowrat and Metternich as permanent members. Within the council Metternich had to struggle to maintain his influence.

The 1848 revolution

With the deposition of the French King and the outbreak of revolution in Paris in late February, 1848, it was only a question of time before matters came to a head in the other European capitals. Vienna, now a city of 400,000, suffered from chronic overcrowding (though this was nothing new), and sporadic food shortages, yet it still came as some surprise when it became the first city to follow in the footsteps of the French. On March 13, the Estates of Lower Austria, consisting of nobles and senior clergy, were due to meet in the Landhaus on Herrengasse (see p.70). They were pressing for various reforms, including the freedom of the press, but top of the agenda was the removal of Metternich. In the morning a crowd gathered outside the Landhaus, and, after listening to a German translation of the inflammatory speech given recently by the Hungarian revolutionary Lajos Kossuth in the Hungarian Diet, forced their way into the building. At around 1pm, a detachment of Italian grenadiers fired into the crowd, killing around thirty unarmed protesters, mostly students, and sparking off a revolution.

That evening, after playing for time, Metternich finally resigned and fled from the capital (disguised as a washerwoman, according to popular legend). The emperor – who when told of the outbreak of revolution had apparently said "but do they have permission?" – immediately made a rapid retreat, declaring "tell the people I agree to everything". A **National Guard** was formed – with Johann Strauss the Younger as *Kapellmeister* – augmented by an academic legion of armed students, with whom they were to man the city in place of the despised imperial troops. In addition, a constitution was promised, and a "Responsible Ministry" of bureaucrats formed to produce it. On April 25, a constitutional monarchy was proposed, with two chambers elected by limited franchise based on property. Not surprisingly, the idea was rejected and rioting, in favour of a single chamber parliament elected by universal suffrage, ensued on May 15. Barricades were erected around the city, and the emperor and his entourage quickly fled to Innsbruck in a stagecoach.

Elections were duly held throughout the empire (with the exception of Italy and Hungary which were busy with their own revolutions) and the first parliament in Habsburg history met in the unlikely surroundings of the Hofburg's Winterreitschule (see p106) on July 22. The deputies were by no means revolutionaries, the majority coming from the educated middle classes, with close to a third of peasant origin. Hampered throughout by disputes between the various nationalities, the assembly did manage to pass one lasting piece of legislation: the emancipation of the peasantry. By August, the court felt secure enough to return to Vienna, bolstered by General Radetzky's military victory over the rebels in Italy and the recapture of Prague by General Windischgrätz.

The spark that lit the final fuse of the Viennese revolution took place on October 6. A battalion, due to be sent to fight against Kossuth's Hungarian revolutionaries, mutinied and joined forces with radicals in the National Guard. Civil war then broke out as some within the National Guard fired on the radicals. In the confusion, the War Minister, General Latour, was lynched by the mob (see p.76) and the imperial family removed themselves once more, this time to Olomouc in Moravia. As Windischgrätz marched his troops towards the capital, the radicals among the academic legion and the National Guard erected barricades and awaited the final showdown. Their only hope lay in the possibility of a Hungarian relief force, which in the event arrived too late. After several days' bombardment and around 2000 casualties, Windischgrätz flushed out the last of the rebels on October 31.

The reign of Franz-Josef I

Meanwhile, back in Olomouc, the Emperor Ferdinand (and his brother Franz Karl) was coerced by the imperial family into renouncing the throne in favour of the latter's eighteen-year-old nephew, **Franz-Josef** (see p.96). A new government was formed under the leadership of the arch-conservative Prince Felix Schwarzenberg, while the assembly continued to meet in the nearby Moravian town of Kremsier (Kroměříž) to try to thrash out a new constitution. Then, to the astonishment of the assembly, on February 28, 1849, Schwarzenberg announced that as the emperor had himself formulated a new constitution, their services were no longer required. Although the new constitution granted equal rights to all, it was anything but liberal, granting the emperor the power of veto over all legislation, the power to dissolve parliament and rule by decree and the power to dismiss and appoint ministers as he saw fit. Meanwhile in Hungary, the Austrians were forced to swallow their pride and enlist the help of the Russians in order to defeat Kossuth's Hungarian revolutionaries once and for all.

In the immediate aftermath of the revolution, it was decided to strengthen the fortifications of the city. Eventually, though, the tide of opinion in the government shifted in favour of tearing down the walls, to prevent a repeat of October 1848 when the revolutionaries had managed to resist the forces of law and order. Finally, in 1857, the emperor decreed that the walls were to come down, and in their place a **Ringstrasse**, lined with noble institutions, was to be constructed (see p.119). This wide boulevard remains the most significant architectural legacy of Franz-Josef's, though it wasn't until the last decade of the emperor's reign that the final sections were completed.

1866 and all that

After some ten years of relative peace, Franz-Josef suffered his first of many embarrassing military setbacks at the Battle of Solferino in 1859. It was not so much the resultant loss of Lombardy that was the problem, but the opportunity it gave the Hungarians to demand their independence once more. In an attempt to placate them, Franz-Josef agreed in 1861 to establish a two-chamber parliament in Vienna. The Hungarians remained unimpressed and failed to send delegates to fill any of their 85 allotted seats in the lower house.

Five years later, the empire was rocked by an even greater crisis with its army's humiliating defeat at the **Battle of Königgrätz** in the Austro-Prussian War. Not only did the Habsburgs lose forever the battle for hegemony over the rest of Germany, but they were finally forced to strike a deal with the Hungarians (while studiously ignoring the demands of the empire's other nationalities).

With the 1867 **Ausgleich** or Compromise the so-called Dual Monarchy of Austria-Hungary was established. According to this new arrangement, Franz-Josef was to be crowned King of Hungary (he was already Emperor of Austria), and the Hungarians were to get their own parliament in Budapest, with autonomy over everything except defence, foreign affairs and the overall imperial budget. Everything within Hungary was to be prefaced with a "k." for *königlich*, everything in the rest of the empire was to be prefaced with the initials "k.k." or *kaiserlich-königlich* (imperial-royal), while everything Austro-Hungarian was prefaced with "k.u.k." or *kaiserlich-und-königlich*.

Meanwhile, delegates from the "Austrian" half of the empire met in Vienna's **parliament** (see p.128). Among the delegates were Czechs, Poles, Croats, Slovenes, Italians and German-speakers from every corner of the empire, who spent most of their time arguing over language issues and abusing each other both verbally and physically. The number of people eligible to vote increased gradually until universal male suffrage was finally introduced in 1907, but in reality, the emperor still ruled supreme since he and his ministers could pass any laws they wanted as "emergency measures", not to mention dissolve parliament and rule by decree (which they did on numerous occasions).

To make matters worse, the economy suffered its worst financial crisis ever in the crash of May 1873, shortly after the opening of Vienna's **Weltausstellung** or World Exhibition in the Prater (see p.209). The 72 banks in Vienna were reduced to eight in the decade following the crash; construction of the Ring was halted and the big projects – the Parliament, Rathaus, Burgtheater and Universität – were only completed in the 1880s. The empire's industrialization was also affected, with railway construction reaching an annual low of 75km of new track in 1880, which had a severe knock-on effect on the other heavy industries.

Fin-de-siècle Vienna

From 1860 to the turn of the century, Vienna more than trebled in size, its population topping two million. Like most industrialized cities of the period, it was a city of enormous contrasts. Wealth and power were in the hands of the upper aristocracy, who alone had an entrée into court society, and exercised enormous influence over the careers of individuals through the system of *Protektion* or patronage. Meanwhile, the bulk of the population, many of them recently arrived immigrants from other parts of the empire, were packed like sardines in the *Mietkaserne* (rent barracks) of the newly built suburbs. At the bottom of the heap were the nocturnal *Bettgeher*, the five percent of the population who could afford only to rent someone else's bed from them during the day.

A significant proportion of the new immigrants were Jews from the empire's rural *shtetls* (small, predominantly Jewish towns). By the turn of the century they made up nearly ten percent of the population. In some walks of life, they comprised an even greater percentage: more than half of the all the city's doctors and lawyers were Jews, as were most of its journalists and bankers. The Jew had long been a stock Viennese scapegoat (see p.78). Now with the 1873 crash – the fault, it was said, of Jewish financiers – and the continuing influx of Orthodox Jews into the city, **anti-Semitism** began to flourish. It found a spokesman in the figure of the pan-German nationalist **Georg von Schönerer**, whose fanatical followers used to wear the effigy of a hanged Jew on their watch chains. Schönerer's political career faltered, however, after 1888 when he was sent to prison for breaking into the offices of the Jewish-owned newspaper, the *Neues Wiener Tagblatt*.

Anti-Semitism was given a more respectable, populist twist by **Karl Lueger** (see p.127). This Vienna-born politician became leader of the Christian Social Party, whose combination of Catholicism, anti-Semitism and municipal socialism went down alarmingly well with the Viennese electorate. In 1897, Lueger became Mayor of Vienna, and the crowd that turned out for his funeral in 1910 was the largest the city had ever seen – among the mourners was the young **Adolf Hitler** (see p.137).

Most middle-class Jews, understandably, gravitated towards the other side of the political spectrum, dominating the upper echelons of the

Social Democratic Workers' Party (SDAP), after it was founded in 1889. The party's chief ideologue before World War I was the Prague-born Jew Viktor Adler, whose peculiar ideology of **Austro-Marxism** was to dominate the party's thinking for the next half century. As far as Adler was concerned capitalism was doomed to failure, so the party could afford to adopt a peaceful approach to politics until the time was right for revolution.

In among all the tensions between Right and Left, Jew and Gentile, rich and poor, **fin-de-siècle Vienna** also succeeded in nurturing intellectual and artistic creativity such as the city had never known, much of it inspired by the city's assimilated Jews. In music, **Arnold Schönberg**, and his followers **Alban Berg** and **Anton Webern**, changed the face of classical music with their atonal – or as Schönberg preferred, "pantonal" – revolution (see p.143). **Gustav Mahler**, meanwhile, turned heads both as a composer and as boss of the Staatsoper. In medicine, **Sigmund Freud** (see p.200) coined the term "psychoanalysis", and expounded on the new discipline in his seminal *Interpretation of Dreams*. In 1897 the artist **Gustav Klimt** led a revolt against the artistic establishment, known as the Secession (see p.140); following in his footsteps were the likes of **Egon Schiele** and **Oskar Kokoschka**. Otto Wagner left the most visible legacy of this period, in the **Jugendstil** and early modernist buildings which can still be seen on the streets of Vienna today.

World War I

On June 28, 1914, the heir to the throne, the **Archduke Franz Ferdinand** and his wife, Sophie, were assassinated in Sarajevo by Bosnian Serbs, with weapons supplied by the chief of Serbia's army intelligence. There was little genuine sadness in court circles, for as Stefan Zweig bluntly put it, "the archduke Franz Ferdinand lacked everything that counts for real popularity in Austria: amiability, personal charm and easy-goingness". Even his uncle, the Emperor Franz-Josef, was more relieved than anything else, as the two got on famously badly.

To begin with, there was also very little action by Austria on the diplomatic front, but eventually on July 28 Franz-Josef and his ministers sent an ultimatum to Serbia, with an impossible set of conditions and a 48-hour time limit. As Serbia could not agree to all the conditions, Austria-Hungary declared war on her, without consulting

its German or Italian allies. The Russians immediately mobilized to defend their Slav brothers, with Britain and France, Russia's allies, following suit. By August 12, the major European powers were at war.

Perhaps surprisingly, the outbreak of war brought patriotic crowds on to the streets of Vienna, and other cities around the empire, with Left and Right alike rallying round the Habsburg cause. Of course, everyone thought the war would be over by Christmas; it was only after years of military defeats, huge casualties and food shortages, that the population began to turn against the war. On October 21, 1916, Viktor Adler's son Friedrich took matters into his own hands and assassinated the Austrian Prime Minister, **Count Karl Stürgkh** (see p.60). At his trial in May the following year, Friedrich Adler gave such a damning indictment of the war that his execution was postponed so as not to boost the anti-war cause further. On November 21, 1916, Franz-Josef finally died at the age of 86, leaving the throne to his 29-year-old great-nephew Karl.

The **Emperor Karl I** is perhaps best-known for his bungled attempt at negotiating a separate peace for his empire with the western allies in March 1917. The approach was rebuffed at the time and a year later became public knowledge, causing huge embarrassment to all concerned. Only victory on the battlefield could now save the dynasty, but it was not to come.

In October 1918, the empire began to crumble from within, with national committees taking over the regional capitals. In Vienna, the Social Democrats, who were in favour of self-determination for the empire's various nationalities, set up a provisional government under Karl Renner. On November 2, 1918, with the end of the war in sight, the Hungarian battalion guarding Schönbrunn upped and left, leaving the imperial family and their servants unguarded. The next day an armistice was signed, and eight days later, the Emperor Karl I agreed to sign away his powers (see p.229), withdrawing first to Eckartsau outside Vienna, and eventually, in 1919, going into exile in Switzerland.

The First Republic

The Austrian Republic – or more correctly **Deutsch-Österreich** or "German Austria" – was proclaimed from the steps of Vienna's parliament on November 12, 1918 (see p.128); the colours chosen for the national flag – red, white, red – were those of the Babenbergs. At first, however, there was precious little enthusiasm for the new country among its people. The Christian Socials wanted a constitutional monarchy, the Pan-Germans wanted Anschluss with Germany, while the Socialists wanted Anschluss with a Socialist Germany. In the proclamation of November 12, the country was even described as "a constituent part of the German Republic". In the regions, both the Tyrol and Salzburg voted overwhelmingly in favour of Anschluss with Germany (requests which were denied by the international community), while the Vorarlberg voted to join the Swiss.

In February 1919, the first national elections took place, creating a coalition government of the SDAP and the Christian Socials under the chancellorship of Social Democrat **Karl Renner**. Nevertheless a political vacuum continued until the end of the year, with soldiers' and workers' councils threatening to follow the revolutionary

soviet example of neighbouring Bavaria and Hungary. There were even two unsuccessful attempts by the newly-formed Austrian Communist Party (KPÖ) to stage a putsch, in April and June 1919.

The new government's foremost task was to feed the population, particularly that of Vienna. Deprived of its former territories, and hampered by a bad harvest, they managed it only with the help of the Allied Famine Relief programme. The government's next most arduous job was to negotiate the **Treaty of St-Germain** with the victorious allies. Many in the delegation still hoped for Anschluss with Germany, but it was not to be. The Austrians (along with the Hungarians) were branded an "enemy state", while the rest of the so-called "successor states" like Czechoslovakia, were not, and were expressly forbidden ever to undertake Anschluss with Germany. With his oft-quoted remark, Georges Clemenceau summed up the Austrians' lack of a bargaining position when he pointed to the map and said "What's left is Austria".

THE BREAK-UP OF THE
AUSTRO-HUNGARIAN
EMPIRE 1918

Red Vienna

Vienna began the war with an ethnically diverse population of 2.1 million, as imperial capital of a multi-national empire of 52 million; by the end of the war, the city's population was down to 1.8 million, and it was head of a country of just 6.4 million. Only two significant minorities remained: Czechs and Jews, who together made up around twenty percent of the total population. The Czechs, who now had their own independent motherland, enjoyed the status of a protected minority, leaving the Jews to serve once more as the chief scapegoat.

This situation was exacerbated by the very visible presence of around 25,000 Jewish refugees from Galicia, an army of poverty-stricken peddlers whose Orthodox garb made them all the more conspicuous. At the same time, the much larger assimilated Jewish population, who were prominent in the arts, the media and the SDAP, became the target of a vicious, anti-Semitic campaign led by the Christian Social and Pan-German parties. The cleric Ignaz Seipel, head of the Christian Socials, was one of the most vociferous anti-Semites, who flirted with the idea of re-ghettoizing the Jews. This sort of rhetoric was a permanent feature of the First Republic, and one which the SDAP consistently failed to tackle head on.

In the municipal elections of May 1919, the Social Democrats won 54 percent of the vote, and Vienna got its first Socialist mayor, **Jakob Reumann**. The party held power in the capital for nearly fifteen years, a period which has gone down in history as **Rotes Wien** or "Red Vienna" (see p.251). Their social reforms have since become legendary, but their most visible legacy is the huge housing estates like the Karl-Marx-Hof (see p.250) that ring the city.

Meanwhile, in the national elections of June 1920, the SDAP-Christian Social coalition broke down, and in fresh elections in October that year, the latter came out as the biggest single party. The two parties remained at loggerheads throughout the 1920s, with the extremist Pan-German Greater German People's Party a further destabilizing element.

Paramilitary politics

For most of the First Republic, then, the country remained split between the heavily industrialized Social Democrat capital of Vienna, where some thirty percent of the population lived, and the deeply conservative Catholic rural *Länder* where the Christian Socials dominated. What made this political polarization all the more dangerous was that by the mid-1920s both sides were backed up by paramilitary organizations, as if the country were at civil war.

On the one hand, the right-wing **Heimwehr** had their origins in armed groups which defended Austria's borders in the chaotic early days of the republic. Based on individual *Länder* and each with their own leader, the Heimwehr organizations didn't share a political platform but were united in their opposition to the Left. On the other hand, the Social Democrats had created the republic's first ad hoc army, the Volkswehr, in the last weeks of the war. They continued to dominate the Volkswehr until it was replaced by the establishment of the official Austrian army or Bundeswehr. As a result, the SDAP eventually formed its own armed division, the **Schutzbund**, in 1923. Throughout the 1920s the party mouthed the rhetoric of class war, while pursuing moderate, social democratic policies. In 1926, the party went even further and declared itself ready to use force if necessary to protect the interests of the workers. The bourgeois press interpreted this as a call for revolution, though the slogan coined by Otto Bauer was "democratic as long as we can be; dictatorship only if we are forced to it, and insofar as we are forced". To the dismay of many on the left, the SDAP proved itself much less willing to resort to violence than its right-wing foes.

On July 14, 1927, three right-wing activists were acquitted of murdering a socialist man and boy. The following day several thousand workers spontaneously descended on the **Justizpalast** (see p.130) and set fire to it. Taken by surprise by the size of the demonstration, the mounted police panicked and fired point-blank into the crowd. In the ensuing chaos, 89 people were killed, and up to 1000 wounded, and the Justizpalast burned to the ground. The SDAP called an indefinite national strike, but refused to call out the Schutzbund. With the heavily armed Heimwehr acting as strike breakers, the general strike was easily crushed and civil war was postponed for a few more years.

Austro-fascism

The onset of the Great Depression further destabilized what was already a fragile democracy. In the elections of November 1930, the Heimwehr, under Prince Starhemberg, won its first parliamentary seats for its newly formed political wing, the Heimatblock. The Social Democrats, meanwhile, emerged for the first time since 1919 as the largest single party, with 41 percent of the vote, but once more it was the Christian Socials who went on to form a series of weak coalition governments. The last of these was formed in May 1932 under the chancellorship of **Engelbert Dollfuss**, with a parliamentary majority of just one.

On March 4, 1933, in an attempt to break a tied vote in parliament, the Social Democrat Karl Renner resigned as speaker in order to free himself to vote. When Renner's two deputy speakers from the Christian Social and Pan-German parties both followed suit, Dollfuss seized the opportunity to dissolve parliament, claiming it could no longer function properly. The same weekend, Adolf Hitler won an absolute majority in the German parliament. The onset of Nazism had a sobering effect on the majority of Austrians, particularly the SDAP, which immediately dropped their call for Anschluss.

On March 15, Dollfuss sent the police in to prevent parliament from reconvening. In response, the SDAP leadership procrastinated and held back from calling in the Schutzbund; two weeks later the latter was outlawed. Dollfuss was determined to combat the threat from Nazi Germany, but instead of agreeing to an anti-Nazi alliance with the SDAP, the chancellor threw in his lot with Mussolini, holding the first of many meetings with the Italian dictator in April. On May 21, no doubt prompted by Mussolini, Dollfuss established the Austro-fascist **Fatherland Front** (Vaterländische Front or VF), under the slogan "Austria Awake!".

In May the Communist Party was banned and in July the Austrian Nazi Party was outlawed. A violent showdown with the Social Democrats, who still controlled the Vienna city council, followed in February 1934. The first incident took place in Linz, where the local Schutzbund on their own initiative opened fire on the police. A three-day battle ensued, with the bloodiest set-to in Vienna's **Karl-Marx-Hof** housing estate, which Dollfuss eventually ordered the army to bomb into submission. The SDAP had stumbled into civil war and it was soundly beaten. The party was swiftly outlawed, and its leaders fled abroad or were imprisoned.

Just as it appeared he had successfully established an Austro-fascist state, Dollfuss was assassinated on July 25, 1934 (see p.72), during the **Juliputsch**, an abortive coup d'etat staged by Austrian Nazis, apparently without the knowledge of Hitler. His successor, **Kurt Schuschnigg**, was forced to rely ever more heavily on Mussolini for support. As a foreign policy this proved disastrous, for in 1935 Hitler and Mussolini began to patch up their differences, and suddenly Schuschnigg found himself being urged by Mussolini to come to an agreement with Hitler. Schuschnigg did just that in the Austro-German agreement of July 11, 1936. In return for Hitler's recognition of Austria's "full sovereignty", Schuschnigg agreed to an amnesty of all Nazi prisoners, and the appointment of various "prominent nationalists" – not Nazis, but fellow travellers – to his government.

In January 1938, the Austrian police raided the apartment of Leopold Tavs, one of Schuschnigg's deputies, and discovered a plan to overthrow the government with German help. As tension between the two countries mounted, the Nazi ambassador, Franz von Papen, suggested Schuschnigg should visit Hitler at his mountain retreat at Berchtesgaden near the Austrian border. At this meeting, Schuschnigg was given one of Hitler's command performances in which he ranted and raved and eventually demanded, among other things, that Schuschnigg hand over yet more key governmental posts to the Austrian Nazi Party. Schuschnigg acquiesced and agreed to appoint the Nazi **Dr Arthur Seyss-Inquart** Interior Minister.

As the Austrian Nazis increased their activities, Schuschnigg decided to chance his arm with a plebiscite to decide the country's future, reckoning (probably correctly) that the majority would vote against the Anschluss. Hitler was certainly not prepared to risk electoral defeat and swiftly demanded the resignation of Schuschnigg and his entire government. Schuschnigg announced his resignation over the radio, in order to avoid "spilling German blood", and Seyss-Inquart took over the chancellorship. President Wilhelm Miklas refused to agree to the latter's appointment and resigned, and Seyss-Inquart wasted no time in inviting the German army into the country on the pretext of preventing civil war.

Anschluss and World War II

In the event, there was no bloodshed: German troops crossed the border into Austria on March

12, 1938, and encountered no resistance whatsoever. Hitler himself began his slow and triumphant journey to the capital in the wake of his troops. First he visited his birthplace of Braunau-am-Inn, then he moved on to his "home town" of Linz, where he was received with such enthusiasm by the locals that he decided there and then to immediately incorporate Austria into the Greater German Reich, rather than pursue the more conciliatory path of preserving Austrian autonomy. Eventually on March 15, Hitler appeared on the balcony of the Hofburg before thousands of jubilant Viennese.

As a propaganda exercise, Hitler also decided to go ahead with Schuschnigg's plebiscite, which took place on April 10. The 99 percent "Yes" vote in favour of the **Anschluss** came as no surprise, with less than two thousand Viennese voting "No". To be fair, those known to be opposed to the Nazis, including Schuschnigg and his followers, had already been arrested – some 76,000 by the time Hitler arrived in Vienna – while Jews and other "undesirables" were barred from voting. On the other hand, many whom one would expect to have opposed the Anschluss, publicly declared themselves in favour, including the Archbishop of Vienna, Cardinal Theodor Innitzer, and the Social Democrat, Karl Renner.

Although the Treaty of St-Germain precluded any Anschluss with Germany, only the Soviet Union and Mexico lodged any formal international protest against the invasion. Meanwhile, the very name of Austria was wiped off the map, initially replaced by the term "**Ostmark**", but eventually simply divided into seven *Gaue* or districts, ruled by Nazi *Gauleiter*.

The fate of Vienna's Jews

In the words of eye-witness George Clare, the Anschluss unleashed a "volcanic outburst of popular anti-Semitism". Jews were dragged out into the street, physically assaulted and humiliated, and then forced to scrub Schuschnigg slogans off the walls. In one instance in the well-to-do suburb of Währing, a group of Nazis urinated on local Jewish women as they forced them to scrub the streets in front of cheering onlookers. A large number of the city's most prominent Jews were arrested immediately, and either sent to concentration camps, or released with orders to leave the country.

In May, without warning, 2000 Jews were arrested and shipped off to Dachau, primarily to encourage still more Jews to emigrate. On the night of November 10–11 – dubbed **Kristallnacht** or "Crystal Night" – the majority of synagogues in the Reich were torched, and numerous Jewish premises ransacked. Another 7800 Jews were arrested that night, 4600 of whom were sent to Dachau. By the outbreak of World War II, more than half of Vienna's Jews had emigrated.

Once the Nazis had invaded Poland, their policy towards the Jews changed, with deportation to the death camps via ghettos, favoured over forced emigration. The deportations began in earnest in February 1941, while emigration came to a complete standstill in November 1941. Of the 57,000 Jews now left in Austria, more than half had been sent to the death camps by June 1942. By the end of the war, around 200 or so Austrian Jews had managed to survive in hiding, with just over 2000 returning from the camps after the war.

Collaboration and resistance

Seyss-Inquart was initially appointed *Reichsstatthalter* (governor) of Vienna, but was transferred to Poland after the outbreak of the war, and eventually ended up in control of the Netherlands, where as *Reichskommissar* he oversaw countless atrocities for which he was hanged at the Nuremberg war trials. Control of Vienna was eventually handed over to the dashing young German lieutenant, **Baldur von Schirach**, whose artistic pretensions – he wrote poetry – were considered highly suitable for Viennese sensibilities. Schirach made the most of his position, moving into the sumptuous governmental offices on Ballhausplatz, employing no fewer than seventeen chambermaids, and entertaining official visitors in lavish style in the Hofburg.

Although Hitler preferred to import German Nazis to many positions within the Austrian Nazi hierarchy, party membership was higher in Austria than in Germany, and Austrians themselves provided more than their ten percent population ratio of concentration camp guards. The Linz-born Nazi **Adolf Eichmann**, who ran Vienna's "Central Office for Jewish Emigration" (see p.187) and was one of the architects of the "Final Solution", is probably the most infamous, though *Schindler's List* has also increased the notoriety of the Vienna-born camp commandant Amon Goeth. Another Linz-born Nazi, Ernst Kaltenbrunner, rose to Heinrich Himmler's number two in the SS, while the Carinthian Odilo Globocnik – one-time *Gauleiter* of Vienna – with ninety other fellow Austrians on his staff, supervised the death of some two million Jews in the extermination camps of Sobibor, Treblinka and Belzec.

Organized resistance to Hitler was, it has to be said, extraordinarily difficult for anti-Nazi Austrians, given the level of collaboration among their fellow citizens, and the efficient way in which the Nazis had wiped out the potential leadership. Aside from individual acts of heroism, there was very little significant non-Communist resistance within Austria. Partisan activity was restricted to a few remote alpine areas, and it wasn't until the spring of 1944 that an organized home resistance, code-named **05**, began to emerge.

Unlike every other Nazi-occupied country, however, the Austrians had no official government-in-exile. Exiled Austrian politicians spent their time bickering, split between an unlikely alliance between the son of the last emperor, Otto von Habsburg, and the Communists, and the two mainstream political parties. The most significant diplomatic step took place in November 1943, when the Allied powers published the **Moscow Declaration** stating that Austria was a "victim" of Nazi aggression and that it should be re-established as a "free and democratic state".

The liberation of Vienna

Vienna itself remained relatively free from direct contact with the war until 1944, when Allied bombing raids intensified. Over the next fourteen months, they were responsible for the deaths of some 9000 Viennese civilians. Among the most important buildings hit were the Staatsoper, the Belvedere, the Burgtheater, Schönbrunn, the Rathaus, Parlament and the Universität; Stephansdom fell victim to Soviet artillery in the last few days of the city's liberation.

By April 5, 1945, the Red Army was nearing the outskirts of the city. The 05 leadership under Major Szokoll had planned to initiate an uprising against the Nazis the very next day, but were betrayed by a junior officer, Lieutenant Walter Hanslick. Several of the 05 leaders were arrested, tortured and publicly hung. The revolt had failed and it took the Russians another three days to reach the Gürtel, and another five days' street fighting to finally win control of the city.

The commander-in-chief of the Russian troops in Austria, **Marshal Tolbukhin**, gave his assurances that the Soviets would liberate the country, respect the social order and refrain from appropriating any territory. In reality, Soviet troops spent much of the next few months raping Austrian women and stealing anything they could find. The actions of the Red Army during this period gave rise to the grim Viennese joke that Austria could probably survive a third world war, but it could never endure a second liberation.

Allied Occupation (1945–55)

On April 27, the Soviets sponsored the formation of a provisional government under the veteran Social Democrat **Karl Renner**, causing widespread alarm about Soviet intentions among the western Allies. Although Renner's cabinet was made up, for the most part, of Socialists and members of the newly founded right-wing People's Party or ÖVP, the Communists were given three posts, including the key positions of Interior Minister and Education and Information Minister. As a form of protest at this unilateral action, the western Allies refused to recognize the Renner government.

Meanwhile, there was continuing confusion over the occupation zones. Although the Moscow Declaration had stated that Austria was a victim of Nazi aggression, the country was nevertheless to be divided just like Germany, with Vienna, as Berlin, lying deep within the British sector. However, controversy over the exact zoning of Vienna helped delay the arrival of western troops in the capital until late August. The Russians took the opportunity of fleecing the capital and eastern Austria of all they could. Vienna, it was agreed, was to be divided between the four Allies, with the Innere Stadt preserved as an international sector, patrolled by one representative of each of the occupying powers. This comical sight on the streets of Vienna became the hallmark of the so-called "four-in-a-jeep" period – and the setting for the famous film *The Third Man* – when, as Karl Renner put it, Vienna was a like a small rowing boat in which four elephants sat at the oars pulling in various directions.

Elections and de-Nazification

In October the western Allies finally recognized the Renner government, and the Russians, for

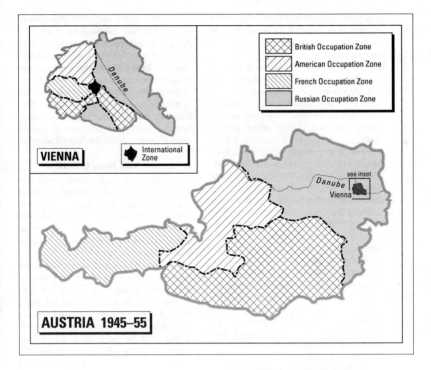

British Occupation Zone
American Occupation Zone
French Occupation Zone
Russian Occupation Zone

VIENNA

International Zone

Danube

see inset

Danube
Vienna

AUSTRIA 1945–55

their part, agreed to free elections. However, whatever hopes they might have had of the Communists gaining power in Austria were dashed by the results of the November 1945 elections. The Communists won a derisory 5.4 percent of the vote, up from their previous high of 1.9 percent in 1932, but earning them just four seats in the 165-seat parliament, and the consolation prize of the Ministry of Electrification. In an almost exact repeat of the election results of the 1920s, the country remained split down the middle between Left and Right. Although the ÖVP won almost fifty percent of the vote, it was Renner who headed the new coalition government of the Socialist Party (SPÖ) and the ÖVP.

One of the most pressing and controversial tasks of the postwar era was the **de-Nazification** process. Initially, this was the responsibility of the Allied powers: the Americans and the British busied themselves by handing out forms in which the respondents were invited to confess; the French, with collaborators of their own back home, were less keen

to get involved; the Russians, predictably, were the most assiduous, though they were as concerned to remove political opponents as ex-Nazis. Of the half a million Austrians who were Nazi party members, only a handful were executed at Nuremberg (for crimes committed outside of Austria); von Schirach was given twenty years. Back in Austria itself, the government took over the de-Nazification process, condemning 38 Nazis to death, and depriving the rest of their civil rights for a brief period before an amnesty was agreed in 1948. Some attempt was made to rid the state bureaucracy of its ex-Nazis, but inevitably many slipped through the net, Eichmann among them, though he was later kidnapped, tried and executed in Israel in 1962.

Communist agitation

When the Red Army liberated Vienna in April 1945, few people thought that the city and the country would remain under Allied occupation for ten years. However, the Soviets were keen to pay back the Austrians for their mass participation in the Nazi armed forces. At the postwar Potsdam conference, the Soviets were granted, instead of cash reparations for war damage, the right to all external German assets in eastern Austria. Over the next ten years, the Russians took this as a carte blanche to asset-strip the entire region of eastern Austria, transporting factories piece by piece back to the Soviet Union, and all in all reaping some half a billion dollars' worth of assets.

Soviet control of eastern Austria – the country's agricultural heartland – also gave them considerable political leverage. With the entire country suffering chronic food shortages, the Soviets deliberately hoarded supplies from their sector, supplying them direct to workers in Soviet-run industries. This won them considerable support in the eastern zone, and increased unrest in the western zones. For despite the Communists' electoral setback, the Russians still had hopes of taking control of Austria. The winter of 1946–47 was particularly harsh, and the Communists took advantage of this by fomenting food riots in May 1947. The rioters besieged the Austrian chancellery and called for a national strike. In the end the putsch failed, because the Socialist trade union leaders refused to support the strike, and the Russians held back from using military force.

While **Marshall Plan** aid from the west helped ease conditions throughout Austria from the summer of 1947 onwards, the Communist coup in Czechoslovakia in February 1948 and the Berlin blockade (June 1948–May 1949) only increased political tensions. Despite their recent setbacks, the Communists had high hopes for the national elections of October 1949. However, though the ruling coalition lost ground, it wasn't to the Communists, who remained on a derisory five percent, but to the newly formed extreme right-wing **Union of Independents** (VdU), who scored 11.6 percent of the vote, attracting the support of the majority of ex-Nazi Party members, who had recently been given back their voting rights.

In the autumn of 1950, Marshall Plan aid was cut back drastically. With the Austrian government forced to increase sharply the price of food, coal and electricity, strikes broke out among workers in cities across Austria. Seizing the moment, the Communists staged their second and most serious coup attempt. Once again, it began with a Communist-inspired mass demonstration outside the chancellery, after which bar-

ricades were erected, roads blocked, tram tracks cemented up and bus windows broken. The Russians stopped police reinforcements in their sector from being called up, and it was only with great difficulty that the situation was kept under control. In the end, however, the Socialist trade unions and the government took sufficient steps to stem the tide, and the general strike held on October 4, though heeded by large numbers of workers in the Russian sectors of the city and eastern Austria, was called off the following day.

The Austrian State Treaty of 1955

The withdrawal of the four Allied powers from Austria in 1955 – or more specifically the Soviet withdrawal – was something of a unique event in the otherwise grim history of the Cold War. And something of a surprise, given the previously unscrupulous behaviour of the Soviets in Austria (and elsewhere in Europe).

For nearly ten years negotiations over a peace treaty with Austria were at a stalemate, with the Soviets insisting that a German peace treaty be prerequisite to an Austrian treaty. The Soviet threat over the future of Austria was used by them to try and forestall German rearmament. However, with the establishment of the Federal Republic of Germany in 1949, it was clear that this policy had failed. A struggle within the Kremlin then ensued over Soviet policy towards Austria. Following the death of Stalin, this struggle intensified and was eventually won by Krushchev, who decided to use the **Austrian State Treaty** as a way of initiating a period of détente.

Other factors influenced Soviet policy. Hopes of creating a Communist Austria had died with the failure of the 1950 putsch. The Soviet sector meanwhile had been bled dry and was no longer of any great economic benefit. A neutral Austria, on the other hand, created a convenient buffer that split NATO's northern and southern flanks. And so on May 15, 1955, the Austrian State Treaty or Staatsvertrag was signed by the four powers in Vienna's Belvedere. The Austrian chancellor, Leopold Figl, waved the treaty triumphantly from the balcony and over half a million Austrians celebrated in the streets of the capital.

1955–83: consensus politics

With the popular vote split between Left and Right, the two main parties of the ÖVP and the

SPÖ formed a succession of coalitions which lasted until 1966. To avoid repeating the mistakes of the past, and to placate the occupying powers, a system of *Proporz* was established, whereby each party shared equally every governmental and state post. In some ways institutionalized political corruption, this process began at the top among the ministries, and continued right down to the local post office. At the same time, various special bodies or chambers representing the various interest groups – the Chamber of Trade, the Chamber of Labour and so on – were established. Like *Proporz*, these new institutions ensured that the country enjoyed an unprecedented period of political and social stability, but left the parliament without an effective opposition and created a system open to widespread abuse. Like the Germans, though, the Austrians enjoyed a period of economic growth and prosperity, and there were few voices of complaint.

In the elections of 1966, the People's Party at last achieved an absolute majority and formed the first one-party government of the postwar era. Many Austrians feared a repeat of the 1920s, but in practice little changed. The system of *Proporz* and the institutions of the corporate state continued to hand out "jobs for the boys", and only at the very top level of government were the Socialists excluded from power. Their turn came, though, in 1970, when a slight economic downturn gave the SPÖ a narrow victory, followed by an outright majority in elections the following year. Under the chancellorship of **Bruno Kreisky**, the Socialists enjoyed thirteen years of power, during which Kreisky carried the SPÖ further away from their radical Marxist past than ever before. The end came in the elections of 1983 when the SPÖ lost its overall majority and was forced into a coalition government with the far-right Freedom Party (FPÖ), successor to the postwar VdU (see opposite).

The Waldheim affair

Having struggled to make the headlines of the international press in the 1960s and 1970s, Austria was catapulted onto the world media stage in 1986 during the campaign for the Austrian presidency. The candidate for the ÖVP was **Kurt Waldheim**, a figure of some international stature who had been UN Secretary-General for ten years (1972–82). However, during the campaign, Waldheim's war record was called

into question. From the summer of 1942 until the end of the war, he had served as a lieutenant in the Balkans with the German Army. Waldheim was never a member of the Nazi Party (one of the initial charges) and there was never any clear evidence that he was directly involved in the atrocities committed by the army in the Balkans, though he was formally charged with (but never tried for) war crimes by the Yugoslavs after the war. What was more difficult to believe, however, was his claim that he had no knowledge of the deportation of Greek Jews to the death camps, despite being an interpreter for the Italian Army in Greece for much of the war.

To the dismay of many around the world, these charges, albeit unproven, did Waldheim's candidacy no harm at all domestically, and he was duly elected to the Austrian presidency with 54 percent of the vote. The international campaign against Waldheim began with the boycott of his swearing-in ceremony by the US ambassador, and culminated in his being put on the US Department of Justice's "Watch List" of undesirable aliens. Waldheim – and by association Austria – became an international pariah, restricted in his state visits to Arab countries. At Waldheim's suggestion, a commission was set up to investigate the charges against him; however, far from exonerating him, the commission's report found him guilty of "proximity to legally incriminating acts and orders", a somewhat woolly phrase that could be applied to just about any Austrian who'd served in the German Army. The British government, meanwhile, followed up the Yugoslav charge that Waldheim had been involved in war crimes against British commandos in the Balkans. The British enquiry concluded that Waldheim's rank was too junior to have had any influence over the fate of the commandos, adding that "knowledge is not itself a crime".

The political present

As if the Waldheim affair were not bad enough, the country has also had to contend with the rise of the FPÖ under their charismatic leader **Jörg Haider**. A strange grouping of free-market liberals and ultra-conservatives, the FPÖ was very much a fringe player in Austrian politics until the mid-1980s, when Haider began to turn it into an effective vehicle for right-wing populism. In his first stab at the polls, in 1986, Haider won nearly ten percent of the vote, frightening the two main parties back into the grand SPÖ–ÖVP coalition of the postwar years under the Socialist Franz Vranitzky. Unfortunately, this only served to play into Haider's hands, increasing popular resentment against the system of *Proporz* (from which the FPÖ is excluded) and thus boosting support for the FPÖ.

A dapper character with a sporty image (a keen skier and jogger, he's the only Austrian party leader to have attempted a bungee-jump), Haider presented himself as something new in national politics, free from the cynical power-sharing manoeuvres of the two main parties. He attended carnival celebrations dressed as Robin Hood in order to press the point home, and campaigned under the slogan "Haider: the only politician whose handshake you can trust" in order to emphasize his disdain for the wheeling and dealing of the Viennese political elite. Both of his parents were Nazi party members who had felt sidelined by post-war Austrian society, and Haider himself deliberately courted far-right support in an attempt to gain notoriety. Elected provincial governor of Carinthia in 1990, Haider expressed enthusiasm for Nazi employment policy in a speech a year later – precipitating his fall from office, but not his fall from popularity.

Haider's main electoral plank was to exploit the fears shared by many Austrians over the country's new wave of **immigrants**, who arrived from the former eastern bloc and war-torn Yugoslavia in considerable numbers in the 1990s. Nationalist frustrations were compounded by the country's entry into the **European Union** in 1995. Although in a referendum sixty percent voted in favour of joining, the austerity measures the country needed to implement in order to meet the criteria necessary for joining a single European currency convinced many that it had been the wrong decision.

In the national **elections in 1994 and 1995**, popular dissatisfaction was publicly registered, with Haider's FPÖ taking a staggering 22 percent of the vote, behind the ÖVP (with 28 percent) and the Socialists (on 38 percent). The biggest shock, though, was in Vienna, where the SPÖ lost its overall majority for the first time in the city's history, with the FPÖ receiving 27 percent of the vote and becoming the main opposition in the Rathaus, ahead of the ÖVP.

Franz Vranitzky's successor as chancellor, **Viktor Klima**, soon established himself as a pop-

ular and trusted figure, and for a time things seemed to carry on as normal, with Klima presiding over an SPÖ/ÖVP government that included ÖVP leader **Wolfgang Schüssel** as foreign minister. However neither Klima nor Schüssel seemed capable of reversing the gradual decline of their respective parties in the polls.

The 1999 election and after

In **October 1999**, campaigning on an openly xenophobic platform – with posters reading "Stop der Überfremdung. Österreich zuerst" ("Stop the foreign tide. Put Austria first") setting the tone – the FPÖ surpassed even their own wildest dreams by squeezing into second place, beating the ÖVP into third by a margin of 415 votes (both the FPÖ and the ÖVP were awarded 52 seats in parliament). Most observers assumed that the SPÖ and the ÖVP would once again close ranks to deny Haider a role in government, but negotiations on the formation of a new coalition dragged on inconclusively, with the ÖVP demanding control of the finance ministry in order to force through economic austerity measures, and sitting chancellor Viktor Klima refusing to concede it. With talks between the two parties breaking down in January 2000, President Klestil had no choice but to invite the ÖVP to enter talks with the FPÖ in the hope of forming a government. Klestil – himself no big fan of Haider – knew that if he dissolved parliament and called new elections, the FPÖ would only get stronger.

Eager to fulfil his dream of becoming chancellor, ÖVP leader Schüssel put together a cabinet in which several top posts went to the FPÖ. Fearful of how the international community would react, however, he succeeded in persuading Haider himself to remain in Carinthia rather than take up a ministerial job. The **new government** was sworn in by an unenthusiastic Klestil on February 2, 2000. All other EU states immediately froze bilateral relations with Austria in protest at the FPÖ's inclusion in government. In a cosmetic excercise designed to placate world opinion, Haider unexpectedly quit the FPÖ leadership in April, to be replaced by the less openly extremist Susanne Riess-Passer. The new government's programme – centred on promises to cut government spending and pave the way for tax cuts – carefully avoided any reference to the FPÖ's pre-election rhetoric, and the EU withdrew their sanctions after six months. Those Austrians who had voted for the ÖVP or the FPÖ were in any case resentful of the outside world's attempts to meddle in the nation's affairs. Others were deeply shamed by the FPÖ's accession to power, and launched the **Widerstand** (Resistance), a rolling campaign of demonstrations and cultural events designed to show that the liberal, tolerant values of centre-left Austria were still very much alive.

Paradoxically, the ÖVP profited more from the new situation than the cock-sure FPÖ. Chancellor Schüssel, together with ÖVP foreign minister Benita Ferrero-Waldner, won popular support for the way in which they appeared to defend Austria's dignity against a hostile EU. The unpopular elements of government policy – cuts in public spending and the introduction of university fees for students – tended to be blamed on their more radical coalition allies. Provincial elections in Styria in October and in Burgenland two months later saw the FPÖ vote collapse, suggesting that a large body of the Austrian electorate was happy to register a protest vote for the FPÖ when it was in opposition, but saw no further use for it now it was in power. The decision by Jörg Haider – the FPÖ's only genuinely charismatic leader – to remain in Carinthia now looked like a tactical mistake, and there was much talk of whether he would return to the national stage. As it was, Haider had his own problems: in late summer 2000, when former FPÖ supporter Josef Kleindienst alleged that Haider and his circle had consistently bribed police officers to provide confidential information on FPÖ opponents. Haider countered that the police apparatus was still dominated by SPÖ appointees who were out to smear him, but the fuse for a long-running scandal had been lit. Having consistently posed as the clean man of Austrian politics, Haider entered 2001 looking exceedingly vulnerable.

The ÖVP/FPÖ coalition may turn out to be a short-term exercise in political pragmatism rather than the opening of a new dark age, but the persistence of xenophobic attitudes in Austria – and their exploitation by the populist right – will continue to be a source of concern for both the international community and the Austrians themselves. The Waldheim Affair and the rise of the FPÖ have proved a **PR disaster** for the country, and in Austria itself there's a growing sense of bewilderment that a nation that promoted itself so successfully as the home of Lipizzaner horses and happy alpine holidays should nowadays be internationally notorious for something entirely different.

Books

There's quite a number of books in print about the Habsburgs and the various artistic figures from Vienna's glorious past, but precious little written in English about the country in the twentieth century and not much fiction in translation – hence the rather uneven selection below. We've listed a few books that are currently out of print (o/p), but you might be able to pick them up in secondhand bookshops. For books in print, we've listed UK publishers first, then US; wherever we've cited a single publisher, it's the same publisher in both territories, unless we've specified UK or US after it.

These days, of course, it's not so important where a book is printed, as any online bookshop can ship you a copy out in very little time. The best-known one is *www.amazon.co.uk* (for the UK) and *www.amazon.com* (for North America), but if you're looking for a specific title, a book search engine like *www.bookbrain.co.uk* will tell you which online bookshop is selling it for the cheapest price

History and society

Steven Beller, *Vienna and the Jews, 1867–1938* (CUP). Beller shows how the Jews played a central role in the vibrant cultural life of Vienna at the turn of the last century. Thorough, but rather on the dry side.

Gordon Brook-Shepherd, *The Austrians* (HarperCollins; Carroll & Graf). Readable, if a little over-earnest history, which attempts to trace the Austrian-ness (or lack of it) in the country's history from the Babenbergs to entry into the EU in 1994. Brook-Shepherd draws on his experience as a *Telegraph* correspondent and as someone who worked in the Allied High Commission in Vienna after World War II.

Frederic V. Grunfeld, *Prophets without Honour* (Kodansha). A useful insight into the intellectual figures of *fin-de-siècle Mitteleuropa*, including Freud, Kafka and Einstein.

William M. Johnston, *The Austrian Mind: An Intellectual and Social History 1848–1938* (University of California Press). Johnston knows his stuff, and though this is a pretty academic approach, it's a fascinating insight into *fin-de-siècle* Vienna.

Robert A. Kann, *History of the Habsburg Empire 1526–1918* (University of California Press). Weighty and wide-ranging 600-page account of the empire, written in the 1970s.

Robert Knight, *Contemporary Austria and the Legacy of the Third Reich 1945-95* (UCL). Highlights the failure of de-Nazification and the subsequent rise of Haider's FPÖ, the consequences of which were partly obscured by the country's postwar prosperity.

Elisabeth Lichtenberger, *Austria: Society and Regions* (Austrian Academy of Science). A scholarly account of the awkward twentieth-century history of Austria, taking the reader right up to the late 1990s.

Frederic Morton, *A Nervous Splendor: Vienna 1888/1889* (Viking); *Thunder at Twilight: Vienna 1913–1914* (P. Owen). Morton has trawled through the newspapers of the time to produce two very readable dramatized accounts of two critical years in the city's history. The first centres on the Mayerling tragedy, the second on the Sarajevo assassination.

Hella Pick, *Guilty Victim: Austria from the Holocaust to Haider* (I.B. Tauris). Probably the best book on postwar Austria, both as a political history and a meditation on the country's (often half-hearted) attempts to come to terms with the darker elements of its past.

Carl E. Schorske, *Fin-de-Siècle Vienna* (Phoenix; Random). Fascinating scholarly essays on, among other things, the impact of the building of the Ringstrasse, and of Freud, Klimt, Kokoschka and Schönberg on the city's culture.

A.J.P. Taylor, *The Habsburg Monarchy 1809–1918* (Penguin, o/p). Readable, forthright as ever and thought-provoking account of the demise of the Habsburgs.

Andrew Wheatcroft, *The Habsburgs* (Penguin). Wheatcroft's intriguing history traces the rise and fall of the Habsburgs from their modest origins in Switzerland to their demise at the head of the Austro-Hungarian empire, looking closely at individual family members, and the promotion of its dynastic image.

Memoirs and travel

George Clare, *Last Waltz in Vienna; The Destruction of a Family 1842–1942* (Papermac). Incredibly moving – and far from bitter – autobiographical account of a Jewish upbringing in inter-war Vienna that ended with the Anschluss.

Edward Crankshaw, *Vienna: The Image of a Culture in Decline* (Macmillan, o/p); *Fall of the House of Habsburg* (Penguin). Part travel journal, part history, and first published in 1938, this is a nostalgic, but by no means rose-tinted, look at the city. The same author's *Fall of the House of Habsburg* is an accessible popular history of the Empire's last days.

Helen Fremont, *After Long Silence* (Judy Piatkus Publishers). Fremont was raised as a Roman Catholic in the US only to discover as an adult that her parents were Austrian Jews who survived the Holocaust, but kept silent about it for forty years.

Patrick Leigh Fermor, *A Time of Gifts* (Penguin). The first volume of Leigh Fermor's trilogy based on his epic walk along the Rhine and Danube rivers in 1933–34. Written forty years later in dense, luscious and highly crafted prose, it's an evocative and poignant insight into the culture of *Mitteleuropa* between the wars.

Claudio Magris, *Danube* (Harvill). In this highly readable travel journal from the 1980s, Magris, a wonderfully erudite Trieste-based academic, traces the Danube, passing through Austria along the way.

Reinhard Spitzty, *How We Squandered the Reich* (Clocktower). Chilling and frank autobiographical account of a young Austrian idealist who became a member of the SS.

Simon Wiesenthal, *Sunflower* (Henry Holt; Schocken). Wiesenthal relates an instance from his time at Mathausen when an ailing SS guard called him to his bedside and asked for forgiveness. In the second half of the book, Wiesenthal asks leading intellectuals to respond to the dilemma of forgiveness.

Stefan Zweig, *The World of Yesterday* (University of Nebraska Press, o/p). Seminal account of *fin-de-siècle* Vienna written just before Zweig was forced by the Nazis into exile in South America, where he and his wife committed suicide.

Biography

The Habsburgs

Steven Beller, *Franz Joseph* (Addison Wesley). Shortest and most portable of the books on Franz-Josef; more of a political than a biographical account, it's a bit short on personal history.

T.C.W. Blanning, *Joseph II* (Longman). Aimed at the general reader, this tells the story of Joseph and his attempts at reform against the background of the Austrian enlightenment.

Jean Paul Bled, *Franz Joseph* (Blackwell, o/p). Well-rounded account of the old duffer, with a smattering of the sort of scurrilous gossip missing in some other biographies.

Katerina von Burg, *Elisabeth of Austria* (Windsor Publications, UK). Recent biography of the endlessly fascinating empress who was assassinated by an Italian anarchist in 1898.

Edward Crankshaw, *Maria Theresa* (Constable). Readable account of the "Virgin Empress", though disappointingly short on light touches.

Brigitte Hamann, *The Reluctant Empress* (Taschen, Köln o/p); *Hitler's Vienna* (OUP). The former is a surprisingly even-handed account of the Empress Elisabeth's extraordinary life, warts and all. Only usually available in Vienna. *Hitler's Vienna* is a newly published account of Hitler's early youth in Vienna, which played an important part in helping form the prejudices of the Nazi leader.

Joan Haslip, *The Emperor and the Actress* (Weidenfeld & Nicolson, o/p); *Lonely Empress: Elizabeth of Austria* (Phoenix, UK). The first is a detailed, steamy account of Franz-Josef's relationship with his long-term mistress, the actress Katharina Schratt. Retreading some of the same material, Haslip's *Lonely Empress* is a sympathetic portrayal of the Kaiser's unhappy spouse.

Alan Palmer, *The Twilight of the Habsburgs: The Life and Times of the Emperor Francis Joseph*; and *Metternich* (both Phoenix; Grove-Atlantic). The first is the latest scholarly and somewhat weighty tome on this much-biographied emperor; the latter a solid account of the arch-conservative who ruled the roost in Vienna from 1815 to 1848.

Music

Peter Franklin, *The life of Mahler* (CUP). A very accessible account of Mahler's life, in Cambridge UP's excellent "Musical Lives" series.

Egon Gartenberg *Johann Strauss, End of an Era* (Da Capo). The story of the waltz king and his world, originator of the Blue Danube, as well as *Die Fledermaus*.

Peter Gay, *Mozart* (Penguin; Viking). A slim, easy-to-read volume which nevertheless includes a good deal of stimulating analysis. Easily the best compact Mozart biography you can get.

Malcolm Hayes, *Anton von Webern* (Phaidon). Not as well known as Schönberg, or as successful as Berg, Webern is seen by some as a progressive, and accused by others of being a Nazi sympathizer. Hayes, understandably, sits on the fence.

Alma Mahler-Werfel, *Diaries 1896–1902* (Faber). Gushingly frank diaries of a supremely attractive young woman, courted by the likes of Klimt and Zemlinsky. The period covered tracks Alma until shortly after her marriage to the composer, Gustav Mahler.

Donald Mitchell, *Gustav Mahler* (Faber; University of California Press). Mitchell's three-volume life of Mahler is a bench-mark biography, as dense and wide-ranging as one of its subject's colossal symphonies.

Elizabeth Norman McKay, *Franz Schubert: A Biography* (Clarendon Press). Straightforward biography of Schubert, which does the best it can to unravel the composer's brief life from the limited source material available.

H.C. Robbins Landon, *Mozart, the Golden Years 1781–1791* (Thames & Hudson; Macmillan). Big, illustrated romp through the composer's mature, Vienna years; a mixture of biography and musicology.

Freud

Frederick C. Crews (ed), *Unauthorized Freud* (Penguin). Crews is virulently against psychoanalysis and has gathered together a whole host of Freud critics to put forward the revisionist case.

Sigmund Freud (ed. Peter Gay), *The Freud Reader* (Vintage; WW Norton). A comprehensive selection of Freud's writings on art, literature and religion, as well as the usual dreams and sexuality. Spans his entire career with useful introduction.

Peter Gay, *Freud* (Papermac; WW Norton). Big tome, a healthy mixture of biography and philosophy, with a bit of spicy drama for good measure.

Michael Jacobs, *Sigmund Freud* (Sage, UK). Brief biography of the bearded one, a quick trot through his ideas and the subsequent criticisms thereof.

Ernest Jones, *Life and Work of Sigmund Freud* (Basic Books). Abridged version of the definitive three-volume biography that Jones – one of Freud's disciples – published in the 1950s just before he died.

Wiesenthal

Alan Levy, *The Wiesenthal File* (Constable, UK). Thoroughly entertaining account of the controversial Vienna-based Nazi-hunter and the various Nazis he has helped to pursue, plus an account of the Waldheim affair.

Hella Pick, *Wiesenthal* (Phoenix; Northeastern UP). The most recent of the Wiesenthal biographies, made with the subject's co-operation. In tracking his wartime sufferings and cataloguing his postwar activities, Pick is sympathetic yet objective, and gives a rare glimpse into the octogenarian Nazi-hunter's personal life.

Wittgenstein

Kimberley Cornish, *The Jew of Linz: Hitler, Wittgenstein and their Secret Battle for the Mind* (Arrow). Utterly wacky book that in effect blames "complex, prickly" Wittgenstein for turning his schoolmate Hitler into an anti-Semite. The philosopher then recruited Kim Philby and his circle for the Russians, to make up for his role in precipitating the Holocaust. The author appears to be serious.

John Heaton & Judy Groves, *Wittgenstein for Beginners* (Icon Books). Even this accessible, irreverent series fails to shed much light on the great philosopher's complex thinking.

Ray Monk, *Ludwig Wittgenstein: The Duty of Genius* (Vintage; Viking Penguin). Exhaustive biography of the perplexing philosopher; a model of its kind, Monk's book interweaves Wittgenstein's life and thought into an inseparable entity.

Austrian fiction

Ingeborg Bachmann, *Songs in Flight* (Marsilio), *The Thirtieth Year* (Holmes & Meier). An acclaimed poet, novelist and short-story writer from the 1950s, Bachmann was fascinated by the impotence of language and developed a voice of her own. For a flavour of her work, try the bilingual edition of her poems, *Songs in Flight*.

Thomas Bernhard, *Cutting Timber* (Vintage; Quartet), *Wittgenstein's Nephew* (University of Chicago) and *Extinction* (Penguin/University of Chicago), *Concrete* (University of Chicago) and *The Voice Imitator* (University of Chicago). Dense, stream-of-consciousness ruminations from the leading critic of the hypocrisy and mediocrity of postwar Austria. Any of the above will prove to be a good introduction to his inimitable style.

Hermann Broch, *The Death of Virgil* (Vintage); *The Guiltless* (Marlboro). With the Anschluss, Broch, who was of Jewish parentage, was briefly interned in a camp, where he began *The Death of Virgil*, which focuses on the last hours of Virgil's life and his questioning of the role his art has given him in society. *The Guiltless* is a more direct and readable examination of the dark side of mid-twentieth-century German culture.

Lilian Faschinger, *Vienna Passion* (Headline). A complex tale, whose black New Yorker heroine, researching into Anna Freud in Vienna, comes across the fascinating story of Rosa Havelka, servant to the Empress and mistress to the heir to the throne at the end of the nineteenth century.

Peter Handke, *Plays 1* (Methuen). Handke is Austria's most provocative contemporary playwright, whose partnership with Wim Wenders has brought him international recognition. This volume gives you six of his best from the 1960s and 1970s, including *Kaspar* and *Offending the Audience*, Handke's favourite pastime.

Elfriede Jelinek, *Wonderful, Wonderful Times*, *The Piano Teacher* and *Lust* (all Serpent's Tail). From one of the best writers to come out of Austria for some time, *The Piano Teacher* is an unsentimental look at Vienna from a woman's perspective, while *Wonderful, Wonderful Times*, which takes place in the late 1950s, digs up the city's murky past. *Lust* takes a dark and disturbing look at small-town life in the Austrian provinces.

Robert Musil, *The Man Without Qualities* (Picador; Vintage); *Diaries 1899-1941* (Harper Collins; Basic Books). Often compared with Joyce and Proust's great works, Musil's 1000-page unfinished novel, *The Man Without Qualities*, takes place at the twilight of the Habsburg Empire. This translation, by Sophie Wilkins, includes a massive amount of material that has never appeared in English before; unfortunately, the UK paperback reprint omits this text in order to squeeze the novel into a single volume – so if UK readers want to read the whole thing, they have to hunt out the two-volume hardback. Those addicted to Musil's irony-drenched, essayistic prose should also dip into his diaries.

Josef Roth, *Radetsky March* (Penguin; Overlook Press). Pitifully underrated, this is Roth's finest work – a nostalgic and melancholic portrait of the moribund Vienna of Franz-Josef. Check also the secondhand stores for Roth's masterful short novels *Job*, *The Emperor's Tomb* and – above all – *Flight Without End*, a heartbreaking tale of dislocation and world-weariness.

Arthur Schnitzler, *Hands Around* (Dover, UK); *Dream Story* (Penguin). Schnitzler's play features ten seductions, each of which shares at least one character with the next one until the circle is complete. A classic portrayal of decadent Viennese *fin-de-siècle* society, it came back to prominence in the 1950s after being filmed as *La Ronde* by Max Ophüls, and enjoyed a comeback in the late 1990s on the stage in an adaptation called *The Blue Room* by David Hare. *Dream Story* was the inspiration for Stanley Kubrick's last film *Eyes Wide Shut*.

Harold B. Segel (ed), *The Vienna Coffeehouse Wits 1890–1938* (Purdue University Press). A rare opportunity to read translated snippets of work by *Kaffeehaus* regulars such as Karl Kraus, Peter Altenberg and Felix Salten (the little-known author of *Bambi* and *The Story of a Vienna Whore*, one of which was made into a Disney cartoon).

Stefan Zweig, *The Burning Secret and Other Stories* (Penguin). Exquisitely wrought tales from *fin-de-siècle* Vienna, including *Letter from an Unknown Woman*, best and most poignant of Zweig's tales.

Literature by foreign writers

Richard & John Lehmann Bassett, *Vienna, a travellers' companion* (Constable, o/p). Out of print but, if you can get hold of a copy, it features some interesting travellers' impressions from over the centuries.

Graham Greene, *The Third Man* (Penguin). *The Third Man* was written by Greene as a film treatment but differs quite a bit from the eventual celluloid version; it's printed along with *Fallen Idol*, a story set in London.

John Irving, *Setting Free the Bears* (Corgi; Ballantine Books). Stream-of-verbiage novel centred (vaguely) on Vienna's zoo after the war.

Philip Kerr, *A German Requiem* (Penguin). Last volume of a gripping spy trilogy set in postwar Vienna.

Mary Stewart, *Airs Above the Ground* (Hodder). Murder mystery written in the 1960s and set in and around Vienna's Spanish Riding School.

Art and architecture

Alessandra Comini, *Egon Schiele* (Thames and Hudson). Contains a good selection of full colour reproductions, as well as an account of Schiele's life set into its cultural context..

Gabriele Fahr-Becker, *Wiener Werkstätte 1903–1932* (Taschen) and *Hundertwasser* (Taschen). Two definitive and copiously illustrated volumes, the first showing in colour and in black and white the enormous breadth of WW's output, and the second taking a close look at Hundertwasser's later ventures into architecture.

Benedetto Gravagnolo, *Adolf Loos* (Art Data). A wonderfully illustrated book for the general reader, covering the life and works of the "father of modernism".

Peter Haiko and Roberto Schezen, *Vienna 1850–1930 Architecture* (Rizzoli). The ultimate coffee-table book on Vienna's most important works of architecture, beautifully photographed (by Schezen) and intelligently discussed.

Ingrid Helsing Almaas, *Vienna: A Guide to Recent Architecture* (Ellipsis; Könemann). Dinky, illustrated pocket guide to Vienna's modern architecture of the last couple of decades, with forthright accompanying critiques and interviews.

Robert Lustenberger, *Adolf Loos* (Birkhauser o/p). One of the Studio Paperback series, illustrated with black-and-white photos.

Erwin Mitsch, *Egon Schiele* (Phaidon). Nicely produced, with a short introduction, then eighty colour plates and eighty more black-and-white photos.

Gilles Néret, *Klimt* (Taschen). Good-value A4-format book, with a fair sprinkling of colour and black-and-white photos, and a succinct text outlining Gustav Klimt's artistic development.

Rolf Toman (ed), *Vienna Art and Architecture* (Könemann). A huge coffee-table volume covering the city from the Middle Ages to the present day, with numerous colour illustrations, accompanied by lots of informative text.

Peter Vergo, *Art in Vienna 1898–1918* (Phaidon). Deals with the major artists of the Secession, including Klimt, Kokoscka and Schiele, and the development of the Wiener Werkstätte.

Alfred Weidinger, *Kokoschka and Alma Mahler: Testimony to a Passionate Relationship* (Prestel Verlag, available in UK). Detailed account of the artist's doomed relationship with Mahler's widow, illustrated with lots of Kokoschka's drawings and paintings from the period.

Patrick Werkner, *Austrian Expressionism: The Formative Years* (University of Washington Press). Interesting articles on Schönberg, Schiele, Kokoschka, Gerstl and Kubin; black-and-white illustrations only.

Language

Although a high proportion of Austrians speak some English, any attempts at learning a few phrases of **German** will be heartily appreciated. That said, German is a highly complex language which you can't hope to master quickly. The biggest problem for English-speakers is that German words can be one of three genders: masculine, feminine or neuter. Each has its own ending and corresponding ending for attached adjectives, plus its own definite article. If in doubt, it's safest to use either the neuter or male forms.

Pronunciation (and spelling) is less of a problem, as individual syllables are generally pronounced as they're printed – the trick is learning how to place the stresses in the notoriously lengthy German words. Though Austrians speak German with a distinct accent, and the Viennese have their own dialect, when speaking to a foreigner most folk will switch to standard German.

The following is a rundown of the basics you'll need on a city break to Vienna. For more detail, check out the *Rough Guide German phrasebook*, set out dictionary-style for easy access, with English–German and German–English sections, cultural tips for tricky situations and a menu reader.

Vowels and umlauts

a as in r**a**ther

e as in g**ay**

i as in f**ee**t

o as in n**o**se

u as in b**oo**t

ä is a combination of a and e, sometimes pronounced like **e** in b**e**t (eg Länder) and sometimes like **ai** in p**ai**d (eg spät).

ö is a combination of o and e, which has no real English equivalent, but is similar to the French *eu*

ü is a combination of u and e, like bl**ue**

Vowel combinations

ai as in wh**y**

au as in m**ou**se

ie as in tr**ee**

ei as in tr**i**al

eu as in b**oi**l

Consonants

Consonants are pronounced as they are written, with no silent letters. The differences from English are:

j pronounced similar to an English y

r is given a dry throaty sound, similar to French

s pronounced similar to, but slightly softer than an English z

v pronounced somewhere between f and v

w pronounced same way as an English v

z pronounced ts.

The German letter **ß** usually replaces ss in a word: pronunciation is identical.

ch is a strong back-of-the-throat sound as in the Scottish loch

sp (at the start of a word) is pronounced shp

st (at the start of a word) is pronounced sht

GERMAN WORDS AND PHRASES

Basics

Ja, Nein	Yes, No	*Jenes*	That one
Bitte	Please/ You're welcome	*Gross, Klein*	Large, small
Bitte schön	A more polite form of *Bitte*	*Mehr, Weniger*	More, less
		Wenig	A little
Danke, Danke schön	Thank you, Thank you very much	*Viel*	A lot
		Billig, Teuer	Cheap, expensive
Wo, Wann, Warum?	Where, when, why?	*Gut, Schlecht*	Good, bad
Wieviel?	How much?	*Heiss, Kalt*	Hot, cold
Hier, Da	Here, there	*Mit, Ohne*	With, without
Geöffnet, Offen, Auf	All mean "open"	*Rechts*	Right
Geschlossen, Zu	Both mean "closed"	*Links*	Left
Da drüben	Over there	*Gerade aus*	Straight ahead
Dieses	This one	*Geh weg*	Go away

Greetings and Times

Grüss Gott	Good day	*Übermorgen*	The day after tomorrow
Guten Morgen	Good morning	*Tag*	Day
Guten Abend	Good evening	*Nacht*	Night
Gute Nacht	Good night	*Mittag*	Midday
Auf Wiedersehen	Goodbye	*Mitternacht*	Midnight
Auf Wiederhören	Goodbye (on the telephone)	*Woche*	Week
		Wochenende	Weekend
Tschüs	Goodbye (informal)	*Monat*	Month
Servus	Hello/Goodbye	*Jahr*	Year
Wie geht es Ihnen?	How are you? (polite)	*Am Vormittag/ Vormittags*	In the morning
Wie geht es dir?	How are you? (informal)		
Heute	Today	*Am Nachmittag/ Nachmittags*	In the afternoon
Gestern	Yesterday		
Morgen	Tomorrow	*Am Abend*	In the evening
Vorgestern	The day before yesterday		

Days, Months and Dates

Montag	Monday	*September*	September
Dienstag	Tuesday	*Oktober*	October
Mittwoch	Wednesday	*November*	November
Donnerstag	Thursday	*Dezember*	December
Freitag	Friday	*Frühling*	Spring
Samstag	Saturday	*Sommer*	Summer
Sonntag	Sunday	*Herbst*	Autumn
Jänner	January	*Winter*	Winter
Februar	February	*Ferien*	Holidays
März	March	*Feiertag*	Bank holiday
April	April	*Montag, der erste April*	Monday, the first of April
Mai	May		
Juni	June	*Der zweite April*	The second of April
Juli	July	*Der dritte April*	The third of April
August	August		

Some Signs

Damen/Frauen	Women's toilets	*Notausgang*	Emergency exit
Herren/Männer	Men's toilets	*Krankenhaus*	Hospital
Eingang	Entrance	*Polizei*	Police
Ausgang	Exit	*Nicht rauchen*	No smoking
Ankunft	Arrival	*Kein Eingang*	No entrance
Abfahrt	Departure	*Drücken*	Push
Ausstellung	Exhibition	*Ziehen*	Pull
Autobahn	Motorway	*Frei*	Vacant
Umleitung	Diversion	*Besetzt*	Occupied
Achtung!	Attention!	*Verboten*	Prohibited
Vorsicht!	Beware!	*Kasse*	Cash desk/ticket office
Not	Emergency		

Questions and Requests

All enquiries should start with the phrase *Entschuldigen Sie bitte* (Excuse me, please). Though strictly you should use *Sie*, the polite form of address, with everyone except close friends, young people often don't bother with it. However, the older generation and anyone official will certainly be offended if you address them with the familiar *Du*.

Sprechen Sie Englisch?	Do you speak English?	*Die Rechnung bitte*	The bill please
Ich spreche kein Deutsch	I don't speak German	*Ist der Tisch frei?*	Is that table free?
Sprechen Sie bitte langsamer	Please speak more slowly	*Die Speisekarte bitte*	The menu please
Ich verstehe nicht	I don't understand	*Fräulein . . .!*	Waitress . . . ! (for attention)
Ich verstehe	I understand	*Herr Ober . . .!*	Waiter . . . ! (for attention)
Wie sagt man das auf Deutsch?	How do you say that in German?	*Haben Sie etwas billigeres?*	Have you got something cheaper?
Können Sie mir sagen wo . . . ist?	Can you tell me where . . . is?	*Haben Sie Zimmer frei?*	Are there rooms available?
Wo ist . . .?	Where is . . .?	*Wo sind die Toiletten bitte?*	Where are the toilets?
Wieviel kostet das?	How much does that cost?	*Ich hätte gern dieses*	I'd like that one
Wann fährt der nächste Zug?	When does the next train leave?	*Ich hätte gern ein Zimmer für zwei*	I'd like a room for two
Um wieviel Uhr?	At what time?	*Ich hätte gern ein Einzelzimmer*	I'd like a single room
Wieviel Uhr ist es?	What time is it?	*Hat es Dusche, Bad, Toilette . . .?*	Does it have a shower, bath, toilet . . .?
Sind die Plätze noch frei?	Are these seats taken?		

Numbers

0	*null*	10	*zehn*	20	*zwanzig*	80	*achtzig*
1	*eins*	11	*elf*	21	*ein-und-zwanzig*	90	*neunzig*
2	*zwei*	12	*zwölf*	22	*zwei-und-zwanzig*	100	*hundert*
3	*drei*	13	*dreizehn*	30	*dreissig*	1000	*tausend*
4	*vier*	14	*vierzehn*	40	*vierzig*	1997	*neunzehn-hundert-sieben-und-neunzig*
5	*fünf*	15	*fünfzehn*	50	*fünfzig*		
6	*sechs*	16	*sechszehn*	60	*sechzig*	1998	*neunzehnhundert-acht-und-neunzig*
7	*sieben*	17	*siebzehn*	70	*siebzig*		
8	*acht*	18	*achtzehn*				
9	*neun*	19	*neunzehn*				

Glossary

German terms

Ausstellung Exhibition.

Bahnhof Station.

Bau Building.

Beisl Pub.

Berg Mountain, hill.

Bezirk City district.

Brücke Bridge.

Brünn Brno, capital of Moravia (Czech Republic).

Brunnen Fountain.

Burg Castle.

Denkmal Memorial.

Dom Cathedral.

Donau River Danube.

Dorf Village.

Durchgang Passageway.

Durchhaus Literally a "through-house" – a house whose ground floor is open, allowing access to a street or courtyard.

Einbahnstrasse One-way street.

Erzherzog Archduke.

Fasching Carnival.

Feiertag Holiday.

Flughafen Airport.

Friedhof Cemetery.

Fussgängerzone Pedestrian zone.

Gasse Alley.

Gemälde Painting.

Gemütlich Snug or cosy.

Grab Grave.

Gürtel The city's outer ring road.

Haltestelle Bus/tram stop.

Haus House.

Herzog Duke.

Heuriger Wine tavern.

Hof Court, courtyard, mansion, housing complex.

Innere Stadt Vienna's first district, the "Inner City".

Jugendherberge Youth hostel.

Kaffeehaus Café.

Kaiser Emperor.

Kapelle Chapel.

Kärnten Carinthia.

Kaserne Barracks.

Kino Cinema.

Kirche Church.

Kloster Monastery, convent.

König King.

Kunst Art.

Kunstkammer Cabinet of curios.

Land (pl Länder) Name given to each of the nine federal provinces of Austria.

Niederösterreich Lower Austria.

Not Emergency

Oberösterreich Upper Austria.

Palast Palace.

Platz Square.

Pressburg Bratislava, capital of Slovakia.

Prinz Prince.

Rathaus Town hall.

Reich Empire.

Residenz Palace.

Ring The Ringstrasse, built on the old fortifications in 1857.

Ritter Knight.

Saal Hall.

Sammlung Collection.

Säule Column.

Schanigarten Summer terrace/backyard.

Schatzkammer Treasury.

Schloss Castle.

Stadt Town.

Steiermark Styria.

Stift Collegiate church.

Strasse Street.

Tor Gate.

Trakt Wing (of a building).

Turm Tower.

Viertel Quarter, district.

Volk People, folk.

Vororte The outer suburbs which lie beyond the Gürtel: Vienna's tenth to twenty-second districts.

Vorstädte The inner suburbs which lie between the Ring and the Gürtel: Vienna's third to ninth districts.

Wald Forest.

Wien Vienna.

Zimmer Room.

Political terms and acronyms

Anschluss Literally a "joining together" or "union" – the euphemism coined by the Nazis for the invasion and annexation of Austria in March 1938.

Austro-fascism Term to describe the one-party state set up by Engelbert Dollfuss in 1934. Dollfuss headed the Fatherland Front, a non-Nazi clerical-fascist movement which lasted until the Anschluss in 1938.

Austro-Marxism Philosophy expounded by SDAP theorists such as Otto Bauer in the early twentieth century. While still adhering to the language of class war, its programme was essentially revisionist, arguing that the downfall of capitalism was inevitable, and didn't have to be brought about by violence.

Babenburgs Dynasty who ruled over Austria from 976 to 1246.

Biedermeier The term (*Bieder* means "upright") derives from the satiric figure of Gottlieb Biedermeier, a Swabian schoolmaster created in 1850 by Ludwig Eichrocht, modelled on Eichrocht's own pious, law-abiding teacher in Baden-Baden, Samuel Sauter. It has come to be applied retrospectively to the period between 1815 and 1848 when Austria was under the sway of Prince Metternich. The era came to symbolize a safe, bourgeois, cosy lifestyle, and was applied to the history, art and culture of the period.

CSP (Christlichsoziale Partei) The Christian Social Party was founded in the 1890s by Karl Lueger, who later became Mayor of Vienna. The Christian Socials' combination of Catholicism, municipal socialism and anti-Semitism proved very popular with the Austrians. They were the main party of government in the 1920s and from their ranks rose Engelbert Dollfuss, who later introduced Austro-fascism in 1933.

FPÖ (Freiheitliche Partei Österreichs) The Austrian Freedom Party was the successor to the postwar VdU (see p.372). A far-right party which rose to prominence in the 1980s and scored spectacular

electoral success under the charismatic and controversial leadership of Jörg Haider.

Habsburg Royal dynasty whose powerbase was Vienna from 1273 to 1918. They also held the office of Holy Roman Emperor from 1452 to 1806, and by marriage, war and diplomacy acquired territories all over Europe.

Heimwehr Right-wing militia whose origins lay in the local armed groups formed after the collapse of the empire in 1918. After 1927, these regional militias joined together and created a political wing, the Heimatblock, which supported the onset of Austro-fascism in 1933.

Holy Roman Empire Revived title of the Roman Empire first bestowed by the Pope on Charlemagne in 800. The emperor was chosen by the seven electors and passed around between the Hohenstaufen, Luxembourg and Habsburg families until 1438, when the Habsburgs made the title hereditary. It was dissolved on the orders of Napoleon in 1806.

Josephine Of or pertaining to the reign of Emperor Josef II (1780–1790).

KPÖ (Kommunistische Partei Österreichs) Austrian Communist Party.

Kristallnacht Literally "Crystal Night", after the broken glass which was strewn across the streets during the pogrom of November 9–10, 1938. On this one night the majority of Jewish shops and institutions in the Third Reich – and all but one of the synagogues in Vienna – were destroyed by the Nazis.

k.u.k. kaiserlich und königlich (Imperial and Royal) – a title used after 1867 to refer to everything in the Austro-Hungarian empire. Everything within Hungary was prefaced with a **k** for königlich, everything in the rest of the empire **K. K.** (kaiserlich-königlich; Imperial-Royal). For more details, see p.350.

NSDAP (National Sozialistische Deutsche Arbeiterpartei) National Socialist German Workers' Party, the official name for the German Nazi Party.

ÖVP (Österreichische Volkspartei) Austrian People's Party, the postwar descendant of the Christian Socials, and the principal postwar centre-right party.

Pan-German This adjective covers a whole range of far-right political parties, who advocated Anschluss with Germany, many of whom came together in the 1920s under the banner of the

Greater German People's Party (Grossdeutsche Volkspartei, GDVP).

Red Vienna The period of Socialist municipal government in Vienna which lasted from 1919 to 1934.

Schutzbund SDAP militia founded in 1923.

SDAP (Sozial-Demokratische Arbeiterpartei) Social Democratic Workers' Party, the name given to the Socialist Party, prior to World War II.

SPÖ (Sozialistische Partei Österreichs) The post-war Austrian Socialist Party, later changed to the Sozialdemokratische Partei Österreichs, but keeping the same acronym.

Staatsvertrag The Austrian State Treaty of 1955, which signalled the withdrawal of Allied troops – American, British, French and Soviet – from Austria, in return for Austrian neutrality.

Toleranzpatent The Patent of Tolerance decreed by Josef II in 1782 which allowed freedom of religious observance to Lutherans, Jews and, to a lesser extent, Protestants.

VdU (Verband der Unabhängigen) Union of Independents. Extreme nationalist party formed in 1949 and precursor of the FPÖ.

VF (Vaterländische Front) The Fatherland Front was founded in 1934 by Engelbert Dollfuss, the Christian Social Austrian chancellor who dissolved parliament and introduced Austro-fascism in 1933. The Front was a patriotic, clerico-fascist organization aimed at preventing the Nazis from seizing power.

Architectural terms

Ambulatory Passage round the back of a church altar, in continuation of the aisles.

Art Nouveau Sinuous and stylized form of architecture and decorative arts, known as Secession or Jugendstil in Austria.

Atlantes Pillars in the shape of musclemen, named after the Greek god Atlas whose job it was to hold up the world.

Baldachin A canopy over an altar, tomb, throne or otherwise.

Baroque Expansive, exuberant architectural style of the seventeenth and eighteenth centuries, characterized by ornate decoration, complex spatial arrangement and grand vistas.

Biedermeier Simple, often Neoclassical, style of art and architecture popular from 1815 to 1848

(see also p.371) and in part a reaction against the excesses of the Baroque period.

Caryatid Sculptured female figure used as a column. Similar to Atlantes (see above).

Chancel Part of the church where the main altar is placed, usually at the east end.

Diapers Ornamental patterning in brickwork.

Empire Neoclassical style of architecture and decorative arts practised in the first half of the nineteenth century.

Filigree Fanciful delicate ornamental decoration in stone or metal.

Fresco Mural painting applied to wet plaster, so that the colours immediately soak into the wall.

Glacis Sloping ground between walls of Vienna's Innere Stadt and the suburbs prior to 1857.

Gothic Architectural style prevalent from the twelfth to the sixteenth centuries, characterized by pointed arches and ribbed vaulting.

Historicism Style of architecture which apes previous styles – ie neo-Baroque, neo-Renaissance, neo-Gothic – also known as Ringstrasse style.

Jugendstil German/Austrian version of Art Nouveau, literally "youthful style" – see also Secession, opposite.

Loggia Covered area on the side of a building, usually arcaded.

Lunette An oval or semi-circular opening to admit light into a dome.

Nave Main body of a church, usually the western end.

Neoclassicism Late eighteenth- and early nineteenth-century style of architecture and design returning to classical Greek and Roman models as a reaction against the excess of Baroque and Rococo.

Oriel A bay window, usually projecting from an upper floor.

Quoins External corner stones of a wall.

Ringstrasse Pompous historicist style of architecture which aped Gothic, Renaissance, Baroque and Classical architecture, and which was very popular during the construction of Vienna's Ringstrasse.

Rococo Highly florid style of architecture and design, forming the last phase of Baroque.

Romanesque Solid architectural style of the late tenth to thirteenth centuries, characterized by round-headed arches and geometrical precision.

Secession Movement of artists who split (seceded – hence the term) from the city's Academy of Arts in 1897. Also used more generally as a term synonymous with Jugendstil.

Sgraffito Monochrome plaster decoration effected by means of scraping back the first white layer to reveal the black underneath.

Spandrel The surface area between two adjacent arches.

Stucco Plaster used for decorative effects.

Transepts The wings of a cruciform church, placed at right angles to the nave and chancel.

Trompe l'oeil Painting designed to fool the onlooker into thinking that it is three-dimensional.

Wiener Werkstätte (Vienna Workshops) A group of Secession artists founded in 1903.

Index

Europe,
with
Rough
Guides

THE ROUGH GUIDE TO Berlin

THE MINI ROUGH GUIDE TO Copenhagen

THE ROUGH GUIDE TO London

THE ROUGH GUIDE TO Vienna

THE ROUGH GUIDE TO St Petersburg

THE ROUGH GUIDE TO Paris

THE ROUGH GUIDE TO Amsterdam

Prague
THE ROUGH GUIDE

Venice
& the Veneto

Barcelona

THE ROUGH GUIDE TO Europe
2001 EDITION
31 Countries • 100 Maps
Turkey, Morocco, the Baltic States

ROUGH GUIDES: Mini Guides, Travel Specials and Phrasebooks

MINI GUIDES

Antigua
Bangkok
Barbados
Beijing
Big Island of Hawaii
Boston
Brussels
Budapest
Cape Town
Copenhagen
Dublin
Edinburgh

Florence
Honolulu
Ibiza & Formentera
Jerusalem
Las Vegas
Lisbon
London Restaurants
Madeira
Madrid
Malta & Gozo
Maui
Melbourne
Menorca

Montreal
New Orleans

Paris
Rome
Seattle
St Lucia
Sydney
Tenerife
Tokyo
Toronto
Vancouver

TRAVEL SPECIALS

First-Time Asia
First-Time Europe
Women Travel

PHRASEBOOKS

Czech
Dutch
Egyptian Arabic
European
French
German
Greek

Hindi & Urdu
Hungarian
Indonesian
Italian
Japanese
Mandarin
  Chinese
Mexican
  Spanish
Polish
Portuguese
Russian
Spanish
Swahili
Thai
Turkish
Vietnamese

ROUGH GUIDES:
Reference and Music CDs

REFERENCE

Blues:
  100 Essential CDs
Classical Music
Classical:
  100 Essential CDs
Country Music
Country:
  100 Essential CDs
Drum'n'bass
House Music
Hip Hop
Irish Music
Jazz

Music USA
Opera
Opera:
  100 Essential CDs
Reggae
Reggae:
  100 Essential CDs
Rock
Rock:
  100 Essential CDs

Soul:
  100 Essential CDs
Techno
World Music

World Music:
  100 Essential CDs
English Football
European Football
Internet
Money Online
Shopping Online
Travel Health

ROUGH GUIDE MUSIC CDs

Music of the Andes
Australian Aboriginal
Bluegrass
Brazilian Music
Cajun & Zydeco
Music of Cape Verde
Classic Jazz
Music of
  Colombia
Cuban Music
Eastern Europe

Music of Egypt
English Roots Music
Flamenco
Music of Greece
Hip Hop
India & Pakistan
Irish Music
Music of Jamaica
Music of Japan
Kenya & Tanzania
Marrabenta
  Mozambique
Native American
North African
Music of Portugal
Reggae
Salsa
Samba
Scottish Music
South African Music
Music of Spain
Sufi Music
Tango

Tex-Mex
West African Music
World Music
World Music Vol 2
Music of Zimbabwe

AVAILABLE AT ALL GOOD BOOKSHOPS

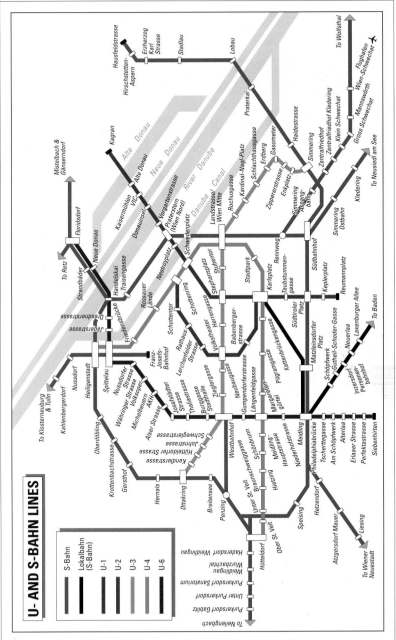

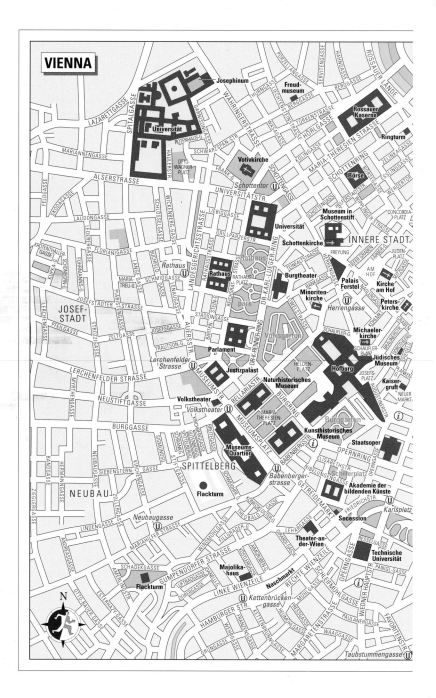

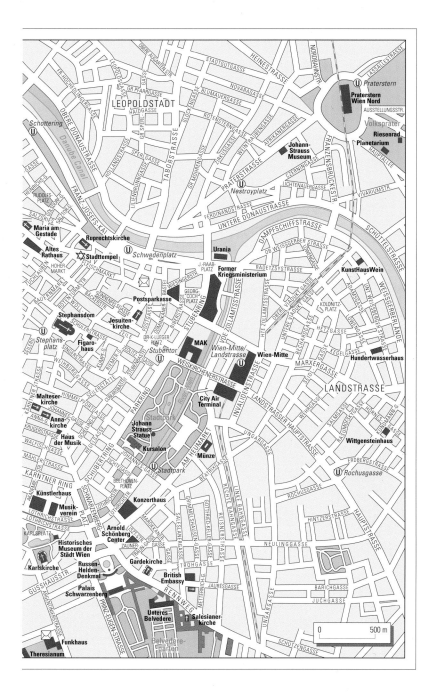

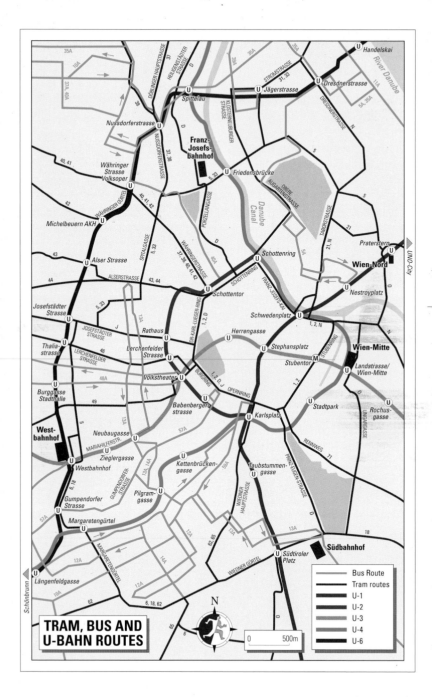

TRAM, BUS AND
U-BAHN ROUTES

Bus Route
Tram routes
U-1
U-2
U-3
U-4
U-6

0   500m